The Total Spectrum of Technology

Personal Trainer®

Eliminate Grading Homework!

Instructors consistently cite reading the text and completing graded homework assignments as a key to student success in managerial accounting; however, finding time to grade homework is difficult. Personal Trainer solves this time problem by allowing professors to assign textbook exercises and problems. Personal Trainer will grade the homework and then post the grade into a full-blown gradebook, all real time! Personal Trainer is an Internet-based homework tutor where students can complete the textbook homework assignments, receive hints, submit their answers and then receive immediate feedback on their answers.

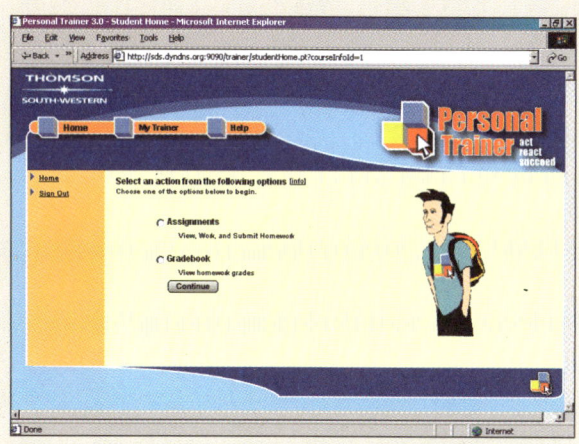

Xtra!

This online resource provides lecture enhancement resources and access to games and quizzes so that students can test their understanding of the content. Xtra! access is available as an optional package with new textbooks. To purchase online, go to http://jacksonxtra.swlearning.com.

To order call 1.800.423.0563
or http://jackson-managerial.swlearning.com

Chapter 2
CHERYL'S BIKE SHOP *is a retailer of bikes and parts and accessories for bikes.*

Chapter 2
NORTHERN LIGHTS CUSTOM CABINETS *manufactures and sells custom-ordered kitchen and bathroom cabinets. The company sells primarily to building contractors, but occasionally deals directly with homeowners.*

Chapter 3
CHARLES' CUSTOM FURNITURE *(CCF) manufactures custom furniture. The company uses job costing to accumulate, track, and assign costs to these pieces of furniture.*

Chapters 4, 8, and 12
BIG AL'S PIZZA, INC., *a subsidiary of Big Al's Pizza Emporium, has been established to produce partially baked, flash-frozen, 16-inch meat pizzas to be sold wholesale to grocery and convenience stores and school cafeterias.*

Chapters 4 and 13
TOP SAIL CONSTRUCTION *is a beach-house contractor based in North Carolina. The company usually builds about 30 houses per year.*

Chapter 5
KENCOR PIZZA EMPORIUM *has been in business for one month, during which it made 2,100 pizzas. The company is expecting to increase its production of pizzas to 2,600.*

Chapter 6
CHERI'S CHIPS *is a manufacturer of banana chips.*

Chapter 6
HAPPY DAZE GAME COMPANY *produces a single game; but the company is considering expanding its product line.*

Chapter 6
ZIA MOTORS *manufactures a single auto, called the Zoomer, which provides basic transportation and sells at the low end of the price range.*

Chapter 7
ACE PUTTERS, INC. *is a manufacturer of custom putters that sells its products to other manufacturers of golf clubs as well as to retailers.*

Chapters 7, 11, and 13
BIRDIE MAKER GOLF COMPANY *is a manufacturer of custom sets of golf clubs that it markets as being superior to other golf clubs.*

Chapter 7
SUNSET AIRLINES *is a major air carrier. Like other air carriers, Sunset's challenge is to discount its tickets enough to fill its planes without losing money by doing so.*

Chapter 7
CLAYTON HERRING TIRE COMPANY *manufactures and sells 10 different models of tires. Sales of a s pecial mud and snow tire have not met the company's expectations.*

Chapter 8
AMBER VALLEY SKI RESORT *is considering the purchase of a new chair lift and opening new ski slopes that will attract more skiers to the resort.*

Chapter 8
BUD & ROSE'S FLOWER SHOP *is a retailer of flowers for all occasions. Bud & Rose's is considering the purchase of a refrigerated deliver van that will allow the company to accept large orders for weddings, receptions, etc.*

Chapter 9
TINA'S FINE JUICES, *located in the Northeast, is a bottler of orange juice. Tina's produces orange juice from fruit concentrate purchased from suppliers in Florida, Arizona, and California. The only ingredients in the juice are water and the concentrate. The juice is blended, pasteurized, and bottled for sale in 12-ounce plastic bottles.*

Chapter 10
CORINNE'S COUNTRY ROCKERS *builds a high-quality rocking chair with a reputation for lasting a lifetime. The company uses a patented rocking mechanism that is not found on other rockers. The chairs are sold through mail order and the Internet.*

Chapter 11
CAMELBACK MOUNTAIN COMMUNITY BANK *is headquartered in Phoenix, Arizona, and has six branches located in and around the Phoenix metropolitan area.*

Chapters 11 and 12
GARCIA & BUFFETT, CPAS, *is a full-service public accounting firm that offers tax, audit, and consulting services.*

Chapters 15 and 16
ROBYN'S BOUTIQUE *is a retail store specializing in children's clothes.*

Solutions designed for the way you teach today's students...

From the day you choose to adopt a Thomson South-Western text through the final exams, we are committed to providing the best materials available to support your teaching *and* your students' learning. That's why this text is supported by two **FREE** resources that provide great educational value while making your own course preparation easier than ever before.

Book Companion Website

Available 24 hours a day from any computer with Internet access, the *Book Companion Website* for this text provides invaluable resources that you and your students can access anytime, anywhere.

Students can access an unmatched array of interactive learning tools – for instance, self-testing, reinforcement activities, and links to the best and most relevant information on the Internet. For instructors, the site can feature course outlines and learning objectives, suggested activities and exercises, and much more.

* Specific resources can vary by title. For detailed information or a demonstration, contact your Thomson South-Western sales representative.

Resource Integration Guide

Your one-stop source for course organization and preparation!

Accessible from the *Book Companion Website*, the *Resource Integration Guide* is an indispensable tool that helps you get the most from your textbook and its supplementary package.

A detailed grid lists all of the resources you can use to enhance your course – such as lecture outlines, PowerPoint® presentations, animations and video clips, online resources, testing options, and much more. You'll soon wonder how you ever did without this valuable course preparation tool!

THOMSON
SOUTH-WESTERN

Preview the companion site for this text and download your *Resource Integration Guide* at:

http://jackson-managerial.swlearning.com

ISBN 0-324-31231-8

Managerial Accounting

3e

WAKE TECHNICAL COMMUNITY COLLEGE LIBRARY
9101 FAYETTEVILLE ROAD
RALEIGH, NORTH CAROLINA 27603

Steve Jackson
Loyola University New Orleans

WITHDRAWN

Roby Sawyers
North Carolina State University

Contributing Author
Greg Jenkins
North Carolina State University

THOMSON
SOUTH-WESTERN

Australia · Canada · Mexico · Singapore · Spain · United Kingdom · United States

Managerial Accounting: A Focus on Decision Making, 3e
Steve Jackson, Roby Sawyers, Greg Jenkins

VP/Editorial Director:
Jack W. Calhoun

Publisher:
Rob Dewey

Executive Acquisitions Editor:
Sharon Oblinger

Developmental Editor:
Ken Martin

Marketing Manager:
Chip Kislack

Production Editor:
Heather A. Mann

Manager of Technology, Editorial:
Vicky True

Technology Project Editor:
Robin Browning

Manufacturing Coordinator:
Doug Wilke

Production House:
Pre-Press Company, Inc.

Printer:
Transcontinental Printing
Beauceville, QC

Art Director:
Chris A. Miller

Internal Designer:
Knapke Design, Cincinnati

Cover Designer:
Knapke Design, Cincinnati

Cover Images:
© Getty Images and Alamy

Photography Manager:
Deanna Ettinger

Photo Researcher:
Terri Miller

COPYRIGHT © 2006
Thomson South-Western, a part of The Thomson Corporation. Thomson, the Star logo, and South-Western are trademarks used herein under license.

Printed in Canada
1 2 3 4 5 07 06 05 04

Student Edition:
ISBN 0-324-30416-1
Instructor's Edition:
ISBN 0-324-31231-8

ALL RIGHTS RESERVED.
No part of this work covered by the copyright hereon may be reproduced or used in any form or by any means—graphic, electronic, or mechanical, including photocopying, recording, taping, Web distribution or information storage and retrieval systems, or in any other manner—without the written permission of the publisher.

For permission to use material from this text or product, submit a request online at http://www.thomsonrights.com.

Library of Congress Control Number:
2004114626

For more information about our products, contact us at:
Thomson Learning Academic Resource Center
1-800-423-0563

Thomson Higher Education
5191 Natorp Boulevard
Mason, OH 45040
USA

Asia (including India)
Thomson Learning
5 Shenton Way
#01-01 UIC Building
Singapore 068808

Australia/New Zealand
Thomson Learning Australia
102 Dodds Street
Southbank, Victoria 3006
Australia

Canada
Thomson Nelson
1120 Birchmount Road
Toronto, Ontario
M1K 5G4
Canada

Latin America
Thomson Learning
Seneca, 53
Colonia Polanco
11560 Mexico
D.F.Mexico

UK/Europe/Middle East/Africa
Thomson Learning
High Holborn House
50/51 Bedford Row
London WC1R 4LR
United Kingdom

Spain (including Portugal)
Thomson Paraninfo
Calle Magallanes, 25
28015 Madrid, Spain

Preface

"If by education we mean the cramming of a pupil's mind with facts or rules, without any real conception of their meaning or of the relations in which they stand to each other, it is perfectly safe to say that it is a waste of time. This kind of education fits a man for a certain groove, in which he moves in a routine way, a mere piece of mechanical machinery, incapable of independent thought or action. If confronted with a new condition, to which his rules do not apply, he is helpless, and is liable to make mistakes that are disastrous, because his action is based on insufficient knowledge of the foundation principles." (*Journal of Accountancy*, 1917).

While 1917 may seem a little dated, more recently the Institute of Management Accountants has stressed that accounting programs should redirect their focus away from curricula that emphasize in-depth, technical, and procedural subject matter to a more general approach that emphasizes concepts and problem-solving skills. Similar sentiments are echoed in the American Institute of Certified Public Accountants' *CPA Vision Project* and in the monograph *Accounting Education: Charting a Course through a Perilous Future*.

These views provide the underlying motivation for this textbook. That is, we believe that it is critical to educate students in the principles and concepts of managerial accounting in a way that teaches and improves their problem-solving skills. While we believe that students should be exposed to traditional concepts and tools in learning to make good decisions, we also feel strongly that an accounting education in the new millennium demands that students be able to apply critical-thinking skills in unstructured settings.

The third edition of **Managerial Accounting** provides students with the necessary understanding of fundamental accounting concepts and tools, while simultaneously emphasizing the analysis and interpretation of information rather than its preparation. This approach enables us to teach students to think not only about "how" the accounting takes place, but also "why" that accounting takes place and how the resultant information improves the decision-making process. Our approach does not rely on the extensive use of journal entries or other accounting procedures because our primary focus is on the use of accounting information by managers in organizations. Accordingly, we provide numerous business examples throughout the text of how actual companies are using managerial accounting in strategic ways to improve their business. We also took care to maintain and improve the understandability and readability of the text—an important feature of the first two editions.

We present an approach that we eagerly invite you to explore—an approach that allows students to discover an understanding of business decision making and prepare for success in their business careers.

This third edition is intended for all students who wish to gain a greater understanding of business and how accounting information is used by managers to make decisions. The text is written in a manner that uses real-world companies to present information that appeals to a wide audience, including students who are studying accounting, management, marketing, finance, human resources, general business, and even students who are not pursuing business degrees. Indeed, the text is intended for all who will *use* accounting information to make decisions.

We anticipate that most students taking a course in managerial accounting have taken one financial accounting course. As such, the text is designed to stand alone and work well in succession to any of the popular financial accounting texts currently on the market. However, with supplemental instruction in basic financial accounting transaction analysis and an introduction to financial statements, **Managerial Accounting** serves equally well as the primary text for students who take managerial accounting first or only take one accounting course.

New to This Edition

- *End-of-Chapter Assignments* have been substantially revised and now include a variety of formats: **Multiple Choice Questions, Concept Questions, Exercises, Problems, Cases,** and **Group and Internet Exercises.** The Cases are designed to allow students to work with less structured contexts. Also, all assignments are identified by learning objective, and most chapters include **spreadsheet assignments** and questions related to **decision making** and **ethics,** all of which are identified by unique icons.

3 Units started and completed: $90,000

51. The Meekma Beverage Corporation manufactures flavored bottled water and uses process costing to account for the cost of the products manufactured. Raw materials and labor are incurred at the same rate during the production process. Data for Meekma's mixing department for March are as follows:

	Units	Production Costs
Work in process, March 1 (80% complete)	5,000	$ 60,000
Started during March	100,000	1,187,500

- *Hitting the Bottom Line* features short discussions of how managerial accounting decisions impact a company's financial health. The discussions are based on real-world events and feature a broad range of companies, including American Airlines, Volkswagen AG, General Electric, and the Royal Dutch/Shell Group. The intent of *Hitting the Bottom Line* is to encourage students to understand the links between managerial accounting, financial accounting, and business decision making.

Hitting the Bottom Line.

"DON'T CHANGE THAT LIGHT BULB!"

One thing is true about flying an airplane—the gas tank has to be full whether there are 15 passengers or 75 passengers. This is the brutal reality of operating an airline—there are many fixed costs. Few airlines have faced this reality like American Airlines, which has lost more than $6.6 billion since late 2001. The company is now taking steps to curb its losses and is finding that questioning long-held beliefs about the industry can pay dividends. For example, the company has decided to spread out its schedule, rather than bunch flights close together, which required employees to staff gates and aircraft at the same time. Also, the company now purchases less expensive blankets for first-class passengers from China rather than Italy, and lightbulbs over seats are changed less frequently than they once were. Other cost savings efforts include replacing passenger windows less frequently—each window costs $1,000, and polishing the exterior of airplanes every two years rather than every year as done in the past. These and other cost savings efforts have allowed American Airlines to slash its annual costs by an astounding $2.2 billion! However, if schedules are less convenient, layovers are longer, passengers are left sitting in the dark, or passengers become concerned about safety, short-term savings may result in long-term costs.

- ***The Ethics of Business*** features discussions of companies whose employees have behaved unethically in the conduct of business. Each of these discussions is followed by "*It's Your Choice*," a series of short questions designed to encourage students to think about how they would act in similar circumstances. Companies that are included in *The Ethics of Business* features include Ford Motor Company, Gillette, Philip Morris USA, and WorldCom (now MCI).

THE ETHICS OF BUSINESS
Cut Your Price or Else!

The Big Three U.S. automakers (Ford, GM, and DaimlerChrysler) have been under tremendous competition from foreign manufacturers for the last decade. Unable to cut labor costs because of collective bargaining agreements with employee labor unions, the companies have turned their attention to their suppliers. For example, Ford and GM contacted Superior Industries International, a supplier of wheels for the companies, and requested that Superior match the price offered by a potential new supplier located in China. The only way that Superior Industries can meet the price is by outsourcing some of their own labor. Essentially, while GM and Ford cannot outsource their labor and reduce that component of product cost, they have forced their suppliers to cut costs for them.

It's Your Choice—Imagine you are the owner of a company that supplies components to Ford and GM and you are approached with the above dilemma. What would you do? What are your ethical obligations to your company, family, employees, community, and customers? What do you think is the ultimate impact of this type of forced outsourcing?

- ***Doing Business*** features short discussions of how real-world companies are using managerial accounting concepts to think about and solve everyday business problems.

Doing Business.
TERRORIST ATTACKS WREAK HAVOC ON SUPPLY CHAINS

Disruptions in shipments of air freight and heightened security at border crossings following the World Trade Center terrorist attacks exposed one of the risks facing companies operating just-in-time factories. Without needed parts, several auto makers were forced to temporarily shut down assembly lines in the days immediately following the attacks. New transportation security rules enacted in October 2003 further tighten border security by requiring companies to provide the U.S. government with advance notification for incoming shipments of international cargo. These notification requirements range from 30 minutes for trucks to 24 hours for ships and may result in goods sitting in port waiting for approval and or inspection. Companies must factor in the risks of the interruption of deliveries into the supply chain management process and either have an alternative source and/or have a buffer like that in a traditional manufacturing system ("Flight Ban Slows 'Just in Time' Factories," *Wall Street Journal*, September 13, 2001, B3 and "Shippers Say New Border Rules Could Delay Just-in-Time Cargo," *Wall Street Journal*, August 29, 2003, A1)

- **Chapter 11—Decentralization and Performance Evaluation** This chapter now includes a discussion of performance evaluation in a multinational environment and the use of cash-based, stock-based, and other forms of managerial compensation to motivate managers.

- **Chapter 12—Performance Evaluation Using the Balanced Scorecard** This chapter includes a new section on measuring and controlling environmental costs.

- **Chapter 13—The Strategic Use of Managerial Accounting Information** This new chapter examines how managerial accounting information is used by companies in developing, monitoring, and maintaining a long-term competitive strategy.

- **Chapter 14—Internal Control, Corporate Governance, and Ethics** This new chapter includes revised and expanded coverage of fraud and internal control and up-to-date coverage of the forces shaping corporate governance and business ethics. Unique to managerial accounting textbooks, the material in this chapter exposes students to some of the most significant issues affecting the business profession today. Topical coverage includes fraudulent financial reporting, misappropriation of assets, common methods of perpetrating fraud, elements of internal control, common control activities, corporate governance practices, ethics programs, codes of ethics, and appropriate responses to ethics violations.

Specific Chapter Coverage

Managerial Accounting is organized into five parts and follows a logical progression of topics. After an introductory chapter dealing with accounting information systems and managerial decisions, Part I consists of Chapters 2 though 4 and includes a variety of topics focused on the costing of products and services. Chapter 2 discusses manufacturing processes, cost terminology, and cost flows, Chapter 3 discusses the use of job, process, and operations costing, and Chapter 4 discusses activity-based costing. Part II of the text consists of Chapters 5 though 8 and includes material on cost behavior and relevant costs (Chapter 5), cost-volume-profit analysis and variable costing (Chapter 6), short-term tactical decision making (Chapter 7) and long-term capital investment decisions (Chapter 8). Part III of the text consists of Chapters 9 through 12 and includes the preparation and use of budgets in planning and decision making (Chapter 9), variance analysis (Chapter 10), decentralization and performance evaluation (Chapter 11), and performance evaluation using the balanced scorecard (Chapter 12). Part IV of the text includes two capstone chapters dealing with strategic decision making. Chapter 13 introduces the concept of the strategic use of managerial accounting information, and Chapter 14 deals with issues of internal control, corporate governance, and ethics. Part V includes chapters on financial statement analysis (Chapter 15) and the statement of cash flows (Chapter 16).

Chapter 1 Accounting Information and Managerial Decisions

This chapter defines accounting information and contrasts the needs for accounting information by internal and external users. The third edition includes significant new coverage of the importance of knowledge management in the business environment and the use and benefits of knowledge warehouses, enterprise resource planning (ERP), and electronic data interchange (EDI) as knowledge management tools. The chapter also discusses the decision-making role of management in planning, operating, and controlling, describes the various functional areas of management, and provides a decision framework for assessing decisions that commonly face managers of organizations.

Chapter 2 Product Costing: Manufacturing Processes, Cost Terminology, and Cost Flows

This chapter begins with a description of basic production processes used by manufacturing companies and identifies the benefits and costs of implementing a just-in-time production system. The chapter provides an introduction into basic cost terminology applicable to manufacturing companies, merchandising companies, and service providers and concludes with a description and analysis of cost flows. The third edition includes relevant journal entries associated with the purchase of raw materials, the transfer of raw materials into work in process, the incurrence of overhead costs, the transfer of work in process to finished goods, and the sale of finished goods.

Chapter 3 Job Costing, Process Costing, and Operations Costing

This chapter begins with a discussion of the basic systems that companies use to accumulate, track, and assign costs to products and services and contrasts and compares job costing, process costing, and operations costing. The chapter introduces the concept of cost pools and cost drivers and how they are used to allocate overhead, using plantwide and departmental overhead rates. The chapter includes a discussion of the use of overhead estimates (predetermined overhead rates) in product costing and the treatment of over- or under-applied overhead. The appendix to the chapter includes a detailed discussion of process costing.

Chapter 4 Activity-Based Costing

In this chapter, we revisit the problems of overhead application and discuss the use of activity-based costing (ABC). We define and identify typical activities and cost drivers in an ABC system and demonstrate the costing of products, using ABC as compared to traditional volume-based costing systems. The benefits and limitations of ABC are discussed, as is the application of ABC to nonmanufacturing activities and in a JIT environment.

Chapter 5 Cost Behavior and Relevant Costs

This chapter introduces concepts and tools that will be used in Chapter 6 through Chapter 8. Chapter 5 begins with a definition of cost behavior and illustrates the concepts of fixed costs, variable costs, and mixed costs. Mixed costs are analyzed using both the high/low method and regression analysis. Next, the chapter revisits the concept of relevant costs as they apply to variable and fixed costs and describes the impact of income taxes on costs.

Chapter 6 Cost-Volume-Profit Analysis and Variable Costing

In this chapter, we develop a set of tools that focus on the distinction between fixed and variable costs. These tools include measures of a company's contribution margin, contribution margin ratio, and operating leverage—the cornerstones of cost-volume-profit (CVP) analysis. The chapter illustrates the use of break-even analysis in both a single and multiproduct environment and discusses the impact of income taxes on CVP analysis.

Chapter 7 Short-Term Tactical Decision Making

In Chapter 7 we analyze a variety of short-term decisions, including the pricing of special orders, the decision to outsource labor, the decision to make or buy a component, the decision to drop a product or service, the utilization of limited resources, and the decision to sell or process further. The theory of constraints is also introduced.

Chapter 8 Long-Term (Capital Investment) Decisions

In this chapter, we develop tools that aid managers in making long-term decisions to purchase new property, plant, and equipment (capital investment decisions). The use of the net present value and internal rate of return methods in both screening decisions and preference decisions is discussed, as is the impact of income taxes on the analysis. The impact of new manufacturing techniques on capital investment decisions and the importance of qualitative factors in the analysis are also discussed. The payback method, an approach to long-term purchasing decisions that does not take into consideration the time value of money, is also mentioned. The appendix of the chapter provides a detailed introduction to time value of money concepts for students that have not been previously exposed to these concepts.

Chapter 9 The Use of Budgets in Planning and Decision Making

In this chapter, we introduce the concept of budgeting and discuss how budgets assist managers in planning and decision making. We discuss and demonstrate the preparation of budgets for a traditional manufacturing company with inventory, as well as for a company operating in a JIT environment. This chapter also covers the use of budgets in merchandising and service companies. We pay special attention to the preparation and use of the cash budget for managerial decision making and tie it into the preparation of the statement of cash flows. Finally, we discuss static and flexible budgets, with particular emphasis on the impact of ABC on flexible budgets and the preparation and use of nonfinancial budgets.

Chapter 10 Variance Analysis—A Tool for Cost Control and Performance Evaluation

In this chapter, we expand the discussion of flexible budgeting and introduce the concept of standard costs and variance analysis as tools to help managers "manage by exception" and evaluate performance in their control function. Included is a discussion of the overall flexible budget variance, the sales price variance, price (rate) and usage (efficiency) variances for direct material, direct labor, and variable overhead, and fixed overhead spending and volume variances. The chapter ends with a discussion of considerations in using and interpreting variances.

Chapter 11 Decentralization and Performance Evaluation

In this chapter, we discuss the structure and management of decentralized organizations, with an emphasis on the impact of responsibility accounting and segment reporting on decision making in decentralized organizations. We discuss performance evaluation in cost, revenue, profit, and investment centers and introduce measures of performance such as return on investment (ROI), residual income, and economic value added (EVA), commonly used in investment centers. New material in the third edition includes a discussion of performance evaluation in a multinational environment and the use of cash-based, stock-based, and other forms of managerial compensation to motivate managers. We conclude the chapter with a discussion of transfer pricing, including a discussion of international issues.

Chapter 12 Performance Evaluation Using the Balanced Scorecard

In this chapter, we introduce the concept of the balanced scorecard and discuss how the balanced scorecard integrates financial and nonfinancial measures of performance. We discuss the four perspectives of the balanced scorecard approach: the financial perspective, the customer perspective, the internal business perspective, and the learning and growth perspective. The chapter defines quality costs and explains the tradeoffs among prevention costs, appraisal costs, internal failure costs, and external failure costs. We relate measures of quality, environmental impact, productivity, efficiency, timeliness, and marketing effectiveness to each perspective of the balanced scorecard. New to the third edition is a section on measuring and controlling environmental costs.

Chapter 13 The Strategic Use of Managerial Accounting Information

In this new chapter, we examine the strategic use of managerial accounting information; that is, how managerial accounting information is used by companies in developing, monitoring and maintaining a long-term competitive strategy. In the first section of the chapter, we discuss the general strategies used by companies in creating a competitive advantage. In the second section, we discuss pricing and strategy, including the use of cost-based pricing and target pricing. In the third section, we discuss the influence of cost management on strategy, including such topics as value chain analysis, supply chain management, customer relationship management, and activity-based management.

Chapter 14 Internal Control, Corporate Governance, and Ethics

This chapter includes revised and expanded coverage of fraud and internal control and up-to-date coverage of the forces shaping corporate governance and business ethics. Unique to managerial accounting textbooks, the material in the chapter exposes students to some of the most significant issues affecting the business profession today. Topical coverage includes fraudulent financial reporting, misappropriation of assets, common methods of perpetrating fraud, elements of internal control, common control activities, corporate governance practices, ethics programs, codes of ethics, and appropriate responses to ethics violations.

Chapter 15 Financial Statement Analysis

In this chapter, we discuss the use of analytical tools in financial statement analysis. Included is a discussion of the limitations of financial statement analysis, the use of comparative and common-size financial statements, liquidity ratios, solvency ratios, and profitability ratios.

Chapter 16 The Statement of Cash Flows

In this chapter we present an in-depth discussion of the preparation and use of the cash flow statement. While this statement is primarily used by parties external to the organization, we discuss its importance to managerial decision making and its links to the cash budget produced for internal purposes.

Supplements for Instructors

- **Solutions Manual** This comprehensive manual contains all the solutions to the end-of-chapter items.
- **Instructor's Manual** This resource provides teaching tips and chapter outlines.
- **Test Bank** Completely revised for the third edition, the Test Bank contains more than 1,500 questions to evaluate students' progress through the course material. A selection of various question types is available, including multiple choice, short answer exercises, and short problems. The printed Test Bank is also available in electronic format, **ExamView® Pro,** which enables instructors to preview and edit questions and add their own questions.
- **Instructor's Resource CD-ROM** This CD is a convenient source for instructor materials, including the Solutions Manual, Instructor's Manual, Test Bank with Exam View, and PowerPoint presentations.
- **WebTutor™ Advantage on WebCT™ and WebTutor Advantage on Blackboard®** are platform-driven systems for complete Web-based course management and delivery. WebTutor Advantage provides a concept review and reinforcement in the form of quizzing, videos, and much more. When students purchase this product, they also get automatic access to Personal Trainer.
- **Product Support Web Site at http://jackson-managerial.swlearning.com** A variety of instructor resources are available through South-Western's password-protected Web site. Downloadable instructor supplement files are available for the Solutions Manual, Instructor's Manual, Test Bank, ExamView, and PowerPoint, each organized by chapter.

Supplements for Students

- **Personal Trainer** Specifically designed to ease the instructor's time-consuming task of grading homework, Personal Trainer 3.0 lets students complete online their assigned homework from the text or practice on unassigned homework. The results are instantaneously entered into a gradebook. Personal Trainer provides an unprecedented real-time, guided, self-correcting learning reinforcement system outside the classroom.

- **Xtra!** Available as an optional, free bundle with every new textbook, Xtra! Gives students FREE access to the following online learning tools:
  —**Quizzes** that measure a student's "test readiness" on the concepts in the chapter.
  —**Quiz Bowl** is a fun way for students to test their understanding of a chapter's material.
  —**Crossword Puzzles** is excellent for students to review their understanding of the key terms in a chapter.
  —**PowerPoint** provides a quick review of the chapter material.

- **Product Support Web Site at http://jackson-managerial.swlearning.com** provides students with a wealth of resources, including quizzing, Internet applications questions, and a review of the chapter concepts.

- **Management Accounting Course Guide** provides tips for successfully completing the managerial accounting course. It includes multiple choice questions for students to use in testing their understanding of a chapter's concepts.

Acknowledgments

We appreciate the assistance of those who worked on the text and ancillary package to ensure accurate information. We are also grateful to the editorial, production, and marketing team at Thomson/South-Western for their invaluable efforts: Sharon Oblinger, Chip Kislack, Ken Martin, and Heather Mann.

    We greatly appreciate the feedback provided by the professors who responded to surveys and answered questions about the revision of this text. In addition, we are indebted to the following professors who reviewed manuscript and submitted useful comments that assisted us in refining our ideas for this revision.

Norma Jacobs
Austin Community College

Mark Myring
Ball State University

Dennis Hwang
Bloomsburg University

Patricia Doherty
Boston University

Stephen Schepman
Central Washington University

Paula Cardwell
Elon University

Betty Nolen
Floyd College

Constance Malone-Hylton
George Mason University

Hubert Glover
Georgia State University

Richard Veazey
Grand Valley State University

Khalid Razaki
Illinois State University

Susan Minke
Indiana University-Purdue University at Ft. Wayne

Wendy Teitz
Kent State University

Suneel Maheshwari
Marshall University

Tom Olach
Mississippi State University

John Giles
North Carolina State University

Karen N. Russom
North Harris College

Linda Marquis
Northern Kentucky University

Rama Ramamurthy
Ohio State University

Joann Pacenta
Pennsylvania College of Technology

Greg Burbage
Sacramento City College

Robert Burdette
Salt Lake Community College

Roger Gee
San Diego Mesa Community College

Mike Costigan
Southern Illinois University–Edwardsville

Sol Ahiarah
SUNY–Buffalo

Alex Ampadu
SUNY–Buffalo

Mary Krygiel
Towson University

Phillip Blanchard
University of Arizona

David Dearman
University of Arkansas–
Ft. Smith

SungWook Yoon
University of Colorado

Marvin Williams
University of Houston–Downtown

Bruce Lubich
University of Maryland

James Lukawitz
University of Memphis

Andrew Morgret
University of Memphis

Karen S. Bird
University of Michigan

Diane Tanner
University of North Florida

Robert Scharlach
University of Southern California

Frank Mayne
University of Texas at El Paso

Kathleen Fitzpatrick
University of Toledo

David Remmele
University of Wisconsin–Whitewater

Carolyn Strand-Norman
Virginia Commonwealth University

Samantha Cox
Wake Technical Community College

Frank A. DeGeorge
West Virginia University

M.A. Houston
Wright State University

Harold Little
Western Kentucky University

To those who influence our decisions:
Cheryl, Christina, Kent, and Ben
Amber and Robyn
Elaine, Anna, and Claire

Brief Contents

Chapter 1   Accounting Information and Managerial Decisions   2

Part 1   The Costing of Products and Services   25

Chapter 2   Product Costing: Manufacturing Processes, Cost Terminology, and Cost Flows   26

Chapter 3   Job Costing, Process Costing, and Operations Costing   64

Chapter 4   Activity-Based Costing   102

Part 2   Costs and Decision Making   159

Chapter 5   Cost Behavior and Relevant Costs   140

Chapter 6   Cost-Volume-Profit Analysis and Variable Costing   174

Chapter 7   Short-Term Tactical Decision Making   214

Chapter 8   Long-Term (Capital Investment) Decisions   246

Part 3   Planning, Performance, Evaluation, and Control   293

Chapter 9   The Use of Budgets in Planning and Decision Making   294

Chapter 10   Variance Analysis—A Tool for Cost Control and Performance Evaluation   336

Chapter 11   Decentralization and Performance Evaluation   372

Chapter 12   Performance Evaluation Using the Balanced Scorecard   412

Part 4   The Impact of Management Decisions   443

Chapter 13   The Strategic Use of Managerial Accounting Information   444

Chapter 14   Internal Control, Corporate Governance, and Ethics   470

Part 5   Other Topics   497

Chapter 15   Financial Statement Analysis   498

Chapter 16   The Statement of Cash Flows   530

Glossary   557

Company Index   562

Subject Index   563

Contents

Chapter 1   **Accounting Information and Managerial Decisions**   2

Introduction   4
Accounting Information   4
Knowledge Management Tools   5
    Data and Knowledge Warehouses   5
    Enterprise Resource Planning Systems   6
    Electronic Data Interchange   7
The Users of Accounting Information   8
    External Users   8
    Internal Users   9
The Functional Areas of Management   10
    The Operations and Production Function   10
    The Marketing Function   10
    The Finance Function   10
    The Human Resource Function   10
The Role of the Managerial Accountant   11
The Information Needs of Internal and External Users   11
An Introduction to Decision Making   11
A Decision-Making Model   13
    Step 1: Define the Problem   13
    Step 2: Identify Objectives   13
    Step 3: Identify and Analyze Available Options   13
    Step 4: Select the Best Option   14
Relevant Factors and Decision Making   14
Risk and Decision Making   15
Ethics and Decision Making   15

Part 1   The Costing of Products and Services   25

Chapter 2   **Product Costing: Manufacturing Processes, Cost Terminology, and Cost Flows**   26

Introduction   28
Manufacturing, Merchandising, and Service Companies   28
The Production Process   28
    Manufacturing in a Traditional Environment   28
    Manufacturing in a JIT Environment   29
Product Costs in a Manufacturing Company   31
    Direct Materials   32
    Direct Labor   32
    Manufacturing Overhead   33
Nonmanufacturing Costs   33
Life-Cycle Costs and the Value Chain   34
Cost Flows in a Manufacturing Company-Traditional Environment with Inventory   35

The Cost-of-Goods-Sold Model for a Traditional Manufacturing Company with Inventory 36
Cost Flows in a Manufacturing Company—JIT Environment 41
Merchandising Companies and the Cost of Products 42
Service Companies and the Cost of Services 43
Product Costs and Period Costs 43

Chapter 3   Job Costing, Process Costing, and Operations Costing 64

Introduction 66
Product-Costing Systems 66
    Job Costing 66
    Process Costing 67
    Operations Costing 67
Basic Job-Order Costing for Manufacturing and Service Companies 68
    Measuring and Tracking Direct Material 68
    Measuring and Tracking Direct Labor 70
    Manufacturing Overhead 71
Cost Drivers and Overhead Rates 71
    Plantwide Overhead Rates 72
    Departmental Overhead Rates 73
The Use of Estimates 75
    Predetermined Overhead Rates 76
    The Problem of Over- and Underapplied Overhead 77
Basic Process Costing 80
Backflush Costing 81
Appendix—Additional Topics in Process Costing 83
    First-In, First-Out (FIFO) 84
    Weighted Average Method 85

Chapter 4   Activity-Based Costing 102

Introduction 104
Activity-Based Costing 104
    Unit-, Batch-, Product-, and Facility-Level Costs 105
    Stage 1- Identification of Activities 105
    Stage 2- Identification of Cost Drivers 106
ABC and Just in Time (JIT) 106
Cost Flows and ABC 108
Traditional Overhead Allocation and ABC-An Example 108
Topsail's Stage 1: Identification of Activities 110
Topsail's Stage 2: Identification of Cost Drivers and Allocation of Costs 110
ABC Systems in Service Industries 114
ABC and Nonmanufacturing Activities 114
Benefits and Limitations of ABC 115

Part 2 Costs and Decision Making 139

Chapter 5   Cost Behavior and Relevant Costs 140

Introduction 142
The Behavior of Fixed and Variable Costs 142

The Cost Equation 145
Cost Behavior and Decision Making 145
Step Costs 147
Mixed Costs 148
    Separating Mixed Costs into Their Fixed and Variable Components 149
Regression Analysis 151
    Using a Spreadsheet Program to Perform Regression Analysis 151
    Regression Statistics 154
    Other Uses of Regression Analysis 155
Estimating Regression Results Using the High/Low Method 155
Cost Behavior, Activity-Based Costing, and Activity-Based Management 156
Relevant Costs and Cost Behavior 156
The Impact of Income Taxes on Costs and Decision Making 157
    Taxes and Decision Making 157
    After-Tax Costs and Revenues 157
Before- and After-Tax Income 158

Chapter 6 Cost-Volume-Profit Analysis and Variable Costing 174

Introduction 176
The Contribution Margin Income Statement 176
    Contribution Margin per Unit 177
    Contribution Margin Ratio 179
The Contribution Margin and Its Uses 179
What-If Decisions Using CVP 180
    Option 1- Reduce Variable Costs 180
    Option 2- Increase Sales Incentives (Commissions) 181
    Option 3- Increase Advertising 182
Changes in Price and Volume 182
Changes in Cost, Price, and Volume 183
Break-Even Analysis 185
Break-Even Calculations with Multiple Products 186
Break-Even Calculations Using Activity-Based Costing 188
Target Profit Analysis (Before and After Tax) 189
The Impact of Taxes 190
Assumptions of CVP Analysis 191
Costing Structure and Operating Leverage 192
    Operating Leverage 192
Variable Costing for Decision Making 194

Chapter 7 Short-Term Tactical Decision Making 214

Introduction 216
Special Orders 216
Outsourcing and Other Make-or-Buy Decisions 218
    Strategic Aspects of Outsourcing and Make-or-Buy Decisions 219
    The Make-or-Buy Decision 220
The Decision to Drop a Product or a Service 223
Resource Utilization Decisions 224
The Theory of Constraints 226
Decisions to Sell or Process Further 227
ABC Relevant-Cost Analysis 229

Chapter 8 Long-Term (Capital Investment) Decisions 246

Introduction 248
Focus on Cash Flow 248
Discounted Cash Flow Analysis 249
Net Present Value 250
Internal Rate of Return 251
The Problem of Uneven Cash Flows 252
Screening and Preference Decisions 253
The Impact of Taxes on Capital Investment Decisions 256
An Extended Example 259
The Impact of Uncertainty on Capital Investment Decisions 261
Sensitivity Analysis 262
The Impact of the New Manufacturing Environment on Capital Investment Decisions 262
The Payback Method 263
Appendix: Time Value of Money and Decision Making 265
    Future Value 265
    Present Value 268
    Annuities 273

Part 3 Planning, Performance, Evaluation, and Control 293

Chapter 9 The Use of Budgets in Planning and Decision Making 294

Introduction 296
The Budget Development Process 296
    Budgets for Planning, Operating, and Control 296
    Advantages of Budgeting 298
The Master Budget 298
Budgeting for Sales 300
Operating Budgets–An Example 301
    Production Budget 301
    Material Purchases Budget 303
    Direct Labor Budget 305
    Manufacturing Overhead Budget 305
    Selling and Administrative Expense Budget 308
Cash Budgets 308
    Why Focus on Cash? 308
    The Cash Receipts Budget 309
    The Cash Disbursements Budget 309
    Summary Cash Budget 310
Budgeted Financial Statements 312
Budgets for a Manufacturing Company in a JIT Environment 316
Budgets for Merchandising Companies and Service Companies 316
Nonfinancial Budgets 316
Budgeting in an International Environment 316
Static versus Flexible Budgets 317
ABC and Flexible Budgets 319

Chapter 10 Variance Analysis—A Tool for Cost Control and Performance Evaluation 336

Introduction 338
Standard Costing 338
    Ideal versus Practical Standards 339
Use of Standards by Nonmanufacturing Organizations 340
Flexible Budgeting with Standard Costs 340
    Sales Volume Variance 341
    Flexible Budget Variance 342
    Sales Price Variance 343
Variable Manufacturing Cost Variances 343
    Analyzing Variable Manufacturing Cost Variances 345
    Direct Material Variances 345
Direct Labor Variances 347
Variable Overhead Variances 348
Fixed Overhead Variances 350
Overhead Variance Analysis Using Activity-Based Costing 351
Selling and Administrative Expense Variance 352
Interpreting and Using Variance Analysis 353
    Management by Exception 354
    Interpreting Favorable and Unfavorable Variances 354
    Behavioral Considerations 355

Chapter 11 Decentralization and Performance Evaluation 372

Introduction 374
Management of Decentralized Organizations 374
Responsibility Accounting and Segment Reporting 376
Cost, Revenue, Profit, and Investment Centers 376
Profit Center Performance and Segmented Income Statements 378
    The Segmented Income Statement 379
    Segment Performance and Activity-Based Costing 381
Investment Centers and Measures of Performance 381
    Return on Investment 382
    Residual Income 385
    ROI vs. Residual Income 386
    Economic Value Added (EVA) 386
    Decentralization and Performance Evaluation in a Multinational Company 389
Performance and Management Compensation Decisions 390
    Cash Compensation 390
    Stock-Based Compensation 391
    Noncash Benefits and Perks 392
    Measuring and Rewarding Performance in a Multinational Environment 392
Segment Performance and Transfer Pricing 393
General Model for Computing Transfer Prices 393
    International Aspects of Transfer Pricing 395

Chapter 12 Performance Evaluation Using the Balanced Scorecard 412

Introduction 414
    The Balanced Scorecard 414

Financial Perspective 415
Customer Perspective 415
Internal Business Perspective 415
Learning and Growth Perspective 415
Measuring and Controlling Quality Costs 416
The Costs of Quality 418
Minimizing Quality Costs 419
Measuring and Controlling Environmental Costs 422
Environmental Costing 423
Productivity 425
Efficiency and Timeliness 426
Marketing Effectiveness 428
A Summary of Key Nonfinancial Measures of the Balanced Scorecard 429

Part 4 The Impact of Management Decisions 443

Chapter 13 The Strategic Use of Managerial Accounting Information 444

Introduction 446
Strategy and Creating a Competitive Advantage 446
Pricing of Products and Services 447
    Economic Concepts and Pricing 447
    Costs and Pricing 447
    Target Pricing 448
    Cost-Plus Pricing 449
    Time and Material Pricing 451
    Value Pricing 451
    Other Pricing Policies 451
    Legal and Ethical Issues in Pricing 451
Cost Management and Strategy 452
    The Value Chain 452
    Supply-Chain Management 454
    Customer Relationship Management 456
    Activity-Based Management and the Value Chain 457

Chapter 14 Internal Control, Corporate Governance, and Ethics 470

Introduction 472
Fraud 472
    Sarbanes-Oxley Act of 2002 472
Types of Fraud 473
    Misappropriation of Assests 475
Causes of Fraud 476
    Situational Pressures and Incentives 477
    Opportunities 477
    Personal Characteristics and Attitudes 478
Combating Fraud 478
Internal Control 479
    Control Environment 480

Risk Assessment 481
Control Activities 481
Information and Communication 482
Monitoring 482

The Impact of Information Technology on Internal Control 482

Corporate Governance 484

The Need for Ethics 486
Ethics Programs 487
Codes of Ethics 487
Responding to Ethics Violations 489

Part 5 Other Topics 497

Chapter 15 Financial Statement Analysis 498

Introduction 500

Why Analyze Financial Statements? 500
Limitations of Financial Statement Analysis 501
The Impact of Inflation on Financial Statement Analysis 501

Horizontal Analysis 501

Vertical Analysis 505

Ratio Analysis 507
Ratio Analysis and Return on Investment 507
Current Ratio 508
Acid-Test Ratio 509
Cash Flow from Operations to Current-Liabilities Ratio 509
Accounts Receivable Analysis 511
Inventory Analysis 511
Cash-to-Cash Operating Cycle Ratio 513
Debt-to-Equity Ratio 513
Times-Interest-Earned Ratio 513
Debt Service Coverage Ratio 513
Cash Flow from Operations to Capital Expenditures Ratio 514
Return on Assets 515
Return on Common Stockholders' Equity 516
Earnings per Share 517
Price Earnings Ratio 517

Chapter 16 The Statement of Cash Flows 530

Introduction 532

Purpose of the Statement of Cash Flows 532
The Composition of the Statement of Cash Flows 532
Operating Activities 533
Investing Activities 533
Financing Activities 533

The Definition of Cash: Cash and Cash Equivalents 535

Noncash Transactions 535

Cash Flows from Operating Activities 536
Direct Method 536
Indirect Method 537

The Statement of Cash Flows and the Accounting Equation 537

Preparing the Statement of Cash Flows 538
        Direct Method 540
        Indirect Method 541

Using the Cash Flow Statement in Decision Making 545

Cash Flow Adequacy 545

Glossary 557

Company Index 562

Subject Index 563

About the Authors

Steve Jackson, C.P.A.

Steve Jackson, C.P.A., is an Associate Professor at Loyola University New Orleans, where he is the accounting area chairperson. He earned a Ph.D. from Arizona State University and a B.S. from the University of Montana.

Professor Jackson has published articles in such refereed journals as *Journal of Accounting and Finance Research, Journal of Economic and Social Measurement, Journal of Economic and Business Perspectives, Journal of Business and Economic Research, Accounting Educators Journal,* and *Journal of Accountancy.* His research interests are in accounting education and behavioral issues. He has more than 20 years of teaching experience and has held faculty positions at Northern Arizona University, Western New England College, the University of Southern Mississippi, the University of Southern Maine, and the University of Tennessee at Martin. Dr. Jackson has taught courses in managerial and strategic cost management, auditing and assurance, and financial accounting at both the undergraduate and graduate levels.

Professor Jackson has received numerous teaching awards, including three excellence-in-teaching awards while a doctoral student at Arizona State University. He was named outstanding faculty member by the University of Southern Mississippi Gulf Coast Accounting Society. He was the recipient of the Faculty Senate Intellectual Contributions award while at the University of Southern Maine and the Excellence in Research award at the University of Tennessee at Martin.

Dr. Jackson's professional activities include membership in the American Institute of Certified Public Accountants, the American Accounting Association, the Institute of Management Accountants, and the Institute of Internal Auditors. He is a former staff accountant with Touche Ross & Co. in Seattle and has more than 12 years of public accounting experience.

Professor Jackson and his wife Cheryl live in D'Iberville, Mississippi. They have three grown children, Christina, Kent, and Benjamin, and a grandson Charles.

Roby Sawyers, C.M.A., C.P.A.

Roby Sawyers, C.M.A., C.P.A., is Professor of Accounting at North Carolina State University. He earned a Ph.D. from Arizona State University, a master's in accounting from the University of South Florida, and a B.S.B.A. from the University of North Carolina at Chapel Hill.

Professor Sawyers has published articles in a variety of journals, including *Journal of Accountancy, Journal of Business Ethics, Journal of the American Taxation Association, Advances in Taxation, National Tax Journal, The Tax Adviser, Tax Notes, The CPA Journal,* and *Auditing: A Journal of Practice and Theory.* He is a contributing author of *Advanced Business Entity Taxation* and was the primary author of a monograph on the future of the estate tax, published by the American Institute of Certified Public Accountants. His research interests include individual behavior and decision making in a variety of contexts, as well as corporate ethics. He has more than 15 years of teaching experience and has taught courses in managerial and cost accounting, strategic cost management, individual and business taxation, and the taxation of estates, gifts, and trusts.

Professor Sawyers has served as a visiting professor in the International Management Program at the IESEG School of Management, Catholic University, Lille, France, and as an adjunct professor at the University of North Carolina at Chapel Hill. He has also taught or developed a variety of continuing education courses for the American Institute of CPAs, the Institute of Management Accountants, McGladrey and Pullen, LLP, BDO Seidman, LLP, and PricewaterhouseCoopers. He has received awards for both outstanding teaching and outstanding extension service from the College of Management at North Carolina State University.

Dr. Sawyers' professional activities include membership in the American Accounting Association, the Institute of Management Accountants, and the American Taxation Association. He has served as an appointed member of the American Institute of CPAs tax division and as chair of the AICPA Trust, Estate and Gift Tax Technical Resource Panel. He is a member of the North Carolina Association of CPAs, and he has worked in public accounting and in providing tax and consulting services to a variety of individual and business clients.

Professor Sawyers lives with his wife and daughter in Raleigh, North Carolina.

Greg Jenkins, C.P.A.

Greg Jenkins, CPA, is Associate Professor of Accounting at North Carolina State University. He earned a Ph.D. from Virginia Polytechnic Institute and State University, and an M.S. in accounting and a B.S.B.A. from Appalachian State University.

Professor Jenkins has published articles in *Auditing: A Journal of Practice and Theory, Internal Auditing, Journal of Accountancy, Journal of Business and Economic Perspectives, Journal of Forensic Accounting, Strategic Finance, The Journal of Applied Business Research,* and *The CPA Journal.* His primary research interests include auditor judgment and behavior and business ethics. He is also a co-author of *Comprehensive Assurance & Systems Tool*, an integrated practice set, and the author of *The Enron Collapse*. He has more than ten years of teaching experience and has taught courses in accounting information systems, undergraduate and graduate auditing, business ethics, managerial and financial accounting principles, and survey of accounting. Professor Jenkins has received the University Outstanding Teacher Award at North Carolina State University and is a member of the Academy of Outstanding Teachers.

Dr. Jenkins' professional activities include membership in the American Accounting Association and the American Institute of Certified Professional Accountants. He previously served as an auditor with Ernst & Young, LLP, and McGladrey & Pullen, LLP, and he has provided consulting services to the furniture industry.

Professor Jenkins lives with his wife and two daughters in Raleigh, North Carolina.

Managerial Accounting

Chapter 1 Accounting Information and Managerial Decisions

The main focus of accounting is decision making. In fact, the American Accounting Association defines accounting as "the process of identifying, measuring and communicating economic information to permit informed judgments and decisions by users of information" *(A Statement of Basic Accounting Theory, 1966, 1).* All organizations—large and small; manufacturing, merchandising, or service; profit or nonprofit—have a need for accounting information. The primary role of accounting is to provide useful information for the decision-making needs of investors, lenders, owners, managers, and others both inside and outside the company. However, the needs of internal users and external users often differ. This chapter defines accounting information and its application by both external and internal users. We also introduce the concept of knowledge management—the process of formally managing information and knowledge resources in order to facilitate access and reuse of that information and knowledge. Information and knowledge resources may vary for each company but include traditional sources of data provided by the accounting information system, as well as internal memos, training manuals, and information customers and suppliers supply. The chapter then describes the decision-making role of management in planning, operating, and controlling and provides a framework for assessing decisions that managers of organizations commonly face. The chapter also provides a discussion of the role of relevant factors, risk, and ethics as they pertain to decision making.

Learning Objectives

After studying the material in this chapter, you should be able to:

1. Define the uses and users of accounting information and the demand for effective information and knowledge management in the business environment

2. Explain the use and benefits of knowledge warehouses, enterprise resource planning systems, and electronic data interchange as knowledge management tools

3. Compare and contrast managerial accounting with financial accounting and distinguish between the information needs of external and internal users

4. Describe the three primary activities of managers

5. Identify the primary functional areas of an organization

6. Explain the role of the managerial accountant

7. Apply a basic four-step decision-making model

8. Recognize the role of relevant factors in decision making

9. Recognize the role of risk in decision making

10. Recognize the significance of ethics in decision making

Introduction

Business environments have changed dramatically in the past few decades. Companies of all sizes can now compete in a dynamic global marketplace through electronic commerce (e-business) and other emerging technologies. Downsizing, combined with a more mobile workforce, has placed a premium on retaining talented, knowledgeable employees. Customers demand specialized products and services and real-time information concerning product availability, order status, and delivery times. Suppliers need information on their buyers' sales and inventory levels in order to tailor their production schedules and delivery times to meet the buyers' demands. Shareholders demand greater value from their investments. Although these changes have provided opportunities for those companies able to adapt and take advantage of them, they have also resulted in challenges. Above all else, these changes require more effective management of knowledge within an organization. In today's business environment, knowledge is power and must be managed for companies to remain competitive.

Although sometimes used interchangeably, the term *knowledge* should not be confused with *data* or *information*. Companies generate literally tons of **data**—financial statements, customer lists, inventory records, and the number and type of products and services sold. However, translating that data into an accessible and usable form is another matter. When data are organized, processed, and summarized, they become **information.** When that information is shared and exploited so that it adds value to an organization, it becomes **knowledge.**

> **KEY CONCEPT**
>
> *Data become information when organized, processed, and summarized and information becomes knowledge when it is shared and exploited to add value to an organization.*

All types of organizations, from large multinational manufacturing companies like Ford Motor Company to small custom-furniture manufacturers, have a need for accounting information. Retailers, such as Wal-Mart and locally owned hardware stores; large service companies, such as FedEx and local CPA and law firms; and even nonprofit organizations, such as the American Red Cross and small local museums and homeless shelters, need accounting information. Accounting information is used by internal managers in their day-to-day decision making and also by external users, such as investors, creditors, donors, and even the Internal Revenue Service.

Accounting Information

Objective 1

Define the uses and users of accounting information and the demand for effective information and knowledge management in the business environment

Accounting information is provided by a company's **accounting information system (AIS).** Traditionally, the AIS was simply a transaction processing system that captured financial data resulting from accounting transactions. For example, the AIS would document a transaction to purchase materials by recording a journal entry showing the date of purchase, an increase to raw materials inventory, and a corresponding increase to accounts payable or decrease in cash.

Under this view of AIS, accounting information was simply financial information (sales, net income, total assets, costs of products, etc.) expressed in terms of dollars or other monetary units (e.g., yen, euros, pesos). Other nonfinancial information—such as (1) the number of units of materials or inventory on hand, (2) the number of budgeted labor hours to produce a product, (3) the number of units necessary to break even, and (4) the time it takes to manufacture a product—were likely collected and processed outside the traditional accounting information system. The use of multiple information systems within a company causes a number of problems. It is costly to support multiple systems. Perhaps more important, it is difficult to integrate information coming from various systems and to make decisions for a company with multiple sources of information. In addition, other useful transaction information—such as the quality of the material purchased, the timeliness of its delivery, or customer satisfaction with an order—might not be captured at all and therefore not evaluated by management.

Over the past few years, **enterprise resource planning (ERP) systems** have been developed in an attempt to address these shortcomings. ERP systems integrate the traditional AIS with other information systems to capture both quantitative and qualitative data, to collect and organize that data into useful information, and to transform that information into knowledge that can be communicated throughout an organization.

Throughout our study of accounting information and its use in decision making, the importance of considering both quantitative and qualitative information is emphasized. In order to provide managers with the information they need to make effective business decisions, financial data must be linked to nonfinancial data, transformed into useful information and knowledge, and communicated throughout an organization (see Exhibit 1-1).

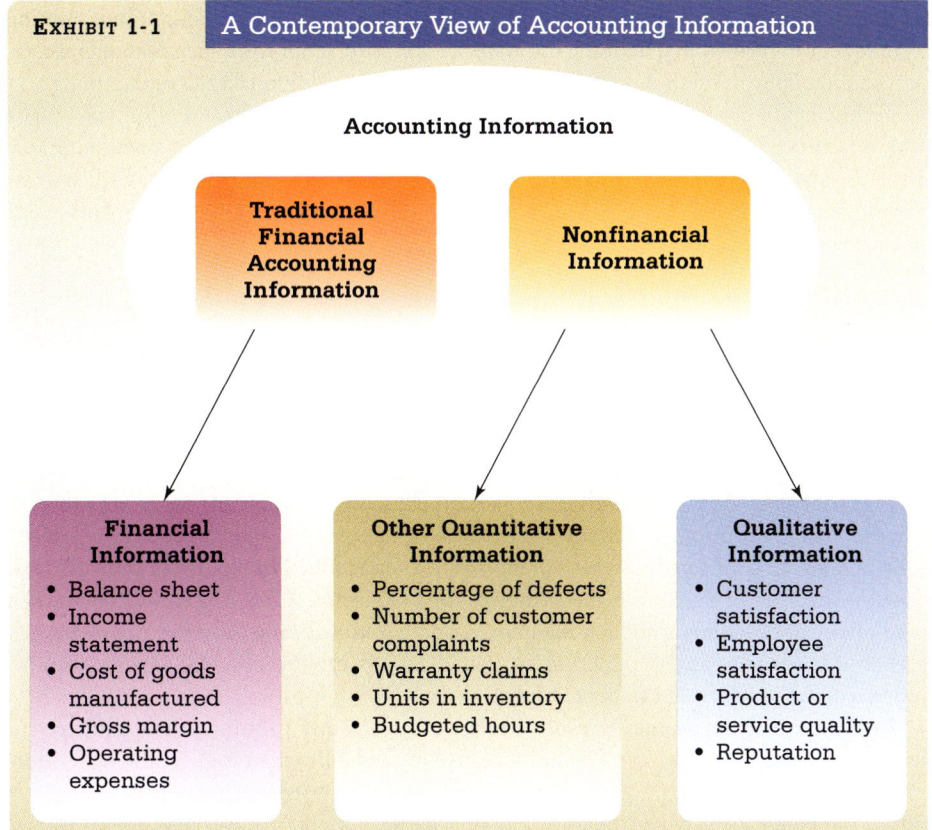

EXHIBIT 1-1 A Contemporary View of Accounting Information

Accounting information includes both financial and nonfinancial information used by decision makers.

Knowledge Management Tools

Effective knowledge management can result in faster and better business decisions, leading ultimately to increased profitability through better strategic planning, more timely development of products and completion of projects, improved customer service, and cost savings. A variety of knowledge management tools, including data and knowledge warehouses, enterprise resource planning systems, and electronic data interchange (EDI) facilitate effective knowledge management.

Data and Knowledge Warehouses

Data warehouses are simply central depositories for electronic data. Data warehouses often contain many years of transactions, which can be accessed and browsed electronically. Although data warehouses contain the ingredients for good business decisions, turning that data into information and knowledge requires other tools. A variety of technological tools are available to help managers uncover the information they need to make business decisions. The term **data mining** was coined as a way to express, in modern-day technical terms, how a manager can search for and extract information from the corporate computer system, much like a coal miner searches for and extracts coal from a mine. Data mining software is used to help find business opportunities in large amounts of data. For example, every time you make a purchase using a value card at a grocery store, the grocery store collects data on what you purchase, how much you purchase, whether you use coupons, and whether you pay with cash, check, or credit card. Data-mining software looks for data patterns that can be used to help

Objective 2

Explain the use and benefits of knowledge warehouses, enterprise resource planning systems and electronic data interchange as knowledge management tools

managers make decisions concerning product placement, product pricing, inventory management, and advertising campaigns.

Knowledge warehouses are organized to provide access to a wide variety of qualitative data. Memos, news articles, client and customer notes, product specifications, documentation of problem resolution, employee information (education, skills, and specialty areas), and competitor intelligence may all be part of a searchable knowledge warehouse. Data-mining techniques can be used to determine the available skill set of employees, identify untapped expertise and opportunities for growth, and identify needs for additional skills and training.

Technological tools, such as Lotus Notes, were traditionally used to store this type of data and to facilitate its access and use. Today, Web-based tools, such as Internet newsgroups, are often used to collect and to share knowledge. As discussed in the next section, ERP systems are another tool enabling organizations to gather information and to disseminate knowledge to their employees.

Enterprise Resource Planning Systems

Companies use enterprise resource planning (ERP) systems to collect, organize, report, and distribute data throughout an organization and to transform that data into the usable knowledge necessary for managers to make informed business decisions. These systems typically integrate payroll, purchasing, sales, manufacturing, inventory, product costing, and billing, providing a more comprehensive view of the organization.

An ERP system digitally records every business transaction a company makes, regardless of whether it is input through accounting, purchasing, sales, or manufacturing, and automatically updates all connected systems to reflect each transaction. This approach provides real-time information to decision makers throughout a company. When a sales associate on the road places an order for a product, the information is automatically conveyed to purchasing, accounts receivable, and production so that materials can be ordered, invoices can be processed, and production can be scheduled.

ERP systems help businesses evolve from data generators to information gatherers to knowledge creators and sharers. The ultimate goal of the ERP system is to get the right information to the right people at the right time. With better knowledge management, an organization can better identify its strengths, pinpoint its weaknesses, uncover new opportunities, capitalize on trends, and make better business decisions.

When used effectively, ERP systems can allow an organization to achieve higher levels of profitability. They can provide more accurate and complete information, resulting in reduced purchasing and manufacturing costs, reduced customer response time, increased quality of products and services, increased customer satisfaction, and better business decisions. The benefits of ERP are not limited to manufacturing companies. Service organizations have also come to realize the increased benefits of ERP systems. Organizational efficiencies, such as improved customer service and better communication, provide benefits to all types of companies.

Although ERP systems have provided benefits to many companies, they are not without their costs. ERP systems tend to involve large-scale financial, human resource, time, and information technology costs. When glitches occur in the systems, the results can be disastrous. In 1999, Hershey Foods (the nation's largest candy producer) went online with its $112 million ERP system designed to track raw ingredients, schedule production, set prices, measure the effectiveness of promotional campaigns, schedule delivery, and decide how to stack products inside trucks. However, glitches in the system left many distributors and retailers with empty candy shelves in the season leading to Halloween. At one point, Hershey could not even tell what had been shipped or to whom it had been shipped ("Hershey's Biggest Dud Has Turned Out to be New Computer System," *Wall Street Journal*, October 29, 1999, A1).

ERP systems are generally not meant to solve business inefficiencies. Rather, they can point to where inefficiencies exist within an organization and allow corporate decision makers to take appropriate corrective measures. A number of companies have reengineered their business processes through involvement with ERP systems, resulting in substantial returns from their ERP investments.

The success of an ERP system usually depends on how quickly it can provide useful information for managerial decision making. This need favors rapid implementation, which shortens the time needed to recapture the investment. However, the average implementation time of a system is 23 months. In addition, it can take up to two years after implementation for a company to achieve a quantifiable return on investment.

Many small corporations have been reluctant to invest in ERP systems, owing to the high cost and the implementation time involved. However, several of the larger ERP system vendors have begun to market scaled-down versions of their ERP packages in order to tap the small- to medium-sized-company market. Companies that either could not afford ERP systems in the past or were merely too small to integrate the applications can now compete with their larger counterparts.

ERP Systems

Historically, the implementation of ERP systems in service companies and small and midsize companies of all types has lagged behind that of manufacturing companies and very large companies. While 85 percent of Fortune 1000 companies have implemented ERP systems, ERP implementation has been much slower in smaller companies. A survey conducted in 2001 indicated that while 40 to 50 percent of manufacturing companies were utilizing ERP software systems, less than 15 percent of health care, insurance, utility, and government organizations had operational ERP systems at that time. However, sales of ERP systems are expected to increase sharply over the next several years. Much of the growth is expected to come from midsize companies, government agencies, and industries related to health care as these organizations replace outdated systems ("Rebound seen for resource management software," by Dawn Kawamoto, CNET News.com, May 17, 2004).

Electronic Data Interchange

Electronic data interchange (EDI) allows suppliers and customers to be brought into the ERP network so that online orders from customers initiate a series of highly integrated transactions that ultimately fulfill the request—from materials acquisition to manufacturing to shipping. EDI is simply the electronic transmission of data, such as purchase orders and invoices. Although originally limited to large companies with a direct data connection or companies on the same network, the Internet has made EDI technology available to a wide range of medium and small businesses. EDI has several benefits. It increases the speed and quality of information exchange, reduces lead times, and reduces processing costs. For example, Nabisco estimates that the cost of processing a paper-based purchase order is $70, whereas the same transaction performed through EDI costs less than $1 (Millman, Howard, "A Brief History of EDI," *Infoworld*, April 6, 1998, 83).

Knowledge management tools such as knowledge warehouses, enterprise resource planning systems and electronic data interchange can reduce costs and result in faster and better decisions.

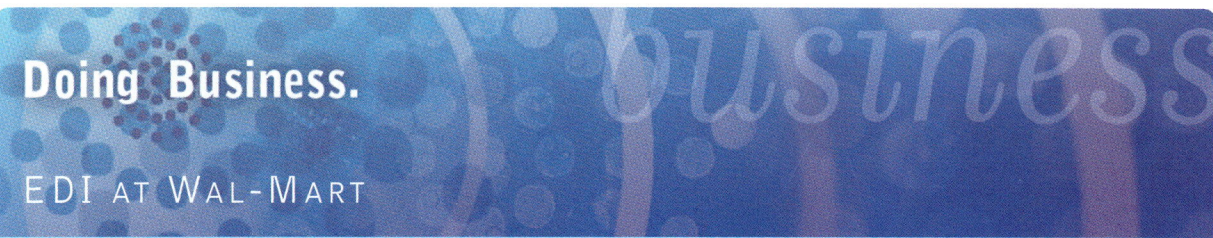

EDI at Wal-Mart

Wal-Mart Stores, Inc. pioneered the idea of retailer and supplier sharing sales data. Wal-Mart shares data on sales, profit margin, and inventory levels with more than 7,000 suppliers that access Wal-Mart's database 120,000 times per week ("Wal-Mart Expands Access to Product Sales History," *Wall Street Journal*, August 18, 1999, B8).

Objective 3

Compare and contrast financial accounting with managerial accounting and the information needs of external and internal users

The Users of Accounting Information

Financial accounting is the area of accounting primarily concerned with the preparation of general use financial statements for use by creditors, investors, and other users outside the company (external users). On the other hand, **managerial accounting** is primarily concerned with generating financial and nonfinancial information for use by managers in their decision-making roles within a company (internal users). This information typically is not shared with those outside the company. While both financial accounting information and managerial accounting information is generated from the same AIS, the information is used in a variety of ways by different users.

External Users

Stockholders, potential investors, creditors, government taxing agencies and regulators, suppliers, and customers are all **external users.** What type of information do external users need? Stockholders and potential investors want information to help them analyze the current and future profitability of an organization. Companies that have issued stock to the public (or those that plan to) provide this information in the form of annual reports, registration statements, prospectuses, and other reports issued to shareholders, potential investors, and the Securities and Exchange Commission (SEC). The information required in these reports and the accounting methods used to prepare them are governed by the Financial Accounting Standards Board (FASB) and SEC. Although this information is primarily financial (sales and net income), it also may include nonfinancial information, such as units shipped and market share. It also may include qualitative information, such as Management's Discussion and Analysis of Financial Condition and Results of Operations, which is found in annual reports.

What about smaller companies that are owned by just a few members of a family (called closely held) or nonprofit organizations, such as the Red Cross? External users of financial information, such as banks or potential donors to nonprofit organizations, still need accounting information to make the proper decision about lending or donating money. However, their needs may differ from those of stockholders and potential investors. Creditors generally want to assess a company's overall financial health and may be particularly interested in a company's cash flow or ability to repay their loans. Potential contributors to nonprofit organizations may have a need for both financial information, such as how much of the Red Cross's budget is spent for charitable purposes, and nonfinancial information, such as how many women with children are served by the local homeless shelter.

Government agencies (federal, state, and local) have very specific information needs, including the measurement of income, payroll, and assets for purposes of assessing taxes. This accounting information is typically provided on income tax returns, payroll reports, and other forms designed specifically to meet the requirements of each agency.

Generally, accounting information provided to shareholders, creditors, and government agencies is characterized by a lack of flexibility (its content is often dictated by the user), the reporting of past events using historical costs (financial statements for the previous three years), and an emphasis on the organization as a whole.

Automobile manufacturers must provide suppliers with detailed inventory records so that parts, such as these engine blocks, can be provided on a timely basis.

Suppliers and customers are also external users. However, their accounting information needs are likely to be very different from those of other external users and may be more clearly aligned with the needs of internal users. For example, suppliers of car parts to General Motors need detailed information on inventory levels of specific parts in order to know when to manufacture and ship parts. Bank customers may want to check on their account or loan balances before making a major purchase. Someone buying a new computer may want to check on the expected delivery date or whether a product is back-ordered before placing an order. This type of information needs to be much more detailed and timely than that provided to most other external users.

Internal Users

Internal users of accounting information include individual employees as well as teams, departments, regions, and top management of an organization. For convenience, these internal users are often referred to as managers. Managers are involved in three primary activities—commonly referred to as planning, operating, and controlling.

Planning involves the development of both the short-term (operational) and the long-term (strategic) objectives and goals of an organization and an identification of the resources needed to achieve them. **Operational planning** involves the development of short-term objectives and goals (typically, those to be achieved in less than one year). Examples of operational planning for Ben & Jerry's include planning the raw material and production needs for each type of ice cream for the next four quarters or determining the company's short-term cash needs. Operational planning for a hospital would include budgeting for the number of physicians, nurses, and other staff needed for the upcoming month or determining the appropriate level of medical supplies to have in inventory. Operational planning also involves determining short-term performance goals and objectives, including meeting customer service expectations, sales quotas, and time budgets.

Strategic planning addresses long-term questions of how an organization positions and distinguishes itself from competitors. For example, Ben & Jerry's strategy for producing high-quality ice cream is very different from that used for producing a store brand of lower-priced ice cream. Long-term decisions about where to locate plants and other facilities, whether to invest in new state-of-the-art production equipment, and whether to introduce new products or services and enter new markets are strategic planning decisions. Strategic planning also involves the determination of long-term performance and profitability measures, such as market share, sales growth, and stock price.

Operating activities encompass what managers must do to run the business on a day-to-day basis. Operating decisions for manufacturing companies include whether to accept special orders, how many parts or other raw materials to buy (or whether to make the parts internally), whether to sell a product or process it further, whether to schedule overtime, which products to produce, and what price to charge. Other operating decisions affecting all organizations include assigning tasks to individual employees, whether to advertise (and the corresponding impact of advertising on sales and profits), and whether to hire full-time employees or to outsource.

Controlling activities involve the motivation and monitoring of employees and the evaluation of people and other resources used in the organization's operations. The purpose of control is to make sure that the goals of the organization are being attained. It includes using incentives and other rewards to motivate employees to accomplish an organization's goals and mechanisms to detect and correct deviations from those goals. Control often involves the comparison of actual outcomes (cost of products, sales, etc.) with desired outcomes as stated in the organization's operating and strategic plans. Control decisions include questions of how to evaluate performance, what measures to use, and what types of incentives to implement. For example, a company that emphasizes high-quality products and excellent customer service may evaluate and reward production workers who have exceeded goals based on these virtues (such goals, for example, may involve specifying the percentage of allowable defective units or scrap, monitoring customer complaints, or myriad other factors).

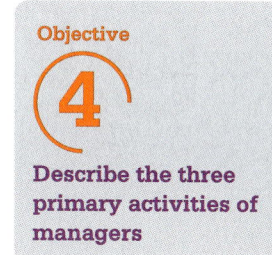

> **Objective 4**
> Describe the three primary activities of managers

> **KEY CONCEPT**
> *The three primary activities of managers are planning, operating and controlling.*

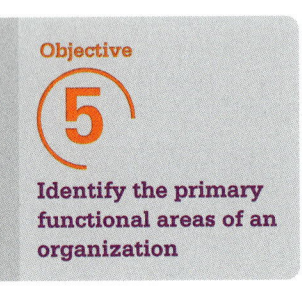

The Functional Areas of Management

Managers are found in all functional areas of an organization, including operations/production, marketing, finance and human resources. Although managers rely on the same information provided to external users, they have other needs as well.

The Operations and Production Function

The **operations and production function** produces the products or services that an organization sells to its customers. Production and operations managers are concerned with providing quality products and services that can compete in a global marketplace. They need accounting information to make planning decisions affecting how and when products are produced and services are provided. They need to know the costs of producing and storing products in order to decide how much inventory to keep on hand. They need to know the costs of labor when making decisions to schedule overtime to complete a production run or when deciding how many physicians are needed in the emergency room. These decisions are also influenced by information provided by the marketing managers, including the expected customer reaction if products are not available when orders are placed or if doctors are not available when patients need them.

Operations and production managers have been forced by a global economy and increasing customer demands to change the methods used to provide products and services. As a consequence, they have placed demands on accounting information systems to provide even more timely and accurate information for decision making as well. The information provided by accounting information systems is continually evolving to meet the demands of its users.

The Marketing Function

The **marketing function** is involved with the process of developing, pricing, promoting and distributing goods and services sold to customers. Marketing managers need to know how much a product costs in order to help establish a reasonable selling price. They need to know how a given advertising campaign and its resulting impact on the number of units sold is expected to affect income. They need to know how enhancing a product's features or changing its packaging will influence its cost. Commissions paid to sales representatives may be based on a company's profits. All these marketing decisions require accounting information.

The Finance Function

The **finance function** is responsible for managing the financial resources of the organization. Finance managers make decisions about how to raise capital as well as where and how it is invested. Finance managers need accounting information to answer such questions as whether money should be raised through borrowing (issuing bonds) or selling stock. Finance managers make decisions concerning whether a new piece of manufacturing equipment should be purchased or leased and whether a plant expansion should be paid for in cash or by borrowing money from the bank.

The Human Resource Function

Although all managers who supervise, motivate, and evaluate other employees are human resource managers, the **human resource function** is concerned with the utilization of human resources to help an organization reach its goals. More specifically, human resource managers support other functions and managers by recruiting and staffing, designing compensation and benefit packages, ensuring the safety and overall health of personnel, and providing training and development opportunities for employees. These decisions require input from all other functional areas. What kind of accounting information do human resource managers need? Human resource decisions, such as hiring new employees, are often made under budget constraints. Ensuring safe workplaces for employees may involve the redesign of manufacturing processes. Accountants can provide information regarding the cost of the redesign. The decision to train employees to use new equipment may require an analysis of the costs and benefits of the new program.

Objective 5

Identify the primary functional areas of an organization

The Role of the Managerial Accountant

What is the role of the managerial accountant in providing information to this diverse group of internal users? Managerial accountants have traditionally been thought of as the bean counters or number crunchers in an organization. However, advances in accounting information systems and other changes in the past five or ten years have resulted in the automation of traditional accounting functions involving data collection, data entry, and data reporting and a corresponding shifting of those functions from management accounting to clerical staff.

As a result, managerial accountants in many companies now focus on analyzing information and creating knowledge from that information rather than collecting data. Managerial accountants have become decision-support specialists who see their role as interpreting information, putting it into a useful format for other managers, and facilitating management decision making ("Counting More, Counting Less: The 1999 Practice Analysis of Management Accounting," Institute of Management Accountants).

Objective 6
Explain the role of the managerial accountant

KEY CONCEPT
Managerial accountants facilitate management decision making.

The Information Needs of Internal and External Users

As you can see, the information needs of internal users and external users differ in significant ways. Due to the varying needs of internal users, managerial accounting is more flexible than financial accounting. While financial accounting is geared toward the preparation of financial statements and other reports according to generally accepted accounting principles (GAAP) and other rules, managerial accounting can be customized to a specific company or segment of a company. While financial accounting is primarily concerned with reporting on the company as a whole, managerial accounting emphasizes the various segments of a company such as divisions, departments, sales regions, and product lines.

Because of the decision focus of internal managers, managerial accounting information must focus on the future rather than the past. Planning is an integral part of the manager's job. In order to plan effectively, managers need up-to-date information. While the timeliness of information is paramount, managerial accounting information frequently is less precise than financial accounting information and frequently includes the use of estimates.

Exhibit 1-2 summarizes the external and internal users of accounting information, the type of information typically needed by these users, and the source of the information.

KEY CONCEPT
The information needs of external users and internal users differ in significant ways.

An Introduction to Decision Making

Although the problems and questions facing marketing, production, finance, and human resource managers of organizations differ, the decision-making process that they follow is remarkably uniform. In fact, it is the same decision-making model that you are likely to use when making nonbusiness decisions. Do you remember the decision-making process you went through the last time you made a major decision? It could have been a decision to purchase or sell a car, a computer, or a stereo system. It could have been a decision to attend a particular college, accept a summer job, or perhaps even get married.

Decisions have many variables or factors that must be considered. If you were making a decision to purchase a car, you would consider such variables as its cost, features, color, and financing options. If you were making a decision about what college to attend, factors might include the cost, proximity to your home, and academic reputation. Different decision makers might even consider different factors for the same decision situation. For example, the color of a car may not be important to one buyer but critical to another. The number and type of variables considered might differ for each individual and for each decision the individual makes.

Decisions may have to be made under time, budget, or other constraints. Your choice of a car may be limited to those that cost under $10,000. Your decision to accept a summer job may be limited to those that are within 30 miles of your home. Your decision to attend a college may have to be made by a certain date. In addition, many decisions are made with

Exhibit 1-2 External and Internal Users of Accounting Information

	Users	Type of Accounting Information Needed	Source
External	Shareholders and creditors	Sales, gross profit, net income, cash flow, assets and liabilities, earnings per share, etc. Although this information is primarily financial, it may also include nonfinancial information (units in inventory). This information is often provided in summary form (for the company as a whole) and typically is historical in nature.	Annual reports, financial statements, and other available documents
External	Government agencies	Varies by agency but includes taxable income, sales, assets, comparisons of actual expenditures to budgets, etc. This information is usually provided for the company as a whole and is historical in nature. It can include both financial and nonfinancial information.	Tax returns and other reports
External	Customers and suppliers	Order status, shipping dates, inventory levels, etc. This information must be very detailed and timely to be useful.	Limited-access databases available to specific customers and suppliers
Internal	Marketing, operations and production, finance, and human resource managers	Timely and detailed information on sales and expenses, product costs, budget information, and measures of performance. Often includes nonfinancial data (direct labor hours, units to break even, etc.). Accounting information is often needed for segments of an organization and is more likely future oriented than historical.	Cost reports, budgets, and other internal documents

missing information or at least with imperfect information. In deciding which car to buy, you would probably want to consider the cost of future repairs for various models. Although you might estimate these costs by using such sources as *Consumer Reports,* you will not know the costs with certainty. Decisions may not be perfect, but they should be the best you can make given the information that is available to you at the time. The process you go through is to gather all the information you can to reduce the risk of an incorrect or less than optimal decision.

Decisions often lead to other decisions. Once you have decided to buy a car or a stereo, you need to make other decisions, such as whether to pay cash or to finance the purchase or whether to buy an extended warranty. It does seem as though life is a never-ending string of decisions.

Decision making is the process of identifying different courses of action and selecting one appropriate to a given situation. All decisions require using judgment. The quality of the decision often depends on how good that judgment is. Judgment refers to the cognitive aspects of the decision-making process. By cognitive, we mean taking a logical, thinking approach to making decisions rather than just making decisions on the spur of the moment. In this section of the chapter, we learn how to structure a decision problem so that we will use better judgment when making decisions.

A Decision-Making Model

In this chapter, we discuss decision problems in general and how to gather as much relevant information as possible to reduce the risk of incorrect decisions. The decision-making model presented here will allow you to approach complex decisions in an orderly fashion.

Using a basic decision-making model does not guarantee that all our decisions will be correct, but it will allow us to increase the odds of making a good decision. A lot of decisions have more than one acceptable solution, as do a lot of the problems and cases in this textbook. The trick is to pick the *best* solution for each particular decision-making situation.

Exhibit 1-3 shows a four-step decision-making model that we will use throughout this book. Each step is described in the following paragraphs.

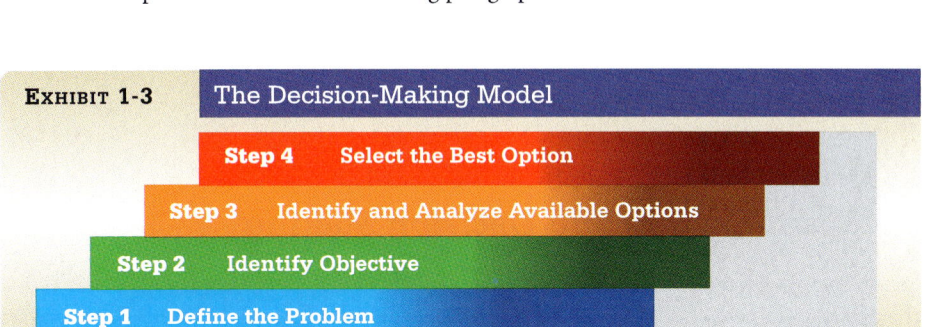

Objective 7

Apply a basic four-step decision-making model

EXHIBIT 1-3   The Decision-Making Model

- Step 4   Select the Best Option
- Step 3   Identify and Analyze Available Options
- Step 2   Identify Objective
- Step 1   Define the Problem

Step 1: Define the Problem

When faced with a problem, the first step is to define it accurately. Managers (and students) often act without a clear understanding of the real problem. In fact, many bad decisions are made simply because the decision maker is trying to solve the wrong problem. For example, a company experiencing a reduction in sales might erroneously define the problem as low sales volume (and attempt to solve the problem by providing increased sales incentives) when the real problem is poor quality of the product sold. Problem definition requires the cooperation of managers in all functional areas of an organization. Whereas a single manager might focus on the reduction in sales, input by accounting, operations, marketing, and sales managers will most likely result in a clearer picture of the underlying problem (poor quality) causing the reduction in sales. Defining the problem may lead to even further refinements, such as identifying the specific type of material that is causing the quality problem. Accurately defining a problem requires a willingness to listen to others, good judgment, and lots of practice.

Step 2: Identify Objectives

The second step in the decision-making process is to identify the objectives in finding a solution to the problem. Objectives may be **quantitative** (to buy at the best price or to increase net income), **qualitative** (to buy the highest-quality component or to increase customer satisfaction), or a combination of the two.

Step 3: Identify and Analyze Available Options

The third step in the decision-making process is to identify the options available to achieve your objectives and analyze those options. This step requires the consideration of relevant variables affecting the problem and of alternative courses of action. Most decisions require the decision maker to consider more than one option and multiple variables. These variables should include both quantitative and qualitative factors. The key here is to identify only the variables that are relevant to a particular decision.

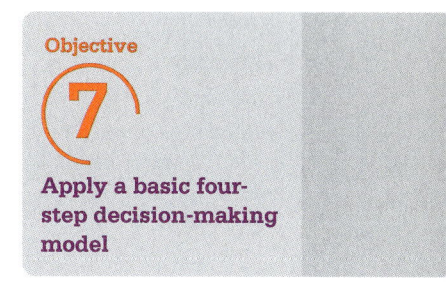

KEY CONCEPT

Never make decisions with just the numbers! Always consider nonnumerical (qualitative) information.

Step 4: Select the Best Option

The fourth and last step is to select the best option. We need to answer the question of how well each of our options will achieve our objective or objectives. This is sometimes the most difficult step in the process. Just as our options and variables included both quantitative and qualitative factors, our solution should consider both as well. As a general rule, you should never make decisions based only on quantitative information. Often, qualitative information is at least as important as or more important than quantitative information.

At this stage, the decision maker must also recognize that decisions are often made in the face of uncertainty. This step in the decision process will involve our preference for risk and our estimate of what chance the future events have of happening. The impact of risk on decision making is discussed more completely on the next page.

Once we have completed the preceding process and chosen the best option, we must then implement our decision and evaluate the results. We may have to go back to Step 1 and repeat the process if the decision turns out to be less than optimal.

Relevant Factors and Decision Making

Objective 8: Recognize the role of relevant factors in decision making

Step 3 in our decision-making model was to identify and analyze relevant factors affecting the decision. How do decision makers determine whether a factor is relevant? Relevant factors are those that affect a particular decision. Therefore, they must be factors that differ between alternatives. In deciding between automobiles, if they all have the same options at the same cost (air conditioning, CD player, etc.), those options are not relevant to the decision. Very often, costs are key factors that must be considered in decisions. As with other factors, **relevant costs** are those that differ between alternatives. Another way to view relevant costs is to identify those that are avoidable or can be eliminated by choosing one alternative over another. In choosing between automobiles, if one car has air conditioning and another does not, the cost of air conditioning is relevant because choosing one of the alternatives could eliminate that cost.

Sunk costs are costs that have already been incurred. Because sunk costs cannot be avoided, they are not relevant in decisions. In your decision to trade in your old vehicle, the amount that you paid for it may appear to be important. However, because that cost is sunk, it cannot be avoided, is not relevant, and should not be considered in your decision.

As another example, assume you are the production manager of a company and that you have the opportunity to purchase a new piece of equipment that can reduce the cost of making a product by 30 percent. However, your boss says that you can't buy the new equipment until the old equipment is fully depreciated in two more years. Is the depreciation on the old machine a relevant cost? As was the case in the previous scenario, the cost of the old equipment (and the corresponding depreciation) is a sunk cost, cannot be avoided, is not relevant, and should not be considered in the decision.

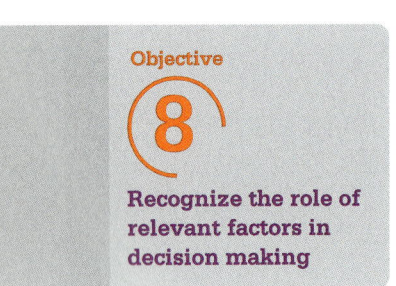

If sunk costs are not relevant, what about other costs that will be incurred in the future? Are all costs that are not sunk relevant? Again, the key is that relevant costs are avoidable costs. If future costs do not differ between alternatives, they are not avoidable (they will be incurred regardless of the alternative chosen) and therefore are not relevant. In your choice of an automobile, if the cost of an option is the same, that cost is not relevant in your decision.

Opportunity costs are the benefits forgone by choosing one alternative over another and are relevant costs for decision-making purposes as well. For example, in choosing to go to college, you are forgoing the salary you could receive by working full time. Almost all alternatives have opportunity costs. In choosing to work instead of going to school, the opportunity cost is the higher salary that you might earn if you choose to go to school. Opportunity costs are sometimes difficult to quantify but nevertheless should be considered in making decisions (see Exhibit 1-4).

KEY CONCEPT

Sunk costs are not relevant.

KEY CONCEPT

Future costs that do not differ between alternatives are not relevant.

KEY CONCEPT

Opportunity costs are relevant.

EXHIBIT 1-4   Relevant and Irrelevant Costs

Relevant Costs		Irrelevant Costs	
Future costs that differ among alternatives	Opportunity costs—benefits that are forgone by choosing one alternative over another	Future costs that do not differ among alternatives	Sunk costs—costs that have already been incurred

Risk and Decision Making

As mentioned earlier, most decisions involve **risk.** A decision maker's goal is to consider (and possibly to minimize) the risk of decisions. One of the factors that comes into play when selecting the best option (Step 4) is the attitude toward risk. If the decision makers are risk seekers, they will rate the alternatives one way. If they are risk averse, they will probably rate the alternatives differently. For example, risk-averse decision makers may rate more highly an automobile that has been in production a couple of years and has a history of being reliable than a brand new model with no track record.

A quantitative method of considering the risk of decision factors is by adjusting the discount rate used in time value of money calculations (see Chapter 8 for a more detailed discussion of this important concept). Cash flows occurring farther in the future might be discounted at a higher interest rate than cash flows occurring in the next year or two. Increasing the interest rate in present-value calculations has the impact of decreasing the present value of those cash flows.

A second way of adjusting for risk is by considering the probability that certain events will occur. For example, in the choice of an automobile, the interest rate on the loan may be an important factor. However, a particular dealer may not guarantee the interest rate before the loan is approved. Knowing that the probability of the rate's changing is 50 percent, you can adjust the rating accordingly to take this risk into account.

A third method of considering risk is through **sensitivity analysis.** Sensitivity analysis is the process of changing the values of key variables considered in the analysis to determine how sensitive decisions are to those changes. For example, if the purchaser of an automobile is not 100 percent sure of qualifying for the best possible loan package at all the dealers, he or she may want to consider the cost of that automobile, taking into account all possible finance packages. If this adjustment changes the decision, the decision is sensitive to changes in that variable. If it does not change the decision, the decision is not sensitive to that variable.

Objective 9

Understand and evaluate the role of risk in decision making

Ethics and Decision Making

Business managers make ethical decisions each and every day. While some might point out that business decisions are simply a matter of economics, there are also ethical dimensions to most of these decisions. In today's business environment, companies not only have to be aware of the economic impact of their decisions, but also the ethical impact. For example, in the late 1990s, Nike encountered a firestorm of controversy related to its overseas manufacturing operations. Reports by CBS recounted some of the conditions in Nike's Vietnamese and Indonesian facilities including the payment of below minimum wages, physical abuse of employees by supervisors, and the forced running of laps by employees who wore nonregulation shoes to work. During the height of the controversy Nike's stock price plunged by more than 40 percent, sales decreased, customers cancelled orders, and numerous colleges and universities ended relationships with Nike. In light of Nike's experience, it is difficult to justify the view that business decisions are merely economic ones.

Ethical problems arise in organizations for a variety of reasons. For example, undue pressure to achieve short-term productivity and profitability goals may lead to unethical behavior

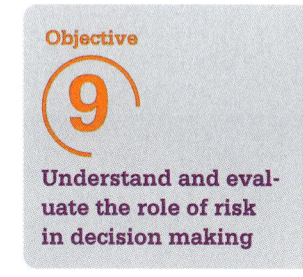

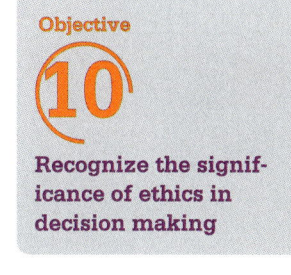

Objective 10

Recognize the significance of ethics in decision making

such as requiring employees to work long hours that exceed limits set by state and federal agencies, intentionally ignoring product safety concerns, and falsifying accounting records or other documentation. Such unethical behavior often occurs in corporate environments in which employees feel as though they have no choice but to follow their superiors' orders and directives. Strictly adhering to an organizational hierarchy can be problematic when employees blindly follow orders.

Famed economist Milton Friedman once made the point that the only social responsibility of corporations was to increase their profits. Further, he stated that business managers should not be expected to make socially responsible decisions because they are not trained to do so. Given the world in which we now live, this perspective is, to say the least, antiquated. Managers simply cannot make business decisions without carefully considering their ethical dimensions. As you continue this study of managerial accounting, thoughtfully consider how managers can use information for both good and bad. Doing so will increase the likelihood that you will be prepared to make informed and ethical choices as a business manager.

Hitting the Bottom Line.

THE "SHELL" GAME LEADS TO RESTATEMENT

In early 2004, a report issued by Royal Dutch/Shell's audit committee and outside attorneys found that engineers and other managers within Shell dramatically overstated the company's oil and gas reserves. The company announced that it was revising downward its oil and natural gas reserves for 2002 and 2003 by almost 5 billion barrels of oil. These revelations not only had a negative impact on the company's reputation, but also negatively impacted its financial statements and share price. The following table provides data to show the effects of the restatement on net income.

	2003	2002	2001	2000
Effect of restatement on net income	($130 million)	($100 million)	($40 million)	($90 million)

Within the first week of 2004, the price of Royal Dutch shares fell from $52.75 to $48.61 and the price of Shell shares fell from $51.69 to $45.29 ("Report of Davis Polk & Wardwell to the Shell Group Audit Committee," available at www.shell.com).

Summary of Key Concepts

- *Data become information when organized, processed, and summarized and information becomes knowledge when it is shared and exploited to add value to an organization. (p. 4)*
- *Accounting information includes both financial and nonfinancial information used by decision makers. (p. 5)*
- *Knowledge management tools such as knowledge warehouses, enterprise resource planning (ERP) systems and electronic data interchange (EDI) can reduce costs and result in faster and better decisions. (p. 7)*
- *The three primary activities of managers are planning, operating, and controlling. (p.9)*
- *Managerial accountants facilitate management decision making. (p. 11)*
- *The information needs of external users and internal users differ in significant ways. (p. 11)*

- *Never make decisions with just the numbers! Always consider nonnumerical (qualitative) information. (p. 14)*
- *Sunk costs are not relevant. (p. 14)*
- *Future costs that do not differ between alternatives are not relevant. (p. 14)*
- *Opportunity costs are relevant. (p. 14)*

Key Definitions

Accounting information system (AIS) A transaction processing system that captures financial data resulting from accounting transactions within a company (p. 4)

Enterprise resource planning (ERP) systems Systems used to collect, organize, report, and distribute organizational data and transform that data into critical information and knowledge (p. 4)

Data Reports, such as financial statements, customer lists, and inventory records (p. 4)

Information Data that have been organized, processed, and summarized (p. 4)

Knowledge Information that is shared and exploited so that it adds value to an organization (p. 4)

Data warehouses Central depositories for electronic data (p. 5)

Data mining A process of searching for and extracting information from data (p. 5)

Knowledge warehouses Used to store and provide access to a wide variety of qualitative data (p. 6)

Electronic data interchange (EDI) The electronic transmission of data, such as purchase orders and invoices (p. 7)

Financial accounting The area of accounting primarily concerned with the preparation and use of general use financial statements for use by creditors, investors, and other users outside the company (p. 8)

Managerial accounting The area of accounting primarily concerned with generating financial and nonfinancial information for users by managers in their decision-making roles within a company (p. 8)

External users Stockholders, potential investors, creditors, government taxing agencies, regulators, suppliers, customers, and others outside the company (p. 8)

Internal users Individual employees, teams, departments, regions, top management, and others inside the company—often referred to as managers (p. 9)

Planning The development of both the short-term (operational) and the long-term (strategic) objectives and goals of an organization and an identification of the resources needed to achieve them (p. 9)

Operational planning The development of short-term objectives and goals (typically, those to be achieved in less than one year) (p. 9)

Strategic planning Addresses long-term questions of how an organization positions and distinguishes itself from competitors (p. 9)

Operating activities The day-to-day operations of a business (p. 9)

Controlling activities The motivation and monitoring of employees and the evaluation of people and other resources used in the operations of the organization (p. 9)

Operations and production function Produces the products or services that an organization sells to its customers (p. 10)

Marketing function Involved with the process of developing, pricing, promoting and distributing goods and services sold to customers (p. 10)

Finance function Responsible for managing the financial resources of the organization (p. 10)

Human resource function Concerned with the utilization of human resources to help an organization reach its goals (p. 10)

Decision making The process of identifying alternative courses of action and selecting an appropriate alternative in a given decision-making situation (p. 12)

Quantitative Can be expressed in terms of dollars or other quantities (units, pounds, etc.) (p. 13)

Qualitative Deals with nonnumerical attributes or characteristics (p. 13)

Relevant costs Those costs that differ between alternatives (p. 14)

Sunk costs Costs that have already been incurred (p. 14)

Opportunity costs The benefits forgone by choosing one alternative over another (p. 14)

Risk The likelihood that an option chosen in a decision situation will yield unsatisfactory results (p. 15)

Sensitivity analysis The process of changing the values of key variables to determine how sensitive decisions are to those changes (p. 15)

Multiple Choice

1. Which of the following statements is true?
    a. Production managers find managerial accounting information useful.
    b. Marketing managers would not find managerial accounting information useful.
    c. Corporate managers rarely consider managerial accounting information in their decision-making process.
    d. The costs of managerial accounting information often exceed the benefits.

2. Customers in today's competitive marketplace demand information about:
    a. product availability
    b. order status
    c. delivery times
    d. all of the above

3. Which of the following definitions is correct?
    a. Data that are organized and summarized become knowledge.
    b. Data that are shared and add value to the company create knowledge.
    c. Information that is shared and leveraged such that it creates value is the foundation of knowledge.
    d. None of the above statements is correct.

4. Data and knowledge warehouses are examples of:
    a. operating systems
    b. knowledge management tools
    c. accounting information systems
    d. Internet facilities

5. Which of the following statements regarding ERP systems is not true?
    a. ERP systems provide real-time information to decision makers throughout a company.
    b. The ultimate goal of the ERP system is to reduce production costs.
    c. ERP systems are costly to implement.
    d. The benefits of ERP are not limited to manufacturing companies

6. Which of the following statements about EDI is not true?
    a. EDI increases lead times and reduces processing costs.
    b. The Internet has made EDI technology available to a wide range of small- and medium-size businesses.
    c. EDI increases the speed and quality of information exchange.
    d. EDI and e-business via the Internet allow suppliers and customers to be brought into an ERP network so that online orders from customers initiate a series of highly integrated transactions.

7. Managerial accounting information is:
   a. generated based on generally accepted accounting principles.
   b. used extensively by internal managers for decision-making purposes.
   c. commonly shared with external parties such as stockholders.
   d. primarily geared toward the preparation of financial statements.

8. Operational planning most commonly addresses:
   a. long-term investment decisions related to production equipment.
   b. measurement of growth in market share.
   c. the current quarter's production requirements.
   d. each of the above planning issues.

9. The _____ function is primarily responsible for managing the financial resources of the organization.
   a. finance
   b. marketing
   c. accounting
   d. human resources

10. Advances in accounting information systems and other changes in the past decade have resulted in managerial accountants to view their roles as including:
    a. the interpretation of information.
    b. creation of useful information for other managers.
    c. facilitators of management decision-making processes.
    d. each of the above roles.

11. Which of the following sequences of steps in the decision-making process is correct?
    a. define the problem, identify objectives, identify and analyze available options, select the best option
    b. identify objectives, define the problem, identify and analyze available options, select the best option
    c. select the best option, identify objectives, define the problem, identify and analyze available options
    d. define the problem, identify and analyze available options, select the best option

12. Relevant costs:
    a. will not differ between decision alternatives.
    b. include those costs that are avoidable when one alternative is chosen rather than another.
    c. have already been incurred and cannot be avoided regardless of a future decision.
    d. should either be considered or ignored based on the circumstances.

13. Opportunity costs:
    a. are never relevant in a decision-making context.
    b. may include costs that have already been incurred and will not change as a consequence of future decisions.
    c. are often difficult to quantify, but should be considered in a decision-making context.
    d. include all past costs regardless of their nature.

14. Most decisions involve risk. Which of the following is true with respect to considering risk in a decision-making context?
    a. Risks cannot be controlled and should be given only minimal attention when making decisions.
    b. Risks are present in most business contexts, but managers generally do not revise plans to counteract those risks.
    c. Risks should be evaluated and their impact on decision alternatives carefully weighed before final decisions are made.
    d. Each of the above statements is true.

15. Which of the following statements about ethics is true?
    a. Business decisions are solely economic and do not require consideration of ethical issues.
    b. Ethical issues frequently arise in decision-making contexts.
    c. Companies can and should operate without consideration to the ethical implications of their decisions.
    d. None of the above statements is true.

Concept Questions

16. *(Objective 1)* Discuss the relationships among data, information, and knowledge.
17. *(Objective 2)* Discuss how ERP systems can enhance effective knowledge management.
18. *(Objective 3)* What is the primary purpose of financial accounting and managerial accounting?
19. *(Objective 4)* Define strategic and operational planning.
20. *(Objective 5)* Briefly describe the role of the finance function within an organization.
21. *(Objective 6)* Why has the role of the managerial accountant changed in recent years?
22. *(Objective 7)* Briefly describe the decision-making model discussed in the chapter.
23. *(Objective 8)* Define sunk costs and opportunity costs, and discuss their importance in decision making.
24. *(Objective 9)* How can managers "adjust" for risk?
25. *(Objective 10)* "Businesses must first do well before they can do good." Do you agree or disagree with the preceding statement? Why or why not?

Exercises

26. Accounting information is used by a variety of individuals and organizations for numerous purposes. Below is a small set of potential users of accounting information.
    a. Bank loan officer
    b. An employee labor union
    c. Production manager
    d. Current stockholder
    e. Sales manager
    f. Company president

    Required

    Identify the types of accounting information that may be of interest to each of the above potential users. Be specific if possible.

27. It is often said that "accounting is the language of business." If that statement is true, business students should be knowledgeable about that language. Consider the following terms commonly used in accounting and business contexts.

Enterprise resource planning system	Sunk costs
Information	Data warehouse
Electronic data interchange	Knowledge warehouse
Data mining	Knowledge
Operational planning	Sensitivity analysis
Opportunity costs	

    Required

    Choose the term from the list above that most appropriately completes the following statements.

a. Frequently containing many years of transactions, a _____ often serves as a central depository for electronic data.
b. _____ is the process of changing the values of key variables considered in an analysis to determine how sensitive decisions are to those changes.
c. Managers who actively search for and extract data and information from computer systems are said to be _____.
d. Data become _____ when organized, processed, and summarized.
e. _____ are costs that have already been incurred and cannot be changed regardless of future decisions.
f. Benefits forgone by choosing one alternative over another are typically called _____.
g. The ultimate goal of a(n) _____ is to get the right information to the right people at the right time.
h. Benefits of _____ include increased speed and quality of information exchange, reduced lead times, and reduced processing costs.
i. Client and customer notes, product specifications, documentation of problem resolution, new articles, and memos may all be part of a searchable _____.
j. Information becomes _____ when it is shared and exploited to add value to an organization.
k. Determining short-term objectives and goals is often called _____.

28. Knowledge management is an often used term in today's business environment. There is little question that some companies more effectively leverage their accumulated knowledge than others.

Required

Briefly describe the goal of "effective knowledge management." Provide an example of a company that has effectively leveraged knowledge and an example of a company that has not effectively leveraged knowledge.

29. Financial and managerial accounting information serve different purposes. The following phrases are commonly used to describe either financial or managerial accounting.

Must follow GAAP   Future orientation
Focused on past performance   Information is often "old"
Timeliness is critical   Reports results by segments
Emphasizes reporting on the whole company   Highly customizable
Information is often less precise

Required

Indicate whether each of the above phrases describes financial accounting or managerial accounting.

30. All business managers do not have the same information needs. Some require detailed production data, while others require detailed data about sales and marketing performance. Read the following statements that describe business managers.
a. These managers make decisions about how to raise capital as well as where and how it is invested.
b. These managers need to know how much a product costs in order to help establish a reasonable selling price.
c. These managers support other managers by recruiting and staffing, designing compensation and benefit packages, and providing training and development opportunities for employees.
d. These managers make decisions about how and when products and services are produced or provided.

Required

Identify the type of business manager described in each of the above statements.

31. A friend has informed you of an opportunity for a part-time job that you are considering accepting during your last semester before graduation. It would start at the beginning of your last semester and require working 20 hours per week at a rate of $15 per hour. It would also provide some good experience that could lead to a full-time job after graduation. However, it would require a 2-hour round-trip commute four days a week. In addition, you currently receive a monthly scholarship of $1,000 that stipulates that you cannot work off campus. Consequently, if you accept the job, you will have to give up the scholarship. You expect to register for 15 credit hours (five classes) during your last semester and have been told that each of the courses is very demanding. In addition to class time, you expect to study about 30 hours each week.

Required

Based on the decision-making model introduced in the chapter:
A. Define the problem you face in deciding whether to accept the job.
B. Based on your personal situation, define your objectives related to the problem you identified in part A.
C. What are your options? And, what factors are likely to be relevant in making your decision?
D. What opportunity costs are associated with the decision?
E. Is the decision risky? How would you take risk into account when making your decision?

32. Walter Meyer Inc. produces batteries for riding lawn mowers. The company provides the batteries to some of the largest manufacturers of riding lawn mowers in the United States. In the last few months, the company has received reports of batteries exploding from high heat. The incidents have all been in southern states and have occurred with only one particular brand and model of lawn mower. In these models, the batteries are installed beneath the seats of the mower. In more than one case, the exploding batteries have resulted in serious injuries. Meyer officials are aware of the potential danger, but have been unable to determine the cause of the problem. Some company officials think that the problem may be with the lawn mower and not with the batteries. Internal testing has been inconclusive.

Required

A. In your opinion, what responsibility does the company bear for the potential dangers of the battery?
B. Should company officials try to shift blame to the manufacturer of the lawn mower, as the problems are only with one particular brand of mower?
C. Discuss ethical considerations faced by company officials in this situation.

Problems

33. Technology has changed the way in which accounting information is generated and used. Today's accounting information systems generate vast amounts of data in a fraction of the time required a few years ago. Most companies now have access to technologies that were prohibitively expensive in the recent past. Today's fast-paced business environment has caused some business leaders to wonder whether accounting information is as relevant to decision making as it once was.

Required

A. Has e-commerce changed the role of accounting information? How?
B. Do you believe that accounting information is more or less relevant today than in the past? Why?

34. Effective knowledge management leads to faster and better business decisions. Two knowledge management tools that are commonly used today are data warehouses and knowledge warehouses. Although some may use these terms synonymously, they are not the same.

Required
- A. Describe data warehouses and knowledge warehouses.
- B. Data mining is a technique commonly used by companies to unlock the value in their data warehouses. Explain how data mining is accomplished.
- C. Give several examples of the ways in which information stored in knowledge warehouses can be used.

35. Imagine that you are home during a break from school and are talking to a friend about classes. You tell your friend, who is not a college student, that you are taking managerial accounting this term. Your friend says that she remembers you took accounting last term and wonders why you have to take another accounting course. You look a little perplexed and decide to give that question some thought.

Required

As you think about your friend's question, you decide to answer the following questions:
- A. Explain in a concise manner the differences between financial and managerial accounting.
- B. Why do the two types of accounting exist?
- C. Who are the users of financial accounting information? Who are the users of managerial accounting information?

36. You have an opportunity to choose a new car. After a lot of thought and research, you have narrowed your options to four different cars. Basic information about each car is presented in the following table:

	Car 1	Car 2	Car 3	Car 4
Base Price	$ 12,000	$ 13,000	$ 14,000	$ 15,000
Audio System	Radio ($250)	Radio, CD Player ($350)	Radio, CD Changer ($500)	Radio, CD Changer, Satellite Radio ($750)
Air Conditioning	None	$ 1,200	$ 1,250	$ 1,200
Automatic Transmission	$ 1,000	$ 1,200	$ 1,250	$ 1,500
Power Package	None	$ 850	$ 1,250	$ 500
Side Curtain Airbags	None	$ 1,400	$ 1,000	$ 1,150
Total Price (all options)	$ 13,250	$ 18,000	$ 19,250	$ 20,100

Required
- A. Define the decision problem that you face in choosing a car from among the options available to you.
- B. What are your objectives in choosing a car? Identify quantitative and qualitative objectives separately. What is the most important objective to you? Why?
- C. The decision model discussed in the chapter requires you to identify all available options (i.e., alternatives) as part of the decision-making process. Given your specific circumstances (e.g., lifestyle, geographic location, etc.), what are your available options in choosing a new car? What are the relevant quantitative and qualitative factors affecting these options?
- D. If you were to choose from among the four cars, which is the best choice? Why?
- E. How important are qualitative factors in choosing from among the four cars? Are qualitative factors more important than quantitative factors? Why?

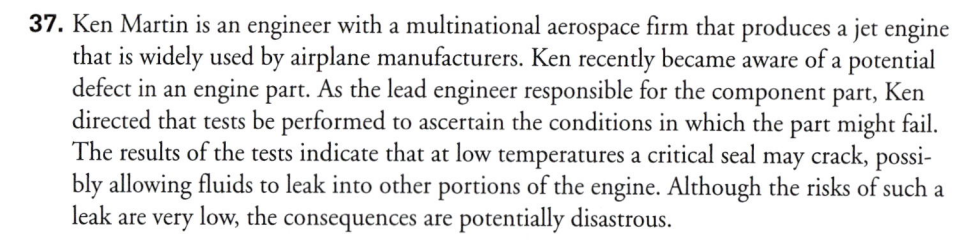

37. Ken Martin is an engineer with a multinational aerospace firm that produces a jet engine that is widely used by airplane manufacturers. Ken recently became aware of a potential defect in an engine part. As the lead engineer responsible for the component part, Ken directed that tests be performed to ascertain the conditions in which the part might fail. The results of the tests indicate that at low temperatures a critical seal may crack, possibly allowing fluids to leak into other portions of the engine. Although the risks of such a leak are very low, the consequences are potentially disastrous.

Required

A. What risks are involved in this scenario? Who bears these risks?
B. Does the company have a responsibility to "manage" risks for others (e.g., company stockholders, airline companies, and passengers) who may not be aware that such risks even exist?
C. Does the company have an ethical responsibility to fix the component part? Should the company consider the estimated cost of fixing the component part in its decision-making process? Why or why not?

Group and Internet Exercises

38. A variety of companies have developed enterprise resource planning software. One of the most well known of these companies is Oracle. On its website, Oracle provides customer stories that are intended to convince potential customers that Oracle's products and services can create significant value and cost savings for them. Visit Oracle's website and review some of these stories. Prepare a brief report of one to two pages that describes several of Oracle's success stories. Do you believe that sharing this type of information is an effective marketing technique for Oracle?

39. More companies than ever before conduct business with companies in other countries. For example, consider the following information: General Electric has more than 350,000 employees, half of whom live outside the United States. In 2003, the company earned more than 50 percent of its revenues, approximately $61 billion, from its international operations. Wal-Mart generates $50 billion in annual sales in some 1,500 international stores. McDonald's has more than 30,000 restaurants in over 100 countries with total global revenues of $17 billion. Some foreign countries have business cultures and ethical beliefs that are not consistent with those of the United States. In some cases, U.S. companies have found themselves faced with circumstances in which foreign government officials expected, or explicitly requested, that they be paid to allow the company to do business in the official's country. Within your group, discuss the ethicality of paying bribes to foreign government or foreign company officials. After discussing the issues surrounding the payment of bribes, prepare a short memo outlining your group's views.

Part 1: The Costing of Products and Services

Chapter 2 Product Costing: Manufacturing Processes, Cost Terminology, and Cost Flows

Chapter 3 Job Costing, Process Costing, and Operations Costing

Chapter 4 Activity-Based Costing

Chapter 2
Product Costing: Manufacturing Processes, Cost Terminology, and Cost Flows

Chapter 2 Product Costing: Manufacturing Processes, Cost Terminology, and Cost Flows

Product (and service) costing is important for both external users and managerial decision making. Externally, the cost of products must be known to value inventory and to determine the gross profit on sales. Internally, managers must know the costs of products and services for a variety of reasons, including making pricing decisions and budgeting for expected cash disbursements. The costing of products and services is described in Chapters 2, 3, and 4. Chapter 2 begins with a description of the production process for both traditional manufacturing companies with inventory and manufacturing companies with little or no inventory. The chapter also provides an introduction to basic cost terminology applicable to manufacturing companies, merchandising companies, and service providers and concludes with a description of cost flows in each type of company. In Chapter 3, we discuss systems that companies use to accumulate, track, and assign costs to specific products and services and some of the issues related to measuring and allocating overhead and other product costs. In Chapter 4, we discuss some of the problems inherent in traditional methods of overhead allocation and describe a contemporary costing system, called activity-based costing, that may be more appropriate for internal decision making.

Learning Objectives

After studying the material in this chapter, you should be able to:

1. Describe basic production processes used by manufacturing companies

2. Identify the benefits and potential costs of implementing a just-in-time (JIT) production system

3. Distinguish manufacturing costs from nonmanufacturing costs and classify manufacturing costs as direct materials, direct labor, or overhead

4. Diagram the flow of costs in manufacturing, merchandising, and service companies and calculate the cost of goods manufactured and cost of goods sold for each

5. Evaluate the impact of product costs and period costs on a company's income statement and balance sheet

Introduction

Regardless of the type of company involved, costs are associated with the products and services produced and sold. Although it might appear simple to determine the cost of a product or service, the process can be quite complicated, as you will see in the next few chapters. How should companies determine the costs of producing products and providing services? What costs should be included? Before we can answer these questions, we should also ask why companies want to determine their product costs. For example, a company might be preparing financial statements for a bank to use in determining whether to make a loan to the company or may be filing its income tax return for the year. Generally accepted accounting principles (GAAP) and tax laws govern costing for financial statement purposes and for tax purposes, respectively. On the other hand, a company might want to determine the cost of a particular product in order to determine its sales price or to estimate a product's profitability. Cost information is also helpful for budgeting and evaluation purposes. Costing for internal decision making is the focus of Chapters 2, 3, and 4.[1]

MANUFACTURING, MERCHANDISING, AND SERVICE COMPANIES

Every company provides a product or a service to customers and clients. **Manufacturing companies** (such as Toyota and Bassett Furniture) take raw materials and produce new products from them. **Merchandising companies** sell products that someone else has manufactured. Examples are large department stores, such as Wal-Mart and Target, as well as the independent record shop or clothing store on the corner. In contrast to manufacturing and merchandising companies, **service companies** do not sell a tangible product as their primary business. Service providers are the fastest-growing segment of the U.S. economy, employing roughly 75 percent of the workforce. Service providers include such diverse companies and industries as airlines, hospitals, automobile repair shops, brokerage firms, law firms, and CPA firms.

The Production Process

> **Objective 1**
>
> Describe basic production processes used by manufacturing companies

Manufacturing companies purchase raw materials from other companies and transform them into a finished product. This transformation typically requires labor and the incurring of other costs, such as utilities, the depreciation of factory equipment, or supplies. Manufacturing companies may produce a single product or many products. Likewise, companies may have only a few customers or many thousands. The process used to manufacture these products depends on the specific product or products made, the customers who buy the product(s), and the company itself. Some companies are very labor intensive, whereas others rely heavily on automation. Some companies choose to make very high quality products, whereas other companies emphasize low cost. Some companies choose to carry large amounts of inventory, whereas others manufacture their products in small batches and make their products just in time to meet customer demand.

Manufacturing in a Traditional Environment

Traditionally, the factory of a manufacturing company is organized so that similar machines are grouped together. For example, a furniture manufacturer might have areas devoted to cutting and rough sanding, shaping the cut lumber into furniture pieces (such as chair legs), using lathes and routers, drilling holes and dovetailing joints, assembling the furniture pieces, and finishing. As raw material (in this case, lumber) is processed in each area, it is "pushed" to the next area for further processing. Lumber is brought into the factory from the warehouse

---

[1] It should be noted that companies might want to cost other objects in addition to products. For example, a company might want to know the costs of a particular department or division or even the costs of servicing a particular customer.

and is cut and rough sanded according to specifications for specific products. It is then moved to another area in the factory for shaping the rough lumber into chair legs, bed posts, and tabletops. Next, the lumber might move to an area containing drill presses and machines to make dovetail joints. After drilling and jointing, it would be moved to still another area for assembly. In this area, workers glue or screw the various parts together and attach necessary hardware and glass. After assembly, the furniture is moved to an area where it is sanded again and varnish or paint finishes applied. It would not be unusual for one or more of these areas to be in different buildings or sometimes in entirely different plants. After leaving the finishing department, the furniture is ready for packing and selling to customers.

In this traditional system, it was normal (and perhaps even desirable) to accumulate **raw materials inventory** and finished-products inventory (called **finished-goods inventory**) to serve as buffers in case of unexpected demand for products or unexpected problems in production. It was also normal to accumulate inventories of partially completed products (called **work-in-process inventory,** or WIP). WIP might result, for example, when furniture pieces that have been drilled and jointed are pushed to the assembly area before the workers in that area are ready for them.

Traditional furniture manufacturers, such as this one, may have significant amounts of work in process inventory.

Manufacturing in a JIT Environment

One of the big changes affecting manufacturing companies in the past 20 years or so has been the adoption of **just-in-time (JIT) production systems.** In an effort to reduce costs and become more efficient producers, companies began to focus on the costs and problems associated with the traditional manufacturing facility and the practice of carrying large amounts of inventory.

Carrying large amounts of inventory results in storage and insurance costs. Traditional manufacturing systems may result in other, not-so-obvious problems, including the production of lower-quality products with more defects. The buffers that seem so desirable may in fact lead workers to pay less attention to detail and work less efficiently. In addition, the organization of factories in which similar machines are grouped together greatly increases the time necessary to manufacture products and makes it more difficult to meet special orders or unexpected increases in demand without having large amounts of inventory on hand.

In a just-in-time system, materials are purchased and products are made "just in time" to meet customer demand. Unlike traditional production, the process begins with a customer order, and products are "pulled" through the manufacturing process. Under ideal conditions, companies operating in a JIT environment would reduce inventories of raw materials, work-in-process, and finished goods to very low levels or even zero.

With only a small buffer of extra finished goods and raw materials, it is imperative that companies employing JIT be able to procure supplies and raw materials on a timely basis and

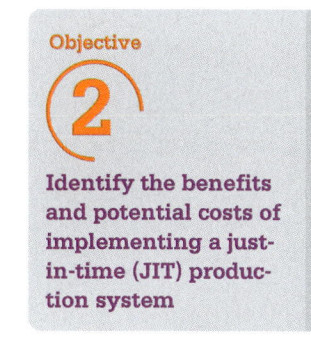

Objective 2

Identify the benefits and potential costs of implementing a just-in-time (JIT) production system

manufacture products very quickly. The first requires that companies work with suppliers that can deliver goods on time and free of defects. Typically JIT companies rely on only a few suppliers that have proven to be highly reliable. The latter often entails restructuring the factory itself. In the traditional factory, similar machines were often grouped together, resulting in raw materials and unfinished products being handled and moved a great deal from area to area. In the traditional factory, it also was difficult and time consuming to switch production from one product to another (from tables to chairs, for example) because the same machines were used for both. In contrast, factories in a JIT environment are typically organized so that all the machinery and equipment needed to make a product is available in one area. These groupings of machines are called manufacturing cells. The use of cells minimizes the handling and moving of products. It also reduces or eliminates setup time (the time needed to switch production from tables to chairs) because we now have one cell devoted just to the manufacture of tables and one cell devoted just to the manufacture of chairs. Sometimes, workers are trained to operate all the machinery in a manufacturing cell, increasing speed and efficiency even more. Dell Computer uses just-in-time manufacturing techniques to assemble build-to-order personal computers. As you can see in Exhibit 2-1, Dell can ship a computer to a customer within 12 hours of receiving an order. The actual assembly takes under 2 hours.

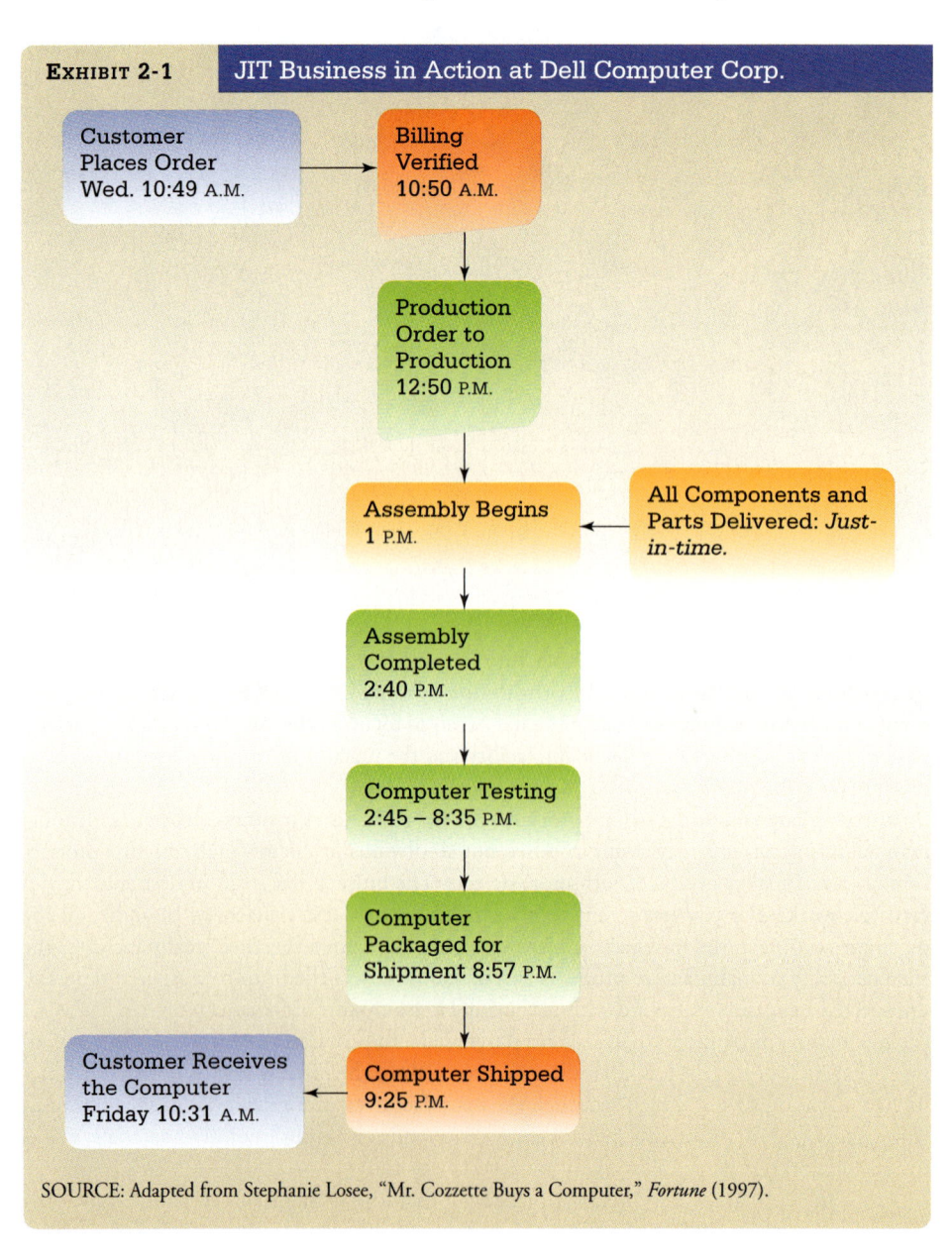

EXHIBIT 2-1 JIT Business in Action at Dell Computer Corp.

- Customer Places Order Wed. 10:49 A.M.
- Billing Verified 10:50 A.M.
- Production Order to Production 12:50 P.M.
- Assembly Begins 1 P.M. ← All Components and Parts Delivered: *Just-in-time.*
- Assembly Completed 2:40 P.M.
- Computer Testing 2:45 – 8:35 P.M.
- Computer Packaged for Shipment 8:57 P.M.
- Computer Shipped 9:25 P.M.
- Customer Receives the Computer Friday 10:31 A.M.

SOURCE: Adapted from Stephanie Losee, "Mr. Cozzette Buys a Computer," *Fortune* (1997).

While it is easy to think of JIT as simply an inventory management tool, JIT has other advantages as well:

1. Reducing the amount of time it takes to produce a product
2. Improving the quality of products by reducing the number of defective units
3. Increasing customer satisfaction
4. Increasing the motivation of the work force

However, JIT does have potential problems. Due to reduced batch sizes and purchasing materials in smaller amounts, some manufacturing costs may actually increase (although total costs are frequently reduced). In addition, disruptions in supply can wreak havoc on companies that rely on just-in-time purchasing of parts and supplies. These disruptions may result from strikes by factory workers of the supplier, natural disasters, and as discussed in "Doing Business," the unexpected closing of national borders when suppliers are located in other countries.

KEY CONCEPT

JIT is more than an inventory management tool

Doing Business.

TERRORIST ATTACKS WREAK HAVOC ON SUPPLY CHAINS

Disruptions in shipments of air freight and heightened security at border crossings following the World Trade Center terrorist attacks exposed one of the risks facing companies operating just-in-time factories. Without needed parts, several auto makers were forced to temporarily shut down assembly lines in the days immediately following the attacks. New transportation security rules enacted in October 2003 further tightened border security by requiring companies to provide the U.S. government with advance notification for incoming shipments of international cargo. These notification requirements range from 30 minutes for trucks to 24 hours for ships and may result in goods sitting in port waiting for approval and/or inspection. Companies must factor in the risks of the interruption of deliveries into the supply chain management process and either have an alternative source and/or have a buffer like that in a traditional manufacturing system. ("Flight Ban Slows 'Just in Time' Factories," *Wall Street Journal*, September 13, 2001, B3 and "Shippers Say New Border Rules Could Delay Just-in-Time Cargo," *Wall Street Journal*, August 29, 2003, A1)

Product Costs in a Manufacturing Company

Regardless of the size of the company involved, the number of products made, or the type of manufacturing system used, manufacturing companies must know how much their products cost. It is convenient to distinguish costs incurred in the manufacture of a product (manufacturing costs) from those incurred elsewhere in the company (nonmanufacturing costs). It is also useful to distinguish between direct and indirect costs. **Direct costs** are costs that are directly attached to the finished product and can be conveniently traced to the product. **Indirect costs** are costs that are attached to the product but cannot be conveniently traced to each separate product. **Manufacturing costs** are costs incurred in the factory or plant and typically consist of three components: *direct materials, direct labor,* and *manufacturing overhead* (see Exhibit 2-3 on page 33).

Objective 3

Distinguish manufacturing costs from nonmanufacturing costs and classify manufacturing costs as direct materials, direct labor, or overhead

Hitting the Bottom Line.

JIT AND THE OPERATING CYCLE

Just-in-time (JIT) inventory management increases cash flow by reducing the operating cycle of a company. The operating cycle begins with the purchase of raw materials and ends with the collection of cash from a customer. The focus of the operating cycle is cash flow and the length of time between the disbursement of cash for manufacturing costs or the purchase of inventory and the collection of cash from customers (see Exhibit 2-2).

If a company typically holds inventory for 60 days and collects cash from customers 30 days after sale, the operating cycle would be 90 days. If the company reduces the number of days inventory is held from 60 days to 5 days after adopting a JIT inventory management system, the operating cycle is shortened to 35 days.

What does that mean in terms of cash flow? If the company normally carries $1,000,000 in inventory, the company could invest that $1,000,000 for 55 extra days per cycle. At 5 percent interest, the reduction in the operating cycle would add over $7,500 in interest income per cycle ($1,000,000 x 5 percent x 55 days/365 days). As you can see, reducing the operating cycle can be very profitable.

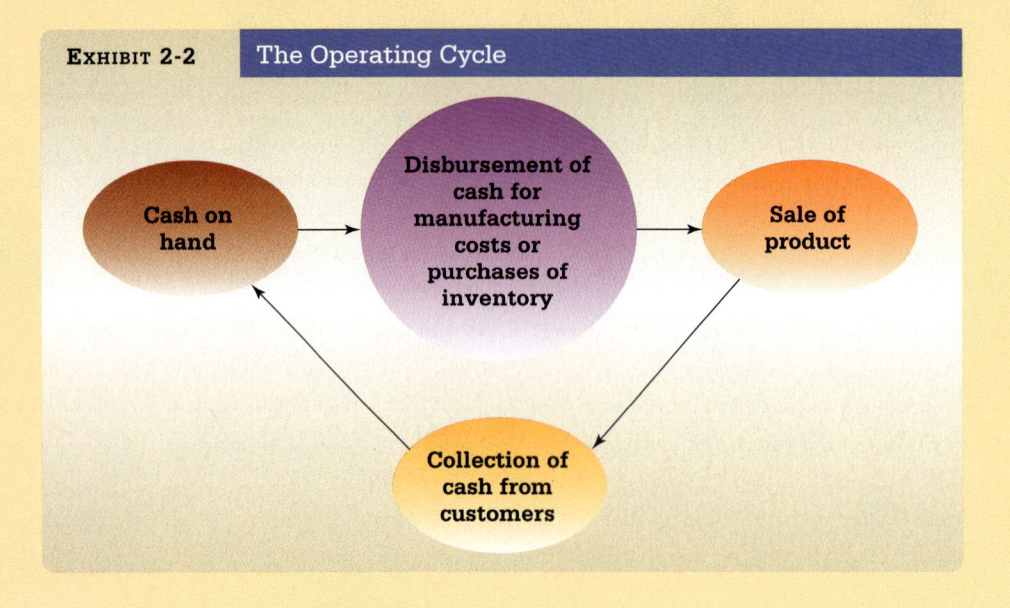

EXHIBIT 2-2 The Operating Cycle

Cash on hand → Disbursement of cash for manufacturing costs or purchases of inventory → Sale of product → Collection of cash from customers → (back to Cash on hand)

Direct Materials

Direct materials are defined as materials that can be directly and conveniently traced to a particular product or other cost object *and* that become an integral part of the finished product. At Ford Motor Company, sheet metal and tires are direct materials. At Dell Computer, the computer chips made by Intel and used in Dell computers are direct materials.

Direct materials typically cause few problems in the costing of products. The amount of direct material used in making products can usually be accurately measured by using engineering studies, and the accounting systems of most companies are capable of tracing the materials used and the costs of those materials to specific products. However, questions do arise and judgment is often needed to correctly classify materials as direct or indirect.

Direct Labor

Direct labor is the labor cost (including fringe benefits) of all production employees who work directly on the product being made or service being provided. Sometimes, direct labor is called *touch labor* to reflect the hands-on relationship between the employee and the product or service. Assembly-line workers are the clearest example of direct labor. As with direct material, identifying direct labor cost is usually straightforward and accurate. Time sheets may be used to keep track of the work employees perform on different products and the wages they are paid.

Manufacturing Overhead

All costs incurred in the factory that are not properly classified as direct material or direct labor are called **manufacturing overhead.** Manufacturing overhead includes both **indirect materials** and **indirect labor.** Materials that we know are used in the manufacture of products but cannot be measured with reasonable accuracy and easily and conveniently traced to a particular product are called indirect materials. For example, the rivets and welding materials used by an automobile manufacturer and the screws and glue used by a furniture manufacturer would probably be classified as indirect materials. Likewise, certain labor costs that are not directly associated with production are classified as indirect labor and included in manufacturing overhead. Examples include labor costs of janitorial staff and maintenance workers in a factory and supervisors who do not directly work on a product.

Manufacturing overhead also includes utilities, depreciation of factory equipment and buildings, rent, repairs and maintenance, insurance, and other factory costs. In a traditional manufacturing environment, the costs included in manufacturing overhead are most often indirect in nature and cannot be conveniently and accurately traced and assigned to a specific product. Remember, the machinery and equipment was typically used to make multiple products, making it difficult to trace the cost of a machine to a specific product. Although many overhead costs in a JIT environment will also be indirect in nature (rent and utilities, for example), more of the costs are likely to be direct in nature. For example, in a JIT environment, the cost of machinery in a manufacturing cell can be traced to a specific product (tables) if it is used only to make tables.

Because of the indirect nature of most overhead costs and the inability of companies to directly measure the amount of overhead included in products or to trace manufacturing overhead to products, accountants have come up with various methods of allocating manufacturing overhead to products. Traditional methods of allocating overhead using job and process costing are discussed in Chapter 3. A contemporary method, called activity-based costing, is discussed in Chapter 4.

Exhibit 2-3 Manufacturing Costs

Direct Materials	Direct Labor	Manufacturing Overhead
Various materials that can be directly and conveniently traced to a product	Labor costs of assembly line workers	Indirect materials such as welding material, glue, screws, etc.
		Indirect labor such as factory maintenance workers and factory janitors
		Other factory costs

Manufacturing costs are also called **product costs** or inventoriable costs because they attach to products as they go through the manufacturing process. Direct material, direct labor, and overhead costs remain with the product until it is sold. Only when the product is sold are these costs expensed on the income statement as cost of goods sold.

Nonmanufacturing Costs

Nonmanufacturing costs consist of those costs that are incurred outside the plant or factory and typically are categorized as selling and administrative costs. Although nonmanufacturing costs are necessarily incurred in running a business, they are not directly incurred in the production of products. A general rule of thumb is to imagine the product not being produced. If a particular cost would still occur, it is generally a nonmanufacturing cost. Common examples of nonmanufacturing costs include advertising costs, commissions paid to salespersons, administrative and accounting salaries, and office supplies. Nonmanufacturing costs also include rent, insurance, taxes, utilities, and depreciation of equipment when used in selling and administrative activities. Nonmanufacturing costs are called **period costs**. In contrast to manufacturing costs, nonmanufacturing costs are expensed on the income statement in the period incurred. Exhibit 2-4 lists several examples of manufacturing and nonmanufacturing costs.

EXHIBIT 2-4 Manufacturing and Nonmanufacturing Costs

Description	Manufacturing Cost	Nonmanufacturing Cost
Depreciation of factory machinery	XX	
Depreciation of vehicles used by sales staff		XX
Lease expense on factory equipment	XX	
Lease expense on office computer		XX
Lubricants used for maintenance of factory machinery (indirect materials)	XX	
Supplies used in the human resources office		XX
Utilities used in the factory building	XX	
Utilities used in the administrative headquarters		XX
Salary of a supervisor in the factory (indirect labor)	XX	
Salary of a supervisor in the marketing department		XX

Life-Cycle Costs and the Value Chain

The classification of costs as manufacturing or nonmanufacturing fails to address some important issues. For example, how should costs associated with research and development be classified? What about costs that are incurred in the engineering and design of products or costs that are incurred after the sale, due to warranty work or providing post-sale customer service? **Life-cycle costing** takes into account costs incurred in all activities in an organization's value chain. The **value chain** of an organization is simply the set of activities that increase the value of an organization's products and services. A typical value chain includes upstream costs such as research and development and design, production costs, and downstream costs such as marketing, distribution, and customer service activities (see Exhibit 2-5). Life-cycle costing includes all the costs incurred throughout a product's life, not just in the manufacture of the product.

Chapter 2 Product Costing: Manufacturing Processes, Cost Terminology, and Cost Flows

EXHIBIT 2-5 Life-Cycle Costs and the Value Chain

← Upstream Costs → ← Downstream Costs →

Research and Development	Product Development	Production	Marketing	Distribution	Customer Service
• R & D costs • Salaries of scientists and engineers	• Development costs • Engineering costs	• Direct materials • Direct labor • Manufacturing overhead	• Advertising and promotion costs • Salaries of sales staff	• Shipping costs • Trucks • Drivers	• Call center personnel • Phone and computer equipment

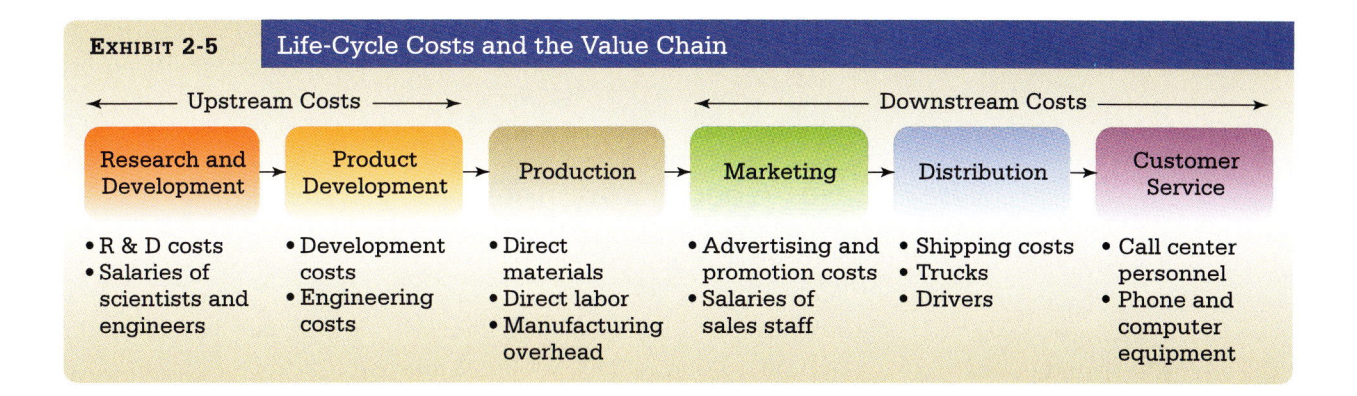

Cost Flows in a Manufacturing Company—Traditional Environment with Inventory

If companies simply used all the materials they purchased to make one product, finished making all the units of that product that they started, and sold everything they finished, calculating the income or loss from selling the product would be relatively easy. However, when multiple products are made or when materials are not all used, goods are not all finished, or products are not all sold, the process becomes more difficult.

To accurately determine the cost of manufactured products, you must trace or allocate manufacturing costs to each individual product as it is being produced and then follow those costs through various inventory accounts as the product progresses toward eventual completion and sale. At the point of sale, the cost of producing the product (the cost of goods sold) must be matched with the sales price to compute a profit or loss on the sale (called gross margin, or gross profit). Subtracting nonmanufacturing costs from the gross margin provides a measure of profitability for the company as a whole. When materials are not all used in production, goods are not finished, or finished goods are not all sold, costs must be accounted for in the appropriate raw material, work-in-process, or finished-goods inventory accounts.

Manufacturing costs include direct material, direct labor, and manufacturing overhead. These costs are also called product costs because they attach to the product as it goes through the production process. Picture a product moving down an assembly line. As labor, material, and overhead costs are incurred, they attach to the product being produced and remain with that product (in an inventory account) until it is sold. Costs flow in the same way that products flow through a production facility (see Exhibit 2-6).

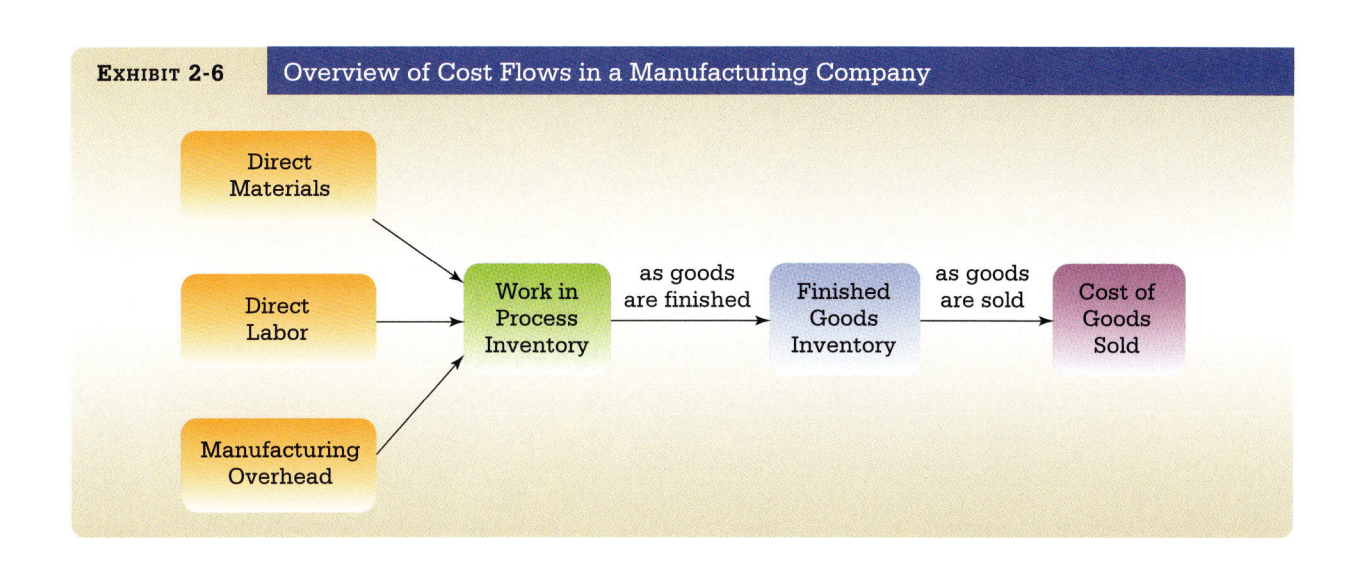

Objective 4

Diagram the flow of costs in manufacturing, merchandising, and service companies and calculate the cost of goods manufactured and cost of goods sold for each

KEY CONCEPT

Costs flow in the same way that products flow through a production facility.

EXHIBIT 2-6 Overview of Cost Flows in a Manufacturing Company

Direct Materials, Direct Labor, Manufacturing Overhead → Work in Process Inventory —as goods are finished→ Finished Goods Inventory —as goods are sold→ Cost of Goods Sold

This basic cost flow model is appropriate (with slight variations) for companies using either job costing or process costing systems. The differences between job costing and process costing systems are discussed more fully in Chapter 3.

The Cost-of-Goods-Sold Model for a Traditional Manufacturing Company with Inventory

To illustrate the production process and some of the associated problems with costing products, we will use a fictional company called Northern Lights Custom Cabinets. Northern Lights Custom Cabinets manufactures and sells custom-ordered kitchen and bathroom cabinets. The company sells primarily to building contractors but occasionally deals directly with homeowners. Northern Lights is located in Anchorage, Alaska, and has been in business only a few years, so management is still learning the business and how to properly determine the cost of each cabinet.

Northern Lights has an engineering and design division, which is involved in all custom-cabinet jobs. Quality control dictates that the engineering and design division must design all cabinets. Northern Lights strives to minimize the costs of production without sacrificing quality. Once the design phase of each cabinet job is complete, the material must be ordered. The material is stored in the raw materials warehouse until needed for each job and is then moved to the production area.

The production factory is separated into three distinct areas (see Exhibit 2-7): (1) cutting, (2) assembly, and (3) finishing. In the cutting area, all wood is cut into the required pieces, based on the plans from the engineering and design division. The pieces are all numbered and bundled for each particular section of the cabinet job. After cutting is completed, the bundles are moved to the assembly area, where the cabinets are constructed using glue and wood dowels. The assembled cabinets are moved to the finish area, where they are finished and stored for delivery to the home. This process can take up to one month to complete and is very labor intensive. After the cabinets have been completed, they are delivered to the home. Because each job is custom, Northern Lights also provides installation services for an extra charge.

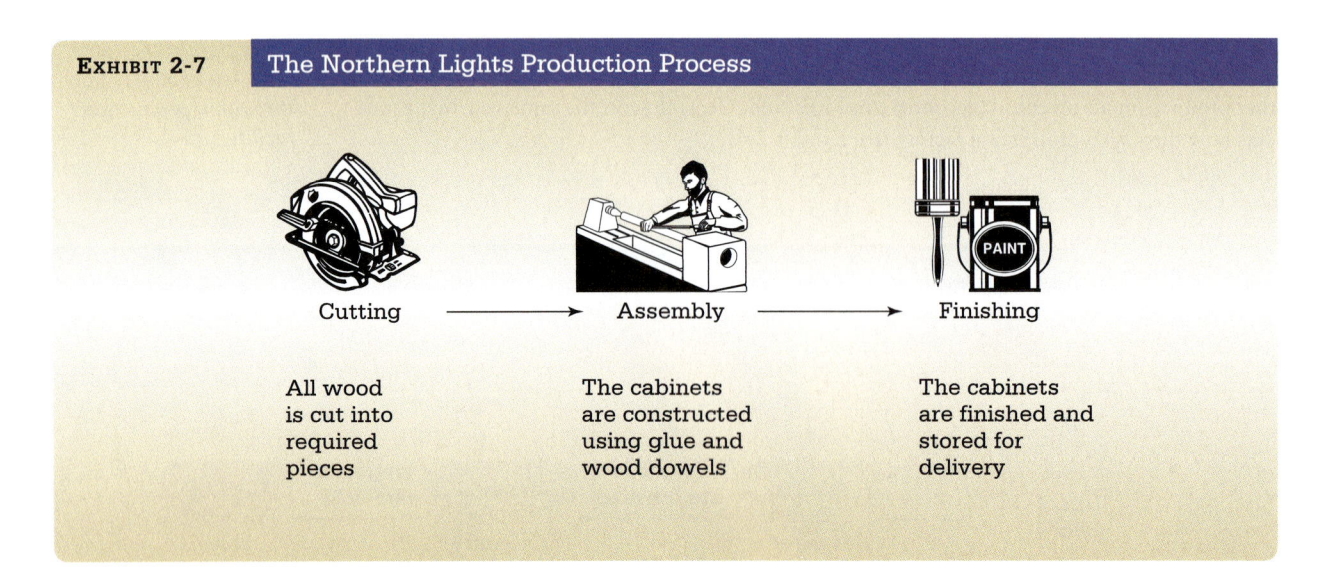

EXHIBIT 2-7   The Northern Lights Production Process

Cutting → Assembly → Finishing

All wood is cut into required pieces

The cabinets are constructed using glue and wood dowels

The cabinets are finished and stored for delivery

Northern Lights purchases raw materials and stores the materials in a warehouse that is separate from the production facility or factory. While these materials are in the warehouse, the costs of the raw materials are included in a raw material inventory account. Northern Lights began 2004 with raw materials costing $10,000 on hand and purchased an additional

$40,000 of raw materials during the year. Therefore, the company had $50,000 of raw materials available for use during the year.

The Purchase of Raw Materials

Description	Item	Amount
Raw materials on hand to start the period	Beginning inventory of raw materials	$10,000
Purchases of raw materials during the period	+ Cost of raw materials purchased	+ 40,000
The pool of raw materials available for use during the period	= Raw materials available for use	= $50,000

The journal entry to record the purchase of raw materials is:

Raw materials inventory	$40,000	
Accounts payable (or cash)		$40,000

When the raw material is moved to the factory, the raw material costs move with the material to a work in process inventory account. Any raw materials not used during the year remain in the raw materials inventory account. Northern Lights moves $45,000 of raw materials to the factory for use in manufacturing cabinets; $5,000 of raw materials remains in raw materials inventory.

Transferring Raw Materials to Work in Process

Description	Item	Amount
The pool of raw materials available for use during the period	Raw materials available for use	$50,000
The amount of raw materials used in production (and moved to a WIP account)	− Raw materials used in production	− 45,000
Raw materials on hand at the end of the period	= Ending inventory of raw materials	= $ 5,000

```
      Raw Materials              Work in Process
   $10,000  | −$45,000 ─┐
   + 40,000 |            └─→ +$45,000
   ─────────
   =$ 5,000
```

The journal entry to record the transfer of raw materials from raw materials inventory to work in process inventory is:

Work in process inventory	$45,000	
Raw materials inventory		$45,000

As direct labor costs of $65,000 are incurred (factory workers work on the cabinets), the cost of the workers is added to the raw material cost in the work in process inventory account. Likewise, as manufacturing overhead costs ($85,000 of machine costs, rent, depreciation, utilities, indirect material, etc.) are incurred, they are added to the work in process account. As long as each set of cabinets remains in the factory, the costs associated with them are recorded in the work in process account.

The journal entry to record the incurrence of direct labor costs is:

Work in process inventory	$65,000	
Salaries and wages payable (or cash)		$65,000

The journal entry to record the incurrence of manufacturing overhead costs is:

Work in process inventory	$85,000	
Accounts payable or cash		$85,000

Note that as the actual manufacturing overhead costs are incurred, they are entered directly into the WIP account with corresponding credits to accounts payable or cash. This system of product costing using the actual overhead costs incurred is called **actual costing.** For a number of reasons discussed in Chapter 3, most companies use a system of product costing called **normal costing** in which estimated or predetermined overhead rates are used to apply overhead to the WIP account.

If there is no beginning inventory of work in process and everything that is started in 2004 is finished (there is no ending inventory of WIP), the cost of goods manufactured is simply the sum of raw materials used, direct labor, and manufacturing overhead. When beginning or ending inventories exist, the cost of goods manufactured must be adjusted accordingly. At the beginning of 2004, Northern Lights had $15,000 of unfinished cabinets (started in 2003) in the factory. These cabinets were completed in early 2004. However, the company got even further behind in 2004, resulting in $20,000 of cabinets being partially finished at the end of 2004. Therefore, the cost of goods (cabinets) manufactured in 2004 and transferred to finished goods was $190,000.

The Calculation of Cost of Goods Manufactured

Description	Item	Amount
Work in process on hand at the beginning of the period	Beginning inventory of WIP	$ 15,000
The amount of raw materials used in production	+ Raw materials used	+ 45,000
The amount of direct labor cost incurred	+ Direct labor	+ 65,000
The amount of manufacturing overhead incurred	+ Manufacturing overhead	+ 85,000
Work in process at the end of the period	− Ending inventory of WIP	− 20,000
The cost of goods manufactured during the period	= Cost of goods manufactured	= $190,000

Work in Process		Finished Goods
$15,000 + 45,000 + 65,000 + 85,000	−$190,000	
		+$190,000
= $20,000		

The journal entry to record the transfer of finished goods from WIP to finished goods inventory is:

Finished goods inventory	$190,000	
Work in process inventory		$190,000

When a cabinet is sold, the accumulated costs in the finished goods inventory account are moved to the cost of goods sold account. If there is no beginning inventory of finished goods and all the goods finished in the current year are sold (there is no ending inventory), the cost of goods sold is equal to the cost of goods manufactured. However, when beginning and ending inventories exist, the cost of goods sold must be adjusted accordingly. Northern Lights had one order (costing $30,000) that was not delivered to customers by the end of 2003. Likewise, at the end of 2004, the company had $5,000 of cabinets that were finished but not sold. Therefore, the cost of goods (cabinets) sold during 2004 was $215,000.

The Calculation of Cost of Goods Sold

Description	Item	Amount
Finished goods on hand at the beginning of the period	Beginning inventory of finished goods	$ 30,000
The cost of goods manufactured during the period	+ Cost of goods manufactured	+ 190,000
Finished goods on hand at the end of the period	− Ending inventory of finished goods	− 5,000
The cost of goods sold during the period	= Cost of goods sold	= $215,000

Finished Goods		Cost of Goods Sold	
$ 30,000	−$215,000		
+ 190,000		+ $215,000	
= $ 5,000			

The journal entry to record the cost of goods sold and the transfer of goods out of finished goods inventory as the product is sold is:

Cost of goods sold	$215,000	
Finished goods inventory		$215,000

In summary, the flow of costs from the raw materials storeroom to work in process inventory, from work in process inventory to finished goods inventory, and from finished goods inventory to cost of goods sold is accounted for as shown in Exhibit 2-8.

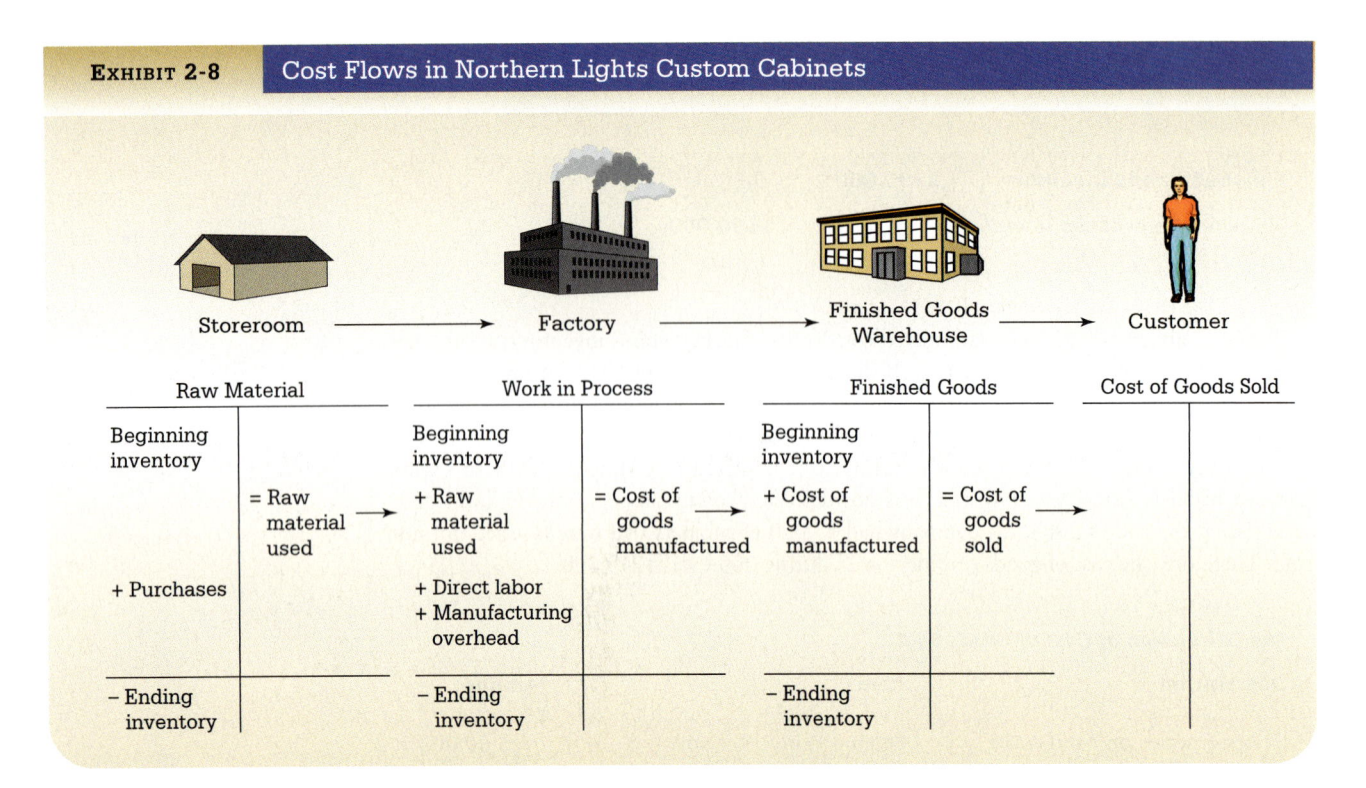

EXHIBIT 2-8 Cost Flows in Northern Lights Custom Cabinets

Storeroom → Factory → Finished Goods Warehouse → Customer

Raw Material
- Beginning inventory
- + Purchases
- − Ending inventory
- = Raw material used

Work in Process
- Beginning inventory
- + Raw material used
- + Direct labor
- + Manufacturing overhead
- − Ending inventory
- = Cost of goods manufactured

Finished Goods
- Beginning inventory
- + Cost of goods manufactured
- − Ending inventory
- = Cost of goods sold

Cost of Goods Sold
- = Cost of goods sold

A schedule of cost of goods manufactured and a schedule of cost of goods sold for Northern Lights Custom Cabinets is presented in Exhibit 2-9.

EXHIBIT 2-9 Schedule of Cost of Goods Manufactured and Schedule of Cost of Goods Sold for a Manufacturing Company

Northern Lights Custom Cabinets
Schedule of Cost of Goods Manufactured
For the year ended December 31, 2004

Beginning raw materials	$10,000	
Add: Raw materials purchased	40,000	
Raw materials available	50,000	
Deduct: Ending raw materials	5,000	
Raw materials used in production		$ 45,000
Direct labor		65,000
Manufacturing overhead		85,000
Total manufacturing costs		195,000
Add: Beginning work in process		15,000
		210,000
Deduct: Ending work in process		20,000
Cost of goods manufactured		$190,000

Northern Lights Custom Cabinets
Schedule of Cost of Goods Sold
For the year ended December 31, 2004

Beginning finished goods inventory	$ 30,000
Add: Cost of goods manufactured	190,000
Goods available for sale	$220,000
Deduct: Ending finished goods inventory	5,000
Cost of goods sold	$215,000

Assuming that Northern Lights had sales of $500,000 and selling and administrative expenses of $175,000, the company's 2004 income statement is presented in Exhibit 2-10.

EXHIBIT 2-10 Income Statement for a Manufacturing Company

Northern Lights Custom Cabinets
Income Statement
For the year ended December 31, 2004

Sales		$500,000
Cost of goods sold:		
Beginning finished goods inventory	$ 30,000	
Add: Cost of goods manufactured	190,000	
Goods available for sale	$220,000	
Deduct: Ending finished goods inventory	5,000	215,000
Gross Margin		285,000
Less: Selling and administrative expense		175,000
Net operating income		$110,000

Cost Flows in a Manufacturing Company— JIT Environment

How do cost flows differ in a manufacturing company utilizing JIT? Remember, in a JIT environment, the physical flow of goods is streamlined by the use of manufacturing cells that largely eliminate inventories of raw materials, WIP, and finished goods. Cost flows are streamlined as well. Although the mechanics of an accounting system for companies utilizing JIT are covered more fully in Chapter 3, direct materials, direct labor, and overhead costs can essentially be accumulated directly in a cost of goods sold account. Because raw materials are immediately placed into production when purchased, there is no need to record their purchase in a separate raw materials inventory account. Likewise, because all goods are typically finished and shipped out immediately to customers, there is no reason to keep track of WIP or finished goods inventories.

The Calculation of Cost of Goods Sold—JIT Environment

Description	Item	Amount
The amount of raw materials purchased and used in production	Raw materials purchased and used	$ 50,000
The amount of direct labor costs incurred	+ Direct labor	+ 65,000
The amount of overhead cost incurred	+ Manufacturing overhead	+ 85,000
The cost of goods sold during the period	= Cost of goods sold	=$200,000

Merchandising Companies and the Cost of Products

Wholesalers and retailers purchase merchandise in finished form from other companies. With the exception of packaging and other minor changes, they simply offer the products for resale to other companies (wholesalers) or to the ultimate consumer (retailers). Therefore, the product cost of a wholesaler or a retailer is simply the purchase price of the merchandise the wholesaler or retailer sells.

Because merchandising companies simply purchase goods for resale, the flow of costs in a retail or a wholesale establishment is fairly simple. On the balance sheet, merchandising companies use a single account for inventory, called merchandise inventory. The costs incurred in inventory are simply the costs to purchase the inventory.

How are the costs incurred in purchasing inventory for resale expensed? You may recall from financial accounting that the principle of matching revenue from sales with the costs associated with that revenue means that the cost of purchasing merchandise is expensed as cost of goods sold as the merchandise is sold. However, the cost of goods sold is not necessarily equal to the cost of merchandise purchased during the period. If merchandise is purchased and not sold or if merchandise that was purchased in another period is sold in the current period, cost of goods sold must be adjusted accordingly.

In the following example, Cheryl's Bike Shop begins 2004 with beginning inventory of bikes and parts of $15,000. During the year, the company purchases $63,000 of merchandise and has merchandise available for sale of $78,000. $18,000 of merchandise inventory remains on hand at the end of 2004 resulting in $60,000 of cost of goods sold. The company's Schedule of Cost of Goods Sold is shown in Exhibit 2-11.

The Calculation of Cost of Goods Sold for a Merchandising Company

Description	Item	Amount
Merchandise on hand to start the period	Beginning inventory	$15,000
Acquisitions of merchandise during the period	+ Cost of goods purchased	+ 63,000
The pool of merchandise available for sale during the period	= Cost of goods available for sale	= $78,000
Merchandise on hand at the end of the period	− Ending inventory	− (18,000)
The expense recognized on the income statement	= Cost of goods sold	= $60,000

EXHIBIT 2-11 Schedule of Cost of Goods Sold for a Merchandising Company

Cheryl's Bike Shop
Schedule of Cost of Goods Sold
For the year ended December 31, 2004

Beginning merchandise inventory	$ 15,000
Add: Purchases	63,000
Goods available for sale	$ 78,000
Deduct: Ending merchandise inventory	18,000
Cost of goods sold	$ 60,000

With sales of $175,000 and selling and administrative expenses totaling $40,000, the income statement is shown in Exhibit 2-12.

EXHIBIT 2-12 — Income Statement for a Merchandising Company

Cheryl's Bike Shop
Income Statement
For the year ended December 31, 2004

Sales		$ 175,000
Cost of goods sold:		
Beginning merchandise inventory	$ 15,000	
Add: Purchases	63,000	
Goods available for sale	$ 78,000	
Deduct: Ending merchandise inventory	18,000	60,000
Gross margin		115,000
Less: Selling and administrative expense		40,000
Net operating income		$ 75,000

Service Companies and the Cost of Services

Many similarities exist between the costing of products in a manufacturing company and the costing of services. Like product costs, the cost of services includes three components: direct materials, direct labor, and overhead. However, the proportions of each may vary dramatically. Service companies typically have few material costs and large amounts of labor and overhead.

Although service companies have both direct and indirect costs, they generally have larger proportions of indirect costs. For example:

- In a movie studio, costumes and props are direct materials and the salaries of actors and directors are direct labor. Overhead would include the costs of the studio itself and all the recording and production equipment. Camera operators and other support people would more than likely be classified as indirect labor because they would likely work on more than one film at a time.

- In a CPA firm, material costs would likely be very small. While paper and other materials are used in the preparation of tax returns, the material would likely be considered an indirect cost and classified as overhead. On the other hand, direct labor costs for a CPA firm would be very large.

- In a hospital, although the costs of specific drugs and special tests or X-rays can be traced to a specific patient, the costs of operating rooms and equipment and the salaries of administrators, discharge personnel, orderlies, and maintenance workers would all be indirect.

While service companies typically have little need for raw materials and finished goods inventory accounts, work in process (WIP) accounts are commonly used on projects that were incomplete at month end, such as audits by CPA firms, lengthy legal cases by law firms, and consulting engagements that are long term.

Product Costs and Period Costs

As previously discussed, manufacturing costs or **product costs** attach to products as they go through the manufacturing process. Until the sale of the product, the costs of manufacturing are included in one of three inventory accounts: raw materials, work in process, and finished

Objective 5

Evaluate the impact of product costs and period costs on a company's income statement and balance sheet

KEY CONCEPT

Product costs attach to the product and are expensed only when the product is sold, whereas period costs are expensed in the period in which they are incurred.

goods. These inventory accounts appear on the balance sheet along with other assets and liabilities. Only when a product is sold are manufacturing costs expensed as cost of goods sold on the income statement. On the other hand, nonmanufacturing costs or **period costs** are expensed immediately on the income statement in the period in which they are incurred (see Exhibit 2-13).

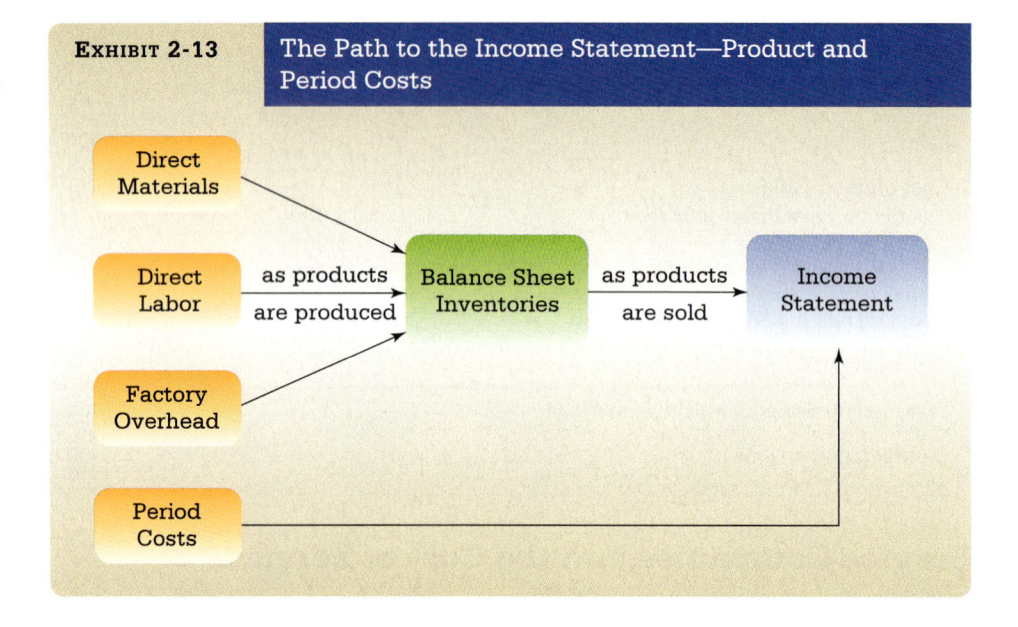

EXHIBIT 2-13 The Path to the Income Statement—Product and Period Costs

Direct Materials, Direct Labor, Factory Overhead → as products are produced → Balance Sheet Inventories → as products are sold → Income Statement

Period Costs → Income Statement

For external financial reporting purposes, information on the cost of goods sold and the amount of inventory owned by a company is provided in financial statements and included in the company's annual report.

THE ETHICS OF BUSINESS
To Expense or Not to Expense

Every company must make decisions about how to report their expenditures. For external financial reporting purposes, companies are expected to follow GAAP to determine whether expenditures should be reported on the income statement or the balance sheet. Expenditures that are reported on the income statement are expenses that result in immediate decreases in net income, or profits; while those that appear on the balance sheet are assets. Companies often prefer to report expenditures as assets rather than as expenses because they feel pressure to increase net income. Such was the case at WorldCom, which improperly reported more than $3.5 billion of expenditures as assets on its balance sheet. By misreporting these expenditures WorldCom's financial statements made it appear as though the company were profitable when that was not the case. Essentially, several highly placed members of WorldCom's management made the decision to report expenditures as assets when they should have been reported as expenses. Many observers consider the accounting shenanigans at WorldCom to have been the result of intentional deceit by management.

It's Your Choice—Imagine the stress that management often feels to show growth and profits. Very often members of management receive bonuses based on the company's financial performance and stock price. Is it surprising that these individuals may intentionally misreport events to protect their bonuses? Would you?

Balance sheets and income statements of a manufacturing company (Bassett Furniture Industries) and a merchandising company (Wal-Mart) are shown in Exhibits 2-14 and 2-15. Note that the balance sheets provided to external users show only a total cost for inventories, rather than a breakdown into raw material, work in process and finished goods. Likewise, the income statements show the overall cost of goods sold (called the cost of sales) and the period costs incurred during the year (called selling, general and administrative expenses by Bassett and operating, selling, general and administrative expenses by Wal-Mart).

EXHIBIT 2-14 Balance Sheets (partial)

Wal-Mart
January 31
(Amounts in millions)

Assets	2004	2003
Current Assets:		
Cash and cash equivalents	$ 5,199	$ 2,736
Receivables	1,254	1,569
Inventories	26,612	24,401
Prepaid expenses and other	1,356	837
Current assets of discontinued operation	–	1,179
Total Current Assets	34,421	30,722
Property, Plant and Equipment, at Cost:		
Land	12,699	11,202
Buildings and improvements	38,966	33,345
Fixtures and equipment	17,861	15,640
Transportation equipment	1,269	1,099
	70,795	61,286
Less accumulated depreciation	15,594	13,116
Property, plant and equipment, net	55,201	48,170
Property Under Capital Lease:		
Property under capital lease	5,092	4,814
Less accumulated amortization	1,763	1,610
Property under capital leases, net	3,329	3,204
Other Assets and Deferred Charges:		
Goodwill	9,882	9,389
Other assets and deferred charges	2,079	2,594
Other assets of discontinued operation	–	729
Total Assets	$104,912	$ 94,808

Bassett Furniture Industries
November 29, 2003, and November 30, 2002
(Amounts in thousands)

Assets	2003	2002
Current assets		
Cash and cash equivalents	$ 15,181	$ 1,371
Accounts receivable, net	39,230	44,806
Inventories	36,454	43,449
Refundable income taxes	–	2,924
Deferred income taxes	5,307	3,600
Other current assets	4,525	6,816
Total current assets	100,697	102,966
Property and equipment, net	50,681	59,365
Investments	65,151	63,248
Retail real estate, net	32,930	31,177
Notes receivable, net	15,399	18,761
Other, net	15,522	15,363
	129,002	128,549
Total Assets	$280,380	$290,880

Exhibit 2-15 Income Statements (partial)

Wal-Mart
Fiscal years ended January 31
(Amounts in millions)

	2004	2003	2002
Revenues:			
Net sales	$ 256,329	$ 229,616	$ 204,011
Other income, net	2,352	1,961	1,812
	258,681	231,577	205,823
Costs and Expenses:			
Cost of sales	198,747	178,299	159,097
Operating, selling, general and administrative expenses	44,909	39,983	35,147
Operating Profit	$ 15,025	$ 13,295	$ 11,579

Bassett Furniture Industries
For the years ended November 29, 2003, November 30, 2002, and November 24, 2001
(Amounts in thousands)

	2003	2002	2001
Net sales	$ 316,857	$ 323,487	$ 305,676
Cost of sales	234,861	254,993	254,456
Gross profit	81,896	68,494	51,220
Selling, general and administrative expenses	80,026	60,987	54,477
Gains on sales of property and equipment, net	–	–	(5,297)
Restructuring and impaired asset charges	3,200	1,251	6,952
Income (loss) from operations	$ (1,230)	$ 6,256	$ (4,912)

Note that the information provided in the financial statements is historical in nature, is in summary form, and is provided for the company as a whole. This is typical of information provided to external users.

In contrast, internal managers require very detailed information on various segments of a company. For example, a manager of a local Wal-Mart store would want to know detailed information on sales and inventory levels of specific merchandise (children's clothing, electronics, household goods, etc.), including how long a product had been on the shelf, while a divisional manager would want sales information for each store in his or her region. Marketing and production managers need to know the cost of goods sold and accompanying gross margin for each product, not just for the company as a whole.

Summary of Key Concepts

- *JIT is more than an inventory management tool. (p. 31)*
- *Costs flow in the same way that products flow through a production facility. (p. 35)*
- *Product costs attach to the product and are expensed only when the product is sold, whereas period costs are expensed in the period in which they are incurred. (p. 44)*

Key Definitions

Manufacturing companies Companies that purchase raw materials from other companies and transform those raw materials into a finished product (p. 28)

Merchandising companies Companies that sell products that someone else has manufactured (p. 28)

Service companies Companies that do not sell a tangible product as their primary business (p. 28)

Raw materials inventory Inventory of materials needed in the production process but not yet moved to the production area (p. 29)

Finished goods inventory Inventory of finished product waiting for sale and shipment to customers (p. 29)

Work in process inventory Inventory of unfinished product (in other words, what is left in the factory at the end of the period) (p. 29)

Just-in-time (JIT) production systems The philosophy of having raw materials arrive just in time to be used in production and for finished goods inventory to be completed just in time to be shipped to customers (p. 29)

Manufacturing costs Costs incurred in the factory or plant to produce a product; typically consists of three elements: direct materials, direct labor, and manufacturing overhead (p. 31)

Direct materials Materials that can easily and conveniently be traced to the final product (p. 32)

Direct labor Labor that can easily and conveniently be traced to particular products (p. 32)

Manufacturing overhead Indirect material and labor and any other expenses related to the production of products but not directly traceable to the specific product (p. 33)

Indirect materials Materials used in the production of products but not directly traceable to the specific product (p. 33)

Indirect labor Labor used in the production of products but not directly traceable to the specific product (p. 33)

Nonmanufacturing costs Costs that include selling and administrative costs (p. 33)

Product costs Costs that attach to the products as they go through the manufacturing process; also called inventoriable costs (p. 33)

Period costs Costs that are expensed in the period incurred; attached to the period as opposed to the product (p. 34)

Life-cycle costing A costing system that includes all the costs incurred throughout a product's life, not just in the manufacturing and selling of the product (p. 34)

Value chain The set of activities that increase the value of an organization's products and services: research and development, design, production, marketing, distribution, and customer service activities (p. 34)

Actual costing A product costing system in which actual overhead costs are entered directly into work in process (p. 38)

Normal costing A product costing system in which estimated or predetermined overhead rates are used to apply overhead to work in process (p. 38)

Multiple Choice

1. Which of the following statements regarding the traditional manufacturing environment is *not* true?
   a. Factories were organized so that similar machines were grouped together.
   b. Finished goods inventories were accumulated in case of unanticipated demand.
   c. Raw materials were purchased "just in time" to meet customer demand.
   d. Products were "pushed" through the production process to maximize output.

2. Traditional manufacturing facilities typically have machines organized in which of the following ways?
   a. Similar machines are grouped together.
   b. Similar and dissimilar machines are grouped together.
   c. Machines are grouped in work cells that produce a limited number of products.
   d. Machines are grouped linearly in a traditional manufacturing facility.

3. Just-in-time environments can most accurately be described by which of the following terms?
   a. Iterative production
   b. Push production
   c. Pull production
   d. Supply production

4. Which of the following is least likely to be a benefit associated with just-in-time techniques?
   a. Improved customer satisfaction
   b. Reduced production time
   c. Reduced production costs
   d. Improved product quality

5. Which of the following statements concerning manufacturing cells is false?
   a. Manufacturing cells can reduce machine setup times.
   b. Manufacturing cells typically have highly trained employees who are allowed to specialize in one process.
   c. Manufacturing cells reduce the time required to move materials and products.
   d. Manufacturing cells accomplish each of the above objectives.

6. Jill Garrett owns a company that manufactures women's clothing. In the most recent year, wage and salary expenses included the following:

Machine operators	$200,000
Quality control supervisors	100,000
Fabric cutters	75,000
Factory janitor	18,000
Company president	150,000

What amount of indirect labor costs were incurred during the year?
   a. $75,000
   b. $118,000
   c. $250,000
   d. $543,000

7. Which of the following costs is least likely to be a manufacturing cost?
   a. Depreciation of production machinery
   b. Production supervisor's salary
   c. Depreciation of sales office computer equipment
   d. Purchase price of wood used to produce tables

Use the following information to answer questions 8 and 9.

University Novelties manufactures key chains for college bookstores. During the year the company incurred the following costs in producing 35,000 units:

Direct materials used	$31,000
Direct labor	18,000
Factory rent	12,000
Depreciation on factory equipment	2,000
Depreciation on office equipment	750
Marketing expenses	2,500
Administrative expenses	40,000

8. What is the product cost per unit?
   a. $1.24
   b. $1.80
   c. $3.04
   d. $2.85

9. What is the company's net income for the year if 30,000 units are sold for $3.50 each?
   a. $122,000
   b. $105,000
   c. $7,750
   d. ($1,250)

   ✓ Gross margin: $51,000

10. Cost of goods manufactured equals:
    a. beginning direct materials inventory plus all production costs incurred less ending direct materials inventory
    b. beginning direct materials inventory plus all production costs incurred less ending work in process inventory
    c. beginning work in process inventory plus direct materials used plus direct labor used plus manufacturing overhead used less ending work in process inventory
    d. beginning work in process inventory plus direct materials used plus direct labor used plus manufacturing overhead used plus beginning finished goods inventory

11. The production cost flow model is best described as:
    a. Raw materials storeroom, work in process, finished goods inventory
    b. Raw materials storeroom, partially finished goods, finished goods inventory
    c. Work in process, raw materials storeroom, finished goods inventory
    d. All of the above

12. Pottery Works, which produces pottery bowls, had the following summary cost information (Note: 15,000 units were produced):

   ✓ Total manufacturing costs: $37,500

Direct materials used	$14,000
Direct labor	12,000
Factory rent	4,000
Equipment depreciation	7,500
Marketing expenses	15,000
Administrative expenses	13,000
Shipping charges	5,000

If 14,500 of the 15,000 units are sold, what is the cost of goods sold?
a. $68,150
b. $25,085
c. $36,250
d. $37,500

Use the following information to answer questions 13 through 15.

Pilar's Creations had the following information available for January:

	Beginning	Ending
Raw materials inventory	$110,000	$115,000
Work in process inventory	55,000	58,000
Finished goods inventory	41,000	37,000
Raw materials purchased		121,000
Direct labor (2,500 hours at $12.00)		30,000
Manufacturing overhead		53,000

13. Raw materials used in January are:
    a. $5,000
    b. $116,000
    c. $121,000
    d. $126,000

14. Pilar's cost of goods manufactured in January is:
    a. $196,000
    b. $199,000
    c. $254,000
    d. $364,000

    ✓ Total manufacturing cost: $199,000

15. Pilar's cost of goods sold for January is:
    a. $4,000
    b. $37,000
    c. $196,000
    d. $200,000

Concept Questions

16. *(Objective 1)* What has changed in the manufacturing environment in the past 20 years or so that has caused some companies to reevaluate their product costs?
17. *(Objective 2)* Briefly describe a just-in-time (JIT) system.
18. *(Objective 2)* What are some of the advantages and disadvantages of making a product in a JIT environment?
19. *(Objective 3)* Compare the terms *direct cost* and *indirect cost*.
20. *(Objective 3)* Define the three components of manufacturing costs.
21. *(Objective 3)* Define nonmanufacturing costs.
22. *(Objective 4)* Briefly describe the flow of costs in a manufacturing company.
23. *(Objective 5)* Are the terms cost and expense synonymous? Why or why not?
24. *(Objective 5)* Compare product and period costs. Why is the designation important?
25. *(Objective 5)* Why do companies need to determine accurate product costs?

Exercises

26. Just-in-time (JIT) production systems are widely viewed as improving the competitive position of companies. However, these systems do have advantages and disadvantages. The following sentences partially describe the effects of JIT systems on a business.
  a. JIT systems _____ storage and other inventory carrying costs.
  b. Time required to produce products typically _____.
  c. Customer satisfaction usually _____.
  d. The cost of raw materials often _____.
  e. Product quality improves because the number of defective products is _____.
  f. Production flexibility _____ because employees are highly trained.
  g. The number of suppliers is often _____ because companies must have highly reliable suppliers to deliver raw materials whenever needed.

Required

Complete each of the above partially descriptive statements by inserting one of the following words: *reduce, increased, improves, decreases, reduced,* or *increases*. Only one of the preceding words correctly completes a statement. Words may be used more than once.

27. Business managers often misunderstand just-in-time (JIT) systems. Often these misunderstandings lead to unreasonable expectations or erroneous conclusions. The following sentences describe some aspects of JIT systems.
  a. Materials are purchased and products are made so that the company has finished goods inventory available to be shipped to a customer on a moment's notice.
  b. Partly because of more frequent delivery of raw materials, direct materials cost will generally increase.
  c. Manufacturing cells often lead to an increase in the number of times materials and work in process inventory must be handled.
  d. Companies that implement just in time often have more disgruntled employees because there are fewer training opportunities for them.
  e. When implemented properly, JIT should result in higher quality products with fewer defects.
  f. The number of machine setups usually increases when a company implements JIT.

Required

Indicate whether each of the above statements is "true" or "false."

28. The Quilt Shop manufactures decorative quilts and incurred the following wage and salary expenses for the most recent year.

Machine operators	$ 100,000
Quality control supervisors	50,000
Fabric cutters	25,000
Factory janitor	8,000
Company president	100,000

Required

Determine the amount of direct labor incurred during the year.

29. The Smiling Place manufactures extra-whitening toothpaste. During the year the company had the following costs:

Direct materials used	$ 41,000	Office depreciation	$ 4,050
Direct labor	28,000	Selling expenses	3,500
Factory rent	12,000	Administrative expenses	50,000
Factory depreciation	9,000		

The Smiling Place produced 45,000 units during the year.

Required

A. Calculate the total product costs for the year.
B. Calculate the product cost on a per unit basis.

30. Deskmakers is a new company that manufactures desks. In its first month of operation, it began and completed 500 desks. The following production information has been provided:

Direct material cost per unit	$ 18
Indirect labor costs	400
Indirect material costs	220
Marketing expenses	750
Cost per direct labor hour	15
Factory rent	2,000
Administrative expenses	1,600
Direct labor per unit	4 hours

Required

A. Calculate the cost of direct labor for one desk.
B. Calculate the total overhead costs for the first month of production.
C. Calculate the total product costs for the first month of production.

✓ Total direct labor: $30,000

31. Fun Times Games produces a variety of popular board games. The company has decided to strategically position itself in the industry with unique handcrafted game boards and game pieces. The company's controller has accumulated the following data regarding raw materials used in production.

Pounds of laminated corrugated material purchased	15,000
Board games produced	10,000
Average pounds of laminated corrugated material per board	0.80
Average cost per pound of laminated corrugated material	$ 1.24
Board games sold during the period	7,850

Required

Assuming the company did not have any laminated corrugated board at the beginning of the period, calculate the amount of raw materials cost that is included in product cost for the period.

32. The following costs were incurred by a manufacturer of breakfast cereals.
   a. Heat, water, and power used in the factory
   b. Cost of repairing mixing machines and ovens
   c. Wheat, sweetener, and artificial colors used in production
   d. Lease payments for salespersons' company cars
   e. Wax paper used to package cereals
   f. Cardboard boxes used to ship packaged cereals to grocery stores
   g. Overtime paid to office employees

Required

Indicate whether each of the above costs is a manufacturing cost or a nonmanufacturing cost.

33. The following costs are manufacturing costs for a producer of personal computers.
   a. Wages of employees who conduct quality testing
   b. Purchase cost of processor chips included in the company computer
   c. Wages paid to maintenance workers
   d. Property taxes paid for the manufacturing facility
   e. Salaries paid to a staff nurse who provides care for manufacturing employees
   f. Wages paid to assembly line employees
   g. Small screws and fasteners

Required

Indicate whether each of the above costs is direct material (DM), direct labor (DL), indirect material (IM), indirect labor (IL), or another manufacturing overhead cost (MOH).

34. Melinda's Bakery had the following information available for the month of January:

	Beginning	Ending
Raw materials inventory	$ 110,000	$ 115,000
Work in process inventory	55,000	58,000
Finished goods inventory	41,000	37,000
Raw materials purchased		121,000
Direct labor (2,500 hrs@$12)		30,000
Overhead		53,000

✓ Raw materials used: $116,000

Required

Calculate the cost of goods manufactured for the month.

35. Perfect Pictures, which produces specialty picture frames, had the following summary cost information:

Direct materials used	$ 24,000
Direct labor	22,000
Factory rent	6,000
Equipment depreciation	7,500
Marketing expense	15,000
Administrative expense	13,000
Shipping charges	5,000
Number of units produced	25,000

✓ Ending finished goods: $2,380

Required

Calculate the cost of goods sold if 24,000 units are sold.

36. Sharon's Department Store features women's fashions. At the beginning of the year, the store had $514,000 in merchandise. Total purchases for the year were $463,000.

Required

A. Calculate cost of goods sold for the year assuming the year-end inventory was $488,000.
B. What was the total amount of merchandise available for sale during the year?

37. Joe's Slacks is a local men's clothing store. Joe buys clothing and accessories from manufacturers and marks them up by 55 percent. Joe began the year with $155,000 worth of items ($240,250 retail value) and bought $350,000 (retail value $542,500) worth of items during the year. Ending inventory is $95,000 (retail value $147,250).

✓ *Gross margin: $225,500*

Required

A. Calculate Joe's cost of goods sold for the year.
B. Calculate Joe's sales for the year.

38. You are the president of Chocolate Creations. Your new accountant, who recently graduated from a local university, presented you with the following income statement for the month of January:

✓ *Gross profit: $220,000*

Sales Revenues	$660,000
Total January Expenses	595,000
Net Income	$ 65,000

By talking to the production departments, you learn that 60,000 units were produced in January at a total cost of $420,000. The sales department notes that 55,000 units were sold for $11 each. Monthly administrative and marketing expenses totaled $75,000.

Required

Based on the above information calculate the correct amount of net income for January.

39. McDonald Inc., a manufacturing company, prepays its insurance coverage for a three-year period. The premium for the three years is $21,000 and is paid at the beginning of the first year. Three-fourths of the premium relates to factory operations and one-fourth relates to selling and administrative activities.

Required

A. Calculate the amount of the premium that should be recorded as a product cost each year.
B. Calculate the amount of the premium that should be recorded as a period cost each year.

40. Campus Coolers manufactures portable coolers adorned with college logos. During the first quarter of the year the company had the following costs:

Direct materials used	$ 56,000
Direct labor	38,000
Factory rent	24,000
Factory equipment depreciation	10,000
Office equipment depreciation	1,400
Marketing expenses	5,500
Administrative expenses	12,000

✓ Cost per unit: $16

Although 8,000 units were produced during the quarter, just 5,300 were sold for an average price of $25 each.

Required

Calculate Campus Cooler's net income for the first quarter.

Problems

41. Tony's Pizza has been established to produce fresh, packaged 16-inch pizzas to be sold wholesale to grocery stores, convenience stores, and school cafeterias. Tony's will have 10 production lines with 5 workers on each line. Each worker is responsible for 1 of the five stages of production: dough, sauce, cheese, toppings, or packaging. The following flowchart of the production lines shows the time needed at each workstation. These time estimates include normal downtime, breaks, and so on. Moving products between stations takes approximately 30 seconds. So the total time to produce 1 pizza is the total of all the time needed at each step plus 2 minutes for product movement (4 movements at ½ minute each), or 13½ minutes per pizza. Tony's production facility is organized in a very traditional fashion. Dough preparation, sauce preparation, cheese preparation, topping preparation, and packaging are all done in separate areas of the factory. In addition, employees on the production lines are responsible for only one task.

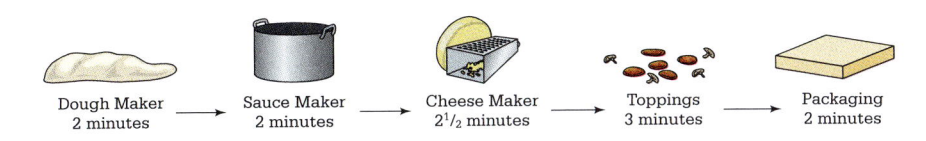

Dough Maker (2 minutes) → Sauce Maker (2 minutes) → Cheese Maker (2½ minutes) → Toppings (3 minutes) → Packaging (2 minutes)

Required

A. Why would Tony's choose to arrange their production facility as described?
B. What options might Tony's consider to improve manufacturing efficiency?
C. What changes to Tony's manufacturing processes are needed if just-in-time practices are adopted?

42. The accounting information system of Evans Co. reported the following cost and inventory data for the year.

Costs Incurred	
Raw material purchased	$ 125,000
Direct labor	75,000
Indirect labor	40,000
Equipment maintenance	10,000
Insurance on factory	12,000
Rent on factory	30,000
Equipment depreciation	20,000
Factory supplies	11,000
Advertising expenses	15,000
Selling and administrative expenses	21,000

Inventories	Beginning Balance	Ending Balance
Raw materials	$ 10,000	$ 17,000
Work in process	20,000	31,000
Finished goods	30,000	25,000

✓ Manufacturing overhead: $123,000

Required

A. Calculate the cost of goods manufactured.
B. Calculate the cost of goods sold.
C. List the costs not included in the calculations of cost of goods manufactured and cost of goods sold, and discuss why you excluded them from those calculations.
D. If raw material and work in process inventories had decreased during the year, would the financial statements be different? How?

43. Fausel Company manufactures wooden rocking chairs. Fausel purchased the following materials in June:

1,500 springs (part of the rocking mechanism) at a cost of $15,000; each chair uses two springs
Glue at a cost of $1,500 (enough to manufacture 500 chairs)
Stain at a cost of $500 (enough to manufacture 500 chairs)
Wood at a cost of $5,000 (enough to build 1,000 chair frames)

Fausel produced 500 chairs during June and had no beginning balances in raw materials, work in process, or finished goods inventories.

✓ Total manufacturing cost: $14,500

Required

A. Which of Fausel's material costs would likely be classified as direct materials? Which as indirect materials?
B. If Fausel completed only 400 of the 500 chairs on which production was started, what is the finished goods inventory account balance at the end of June?

C. If 380 of the finished chairs were sold, what would be the cost of goods sold?
D. What is the work in process inventory account balance at the end of June?

44. Business Games, Inc. (BGI) has designed the ultimate business board game. The game has been on the market for 10 years and the company has sold more than 20 million games. The game's wholesale price is $9 and the suggested retail price is $15. BGI has computed the cost of producing the game to be $5.40. The cost includes direct materials, direct labor, and overhead. BGI's management has decided that the time is right to produce a special edition of the game in a mahogany collector's box with a special game board and new, limited edition game pieces. Your job is to set a new sales price and decide whether the special game should be produced. You receive the following report from the accounting department to help you with your decision:

	Present Game	Special Game (Estimated)
Direct materials	$1.25	$30.50
Direct labor	2.00	3.50
Overhead	2.15	2.15
	$5.40	$36.15

Required

A. Is the above cost information sufficient to determine a sales price for each game? Why or why not?
B. What qualitative factors should be considered in deciding whether to produce and sell the special game?

45. Fletcher & Fuller, LLP is a local CPA firm that prepares approximately 1,000 tax returns each year for its clients. The managing partner of the firm has asked for information concerning the costs of preparing tax returns. He has been provided with the following data:

Average wage per hour of tax preparation staff	$ 35
Average wage per hour of clerical staff	$ 12
Average number of hours per return (preparation)	10
Average number of hours per return (clerical)	2

Required

A. What is Fletcher & Fuller's average direct labor cost of preparing a tax return?
B. Think creatively about options that might be used to reduce the cost of preparing tax returns. What are the implications of the options you suggest?
C. Fletcher & Fuller has an opportunity to purchase tax preparation software for $5,000 per year. If the software is used, the hours needed to prepare the return would decrease to 3 hours per return and the clerical time would increase to 4 hours because of additional computer operator time. How would the purchase affect the cost of labor on a per tax return basis?
D. Does it appear to be a good business decision to purchase the software? What other costs must be considered?
E. What are the qualitative aspects of the preceding decision?

46. Porter Manufacturing was organized on January 1 of the current year. Outside investors who financed the business stipulated that the company must show a profit by the sixth month or the financing will be stopped. Porter reported losses for the first four months, but expected to show a profit in the fifth and current month. After reviewing the income statement for the fifth month (May), the president, Craig, was disappointed with the performance and called an employee meeting. At the meeting, Craig informed the employees that based on the performance for the first five months and in particular the month of May, he saw very little hope of a profit by the sixth month. He also informed the employees that they should prepare to close the business. After the meeting, the controller quit, leaving you in charge of the accounting function. The latest financial information is as follows:

✓ Gross margin: $85,500

Porter Manufacturing
Income Statement
For the Month Ended May 31

Sales		$ 325,000
Less: Raw materials purchased	$140,000	
Direct labor	75,000	
Indirect labor	10,000	
Utilities	25,000	
Depreciation	30,000	
Insurance	15,000	
Rent	12,000	
Selling & administrative	30,000	
Advertising	25,000	
		362,000
Net loss		$ (37,000)

Other Information

Inventory	May 1 Balance	May 31 Balance
Raw material	$ 10,000	$ 30,000
Work in process	15,000	22,000
Finished goods	50,000	70,000

Seventy-five percent of utilities, depreciation, insurance, and rent are related to production operations, whereas 25 percent of those costs are related to selling and administrative activities.

Required

A. Prepare the income statement for May based on the information provided above. (Include a statement of cost of goods manufactured and a statement of cost of goods sold.)
B. Do you agree with the president's assessment of the situation? Why or why not?
C. How will you explain to the investors why your income statement is different from the one prepared by the controller?

47. Northern Lights Custom Cabinets manufactures and sells custom-ordered kitchen and bathroom cabinets. The company sells primarily to building contractors but occasionally deals directly with homeowners. Following is a summary of inventory and cost information for the year:

	Beginning Balance	Ending Balance
Raw material inventory	$ 10,000	$ 15,000
Work in process inventory	15,000	12,000
Finished goods inventory	30,000	32,000

During the year, raw material purchases totaled $350,000. Northern Lights incurred $200,000 for labor costs in the factory and $175,000 in manufacturing overhead for the year.

Required

A. Calculate the amount of direct materials transferred to work in process during the year.
B. Calculate total manufacturing costs for the year.
C. Calculate total cost of goods manufactured for the year.
D. Calculate cost of goods sold for the year.

48. Business managers frequently operate in a world where data are not readily available. Imagine a situation in which a company experiences a catastrophic event (for example, a hurricane, flood, or fire) and must reconstruct its accounting data. Consider the following independent situations in which selected data are missing:

	Company 1	Company 2
Direct materials used	$ 9,000	$ 19,000
Direct labor	4,000	14,000
Manufacturing overhead	11,000	?
Total manufacturing costs	?	35,000
Beginning work in process	?	11,000
Ending work in process	6,000	13,500
Cost of goods manufactured	$ 21,000	?
Sales	$ 35,000	$ 50,000
Beginning finished goods inventory	7,000	?
Cost of goods manufactured	?	?
Goods available for sale	?	?
Ending finished goods inventory	10,000	14,000
Cost of goods sold	?	25,500
Gross margin	?	?
Selling and administrative expenses	7,000	?
Net income	$?	$ 15,500

Required

A. Supply the missing data for each independent situation.
B. Prepare an income statement for each independent situation.

LO 4 5

✓ Cost of goods sold: $280,820

49. Hampton Corporation's accounting manager recently left the company without completing the company's schedule of cost of goods manufactured. The company's president is unsure what to do. He is unable to complete the schedule and has turned to you for help.

Hampton Corporation
Schedule of Cost of Goods Manufactured
For the month ended December 31, 2005

Direct Materials:		
Beginning raw materials	$ 16,000	
Raw materials purchases	?	
Raw materials available	164,000	
Ending raw materials	?	
Raw materials used in production		$ 154,500
Direct Labor		?
Manufacturing Overhead:		
Indirect labor	?	
Glue and fasteners	1,080	
Equipment depreciation	11,210	
Factory depreciation	4,300	
Factory insurance	2,420	
Property taxes	3,600	
Utilities	2,100	
Total manufacturing overhead		52,010
Total manufacturing costs		269,760
Add: Beginning work in process		?
		288,590
Deduct: Ending work in process		12,940
Cost of goods manufactured		$?

Inventories	Beginning Balance	Ending Balance
Raw materials	$ 16,000	?
Work in process	?	$ 12,940
Finished goods	23,000	17,830

Required

A. Supply the missing data.
B. Prepare an income statement for the month. Sales totaled $415,000 for December and selling and administrative expenses were $31,900.

LO 4 5

50. Dunn Computer Company began manufacturing personal computers for small businesses at the beginning of 2005. During the year, Dunn purchased 30,000 mouse pads with the company's name and logo at a cost of $2.50 each. The marketing manager used 2,500 of the pads as an advertising gimmick at a local trade show, and 25,000 of the pads were packaged with computers that were manufactured during 2005. Eighty percent of the computers were finished during the year; of that amount, 90 percent were sold.

Required

A. Determine the cost of the mouse pads that would be included in the following accounts as of December 31, 2005:
  a. Raw materials
  b. Work in process
  c. Finished goods

d. Cost of goods sold
   e. Advertising expense
   B. On which basic financial statement do the accounts in question A appear? Why does it matter on which basic financial statement the amounts associated with purchasing the computer mouse pads appears?

Cases

51. You recently began work at Martin & Oblinger Ltd. The company is a well-known distributor of gourmet foods. Like many similar companies, Martin & Oblinger currently maintain a relatively large warehouse in which a wide variety of products are stored. Most other food wholesalers maintain large warehouses; however, Sharon Oblinger, the company's president, is very concerned about the company's ability to maintain and sell the freshest products. She has also grown increasingly concerned about the company's cash management practices. She has accumulated the following inventory data:

Spices	$ 28,000
Coffee and tea	61,060
Pasta	32,140
Vegetables	108,460
Health supplements	84,700
Dairy	46,975
Meats	185,610
Personal products	71,440
Household	88,200
Pet care	15,920

Ken Martin, cofounder and chief strategist, is equally concerned about the company, but he believes that specialty food shops that sell the company's products expect to be able to order items from Martin & Oblinger and have them shipped immediately. In short, Ken thinks that maintaining an adequate inventory is crucial to the company's future. Sharon and Ken have set a meeting for late next week to decide on the company's adoption of a just-in-time inventory management system. Sharon is proposing that inventory be reduced by 80 percent and that warehouse employment be decreased by 30 percent. Currently, the 10 warehouse employees earn an average gross pay of $350 per week.

Required

A. What impact will reducing inventory by 80 percent have on Martin & Oblinger's ability to meet its customer demand?
B. If Sharon and Ken agree to reduce inventory, how should the company accomplish the reduction?
C. Assume that Martin & Oblinger can invest cash that would otherwise be "tied up" in inventory. Calculate the potential interest income if the company were to receive an annual interest rate of 3.5 percent on the cash that would otherwise be invested in the inventory represented by the 80 percent reduction.
D. While annual sales are currently $3,800,000, Ken believes that adopting a just-in-time system will ultimately cause problems such that customers will turn to other wholesalers for their needs. Ken is estimating lost revenues of 20 percent. If the company's gross profit is 30 percent of sales, what impact will the lost revenues have on the company's income statement?

E. Should Martin & Oblinger adopt the just-in-time inventory management system? Why or why not?

52. Crystal Glass is a producer of heirloom quality glassware. The company has a solid reputation and is widely regarded as a model corporate citizen. Your friend began working for the company last year as a financial analyst and has recently begun to question the company's squeaky clean image. Because you graduated with an accounting degree from a well-regarded university, your friend has asked you to look over Crystal's income statement and answer a few questions. The income statement appears as follows:

Crystal Glass, Inc.
Statement of Income
For the year ended October 31, 2005

Sales revenue	$ 12,008,450
Cost of goods sold	8,475,361
Gross profit	3,533,089
Selling & administrative expenses	1,845,902
Net income	$ 1,687,187

Your friend also asked that you look over the following supplementary schedule.

Crystal Glass, Inc.
Manufacturing Overhead Schedule
For the year ended October 31, 2005

Indirect labor	$ 743,012
Supplies	41,950
Advertising	210,375
Equipment depreciation	96,210
Factory depreciation	32,900
Factory insurance	22,420
Property taxes	18,600
Utilities	27,100
Management salary allocation	194,800
Total manufacturing overhead	$ 1,387,367

You are a little surprised to see the inclusion of advertising expense in the manufacturing overhead schedule and you really have no idea why the "management salary allocation" would be considered overhead.

Required

A. Where would you expect to see advertising expense included on an income statement? Does the inclusion of advertising in the overhead amount seem reasonable to you? Why might Crystal Glass want to include advertising expense in manufacturing overhead?

B. Your friend explains to you that the "management salary allocation" is the result of a corporate strategy of requiring that each part of the business bear some of the costs associated with management's functions. You learn that none of the salary allocation relates to management members that are associated with production operations. Is the inclusion of the salary allocation legitimate?

C. What is the financial statement impact of including advertising expenses and an allocation for management's salaries in manufacturing overhead?

Group and Internet Exercises

53. Just-in-time (JIT) techniques encompass a broad range of techniques designed to make businesses more efficient. Companies adopt JIT for a variety of reasons. For example, JIT might be used to simply reduce investments in inventory, strengthen relationships with suppliers, improve worker morale, and increase production efficiency. Within your group, select three companies (one manufacturer, one service-oriented organization, and one merchandiser) and discuss ways in which the companies could effectively implement JIT. Which of the organizations do you believe will benefit most greatly from JIT techniques? Will the companies' customers benefit? How?

54. Finding public information about product cost is not easy. Search the Internet to find annual reports and other financial information for two companies of your choosing. Determine the cost of goods sold for each company. Can you determine the cost of goods manufactured? Why do you suppose companies do not disclose more data about their product costs?

Chapter 3: Job Costing, Process Costing, and Operations Costing

Chapter 3 Job Costing, Process Costing, and Operations Costing

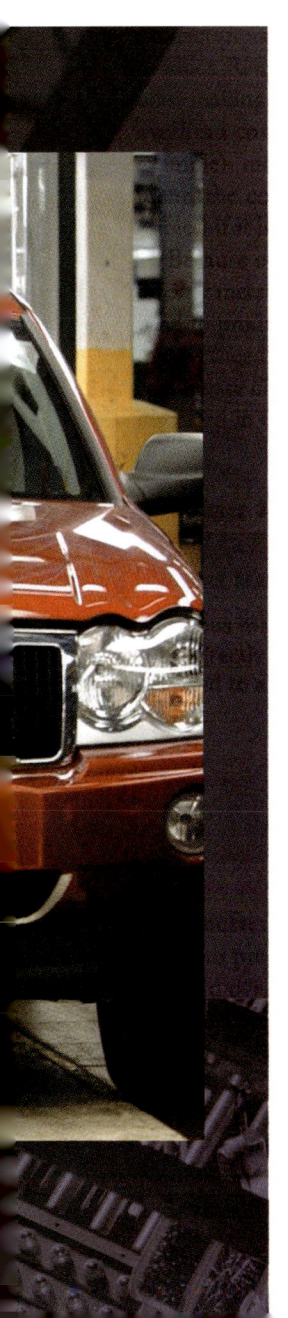

In Chapter 2, we defined product costs and discussed the flow of costs in manufacturing, merchandising, and service companies. Chapter 3 begins with a discussion of the basic systems that companies use to accumulate, track, and assign costs to products and services. These systems are called job costing, process costing, and operations costing. Job, process, and operations costing have the same goals—to accumulate, track, and assign direct material, direct labor, and overhead costs to the products and services a company produces and provides. Direct material and direct labor can usually be traced directly to products and services. But because of their indirect nature, overhead costs must be allocated to the products or services a company provides. Chapter 3 introduces the concept of cost pools and cost drivers and explains how they are used to allocate overhead, using plantwide and departmental overhead rates. The chapter includes a discussion of the use of overhead estimates (predetermined overhead rates) in product costing and the treatment of over- or underapplied overhead. The appendix of the chapter discusses process costing in more detail.

Learning Objectives

After studying the material in this chapter, you should be able to:

1 Contrast job costing, process costing, and operations costing and explain how they are used to accumulate, track, and assign product costs

2 Recognize issues related to the measurement of direct material and direct labor costs in job costing

3 Recognize issues related to the allocation of manufacturing overhead cost to products

4 Define a cost driver and demonstrate the use of cost drivers in calculating overhead rates in order to allocate overhead costs to products

5 Compare plantwide overhead rates to departmental overhead rates and demonstrate the use of each in costing products

6 Explain the need for using predetermined overhead rates and demonstrate the use of predetermined overhead rates in product costing

7 Calculate the amount of applied overhead in a normal costing system

8 Determine whether overhead has been over- or underapplied and demonstrate the alternative treatments of the over- or underapplied amount

9 Describe basic process costing and the calculation of equivalent units of production

10 Describe the use of backflush costing in companies utilizing JIT manufacturing techniques

11 (Appendix) Compare and contrast the weighted average and first-in, first-out (FIFO) methods of process costing and apply each step of the four-step process costing system under both methods

Introduction

One of the most important roles of managerial accountants is to help determine the cost of the products or services being produced and sold by a company. Cost information is equally important for manufacturing and service businesses and is used by managers across the organization. Pricing decisions made by marketing managers, manufacturing decisions made by production managers, and finance decisions made by finance managers are all influenced by the cost of products.

In today's competitive environment, managers must be aware of the impact of financial decisions on the overall success of their business. For example, marketing managers need to set a competitive price that will capture the needed market share and provide a fair profit. If the price of the product is set too low, a larger market share may be captured but the business may not earn a satisfactory profit. On the other hand, if the price of the product is too high, the business may not capture sufficient market share to remain competitive. These pricing decisions require product cost information in order for an optimal price to be set.

Production managers make decisions concerning whether to buy components used in manufacturing a product or to make them internally. For example, an automobile manufacturer could choose to make batteries used in its cars or to buy them from an outside supplier. The cost to make the battery compared to the cost of buying it would be important in this decision. The company would also consider qualitative factors, such as the reliability of the supplier and the quality of the battery. This and other production decisions are discussed in Chapter 7.

Doing Business.

CHASING PROFITS AT FORD

Striking a balance between market share, price, and profit margins is critical for the long-term success of any business. Selling a large volume of cars and trucks has always been important to Ford Motor Company. However, in early 2004, the chairman and chief executive of Ford announced that profits were more important than volume and began reducing capacity at many plants, dropping slow-selling models and models with low margins, and reducing rebates on other models. ("At Ford Motor, High Volume Takes Back Seat to Profits," *Wall Street Journal*, May 7, 2004).

Product-Costing Systems

Just as companies use different techniques to manufacture products or to provide services, companies also use various product-costing systems to accumulate, track, and assign the costs of production to the goods produced and services provided.

Objective 1

Contrast job costing, process costing, and operations costing and explain how they are used to accumulate, track, and assign product costs

Job Costing

Companies that manufacture customized products or provide customized services to clients use a costing system called **job costing,** which accumulates, tracks, and assigns costs for each job. Jobs are simply the individual units of a product. For a builder of custom homes, each house is a job. For a CPA firm, a job might be an individual tax return, an audit engagement, or a consulting engagement for a particular client. For a print shop, each order for wedding invitations, graduation announcements, or custom letterhead is a job. For a hospital, each patient is a job. In general, job costing is used in situations in which a customer initiates an order, which "pulls" the product or service through the process.

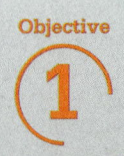

Process Costing

On the other hand, companies that produce a homogeneous product on a continuous basis (oil refineries, breweries, paint and paper manufacturers, for example) use **process costing** to accumulate, track, and assign costs to products. In general, process costing is used by companies that forecast demand and consequently "push" a product through the manufacturing process. Rather than accumulating the costs for each unit produced and directly tracking and assigning costs to each unique unit, process costing accumulates and tracks costs for each process as products pass through the process and then assigns costs equally to the units that come out of each process. A process is simply the work that is performed on a product. For a paint manufacturer, blending and pouring are processes. For a bread baker, mixing, baking, and slicing are processes. The details of process costing are demonstrated in the appendix to this chapter.

In this clothing manufacturer, each batch of T-shirts is costed using operations costing.

Operations Costing

Operations costing is a hybrid of job and process costing and is used by companies, such as clothing or automobile manufacturers, that make products in batches—large numbers of products that are standardized within a batch. For example, a clothing manufacturer might make 5,000 identical shirts in one batch. Each batch is costed like a job in job costing, but each shirt in the batch is costed like a homogeneous product in process costing. Exhibit 3-1 summarizes the types of products that would most likely be costed using job, operations, and process costing.

EXHIBIT 3-1   Product Costing Systems

	Costing System		
	Job Costing	Operations Costing	Process Costing
Type of Product	Custom	Standardized within batches	Homogeneous
Examples	Construction, movie studios, hospitals, print shops, CPA and law firms	Automobile and clothing manufacturers	Beverages, oil refineries, paint, paper, rolled steel

THE ETHICS OF BUSINESS
Paying For The Past

In August 1989, several former employees filed a lawsuit against Northrop Grumman claiming that the company had overcharged the Pentagon millions of dollars for work on fighter jets and bombers by falsely inflating, recording, and presenting costs that were not actually incurred. The fraudulent nature of the cover-up is captured in a sentence found in a 1986 memo distributed to company managers reading "We can't tell the truth."

Although this happened more than 15 years ago, Northrop Grumman's 2003 annual report disclosed that the U.S. government is seeking damages that could exceed $1.1 billion, asserting that the company failed to fix a faulty cost accounting system.

As of December 31, 2003, the company reported total assets of $33 billion and total revenue of $26.2 billion. While the company has significant resources, there is only $342 million in cash! Much of the company's balance sheet is not "liquid," meaning that most of the assets cannot be easily converted into cash. ("Northrop Papers Indicate Coverup," *Wall Street Journal*, April 19, 2004.)

It's Your Choice—If the Justice Department proves its case against Northrop Grumman, what sanctions are appropriate? Should former and current employees be personally liable for their roles in the cover-up?

Basic Job Costing for Manufacturing and Service Companies

Objective 2

Recognize issues related to the measurement of direct material and direct labor costs in job costing

Charles' Custom Furniture (CCF) uses job costing to accumulate, track, and assign costs to the cabinets it produces. The direct material, direct labor, and overhead costs for a specific job are accumulated on a job cost report. This report may be prepared manually or be totally automated. Regardless, its role is to keep track of the material, labor, and overhead costs that are incurred for a particular job. A job cost report for CCF is shown in Exhibit 3-2.

Measuring and Tracking Direct Material

Direct materials include the costs of the primary materials used in production. In addition to the cost of the materials themselves, the cost of direct materials includes shipping costs (if paid by the purchaser), sales tax paid on the purchase (if any) and other costs incurred in delivering the materials to the factory.

Measuring direct material cost should be a relatively easy task for CCF. The company has to identify only the amount of material actually used in each job and attach the proper cost to it. CCF uses a variety of materials, including wood, fabric, glue, screws, dowels, and stain in constructing a finished piece of furniture. Although some of the more common materials are stored in inventory, exotic and more expensive wood, fabric and hardware, such as handles, are typically purchased just in time for their use in a particular job. As it is needed for a particular job, raw material is recorded on the job cost report.

The amount and type of direct materials used in a job depend on the specific furniture built. Because they differ with each job, they must be accumulated, tracked, and assigned by job. It would not make good business sense for CCF to stock a large amount of expensive hardware items for furniture when some of the special hardware items may be used only once

Exhibit 3-2 Job Cost Report

Charles' Custom Furniture

Job Number: 101
Date Started: March 6
Description: TV Cabinet

Customer: Robyn Gray
Date Finished: March 19

Direct Materials		Direct Labor			Manufacturing Overhead		
Type	Cost	Employee	Hours	Amount	Hours	Rate	Amount
Oak	$ 875	Staley	12.6	$255.15	22.4	$12.50	$280.00
Maple	600	Chen	4.5	91.13			
Particleboard	78	Kent	5.3	107.33			
Glass	330						
	$1,803		22.4	$453.61	22.4		$280.00

Cost Summary

Direct Materials	$1,883.00
Direct Labor	453.61
Manufacturing Overhead	280.00
Total	$2,616.61

a year, so these items are purchased just in time to be used in production. On the other hand, because oak is used in over 50 percent of furniture, CCF chooses to keep enough on hand to meet two to three months of expected demand.

In Exhibit 3-2, you can see that CCF used oak, maple, particleboard, and glass in the manufacture of Job 101. These materials can all be traced directly to Job 101 and are treated as direct materials.

In Job 101, the customer has requested that the door be made of glass, a material that has a tendency to crack while being installed. Sure enough, as the material is being installed, it cracks and has to be discarded. How should the cost of the cracked material (spoilage) be treated? If the spoilage is considered normal, the cost is included in the determination of product costs. **Normal spoilage** results from the regular operation of the production process. If the broken glass is considered normal spoilage, its cost is treated as part of the direct material cost for the job being produced. On the other hand, other reasons, perhaps improper handling, poorly trained craftspeople, or equipment that is in poor condition, cause **abnormal spoilage.** If the glass was broken because a blade has not been properly sharpened, it would probably be considered abnormal spoilage.

How should you treat the cost of abnormal spoilage? Would it be fair to treat it as part of the direct material cost for the job being produced? Should the cost of abnormal waste be passed on to the customer as an increase in the sales price? Abnormal spoilage should be expensed as a period cost or included in manufacturing overhead, where the cost is spread across all jobs completed during the period. Abnormal spoilage should not be treated as direct material cost, where it would be considered in the cost of a specific job.

CCF also uses a variety of wooden dowels, screws, glues, and finishing nails in the construction of Job 101. However, you should note that these items are not listed as direct materials on the job cost report in Exhibit 3-2. Although it may be physically possible to track the specific screws, glue, and nails to a particular job, the cost of doing so is great and the benefits are few. CCF has chosen to treat these materials as indirect material that will be allocated to the job as part of overhead.

Companies that primarily provide services to clients or have minimal material costs may not treat any materials as direct. For example, a law firm that primarily prepares wills and other paper documents may choose to treat the costs of paper as an indirect material (part of overhead). Likewise, although CPA firms may use a lot of paper and other materials processing tax returns for clients, they may not track the paper to specific jobs on a job cost report. On the other hand, a hospital might choose to itemize every pill (even aspirin) and other medication given to a patient and every bandage used in an operation on a patient's job cost report (the patient's case file).

Tracking the use of pills and other medications to a patient provides other valuable benefits to doctors and the hospital. Doctors need to know exactly what medications have been given and when. Although it may also provide a way to charge patients for the cost of medications they consume during a hospital stay, the costing of the medications is probably not as important as the tracking itself.

Measuring and Tracking Direct Labor

The costs of direct labor include the wages earned by production workers for the actual time spent working on a product. The measurement of direct labor cost also should be a relatively easy task. Direct labor cost refers to labor that is directly related to the manufacture of a product or providing a service. Assembly-line workers in a manufacturing setting and CPAs working on tax returns are examples of direct labor. On the other hand, manufacturing supervisors, janitorial staff, and maintenance personnel in a manufacturing company and secretarial staff in a CPA firm are considered indirect labor and are included in overhead. The costs of direct labor for a specific job are accumulated on a job cost report, but most companies keep track of each employee's time by requiring the completion of time sheets. Time sheets may be prepared by hand or be totally automated and integrated with the company's accounting information system. Regardless of the form used, employees must keep track of how much time they spend on specific jobs. For assembly-line workers, management needs to know how much time is spent manufacturing a specific product. For CPAs and attorneys, the managing partner needs to know how many hours are spent servicing a particular client.

The cost of direct labor is simply calculated by multiplying a wage rate for each employee by the number of hours that each employee works on each product.

Fringe Benefits In addition to the hourly cost of labor, wage rates must also include the cost of **fringe benefits.** These fringe benefits include the employer's cost for health, dental, and other insurance; retirement plans; and so on. The employer portion of social security tax and state and federal unemployment taxes would also be included. Studies have shown that fringe benefits typically cost a company 30 to 35 percent of the base wage of each full-time employee. The job cost report in Exhibit 3-2 shows that three employees of CCF worked 22.4 hours on Job 101 at a cost of $20.25 per hour. This cost includes a $15 hourly wage rate plus benefits of $5.25 per hour.

Idle Time As a result of a power outage, CCF incurred idle time while working on Job 101. Would CCF most likely treat this idle time as overhead or an additional cost of direct labor assigned directly to Job 101? Not all the time that direct labor workers are paid for is spent productively. For example, if machinery and equipment break down or if materials are not available when needed, **idle time** results. How should idle time of direct labor workers be treated? Although idle time could be traced to a specific job (the job that is being worked on when the idle time occurs), most companies choose to treat idle time as an overhead cost rather than a cost of a specific job.

Overtime **Overtime premiums** paid to direct labor workers cause similar classification problems. Overtime is typically paid at 150 percent of the normal wage rate (sometimes called "time and a half") for hours worked in excess of 40 per week. For example, let's assume that the hourly pay for an assembly-line worker is $15. An overtime premium for this worker would be $7.50 per hour, increasing the total hourly wage to $22.50. With fringe benefits at 35 percent, the cost of labor rises to $30.38 per hour. Overtime may be incurred for a number of reasons. Sometimes, production problems cause a company to get behind on a job. When this happens, the company may choose to incur overtime costs (work over the weekend) to finish up a job on time. In other situations, a company might accept an order, knowing that it will require the scheduling of overtime.

In practice, the treatment of overtime costs depends on the reason the overhead is incurred. If overtime is incurred as a result of production problems, most companies treat the cost as overhead. On the other hand, if the overtime results from the acceptance of a rush order, most companies would treat the overhead as a direct labor cost that would be assigned directly to the specific job (and would most likely be included in determining its price).

For example, on a Friday morning, the customer who had ordered Job 101 called CCF and said she needed the TV cabinet next Monday instead of next Wednesday. CCF craftspeople worked eight hours on Saturday, and the company incurred overtime premiums in order to finish the job by the new due date. CCF likely would treat the overtime premium as a direct labor cost in this situation.

In highly automated manufacturing environments, the cost of direct labor has been reduced significantly as automated machinery and robotics have replaced direct labor workers. As discussed more thoroughly later in the chapter, this shift in product costs from labor to overhead has had important implications for product costing. Whereas the cost of direct labor is relatively easy to accumulate, track, and assign to products, overhead costs are a different matter.

Manufacturing Overhead

Overhead is the most difficult product cost to accumulate, track, and assign to products. Unlike direct materials and direct labor, overhead is made up of several seemingly unrelated costs—rent, depreciation, insurance, repairs and maintenance, utilities, indirect labor, indirect material, and so on. In addition, most overhead is indirect in nature. As a result, overhead it cannot be directly tracked to products and services but must instead be allocated.[1]

Allocation involves finding a logical method of assigning overhead costs to the products or services a company produces or provides. If a company produces only one product, the allocation would be simple. We could simply divide the total overhead cost by the total number of units produced. If our total overhead costs incurred during the year were $100,000 and we produced 20,000 identical tables during the year, it would be logical to assign $5 of overhead to each table ($100,000/20,000 tables). However, what if we make 10,000 tables and 10,000 chairs? Does it still make sense to allocate overhead based on the number of units produced? Probably not. A more logical approach might be to allocate the overhead to the tables and chairs based on the number of direct labor hours or machine hours consumed in the manufacture of each. If chairs take twice as long to manufacture as tables, twice as much overhead would be allocated to them. The choice of an allocation base requires a thorough understanding of what causes overhead costs to be incurred.

Objective 3

Recognize issues related to the allocation of manufacturing overhead cost to products

KEY CONCEPT

Overhead cannot be directly tracked to products and services but must instead be allocated using cost drivers.

Cost Drivers and Overhead Rates

Understanding what causes overhead costs to be incurred is the key to allocating overhead. The choice of a logical base on which to allocate overhead depends on finding a cause-and-effect relationship between the base and the overhead. A good allocation base is one that drives the incurrence of the overhead cost. Therefore, allocation bases are often referred to as **cost drivers.**

---

[1] Although many overhead costs in a just-in-time (JIT) environment will also be indirect in nature (rent and utilities, for example), more of the costs are likely to be direct. For example, in a JIT environment, the cost of machinery in a manufacturing cell can be traced to a specific product (tables) if it is used only to make tables.

Objective 4

Define a cost driver and demonstrate the use of cost drivers in calculating overhead rates in order to allocate overhead costs to products

KEY CONCEPT

Understanding what causes overhead costs to be incurred (what drives them) is the key to allocating overhead.

A cost driver for overhead is an activity that causes overhead to be incurred. If we wanted to allocate the cost of utilities incurred to run machines in the factory to products, we would want to find a cost driver that causes the utility costs to be incurred. In this case, the time the machines were in use (machine hours) might be an appropriate allocation base. If it takes twice as many machine hours to make chairs as it does to make tables, chairs would correspondingly be allocated twice as much utility cost. Other overhead costs associated with machines, such as depreciation and repairs and maintenance, could be allocated using the same cost driver. In more labor intensive companies, the cost of utilities might be allocated using direct labor hours as the cost driver. In that case, if it takes three labor hours to make a table and only one labor hour to make a chair, a table would be allocated three times as much overhead as a chair. The choice of cost driver depends on the specific company and the processes it utilizes in manufacturing products and providing services to customers.

Overhead consists of a variety of costs with potentially different drivers for each. For example, the salaries of janitors and supervisors in the factory are overhead costs. The costs of rent and insurance for the factory building are overhead costs. The costs of indirect materials are overhead costs. Instead of identifying cost drivers for each component of overhead, companies have traditionally lumped overhead into similar **cost pools** to simplify the task. In the most extreme case, companies lump all overhead costs into one cost pool for the entire factory. Other companies have separate pools of overhead costs for each department. Still others use cost pools for each activity performed in making a product. Regardless of the number of cost pools and method of overhead allocation used, overhead rates are calculated using the same basic formula:

$$\text{Overhead rate} = \text{Manufacturing overhead} / \text{Cost driver}$$

CCF incurs utility costs of $1,000 during the month and starts and finishes 12 jobs. Each job requires machine time, but the time varies greatly, depending on the materials used and the difficulty of the job. Job 101 required 22.4 labor hours, whereas Job 104 required 60 hours. The total labor hours during the month totaled 500. If CCF allocates utility cost using labor hours as the cost driver, how much of the utility cost should be allocated to Job 101? How much to Job 104? The overhead rate for utility costs is $2 per direct labor hour ($1,000/500 direct labor hours). Therefore, $44.80 of utility costs (22.4 × $2 per hour) should be allocated to Job 101, whereas $120 of utility costs (60 hours × $2 per hour) should be allocated to Job 104.

Plantwide Overhead Rates

Objective 5

Compare plantwide overhead rates to departmental overhead rates and demonstrate the use of each in costing products

In labor intensive manufacturing companies and service industries, direct labor hours or direct labor cost have often served as cost drivers. In automated manufacturing environments, machine hours historically have been used as the cost driver. Direct labor hours and machine hours are both volume-based cost drivers—that is, they are directly related to the volume or number of units produced. Allocating overhead based on direct labor hours or machine time works well when companies make only a few products, when they incur relatively small overhead costs compared to labor and material costs, and when that overhead is related to the volume of products produced.

For example, as demonstrated in Exhibit 3-3, a pizza restaurant might apply overhead by using a single predetermined overhead rate for the entire restaurant. The costs of pizza ovens, rent, utilities, and other overhead costs would be lumped into one cost pool and allocated to products (pizzas), based on the amount of labor time (direct labor hours, or DLHs) it takes to make each pizza. In this case, the cost of overhead is relatively small and is likely to be related to the number of pizzas made. In other words, it is volume-based.

In Exhibit 3-4, overhead costs total $8,000 per month. If direct labor hours per month are 800, the overhead rate is equal to $10.00 per direct labor hour. If a thick crust pizza takes 10 minutes of direct labor time to produce, a thin crust pizza takes 6 minutes to produce and a deep dish pizza takes 15 minutes to produce, the amount of overhead allocated to each is $1.66, $1.00, and $2.50, respectively.

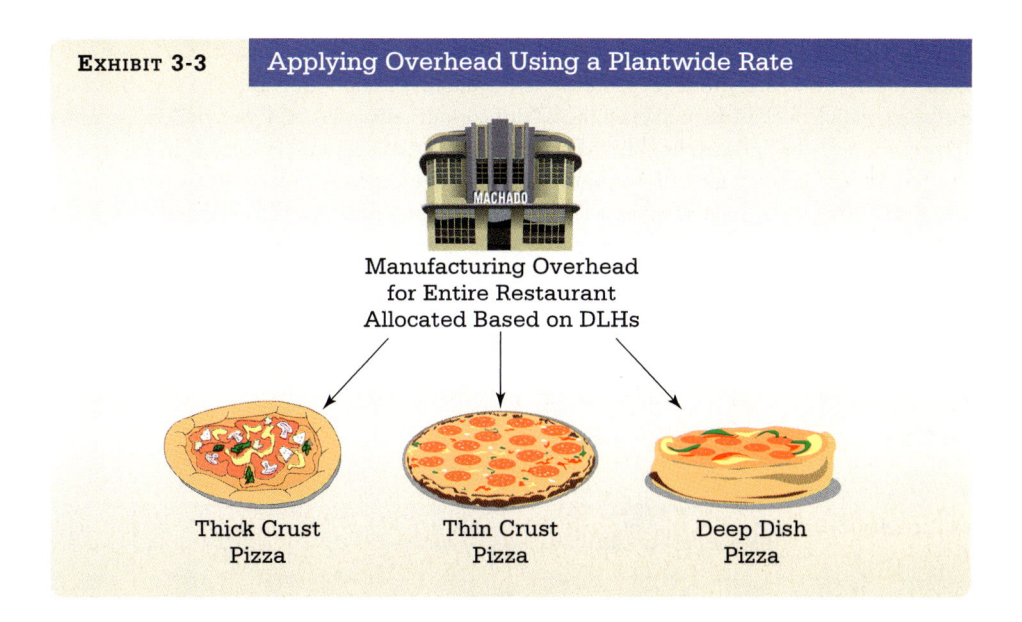

Exhibit 3-3 — Applying Overhead Using a Plantwide Rate

Manufacturing Overhead for Entire Restaurant Allocated Based on DLHs

- Thick Crust Pizza
- Thin Crust Pizza
- Deep Dish Pizza

Exhibit 3-4 — Overhead Allocation Using Direct Labor Hours as the Cost Driver

Overhead costs per month:

Depreciation on pizza ovens	$1,500
Rent	2,000
Utilities	1,000
Other	3,500
Total	$8,000

Direct labor hours (DLHs) per month   800 direct labor hours

Overhead per direct labor hour   ($8,000/800 DLHs) = $10.00 per DLH

Direct labor hours per pizza:
- Thick crust   10 minutes
- Thin crust   6 minutes
- Deep dish   15 minutes

Allocation of overhead for each type of pizza:

Thick crust	$10.00 × 1/6 hour of labor	= $1.66
Thin crust	$10.00 × 1/10 hour of labor	= $1.00
Deep dish	$10.00 × 1/4 hour of labor	= $2.50

Departmental Overhead Rates

As companies make more diverse products and become more heavily automated, the use of plantwide cost pools and single cost drivers may provide less than accurate cost information. Companies using departmental overhead rates form separate cost pools for each department. The overhead in each cost pool can then be applied to products based on different cost drivers. Consider the pizza restaurant again. Let's assume that the restaurant has two primary departments—one that produces pizzas for in-restaurant consumption and a second that produces partially cooked (par-cooked) pizzas for take-out customers and the wholesale market (grocery stores). The process used to make pizzas in the two departments varies. In contrast to the production of pizzas for consumption in the restaurant, production of the par-cooked pizzas is much more automated using an automated mixing machine for dough and an automated oven in which the pizzas move through the oven on a conveyor belt to ensure a uniform level of baking and an automatic wrapping machine.

In this scenario, it would make sense for the restaurant to accumulate overhead costs into two cost pools—one for each department. Although the overhead costs associated with the traditional in-restaurant sales might still be allocated based on direct labor hours incurred, a better driver of the costs associated with the wholesale activities (which is more heavily automated) might be machine hours (see Exhibit 3-5).

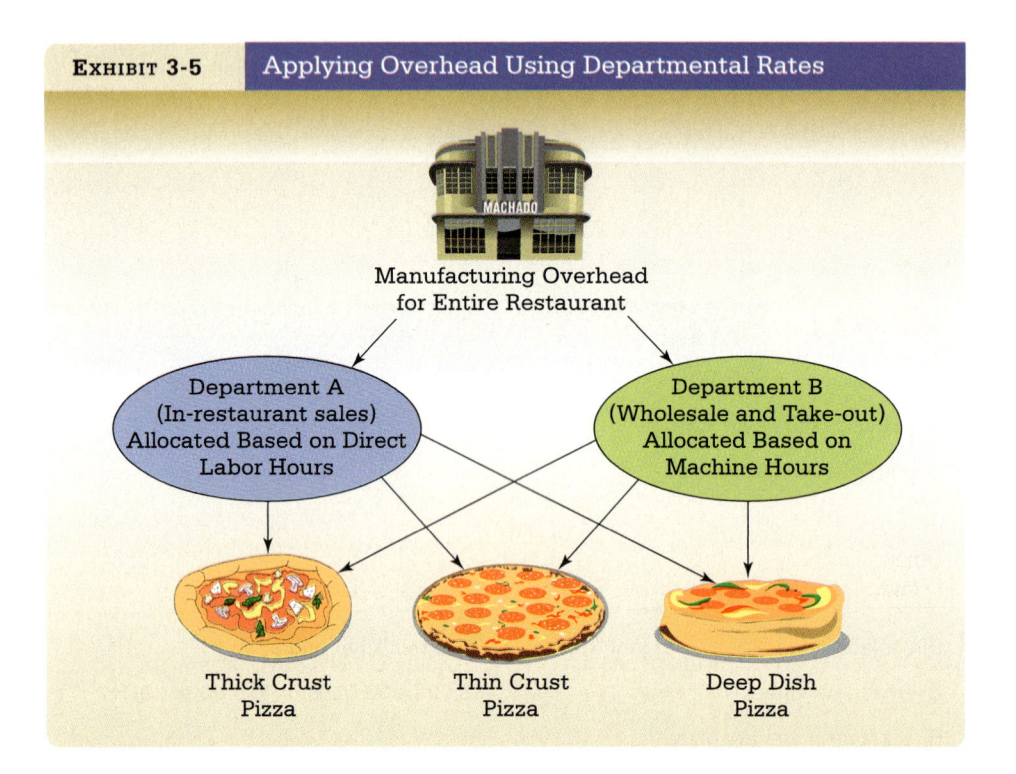

EXHIBIT 3-5 Applying Overhead Using Departmental Rates

Manufacturing Overhead for Entire Restaurant

- Department A (In-restaurant sales) Allocated Based on Direct Labor Hours
- Department B (Wholesale and Take-out) Allocated Based on Machine Hours

Thick Crust Pizza — Thin Crust Pizza — Deep Dish Pizza

In Exhibit 3-6, overhead costs once again total $8,000 per month. However, the restaurant now accumulates the overhead cost by department—$2,000 for Department A and $6,000 for Department B. Department A allocates its overhead based on direct labor hours while Department B allocates its overhead based on machine hours (MHs). The overhead rate for Department A is now $2.50 per direct labor hour ($2,000/800 direct labor hours) while the overhead rate in Department B is $6.00 per machine hour ($6,000/1,000 machine hours).

The choice of a single plantwide overhead rate or multiple overhead rates depends on a variety of factors and an analysis of the costs and benefits of each approach. The use of a single plantwide rate is easier, less time consuming, and cheaper than the use of multiple departmental overhead rates. But departmental rates can provide more accurate cost information. This is particularly true when multiple products are produced, the products consume resources differently, and departments perform very different activities. Regardless of whether a single rate or multiple rates are used, choosing an appropriate cost driver is an important factor.

In heavily automated manufacturing environments, direct labor costs have shrunk to as little as 5 percent of total production costs, whereas overhead costs have soared to 60 percent or more of total product costs. It's not hard to see why. Consider a modern automobile manufacturing plant. High-tech computers control robots that weld, paint, and perform other jobs

KEY CONCEPT

Accuracy in overhead application has become much more important as overhead costs have increased and make up a larger portion of the total costs of products.

Exhibit 3-6: Overhead Allocation Using Departmental Overhead Rates

Department A (In-restaurant sales)	$2,000 per month
Department B (Wholesale and take-out)	6,000 per month
Total overhead per month (see Exhibit 3-4)	$8,000 per month

Department A overhead allocation:

Direct labor hours (DLHs) per month   800 direct labor hours

Overhead per direct labor hour   ($2,000/800 DLHs) = $2.50 per DLH

Direct labor hours per pizza:
 Thick crust   10 minutes
 Thin crust   6 minutes
 Deep dish   15 minutes

Allocation of overhead from Department A for each type of pizza:

Thick crust $2.50 × 1/6 DLH   = $.416
Thin crust $2.50 × 1/10 DLH = $.25
Deep dish $2.50 × 1/4 DLH   = $.625

Department B overhead allocation:

Machine hours (MH) per month   1,000 Machine hours

Overhead per machine hour   ($6,000/1,000 MHs) = $6.00 per MH

Machine hours per pizza:
 Thick crust   15 minutes
 Thin crust   5 minutes
 Deep dish   20 minutes

Allocation of overhead from Department B for each type of pizza:

Thick crust $6.00 × 1/4 MH   = $1.50
Thin crust $6.00 × 1/12 MH = $ .50
Deep dish $6.00 × 1/3 MH   = $2.00

---

that were previously done by humans. These machines are very expensive and are treated as part of overhead cost. As overhead costs have increased and make up a much larger portion of the total costs of products, accuracy in overhead application has become much more important as well. Overhead allocation using multiple cost pools and overhead rates based on the activities performed in a company is discussed in Chapter 4.

KEY CONCEPT

Accuracy in overhead application become much more important as overhead costs have increased and make up a larger portion of the total costs of products.

The Use of Estimates

It is not unusual for managers to want to estimate the cost of a product before it is actually produced. Having timely cost information is useful for pricing decisions as well as for production decisions. However, because the actual amount of many overhead items will not be known until the end of a period (perhaps when an invoice is received), companies often estimate the amount of overhead that will be incurred in the coming period. For example, a manufacturer of computers that are custom made to meet customer requirements needs to know the cost of producing each computer so it can establish a sales price. Customers place orders

Objective 6

Explain the need for using predetermined overhead rates and demonstrate the use of predetermined overhead rates in product costing

24 hours a day, and the company's policy is to ship computers to customers within 48 hours of the order. Although the company has records of each component and other material used in the assembly of the computer and knows the exact amount of time workers spend putting the computer together (remember the job cost report discussed earlier), calculating the actual amount of overhead cost incurred is virtually impossible to do in a timely manner. Why? Because the amount of most overhead items, such as utilities expense, maintenance expense, supplies, and so forth, will not be known until after the computer is assembled and shipped. The only alternative, short of requiring the customer to wait until the end of the period to know the actual price of the computer, is to estimate the amount of overhead on each computer and to set the sales price accordingly. Using estimates has another advantage as well. It is not unusual for overhead to fluctuate during the year. For example, the utilities costs incurred by Ben & Jerry's (whose factory is located in Vermont) during the winter are likely to be higher than those incurred in the summer. If Ben & Jerry's used actual overhead costs to cost products, the ice cream the company makes in February would cost more than the ice cream it makes in May. Using estimates smoothes out, or normalizes, seasonal and random fluctuations in overhead costs. Thus, this method of costing is often called **normal costing.**

Predetermined Overhead Rates

Companies that estimate the amount of overhead cost incurred in costing products allocate overhead by using predetermined overhead rates. **Predetermined overhead rates** are calculated using a slight modification of the basic overhead rate formula:

$$\text{Predetermined overhead rate (for a cost pool)} = \frac{\text{Estimated overhead for the cost pool}}{\text{Estimated units of the cost driver}}$$

Predetermined overhead rates are typically calculated using annual estimates of overhead and cost drivers, although some companies do more frequent calculations.

The Application of Overhead Products The allocation of overhead using predetermined overhead rates is called an application of overhead. The amount of overhead applied to a product is calculated by multiplying the predetermined overhead rate by the actual units of the cost driver incurred in producing the product or service.

$$\text{Applied overhead} = \text{Predetermined overhead rate} \times \text{Actual units of cost driver}$$

The cost of a product or a service for a company utilizing normal costing therefore includes an actual amount of direct material, an actual amount of direct labor, and an applied amount of manufacturing overhead based on estimates.

Calculating predetermined overhead rates is a three-step process. Step 1 involves the identification and estimation of the overhead costs included in the plantwide or departmental cost pool. Step 2 involves the identification and estimation of the appropriate allocation base (the cost driver). Step 3 is the actual computation of the predetermined overhead rate.

As an example, let's assume that CCF has chosen to lump all overhead into one cost pool for the entire factory (a plantwide cost pool). The company identifies overhead costs as including the cost of utilities, insurance, and rent for the factory building; depreciation and repairs and maintenance of manufacturing equipment; supplies used in the factory; and the salaries of a production supervisor and janitor in the factory. The company further estimates that these costs should total about $100,000 in the next year. As CCF is very labor intensive, it has chosen labor hours as the cost driver and estimates using 8,000 labor hours during the next year. Dividing the estimated overhead of $100,000 by the estimated allocation base of 8,000 labor hours results in a predetermined overhead rate of $12.50 per labor hour.

$$\frac{\$100,000}{8,000} = \$12.50 \text{ per labor hour}$$

In other words, for every labor hour worked on a product, the company should apply $12.50 in overhead cost. As shown in Exhibit 3-2 (page 67), since Job 101 required 22.4 labor hours, it was allocated $280.00 of overhead.

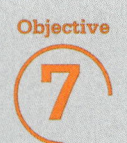

The Problem of Over- and Underapplied Overhead

Because overhead is applied to products using predetermined overhead rates based on estimates, it is likely that actual overhead costs (when they become known) will differ from that applied. If applied overhead is greater than actual overhead, the company **overapplied overhead**. If the applied overhead is less than actual overhead, the company **underapplied overhead** for the period. Over- and underapplied overhead can occur for a couple of reasons—estimating the overhead incorrectly or estimating the cost driver incorrectly. As shown in Exhibit 3-7, CCF had a predetermined overhead rate of $12.50 per direct labor hour based on estimated overhead of $100,000 and estimated direct labor hours of 8,000. If during the year, 8,100 direct labor hours are actually incurred in making furniture, CCF's applied overhead will be $101,250.

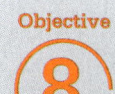

Objective 8

Determine whether overhead has been over- or underapplied and demonstrate the alternative treatments of the over- or underapplied amount

Exhibit 3-7 The Calculation of Applied Overhead

Estimated overhead	$100,000
Estimated units of cost driver	8,000 direct labor hours
Predetermined overhead rate	$12.50 ($100,000/8,000 DLHs)
Applied overhead = Predetermined overhead rate × actual direct labor hours	
Applied overhead	$101,250 ($12.50 per DLH × 8,100 direct labor hours)

Now, assume that the actual overhead costs for CCF total $102,000 and consist of the following:

Indirect labor	$ 25,000
Indirect material	10,000
Utilities expense	30,000
Maintenance expense	25,000
Insurance expense	7,000
Supplies expense	5,000
Total	$102,000

Under a normal costing system, as actual overhead costs are incurred throughout the year, the manufacturing overhead account is increased (debited) for the amount of the actual costs. The journal entry to record the payment of overhead expenses and the transfer of those costs to manufacturing overhead is:

Manufacturing overhead	$102,000	
Accounts payable or cash		$102,000

Likewise, as individual jobs are completed throughout the year, overhead is applied to work in process using the predetermined overhead rate.

As shown in Exhibit 3-7, CCF's applied overhead was $101,250. The journal entry to record the application of overhead to work in process requires a debit to work in process and a credit to manufacturing overhead.

Work in process inventory	$101,250	
Manufacturing overhead		$101,250

The manufacturing overhead account essentially serves as a clearing account. At this point (see Exhibit 3-8) the manufacturing overhead account has a debit balance of $102,000 and a credit balance of $101,250.

EXHIBIT 3-8　The Manufacturing Overhead Account

Manufacturing Overhead	
$102,000	$101,250
Actual overhead costs as incurred	Overhead applied to WIP using the predetermined overhead rate

CCF's actual overhead is greater than the applied overhead by $750. Consequently, CCF has underapplied overhead in the amount of $750. What impact does the underapplied overhead have on the cost of furniture produced by CCF?

Because applied overhead is accumulated in work in process (WIP) and then transferred to finished goods as units are completed and then to cost of goods sold as units are sold, if everything is sold, adjusting for over- or underapplied overhead involves adjusting the balance of the cost of goods sold account. In practice (particularly in a JIT manufacturing environment) this is likely to be the case. Jobs are typically completed and sold before any adjustment could be made to an inventory account. In our case, if CCF sells all the furniture it produces, its cost of goods sold would be understated by $750 and our adjustment would increase cost of goods sold by $750. But what if some of the furniture were not sold or perhaps not even finished? Then, the $750 might be allocated in some fashion to WIP, finished goods, and cost of goods sold to recognize that all three accounts are too low. This allocation is usually based on the amount of overhead in each account. As an alternative, if the amount of the adjustment is immaterial, companies may choose to adjust only the cost of goods sold account. Assume that the amount of overhead in WIP, finished goods, and cost of goods sold is as follows:

Work in process	$ 20,250	(20% of total)
Finished goods	30,375	(30% of total)
Cost of goods sold	50,625	(50% of total)
Total	$101,250	

If the amount of underapplied overhead is considered immaterial, the cost of goods sold is adjusted by the entire $750. The balance after adjustment is $51,375.

	Original Balance		Underapplied Overhead		Adjusted Balance
Cost of goods sold	$50,625	+	$750	=	$51,375*

*Note that the underapplied overhead increases the cost of goods sold amount. If overhead had been overapplied, the adjustment would have decreased the cost of goods sold balance.

The journal entry to record the adjustment to cost of goods sold is:

Cost of goods sold	$750	
Manufacturing overhead		$750

On the other hand, if the amount of underapplied overhead is considered material, the underapplied overhead might be allocated to WIP, finished goods, and cost of goods sold. After adjustment, the amount of overhead in each inventory account is as follows:

	Original Balance		Underapplied Overhead		Adjusted Balance
Work in process	$20,250	+	$150	=	$20,400
Finished goods	30,375	+	225	=	30,600
Cost of goods sold	50,625	+	375	=	51,000
Total	$101,250	+	$750	=	$102,000

The journal entry to allocate the underapplied overhead to the three accounts is:

Work in process	$150	
Finished goods	$225	
Cost of goods sold	$375	
Manufacturing overhead		$750

Hitting the Bottom Line.

THIS CHOICE MAKES A DIFFERENCE

The choice of allocating under- and overapplied overhead to work in process, finished goods, and cost of goods sold versus an adjustment only to cost of goods sold has other implications as well. For example, consider the case of an accounting manager whose compensation is partially based on company net income. Allocating all of the underapplied overhead in Exhibit 3-8 to cost of goods sold reduces net income by $750. Had the manager allocated the underapplied balance to work in process, finished goods, and cost of goods sold, income would have been reduced by only $375. However, the impact on income is only temporary. As work in process is completed and finished goods are sold next year, the remaining costs that are "stuck" in inventory will be expensed.

Objective 9

Describe basic process costing and the calculation of equivalent units of production

Basic Process Costing

Companies that produce beverages and other products (paint, paper, oil, and textiles) in a continuous flow production process typically use process costing. As mentioned previously, instead of accumulating, tracking, and assigning direct material and direct labor costs directly to each job, process costing systems accumulate and track direct material and direct labor costs by department and then assign the costs evenly to the products that pass through each department. Likewise, instead of applying overhead to each specific job, overhead is applied to each department and then assigned evenly to each product that passes through. Although the application to job or department differs, the amount of overhead applied is calculated in exactly the same way. After predetermined overhead rates are developed, overhead is applied by multiplying the predetermined overhead rate by the actual units of cost driver incurred in each department. A comparison of the cost flows in job costing and process costing is shown in Exhibit 3-9.

In companies with no beginning or ending inventories (all units are finished), the mechanics of process costing are very simple. Because all the units produced are identical, costs accumulated and tracked in each department can simply be averaged across all the units that are produced. If $30,000 of direct material costs and $70,000 of direct labor and overhead costs are incurred in the blending department of a paint manufacturer, and 10,000 gallons of product are produced, the cost of blending each gallon is $10 per gallon and the 10,000 finished units cost $100,000 to produce.

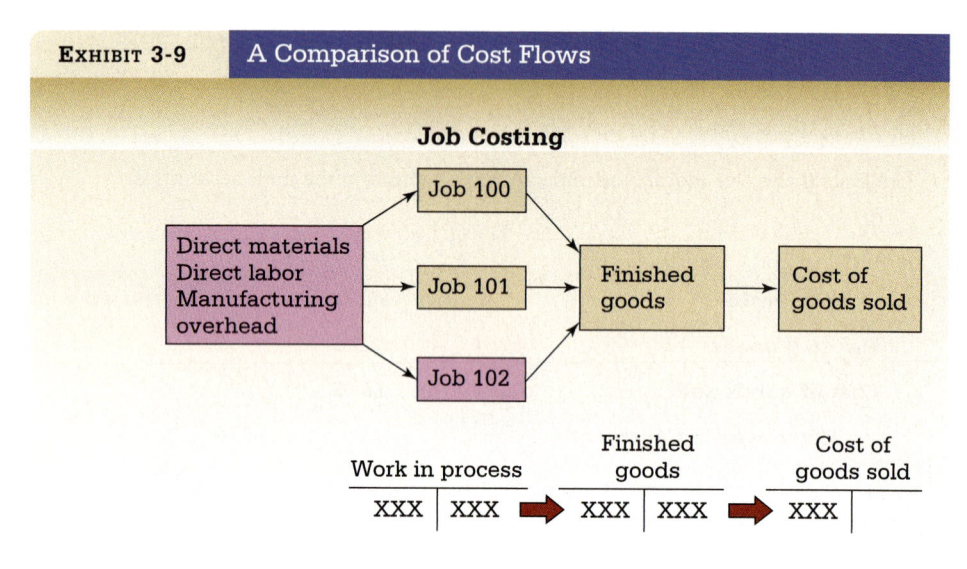

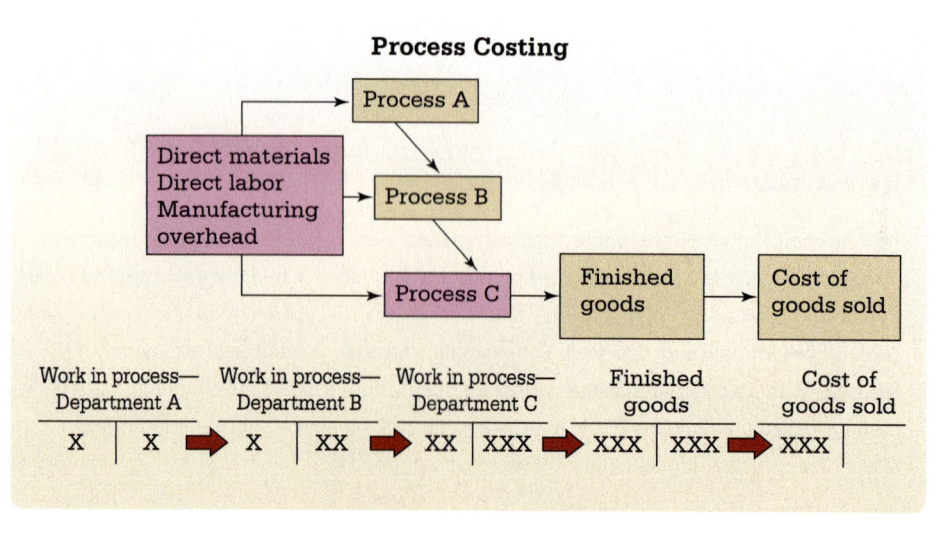

EXHIBIT 3-9 A Comparison of Cost Flows

However, problems quickly arise when companies have inventories. Let's assume that the blending department finishes blending only 8,000 gallons and that 2,000 gallons are left in ending WIP at the end of the year. These 2,000 gallons are 50 percent complete and will require additional materials, labor, and overhead during the next period before they are finished. Should each gallon (finished or unfinished) still cost $10 in this case? That would mean that our 8,000 finished units cost $80,000, whereas our 2,000 unfinished units cost $20,000. Of course, that would not make sense, because we would expect our finished units to cost more per gallon than those that are only half finished!

To get around this problem, we need to calculate the number of **equivalent units** completed during the period. If two units are uniformly 50 percent finished at the end of a period, we have finished the equivalent of one complete unit. In the previous example, we partially finished 2,000 units with each unit uniformly 50 percent complete. How many finished units could we have completed using the same amount of direct materials, labor, and overhead? The 2,000 units that are 50 percent finished are the equivalent of 1,000 finished units. Therefore, our total equivalent units finished during the period equals 9,000—the 8,000 units we actually finished plus another 1,000 equivalent finished units in ending WIP.

Our cost per equivalent unit is therefore $11.11 ($100,000/9,000 equivalent units) and the 8,000 finished units cost $88,880, whereas the 2,000 units in ending inventory (1,000 equivalent units) cost $11,120 ($100,000 − $88,880). Process costing and the calculation of equivalent units are substantially more complicated when companies have both beginning and ending inventories of WIP.

Another difference between job costing and process costing is that process cost systems often require multiple WIP accounts—one for every process. As products are moved from one process to another, the costs of the previous process are simply transferred to the next process. For example, a paint manufacturer accumulates and tracks direct material, direct labor, and overhead costs to a WIP account for each process (blending and pouring). The total costs for each process are then assigned to the paint by dividing by the number of gallons of paint that come out of each process. The total cost of each gallon is therefore the sum of the costs assigned from each process and an average of the costs incurred in each process. For a more detailed discussion of process costing, see the appendix to this chapter on page 80.

Backflush Costing

Companies utilizing just-in-time manufacturing techniques generally have little or no inventory of raw material, WIP, or finished goods. Remember that products are typically produced only after an order has been placed, so theoretically all units produced will be sold. Although managers still need to know the cost of goods produced using JIT techniques, the costing process used is greatly simplified by recording all manufacturing costs directly into cost of goods sold. As can be seen in Exhibit 3-10, instead of sequentially tracking manufacturing costs through raw materials inventory, WIP, finished goods, and cost of goods sold, manufacturing costs are flushed directly into cost of goods sold. At the end of the period, if the company has small amounts of inventory on hand, manufacturing costs are backflushed into the appropriate inventory account. This is the exception rather than the rule. In most cases, we would expect all costs to remain in cost of goods sold.

A chief attraction of **backflush costing** is its simplicity. Simple systems, however, generally do not yield as much information as do more complex systems. Criticisms of backflush costing focus mainly on the inability of the accounting system to pinpoint the uses of resources at each step of the production process. Managers, however, keep track of operations by personal observations, computer monitoring, and nonfinancial measures. In a backflush costing system, control shifts away from accounting numbers toward critical physical measures observable by management in the factory.

> **Objective 10**
>
> Describe the use of backflush costing in companies utilizing JIT manufacturing techniques

EXHIBIT 3-10 | A Comparison of Cost Flows

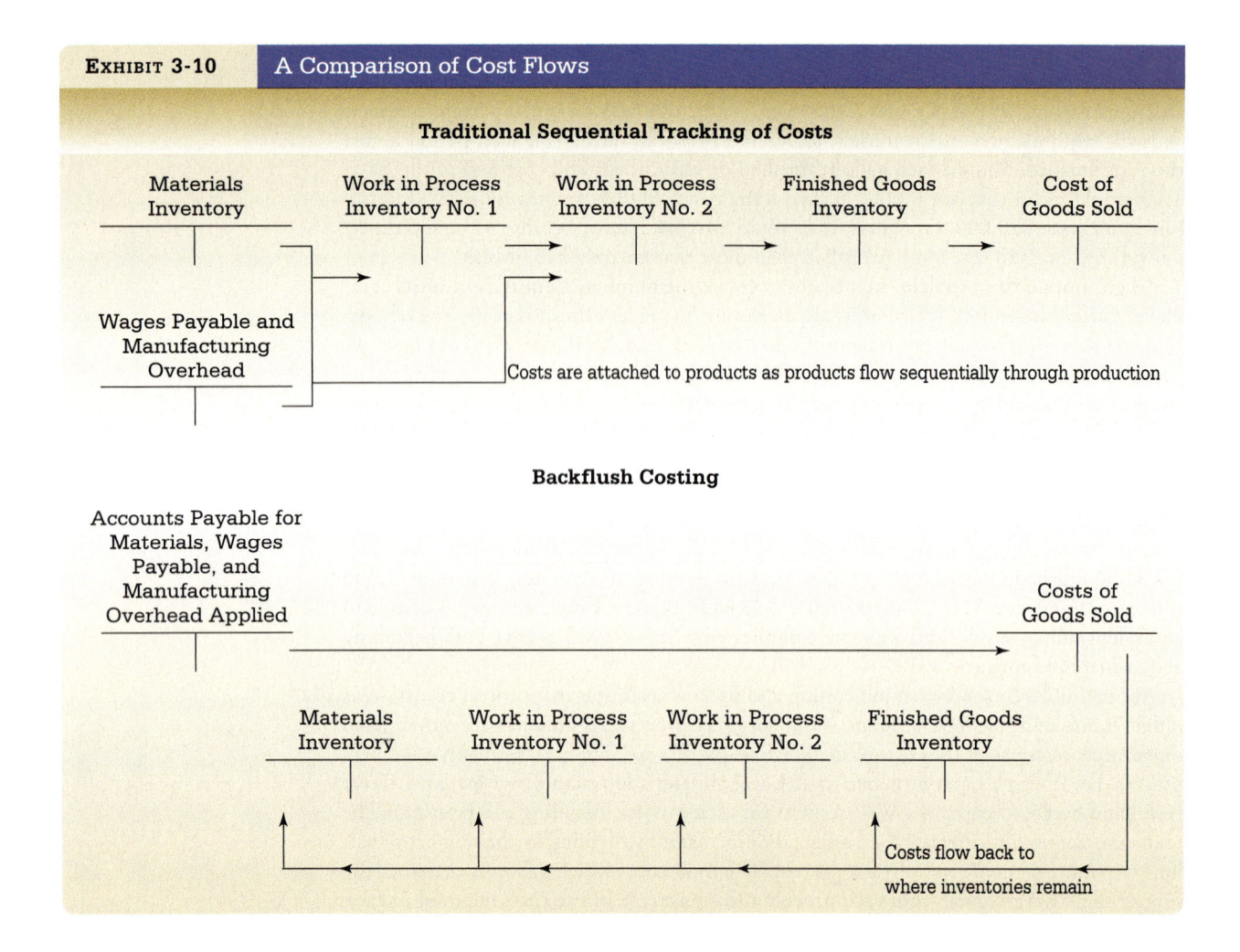

Traditional Sequential Tracking of Costs

Materials Inventory → Work in Process Inventory No. 1 → Work in Process Inventory No. 2 → Finished Goods Inventory → Cost of Goods Sold

Wages Payable and Manufacturing Overhead

Costs are attached to products as products flow sequentially through production

Backflush Costing

Accounts Payable for Materials, Wages Payable, and Manufacturing Overhead Applied → Costs of Goods Sold

Materials Inventory, Work in Process Inventory No. 1, Work in Process Inventory No. 2, Finished Goods Inventory

Costs flow back to where inventories remain

Appendix—Additional Topics in Process Costing

Objective 11

(Appendix) Compare and constrast the weighted average and first-in, first-out (FIFO) methods of process costing and apply each step of the four-step process costing system under both methods

When a company has both beginning and ending inventories of WIP process costing becomes more complicated. In this situation, it is useful to view process costing in four steps. In Step 1, the physical flow of units and their associated costs are analyzed. In this step, it is essential to note the percentage of completion of both the beginning and ending inventories of WIP. For example, let's assume that the blending department of a paint manufacturer has 2,000 gallons of paint that is 80 percent complete in its beginning inventory of WIP. These units were started last period but not completed by the end of the period and will be finished this period. In addition, let's assume that $1,600 of direct material costs and $1,000 of conversion costs (the cost of direct labor and overhead incurred to convert the direct materials to a finished product) have already been incurred in blending these 2,000 gallons of partially completed paint.

During the current period, another 12,000 gallons of paint are started in the blending department so 14,000 gallons are now in process. The company incurs another $20,000 of direct material costs (DM) and $7,370 of conversion costs (CC) working on these 14,000 gallons. The total costs incurred in the blending department now include $21,600 for direct material ($1,600 incurred last period and $20,000 incurred this period) and $8,370 for conversion costs ($1,000 incurred last period and $7,370 incurred this period).

Of the 14,000 gallons of paint now in process in the blending department, 13,000 gallons are finished by the end of the period. Consequently, 1,000 gallons remain in ending inventory. Let's assume that these 1,000 gallons are 50 percent complete (see Exhibit 3-11).

The goal of a process costing system is to allocate the $29,970 of manufacturing costs that have been incurred in the blending department ($21,600 of DM and $8,370 of CC) to the 13,000 gallons of paint that are finished and transferred out (in this case to the next process-

Exhibit 3-11 — Step 1—The Physical Flow of Units and Their Associated Costs

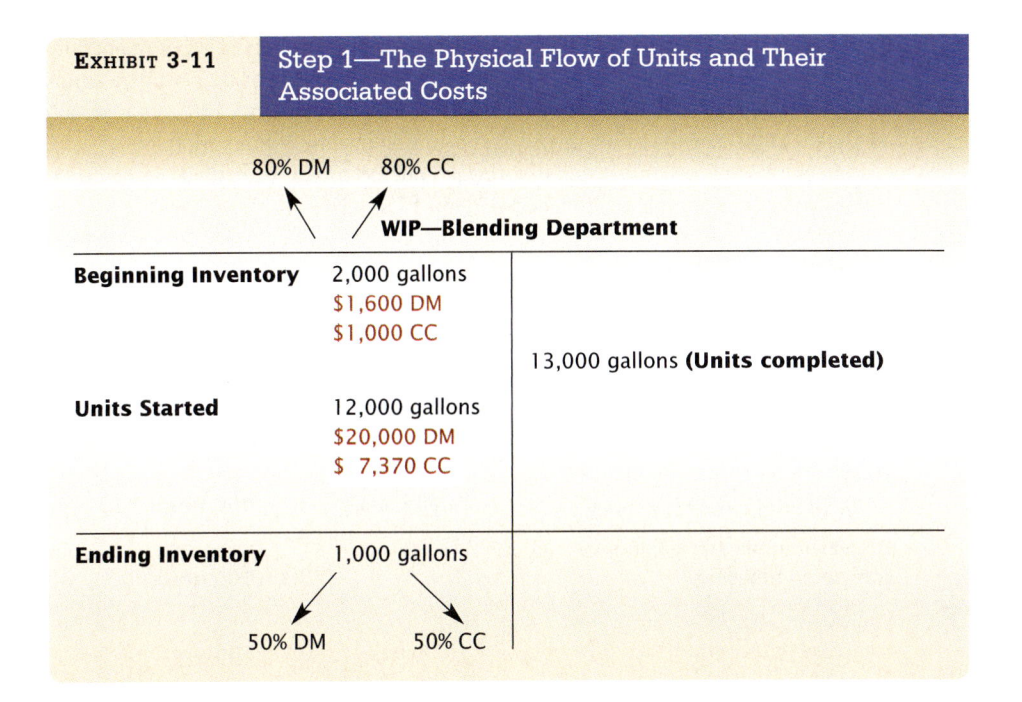

WIP—Blending Department

Beginning Inventory	2,000 gallons (80% DM, 80% CC) $1,600 DM $1,000 CC	13,000 gallons **(Units completed)**
Units Started	12,000 gallons $20,000 DM $ 7,370 CC	
Ending Inventory	1,000 gallons (50% DM, 50% CC)	

ing department) and to the 1,000 gallons of paint that remain in the blending department's ending inventory.

Equivalent units of production can be calculated in two different ways—the first-in, first-out (FIFO) method and the weighted average method. In the FIFO method, the equivalent units and unit costs for the current period relate only to the work done and the costs incurred in the current period. In contrast, in the weighted average method, the units and costs from the current period are combined with the units and costs from last period in the calculation of equivalent units and unit costs.

First-In, First-Out (FIFO)

With the FIFO method, the 2,000 gallons in beginning WIP are assumed to be the first units finished. Consequently, of the 12,000 gallons started this period, 11,000 are finished whereas 1,000 gallons are partially completed and remain in ending WIP (Exhibit 3-12).

Exhibit 3-12 — Step 1—The Physical Flow of Units with FIFO

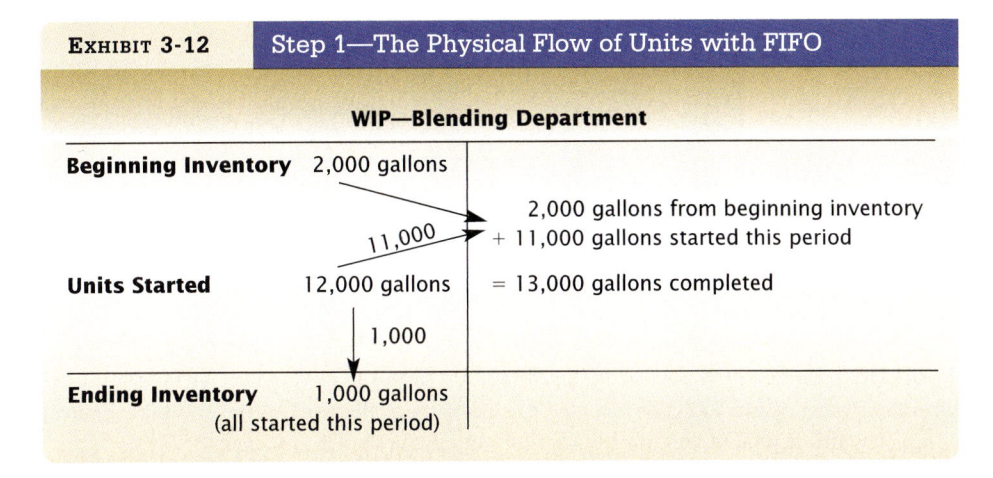

WIP—Blending Department

Beginning Inventory	2,000 gallons	2,000 gallons from beginning inventory + 11,000 gallons started this period = 13,000 gallons completed
Units Started	12,000 gallons (11,000 completed; 1,000 to ending)	
Ending Inventory	1,000 gallons (all started this period)	

In Step 2, equivalent units of production (EU) are calculated. With the FIFO method, the equivalent units in beginning WIP (the units considered already complete at the beginning of the period) are correctly excluded from the calculation of equivalent units of production for the current period. Basically, we want to know the number of equivalent units completed *this* period.

In our example, the 2,000 gallons are 80 percent complete at the beginning of the period. This is equivalent to 1,600 EUs (2,000 × 80 percent). If 80 percent of the work was completed last period, 20 percent will be completed this period. Therefore, we will complete 400 equivalent units (2,000 × 20 percent) out of the beginning inventory *this* period.

What about the 12,000 gallons started new this period? According to Exhibit 3-12, 11,000 of the 12,000 gallons are completely finished (11,000 EUs) while another 1,000 are 50 percent finished (500 EUs). As shown in Exhibit 3-13, the total equivalent units are 11,900 (400 from beginning inventory plus 11,000 units started and completely finished plus 500 units in ending inventory).

Exhibit 3-13 Step 2—Calculation of Equivalent Units with FIFO

Equivalent units of beginning WIP completed this period	2,000 units × 20%* = **400 units**
Equivalent units started and completed this period	**11,000 units**
Equivalent units of ending WIP completed this period	1,000 units × 50% = **500 units**
Total equivalent units	**11,900 units**

*The beginning inventory was 80 percent complete with respect to direct materials and conversion costs so 20 percent is left to complete this period.

If the completion percentage differs for direct materials and conversion costs, this calculation must be done separately for direct materials and conversion costs. However, in our example, the completion percentage is uniform and the calculation of equivalent units for direct material and conversion costs is the same.

In Step 3, manufacturing costs per equivalent unit are calculated (see Exhibit 3-14). With the FIFO method, only the current period costs ($20,000 of DM and $7,370 of CC) are included in the calculation. Last period's costs of $2,600 ($1,600 of DM and $1,000 of CC) are correctly segregated from the costs incurred this period. This allocation is consistent with including only the percentage of beginning inventory completed this period in the calculation of equivalent units.

Exhibit 3-14 Step 3—Calculation of Cost per Equivalent Unit with FIFO

Current period costs	$27,370
Equivalent units of production	÷ 11,900 EUs
Cost per equivalent unit	**$2.30 per EU**

In Step 4, the $29,970 of costs incurred ($2,600 from last period associated with the beginning inventory and $27,370 incurred this period) are allocated to the 13,000 gallons of completely finished paint and the 1,000 gallons of partially finished paint.

Because all 2,000 units in beginning inventory are assumed to be completed this period, the $2,600 of costs associated with those units will be allocated to the costs of the 13,000 finished units. Of course, we incur additional costs this period to finish the 2,000 units and to start and finish another 11,000 units. How much are these additional costs? According to our calculation in Exhibit 3-14, it cost $2.30 per equivalent unit to blend paint this period. As calculated in Exhibit 3-15, the 13,000 gallons of completely finished paint cost $28,820.

EXHIBIT 3-15	Step 4—Allocating Costs to the Finished Units

Cost of the 2,000 units from beginning inventory:	
Cost incurred last period	$ 2,600
Cost to finish the units this period	
DM and CC ($2.30 per EU × 400 EUs*)	$ 920
Cost of the 11,000 units started and finished this period	
DM and CC ($2.30 per EU × 11,000 EUs)	$25,300
Total cost	**$28,820**

*The beginning inventory was 80 percent complete with respect to direct materials and conversion costs, so 20 percent is left to complete this period (2,000 units × 20 percent = 400 EUs).

The 1,000 units in ending work in process inventory are easier to cost. All are considered to come from the 12,000 units started this period and cost $2.30 per equivalent unit. As shown in Exhibit 3-16 the cost of the 1,000 units (500 equivalent units) in ending WIP is $1,150.

EXHIBIT 3-16	Step 4—Allocating Costs to the Ending WIP

Cost of the 1,000 units in ending WIP	
DM and CC ($2.30 per EU × 500 EUs)	$1,150

You should note that the total cost allocated to the 13,000 units of finished units and the 1,000 units of ending WIP must total $29,970. Consequently, if the finished units cost $28,820, the ending inventory must cost $1,150 ($29,970 − $28,820).

Weighted Average Method

In contrast to the FIFO method, the weighted average method treats the units in beginning inventory as if they were started in the current period. That is, we combine the units we know were partially completed last period with the units started this period. Consequently, the 13,000 gallons of completed units and the 1,000 gallons of paint in ending WIP are both assumed to come from the 14,000 units we treat as having been started in the current period (Exhibit 3-17). This simplifies the calculation of equivalent units in Exhibit 3-18.

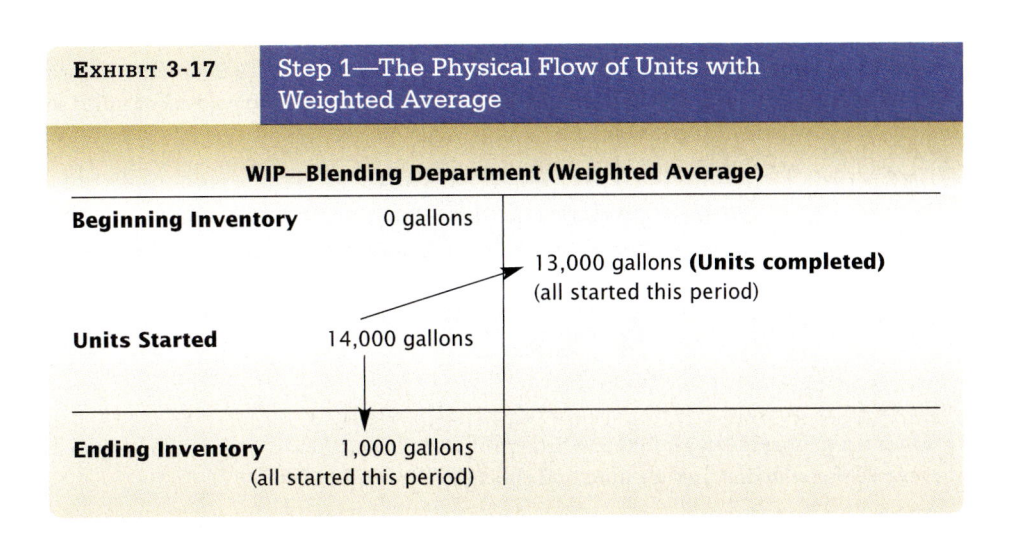

EXHIBIT 3-17	Step 1—The Physical Flow of Units with Weighted Average

WIP—Blending Department (Weighted Average)

Beginning Inventory	0 gallons	
		13,000 gallons **(Units completed)** (all started this period)
Units Started	14,000 gallons	
Ending Inventory	1,000 gallons (all started this period)	

EXHIBIT 3-18	Step 2—Calculation of Equivalent Units with Weighted Average

Equivalent units started and completed this period;	
Units completely finished	13,000 units
Equivalent units of ending WIP completed this period	1,000 units × 50% = 500 units
Total equivalent units	**13,500 units**

With the weighted average method, last period's costs are combined with the current period's costs in the calculation of cost per equivalent unit in Step 3 (see Exhibit 3-19). This is consistent with treating the units in beginning inventory as if they were started this period in the calculation of equivalent units.

EXHIBIT 3-19	Step 3—Calculation of Cost per Equivalent Unit with Weighted Average

Total costs	$29,970
Equivalent units of production	÷ 13,500 EUs
Cost per equivalent unit	**$2.22 per EU**

As with the FIFO method, in Step 4, the $29,970 of costs incurred are allocated to the 13,000 gallons of completely finished paint and the 1,000 gallons of partially finished paint. As calculated in Exhibit 3-20, the 13,000 gallons of completely finished paint cost $28,860.

EXHIBIT 3-20	Step 4—Allocating Costs to the Finished Units

Cost of the 13,000 units started and completely finished DM and CC ($2.22 per EU × 13,000 EUs)	$28,860

The 1,000 units in ending inventory must also have come from the 14,000 units assumed to be started this period. Consequently, the cost of the 1,000 units (500 equivalent units) in ending inventory is $1,110 (see Exhibit 3-21).

EXHIBIT 3-21	Step 4—Allocating Costs to the Ending WIP

Cost of the 1,000 units in ending WIP DM and CC ($2.22 per EU × 500 EUs)	$1,110

Once again, note that regardless of whether FIFO or the weighted-average method is used, the costs allocated to the finished units and ending WIP total $29,970.

Which method is preferable? Although the FIFO method is conceptually superior, the weighted average method will provide similar cost calculations when inventory levels are small (as in a JIT environment) or when costs are relatively stable from period to period.

Summary of Key Concepts

- Overhead cannot be directly tracked to products and services but must instead be allocated using cost drivers. (p. 71)
- Understanding what causes overhead costs to be incurred (what drives them) is the key to allocating overhead. (p. 72)
- Accuracy in overhead application has become much more important as overhead costs have increased and make up a larger portion of the total costs of products. (p. 75)
- In order to provide relevant information for decision making, overhead must often be estimated. (p. 76)
- Under normal costing, the cost of a product includes the actual amount of direct materials, the actual amount of direct labor, and an applied amount of manufacturing overhead. (p. 76)

Key Definitions

Job costing A costing system that accumulates, tracks, and assigns costs for each job produced by a company (p. 66)

Process costing A costing system that accumulates and tracks costs for each process performed and then assigns those costs equally to each unit produced (p. 67)

Operations costing A hybrid of job and process costing; used by companies that make products in batches (p. 67)

Normal spoilage Spoilage resulting from the regular operations of the production process (p. 69)

Abnormal spoilage Spoilage resulting from unusual circumstances, including improper handling, poorly trained employees, faulty equipment, and so on (p. 69)

Fringe benefits Payroll costs in addition to the basic hourly wage (p. 70)

Idle time Worker time that is not used in the production of the finished product (p. 70)

Overtime premiums An additional amount added to the basic hourly wage owing to overtime worked by the workers (p. 71)

Allocation The process of finding a logical method of assigning overhead costs to the products or services a company produces or provides (p. 71)

Cost drivers Factors that cause, or drive, the incurrence of costs (p. 72)

Cost pools Groups of overhead costs that are similar; used to simplify the task of assigning costs to products using ABC costing (p. 72)

Normal costing A method of costing using an estimate of overhead and predetermined overhead rates instead of the actual amount of overhead (p. 76)

Predetermined overhead rates Used to apply overhead to products; calculated by dividing the estimated overhead for a cost pool by the estimated units of the cost driver (p. 76)

Overapplied overhead The amount of applied overhead in excess of actual overhead (p. 77)

Underapplied overhead The amount of actual overhead in excess of applied overhead (p. 77)

Equivalent units The number of finished units that can be made from the materials, labor, and overhead included in partially completed units (p. 81)

Backflush costing A costing system in which manufacturing costs are directly flushed into cost of goods sold instead of flowing through inventory (p. 81)

Multiple Choice

1. Which of the following costing systems often requires multiple work-in-process accounts?
   a. Process costing
   b. Backflush costing
   c. Job costing
   d. Each of the above requires multiple work in process accounts

2. Which of the following organizations would be most likely to adopt a job costing system?
   a. Custom home contractor
   b. Beverage maker
   c. Paint manufacturer
   d. Bakery

3. Job costing systems require which of the following costs to be "tracked" to ensure that all related costs are assigned to a specific job?
   a. Labor of factory maintenance workers
   b. Costs of primary raw materials used in the production process
   c. Utilities expense allocation to the manufacturing space
   d. Salary paid to factory supervisor

4. Normal spoilage:
   a. results from the regular operation of the production process and is treated as a product cost.
   b. results from improper handling, improperly trained employees, and poor equipment conditions and is treated as a period cost.
   c. results from the regular operation of the production process and is treated as a period cost.
   d. results from improper handling, improperly trained employees, and poor equipment conditions and is treated as a product cost.

5. Overtime premiums incurred as a result of receiving a special rush order from a customer should be:
   a. treated as indirect labor and included in manufacturing overhead.
   b. treated as direct labor and included in manufacturing overhead.
   c. treated as direct labor and included in the product's cost.
   d. treated as indirect labor and included in the product's cost.

6. Costs associated with factory insurance, maintenance, rent, property taxes, and other similar items are typically included in manufacturing overhead and assigned to products:
   a. primarily based on whatever technique is easiest.
   b. based on a related cost driver that can be identified and measured.
   c. if not treated as a period cost.
   d. based on the relative sales revenue generated by the product.

7. Cost allocation:
   a. is quite useful for direct material and direct labor costs.
   b. involves the logical assignment of overhead costs to products and services.
   c. is not allowed when a process costing system is selected.
   d. is only required when following generally accepted management accounting practices.

8. Which of the following statements is correct?
   a. Overhead consists of a limited variety of costs that should have the same cost driver.
   b. Overhead consists of a wide variety of costs that should have the same cost driver.
   c. Overhead consists of a variety of costs that may potentially have different cost drivers.
   d. Overhead consists of a limited variety of costs that must each have a unique cost driver.

9. Each of the following statements regarding a plantwide overhead rate is true, except:
   a. The use of a plantwide rate is easy.
   b. A plantwide rate provides less accurate cost information than does a departmental rate.
   c. A plantwide rate is less time consuming to prepare than is a departmental rate.
   d. A plantwide rate is more costly to prepare than is a departmental rate.

10. At the law firm of Kimberly Kanakes and Associates LLP, overhead is assigned to clients based on direct labor hours. At the beginning of the current year, estimated overhead costs were $156,000, and estimated direct labor hours were 20,800. Actual overhead costs for the year amounted to $166,400, and the firm's attorneys worked 20,904 hours on various client issues. How much overhead cost should be assigned to a client whose file indicates that attorneys worked 120 hours on various client issues?
    a. $895.20
    b. $900.00
    c. $955.20
    d. $960.00

11. Refer to question 10 above. How much is overhead overapplied or underapplied?
    a. $9,620 overapplied
    b. $9,620 underapplied
    c. $780 overapplied
    d. $780 underapplied

12. In its initial year of operation, Computer World manufactured 1,000 computer screens and had a batch of 200 more computer screens that were 50 percent complete at year end. Production costs for the year totaled $220,000. How many equivalent units were completed during the year?
    a. 100
    b. 1,000
    c. 1,100
    d. 1,200

13. Mark Goodwin Ltd. has a beginning work in process inventory of 25,000 units, 40 percent complete. During the period, 100,000 units were transferred in from a preceding process. The ending work in process inventory was 20,000 units, 80 percent complete. What are the equivalent units for the conversion costs, assuming that the company uses the weighted-average method?
    a. 106,000
    b. 115,000
    c. 121,000
    d. 131,000

14. Under which of the following conditions will the first-in, first-out method produce the same cost of goods manufactured as the weighted-average method?
    a. There is no ending work in process inventory.
    b. There is no beginning work in process inventory.
    c. The beginning and ending work in process inventories are equal.
    d. The beginning and ending work in process inventories are both 50 percent complete.

15. The costs included in the cost per equivalent unit using the weighted average method are:
    a. current costs and those from beginning work in process inventory.
    b. current costs and those from ending work in process inventory.
    c. current costs only.
    d. costs from beginning and ending work in process inventories.

Concept Questions

16. *(Objective 1)* Explain the importance of product cost information in the context of management decision making.

17. *(Objective 1)* Briefly describe job costing and process costing. Give an example of the type of organization most likely to use job costing and an example of the type of organization most likely to use process costing.

18. *(Objective 2)* What two components of product costs must be carefully measured and tracked when a company uses job costing?

19. *(Objective 2)* Describe the basic elements of a job cost sheet.

20. *(Objective 3, 4)* Why is overhead difficult to track and allocate to products in a traditional manufacturing environment?

21. *(Objective 4, 5)* What should managers look for when trying to choose a cost driver for overhead costs?

22. *(Objective 5)* Briefly explain why the following statement is true. "As companies begin to produce a greater variety of products and become more heavily automated, the use of plantwide cost pools and single cost drivers may provide less accurate cost information."

23. *(Objective 6, 7)* When should a normalized (i.e., predetermined) overhead rate be used?

24. *(Objective 8)* Why would a manager prefer one treatment for overapplied overhead over another?

25. *(Objective 9)* Define the term *equivalent units of production*.

26. *(Objective 10)* Why would a company use backflush costing?

27. *(Objective 11)* Why is the FIFO method preferred for calculating equivalent units and calculating unit costs?

Exercises

28. Product (service) costing systems are customized to provide accurate and timely cost data. A company should select a costing system that is appropriate for its production process. The following is a list of different organizations and selected products or services they provide.
   a. Physical therapy clinic (mobility therapy)
   b. Graphic design studio (logo design)
   c. Auto repair shop (miscellaneous auto repairs)
   d. Local bakery (wheat bread)
   e. Dairy (whole milk)
   f. Oil refinery (motor oil)
   g. Construction contractor (custom built homes)

Required

Indicate whether each of the above organizations would most likely choose *job costing* or *process costing*.

29. Product costing systems are used to accumulate, track, and assign costs to products. The following partially complete statements describe various issues related to product costing systems.
   a. _____ is a hybrid of job and process costing methods.
   b. Process costing accumulates and tracks costs for each _____ as products pass through each process.
   c. Costs of homogeneous products are most appropriately developed with _____.
   d. _____ is a commonly used costing method especially within the automotive industry.
   e. Job cost reports are used to record _____, _____, and _____ in a job costing system.

f. Two methods used to calculate equivalent units of production are _____ and _____.

g. _____ accumulates, tracks, and assigns costs for each job.

Required

Complete each of the above partially descriptive statements by inserting one of the following words or phrases: *process, job costing, operations costing, process costing, direct material, weighted average, direct labor, first-in, first-out (FIFO),* or *overhead*. Only one of the preceding words or phrases correctly completes a statement. Words may be used more than once.

30. Love's Pottery Barn had the following costs for June:

Direct labor	$ 400
Indirect materials	375
Beginning work in process	0
Ending work in process	0
Costs of goods manufactured	1,050
Beginning finished goods	2,450
Ending finished goods	3,400

Required

How much direct material costs were incurred during June?

31. Walter Meyer Productions had the following costs for March:

Purchases of direct materials	$ 30,000
Indirect labor	20,000
Ending direct material inventory	10,000
Beginning direct material inventory	0
Total manufacturing costs	115,000
Direct labor	25,000

Required

How much manufacturing overhead was incurred during March?

32. Jim Wilson is a typical manufacturing employee who commonly works 40 hours per week and is paid $14 per hour. During the last pay period, Jim performed the following activities:

Product assembly	29.5 hours
Cleaning his work area	5.0
Attending a workplace safety meeting	2.5
Talking with a supervisor about football	1.0
Giving a tour of the plant to schoolchildren	2.0

Required

Jim's employer uses job costing to measure and track production costs. The company is very concerned with maintaining accurate cost data. Determine the amount of labor costs that should be allocated to direct labor and indirect labor as manufacturing overhead.

33. Overhead costs are rarely directly linked to the production of a specific product or group of products. Generally, overhead costs are only indirectly linked to production, and so they must be allocated. Understanding the relationship between overhead costs and production activities is challenging for most businesses. Consider the following:
   a. Architectural design firm: designer hours, _____
   b. Caterer and party consultancy firm: number of party guests, _____
   c. Furniture manufacturer: direct labor hours, _____
   d. Printer and copy shop: size of print or copy job, _____
   e. Textbook binder: machine hours, _____
   f. Automobile repair shop: technician labor hours, _____
   g. Winemaker: pounds of grapes used, _____

Required

Identify one additional potential cost driver that each of the above organizations could use to allocate overhead to its products or services.

34. The following statements describe various aspects of overhead costs and the roles of cost pools and cost drivers in the allocation of overhead.
   a. Overhead costs cause cost drivers.
   b. In traditional manufacturing environments, most overhead costs are directly related to production activities.
   c. Overhead rates are calculated by dividing manufacturing overhead costs by the volume of cost pool activity.
   d. Companies that are labor intensive are likely to allocate overhead costs such as utilities expense based on direct labor hours.
   e. More overhead costs in a just-in-time environment are direct in nature as opposed to indirect.
   f. A "good" allocation base is one that drives the incurrence of overhead costs.
   g. Companies generally allocate overhead equally to all products produced during a given period of time.

Required

Indicate whether each of the above statements is true or false.

35. In the recent past, companies commonly used either a plantwide rate or a limited number of departmental rates to allocate overhead to products and services. The following statements describe some of the advantages and disadvantages of using plantwide and departmental rates. Read and consider each of the following statements:
   a. Departmental overhead rates are much simpler to apply than plantwide overhead rates.
   b. Plantwide overhead rates allow companies with a diverse product offering to accurately assign overhead costs.
   c. Companies frequently believe the use of plantwide overhead rates encourages efficient production operations.
   d. The use of a plantwide overhead rate is less time consuming and less expensive than multiple departmental overhead rates.
   e. A plantwide overhead rate can lead to a more accurate identification of a company's cost driver.
   f. As direct labor and direct materials have become a greater proportion of product costs, the assignment of overhead costs has become less critical.
   g. The selection of a cost driver is much more important when a company uses multiple departmental overhead rates than when it uses a plantwide overhead rate.

Required

Indicate whether each of the above statements is true or false.

36. Bostock's Building Blocks uses number of minutes in its firing oven to allocate overhead costs to products. In a typical month, 5,000 firing minutes are expected, and average monthly overhead costs are $3,500. During January, 4,800 firing minutes were used and total overhead costs were $2,750.

✓ Applied overhead rate: $0.70/minute

Required

Compute Bostock's predetermined overhead rate and the amount of applied overhead for January.

37. Enrique Mares Enterprises applies overhead using direct labor hours. The following data are available for the year:

Expected direct labor hours	600,000
Actual direct labor hours	545,000
Overhead applied	$2,937,550
Actual overhead	$2,800,000

Required

What predetermined overhead rate did Enrique Mares use?

38. Ben Whitney manufactures holiday decorations. Overhead is applied to products based on direct labor hours. Last year, total overhead costs were expected to be $85,000. Actual overhead costs totaled $88,750 for 8,400 actual hours. At the end of the year, overhead was underapplied by $4,750.

Required

A. Calculate the predetermined overhead rate.
B. How much overhead should be applied to a job that was completed in three direct labor hours?

39. O'Callahan Snack Company produces gourmet chips and other snack foods. One of the company's most popular snacks is a combination of several varieties of organic potatoes. The snack food goes through several processes including a potato peeling operation. Costs for operations during April are shown below. (Note: Production costs include direct materials and conversions costs for the department.)

	Number of Bags	Production Costs
Beginning work in process (10% complete)	3,000	$ 10,000
Current period production	20,000	70,240
Ending work in process (85% complete)	5,000	

O'Callahan Snack Company uses the first-in, first-out method of computing equivalent units and assigning product costs.

Required

A. How many bags of the popular snack were completed during April?
B. Of the bags completed during April, how many bags were *started and completed* during the month?

40. O'Callahan Snack Company produces gourmet chips and other snack foods. One of the company's most popular snacks is a combination of several varieties of organic potatoes. The snack food goes through several processes including a potato peeling operation. Costs for operations during April are shown below. (Note: Production costs include direct materials and conversions costs for the department.)

✓ Ending WIP equivalent units: 4,250

	Number of Bags	Production Costs
Beginning work in process (10% complete)	3,000	$ 10,000
Current period production	20,000	70,240
Ending work in process (85% complete)	5,000	

O'Callahan Snack Company uses the first-in, first-out method of computing equivalent units and assigning product costs.

Required

A. How many equivalent units did O'Callahan complete during April?
B. Calculate the cost of the ending work in process inventory.

41. Mike Aliscad is widely known as an exceptional winemaker. He has developed a production process that has several distinct processes including "speed crushing," which involves the breaking down of the grapes' skin and pulverizing of the grape fruit to produce a juice-like product. The following data relate to Aliscad's crushing process for October. (Note: Production costs include direct materials and conversions costs for the department.)

	Pounds of Grapes	Production Costs
Beginning work in process (15% complete)	2,000	$ 8,040
Current period production	11,000	22,960
Ending work in process (60% complete)	3,000	

Aliscad uses the weighted average method of computing equivalent units and assigning product costs.

Required

How many equivalent units were produced during October?

42. Arnsparger Outdoors produces climbing gear specially designed to weather the toughest conditions. Arnsparger has developed and patented a process that leads to a substantially stronger rope than its competitors. The strengthening process is complicated and has increased the time required to produce rope, but Arnsparger believes the additional time is worth the effort. The following data relate to the process for the month of June. (Note: Production costs include direct materials and conversions costs for the department.)

	Feet of Rope	Production Costs
Beginning work in process (10% complete)	4,000	$ 4,000
Current period production	13,000	26,000
Ending work in process (50% complete)	4,000	

Arnsparger Outdoors uses the weighted average method of computing equivalent units and assigning product costs.

Required

A. Calculate the number of equivalent units produced during June.
B. What is the production cost per equivalent unit?

Problems

43. The Orville Haberman Company, a small manufacturer, uses a job costing system to measure and track product costs for its line of specialty outdoor clothing. Haberman's management believes that using a job costing system allows the company to track costs more closely even though it could use another costing system. For the coming year, Kristin George, Haberman's controller, estimates total overhead costs to be $100,000. Production manager, Portia Kabler, told Kristin that her best estimate for total production time for the year is 20,000 hours.

Production data for the first quarter of the year is shown below:

	Parkas	Shirts	Pants	Shoes
Direct materials used	$ 16,000	$ 12,000	$ 9,500	$11,500
Direct labor cost	13,000	10,000	7,000	9,500
Direct labor hours	1,500	1,250	850	950

Required

A. Calculate Haberman's predetermined overhead rate based on direct labor hours.
B. Calculate the overhead cost to be assigned to parkas, shirts, pants, and shoes.
C. Calculate the total manufacturing cost of parkas, shirts, pants, and shoes.
D. Based on your knowledge of costing systems described in the chapter, which other method(s) might Haberman consider to measure and track the cost of its products? Why would the company choose to continue using job costing as it currently does?

44. Moody Blues Record Company has several divisions including one that recently began producing CDs for some old favorites. The production division only produces CDs for a select group of artists and is a relatively small part of Moody Blues Record Company. The production division operations data for the first quarter of the year were as follows. (Note: Because the company began operations at the beginning of the quarter, there were no beginning inventory balances.)

✓ *Overhead applied: $90,000*

Materials data:	
Direct materials purchases	$100,000
Direct materials used in production (cost)	85,000
Labor data:	
Direct labor costs	60,000
Indirect labor costs	30,000
Manufacturing overhead data:	
Incurred utilities, rent, and depreciation	50,000
Overhead application rate per machine hour	9.00
Machine hours used	10,000
Inventory data:	
Transferred to finished goods	210,000
Cost of goods sold during quarter	190,000

Required

A. Calculate the direct materials ending inventory.
B. Calculate the work in process ending inventory.
C. Calculate the finished goods ending inventory.
D. Calculate the over- or underapplied overhead for the period.

45. Gordon Mfg. produces a special Florida hammock. The unique hammocks have a special weaving pattern that not only enhance the look, but also increase the stability and strength of the hammocks. Gordon Mfg. experienced the following events during the year:

✓ *Overhead applied: $61,875*

Purchased $100,000 of raw materials
Direct materials used in production amounted to $70,000
Production employees worked 4,500 labor hours
Production employees pay averaged $11 per hour
Applied overhead at the rate of $13.75 per direct labor hour
Indirect labor costs were $25,000
Incurred utilities, rent, and depreciation for production totaling $45,000
$180,000 of completed products were transferred to finished goods
Products costing $160,000 were sold

As this was the first year of operations, there were no beginning inventory balances.

Required

A. Calculate the ending balance of direct materials inventory.
B. Calculate the ending balance of work in process inventory.
C. Calculate the ending balance of finished goods inventory.
D. Calculate the over- or underapplied overhead for the period

46. Grandma Whitney knits made-to-order blankets. The following is an incomplete job cost report for a Flower Petal blanket ordered by Anna Schotten.

	Direct Materials		Direct Labor			Overhead
Type of Yarn	Total Cost	Date	Knitting Hours	Total Cost		Total Applied
Blue—4 skeins	$14.00	January 23	5	$40.00		$4.50
Brown—2 skeins	11.00	January 24	7	?		?
Green—2 skeins	13.00	January 25	3	24.00		2.70

Required

A. What is the direct labor cost per hour?
B. What is the direct labor cost for January 24?
C. Based on this job cost report, how is overhead being assigned to each blanket? Do you believe that the chosen cost driver is appropriate in this instance? Why or why not?
D. How much overhead should be applied on January 24?
E. What is the total manufacturing cost for this blanket?

47. Krall Kabinets produces custom cabinetry for homes, which is sold nationwide. The company adds overhead costs to cabinetry projects at the rate of $7.75 per direct labor hour. The company accumulates overhead costs in a separate manufacturing overhead account and uses normal costing to assign overhead. The following data provide details of the company's activity and balances during the last half of the year:

	July 1	December 31
Direct materials inventory	$60,250	$61,750
Work in process inventory	44,000	43,500
Finished goods inventory	24,150	23,000
Monthly production data:		
Direct materials purchased	$155,000	
Direct labor costs ($15/hr.)	270,000	
Factory utilities	35,000	
Factory rent	52,000	
Factory supervisor	43,000	
Depreciation on factory equipment	25,000	

Required

A. Calculate the cost of direct materials used during the period.
B. Calculate the cost of goods manufactured during the period.
C. Calculate the cost of goods sold during the period. Krall adjusts cost of goods sold at the end of the year for any over- or underapplied overhead.

48. Marc's Pizza Palace has been in business for three months selling a very good three-cheese pizza. Because of customer demand, Marc has decided to introduce a variety of new pizzas including specialty meat pizzas and veggie pizzas next month. Since he opened his business, Marc has allocated overhead to each pizza by simply dividing the estimated total overhead by the estimated number of pizzas. Now, Marc realizes that the new pizzas will require more preparation time and more time in the oven. He does not expect the total volume of pizzas to change; people who now order cheese will simply switch to one of the other options.

Required

A. Does it make sense to still allocate overhead by number of pizzas if the total number of pizzas remains the same? Why or why not?
B. What are Marc's alternatives for allocating his overhead costs?

49. Mollie Schlue started Mollie's Magnets seven years ago. The small company creates special-order magnets with varying logos and designs, and for different purposes. Mollie estimates her overhead costs to be $12,000 per month. In addition, she expects employees to work 2,000 hours and there are usually 1,500 machine hours in a given month. Mollie's Magnets has two departments. The assembly department gives rise to 1,800 of the labor hours, and the finishing department requires 1,200 of the machine hours. The $12,000 in overhead is allocated as follows: $9,000 is traced to the assembly department and $3,000 is traced to the finishing department. During January, the following jobs were completed:

	Job 101	Job 102
Direct materials used	$1,100	$1,450
Direct labor cost	2,300	1,250
Direct labor hours	150	25
Machine hours	25	230

Required

A. What is the company's plantwide predetermined overhead rate using direct labor hours as the base?
B. What is the company's plantwide predetermined overhead rate using machine hours as the base?
C. How much overhead would be applied to each job if direct labor hours were used as the cost driver for overhead?
D. How much overhead would be applied to each job if machine hours were used as the cost driver for overhead?
E. If Mollie's Magnets decides to use department overhead rates, what would the overhead rates be for each department? The assembly department allocates overhead based on direct labor hours and the finishing department allocates overhead based on machine hours.
F. Explain why it is important for Mollie's company to use departmental rates as opposed to a single plantwide rate to allocate overhead costs.

50. Hartselle Enterprises manufactures a variety of hand-finished pottery. Each piece of pottery must go through two critical and relatively standardized processes: molding and firing. Crystal Hartselle, founder of the company, is also responsible for maintaining the company's accounting information system. She currently calculates overhead rates on a monthly basis. Crystal recently prepared the following data for last month:

✓ *Part E–overhead applied in firing: $7,200*

Monthly Costs and Quantities

Direct material	2,500 pounds ($ 0.75 per pound)
Direct labor	200 hours (Pay rate: $7.50 per hour plus benefits at 20 percent of hourly rate)
Overhead per department (estimated)	$6,000
Direct labor hours (estimated)	300 (200 in molding and 100 in firing)
Machine hours (estimated)	200 (50 in molding and 150 in firing)

Actual Overhead Costs

Factory rent	$3,000
Factory utilities	3,700
Advertising	2,500
Factory equipment depreciation	3,000
Sales commissions	2,500

Required

A. Calculate a plantwide predetermined overhead rate using direct labor hours as the cost driver.
B. Calculate a plantwide predetermined overhead rate using machine hours as the cost driver.
C. Using the plantwide rate calculated based on direct labor hours, how much overhead would be applied to a job requiring 225 direct labor hours?
D. Using the plantwide rate calculated based on machine hours, how much overhead would be applied to a job requiring 210 machine hours?
E. Crystal is considering the use of departmental overhead rates. Assume that the cost driver for the molding department is direct labor hours and that the cost driver for the firing department is machine hours. How much overhead would be applied to a job using 180 direct labor hours and 30 machine hours in the molding department and 45 direct labor hours and 180 machine hours in the firing department?

51. The Meekma Beverage Corporation manufactures flavored bottled water and uses process costing to account for the cost of the products manufactured. Raw materials and labor are incurred at the same rate during the production process. Data for Meekma's mixing department for March are as follows:

	Units	Production Costs
Work in process, March 1 (80% complete)	5,000	$ 60,000
Started during March	100,000	1,187,500
Work in process, March 31 (40% complete)	10,000	

Meekma uses the first-in, first-out method to calculate equivalent units.

Required

A. How many units were completed in March?
B. How many equivalent units were completed in March?
C. What is the cost per equivalent unit?
D. What is the cost of the ending WIP?
E. What is the cost of the units transferred out of the mixing department? That is, what is the cost of goods manufactured during March?

52. The Gibson & Zorich Bakery bakes breads and muffins for wholesale to restaurants. The company uses process costing to account for the cost of the breads and muffins that it produces. Raw materials (for example, flour, sugar, flavoring, fruits) and labor are incurred at the same rate during the production process. Data for Gibson & Zorich's blending department for December are as follows:

	Unit	Production Costs
Work in process, December 1 (80% complete)	5,000	$ 140,000
Started during December	100,000	1,060,000
Work in process, December 31 (50% complete)	10,000	

Gibson & Zorich Bakery uses the weighted average method to compute equivalent units.

Required

A. How many units were completed in December?
B. How many equivalent units were completed in December?
C. What is the cost per equivalent unit?
D. What is the cost of the ending WIP?
E. What is the cost of the units transferred out of the blending department? That is, what is the cost of goods manufactured during December?

Cases

53. Bergan Brewery uses the latest in modern brewing technology to produce a prize-winning beer. In both 2005 and 2006, Bergan produced and sold 100,000 cases of beer and had no raw material, work in process, or finished goods inventory at the beginning or end of either year. At the end of 2005, the company installed machines to perform some of the repetitive tasks previously performed with direct labor. At the beginning of 2006, Bergan's bookkeeper estimated that net income would increase from $530,000 in 2005 to $706,000 in 2006.

LO ③ ④ ⑥

Activity Making Decision A

✓ Part C-Gross profit: $535,000

	2005 (Actual)	2006 (Estimated)
Beer sales (100,000 cases)	$1,000,000	$1,000,000
Less: Cost of goods sold:		
Direct material	150,000	150,000
Direct labor	125,000	25,000
Applied overhead*	95,000	19,000
Gross profit	$ 630,000	$ 806,000
Less: Selling and administrative costs	100,000	100,000
Net income	$ 530,000	$ 706,000

*For 2006, overhead was applied at the 2005 rate of $9.50 per direct labor hour for an estimated 2,000 hours of direct labor. A total of 10,000 direct labor hours were worked in 2005. Bergan's bookkeeper estimates that 5,000 machine hours will be worked in 2006.

However, when actual overhead was used to calculate net income at the end of the year, net income decreased from $530,000 in 2005 to $435,000 in 2006.

	2005 (Actual)	2006 (Actual)
Beer sales (100,000 cases)	$1,000,000	$1,000,000
Less: Cost of goods sold:		
Direct material	150,000	150,000
Direct labor	125,000	25,000
Actual overhead:		
Lease expense	25,000	25,000
Utilities expense	15,000	30,000
Depreciation (equipment)	50,000	200,000
Equipment maintenance	5,000	35,000
Gross profit	$ 630,000	$ 535,000
Less: Selling and administrative costs	100,000	100,000
Net income	$ 530,000	$ 435,000

Required

A. What potential problems do you see in the bookkeeper's income estimate for 2006?
B. Based on the information given, would you change the cost driver or predetermined overhead rate for 2006? What cost driver would you suggest? What would be the new predetermined overhead rate?
C. Using the cost driver and predetermined overhead rate you suggested in B, and assuming that 5,000 machine hours will be incurred, recalculate Bergan's estimated net income for 2006.
D. Bergan has set a goal of increasing net income in 2007 to $550,000. However, sales are expected to be flat. Using the decision model introduced in Chapter 1, identify some options for Bergan Brewery. How might it reach its goal of increasing income to $550,000? What qualitative factors should be considered in its decision?

54. Thiel Boots manufactures hunting boots. The company's president, Dick Thiel, has become increasingly doubtful about the company's current overhead allocation. As a consequence, Dick has asked the company's controller to prepare some basic data so that other allocation methods can be investigated. The following estimated income

LO ④ ⑤ ⑥ ⑦ ⑧

statement was prepared under several basic assumptions. The company expects to sell 10,000 pairs of boots in the coming year and estimates that production employees will work 10,000 hours. In total, production equipment is expected to operate 8,000 hours.

Thiel Boots
Estimated Income Statement
For the year ending November 30, 2006

Sales		$1,000,000
Cost of goods sold:		
Direct materials	300,000	
Direct labor	160,000	
Estimated overhead	240,000	700,000
Gross profit		300,000
Selling and administrative expenses		175,000
Net income		$ 125,000

Required

A. Compute the predetermined overhead rate for Thiel using the following three cost drivers: direct labor hours, direct labor dollars, and machine hours.
B. If actual labor cost were $170,000 for 10,500 direct labor hours and actual machine hours used were 7,800, what would be the applied overhead, using the three predetermined overhead rates computed in part A?
C. Compute the amount of the over- or underapplied overhead assuming that actual overhead is $229,000. You should assume that overhead was applied as computed by you in part B.
D. Take a moment to compare the overapplied or underapplied overhead amounts calculated in part C. Why do the different cost drivers result in such different applied overhead amounts? Is there one "best" cost driver? What basis should Dick Thiel use to select a cost driver?
E. What options are available to Thiel Boots to dispose of the over- or underapplied overhead amounts? Which option do you recommend? Why?

Group Exercises

55. Within your group identify two or three local businesspeople that you can interview about how they measure and track product or service costs. Be creative in selecting businesses and try to include a variety of business types. How do the businesses you investigated measure and track direct materials? Direct labor? Overhead? Do the costing systems that are currently being used give accurate data? How does the businessperson verify the accuracy of the cost data? What suggestions does your group have for how the business could improve its costing system?

56. The production manager at Terra Firma is responsible for estimating the percentage of completion for all terra cotta planters, figurines, and yard art. Recently, she determined that the work in process inventory was 40 percent complete with respect to conversion costs. Shortly after the production manager produced her monthly report, she received a call from the company's controller. He asked her to stop by his office for a conversation at the end of the day. Not quite knowing what to expect, she stopped by and found the controller poring over the monthly financial reports. He quickly told her that he was concerned about her estimate of the percentage completion for the work in process inventory. He also told her that he was worried the company would not be receiving the new loan that it so desperately needs. She asked how her report could affect the loan decision. He asked her to reconsider her production report. Before she left his office, he said that it would really help matters if she could see things his way and just increase

the percentage of completion to 60 percent. After all, the inventory will be finished next month.

Each group member should complete the following questions individually and reconvene to discuss their answers after each person is finished.

Required
- A. What impact will increasing the percentage of completion have on Terra Firma's financial statements?
- B. Should the production manager agree with the request?
- C. What actions should the production manager take with respect to discussing her conversation with others? Be sure to consider other employees as well as outside parties (for example, friends, law enforcement, the company's loan officer).

Chapter 4: Activity-Based Costing

In this chapter, we revisit the problems of overhead application and discuss the use of an alternative product-costing system called activity-based costing (ABC). Assigning overhead to products and services using traditional allocation methods and volume-based cost drivers may not provide adequate information to managers to make good decisions. Activity-based costing provides more accurate cost information by focusing on the activities or work that is performed in the manufacturing of a product or providing a service and the cost drivers associated with those activities. The benefits and limitations of ABC are discussed, as is the application of ABC to nonmanufacturing activities and in a just-in-time (JIT) environment.

Learning Objectives

After studying the material in this chapter, you should be able to:

1. Recognize the need for activity-based costing (ABC) systems

2. Classify overhead costs as unit, batch, product, or facility level

3. Define and identify typical activities in an ABC system

4. Define and identity typical cost drivers in an ABC system

5. Calculate the cost of a product using ABC and compare traditional volume-based costing to ABC

6. Recognize that ABC can be applied to non-manufacturing activities

7. Evaluate the benefits and limitations of ABC systems

Introduction

The previous chapter examined a number of problems associated with the application of overhead to products and services. Owing to the indirect nature of overhead and the fact that overhead consists of a variety of seemingly unrelated costs, it is often difficult to determine how much overhead should be included when costing specific products and services. To complicate matters further, overhead costs must often be estimated in order to provide timely cost information to managers.

In the past, overhead typically made up a smaller portion of the total cost of a product or service. The environment was one of "labor-intensive" manufacturing. With labor as the dominant activity and therefore the cost driver, direct labor hours worked was a logical activity base with which to allocate overhead to products. As the manufacturing environment has matured and the use of machines or robotics in production has increased, overhead cost has become a larger percentage of the total manufacturing cost. In heavily automated manufacturing environments, direct labor costs have shrunk to as little as 5 percent of total production costs, whereas overhead costs have soared to 60 percent or more of total product costs (see Exhibit 4-1). It's not difficult to see why. Consider a modern automobile manufacturing plant. High-tech computers control robots that weld, paint, and perform other jobs that used to be done by human labor. High-tech computer-operated equipment, such as robots, is very expensive and is treated as part of overhead cost. As overhead costs increase and make up a larger portion of the total costs of products, accuracy in overhead application has become much more important. At the same time, advances in information technology have allowed even the smallest businesses to take advantage of computers. These advances have provided more and more timely information to managers than ever before.

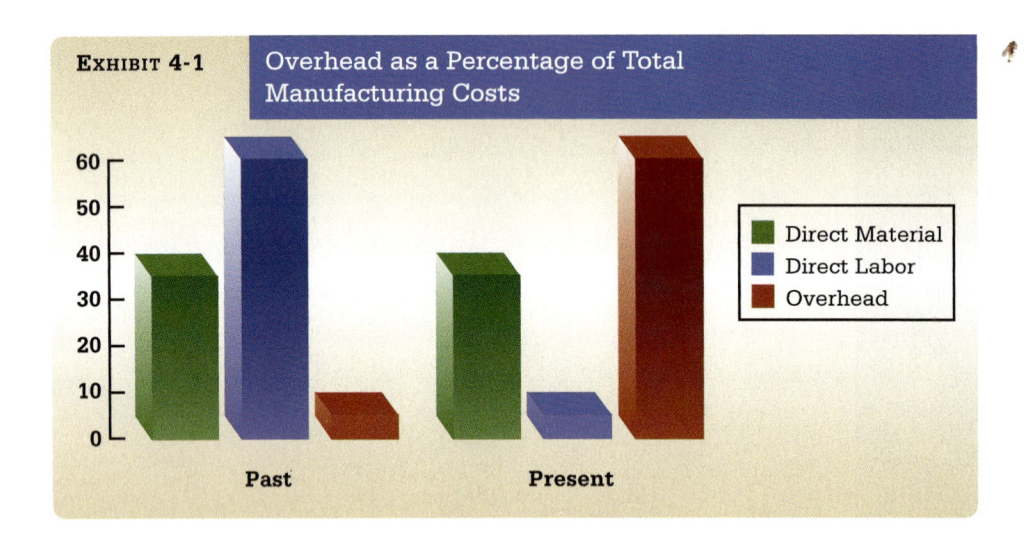

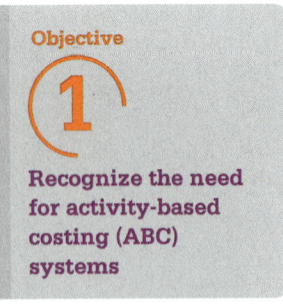

EXHIBIT 4-1 Overhead as a Percentage of Total Manufacturing Costs

Objective 1

Recognize the need for activity-based costing (ABC) systems

Activity-Based Costing

Traditional overhead allocation methods, which use one or two volume-based cost drivers to assign overhead costs to products, can provide misleading product-cost information in heavily automated manufacturing environments in which companies make a variety of diverse products. Volume-based allocation methods work best if the manufacturing environment includes mostly **unit-level costs** (costs that vary with every unit produced or the volume of production).

Unit-, Batch-, Product-, and Facility-Level Costs

Costs incurred in setting up machinery to make different products, costs incurred in designing a new model, and costs incurred in providing manufacturing facilities are not incurred every time an individual unit (a table) is produced. Rather, **batch-level costs,** such as machine setups, are incurred only when a batch of products (100 tables) is produced. Likewise, **product-level costs** (designing a new model) are incurred only when a new product is introduced. Finally, **facility-level costs,** such as the rent on the factory building, are incurred to sustain the overall manufacturing processes and do not vary with the number or type of products produced.[1]

Examples of unit-, batch-, product- and facility-level overhead costs are provided in Exhibit 4-2.

Objective 2
Classify overhead costs as unit, batch, product or facility level

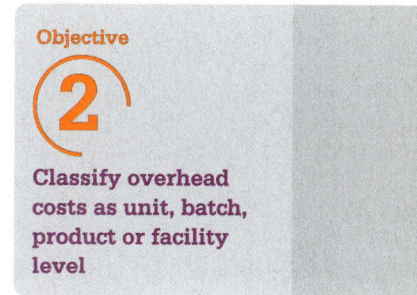

KEY CONCEPT

Unit-level costs are incurred each time a unit is produced. Batch-level costs are incurred each time a batch of goods is produced. Product-level costs are incurred as needed to support the production of each type of product. Facility-level costs simply sustain a facility's general manufacturing process.

EXHIBIT 4-2 Overhead Costs and Cooper's Hierarchy

Unit-Level Costs	Product-Level Costs
Supplies for factory	Salaries of engineers
Depreciation of factory machinery	Depreciation of engineering equipment
Energy costs for factory machinery	Product development costs (testing)
Repairs and maintenance of factory machinery	Quality control costs

Batch-Level Costs	Facility-Level Costs
Salaries related to purchasing and receiving	Depreciation of factory building or rent
Salaries related to moving material	Salary of plant manager
Quality control costs	Insurance, taxes, etc.
Depreciation of setup equipment	Training

When concentrated at the unit level, it makes sense that the number of units produced should be correlated with the amount of overhead costs allocated to each unit. However, as companies incur more and more batch-, product-, and facility-level costs, the correlation between the volume of product produced and the allocation of overhead becomes very fuzzy. **Activity-based costing (ABC),** which is based on the concept of assigning costs based on activities that drive costs rather than on the volume or number of units produced, provides more accurate costing in these situations. **Activities** are procedures or processes that cause work to be accomplished. Activities consume resources, and products consume activities.

Overhead costs are assigned to products in an ABC system in two stages.

KEY CONCEPT

The key feature of an ABC system is allocating overhead costs based on activities that drive costs rather than on the volume or number of units produced.

Stage 1—Identification of Activities

In Stage 1, activities are identified. Examples of typical activities of a company are shown in the first column of Exhibit 4-3. It should be noted that overhead costs can be traced to more than one activity. For example, utilities may be related to purchasing, engineering, and machining activities. An employee who provides maintenance services and runs machines in the factory might have his salary split between machining and maintenance activities. Likewise, whereas depreciation of factory equipment is related to machining, depreciation of other equipment might be related to maintenance or quality control activities.

Objective 3
Define and identify typical activities in an ABC system

---

[1] This classification of unit-level, batch-level, product-level, and facility-level costs is commonly referred to as Cooper's hierarchy.

Exhibit 4-3　Activities and Cost Drivers

Activity	Level	Typical Cost Drivers
Repair and maintenance of factory equipment	Unit	Machine hours, labor hours, or number of units
Energy costs for factory equipment	Unit	Machine hours
Supplies for factory	Unit	Machine hours or number of units
Purchasing	Batch	Number of purchase orders or number of parts
Receiving	Batch	Amount of material or number of receipts
Machine setups	Batch	Number of setups
Product testing	Product	Number of change orders, number of tests, or hours of testing time
Engineering costs	Product	Number of engineering hours or number of products
Product design	Product	Number of new or revised products
Quality control	Unit, batch, product	Number of inspections, hours of inspection, or number of defective units
Plant occupancy costs (rent, taxes, insurance, etc.)	Facility	Square footage, number of employees, labor hours, or machine hours

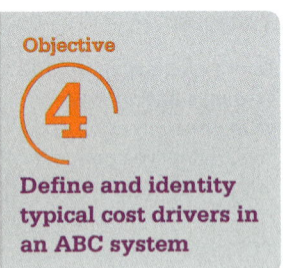

Objective 4

Define and identify typical cost drivers in an ABC system

Stage 2—Identification of Cost Drivers

In Stage 2, cost drivers for activities are chosen. As discussed in Chapter 2, cost drivers should cause, or drive, the incurrence of costs. For example, costs of purchasing might be driven by the number of purchase orders processed, whereas engineering costs might be driven by the number of parts in a product. Typical cost drivers for the activities identified in the exhibit are provided in the third column of Exhibit 4-3.

Unit-, batch-, and product-level activities are assigned to products by using cost drivers that capture the underlying behavior of the costs that are being assigned. Facility-level costs, however, are usually not allocated to products or are allocated to products in an arbitrary manner. For example, plant occupancy is a facility-level activity that would include such costs as plant managers' salaries, depreciation of the factory building, rent, taxes, and insurance. Allocation of these costs would require the use of arbitrary cost drivers, such as square footage, number of employees, labor hours, or machine hours.

It should be recognized that because of different types of production processes and products, every business will have a different set of activities and cost drivers. In addition, the more complex the business or the production process, the more complex the ABC system is likely to be.

ABC and Just in Time

ABC can be used by companies employing traditional manufacturing techniques with inventory and by those utilizing just-in-time (JIT) production systems. JIT systems were described in Chapter 2 as production systems in which materials are purchased and products are produced just in time to be used in production or sold to customers. Because factories are typically redesigned in a JIT environment so that all machinery and equipment needed to make a product is available in one area (a manufacturing cell), overhead costs are more likely to be traced to products as unit-, batch-, or product-level costs. Fewer overhead costs are likely to be considered facility-level costs requiring arbitrary allocation. Although utilizing JIT production techniques does not eliminate all facility-level costs, combining ABC and JIT should result in even more accurate product costing.

Doing Business.

THE ABCs OF ART

While the dot-com craze may be over, some of the companies born in the heady 1990s are still around and learning to flourish in today's business environment. One such company is Art.com. The company, which opened its website in 1998, sells prints, posters, and custom framing. Art.com's management implemented activity-based costing because it saw the approach as a tool to assist them in their decision-making processes. As a first step, the company identified 12 activities that were critical to its success. Even before the company considered the cost-savings potential, it benefited from the activity identification process because functional area managers were able to see and understand the "cost" created by their areas.

Selected Activities from art.com

Service Customers—Servicing customers requires resources of space, phone system and email, and information technology.
- Help customers select products or a mix of products.
- Answer customer questions about the website, product availability, and orders.
- Assist customers in resolving problems related to damaged goods, discontinued prints, and returned items.

Website Optimization—This activity links the business model to the customer and requires resources necessary for an electronic order.
- Design and maintain the website.
- Maintain hardware, software and telephone systems for electronic customer order processing.

Merchandise Inventory Selection and Management—Building and maintaining the inventory on the Web page requires resources such as the computer server and scanning equipment.
- Attend product shows.
- Create and develop new products, such as gifts and gift packages.
- Upload and remove images from the website.

Purchasing and Receiving—Purchasing product inventory, supplies, production tools, and equipment requires resources of space, time and information technology.
- Negotiate prices and order items.
- Respond to suppliers about damaged goods.
- Receive goods and match supplier invoices to purchase orders for goods received.

Customer Acquisition and Retention—Attracting customers requires resources of space, time, and information technology.
- Implement Web marketing through AOL, Yahoo!, etc.
- Pursue traditional marketing such as print, radio, and TV.
- Implement customer awareness programs through email, etc.

"How art.com uses ABC to Succeed," *Strategic Finance*, Volume 82, Issue 9.

Cost Flows and ABC

The flow of costs from raw materials to work in process to finished goods and cost of goods sold is not affected by the implementation of activity-based costing. Although the existence of multiple overhead rates (rather than plantwide or departmental rates) may make the application of overhead more complex, the cost flows remain the same as that described in Chapter 2 for manufacturing companies with inventory, manufacturing companies operating in a JIT environment, service companies, and merchandising companies.

Traditional Overhead Allocation and ABC—An Example

As an example, let's consider TopSail Construction, a beach-housing contractor based in North Carolina. TopSail Construction usually builds about 30 houses per year. On average, it takes about 4 months (16 weeks) to build each house. As in all manufactured products, the cost of a house consists of three main components: direct material, direct labor, and overhead.

Many types of materials are used in the construction of a house. Raw materials needed in home construction range from lumber and roofing to insulation, sheet rock, brick, siding, and more. These types of raw materials can usually be accumulated, tracked, and assigned to specific homes with relative ease and thus are classified as direct materials. Indirect materials would include such things as nails, screws, and glue, which are not worth the effort to try and measure with complete accuracy.

Direct labor is also fairly straightforward in the construction business. Like many building contractors, TopSail does not employ brick masons, electricians, plumbers, sheet rock installers, and painters but rather uses subcontractors to perform this work. Because subcontractor labor can be traced directly to each house built, these costs are classified as direct labor. TopSail has only six full-time employees. Two are carpenters who work directly on houses; they are also classified as direct labor costs. Two are construction supervisors whose primary job is to supervise the subcontractors and inspect the work done on each house. The construction supervisors typically spend their days going from house to house. TopSail consequently classifies their salaries as indirect labor. TopSail also employs a full-time administrative assistant and a secretary in the office to handle the ordering of materials and processing of change orders for each house as well as payroll, billing, accounts payable, and other accounting and administrative tasks related to the business. Because about one-half of the time of the office staff is spent directly on manufacturing duties, one half of the cost of their salaries (indirect labor) and other office expenses, such as rent, insurance, utilities, and supplies (overhead), is treated as a product cost. The other half is related to administrative duties and is treated as a period cost. In addition, TopSail has two part-time employees who deliver materials every morning and clear construction debris after work is complete each day. The salary of these workers is classified as indirect labor.

TopSail Construction incurs other overhead costs, including the cost of tools (saws, drills, etc.) used on the job, trucks used for material delivery and cleanup, trucks used by the construction supervisors, rent of construction trailers used as temporary offices at large construction sites, and so on. TopSail estimates that its overhead costs will total $485,000 in 2005. Exhibit 4-4 provides a breakdown of this estimate.

If TopSail produced only one type of house, the overhead allocation process would be very simple. As discussed in Chapter 3, all the company would have to do is divide the total overhead of $485,000 by the number of houses constructed. If TopSail constructed 30 houses in 2005, each house would be allocated $16,167 of overhead costs. However, to meet the specific needs of customers, TopSail builds both standard homes in large subdivisions and custom homes (on the beach) of different design, size, and features. The construction of custom homes requires TopSail to give more attention to the proper allocation of overhead costs to each house.

Using a traditional volume-based overhead allocation method would result in TopSail Construction using only one predetermined overhead rate, such as direct labor hours, to allocate overhead to houses. If TopSail estimates that the total direct labor hours used in 2005 in

Exhibit 4-4: Estimated Overhead Costs for 2005

Overhead Item	Estimated Cost
Indirect materials	$180,000
Indirect labor:	
Construction supervisors	130,000
Office staff	30,000
Part-time workers	30,000
Other overhead:	
Office expenses	48,000
Tools	15,000
Trucks and other equipment	40,000
Rent on construction trailers	12,000
Total	$485,000

building homes will be 88,000, it would have a predetermined overhead rate of $5.51 per hour of direct labor used to construct each house ($485,000/88,000 direct labor hours). If a standard house takes 2,400 hours of labor to build, it would be allocated $13,224 of overhead costs. Likewise, a custom home requiring 4,000 direct labor hours would be allocated $22,040 of overhead costs. Exhibit 4-5 illustrates the total cost of a standard house and a custom house, using traditional volume-based costing.

Exhibit 4-5: Traditional Volume-Based Allocation Using Direct Labor Hours

Cost	Standard House		Custom House	
Direct material	$ 75,000		$112,500	
Direct labor	60,000	(2,400 hours at $25 per hour)	100,000	(4,000 hours at $25 per hour)
Overhead	13,224	(2,400 hours at $5.51 per hour)	22,040	(4,000 hours at $5.51 per hour)
Total costs	$148,224		$234,540	

    If all the overhead costs were related to the amount of labor hours needed to build the house, a volume-based overhead allocation system would provide management with the information needed to make good decisions.

    However, because TopSail builds two types of houses, a standard house with very few options and a custom home designed for beach property that will have many different options, the traditional volume-based overhead allocation method may not provide the best information to management. The custom house requires much more inspection activity and typically has many more change orders than the standard house. In addition, the materials used in a custom house are more varied, resulting in more frequent purchases and deliveries. The use of an activity-based costing system might be more appropriate. In the next section, we explore TopSail's use of ABC.

TopSail's Stage 1: Identification of Activities

The first step in the implementation of an ABC system is the identification of activities and the tracing of overhead costs to each activity. Remember that activities are processes or procedures that cause work to be accomplished. TopSail Construction identifies five primary activities that consume the resources of the company:

1. Inspections
2. Purchasing
3. Supervision
4. Material delivery and handling
5. Processing of change orders

Exhibit 4-6 provides the overhead costs associated with each activity. Note that the total overhead is $485,000 regardless of whether it is allocated using volume-based drivers or using ABC.

EXHIBIT 4-6 Estimated Overhead Costs for 2004

Activity	Estimated Cost
Inspections	$ 50,000
Purchasing	30,000
Supervision	100,000
Material delivery and handling	225,000
Processing change orders	80,000
Total	$485,000

TopSail's Stage 2: Identification of Cost Drivers and Allocation of Costs

Once the activities have been identified and overhead costs traced to each activity, cost drivers must be identified for each activity. The cost drivers chosen are as follows:

Activity	Cost Driver
Inspections	Number of inspections
Purchasing	Number of purchase orders
Supervision	Hours of supervisor time
Material delivery and handling	Number of deliveries
Processing change orders	Number of change orders

As you can see from the cost drivers chosen, they are more closely related to the activity than to direct labor hours. It simply makes more sense to allocate the cost of processing change orders based on the number of change orders processed rather than on the number of labor hours to build each house.

An example of "standard" houses.

An example of a "custom" beach house.

TopSail estimates that it will build 20 standard houses and 10 custom houses during the next year. TopSail further estimates that each standard house will require weekly inspections over the estimated 16-week construction period (16 per house), whereas the custom homes will require daily inspections (80 per house). Custom homes built on the beach must meet specific state and local building codes to withstand hurricane-force winds and tidal surges. They require more detailed inspections at more frequent time intervals than do TopSail's standard houses.

Standard houses also require less supervision time (100 hours) than does a custom house (150 hours). Custom homes require different and more varied materials than does the standard house. There will be 30 purchase orders issued for standard houses and 60 purchase orders issued for custom houses. TopSail expects that material will be delivered about 24 times over the four-month construction period for a standard house (1.5 times per week on average), whereas the custom house will require about three deliveries per week. Finally, TopSail expects to process considerably more change orders with the custom house (30 per house) compared to only 5 for the standard house. Exhibit 4-7 summarizes the total number of inspections, purchase orders, supervision hours, deliveries, and change orders TopSail expects next year.

Exhibit 4-7: Estimated Cost Driver Activity

Cost Driver	Standard Houses (each)	Standard Houses (total for 20 houses)	Custom Houses (each)	Custom Houses (total for 10 houses)	Total
Number of inspections	16	320	80	800	1,120
Number of purchase orders	30	600	60	600	1,200
Hours of supervision time	100	2,000	150	1,500	3,500
Number of deliveries	24	480	48	480	960
Number of change orders	5	100	30	300	400

In Exhibit 4-8, predetermined overhead rates are calculated for each activity and cost driver, just as we did using a plantwide or departmental overhead rate with volume-based cost drivers.

Exhibit 4-8: The Calculation of Predetermined Overhead Rates

Activity	Total Estimated Cost	Cost Driver and Estimated Amount	Predetermined Overhead Rate
Inspections	$ 50,000	Number of inspections (1,120)	$44.64 per inspection
Purchasing	30,000	Number of purchase orders (1,200)	$25 per purchase order
Supervision	100,000	Hours of supervisor time (3,500)	$28.57 per supervisor hour
Material delivery and handling	225,000	Number of deliveries (960)	$234.38 per delivery
Processing change orders	80,000	Number of change orders (400)	$200 per change order
Total overhead	$485,000		

Exhibit 4-9 illustrates the total cost of a standard house and a custom house using an activity-based costing system.

Exhibit 4-9: Activity-Based Costing

Cost	Standard House	Custom House
Direct materials	$ 75,000	$112,500
Direct labor	60,000	100,000
Inspections	714	3,571
Purchasing	750	1,500
Supervision	2,857	4,286
Material handling and delivery	5,625	11,250
Processing change orders	1,000	6,000
Total costs	$145,946	$239,107

If we compare the two methods of allocating overhead costs to standard and custom houses, we can see why volume-based allocation and activity-based costing resulted in different amounts of overhead being applied to each house. Allocating overhead costs using an activity-based costing system results in greater allocations of overhead to the custom house because it consumes more of the purchasing, inspection, supervision, material handling, and processing change order activities than does the standard house. Although the custom house was also allocated more overhead under the volume-based costing system, the amount is different (as is our rationale for the allocation). Under a traditional volume-based costing system, the custom house was allocated more overhead than the standard house simply because it consumed more direct labor hours. Remember that the custom house required 4,000 direct labor hours, whereas the standard house required only 2,400 direct labor hours. In Exhibit 4-10, notice that using volume-based costing resulted in overcosting the standard house and undercosting the custom house compared to costing under ABC.

EXHIBIT 4-10	Cost Comparison between Traditional and ABC Costing	
	Standard House	**Custom House**
Traditional costing	$148,224	$234,540
ABC costing	$145,946	$239,107
Difference in cost	$ 2,278 lower	$ 4,567 higher

One important aspect of ABC systems is the elimination of cross subsidies between products. Cross subsidies occur when high-volume products, such as the standard house, are assigned more than their fair share of overhead costs. At the same time, more complicated low-volume products, such as the custom house, are allocated too little overhead. This cross subsidy may make high-volume products appear unprofitable when they may not be, or it may make them appear to show less profit than they actually do. Activity-based costing systems eliminate the cross subsidy between high- and low-volume products.

Volume-based costing and activity-based costing result in different allocations of overhead when products consume activities in different proportions. On the other hand, volume-based costing and activity-based costing result in the same allocations of overhead when products consume resources in the same proportions. For example, producing a standard house consumed 2,400 direct labor hours, whereas producing a custom house consumed 4,000 direct labor hours (see Exhibit 4-5). Based on this consumption of resources, the standard house was allocated 37.5 percent, or $13,224 of overhead, whereas the custom house was allocated 62.5 percent, or $22,040 of overhead. If the standard house and the custom house had consumed all resources related to inspections, purchase orders, supervision, deliveries, and processing change orders in the same proportion as they consumed direct labor (37.5 percent for the standard house and 62.5 percent for the custom house), the total overhead allocated to each house using volume-based costing and ABC would be exactly the same.

KEY CONCEPT

Volume-based costing systems often result in overcosting high-volume products and undercosting low-volume products. This cross subsidy is eliminated by the use of ABC.

Although the differences in cost may seem slight, consider the impact on TopSail's pricing policy (see Exhibit 4-11). TopSail typically establishes a sales price equal to 125 percent of total manufacturing costs (rounded up to the nearest thousand). Remember, this is not all profit, as TopSail must still cover all selling and administrative costs (half of its office expenses, advertising, commissions on sales made by real estate agents, etc.).

Under ABC, TopSail would price the standard house at $183,000 instead of $186,000 and the custom house at $299,000 instead of $294,000. In the very price-conscious standard-housing market, overpricing the standard house by $3,000 could result in a loss of sales, which could impact TopSail Construction's profit margin. Likewise, in the more flexible

Exhibit 4-11: Price Comparison between Traditional and ABC Costing

	Standard House	Custom House
Sales price based on traditional costing	$186,000	$294,000
Sales price based on ABC costing	$183,000	$299,000
Difference in sales price	$ 3,000 lower	$ 5,000 higher

custom-home market, TopSail could have likely priced its custom house at a higher price than that indicated by traditional costing methods.

As this example illustrates, the allocation of costs using activity-based costing is more accurate and reflects the consumption of costs based on the activities that drive them rather than on one volume-based cost driver. In addition to providing management with more accurate cost information for pricing decisions, it also affects a variety of other decisions discussed in Part II of this book.

ABC Systems in Service Industries

Service providers currently make up the fastest-growing segment of the U.S. economy, employing almost 75 percent of the workforce. As service companies expand the scope and quality of services offered, the need for fast, accurate costing information becomes more important. Can ABC be used to cost services as well as products? Do the same principles that we learned for manufacturing companies apply to service businesses? The answer is yes! In fact, ABC is every bit as important for service providers as it is for manufacturing companies. Although ABC was developed for use primarily by manufacturing companies, it has gained widespread acceptance in the service sector. Companies in the service sector have been embracing ABC in record numbers over the past decade or so. This trend is especially true of companies whose industry groups (such as airlines, telecommunications, and utilities) have encountered significant changes due to deregulation.

However, implementing ABC in service companies is not without its problems. One common problem is that the type of work done in service companies tends to be nonrepetitive. Unlike highly automated manufacturing companies, analyzing the activities of a service provider can be difficult when the activities differ greatly for each customer or service. In addition, service-oriented companies are likely to have proportionately more facility-level costs than do manufacturing companies. Remember from our earlier discussion that facility-level costs are allocated arbitrarily to goods and services (if at all).

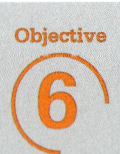

ABC and Nonmanufacturing Activities

Objective 6
Recognize that ABC can be applied to nonmanufacturing activities

The principles of ABC can be applied to nonmanufacturing activities as well. Instead of computing the manufacturing cost of a product or a service, the goal is to determine the total cost of a product or service. ABC can also be used to determine the cost of providing a particular nonmanufacturing activity. For example, a company might use ABC to determine the cost of providing payroll services. This information can be used to help management determine whether to continue processing payroll in-house or whether to outsource.

Doing Business.

ABC IN THE POST OFFICE

The U.S. Post Office used activity-based costing to help determine the costs and benefits of allowing customers to pay with debit and credit cards. In this case, the post office focused on the impact of using debit and credit cards on customer satisfaction even though cost savings were also likely to be seen (Carter, Sedaghat, and Williams, "How ABC Changed the Post Office," *Management Accounting*, February 1998).

Benefits and Limitations of ABC

Because of the increase in global competition, companies must strive to achieve and to sustain a competitive advantage. This requires organizations to continually improve performance in all aspects of their business operations. By focusing on continuous improvement, organizations can minimize scrap in the manufacturing process, reduce lead times for customer deliveries or vendor shipments, increase the quality of products and services produced, and control manufacturing and nonmanufacturing costs.

Activity-based costing systems provide more and more accurate cost information that focuses managers on opportunities for continuous improvement. Throughout their planning, operating, and control activities, managers use the information provided by ABC systems. In Chapter 1, planning was defined as the development of short- and long-term objectives and goals of an organization and an identification of the resources needed to achieve them. Using ABC in the budgeting process provides more accurate estimates of these resources.

One of the biggest advantages of ABC is the increased accuracy of cost information it provides for day-to-day decision making by managers (operating decisions). Managers use ABC information to make better decisions related to adding or dropping products, making or buying components used in the manufacturing process, marketing and pricing strategies, and so forth.

ABC also provides benefits related to the control function of managers. Costs that appear to be indirect using volume-based costing systems now are traced to specific activities using cost drivers. This method allows managers to better see what causes costs to be incurred, leading to better control.

However, ABC is not for everyone, and the benefits of increased accuracy do not come without costs. Accumulating, tracking, and assigning costs to products and services using ABC requires the use of multiple activity pools and cost drivers. High measurement costs associated with ABC systems are a significant limitation. Companies may decide that the measurement costs associated with implementing ABC systems are greater than the expected benefit from having more accurate cost information. For example, if the market dictates prices, such as with commodity products, and companies have little control over pricing their products, highly reliable product costs may not be necessary for pricing. However, ABC may still prove valuable for planning and cost-reduction efforts.

In general, companies that have a high potential for cost distortions are more likely to benefit from ABC. Cost distortions are likely when companies make **diverse products** that consume resources differently. Products that vary a great deal in complexity are typically diverse, but differences in color or other seemingly minor differences in products can lead to product diversity when these differences materially change the products and affect the resources they consume.

Companies that have a large proportion of non-unit-level costs are also likely to benefit from ABC. Remember, unit-level costs vary with the number of units produced and can

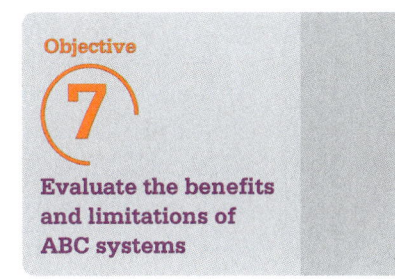

Objective 7

Evaluate the benefits and limitations of ABC systems

be allocated with reasonable accuracy using volume-based cost systems and drivers. On the other hand, volume-based costing systems can result in distortions when allocating batch-, product-, and facility-level costs.

Companies that have relatively high proportions of overhead compared to direct materials and direct labor are likely to benefit from ABC as well. This situation is often the case with highly automated manufacturing companies or companies that have adopted JIT techniques. Note that service companies, such as law or CPA firms, may also have high overhead costs compared to direct material and direct labor and likewise may benefit from the implementation of ABC.

Hitting the Bottom Line.

ABC Can Be Profitable

The bottom-line benefits of ABC can be impressive. A small manufacturer with sales of $10 million reported that profits increased 500 percent on a sales increase of 300 percent since adopting ABC four years earlier. According to the company, the improvement in profitability came from two primary sources—selling a more profitable mix of products as a result of a more accurate costing system and identifying areas for cost control that were hidden under the traditional costing system ("Yes, ABC is for Small Business, Too," *Journal of Accountancy*, Volume 188, Number 2).

Summary of Key Concepts

- Unit-level costs are incurred each time a unit is produced. Batch-level costs are incurred each time a batch of goods is produced. Product-level costs are incurred as needed to support the production of each type of product. Facility-level costs simply sustain a facility's general manufacturing process. (p. 105)

- The key feature of an ABC system is allocating overhead costs based on activities that drive costs rather than on the volume or number of units produced. (p. 105)

- Volume-based costing systems often result in overcosting high-volume products and undercosting low-volume products. This cross subsidy is eliminated by the use of ABC. (p. 113)

Key Definitions

Unit-level costs Costs that are incurred each time a unit is produced (p. 104)

Batch-level costs Costs that are incurred each time a batch of goods is produced (p. 105)

Product-level costs Costs that are incurred as needed to support the production of each type of product (p. 105)

Facility-level costs Costs that are incurred to sustain the overall manufacturing process (p. 105)

Activity-based costing (ABC) A system of allocating overhead costs that assumes that activities, not volume of production, cause overhead costs to be incurred (p. 105)

Activities Procedures or processes that cause work to be accomplished (p. 105)

Diverse products Products that consume resources in different proportions (p. 115)

Multiple Choice

1. Activity-based costing is a method of cost allocation that is useful for assigning _____ costs to products or services.
   a. direct labor
   b. direct material
   c. manufacturing overhead
   d. direct labor and direct material

2. Which of the following statements most accurately describes product-level costs?
   a. Product-level costs occur whenever a unit is manufactured.
   b. Product-level costs are incurred as necessary to support the production of a product.
   c. Product-level costs occur whenever a batch of products is manufactured.
   d. Product-level costs are necessary to sustain the overall manufacturing operations.

3. As the proportion of batch-, product-, and facility-level costs increases relative to unit-level costs, the correlation between the overhead allocation and production volume:
   a. becomes more predictable and stable.
   b. becomes fixed and positive.
   c. becomes less predictable.
   d. becomes variable and negative.

4. Saturation Sprinkler Supply sells sprinkler systems suited for large and small yards. To better estimate costs, the company recently adopted an activity-based costing system. Last year, the company incurred $1,000,000 in overhead costs. Detailed information about these costs is as follows:

   ✓ Overhead rate for purchasing: $10/purchase order

Activity	Allocation Base	Proportion of Overhead Cost
Purchasing	Number of purchase orders	35 %
Material handling	Number of shipments received	20 %
Quality inspection	Number of inspections	45 %

   The numbers of activities for large-yard and small-yard systems were as follows:

	Large	Small
Purchase orders	15,000	20,000
Shipments received	7,500	12,500
Inspections	11,500	11,000

   If a large-yard system requires three deliveries of materials to a job site, what amount of overhead should be assigned to that job with respect to material handling?
   a. $80
   b. $30
   c. $10
   d. $6

LO 3 4 5

✓ Overhead rate for fabric receiving: $8/shipment received

5. The Fancy Drapery Company sells draperies suited for fancy and plain windows. Last year, the company incurred $800,000 in overhead costs. After implementing an activity-based costing system this year, the company's controller identified the following related information:

Activity	Allocation Base	Proportion of Overhead Cost
Customer contact	Number of customer visits	30 %
Fabric receiving	Number of shipments received	40 %
Sales	Number of sales orders	30 %

The numbers of activities for fancy and plain-window draperies were as follows:

	Fancy	Plain
Customer visits	5,000	5,000
Shipments received	8,500	11,500
Sales orders	6,000	9,000

If a customer requested a cost estimate on a specially designed drapery that would require two customer visits, how much customer contact overhead should be included in the cost estimate?
 a. $ 48
 b. $ 24
 c. $ 96
 d. $ 32

LO 4

6. Which of the following statements regarding activity-based costing (ABC) systems in a just-in-time (JIT) environment is true?
 a. ABC should not be utilized in a JIT environment.
 b. ABC can be very successful in a JIT environment because most overhead costs in such a setting are typically facility-level costs.
 c. Combining ABC and JIT should result in very accurate product costing.
 d. Both b and c are true statements.

LO 5

7. Which of the following statements comparing traditional and activity-based costing (ABC) systems is true?
 a. Traditional systems are generally more accurate than ABC systems.
 b. ABC systems are generally more accurate than traditional systems.
 c. ABC and traditional systems often produce similar product-cost information.
 d. Each of the above is true.

LO 5

8. Which of the following statements comparing traditional and activity-based costing (ABC) is true?
 a. ABC systems eliminate cross subsidies.
 b. Traditional systems eliminate cross subsidies.
 c. ABC and traditional systems often produce similar product-cost information.
 d. Each of the above is true.

LO 5

9. Cross subsidies:
 a. occur when high-volume products are assigned less than their fair share of overhead costs.
 b. occur when high-volume products are assigned more than their fair share of overhead costs.
 c. occur regularly with both traditional and activity-based costing systems.
 d. occur when low-volume products are assigned more than their fair share of overhead costs.

10. Implementing an activity-based costing (ABC) system in a service company:
    a. is exactly the same as implementing an ABC system in a manufacturing company.
    b. can be more difficult than implementing an ABC system in a manufacturing company partly because there are fewer repetitive activities.
    c. differs from implementing an ABC system in a manufacturing company because service companies generally have more batch-level costs than do manufacturing companies.
    d. is not possible because of the nature of service companies.
11. Activity-based costing (ABC):
    a. can be applied to selling and administrative activities.
    b. cannot be applied to selling and administrative activities, as they are nonmanufacturing costs.
    c. cannot be applied to service companies.
    d. can be applied only to manufacturing companies.
12. Why would a company choose to apply activity-based costing techniques to its selling and administrative costs?
    a. To obtain a more accurate estimate of various selling and administrative activities.
    b. To develop a thorough understanding of the activities that drive selling and administrative costs.
    c. To estimate the selling and administrative costs associated with a particular company division.
    d. Each of the above is a valid purpose for which activity-based costing may be applied.
13. Which of the following types of companies would be most likely to benefit from activity-based costing?
    a. Companies with a low potential for cost distortions
    b. Companies that have a large proportion of unit-level costs
    c. Companies that have a relatively high proportion of overhead compared to direct materials and direct labor
    d. None of the above
14. Which of the following is not generally believed to be a benefit of an activity-based costing system?
    a. Managers are able to exercise less control over functional areas due to increased complexities associated with cost accumulation and estimation.
    b. Product and services costs are generally more accurately estimated in an activity-based costing system.
    c. Managers' efforts are more focused on continuous improvement.
    d. The budgeting process is enhanced with more detailed and accurate activity data.

Concept Questions

15. *(Objective 1, 2)* Define activity-based costing. Overhead costs are typically identified as belonging to one of four categories. List and briefly describe each category.
16. *(Objective 3, 4)* Identify and describe the two stages of cost allocation in an activity-based costing system.
17. *(Objective 4)* Discuss the importance of choosing the right cost driver and the potential impact of choosing the wrong cost driver.
18. *(Objective 4)* Why would a company that utilizes just-in-time techniques also wish to implement an activity-based costing system?
19. *(Objective 5)* What are "cross subsidies between products" and how can they be controlled?
20. *(Objective 6)* How can activity-based costing techniques be applied to selling and administration activities?

21. *(Objective 6)* Discuss activity-based costing systems in service businesses. Be sure to explain how they differ from those used in manufacturing businesses.
22. *(Objective 7)* What are some of the benefits of activity-based costing systems?
23. *(Objective 7)* What are some of the downsides of activity-based costing systems?

Exercises

24. Hendee Cable Systems manufactures a variety of products for the fiber optic industry in its facility in San Bernadino, California. The following are examples of the activities performed by various personnel at Hendee.
    a. Purchase orders are generated for raw materials purchases from suppliers. Hendee orders raw materials as needed to fill customer orders and maintains a very small amount of raw materials inventory.
    b. Engineers conduct research and development activities aimed at identifying new technologies for data transmission.
    c. Hendee conducts continuous quality inspections during the production process. All cable is 100 percent guaranteed to be free of defects.
    d. Machine operators must calibrate production equipment whenever production is started on a new order.
    e. Maintenance personnel regularly inspect the manufacturing facility's heating and cooling systems to ensure adequate conditions within the manufacturing environment.
    f. Newly purchased production equipment is being depreciated over five years.
    g. Hendee recently hired several new engineers to begin work on development of a new product line.
    h. Accounting personnel received and paid property taxes for the manufacturing facility.
    i. Hendee launched a website to auction excess cable to interested parties.
    j. A new facility was built to house all design engineers in one central location. This new facility will be depreciated over 20 years.

    Required

    Classify each of the activities as unit-level, batch-level, product-level, or facility-level activities.

25. Jakubielski and Martin, CPAs, is a full-service CPA firm that provides accounting, tax, and consulting services to its clients. The firm is considering changing to an activity-based costing system and has asked for your input regarding the design of the system. The firm has identified certain activities that are integral to the practice and would like your suggestions regarding potential cost drivers.

Activity	Cost Driver
a. Client interview	1. Professional staff hours
b. Tax return preparation	2. Transactions
c. Tax return review	3. Number of pages
d. Data input	4. Number of employees
e. Report assembly	5. Machine hours
f. Research	6. Clerical staff hours
g. Report writing	
h. Site visits	

Required

Match each of the activities with a potential cost driver. Please note that you may not use all drivers and some may be used more than once.

26. The University of Tennessee has asked for your help with implementing an activity-based costing system for the admissions office. The following activities and cost drivers were identified by the chief admissions officer for the university.

Activity	Cost Driver
a. Receiving applications	1. Number of students
b. Processing applications	2. Number of acceptances
c. Receiving student inquiries	3. Number of applications
d. Responding to student inquiries	4. Labor hours
e. Accepting students	5. Number of inquiries
f. Enrolling students	

Required

Match each of the activities with a potential cost driver. Please note that you may not use all drivers and some may be used more than once.

27. Tip Top Company sells umbrellas suited for small and large picnic tables. Based on the advice of its accountant, Tip Top is considering whether to adopt an activity-based costing system. To evaluate the possible impact on cost, the company has accumulated the following data from last year:

✓ Overhead assigned to small umbrellas for purchasing: $200,000

Activity	Allocation Base	Overhead Cost
Purchasing	Number of purchase orders	$300,000
Receiving	Number of shipments received	150,000
Sales	Number of sales orders	150,000

The numbers of activities for small and large umbrellas were as follows:

	Small	Large
Purchase orders	10,000	5,000
Shipments received	12,500	7,500
Sales orders	8,500	6,500

Required

A. Calculate the overhead rates for the following activities: purchasing, receiving, and sales.
B. Calculate the dollar amount of overhead that should be assigned to small and large umbrellas for each of the three activities.

28. The Bouncy Baby Crib Mattress Company sells firm and extra-firm mattresses. The company's president, Anna Greer, has become interested in the possibility of improving company performance by more closely monitoring overhead costs. She has decided to adopt an activity-based costing system for the current year. Last year, the company incurred $2,000,000 in overhead costs related to the following activities:

✓ Total overhead for firm mattresses: $1,450,000

Activity	Allocation Base	Overhead Cost
Materials processing	Number of parts	$1,400,000
Firmness testing	Number of tests	400,000
Customer calls	Number of customer calls	200,000

During the year, 100,000 parts were handled (75,000 for firm mattresses and 25,000 for extra-firm mattresses), 20,000 firmness tests were conducted (12,500 for firm and 7,500 for extra-firm), and 10,000 customer calls were answered (7,500 for firm and 2,500 for extra-firm).

Required

A. Based on an activity-based approach, determine the total amount of overhead that should be assigned to firm and extra-firm mattresses.
B. If a firm mattress requires five parts, two tests, and one customer call, then what amount of overhead should be assigned to that mattress?

29. The following overhead cost information is available for the Christopher Corporation for the prior year:

✓ Overhead rate for quality control: $20/inspection

Activity	Allocation Base	Overhead Cost
Purchasing	Number of purchase orders	$400,000
Receiving	Number of shipments received	100,000
Machine setups	Number of setups	400,000
Quality control	Number of inspections	150,000

During the year, 8,000 purchase orders were issued; 25,000 shipments were received; 4,000 machine setups occurred; and 7,500 inspections were conducted. Employees worked a total of 10,000 hours on production. The corporate managers are trying to decide whether they should use a traditional overhead allocation method based on direct labor hours or switch to an activity-based costing system.

Required

A. Determine the overhead rate using the traditional overhead allocation method based on direct labor hours.
B. Determine the overhead rate for each of the activities assuming that activity-based costing is used.

30. The following overhead cost information is available for the Herbert Love Corporation for the prior year:

✓ Traditional predetermined overhead rate: $105/direct labor hour

Activity	Allocation Base	Overhead Cost
Purchasing	Number of purchase orders	$400,000
Receiving	Number of shipments received	100,000
Machine setups	Number of setups	400,000
Quality control	Number of inspections	150,000

During the year, 8,000 purchase orders were issued; 25,000 shipments were received; 4,000 machine setups occurred; and 7,500 inspections were conducted. Employees worked a total of 10,000 hours on production. The corporate managers are trying to decide whether they should use a traditional overhead allocation method based on direct labor hours, or switch to an activity-based costing system. Assume that a batch of products has the following specifications.

Direct labor hours	7
Purchase orders	7
Shipments received	10
Machine setups	3
Inspections	3

Required

A. Determine the overhead allocation for the batch under the traditional overhead allocation based on direct labor hours.
B. Determine the overhead allocation for the batch under activity-based costing.

31. Elise Entertainment is a progressive company that is considering the implementation of activity-based costing techniques to better understand and control costs associated with its human resources (HR) department. Currently, the department incurs annual costs of $750,000. Claire Elise, the company's president, believes there are four primary activities within the department: recruiting new employees, responding to employee questions about benefits, general employee administration, and employee termination/separation. She asked the HR manager to identify possible drivers and costs associated with each of these activities. The manager provided the following data:

✓ *Overhead rate for recruitment: $125/applicant*

Activity	Allocation Base	Overhead Cost
Recruitment	Number of applicants	$250,000
Query response	Number of questions	156,000
Administration	Number of employees	294,000
Separation	Number of terminations/separations	50,000

The HR manager determined that in the most recent year there were 2,000 applications received; 2,400 benefits-related questions from employees; an average monthly employment of 600 individuals; and 100 employees who were either terminated or otherwise left the company.

Required

A. Estimate the overhead cost for each activity.
B. Which activity is the most expensive and which is the least expensive?

32. Claire Elise is not convinced that using activity-based costing techniques allows her to better control the costs in the HR department, so she asked the HR manager to estimate costs based simply on the number of employees. Claire also asked the manager to be prepared to explain why the company should use activity-based costing for her department.

Required

A. Using the data in Exercise 31, calculate the HR department cost per employee for Elise Entertainment.
B. Why should Elise Entertainment use activity-based costing?

Problems

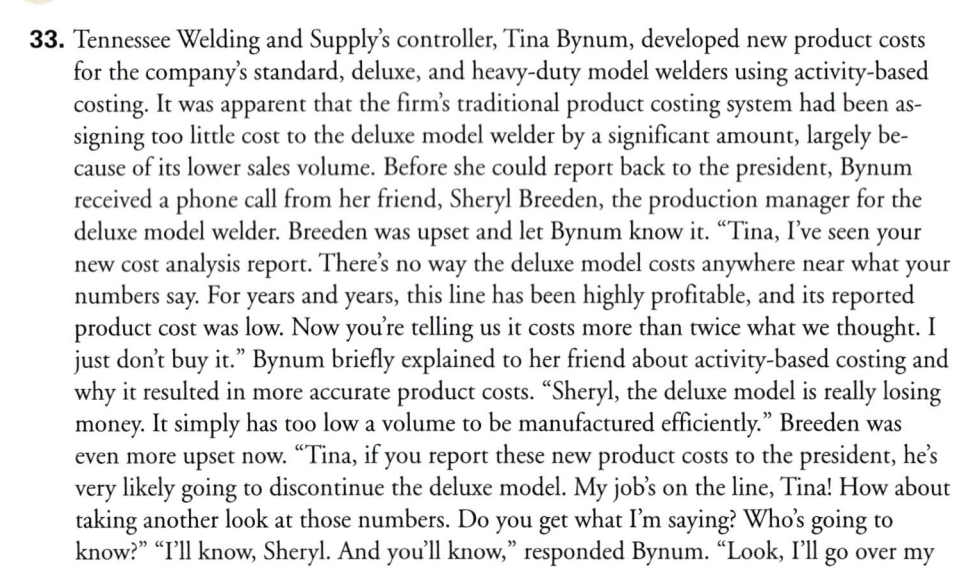

33. Tennessee Welding and Supply's controller, Tina Bynum, developed new product costs for the company's standard, deluxe, and heavy-duty model welders using activity-based costing. It was apparent that the firm's traditional product costing system had been assigning too little cost to the deluxe model welder by a significant amount, largely because of its lower sales volume. Before she could report back to the president, Bynum received a phone call from her friend, Sheryl Breeden, the production manager for the deluxe model welder. Breeden was upset and let Bynum know it. "Tina, I've seen your new cost analysis report. There's no way the deluxe model costs anywhere near what your numbers say. For years and years, this line has been highly profitable, and its reported product cost was low. Now you're telling us it costs more than twice what we thought. I just don't buy it." Bynum briefly explained to her friend about activity-based costing and why it resulted in more accurate product costs. "Sheryl, the deluxe model is really losing money. It simply has too low a volume to be manufactured efficiently." Breeden was even more upset now. "Tina, if you report these new product costs to the president, he's very likely going to discontinue the deluxe model. My job's on the line, Tina! How about taking another look at those numbers. Do you get what I'm saying? Who's going to know?" "I'll know, Sheryl. And you'll know," responded Bynum. "Look, I'll go over my analysis again to make sure I haven't made an error."

Required

A. Is the controller, Tina Bynum, acting ethically by potentially making data known that may lead to job losses?
B. Is the production manager, Sheryl Breeden, acting ethically?
C. What are Bynum's ethical obligations? To the president? To her friend?

34. Bob Haynes is the managing director of Prather Industries, which provides services to both state government agencies and private organizations. Both types of contracts are awarded on the basis of competitive bids. The government agencies require that the cost of the services be calculated using a specific methodology. In the past, Prather has used this methodology for costing both government and private contracts. Bob's contracts with government agencies provide for reimbursement of costs plus a predetermined markup of 30 percent. Bob's contracts with private organizations are based on negotiated fees and are not directly a function of the estimated costs of the service. The relative profitability of the two types of contracts, based on average-cost information, is as follows:

Costs and Revenues	Government Contract	Private Contract	Total
Costs	$ 20,000	$20,000	$40,000
Cost + 30%	26,000		26,000
Negotiated fee		30,000	30,000
Profit	$ 6,000	$10,000	$16,000

Bob's recently completed ABC analysis shows that government contracts are much less costly than estimated previously and that the private contracts are more costly.

Costs and Revenues	Government Contract	Private Contract	Total
ABC costs	$10,000	$30,000	$40,000
Cost + 30%	13,000	—	13,000
Negotiated fee	—	30,000	30,000
Profit	$ 3,000	$ 0	$ 3,000

Required

If Bob uses the ABC analysis for contracting and does not renegotiate the fee for the private contract, overall profitability will decrease. Bob would like to use the old method to cost (and price) the government contracts and to use the ABC information to renegotiate the fee for the private contracts. Is this strategy ethical?

35. Surfs Up manufactures surfboards. The company produces two models: the small board and the big board. Data regarding the two boards are as follows:

Product	Direct Labor Hours per Unit	Annual Production	Total Direct Labor Hours
Big	1.5	8,000 boards	15,000
Small	1.0	40,000 boards	35,000

✓ Total cost to produce one big board: $209.20

The big board requires $75 in direct materials per unit, whereas the small board requires $40. The company pays an average direct labor rate of $13 per hour. The company has historically used direct labor hours as the activity base for applying overhead to the boards. Manufacturing overhead is estimated to be $1,664,000 per year. The big board is more complex to manufacture than the small board because it requires more machine time.

Blake Moore, the company's controller, is considering the use of activity-based costing to apply overhead because the surf boards require such different amounts of machining. Blake has identified the following four separate activity centers.

Activity Center	Cost Driver	Traceable Costs	Volume of Annual Activity Big Board	Volume of Annual Activity Small Board
Machine setup	Number of setups	$100,000	100	100
Special design	Design hours	364,000	900	100
Production	Direct labor hours	900,000	15,000	35,000
Machining	Machine hours	300,000	9,000	1,000

Required

A. Calculate the overhead rate based on traditional overhead allocation with direct labor hours as the base.
B. Determine the total cost to produce one unit of each product. (Use the overhead rate calculated in question A.)

(Continued)

C. Calculate the overhead rate for each activity center based on activity-based costing techniques.
D. Determine the total cost to produce one unit of each product. Use the overhead rates calculated in question C.
E. Explain why overhead cost shifted from the high-volume product to the low-volume product under activity-based costing.
F. Discuss the concept of cross subsidies between products as it applies in this case.

36. The following cost information is available for Senkowski Ltd.:

Activity	Allocation Base	Volume of Activity	Overhead Cost
Purchasing	Purchase orders	30,000	$150,000
Receiving	Shipments received	15,000	60,000
Machine setups	Setups	2,500	200,000
Quality control	Inspections	18,000	90,000

Direct materials are $15 per unit for luxury handbags and $11 per unit for deluxe handbags. There were 12,500 direct labor hours, each of which was charged to inventory at $18 per hour.

Required

A. Management is trying to decide between using the traditional allocation method based on direct labor hours or activity-based costing. Calculate the overhead rates based on each method.
B. One particular batch of 40 luxury handbags had the following specifications:

Direct labor hours	8
Purchase orders	4
Shipments received	3
Setups	2
Inspections	12

Calculate the overhead to be allocated to the bags under traditional and activity-based costing techniques.
C. Which costing method do you think is better for the company? Why?

37. David Mayes, Inc. manufactures plastic and ceramic outdoor dinnerware. The company's western plant has changed from a manual labor operation to a robotics-intensive environment. As a result, management is considering moving from a direct-labor-based overhead rate to an activity-based costing system. The controller has chosen the following activity cost pools and cost drivers for factory overhead:

Overhead Cost Information		Cost Driver	Driver Activity
Purchase orders	$200,000	Number of orders	25,000
Setup costs	300,000	Number of setups	15,000
Testing costs	420,000	Number of tests	16,000
Machine maintenance	800,000	Machine hours	50,000

✓ Traditional overhead allocation for the batch: $320.00

✓ Total overhead assigned: $3,007.75

Required

A. Calculate the overhead rate for each cost driver.
B. An order for 50 ceramic dish sets had the following requirements:

Number of purchase orders	3
Number of setups	20
Number of product tests	7
Machine hours	150

How much overhead should be assigned to this order?
C. Would you expect the new activity-based system to allocate a different amount of overhead?
D. Discuss why using an activity-based system could provide better information to decision makers regarding the setting of sales prices. What other advantages might David Mayes, Inc. realize from the new costing system?

38. Gramercy, Inc. manufactures sailboats and has two major categories of overhead: material handling and quality inspection. The costs expected for these categories for the coming year are as follows:

Material handling (based on 500 material moves)	$100,000
Quality inspection (based on 200 inspections)	$300,000

✓ *Total product cost using ABC: $30,200*

The plant currently applies overhead based on direct labor hours. The estimated amount of direct labor hours is 50,000. Polly Richardson, the plant manager, has been asked to submit a bid and has assembled the following data on the proposed job:

Direct materials	$3,700
Direct labor (1,000 hours)	$17,000
Overhead	?
Number of material moves	10
Number of inspections	5

Polly has been told that many similar companies use an activity-based approach to assign overhead to jobs. Before submitting a bid, Polly wants to assess the effects of this alternative approach.

Required

A. Calculate the total cost of the potential job using traditional overhead application.
B. Calculate the total cost of the job using activity-based costing with the new cost drivers to allocate overhead.
C. Discuss the difference in the costs calculated under the two overhead allocation methods and what impact the change to activity-based costing might have on the pricing decision.

39. The HITEC Company manufactures multimedia equipment designed to be sold to universities. The company's southeastern plant has undergone production changes that have resulted in decreased usage of direct labor and increased usage of automated processes. As a

✓ Total overhead allocated: $24,649

result, management no longer believes that its overhead allocation method is accurate and is considering changing from a traditional overhead allocation to an activity-based method. The controller has chosen the following activity centers and cost drivers for overhead:

Overhead Cost Information		Cost Driver	Driver Activity
Purchase orders	$200,000	Number of orders	25,000
Setup costs	300,000	Number of setups	15,000
Testing costs	420,000	Number of tests	16,000
Machine maintenance	800,000	Machine hours	50,000

Required

A. Calculate the overhead rate for each cost driver.
B. An order for 1,000 video projectors had the following requirements:

Number of purchase orders	3
Number of setups	5
Number of product tests	20
Machine hours	1,500

How much total overhead should be assigned to this order?

C. What could management do to reduce the overhead costs assigned to these video projectors? What would be the impact on company net income of reducing overhead assigned to the video projectors?

40. Pritchett Enterprises manufactures hiking and outdoor equipment. The company's plant in western Colorado has recently seen dramatic changes in manufacturing processes. Management is concerned that the current cost system no longer captures the impact of the diversity of activities involved in its production processes. As a result, management is evaluating whether activity-based costing may provide more accurate and meaningful cost data. The production environment includes the following primary activities and cost drivers:

✓ Total cost savings: $185,000

Activity	Overhead Cost	Cost Driver	Activity Volume
Purchase orders	$200,000	Number of orders	10,000
Receiving orders	25,000	Number of orders	10,000
Setup costs	25,000	Number of setups	5,000
Testing costs	48,000	Number of tests	6,000
Machine maintenance	350,000	Machine hours	10,000

The company has decided to implement just-in-time inventory management techniques. Using JIT will reduce the amount of inventory on hand at any point in time and save approximately $50,000 annually on inventory carrying costs. In addition, there will be 70 percent fewer purchase orders for inventory issued, but twice as many setups for production runs. The company will also be able to receive a 2 percent discount on raw material purchases because of the long-term nature of the orders.

Required

- A. If raw material purchases are $1,000,000 per year (that is, cost before the above changes are implemented), what quantitative impact will the change to JIT have on the overall costs for the company?
- B. What qualitative factors will be impacted by the change to JIT?
- C. Does it appear that the move to JIT will be positive or negative for the company? Why or why not?

41. The following cost information is available for the Stuart and Hahn Corporation:

Activity	Allocation Base	Overhead Cost
Purchasing	Number of purchase orders	$150,000
Receiving	Number of shipments received	50,000
Machine setups	Number of setups	250,000
Quality control	Number of inspections	125,000
Direct material	$14 per unit for deluxe pillows; $10 per unit for regular pillows	
Direct labor	$20 per hour (including benefits)	

During the year, 30,000 purchase orders were issued; 20,000 shipments were received; machine setups numbered 2,500; and 25,000 inspections were conducted.

A customer has contacted the company requesting comparative bids for an order of 100 deluxe pillows and 100 regular pillows. The company adds a 20 percent markup on deluxe pillows and 15 percent on regular pillows for its profits. The company's records indicate that the following activities would be required to complete an order of 100 deluxe and regular pillows:

	Regular	Deluxe
Direct labor hours	7	10
Purchase orders	7	7
Shipments received	10	10
Setups	3	4
Inspections	3	4

Required

Compute the bids for deluxe and regular pillows on a total order basis.

LO 5, 7

Activity Making Decision A

✓ Total overhead allocated to Kennedy Rockers under ABC: $37,500

42. Grandma's Rocking Chair Company produces 1,000 units each of the Kennedy Rocker and the Bentwood Rocker. Currently, the company uses a traditional cost system, but is considering an activity-based cost system. The company is committed to producing only the highest quality chairs. Consequently, the management group wants to know what the cost of inspection would be for both products given the following data:

Number of inspections per unit:	
Kennedy	3
Bentwood	1
Inspection cost (in total)	$50,000
Direct labor hours:	
Kennedy	3,000
Bentwood	2,000

Required

A. Under traditional costing, how much of the inspection cost would be allocated to Kennedy Rockers and Bentwood Rockers, respectively?
B. Using activity-based costing, how much of the inspection cost would be allocated to Kennedy Rockers and Bentwood Rockers, respectively?
C. Discuss what caused the difference. Would this difference affect management decisions? How? What method is more accurate? Why?

LO 5, 7

43. Fairchild Inc. manufactures televisions that are designed for use in sports bars. The company has budgeted manufacturing overhead costs for the year as follows:

Type of Cost	Cost Pools
Electric power	$2,500,000
Inspection	1,500,000

Under a traditional cost system, the company estimated the budgeted capacity for machine hours to be 40,000 hours. The company is considering changing to an activity-based cost system. As part of its consideration of the new costing system, the company developed the following estimates:

Type of Cost	Activity-Based Cost Drivers
Electric power	50,000 kilowatt hours (KWH)
Inspection	10,000 inspections (INSP)

The following information related to the production of 2,000 units of Model #1003 was accumulated:

Direct materials cost	$ 50,000
Direct labor costs	$ 75,000
Machine hours	10,000
Direct labor hours	5,000
Electric power—kilowatt hours	20,000
Number of inspections	1,000

Based on the data, Fairchild's accounting department provided management with the following report:

Traditional Costing System Estimate:

Overhead rate per machine hour		$ 100.00
Manufacturing costs for 2,000 units:		
Direct materials	$ 50,000	
Direct labor	75,000	
Applied overhead	1,000,000	
Total cost	$1,125,000	
Cost per unit		$ 562.50

Activity-Based Costing System Estimate:

Electric power overhead rate (per KWH)		$ 50.00
Inspection cost overhead rate (per INSP)		150.00
Manufacturing costs for 2,000 units:		
Direct materials	$ 50,000	
Direct labor	75,000	
Applied overhead	1,150,000	
Total	$1,275,000	
Cost per unit		$ 637.50

Required

A. Explain the difference between activity-based costing and traditional costing and how ABC might enhance the financial reporting of Fairchild.

B. If Fairchild were setting a sales price based on a 20 percent markup, how would profit be affected if the company did not change to an ABC system?

Cases

44. Duffy and Rowe is a full-service legal firm. During the year, corporate clients required 5,000 hours of legal services, whereas individuals required 3,000 hours. In the past, the firm has assigned overhead to client engagements based on direct labor hours. However, Duffy suspects that legal services to corporate clients drive firm overhead more than legal services to individuals and believes that adopting activity-based costing will allow a more accurate allocation of cost to various clients. The firm's revenues and costs for the year are as follows:

✓ *Total overhead allocated to individual clients under ABC: $21,250*

	Corporate	Individual	Total
Revenue	$150,000	$150,000	$300,000
Expenses			
Lawyers' salaries	100,000	50,000	150,000
Overhead			
Filing			$ 10,000
Quality control			5,000
Data entry			25,000
Total overhead			$ 40,000

Rowe has kept records of the following data for use in the new activity-based costing system:

Overhead Cost	Cost Driver	Activity Level Corporate	Activity Level Individual
Filing	Number of clients	5	5
Quality control	Number of hours spent	75	25
Data entry	Number of pages entered	1,000	1,500

The accounting manager has prepared the following pro forma income statements:

Income Statement Using Traditional Costing

	Corporate	Individual	Total
Revenue	$ 150,000	$ 150,000	$ 300,000
Expenses			
Salaries	100,000	50,000	150,000
Overhead	25,000	15,000	40,000
Total expenses	$ 125,000	$ 65,000	$ 190,000
Operating profit	$ 25,000	$ 85,000	$ 110,000

Income Statement Using Activity-Based Costing

	Corporate	Individual	Total
Revenue	$ 150,000	$ 150,000	$ 300,000
Expenses			
Salaries	100,000	50,000	150,000
Overhead			
Filing ($1,000 × 5)	5,000	5,000	10,000
Quality costs ($50 × 75)	3,750		3,750
($50 × 25)		1,250	1,250
Data entry ($10 × 1,000)	10,000		10,000
($10 × 1,500)		15,000	15,000
Total overhead	$ 18,750	$ 21,250	$ 40,000
Total expenses	$ 118,750	$ 71,250	$ 190,000
Operating profit	$ 31,250	$ 78,750	$ 110,000

Required

Calculate the overhead rate for individual and corporate clients for the traditional income statement. Compare those rates to the rates for the activity-based costing income statement. Discuss the best way to allocate costs in this example, and include the approximate difference in profits between corporate and individual clients. Why would activity-based costing be preferred as a cost allocation method?

45. Worth Hawes Manufacturing has just completed a major change in its quality control (QC) process. Previously, QC inspectors had reviewed products at the end of each major process, and the company's 10 QC inspectors were charged as direct labor to the operation or job. In an effort to improve efficiency and quality, Worth Hawes purchased a computer video QC system for $250,000. The system consists of a minicomputer, 15 video cameras, other peripheral hardware, and software.

The new system uses cameras stationed by QC engineers at key points in the production process. Each time an operation changes or a new operation begins, the cameras are moved, and a QC engineer loads a new master picture into the computer. The camera takes pictures of the unit in process, and the computer compares them to the picture of a "good" unit. Any differences are sent to a QC engineer, who removes the bad units and immediately discusses the flaws with the production supervisors. The new system has replaced the 10 QC inspectors with two QC engineers.

The operating costs of the new QC system, including the salaries of the QC engineers, have been included as overhead in calculating the company's plantwide factory overhead rate, which is based on direct labor dollars.

In short, the company's president is confused. The vice president of production has been commenting on how efficient the new system is, yet the president has observed that there is a significant increase in the factory overhead rate. The computation of the rate before and after implementation of the new QC system is as follows:

	Before	After
Budgeted overhead	$ 1,900,000	$ 2,100,000
Budgeted direct labor	$ 1,000,000	$ 700,000
Budgeted overhead rate	190%	300%

"Three hundred percent," lamented the president. "How can we compete with such a high factory overhead rate?"

Required
   A. Discuss the development of factory overhead rates. Why do we need factory overhead rates, and how are they computed? Discuss the accuracy of the computation of a factory overhead rate.
   B. Explain why the increase in the overhead rate should not have a negative impact on Worth Hawes Manufacturing.
   C. Explain, in the greatest detail possible, how the company could change its overhead accounting system to eliminate confusion over product costs.
   D. Discuss how an activity-based costing system might benefit Worth Hawes Manufacturing.

Group and Internet Exercises

46. Conduct an Internet search for stories about companies or organizations that have implemented activity-based costing. Prepare a one-page summary that briefly describes the organization's experience. Based on your reading of the article, was the implementation successful? What were the factors that resulted in the success or lack of success?

47. Overhead cost is becoming an increasingly significant component of the cost of delivering products and services to consumers. To remain competitive, managers must know and understand these costs and the drivers behind them. Because the business environment has changed so dramatically in the last decade, managers should seek new ways of identifying, evaluating, and leveraging overhead costs. Within your group, select one

manufacturing company and one service-oriented company with which each member of the group is familiar. Next, ask each group member to separately identify traditional cost drivers that the company may use to allocate overhead and then identify potential activities that the company might use to allocate that same overhead if it were to use activity-based costing. Once each group member has identified traditional cost drivers and potential activities, reconvene the group and share the results. What are the similarities and differences among the individuals' cost drivers' and activities? Based on this simple exercise, how difficult would such a process be to complete in an actual business environment?

Big Al's Pizza, Inc.

Part One: Costing of Products Summary Problem

Section A

Big Al's Pizza, Inc., a new subsidiary of Big Al's Pizza Emporium, has been established to produce partially baked, flash-frozen, 16-inch meat pizzas to be sold wholesale to grocery and convenience stores and school cafeterias. As a new entrant to the market, the company's goal is to produce and sell 319,500 pizzas in the first year. Big Al's plans to keep approximately a one-month supply of frozen pizzas in finished goods inventory.

Big Al's Pizza will have 10 production lines. Each of the five workers on each line will be responsible for one of the five stages of production: dough, sauce, cheese, toppings, and packaging. Each of the 10 production lines can produce 20 meat pizzas per hour.

Big Al's deals exclusively with Pizza Products, Inc. to purchase raw materials and equipment. All ingredients (dough, sauce, cheese, meat, etc.) are fresh, and Big Al's generally holds a two- or three-day supply in raw materials inventory.

The projected material costs are as follows:

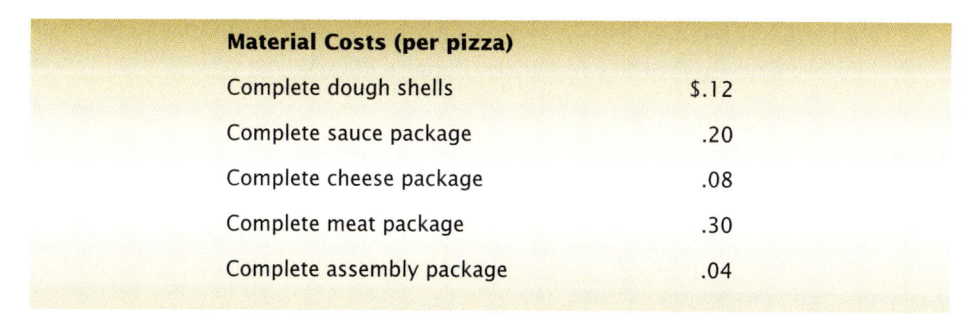

Material Costs (per pizza)	
Complete dough shells	$.12
Complete sauce package	.20
Complete cheese package	.08
Complete meat package	.30
Complete assembly package	.04

Direct labor employees are paid on an hourly basis according to hours worked. Once production-line workers finish a day's scheduled production, they are sent home. They can work a maximum of 8 hours each day without earning overtime. The overtime premium is an additional 50 percent of the basic hourly rate of $7.50 per hour. Supervisors and other indirect labor employees are salaried.

Labor Costs (estimated)	
Rate for direct labor	$7.50 per hour (plus $2.50 per hour in fringe benefits)
Indirect labor (per month):	
Supervisor (including fringe benefits)	$3,000
Other indirect labor (including fringe benefits)	$2,000

Overhead Costs (estimated, per month)	
Rent on production facility	$1,000
Utilities	$1,475
Other overhead:	
Indirect material	$2,500
Maintenance costs	$1,500
Quality inspection costs	$2,000
Equipment (lease costs)	$2,500

Selling and Administrative Costs (estimated, per month)	
Administrative salaries	$4,000
Salaries of sales staff	$5,000
Product promotion and advertising	$2,000
Rent on office space for staff	$2,000
Utilities and insurance	$ 500
Lease of office furniture and equipment	$ 800

During the first year of operation, Big Al's estimated that they would produce 319,500 pizzas but actually produced 309,408 pizzas. Direct material costs were $228,962 and direct labor costs were $773,520 for 77,352 hours worked. Estimated overhead costs for the year were $191,700 while actual overhead was $193,000.

Required:

A. What is an appropriate cost driver for allocating overhead to pizzas in year 1?
B. Using normal costing, compute the cost of each of the 309,408 meat pizzas produced in year 1.
C. Was overhead over- or underapplied during the year? By how much? Why do you think overhead was over- or underapplied during the year?

Section B

In its second year of operations, Big Al's has decided to expand the product line by producing a veggie pizza. This new pizza will require the purchase of a veggie package from Pizza Products at a cost of $.18 per pizza. Of course, the meat package will not be required. All other ingredients and prices remain the same.

The veggie toppings require additional processing time (cutting and dicing) that limits production to 18 veggie pizzas per hour per assembly line. The new veggie pizza is not expected to affect sales of the meat pizza. In the second year of operations, Big Al's expects to produce about 352,800 meat pizzas and 25,200 veggie pizzas.

Increasing production is expected to increase overhead costs by 5 percent in year 2. Direct labor costs per hour are not expected to change, and the number of labor hours is estimated to be 94,500. The costs of product promotion and advertising are expected to increase to $3,000 per month. All other selling and administrative costs are expected to remain the same as in year 1.

Actual production in year 2 was 345,132 meat pizzas and 25,200 veggie pizzas. Direct material costs transferred to WIP were $259,000 for the meat pizzas and $15,624 for the veggie pizzas. Direct labor costs were $862,830 for the meat pizzas and $70,010 for the veggie pizzas, representing 86,283 and 7,001 direct labor hours, respectively. Actual overhead costs were $203,600.

Purchases of raw materials during year 2 were $276,138. Sales during year 2 were $1,701,410 for 340,282 meat pizzas and $121,275 for 23,100 veggie pizzas.

Schedule of beginning and ending inventory amounts for year 2.

	Beginning Inventory	Ending Inventory
Raw materials	$ 1,973	$ 3,487
Work in process	0	0
Finished goods	95,000	121,645

Required:

A. Can Big Al's still allocate overhead based on the number of pizzas produced in year 2?
B. What appears to be the most logical cost driver for allocating overhead in year 2?
C. Compute a predetermined overhead rate for Big Al's in year 2.
D. Using normal costing and the predetermined overhead rate calculated in requirement C, compute the total manufacturing cost for the 345,132 meat and 25,200 veggie pizzas produced in year 2, as well as the cost per pizza for each type. Was overhead over- or underapplied for the year? By how much?
E. Prepare a cost of goods manufactured schedule for year 2 using *actual* overhead.
F. Prepare a cost of goods sold schedule for year 2 using *actual* overhead.
G. Calculate Big Al's operating income (before income taxes) for year 2.
H. The marketing manager of Big Al's estimates year 3 sales of 385,000 meat and 30,000 veggie pizzas. The production manager is concerned about being able to produce that number of pizzas without incurring significant overtime or making changes in the production process. Outline the problem, potential objectives, and options that the management team of Big Al's should consider.

Section C

Charles Jackson, the accounting manager at Big Al's, has just returned from a conference on activity-based costing in Seattle and thinks Big Al's should consider implementing an ABC system at the beginning of year 2. Charles has identified five primary activities taking place in the production facility at Big Al's, has traced overhead costs to each activity, and has identified a cost driver for each activity as follows:

Estimated Year 2 Overhead Costs:

Activity	Monthly Overhead Cost	Cost Driver
Material delivery and handling	$4,620	Number of shipments
Assembly of pizzas	$5,670	Direct labor hours
Packaging	$1,260	Number of pizzas
Storage of materials	$3,150	Refrigerator space
Quality inspections	$2,100	Number of inspections

Big Al's gets material for the veggie pizzas twice per week so the veggies can remain fresh and crisp until used in production. Veggie pizzas are also thicker, due to the height of the toppings, than a one-topping meat pizza so more refrigerator space is estimated to be needed. Big Al's has also determined that meat pizzas need to be inspected more frequently for quality control due to the much higher volume of production. Charles has estimated the activity for each cost driver as follows:

	Meat Pizzas	Veggie Pizzas	Total
Number of material shipments	52	108	160
Direct labor hours	87,500	7,000	94,500
Number of pizzas	352,800	25,200	378,000
Refrigerator space (cubic feet)	2,500	500	3,000
Number of inspections	80,000	4,000	84,000

Required:

A. Using the overhead activity categories identified above, classify Big Al's overhead costs as unit-level, batch-level, product-level, or facility-level.
B. Using the preceding activities and cost drivers, calculate a predetermined overhead rate for each activity.
C. Using ABC, how much estimated overhead would be allocated to a meat pizza and a veggie pizza?
D. Compare the estimated overhead allocation using ABC to the estimated overhead allocation using direct labor hours.
E. What are some of the advantages and disadvantages of using ABC in this case?
F. Would you suggest that Big Al's adopt an ABC system? Why?
G. Does the information provided by the ABC system give you some insight into areas of cost reduction? What areas have the greatest potential for cost reduction, and what are the potential impacts on the business from these cost reductions?

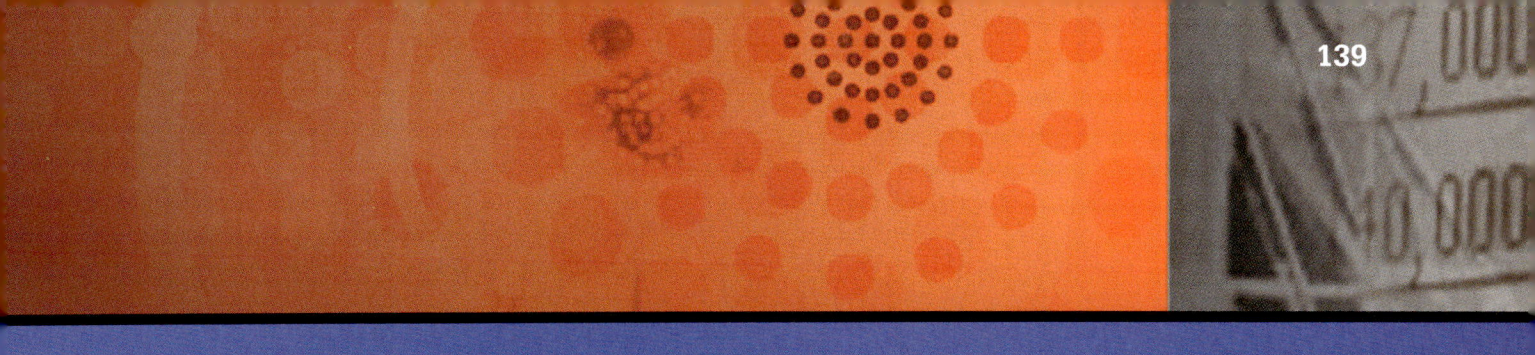

Part 2: Costs and Decision Making

Chapter 5   Cost Behavior and Relevant Costs

Chapter 6   Cost-Volume-Profit Analysis and Variable Costing

Chapter 7   Short-Term Tactical Decision Making

Chapter 8   Long-Term (Capital Investment) Decisions

Chapter 5: Cost Behavior and Relevant Costs

Understanding the behavior of costs is of vital importance to managers. Understanding how costs behave, whether costs are relevant to specific decisions, and how costs are affected by income taxes allows managers to determine the impact of changing costs and other factors on a variety of decisions. This chapter introduces concepts and tools that will be used in Chapters 6 through 8. Chapter 5 begins with a definition of cost behavior and illustrates the concepts of fixed costs, variable costs, and mixed costs. Next, the chapter revisits the concept of relevant costs (introduced in Chapter 1) as it applies to variable and fixed costs. The chapter also describes the impact of income taxes on costs.

Learning Objectives

After studying the material in this chapter, you should be able to:

1 Describe the nature and behavior of fixed, variable, and mixed costs

2 Analyze mixed costs using regression analysis and the high/low method

3 Distinguish between relevant and irrelevant costs and apply the concept to decision making

4 Illustrate the impact of income taxes on costs and decision making

KEY CONCEPT

Costs behave in predictable ways.

Objective 1

Describe the nature and behavior of fixed, variable, and mixed costs

Introduction

In Part I, we defined and determined the cost of a product or a service. We now focus our attention on the nature of those costs and how they are used in decision making. As production volume changes, some costs may increase or decrease and other costs may remain stable, but specific costs behave in predictable ways as volume changes. This concept of predictable **cost behavior** based on volume is very important to the effective use of accounting information for managerial decision making.

The Behavior of Fixed and Variable Costs

Fixed costs are costs that remain the same in total but vary per unit when production volume changes. Facility-level costs, such as rent, depreciation of a factory building, the salary of a plant manager, insurance, and property taxes, are likely to be fixed costs. Summarizing this cost behavior, fixed costs stay the same in total but vary when expressed on a per unit basis.

Rent is a good example. If the cost to rent a factory building is $10,000 per year and 5,000 units of product are produced, the rent per unit is $2.00 ($10,000/5,000). If production volume decreases to 2,500 units per year, the cost per unit will increase to $4.00 ($10,000/2,500). If production volume increases to 7,500 units, the cost per unit decreases to $1.33 ($10,000/7,500) per unit. However, the total rent remains $10,000 per year (see Exhibit 5-1).

On the other hand, **variable costs** vary in direct proportion to changes in production volume but are constant when expressed as per unit amounts. As production increases,

EXHIBIT 5-1 The Behavior of Fixed Costs

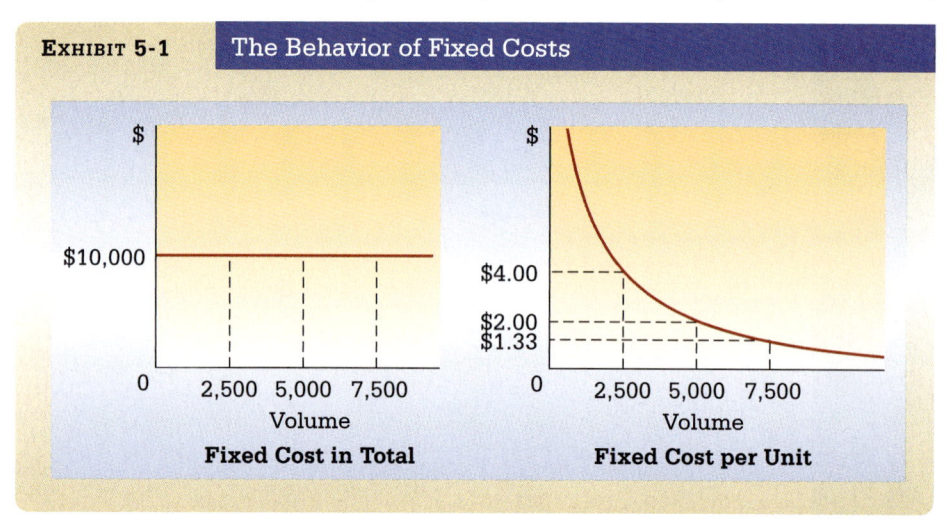

Fixed Cost in Total: horizontal line at $10,000 across volumes 2,500, 5,000, 7,500.

Fixed Cost per Unit: decreasing curve showing $4.00 at 2,500; $2.00 at 5,000; $1.33 at 7,500.

variable costs increase in direct proportion to the change in volume; as production decreases, variable costs decrease in direct proportion to the change in volume. Examples include direct material, direct labor (if paid per unit of output), and other unit-level costs, such as factory supplies, energy costs to run factory machinery, and so on.

Consider the behavior of direct material costs as production increases and decreases. If the manufacture of a standard classroom desk requires $20 of direct material (wood, hardware, etc.), the total direct material costs incurred will increase or decrease proportionately with increases and decreases in production volume. If 5,000 desks are produced, the total direct material cost will be $100,000 (5,000 × $20). If production volume is increased to 7,500 units (a 50 percent increase), direct material costs will also increase 50 percent to $150,000 (7,500 × $20). However the cost per unit is still $20. Likewise, if production volume is decreased to 2,500 desks, direct material costs will decrease by 50 percent to $50,000. But once again, the cost per unit remains $20 (see Exhibit 5-2).

Although direct labor is often treated as a variable cost, in reality it may behave more like a fixed cost in many companies. Companies may be reluctant to lay off highly skilled workers for a short period of time, and labor unions are increasingly successful in negotiating long-term contracts for their members, making it difficult to adjust workforce size as sales

EXHIBIT 5-2 The Behavior of Variable Costs

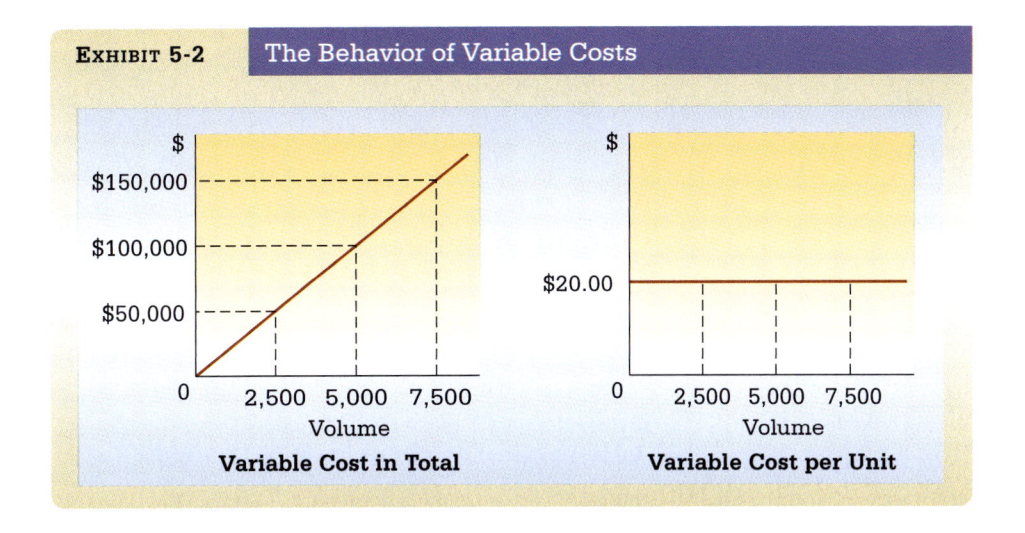

Variable Cost in Total (left graph): Linear increase from 0 through $50,000, $100,000, $150,000 as volume increases from 0 to 2,500, 5,000, 7,500.

Variable Cost per Unit (right graph): Flat line at $20.00 across volumes 0, 2,500, 5,000, 7,500.

(and production) increase or decrease. For example, companies may agree to employment contracts that guarantee workers a minimum number of hours each week. This contract means that even if an employee is not working, direct labor costs are still incurred. On the other hand, if employees are paid only for the actual work hours and not guaranteed a minimum salary, the cost would be considered a variable cost.

In addition, a trend in manufacturing is to automate, or to replace direct factory labor with robotics and other automated machinery and equipment. This trend has the effect of increasing fixed costs (depreciation) and decreasing variable costs (direct labor). Although there are many advantages to automation, the impact of automation on the employee work force and on day-to-day decisions made by managers must not be ignored. The impact of cost behavior on decision making is discussed in more detail in Chapter 6.

THE ETHICS OF BUSINESS

They're Seeing Red in Dearborn

Ford Motor Company is the second largest automobile manufacturer in the world with annual revenues of more than $160 billion. To put that number in perspective, think of this: Ford generated $18.3 million in revenue each hour of the day in 2003! You might think that such a large company would have plenty of profits. Ford did earn $759 million in 2003, but those profits were not earned equally by all of the company's divisions. In fact, in spite of its revenue of some $19 billion, Ford of Europe has not turned a profit in the last three years. The company has slashed costs by reengineering its facilities to reflect capacity consistent with reduced demand for its cars and trucks and cut its workforce by 10 percent in Germany, Britain, and Belgium. The company insists that these actions will benefit the company in the long run and will return the division to profitability.

It's Your Choice—Like many companies, Ford cut its workforce to reduce costs and increase profits. Few days pass without another story of a merger of mega-companies and the requisite employee layoffs due to the inevitable "duplicate positions." What ethical obligations do companies such as Ford have to displaced workers? Do you think such mass layoffs are simply part of the world in which we now live? Why should companies be so concerned with profits? Is Ford Motor Company an end in and of itself, or is the company merely the means by which employees make their living? And, is that enough?

Doing Business.

IT PAYS TO COUNT YOUR BEANS

Due to the higher costs of fertilizer and chemicals, the variable costs of growing soybeans in Brazil are 68 percent higher than the variable costs of growing soybeans in the U.S. heartland. However, the fixed costs in Brazil are 90 percent lower than in the United States, primarily as a result of lower costs of leasing land and lower costs of and less reliance on machinery and equipment. While Brazil's soybean production now rivals that of the United States, much of the cost savings enjoyed by Brazil's soybean farmers is offset by the additional transportation and shipping costs incurred due to poor roads and the increased distance from major markets in Europe and China.

Variable Costs per Acre of Soybeans	U.S. Heartland	Brazil
Seed	$ 19.77	$ 11.23
Fertilizer	8.22	44.95
Chemicals	27.31	39.97
Machinery	20.19	18.22
Labor	1.29	5.58
Other	1.81	12.11
Total variable costs	**$ 78.59**	**$132.06**
Fixed Costs per Acre of Soybeans		
Equipment depreciation	$ 47.99	$ 8.97
Land costs (lease costs)	87.96	5.84
Taxes and insurance	6.97	.55
Farm overhead	13.40	—0—
Total fixed costs	**$156.32**	**$ 15.36**
Average yield per acre (in bushels)	46	41.65
Variable costs per bushel	$ 1.71	$3.17
Fixed costs per bushel	$ 3.40	$ .37
Total costs per bushel	$ 5.11	$ 3.54

Source: "Who Feeds the World," *The News and Observer*, April 11, 2004, Raleigh, NC, 19A.

Strictly speaking, a cost that varies in direct proportion to changes in volume requires a linear (straight-line) relationship between the cost and volume. However, in reality costs may behave in a curvilinear fashion. Average costs or cost per unit may increase or decrease as production increases. For example, utility costs per kilowatt-hour may decrease at higher levels of electricity use (and production). Managerial accountants typically get around this problem by assuming that the relationship between the cost and volume is linear within the relevant range of production. In other words, the cost per unit is assumed to remain constant over the relevant range. The **relevant range** is the normal range of production that can be expected for a particular product and company. The relevant range can also be viewed as the volume of production for which the fixed and variable cost relationship holds true. As you can see in Exhibit 5-3, within this narrower range of production, a curvilinear cost can be approximated by a linear relationship between the cost and volume.

KEY CONCEPT

Within the relevant range, fixed costs are constant in total and vary per unit, and variable costs vary in total and are constant per unit.

EXHIBIT 5-3 Curvilinear Costs and the Relevant Range

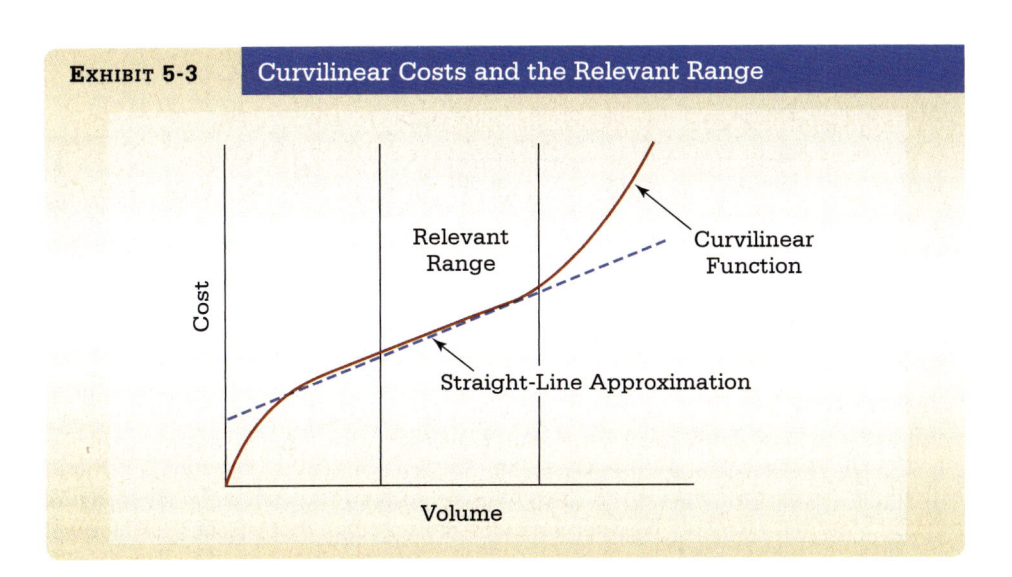

The Cost Equation

Expressing the link between costs and production volume as an algebraic equation is useful. The equation for a straight line is:

$$Y = a + bx$$

The a in the equation is the point where the line intersects the vertical (y) axis and b is the slope of the line. In Exhibit 5-4, if y = total direct material costs and x = units produced, $y = \$0 + \$20x$. The y intercept is zero and the slope of the line is $20. For every one unit increase (decrease) in production (x), direct material costs increase (decrease) by $20. You can see that direct material costs are variable because they stay the same on a per unit basis but increase in total as production increases. Likewise, we can express the fixed-cost line as an equation. If y = rent cost and x = units produced, $y = \$10,000 + \$0x$. In this case, the y intercept is $10,000 and the slope is zero. In other words, fixed costs are $10,000 at any level of production within the relevant range.

Cost Behavior and Decision Making

Understanding how costs behave is vitally important when making production decisions, preparing budgets, and so on. To further explore this idea, let's consider KenCor Pizza Emporium. After operating for one month, the owner of KenCor asked his accountant how

EXHIBIT 5-4 Fixed and Variable Costs

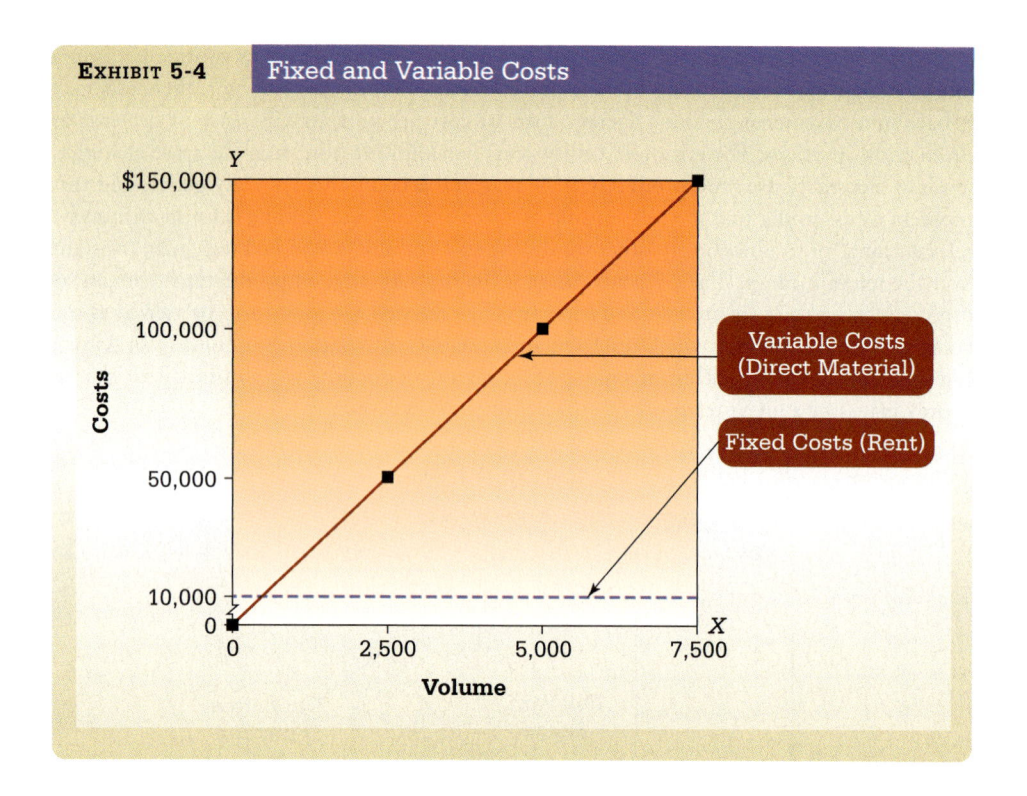

much it cost to make 2,100 pizzas last month. KenCor incurred $4,200 for direct materials (pizza dough, cheese, and other ingredients), $3,150 for direct labor, and $8,400 for overhead (rent, utilities, insurance, depreciation of pizza ovens, supervisor salary, etc.). As shown in the following table, the accountant calculated the cost of a pizza (the cost of goods sold) as $7.50 ($15,750 total costs/2,100 pizzas).

Cost	Amount	Per Unit
Direct materials	$ 4,200	$2.00
Direct labor	3,150	1.50
Overhead	8,400	4.00
Total	$15,750	$7.50

KenCor's owner then estimated that because production was expected to increase to 2,600 pizzas next month, his total cost of goods sold should be $19,500 (2,600 pizzas × $7.50 each). Do you agree with his calculation of cost of goods sold? Why or why not? While it cost $7.50 per pizza to make 2,100 pizzas, this per unit amount is going to change as the volume of pizzas changes if any of the costs of making pizzas are fixed. Remember, fixed costs stay constant in total but vary on a per unit basis. Let's assume that direct materials and direct labor are variable costs and that $6,300 of overhead is fixed. The remainder of the overhead cost is a variable cost of $1.00 per pizza. With this new information, how much total costs should KenCor expect to incur next month if it produces 2,600 pizzas? As you can see in the following table, the total cost of making 2,600 pizzas is expected to be $18,000, or $6.92 per pizza. The cost per pizza has decreased from $7.50 to $6.92 as production volume increased from 2,100 to 2,600 pizzas.

Cost	Amount		Per Unit
Direct materials	$ 5,200	($2.00 × 2,600)	$2.00
Direct labor	3,900	($1.50 × 2,600)	1.50
Variable overhead	2,600	($1.00 × 2,600)	1.00
Fixed overhead	6,300		2.42
Total	$18,000		$6.92

Although the traditional income statement introduced in Chapter 2 is good at separating product and period costs, it commingles fixed and variable costs (see Exhibit 5-5). Therefore, cost of goods sold consists of both fixed and variable costs and will differ at different levels of production. Even though the traditional income statement's focus on cost of goods sold and gross margin is useful for external reporting purposes, an income statement focusing on cost behavior is more useful for internal decision making.

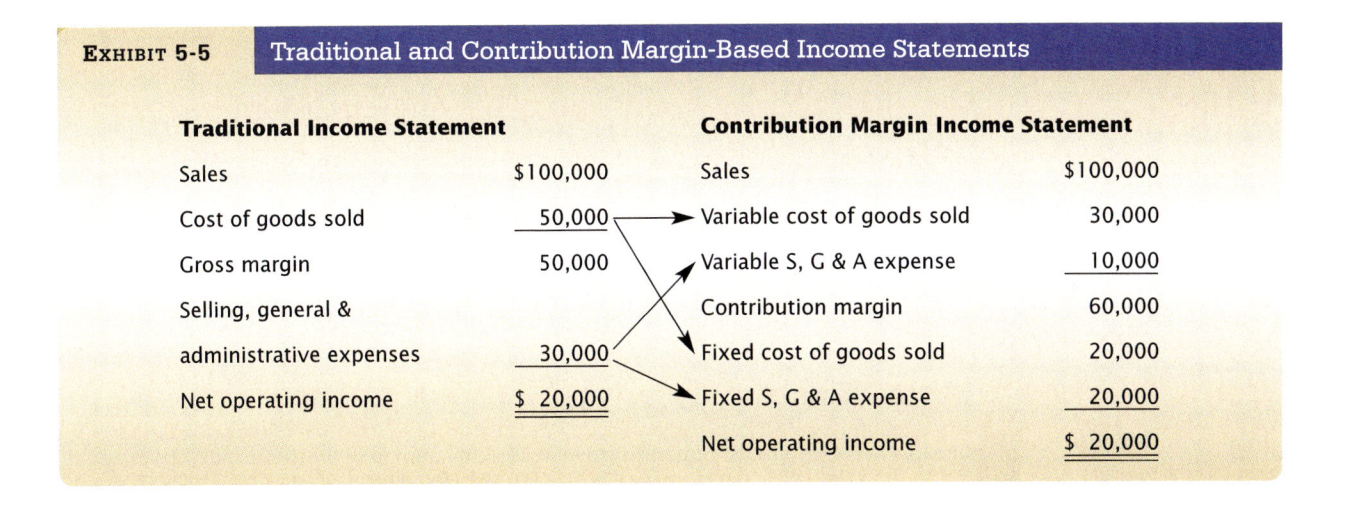

EXHIBIT 5-5 Traditional and Contribution Margin-Based Income Statements

Traditional Income Statement		Contribution Margin Income Statement	
Sales	$100,000	Sales	$100,000
Cost of goods sold	50,000	Variable cost of goods sold	30,000
Gross margin	50,000	Variable S, G & A expense	10,000
Selling, general & administrative expenses	30,000	Contribution margin	60,000
		Fixed cost of goods sold	20,000
Net operating income	$ 20,000	Fixed S, G & A expense	20,000
		Net operating income	$ 20,000

Step Costs

Classification of costs is not always a simple process. Some costs vary but only with relatively large changes in production volume. Batch-level costs related to moving materials may vary with the number of batches of product produced but not with every unit of product. Product-level costs associated with quality control inspections may vary when new products are introduced. Costs like these are sometimes referred to as **step costs**. In practice, step costs may look like and be treated as either variable costs or fixed costs. Although step costs are technically not fixed costs, they may be treated as such if they remain constant within a relatively wide range of production. Consider the costs of janitorial services within a company. As long as production is below 7,500 desks, the company will hire one janitor with salary and fringe benefits totaling $25,000. The cost is fixed as long as production remains below 7,500 units. However, if desk production exceeds

7,500, which increases the amount of waste and cleanup needed, it may be necessary to hire a second janitor at a cost of another $25,000. However, within a relevant range of production between 7,501 and 15,000 units, the cost is essentially fixed ($50,000). A graphical representation of a step (fixed) cost is shown in Exhibit 5-6.

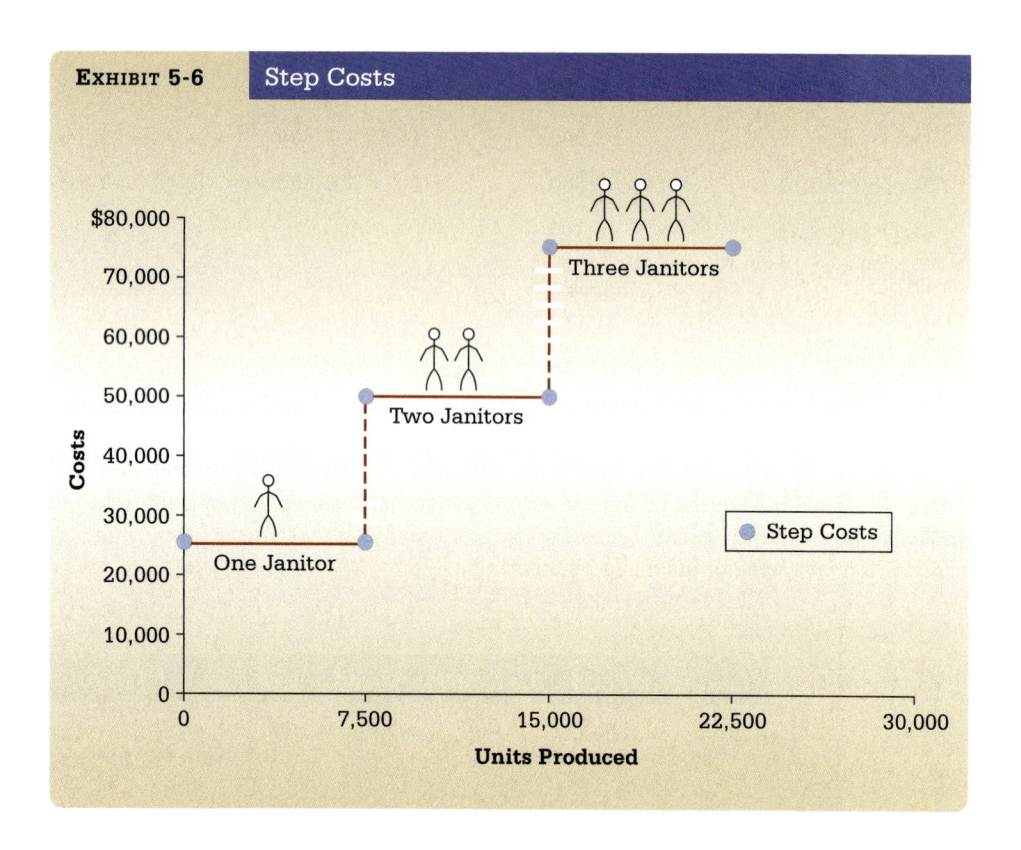

EXHIBIT 5-6 Step Costs

Mixed Costs

Objective 2

Analyze mixed costs using regression analysis and the high/low method

Mixed costs present a unique challenge because they include both a fixed and a variable component. Consequently, it is difficult to predict the behavior of a mixed cost as production changes unless the cost is first separated into its fixed and variable components. A good example of a mixed cost is the cost of a delivery vehicle for KenCor. Let's assume that KenCor enters into a lease agreement that calls for a lease payment of $400 per month for a new delivery van. Every month, KenCor is required to make the $400 payment, regardless of whether any deliveries are made; hence, $400 of the cost is fixed. However, KenCor also incurs costs related to driving the vehicle (gasoline, oil, maintenance costs, etc.) that vary with the number of deliveries made (and miles driven). If these costs average $1.50 per delivery and 200 deliveries are made during the month, KenCor will incur an additional $300 of variable costs for a total cost of $700. If 100 deliveries are made, the additional cost will be $150. Although the variable portion of the cost of the delivery van varies in total as the number of deliveries increases or decreases, it remains fixed when expressed per unit ($1.50 per delivery). On the other hand, the fixed portion of the cost remains constant in total ($400) but varies when expressed per unit.

Although the fixed and variable components of a cost are obvious, they may be difficult to identify. For example, KenCor has incurred the following overhead costs over the last 7 weeks:

Week	Pizzas	Total Overhead Costs	Cost per Unit
1 (Start-up)	0	$ 679	N/A
2	423	1,842	$4.35
3	601	2,350	3.91
4	347	1,546	4.46
5	559	2,250	4.03
6	398	1,769	4.44
7	251	1,288	5.13

Is the overhead cost a fixed, variable, or mixed cost? Clearly, the cost is not fixed, because it changes each week. However, is it a variable cost? Although the cost changes each week, it does not vary in direct proportion to changes in production. In addition, remember that variable costs remain constant when expressed per unit. In this case, the amount of overhead cost per pizza changes from week to week. A cost that changes in total and also changes per unit is a mixed cost. As you can see in Exhibit 5-7, a mixed cost looks somewhat like a variable cost. However, the cost does not vary in direct proportion to changes in the level of production (you can't draw a straight line through all the data points) and if a line were drawn through the data points back to the y-axis, we would still incur overhead cost at a production volume of zero. Like a fixed cost, a mixed cost has a component that is constant regardless of production volume.

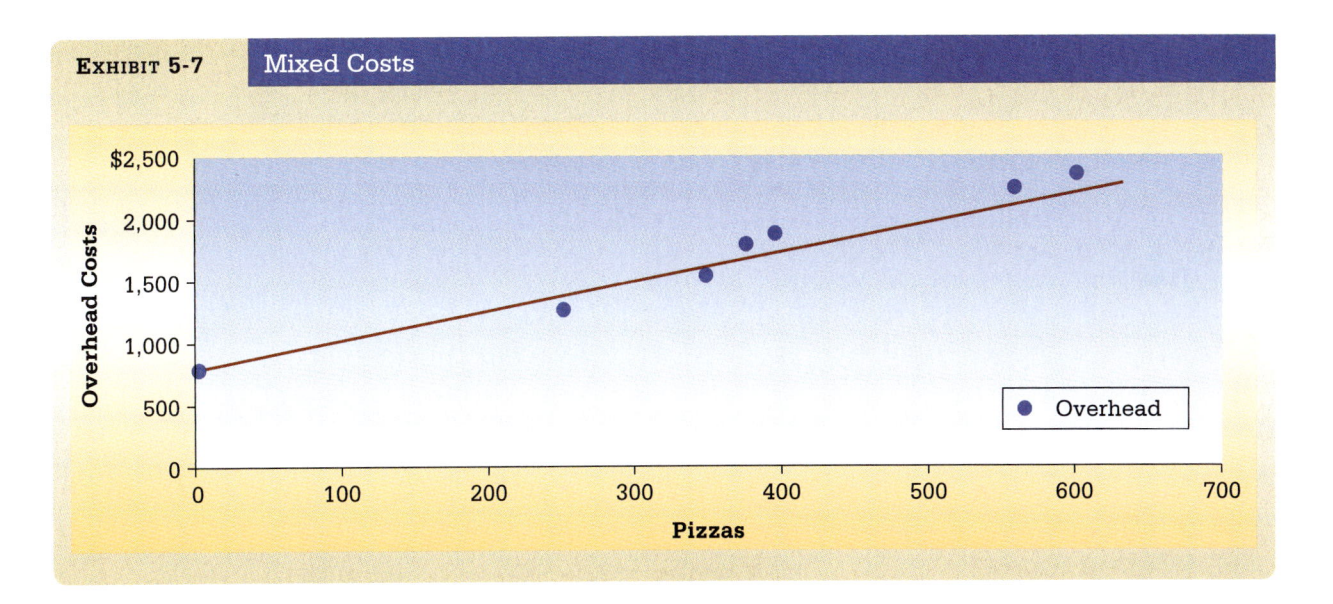

EXHIBIT 5-7 Mixed Costs

Once we know that a cost is mixed, we are left with the task of separating the mixed cost into its fixed and variable components. However, unlike the lease example, it is not clear how much of the overhead cost is fixed and how much is variable. In the next section, we demonstrate the use of a statistical tool called regression analysis to estimate the fixed and variable components of a mixed cost.

Separating Mixed Costs into Their Fixed and Variable Components

A variety of tools can be used to estimate the fixed and variable components of a mixed cost. When we separate a mixed cost into its variable and fixed components, what we are really doing is generating the equation for a straight line, with the *y* intercept estimating the fixed cost and the slope estimating the variable cost per unit.

Continuing our example of KenCor Pizza Emporium, after the initial seven-week start-up period, the company's accountant compiles data regarding the total overhead cost and the number of pizzas produced in the next 12 months (see Exhibit 5-8) As you can see, because the overhead cost varies in total and on a per unit basis, it must be a mixed cost. A graph of the data is shown in Exhibit 5-9.

Exhibit 5-8 Overhead Costs per Pizza

Month	Pizzas	Overhead	Per Pizza
1	2,100	$ 8,400	$4.00
2	2,600	10,100	3.88
3	2,300	8,800	3.83
4	2,450	9,250	3.78
5	2,100	8,050	3.83
6	2,175	8,200	3.77
7	1,450	6,950	4.79
8	1,200	6,750	5.63
9	1,350	7,250	5.37
10	1,750	7,300	4.17
11	1,550	7,250	4.68
12	2,050	7,950	3.88

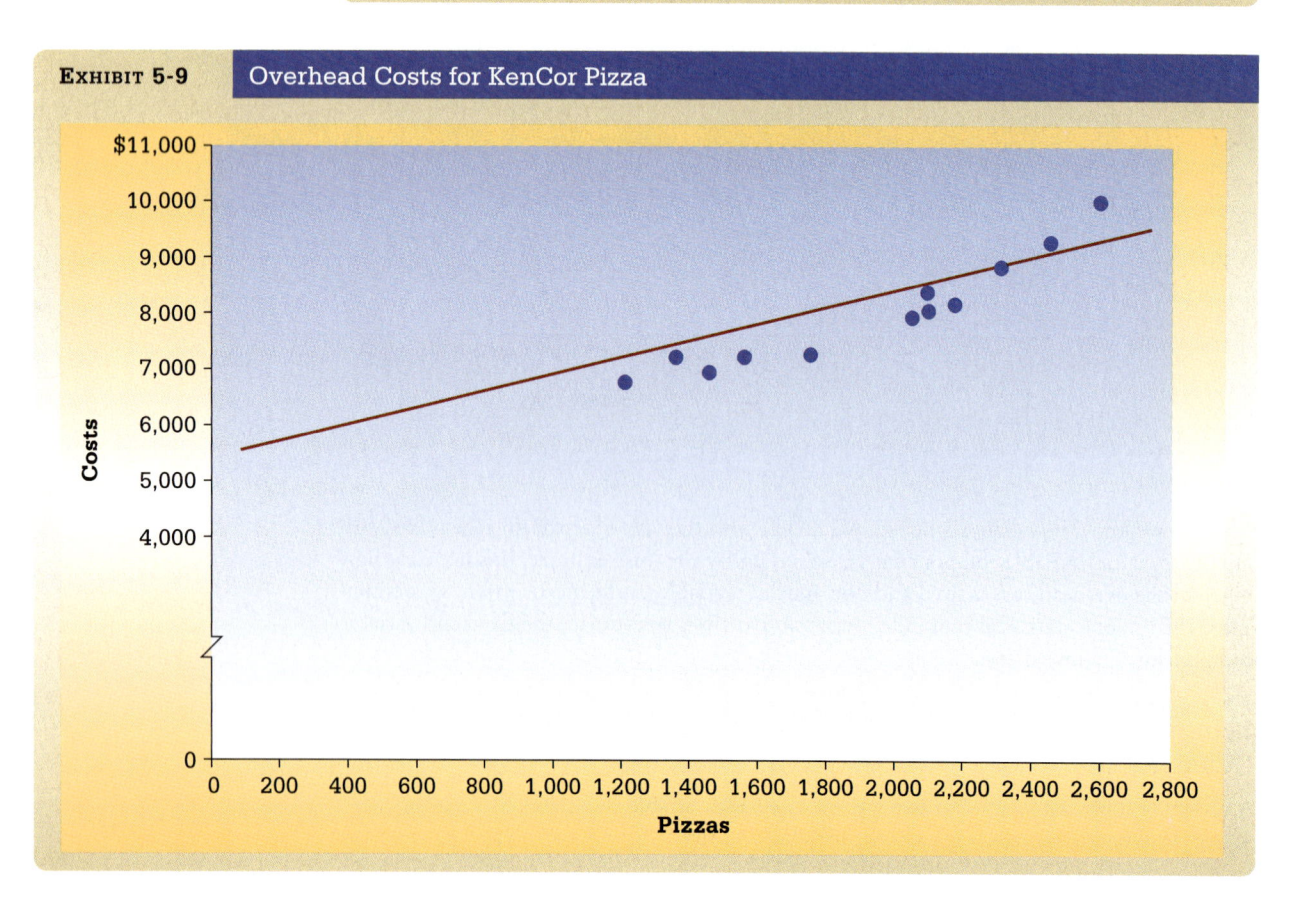

Exhibit 5-9 Overhead Costs for KenCor Pizza

Hitting the Bottom Line.

"Don't Change that Light Bulb!"

One thing is true about flying an airplane—the gas tank has to be full whether there are 15 passengers or 75 passengers. This is the brutal reality of operating an airline—there are many fixed costs. Few airlines have faced this reality like American Airlines, which has lost more than $6.6 billion since late 2001. The company is now taking steps to curb its losses and is finding that questioning long-held beliefs about the industry can pay dividends. For example, the company has decided to spread out its schedule, rather than bunch flights close together, which required employees to staff gates and aircraft at the same time. Also, for first-class passengers, the company now purchases less expensive blankets from China rather than Italy, and lightbulbs over seats are changed less frequently than they once were. Other cost savings efforts include replacing passenger windows less frequently—each window costs $1,000—and polishing the exterior of airplanes every two years rather than every year as done in the past. These and other cost savings efforts have allowed American Airlines to slash its annual costs by an astounding $2.2 billion! However, if schedules are less convenient, layovers are longer, passengers are left sitting in the dark, or passengers become concerned about safety, short-term savings may result in long-term costs.

Regression Analysis

A statistical technique used to estimate the fixed and variable components of a mixed cost is called least squares regression. **Regression analysis** uses statistical methods to fit a cost line (called a regression line) through a number of data points. Note that although the data points in our example do not lie along a straight line, regression analysis statistically finds the line that minimizes the sum of the squared distance from each data point to the line (hence the name least squares regression).

Using a Spreadsheet Program to Perform Regression Analysis

Using a spreadsheet program to estimate regression models is a relatively simple process. We are going to use Excel in this example, but all spreadsheet programs are very similar. The first step is to enter the actual values for our mixed cost (called the **dependent variable** in regression analysis because the amount of cost is dependent on production) and the related volume of production (called the **independent variable** because it drives the cost of the dependent variable) into a spreadsheet using one column for each variable. Using data from KenCor Pizza Emporium for overhead costs incurred and pizzas produced for the first 12 months of operations, the results are shown in the Excel spreadsheet in Exhibit 5-10.

The next step in Excel (see Exhibit 5-11) is to click on the tools option from the toolbar and choose data analysis from the pull-down menu. From the data analysis screen, scroll down, highlight regression, and either double-click or choose OK.

The regression screen will prompt you to choose a number of options. The first is to input the *y* range. The *y* range will be used to identify the dependent variable (overhead costs) found in column C of your spreadsheet. You can either type in the range of cells or simply highlight the cells in the spreadsheet (be sure not to include the column heading), and click on the icon in the *y*-range box. The next step is to select the *x* range for the independent variable (volume of pizzas). Once again, you can enter the cells directly or highlight the cells in the second column of your spreadsheet.

EXHIBIT 5-10　Regression Analysis—Step 1

Month	Pizzas	Overhead
1	2,100	$ 8,400.00
2	2,600	$10,100.00
3	2,300	$ 8,800.00
4	2,450	$ 9,250.00
5	2,100	$ 8,050.00
6	2,175	$ 8,200.00
7	1,450	$ 6,950.00
8	1,200	$ 6,750.00
9	1,350	$ 7,250.00
10	1,750	$ 7,300.00
11	1,550	$ 7,250.00
12	2,050	$ 7,950.00

EXHIBIT 5-11　Regression Analysis—Step 2

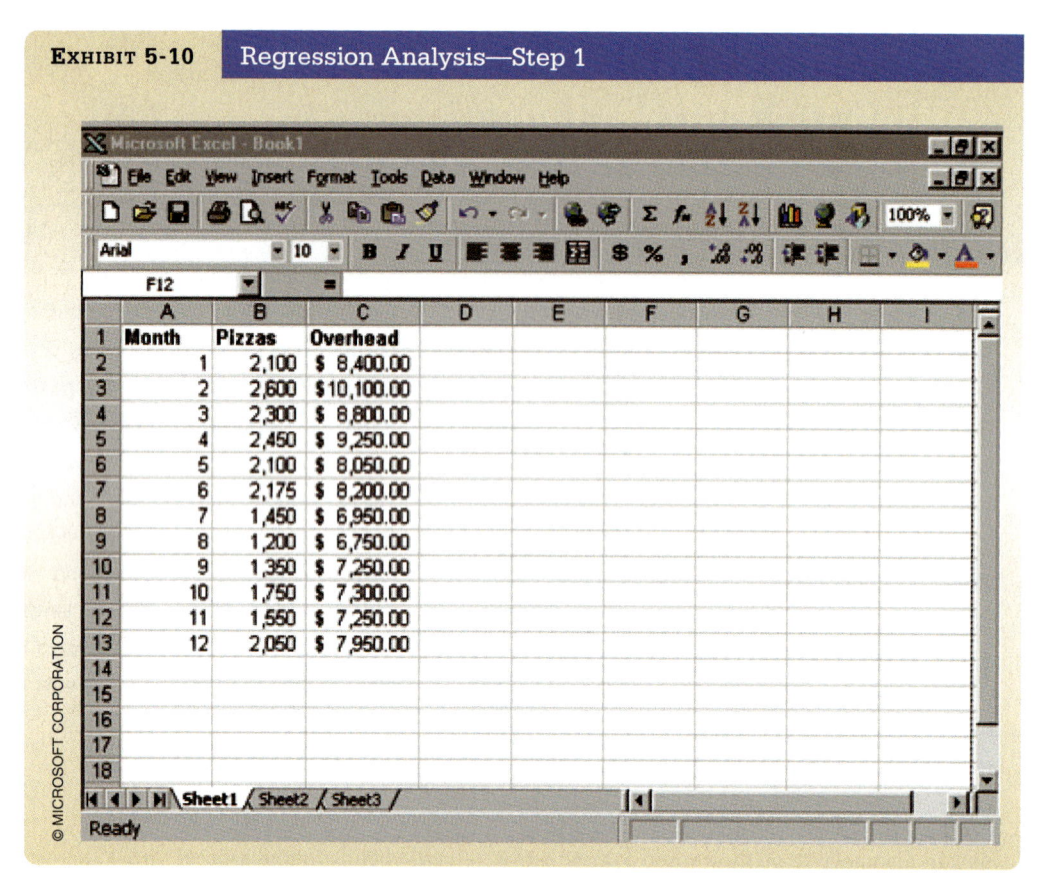

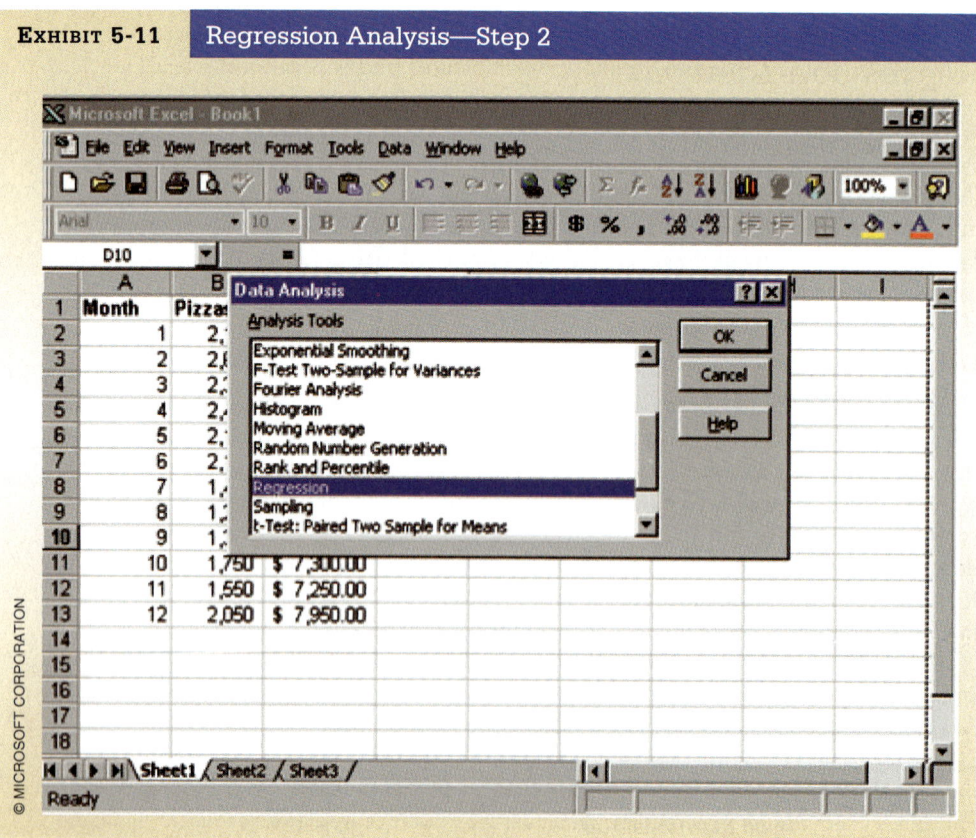

After inputting the appropriate *y* and *x* ranges, your Excel spreadsheet should look like the example shown in Exhibit 5-12. Click OK, and the regression model summary output appears as shown in Exhibit 5-13.

EXHIBIT 5-12 Regression Analysis—Step 2 (continued)

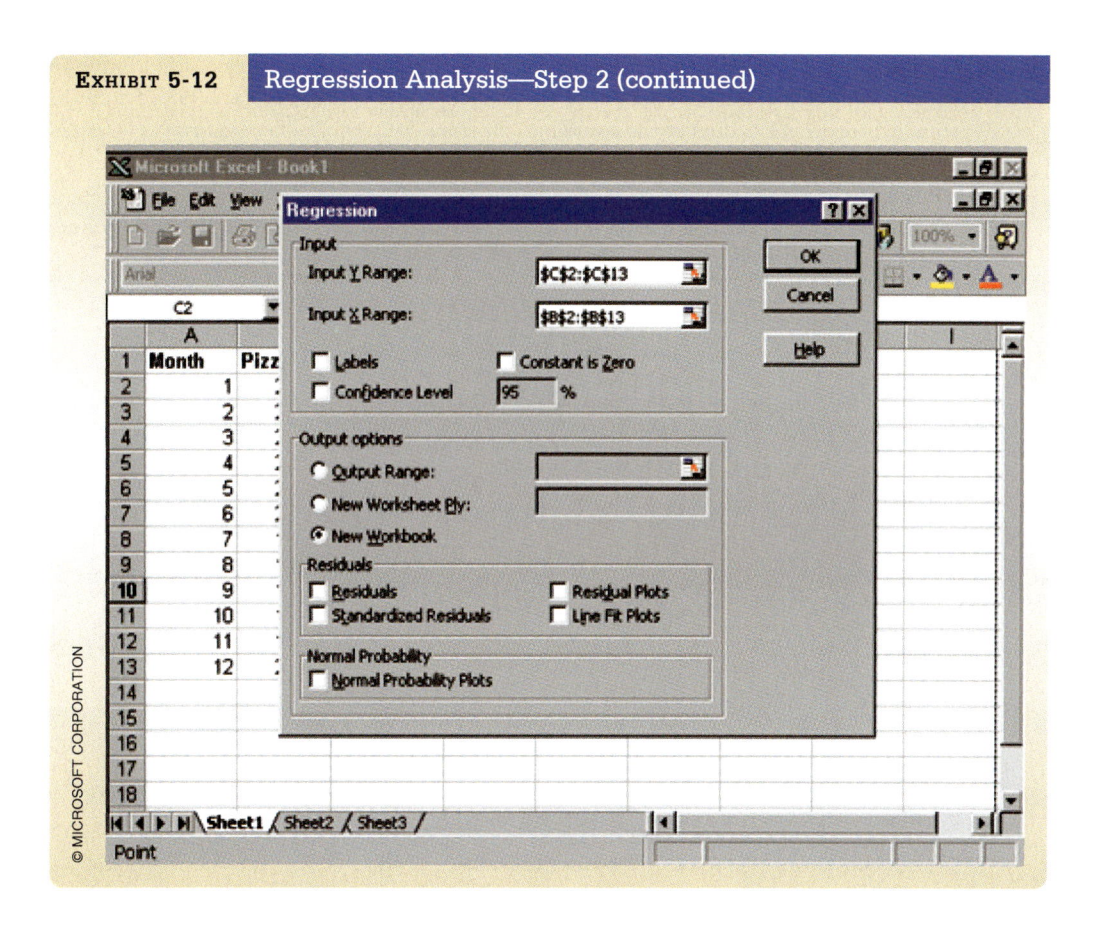

EXHIBIT 5-13 Regression Analysis—Summary Output

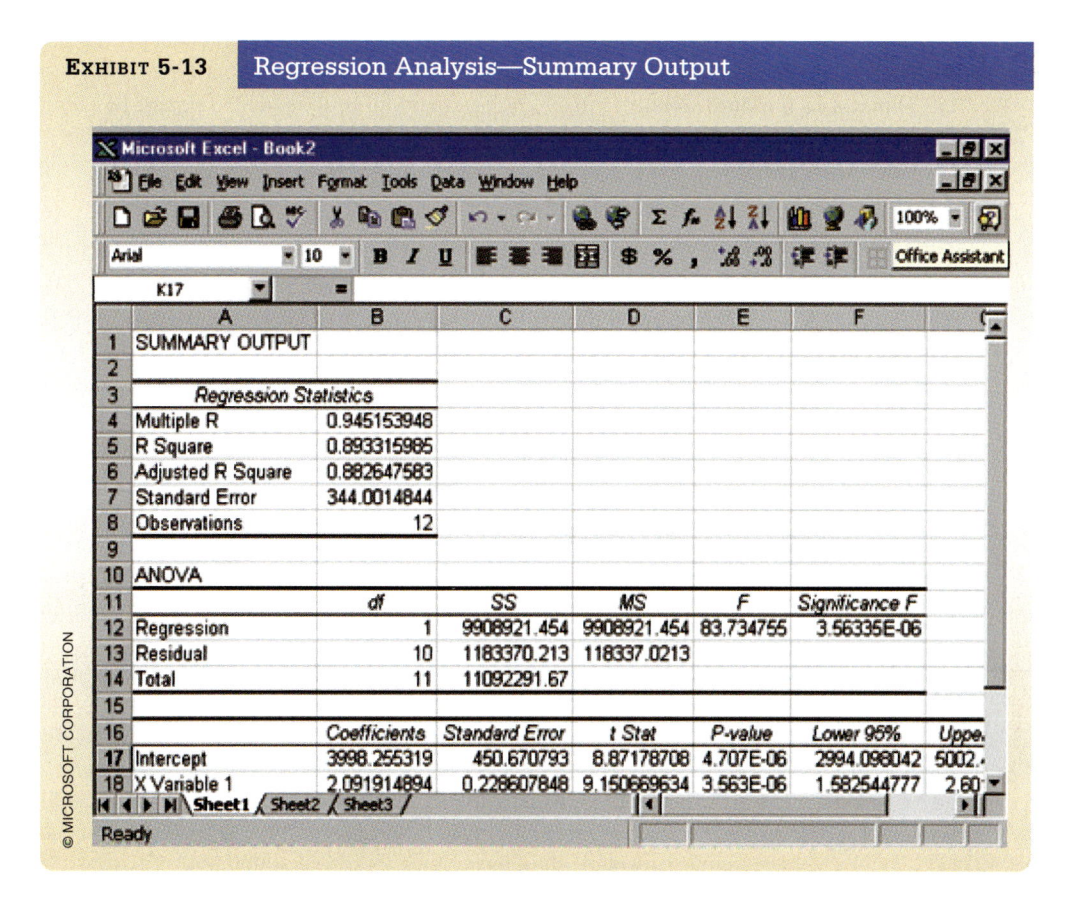

SUMMARY OUTPUT

Regression Statistics	
Multiple R	0.945153948
R Square	0.893315985
Adjusted R Square	0.882647583
Standard Error	344.0014844
Observations	12

ANOVA

	df	SS	MS	F	Significance F
Regression	1	9908921.454	9908921.454	83.734755	3.56335E-06
Residual	10	1183370.213	118337.0213		
Total	11	11092291.67			

	Coefficients	Standard Error	t Stat	P-value	Lower 95%	Upper
Intercept	3998.255319	450.670793	8.87178708	4.707E-06	2994.098042	5002.
X Variable 1	2.091914894	0.228607848	9.150669634	3.563E-06	1.582544777	2.60

How is the summary output interpreted? First, note toward the bottom of Exhibit 5-13 that the estimated coefficient (value) of the intercept (the *y* intercept) is 3,998.25 and the estimated coefficient (value) of the *x* variable (the slope) is 2.09. The fixed-cost component of our mixed overhead cost is estimated to be $3,998.25, and the variable cost component is estimated to be $2.09 per pizza.

Using the least squares regression results, we can compute the regression line for overhead costs at KenCor Pizza Emporium:

Total overhead cost = Fixed cost + (Variable cost per unit × Volume)
Total overhead cost = $3,998.25 + ($2.09 × Volume)

Graphically, the line for the total overhead costs can be expressed as seen in the following illustration.

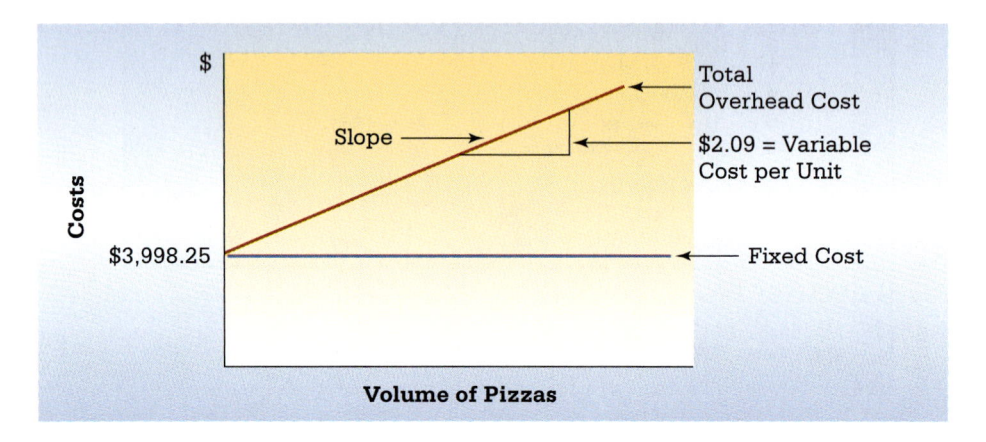

We can use this equation to help predict the amount of overhead costs that will be incurred for any number of pizzas within the relevant range. The relevant range is that range of activity within which management expects to operate, or the range in which this equation is useful or meaningful. Our predictions should be limited to those activity levels within the relevant range. Based on last year's data, KenCor expects to produce between 1,200 and 2,600 pizzas each month. Next month, KenCor expects to produce 1,750 pizzas. Based on the regression equation, KenCor estimates total overhead costs to be $7,655.75 ($3,998.25 + ($2.09 × 1,750 pizzas)).

Regression Statistics

The regression statistics section at the top of Exhibit 5-13 provides useful diagnostic tools. The multiple *R* (called the correlation coefficient) is a measure of the proximity of the data points to the regression line. In addition, the sign of the statistic (+ or −) tells us the direction of the correlation between the independent and dependent variables. In this case, there is a positive correlation between the number of pizzas produced and total overhead costs. The **R square** (often represented as **R^2** and called the coefficient of determination) is a measure of goodness of fit (how well the regression line "fits" the data). An R^2 of 1.0 indicates a perfect correlation between the independent and dependent variables in the regression equation; in other words, 100 percent of the data points are on the regression line. R^2 can be interpreted as the proportion of dependent-variable variation that is explained by changes in the independent variable. In this case, the R^2 of 0.8933 indicates that over 89 percent of the variation in overhead costs is explained by increasing or decreasing pizza production.

A low value of R^2 may indicate that the chosen independent variable is not a very reliable predictor of the dependent variable or that other independent variables may have an impact on the dependent variable. For example, outside temperature and other environmental factors might impact overhead costs incurred by KenCor. Multiple regression is a technique in which additional independent variables are used to help predict changes in a dependent variable. If we added variables to our regression model, we would probably get a better predictive model.

However, it is unlikely that we will ever identify all the relevant variables that cause the total cost to change. Nor is it necessary. The goal of separating a mixed cost into its fixed and variable components is to help managers predict costs in the future, not to compute an exact breakdown.

The presence of outliers in the data may also result in low R^2 values. Outliers are simply extreme observations, that is, observations so far from the normal activity that they may be nonrepresentative of the normal business. Under the least squares method, a regression line may be pulled disproportionately toward the outlier and result in misleading estimates of fixed and variable costs and measures of goodness of fit.

For example, if KenCor were closed for two weeks due to a fire or other unusual circumstance, the number of pizzas produced and the overhead costs incurred that month would not be representative of normal business operations. When there is direct evidence that an outlier has been caused by an extraneous and unusual event, a malfunction of equipment or a similar type of circumstance, the outlier is typically removed from the analysis. However, outliers may convey significant information and the decision to discard them must be considered carefully.

Other Uses of Regression Analysis

Regression analysis can be used in a variety of ways in managerial decision making. For example, marketing managers may be interested in predicting changes in sales based on changes in advertising expenditures and other variables. Production managers interested in quality control might collect data on overtime worked in a factory and compare that to the number of defective items produced to see whether increases in overtime affect the amount of defective goods produced. This analysis could lead management to hire additional workers rather than working existing workers excessive amounts of overtime.

However, regression analysis must be used with caution. The precision of a computerized statistical technique like regression analysis can be misleading. Regression results, after all, are only estimates. First and foremost, high correlations between independent variables and dependent variables and "good" models do not necessarily indicate a cause-and-effect relationship. It is important that managers use common sense and their intimate knowledge of what activities really drive costs before attempting to model cost equations.

Estimating Regression Results Using the High/Low Method

If we did not have access to a computer regression program or for some reason did not want to use this tool, we could estimate the regression equation using a simpler technique called the high/low method. The high/low method uses only two data points (related to the high and low levels of activity) and mathematically derives an equation for a straight line intersecting those two data points. Though technically inferior to regression analysis (which uses all the data points), from a practical perspective, the high/low method can often provide a reasonable estimate of the regression equation.

In Exhibit 5-8 on page 150, the high level of activity occurred in month 2, when 2,600 pizzas were produced and $10,100 of overhead cost was incurred. The low level of activity occurred in month 8, when only 1,200 pizzas were produced and overhead costs totaled $6,750. The slope of the line connecting those two points can be calculated by dividing the difference between the costs incurred at the high and low levels of activity by the difference in volume (number of pizzas at those levels). Remember, the slope of a line is calculated as the change in cost over the change in volume, in this case the difference in cost to produce pizzas over the difference in volume of pizzas made. As with the regression equation, the slope of the line is interpreted as the variable-cost component of the mixed cost:

$$\frac{\text{Change in cost}}{\text{Change in volume}} = \text{Variable cost per unit}$$

Inserting the data for KenCor Pizza Emporium, the variable cost is $2.39 per unit ($10,100 − $6,750)/(2,600 − 1,200). This result compares with our regression estimate of $2.09. We then solve for the fixed-cost component by calculating the total variable cost incurred at either the high or the low level of activity and subtracting the variable costs from the total overhead cost incurred at that level. Mathematically, if

$$\text{Total overhead costs} = \text{Fixed costs} + (\text{Variable cost per unit} \times (\text{number of pizzas}))$$

then

$$\text{Total overhead costs} - \text{Variable costs} = \text{Fixed costs}$$

At the high level of activity, total overhead costs are $10,100 and variable costs equal $6,214 (2,600 pizzas × $2.39 per pizza). Therefore, the fixed-cost component of overhead costs is estimated to be $3,886 (total overhead costs of $10,100 less variable costs of $6,214), and the total overhead cost is estimated to be $3,886 + ($2.39 × (number of pizzas produced)).

Why is this equation different from the least squares regression equation? Regression is a statistical tool that fits the "best" line through all 12 data points, whereas the high/low method mathematically derives a straight line between just two of the data points. By using the two points at the highest and lowest levels of activity, we are forcing a line between those points without regard to the remaining data points. If one or both of these points is unusual (an outlier), the result will be a cost line that is skewed and therefore may not be a good measure of the fixed and variable components of the mixed cost.

In the case of KenCor Pizza Emporium, let's see how the high/low estimate would impact our prediction of total overhead costs next month, when 1,750 pizzas are produced. Using the high/low estimate of the cost equation, we would predict total overhead costs of $8,068.50 ($3,886 + ($2.39 × 1,750 pizzas)). This result compares with our estimate of $7,655.75 using the cost equation generated from the regression analysis.

Given the simplicity of generating regression equations using spreadsheet packages and handheld calculators, the need for using the high/low method for computing cost equations in practice is questionable. However, it remains an easy-to-use tool for estimating cost behavior.

Cost Behavior and Activity-Based Costing

So far, we have examined the behavior of unit-level costs related to changes in production volume (number of pizzas and number of deliveries). However, costs are affected by changes in other cost drivers as well. In Chapters 3 and 4, we introduced the concept of activities as procedures or processes that cause work to be accomplished (purchasing, receiving, production, plant occupancy, etc.) and cost drivers as allocation bases that cause, or drive, the incurrence of costs. Some of these drivers are related to volume (machine hours and labor hours), but drivers of batch- and product-level costs are more likely related to the complexity of a product (number of parts, number of inspections) or product diversity (number of setups, number of purchase orders). Although these costs may not vary in direct proportion to volume, they may vary in direct proportion to other cost drivers.

Regression analysis can be used to help managers identify the "best" cost drivers of activities for use in activity-based costing. For example, the activity of processing customer orders might vary with the number of orders or the number of customers. Regression analysis can be used to identify which of the two possible independent variables better explains the variation in the dependent variable (costs of placing customer orders).

Objective 3

Distinguish between relevant and irrelevant costs and apply the concept to decision making

Relevant Costs and Cost Behavior

As mentioned in Chapter 1, relevant costs are those that are avoidable or can be eliminated by choosing one alternative over another. Relevant costs are also known as differential, or incremental, costs. In general, variable costs are relevant in production decisions because they vary with the level of production. Likewise, fixed costs are generally not relevant, because they typically do not change as production changes. However, variable costs can remain the same between two alternatives, and fixed costs can vary between alternatives. For example, if the direct material cost of a product is the same for two competing designs, the material cost is not a relevant factor in choosing a design. However, other qualitative factors relating to the material, such as durability, may still be relevant. Likewise, fixed costs can be relevant if they vary between alternatives. Consider rent paid for a facility to store inventory. Although the rent is a fixed cost, it is relevant to a decision to reduce inventory storage costs through just-in-time production techniques if the cost of the rent can be avoided (by subleasing the space, for example) by choosing one alternative over another.

KEY CONCEPT

It can be misleading to always view variable costs as relevant and fixed costs as not relevant.

The Impact of Income Taxes on Costs and Decision Making

Taxes and Decision Making

We always need to consider tax laws and the impact income and other taxes have on costs, revenues, and decision making. Just as an individual should consider the impact of income taxes on a decision to hold or to sell a stock, managers must consider the impact of taxes in a variety of decisions. The first key to understanding the impact of taxes on costs and revenues is the recognition that many costs of operating businesses are deductible for income tax purposes and that most business revenues are taxable. Second, the form of a transaction may impact the amount of tax that is paid or whether a cost is tax deductible. For example, structuring a purchase of a building as a lease with a corresponding payment of rent has different tax implications than a purchase of the same building. While both rent and depreciation are deductible business expenses, the amount of the deduction generally will vary. In addition, if the building is purchased, most local governments will assess property tax on the value of the property owned while leased property may escape the assessment of property tax. Third, the payment of taxes requires a cash outflow and reduces the amount of cash available for other purposes in a business organization. For example, purchases of office supplies and other goods will, in most states, result in the payment of a sales tax. If $100 of office supplies are purchased and the sales tax rate is 7 percent, the cash outflow associated with the purchase is $107 ($100 × 1.07). To complicate things further, sales taxes and property taxes are generally deductible in calculating income taxes owed by business entities, so that the income tax burden of the business is reduced accordingly. The impact of taxes must be considered in a variety of managerial decisions, including cost-volume-profit analysis (Chapter 6), the purchase of property and equipment (Chapter 8), and budgeting (Chapter 9).

Objective 4

Illustrate the impact of income taxes on costs and decision making

KEY CONCEPT

Managers must consider the impact of taxes when making decisions.

After-Tax Costs and Revenues

Consider an example in which your current taxable cash revenue is $100 and tax-deductible cash expenses equal $60. As shown in Exhibit 5-14, taxable income therefore equals $40. If the income tax rate is 40 percent, $16 of income taxes will be paid, leaving you with $24 cash after tax. Now consider the impact of spending an additional $20 on tax-deductible expenditures. This reduces your taxable income to $20. With a 40 percent income tax rate, $8 of income taxes will be paid instead of $16 (you saved $8 of income tax) and you will be left with $12 after tax. Even though you spent an additional $20, your cash flow decreased by only $12 ($24 less $12).

EXHIBIT 5-14 | The Impact of Income Taxes on Cash Flow

	Current	Increase Spending by $20	Increase Revenue by $20
Revenue	$100	$100	$120
Expense	− 60	− **80**	−60
Taxable income	$ 40	$ 20	$ 60
Tax (rate = 40%)	− 16	− 8	− 24
After-tax cash flow	$ 24	$ 12	$ 36

Mathematically, the after-tax cost of a tax-deductible cash expenditure can be found by subtracting the income tax savings from the before-tax cost or by simply multiplying the before-tax amount by (1 − tax rate):

$$\text{After-tax cost} = \text{Pretax cost} \times (1 - \text{tax rate})$$

So if the before-tax cost is $20 and the income tax rate is 40 percent, the after-tax cost is $12 ($12 = $20 × (1 − 0.40)). In this case, the impact of income taxes is to reduce the "real" cost of a tax-deductible expense to the business and to increase cash flow.

Income taxes also have an impact on cash revenues received by a business. Continuing our original example in Exhibit 5-14, if taxable cash revenue increases by $20, taxable income will increase to $60 ($120 − $60). After payment of $24 of income taxes, you will be left with $36 of cash. An increase in revenue of $20 increases your cash flow by only $12 ($36 − $24). Why? Because the $20 is taxable and results in the payment of an additional $8 of income tax ($20 × 0.40). Mathematically, the formula to find the after-tax benefit associated with a taxable cash revenue is analogous to the formula for after-tax cost. The after-tax benefit of a taxable cash receipt can be found by subtracting the additional income tax to be paid from the before-tax receipt or by simply multiplying the pretax receipt by (1 − tax rate):

$$\text{After-tax benefit} = \text{Pretax receipts} \times (1 - \text{tax rate})$$

So if the before-tax receipt is $20 and the tax rate is 40 percent, the after-tax benefit is $12 ($12 = $20 × (1 − 0.40)). In this case, the impact of income taxes is to increase the "real" cost to the business and to decrease cash flow.

Before- and After-Tax Income

In a similar fashion, managers can calculate the impact of income taxes on income. If we have an income tax rate of 40 percent and operating income of $1,000,000, we will have a tax liability of $400,000 (40 percent of the $1,000,000) and be left with $600,000 of after-tax income. This is exactly the same thing that happens to our paychecks as individuals. If an individual earns $1,000 per week and faces a 30 percent income tax rate, the individual's take-home pay (after considering income tax withholding) is only $700. Mathematically,

$$\text{After-tax income} = \text{Pretax income} \times (1 - \text{tax rate})$$

Although tax laws are very complex and computing tax due is rarely as simple as applying one rate to income, estimating the impact of income tax and other taxes on cash receipts and disbursements is important in managerial decision making.

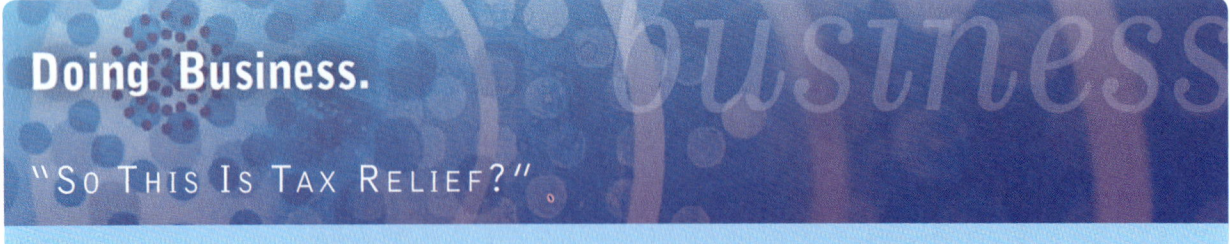

Doing Business.

"So This Is Tax Relief?"

In the past decade, there have been thousands of changes to the Internal Revenue Code, making tax planning a nightmare for many small businesses. Major tax bills during that time include the Taxpayer Relief Act of 1997, the Economic Growth and Tax Relief Reconciliation Act of 2001, the Jobs and Growth Tax Relief Reconciliation Act of 2003, the Working Families Tax Relief Act of 2004, and the American Jobs Creation Act of 2004. Particularly problematic is Congress's habit of making temporary tax changes that expire every few years. Although the changes are made on a temporary basis owing to budget considerations, they are almost always extended at the last minute. Making decisions in an environment characterized by continually changing tax rules is challenging, to say the least.

Summary of Key Concepts

- *Costs behave in predictable ways. (p. 142)*
- *Within the relevant range, fixed costs are constant in total and vary per unit, and variable costs vary in total and are constant per unit. (p. 145)*
- *It can be misleading to always view variable costs as relevant and fixed costs as not relevant. (p. 157)*
- *Managers must consider the impact of taxes when making decisions. (p. 157)*

Key Definitions

Cost behavior How costs react to changes in production volume or other levels of activity (p. 142)

Fixed costs Costs that remain the same in total when production volume increases or decreases but vary per unit (p. 142)

Variable costs Costs that stay the same per unit but change in total as production volume increases or decreases (p. 142)

Relevant range The normal range of production that can be expected for a particular product and company (p. 145)

Step costs Costs that vary with activity in steps and may look like and be treated as either variable costs or fixed costs; step costs are technically not fixed costs but may be treated as such if they remain constant within a relevant range of production (p. 147)

Mixed costs Costs that include both a fixed and a variable component, making it difficult to predict the behavior of a mixed cost as production changes unless the cost is first separated into its fixed and variable components (p. 148)

Regression analysis The procedure that uses statistical methods (least squares regression) to fit a cost line (called a regression line) through a number of data points (p. 151)

Dependent variable The variable in regression analysis that is dependent on changes in the independent variable (p. 151)

Independent variable The variable in regression analysis that drives changes in the dependent variable (p. 151)

R square (R^2) A measure of goodness of fit (how well the regression line "fits" the data) (p. 154)

Multiple Choice

1. You are given the following cost and volume information:

Volume (in units)	Cost (in $)
1	15
10	150
100	1,500

What type of a cost is given?
a. Fixed cost
b. Variable cost
c. Step cost
d. None of the above

2. You are given the following cost and volume information:

Volume (in units)	Cost (in $)
1	150
10	150
100	150

What type of a cost is given?
a. Fixed cost
b. Variable cost
c. Step cost
d. None of the above

3. Hood Company plans to double its advertising budget next year, which will increase its fixed costs by 20 percent while variable costs remain the same. Current year costs include variable costs per unit of $5 and fixed costs of $4,000. If next year's production is 5,000 units, estimated total costs equal:
a. $29,000
b. $29,005
c. $29,800
d. $30,000

4. Staudt Ltd. plans to triple its marketing budget next year, which will increase overall fixed costs by a total of 10 percent. This change will have no effect on variable costs, which will remain $5 for each unit. Fixed costs in the current year are $5,000. If next year's production is 25,000 units, estimated total costs equal:
a. $125,000
b. $125,005
c. $130,000
d. $130,500

5. Which of the following statements best describes variable costs?
a. Costs that vary in total and on a per unit basis.
b. Costs that remain fixed in total, but vary on a per unit basis.
c. Costs that vary in total, but are constant on a per unit basis.
d. Costs that remain constant in total and on a per unit basis.

6. Complete the following statement: "_____ costs vary in _____ to changes in production."
a. Fixed, a constant manner
b. Fixed, proportion
c. Variable, an inverse manner
d. Variable, direct proportion

7. You run a regression analysis and receive the following results (partial results are presented):

Variables in the Equation

Variable	Coefficients
X variable 1	7.94000
Intercept	204.07000

If the preceding analysis were for production costs and 200 units of X are produced, then total production costs should be:
a. $1,700.94
b. $2,004.07
c. $1,588.00
d. $1,792.07

8. Mixed costs are most appropriately described by which of the following statements:
   a. Mixed costs rarely occur and pose few challenges to management.
   b. Mixed costs include mostly fixed costs with some variable costs and are generally understood to behave as fixed costs.
   c. Mixed costs include fixed and variable costs and must be carefully analyzed to understand their behavior.
   d. Mixed costs must be analyzed using regression analysis.

9. C. Martin's Foot Fashions documented its production levels and manufacturing overhead costs for the past five months as follows:

	Production (pairs)	Overhead Cost
January	10,500	$40,250
February	10,675	41,000
March	11,500	44,250
April	12,500	45,250
May	11,000	43,750

   Using the high/low method, what is the overhead cost equation?
   a. $Y = \$7,080 + \$3.83X$
   b. $Y = \$14,000 + \$2.50X$
   c. $Y = \$29,750 + \$3.62X$
   d. $Y = \$8,500 + \$2.35X$

10. Refer to question 9. If C. Martin's production were expected to be 10,850 pairs, how much estimated overhead costs would be incurred?
    a. $48,635.50
    b. $41,125.00
    c. $69,027.00
    d. $33,997.50

11. Which of the following techniques is generally most accurate in estimating the fixed and variable components of a mixed cost?
    a. High/low method
    b. Regression analysis
    c. Spreadsheet analysis
    d. Scattergraph analysis

12. Generally speaking, variable costs are relevant to production decisions, except when:
    a. the variable costs are part of a mixed cost.
    b. the variable costs are unavoidable.
    c. the variable costs do not differ between alternatives.
    d. none of the above; variable costs are always relevant to production decisions.

13. Generally speaking, fixed costs are not relevant to production decisions, except when:
    a. the fixed costs are part of a mixed cost.
    b. the fixed costs are unavoidable.
    c. the fixed costs differ between alternatives.
    d. none of the above; fixed costs are always relevant to production decisions.

14. The after-tax cost of a tax-deductible cash expenditure can be calculated as follows:
    a. After-tax cost = Before-tax cost × (1 − tax rate)
    b. After-tax cost = (Before-tax cost × tax rate) − 1
    c. After-tax cost = Before-tax cost × tax rate
    d. After-tax cost = Before-tax cost × (tax rate − 1)

15. A manager is considering a project that will increase sales revenue by $120,000 without affecting expenses. What is the after-tax revenue given a 30 percent tax rate?
   a. $36,000
   b. $84,000
   c. $120,000
   d. $150,000

Concept Questions

16. *(Objective 1)* Describe the behavior of direct material cost in total and per unit as production volume changes.

17. *(Objective 1)* Describe the relevant range and how it relates to cost behavior.

18. *(Objective 1)* How will fixed costs expressed on a per unit basis react to a change in the level of activity?

19. *(Objective 1)* Give the equation that best describes the fundamental relationship among total costs (*TC*), fixed costs (*FC*), and variable costs per unit (*VC*). Use *TC*, *FC*, and *VC* in formulating your answer.

20. *(Objective 2)* Discuss the meaning of dependent and independent variables in regression analysis.

21. *(Objective 2)* Discuss the meaning of *R* square in regression analysis. What does an *R* square of 1.00 mean?

22. *(Objective 2)* Discuss situations in which the high/low method may provide inaccurate estimates of fixed and variable costs.

23. *(Objective 3)* Why are fixed costs not relevant for most short-term decisions?

24. *(Objective 3)* Compare and contrast the terms *relevant* and *irrelevant* costs as they pertain to decision making.

25. *(Objective 4)* Discuss the impact of taxes on costs and how that impact affects decision making.

Exercises

26. Carron Corp. produces fine porcelain dolls that are sold in exclusive gift shops. The controller and sales manager are discussing potential price increases and have started looking at various costs to consider their potential impact on price. The following are several of the costs they are discussing.
   a. Advertising
   b. Packaging (each doll is carefully packaged in a nicely designed collectible carton)
   c. Supervisors' salaries
   d. Fabric used in production (each doll is adorned in unique fabrics)
   e. Assembly labor
   f. Mortgage payment on the production facility
   g. Production facility utilities
   h. Quality assurance (each doll is carefully inspected)

Required

Assist the controller and sales manager by indicating whether each of the above costs is most likely a fixed cost (*FC*) or a variable cost (*VC*).

27. Ken Washburn and Associates incurred total costs of $10,000 to produce 500 custom mirrors. A total of 550 hours were required for the production of the mirrors. Direct labor is variable and costs $10 per hour.

Required

How much fixed cost did Ken Washburn and Associates incur?

28. Sara Ouellette has leased a new automobile under a special lease plan. If she drives the car 1,000 miles or less during a one-month period, the lease payment is $250. If the mileage ranges between 1,001 and 1,500 miles, the lease payment becomes $300. If the mileage ranges between 1,501 and 2,000 miles, the lease payment rises to $350.

Required

A. What type of cost is the lease?
B. If Sara only drives the car between 1,200 and 1,400 miles per month, then what type of cost does the lease effectively become?

29. Lockwood Lock and Keys provides custom creation of door locks for expensive homes. The company has recently become concerned about its ability to plan and control costs. Howard Lockwood, the company's founder, believes that he can summarize the company's monthly cost with a simple formula that appears as "Cost = $12,800 + $25.00/labor hour."

Required

If Lockwood's employees work 850 hours in a single month, calculate an estimate of the company's total costs.

30. Brunner's Baskets has the following current year costs:

Variable costs	$6 per unit
Fixed costs	$7,000

Brunner and a key supplier have entered into an arrangement that will result in a per unit decrease in Brunner's variable cost of $0.50 next year. Rental space will also be reduced, thereby decreasing fixed costs by 10 percent.

Required

A. If the company makes these changes, what is the new cost equation?
B. Given the new cost equation, determine estimated total costs if production remains at 12,000 units.

31. Sisters, Erin Joyner and Teresa Hayes, have started separate companies in the same city. Each company provides party planning services for weddings, birthday parties, holiday parties, and other occasions. Erin and Teresa graduated from Upper State University and completed a managerial accounting course, so they both understand the importance of managing their company's costs. Erin has estimated her cost equation to be "Total cost = $4,000 + $40/planning hour." On the other hand, Teresa has estimated her cost equation to be "Total cost = $250 + $60/planning hour."

Required

A. What could explain such a difference in the cost equations?
B. If each sister works a total of 135 planning hours, what total costs would each report?

32. Gross's Goodies is a manufacturer of fine chocolates. Recently, the owner, Melinda Gross, asked her controller to perform a regression analysis on production costs. Melinda believes that pounds of chocolate produced drive all of the company's production costs. The controller generated the following regression output:

	R Square	0.50688
	Standard Error	1.43764

Analysis of Variance

	DF	Sum of Squares	Mean Square
Regression	1	418.52992	418.52992
Residual	197	407.16375	2.06682

F = 202.49935   Signif. F = 0.0000

Variables in the Equation

Variable	Coefficients	Standard Error	t-Stat	P-Value
Pounds	7.940	0.055794	14.230	0.0000
Intercept	204.070	0.261513	−0.780	0.4361

Required

Calculate an estimated total cost assuming that Gross's Goodies manufactures 5,000 pounds of chocolate.

33. Refer to exercise 32. Melinda has become more curious about the regression analysis and has asked more questions.

Required

A. Melinda would like to know whether she is correct in assuming that the amount of chocolate is a significant driver of production costs. What can you tell her?
B. What is the company's cost equation?

34. Estes Silver accumulated the following production and overhead cost data for the past five months.

✓ Variable cost per unit: $2.75

	Production (units)	Overhead Cost
January	10,600	$40,250
February	10,500	40,000
March	11,500	44,250
April	12,500	45,500
May	11,000	43,750

Required

A. Use the high/low method to calculate the variable cost per unit and fixed costs for Estes Silver.
B. What are estimated total costs for production of 12,000 units?
C. Prepare a line graph for the total variable costs based on your calculation of variable cost per unit in question A. You will need to graph data for January through May. Does this graph appear as you would expect? (Hint: Set the minimum Y-axis value to $25,000.)

35. Tucker Brothers used the high/low method to derive the cost formula for electrical power cost. According to the cost formula, the variable cost per unit of activity is $3 per machine hour. Total electrical power cost at the high level of activity was $7,600 and was $7,300 at the low level of activity. The high level of activity was 1,200 machine hours.

✓ Fixed costs: $4,000

Required

Calculate the low level of activity.

36. DeLucia, Inc. is preparing a budget for next year and requires a breakdown of the cost of steam used in its factory into fixed and variable components. The following data on the cost of steam used and direct labor hours worked are available for the last six months:

✓ Fixed costs: $5,200

	Cost of Steam	Direct labor hours
July	$ 15,850	3,000
August	13,400	2,050
September	16,370	2,900
October	19,800	3,650
November	17,600	2,670
December	18,500	2,650
	$101,520	16,920

Required

A. Use the high/low method to calculate the estimated variable cost of steam per direct labor hour.

B. Prepare a graph of the cost of steam and the direct labor hours. Show labor hours on the X-axis and costs on the Y-axis. What can you observe from the graph you prepared? (Hint: Set the minimum Y-axis value to $11,000.)

37. Tom Wagner and Jim Wilson are partners in an outdoor equipment store, WW Outdoors. The two partners have been debating whether to keep the store open extra hours on Friday and Saturday. Jim has compiled the following cost data.

Manager salary	$45,000 per year
Assistant manager salary (expected to work extra hours)	$23,000 per year
Store utilities	$900 per month (on average)
After hours security (9 P.M. to 8 A.M.)	$10 per hour
Store rent	$3,500 per month
Shopping center assessment (based on square footage)	$12,000 per year
Sales associates' wages	$8.50 per hour

Tom and Jim do not anticipate hiring additional employees, but would instead ask current employees to work additional hours. No overtime work is expected as all employees currently work a maximum of 32 hours per week.

Required

Which of the above costs are relevant to the decision to stay open extra hours on Friday and Saturday? Why are these costs relevant?

38. Froelich Corporation anticipates net income of $1,200,000 this year. The company is considering signing an equipment lease that would result in a $175,000 deductible expense this year. The company's tax rate is 35 percent.

Required

A. What is the tax expense and net income after taxes for the anticipated net income without the lease of the equipment?

B. What is the tax expense and net income after taxes if the equipment is leased?

39. Ben Rakusin is contemplating an expansion of his business. He believes he can increase revenues by $9,000 each month if he leases 1,500 additional square feet of showroom space. Rakusin has found the perfect showroom. It leases for $4,000 per month. Ben's tax rate is 30 percent.

Required

What estimated after-tax income will Rakusin earn from his expansion?

✓ After-tax revenues increase: $6,300

40. Most business transactions have tax consequences. Understanding the "after-tax" effects of transactions is fundamentally important. Consider the following:

Before-Tax Revenue	Tax Rate	After-Tax Revenue
$ 100,000	40 %	?
200,000	20 %	?
135,000	35 %	?

Before-Tax Cost	Tax Rate	After-Tax Cost
$ 25,000	40 %	?
50,000	20 %	?
35,000	35 %	?

Required

Calculate the after-tax revenue or after-tax cost for each of the above transactions.

Problems

41. Erneston Corporation produces toolboxes used by construction professionals and homeowners. The company is concerned that it does not have an understanding of its utility consumption. The company's president, George, has asked the plant manager and cost accountant to work together to get information about utilities cost. The two of them accumulated the following data for the past 14 months (production volume is presented in units):

✓ Fixed costs: $929

	Production	Utility Cost
January	113,000	$ 1,712
February	114,000	1,716
March	90,000	1,469
April	110,000	1,600
May	112,000	1,698
June	101,000	1,691
July	104,000	1,700

	Production	Utility Cost
August	105,000	$1,721
September	115,000	1,619
October	97,000	1,452
November	98,000	1,399
December	98,000	1,403
January	112,000	1,543
February	107,000	1,608

Required

A. Using the high/low method, what is the company's utility cost equation?
B. What would be the expected utility cost of producing 120,000 units? (The relevant range is 85,000 to 125,000 units of production.)
C. Using the data shown and a spreadsheet program, perform a regression analysis. Discuss any differences in the results and the potential impact on decision making.

42. Kentner Office Services sells various products and services in the greater Wentworth area. Duplicating is one of its most popular services for corporate customers and individuals alike. Selected data from the Duplicating Department for the previous six months are as follows:

	Number of Copies Made	Duplicating Department's Costs
January	20,000	$17,000
February	25,000	19,500
March	27,000	21,000
April	22,000	18,000
May	24,000	19,000
June	30,000	24,000

Regression output based on the previous data is as follows:

Coefficient of intercept	2,807.895
R square	0.967696
Number of observations	6
X coefficient (independent variable)	0.686842

Required

A. What is the variable cost per copy for Kentner Office Services?
B. What is the fixed cost for the Duplicating Department?
C. Based on the limited regression output provided above, what cost formula should be used to compute an estimate of future total costs in the Duplicating Department?
D. If 26,000 copies are made next month, what total cost would be predicted?
E. Based on the information given, how accurate will the cost formula developed in response to question C be at predicting total Duplicating Department cost each month?

LO 1

✓ Housekeeping costs for fall semester: $40,000

43. The chief financial officer of Sawyer College, a small, highly selective liberal arts school, has determined that a member of Wobbekind Cleaning's staff can clean an average of 20 dorm rooms each day. Bay View Dorm, the school's newest dorm, has 100 rooms and is projected to be 80 percent full during the spring semester (January to May). During the summer term (June to August), the dorm is used only for summer camps and so is projected to be only 50 percent full. During the fall semester (September to December), the dorm is projected to be 100 percent full. Each occupied room is cleaned daily. Sawyer College outsources all housekeeping activities to Wobbekind Cleaning. Wobbekind charges Sawyer College $2,000 per month for each janitor employed on the school's behalf. The company's policy is to hire janitors on a full-time basis only. Although this policy results in some inefficiency, the tight labor market dictates this policy.

Required

A. Compute the cost for housekeeping service for Bay View Dorm for the spring semester, summer term, and fall semester.
B. What cost behavior pattern best describes housekeeping costs for Bay View Dorm?
C. What factors are important in predicting housekeeping costs for Bay View Dorm?

LO 1 2

✓ Garfunkel's variable cost component for maintenance per unit: $7.00

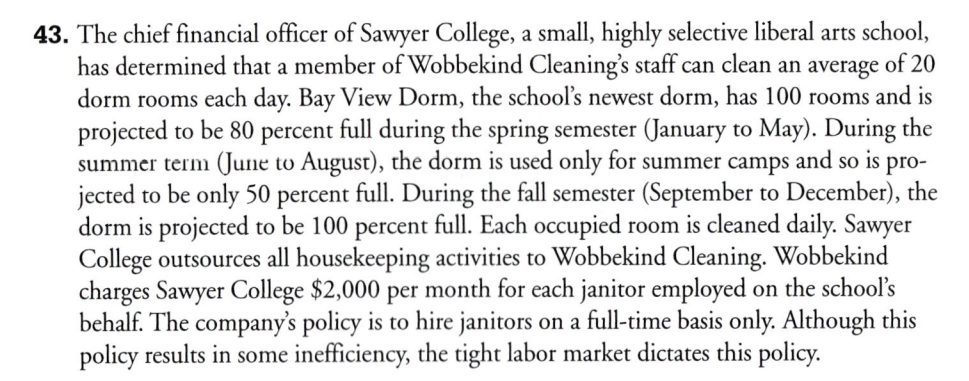

44. Simon and Garfunkel operate separate, but related businesses in the same town. The two have been debating which of them has the least amount of fixed costs. Simon, because he has always come first, believes his business has lower fixed costs than Garfunkel's business. Of course, Garfunkel disagrees saying that his business has lower fixed costs. The two have accumulated the following activity and cost data and have asked that you help them resolve their debate.

Simon's Business Data

Units Produced	Utilities	Rent	Indirect Labor
1,000	$10,000	$15,000	$13,000
1,500	12,500	15,000	15,600

Garfunkel's Business Data

Units Produced	Maintenance Expense	Rent	Indirect Labor
2,000	$24,250	$21,000	$22,000
8,000	66,250	21,000	88,000

Required

A. Classify each of Simon and Garfunkel's expenses as a fixed, variable, or mixed cost.
B. Calculate the total cost formula for each business. Which business has lower fixed costs?
C. If Simon produces 1,300 units, what would his total costs be?
D. If Garfunkel produces 9,000 units, what would his total costs be?

LO 1 2 EXCEL

✓ Fixed costs based on high/low method: $570

45. Manuelidis Rapid Delivery Service wants to determine the cost behavior pattern of maintenance costs for its delivery vehicles. The company has decided to use linear regression to examine the costs. The prior year's data regarding maintenance hours and costs are as follows:

	Hours of Activity	Maintenance Costs
January	480	$4,200
February	320	3,000
March	400	3,600
April	300	2,820

	Hours of Activity	Maintenance Costs
May	500	$4,350
June	310	2,960
July	320	3,030
August	520	4,470
September	490	4,260
October	470	4,050
November	350	3,300
December	340	3,160

Required

A. Perform a regression analysis on the above data. What maintenance costs should be budgeted for a month in which 420 maintenance hours will be worked?
B. What is the percentage of the total variance that can be explained by your analysis?
C. Use the high/low method to estimate a cost formula for Manuelidis. How similar is your high/low solution to the regression solution?

46. Chris Gill founded Gill's Grill over 20 years ago. The business has grown so much and been so successful that Chris is now considering selling franchises. Chris knows that potential franchisees will want access to certain operational data. Gill's Grill is probably best known for its incredible "potato flats," a french fry-like item served with a special secret sauce. Chris is concerned that some of the potato flats data are unusual and out of the ordinary. The following production data related to "potato flats" have been compiled.

	Pounds of Potatoes	Food Preparation Costs
January	20,000	$17,000
February	25,000	11,000
March	27,000	27,000
April	22,000	18,000
May	24,000	30,000
June	30,000	24,000
July	22,000	18,000
August	23,000	18,500
September	34,000	26,000

Regression Output

Coefficient of intercept	4,104.372
R square	0.244367
X coefficient	0.672073

Required

A. Should Chris remove some of the data? In other words, are any of the months unusual relative to the others? If so, identify likely outliers from the data and state reasons why you would remove them.
B. Do you think removing the data points would change the regression output? Perform a regression analysis to find out the correct answer.

LO 1 2

Activity Making Decision A

✓ Fixed costs for number of mats: $2,800

47. Steinhauser Framing is well known for the quality of its picture framing. Lucinda Steinhauser, the company's president, believes that the linear feet of framing used is the best predictor of framing costs for her company. She asked her assistant to accumulate the following data:

	Linear Feet of Framing	Number of Mats	Framing Costs
January	20,000	7,100	$ 17,000
February	25,000	8,120	19,500
March	27,000	8,500	21,000
April	22,000	8,400	18,000
May	24,000	8,300	19,000
June	30,000	10,600	24,000

Required

A. Use the high/low method to develop a total cost formula for Steinhauser Framing. You will need to perform two separate calculations, one for feet of framing and one for number of mats.
B. Compare the cost formulas developed in question A. Why are there differences?
C. On what basis should Steinhauser select a formula to predict framing costs? Would you recommend that Steinhauser rely on the results of the high/low method?

LO 3

48. Mack, a resident of Tennessee, has just returned from his annual one-week trip to Montana to fly-fish for trophy rainbow trout. His wife is trying to convince him that the trip is too expensive. Mack practices "catch and release" fishing, so he brings home only one fish, which he has mounted to display in his den. He caught and released 35 fish per day while on his trip. He goes fishing almost every weekend at home. Mack's wife accumulated the following costs so she could make her point that his fishing trip

Airfare to Montana	$ 350
Resort expenses (room and meals)	1,000
Fishing equipment (three rods and reels with a 20-year life)	2,500
Flies (50 per trip, enough for five fish)	150
Other equipment	350
Montana fishing license	50
Tennessee fishing license	35
Money lost playing backgammon (he plays every weekend)	100
A bottle of Jack Daniels (for warmth during backgammon)	25
Total cost	$ 4,560
Cost per fish ($4,560÷245)	$ 18.61

is too expensive.

Required

A. Assuming that this year's fishing trip is typical, what costs are relevant to a decision to go or not go on the Montana trip every year?
B. If Mack were to catch 300 fish on his next trip to Montana, what would be the additional cost for the extra 55 fish?

C. Which costs are relevant to a decision to give up fishing altogether?

49. Moore Enterprises has five stores, three of which are very profitable and two of which are losing money. The company's president, Karen Moore, is trying to decide whether to close

Store One (in local mall)		Store Two (in strip mall)	
Sales	$1,250,000	Sales	$1,000,000
Cost of sales	800,000	Cost of sales	700,000
Gross margin	$ 450,000	Gross margin	$ 300,000
Rent	250,000	Rent	200,000
Advertising	50,000	Advertising	50,000
Corporate expense	75,000	Corporate expense	75,000
Salaries	125,000	Salaries	90,000
Net income	$ (50,000)	Net income	$ (115,000)

✓ Fixed costs avoided if Store Two is closed: $340,000

one or both of the stores. The following income statements are presented for the two stores: If the two stores are closed, the corporate expense will be allocated to the other three stores, and the salaries for the store managers will be eliminated. The advertising expense is specific to each store, so that expense would be eliminated as well. The rent for Store One is $125,000 per year plus 10 percent of the sales dollars. The lease, signed six months ago, is for five years and cannot be canceled. The rent for Store Two is $16,666.67 per month and can be canceled with 30-days notice.

Required

A. What items on each income statement are relevant to the decision to close each store?
B. What would you recommend that management do? Why?

Cases

50. Claire's Cruise Co. has been operating for more than 20 years. The company has recently undergone several major management changes and needs accurate information to plan new cruises. You have been retained as a consultant to provide a cruise planning model. The company's accounting department provided you with the following data regarding last year's average costs for 12 cruises on the MS Robyn, a cruise ship that has a maximum capacity of

✓ Variable cost per passenger: $481.07

Cruise	Days	Passengers	Total Cost
1	7	455	$315,010
2	7	420	297,525
3	7	473	317,595
4	7	510	326,615
5	7	447	314,510
6	7	435	310,015
7	10	445	365,015
8	10	495	370,015
9	10	480	367,035
10	10	505	375,000
11	10	471	367,500
12	10	439	365,090

525 passengers and a crew of 250. All cruises on the MS Robyn are for either 7 or 10 days. The total cost provided above includes all costs of operating the ship (fuel, maintenance, depreciation, etc.) as well as meals, entertainment, and crew costs.

Required

A. Using the number of passengers as the independent variable, perform a regression analysis to develop the total cost formula for a cruise.
B. How accurate is the model calculated in question A? (Hint: Look at how much variance in total cost is explained by the number of passengers.)
C. What are the total fixed costs per cruise? (Round your answer to the nearest cent.)
D. What are the variable costs per passenger? (Round your answer to the nearest cent.)
E. What other independent variable might Claire's Cruise Co. use to predict total cruise costs? Using regression analysis, develop another total-cost formula based on the new independent variable.
F. Using the best planning model you can develop from the data provided, what is the estimated cost of a 10-day cruise at full capacity of 525 passengers? (Round your answer to the nearest cent.)

✓ Operating cost based on orders: $158,142

51. Adams-Boyd, a major retailing and mail-order operation, has been in business for the past 10 years. During that time, the mail-order operations have grown from a sideline to more than 80 percent of the company's annual sales. Of course, the company has suffered growing pains. There were times when overloaded or faulty computer programs resulted in lost sales. And, hiring and scheduling temporary employees to augment the permanent staff during peak periods has always been a problem.

Gail Lobanoff, manager of mail-order operations, has developed procedures for handling most problems. However, she is still trying to improve the scheduling of temporary employees to take telephone orders from customers. Under the current system, Lobanoff keeps a permanent staff of 60 employees who handle the basic workload. Based on her estimate of the upcoming week's telephone volume, she determines the number of temporary employees needed. The permanent employees are paid an average of $10 per hour plus 30 percent fringe benefits. The temporary employees are paid $7 per hour with no fringe benefits. The full-time employees are seldom sent home when volume is light and they are not paid for hours missed. Temporary employees are paid only for the hours worked. Adams-Boyd normally has three supervisors who earn $1,000 per month, but one additional supervisor is hired when temporary employees are used.

Lobanoff has decided to try regression analysis as a way to improve the prediction of total costs of processing telephone orders. By summarizing the daily labor hours into monthly totals for the past year, she was able to determine the number of labor hours incurred each month. In addition, she summarized the number of orders that had been processed each month. After entering the data into a spreadsheet, Lobanoff ran two regressions. Regression 1 related the total hours worked (permanent and temporary employees) to the total cost to operate the phone center. Regression 2 related the number of

Month	Total Cost	Total Hours	Number of Orders
January	$134,000	9,600	10,560
February	133,350	9,550	10,450
March	132,700	9,500	10,200
April	134,000	9,600	10,700
May	133,675	9,575	10,400
June	139,900	10,100	10,700
July	143,820	10,500	11,100
August	140,880	10,200	10,450

Month	Total Cost	Total Hours	Number of Orders
September	$137,940	9,900	10,200
October	153,620	11,500	12,200
November	163,420	12,500	12,900
December	150,680	11,200	11,490

orders taken to the total cost. The data used and regression output are provided below:
Regression equation: $TC = FC + VC$ (orders), or $TC = FC + VC$ (hours), where

	Regression 1	Regression 2
Intercept (FC)	36,180.42	21,595.15
X Variable (VC)	10.21475	10.95427
R square	0.997958	0.890802

TC = total cost; FC = fixed cost, and VC = variable cost per hour or order.

Required

A. What is the total cost formula for each of the above regressions? State each formula using costs that are rounded to the nearest cent.
B. Gail Lobanoff estimates that 12,470 orders will be received and 12,000 hours will be worked during January. Use each cost formula you developed in question A to predict the total cost of operating the phone center. Round your answers to the nearest dollar.
C. Gail needs to select one of the models for use in predicting total phone center costs for next year's monthly budget.
   (1) What are the objectives in selecting a prediction model?
   (2) What options are available to Gail? That is, what other independent variables might be used to predict the costs of the phone center?

Group and Internet Exercises

52. Search the Internet to find stories about how businesses are managing their fixed and variable costs. Be creative! Companies make decisions on a daily basis that reflect their understanding of cost behavior. You may remember Kmart's decision some years ago to stop sponsoring a PGA golf tournament because the sponsorship was too expensive. The company made this decision with little impact on its employees and an automatic increase in its net income. Consider looking for stories about automobile manufacturers, airlines, and sports teams. Prepare a one-page memo about the story that you find most interesting. Be sure to explain how management is managing the company's costs, rather than letting its costs manage the company.

53. Companies have historically been very concerned with how transactions impact their income tax return. Some companies have become so consumed by a desire to lower their income tax expense that they have entered into tax shelters, transactions specifically designed to achieve some desired income tax effect. Conduct an Internet search on income taxes and decision making. Prepare a memo that explains how business professionals structure transactions and conduct business to achieve a specific goal as it relates to income taxes. Is it ethical for a business to try and minimize its share of income taxes? Do you try to minimize your income taxes?

Chapter 6: Cost-Volume-Profit Analysis and Variable Costing

Chapter 6 Cost-Volume-Profit Analysis and Variable Costing

In Chapter 5, we emphasized the importance of understanding the behavior of costs. In this chapter, we develop a set of tools that focus on the distinction between fixed and variable costs. These tools include measures of a company's contribution margin, contribution margin ratio, and operating leverage—the cornerstones of cost-volume-profit (CVP) analysis. CVP analysis provides marketing and operations managers with useful information concerning sales necessary in order to break even or to earn a target profit and how profit is affected when the costs, volume, or prices of products or services are changed. The effect of income taxes on CVP analysis is also discussed.

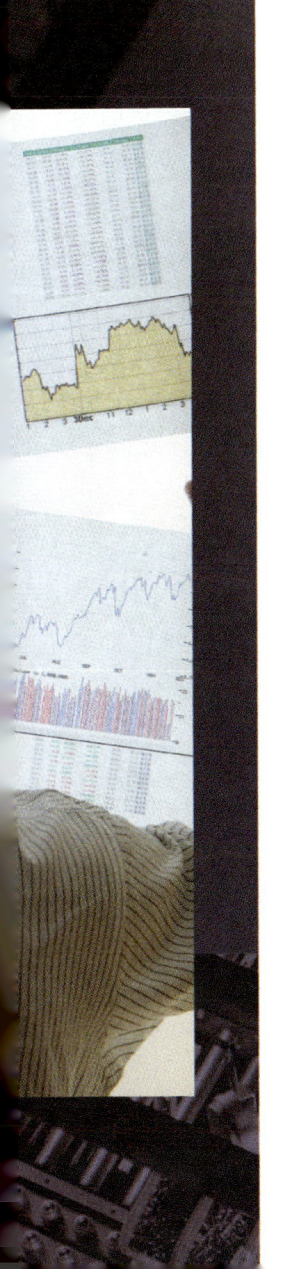

Learning Objectives

After studying the material in this chapter, you should be able to:

1. Determine the format and use of the contribution margin income statement

2. Use the contribution margin per unit and the contribution margin ratio to determine the impact of changes in sales on income

3. Analyze what-if decisions, using contribution margin per unit, contribution margin ratio, and operating leverage

4. Compute a company's break-even point in a single and a multiproduct environment

5. Use break-even analysis in an activity-based costing environment

6. Analyze target profit before and after the impact of income tax

7. Identify the assumptions inherent in CVP analysis

8. Identify the differences between variable costing and absorption costing and recognize the benefits of using variable costing for decision making

Introduction

Some of the more important decisions managers make involve analyzing the relationship among the cost, volume, and profitability of products produced and services provided by a company. **Cost-volume-profit (CVP) analysis** focuses on the relationship among the following five factors and the overall profitability of a company:

1. The prices of products or services
2. The volume of products or services produced and sold
3. The per unit variable costs
4. The total fixed costs
5. The mix of products or services produced

The Contribution Margin Income Statement

Objective 1

Determine the format and use of the contribution margin income statement

As mentioned in Chapter 5, the traditional income statement required for external financial reporting focuses on function (product costs versus period costs) in calculating the cost of goods sold and a company's gross profit. **Gross profit** is the difference between sales and cost of goods sold. However, because cost of goods sold includes both fixed costs (facility-level costs) and variable costs (unit-level costs, such as direct material), the behavior of cost of goods sold and gross profit is difficult to predict when production increases or decreases.

In contrast, the contribution margin income statement is structured by behavior rather than by function. In Exhibit 6-1 a traditional income statement and a contribution margin income statement are shown side by side so you can see the difference.

Exhibit 6-1 Comparison of Income Statements

Traditional			Contribution Margin		
Sales		$1,000	Sales		$1,000
Less: Cost of goods sold:			Less: Variable costs:		
Variable costs	$350		Manufacturing costs	$350	
Fixed costs	150		S, G & A costs	50	
Total cost of goods sold		500	Total variable costs		400
Gross profit		$ 500	Contribution margin		$ 600
Less: S, G & A costs:			Less: Fixed costs:		
Variable costs	$ 50		Manufacturing costs	$150	
Fixed costs	250		S, G & A costs	250	
Total S, G & A costs		300	Total fixed costs		400
Net income		$ 200	Net income		$ 200

KEY CONCEPT

The contribution margin income statement is structured to emphasize cost behavior as opposed to cost function.

As you can see, although the net income is the same for both statements, the traditional statement focuses on the function of the costs, whereas the contribution margin income statement focuses on the behavior of the costs. In the traditional income statement, cost of goods sold and selling, general and administrative (S, G, & A) costs include both variable and fixed costs. In the contribution margin income statement, costs are separated by behavior (variable versus fixed) rather than by function. Note, however, that the contribution margin income statement combines product and period costs. Variable costs include both variable product costs (direct materials) and variable selling, general and administrative costs (commissions on sales), whereas fixed costs likewise include both product and period costs.

Because of the focus on cost behavior, the information in the contribution margin income statement is very useful for managerial decision making. For example, a contribution margin income statement for Cheri's Chips (a manufacturer of banana chips) follows. Note that per unit cost information is also shown in the statement. This information is helpful in understanding the usefulness of the contribution margin income statement.

	Total	Per Unit
Sales (100,000 units)	$200,000	$2.00
Less: Variable costs	80,000	0.80
Contribution margin	$120,000	$1.20
Less: Fixed costs	40,000	
Net income	$ 80,000	

Contribution Margin per Unit

As you can see in the preceding income statement, the contribution margin is $1.20 per bag. What exactly does that tell us? It tells us that every bag of chips sold contributes $1.20 toward the payment of fixed costs. Once fixed costs are covered, each bag sold will contribute $1.20 toward net income. Remember that variable costs vary in total with production and remain constant when expressed as a per unit amount. As long as total sales vary in direct proportion to the number of units sold, **contribution margin per unit** will also remain constant.

Note what happens to the company's contribution margin if one additional bag of chips is produced and sold. Increasing sales by one bag increases contribution margin by $1.20. Assuming that fixed costs don't change, net income increases by the same $1.20.

	Total	Per Unit
Sales (100,001 units)	$200,002.00	$2.00
Less: Variable costs	80,000.80	0.80
Contribution margin	$120,001.20	$1.20
Less: Fixed costs	40,000.00	
Net income	$ 80,001.20	

What happens if sales increase by 100 bags (from 100,000 to 100,100)? As you can see, contribution margin and net income increase by $120 (100 units × $1.20 per unit) to $120,120 and $80,120, respectively. You can also analyze this as a 99-unit change from 100,001 units. Contribution margin and net income increase by $118.80 (99 units × $1.20 per unit).

	Total	Per Unit
Sales (100,100 units)	$200,200.00	$2.00
Less: Variable costs	80,080.00	0.80
Contribution margin	$120,120.00	$1.20
Less: Fixed costs	40,000.00	
Net income	$ 80,120.00	

What happens if sales decrease from the original 100,000 units to 99,000 units (a decrease of 1,000 units)? Contribution margin and net income will decrease by $1,200 (1,000 units × $1.20 per unit). This change can also be viewed as a 1,100-unit decrease from sales of 100,100 units. As you can see, contribution margin and net income will decrease by $1,320 (1,100 units × $1.20 per unit).

	Total	Per Unit
Sales (99,000 units)	$198,000.00	$2.00
Less: Variable costs	79,200.00	0.80
Contribution margin	$118,800.00	$1.20
Less: Fixed costs	40,000.00	
Net income	$ 78,800.00	

As summarized in Exhibit 6-2, the use of contribution margin per unit makes it very easy to predict how both increases and decreases in sales volume impact contribution margin and net income.

EXHIBIT 6-2 The Impact of Changes in Sales on Contribution Margin and Net Income

	Decreased by 1,000 units	Original Total	Increased by 1 unit	Increased by 100 units
	99,000 units	100,000 units	100,001 units	100,100 units
Sales (sales price $2.00/unit)	$ 198,000	$ 200,000	$ 200,002.00	$ 200,200
Less: Variable costs ($.80/unit)	79,200	80,000	80,000.80	80,080
Contribution margin ($1.20/unit)	$ 118,800	$ 120,000	$ 120,120.00	$ 120,120
Less: Fixed costs	40,000	40,000	40,000.00	40,000
Net income	$ 78,800	$ 80,000	$ 80,001.20	$ 80,120
Change in income	Decreased by $1,200 (1,000 units × $1.20)		Increased by $1.20 (1 unit × $1.20)	Increased by $120 (100 units × $1.20)

KEY CONCEPT

For every unit change in sales, contribution margin will increase or decrease by the contribution margin per unit multiplied by the increase or decrease in sales volume.

Note what happens when sales volume decreases to 33,334 units. At this point, the company's net income is zero. The company is at the break-even point when the contribution margin just covers fixed expenses and net income is zero. The calculation of a firm's break-even point is discussed in more detail later in the chapter.

	Total	Per Unit
Sales (33,334 units)	$66,668	$2.00
Less: Variable costs	26,668	0.80
Contribution margin	$40,000	$1.20
Less: Fixed costs	40,000	
Net income	$ 0	

Contribution Margin Ratio

The contribution margin income statement can also be presented using percentages, as shown in the following income statement. The **contribution margin ratio** is calculated by dividing the contribution margin in dollars by sales dollars:

$$\text{Contribution margin ratio} = \frac{\text{Contribution margin (in \$)}}{\text{Sales (in \$)}}$$

The contribution margin ratio can be viewed as the amount of each sales dollar contributing to the payment of fixed costs and increasing net profit—that is, 60 cents of each sales dollar contributes to the payment of fixed costs or increases net income. Like the contribution margin per unit, the contribution margin ratio will remain constant as long as sales vary in direct proportion to volume.

	Total	Percentage
Sales (100,000 units)	$200,000	100
Less: Variable costs	80,000	40
Contribution margin	$120,000	60 ($120,000/$200,000)
Less: Fixed costs	40,000	
Net income	$ 80,000	

Like contribution margin per unit, the contribution margin ratio allows us to very quickly see the impact of a change in sales on contribution margin and net income. As you saw in Exhibit 6-2, a $200 increase in sales (100 units) will increase contribution margin by $120 ($200 × 60%). Assuming that fixed costs don't change, this $120 increase in contribution margin increases net income by the same amount. Likewise, in Exhibit 6-2, we decreased sales by 1,000 units ($2,000), resulting in a decrease in contribution margin and net income of $1,200 ($2,000 × 60%).

The Contribution Margin and Its Uses

To illustrate the many uses of the contribution margin income statement in managerial decision making, let's look at the income statement of Happy Daze Game Company. Happy Daze produces just one game but plans to increase its product line to include more games in the near future. The latest income statement for Happy Daze is as follows:

Happy Daze Game Company

	Total	Per Unit	Percentage
Sales (8,000 units)	$100,000	$12.50	100
Less: Variable costs	72,000	9.00	72
Contribution margin	$ 28,000	$ 3.50	28
Less: Fixed costs	35,000		
Net income (loss)	$ (7,000)		

In this case, Happy Daze is losing $7,000 on sales of $100,000. What would happen if sales were to increase by 3,000 units? Using what we know about the contribution margin income statement, we can see that every unit sold contributes $3.50, or 28 percent of every sales dollar, toward fixed costs. If Happy Daze sells 3,000 more units, contribution margin

KEY CONCEPT

The contribution margin per unit and the contribution margin ratio will remain constant as long as sales vary in direct proportion to volume.

KEY CONCEPT

For every dollar change in sales, contribution margin will increase or decrease by the contribution margin ratio multiplied by the increase or decrease in sales dollars.

Objective 2

Use the contribution margin per unit and the contribution margin ratio to determine the impact of changes in sales on income

and net income will increase by $10,500 (3,000 × $3.50). We can use the contribution margin ratio to arrive at the same solution. Increasing sales by 3,000 units at $12.50 per unit will increase sales dollars by $37,500. With a contribution margin ratio of 28 percent and no changes in fixed costs, a $37,500 increase in sales will increase net income by $10,500 ($37,500 × 28%). What does this mean for Happy Daze? If the company can increase sales volume by 3,000 units (without changing anything else), it will show a profit of $3,500 instead of a loss of $7,000.

However, increases in sales may not happen in isolation. In order for Happy Daze to increase sales by 3,000 units, management might choose to lower the sales price, increase commissions and other sales incentives in order to motivate the sales staff, improve the quality of the product, or perhaps increase the advertising budget. As you will see in the next section, CVP analysis helps managers determine the impact on net income when these and other "what-if" decisions are made.

What-If Decisions Using CVP

In the earlier example, Happy Daze has a net loss of $7,000 when 8,000 units are sold. At that level of sales, the total contribution margin of $28,000 is not sufficient to cover fixed costs of $35,000. The CEO of the company is not happy with the situation and would like to consider options to increase net income while maintaining the high quality of the company's products. After consultation with marketing, operations, and accounting managers, the CEO identifies three options that she would like to consider in more depth:

1. Reducing the variable costs of manufacturing the product
2. Increasing sales through a change in the sales incentive structure or commissions (which would also increase variable costs)
3. Increasing sales through increasing advertising (a fixed cost)

Option 1—Reduce Variable Costs

Objective 3

Analyze what-if decisions using contribution margin per unit, contribution margin ratio, and operating leverage

When variable costs are reduced, contribution margin will increase. So the question becomes: what can be done to reduce the variable costs of manufacturing? Happy Daze could find a less expensive supplier of raw materials. The company could also investigate the possibility of reducing the amount of labor used in the production process or of using lower-wage employees in the production process.

In either case, qualitative factors must be considered. If Happy Daze finds a less expensive supplier of raw materials, the reliability (shipments may be late, causing down time) of the supplier and the quality (paper products are not as good, adhesive is not bonding) of the material must be considered. Reducing labor costs also has both quantitative and qualitative implications. If less labor is involved in the production process, more machine time may be needed. Although this option certainly lowers variable costs, it may also raise fixed costs. Using lower-skilled workers to save money could result in more defective products owing to mistakes made by inexperienced workers. Another possible result of using fewer workers is that it can adversely affect employee morale. Being short-staffed can cause stress on workers, owing to the likelihood that they will be overworked.

Remember that a decision maker should consider only those costs and other factors that are relevant to the decision. In other words, only those costs and other factors that vary between each of the options should be considered.

Happy Daze decides to decrease variable costs by reducing the costs of direct labor. This change reduces variable costs by 10 percent and, as shown in the following analysis, results in an overall increase in net income of $7,200.

Impact of Reducing Variable Costs by 10 Percent

	Current	Option 1
Sales	$100,000	$100,000
Less: Variable costs	72,000	64,800
Contribution margin	$ 28,000	$ 35,200
Less: Fixed costs	35,000	35,000
Net income (loss)	$ (7,000)	$ 200

Option 2—Increase Sales Incentives (Commissions)

The CEO of Happy Daze would also like to consider providing additional sales incentives to motivate the sales staff in an effort to increase sales volume. For example, the marketing manager estimates that if Happy Daze raises the sales commission by 10 percent on all sales above the present level, sales will increase by $30,000, or 2,400 games. (The additional sales commission will be $3,000.) The results of Option 2 are as follows:

Impact of Increasing Sales Incentives (sales increase to $130,000)

	Current	Option 2
Sales	$100,000	$130,000
Less: Variable costs	72,000	96,600
Contribution margin	$ 28,000	$ 33,400
Less: Fixed costs	35,000	35,000
Net income (loss)	$ (7,000)	$ (1,600)

Happy Daze can increase net income by $5,400 by increasing the sales commission by 10 percent on all sales of more than $100,000. The new variable costs are calculated by using a variable-cost percentage of 72 percent on sales up to $100,000 and 82 percent on all sales of more than $100,000. However, note that Happy Daze still has a net loss under this option. In addition, it is important to remember that the increase in sales is an estimate, and actual sales may be higher or lower than $130,000. As you can see in the following income statement, if sales increase by $40,000 instead of $30,000, income will increase by $7,200, and Happy Daze will report net income of $200.

Impact of Increasing Sales Incentives (sales increase to $140,000)

	Current	Option 2a
Sales	$100,000	$140,000
Less: Variable costs	72,000	104,800
Contribution margin	$ 28,000	$ 35,200
Less: Fixed costs	35,000	35,000
Net income (loss)	$ (7,000)	$ 200

In Option 1 and Option 2, the ultimate change in net income can be determined by focusing solely on the change in contribution margin. Fixed costs are not relevant in either analysis because they do not vary. However, as you will see in Option 3, that is not always the case.

Option 3—Increase Advertising

The marketing manager estimates that spending an additional $10,000 on advertising will increase sales by $40,000, or 3,200 games. By spending an additional $10,000 on advertising, the company can reach more potential customers through ads in newspapers or magazines, radio or TV commercials, and other means such as flyers on automobile windshields. Contribution margin is again relevant because it differs between options. In addition, fixed costs are relevant in analyzing Option 3 because the increase in sales will occur only with an increase in advertising (a fixed cost).

What is the impact of Option 3 on the contribution margin and net income of Happy Daze? As shown next, increasing sales by $40,000 (3,200 games) will increase contribution margin by $11,200 (($12.50 − $9) × 3,200), or ($40,000 × 0.28). However, because fixed costs will also increase by $10,000, net income will increase (the net loss will decrease) by only $1,200.

Impact of Increasing Advertising

	Current (8,000 units)	Option 3 (11,200 units)
Sales	$100,000	$140,000
Less: Variable costs	72,000	100,800
Contribution margin	$ 28,000	$ 39,200
Less: Fixed costs	35,000	45,000
Net income (loss)	$ (7,000)	$ (5,800)

How well does each option meet the stated objectives of increasing net income while maintaining a high-quality product? The CEO of Happy Daze should analyze each alternative solution in the same manner and choose the best course of action based on both quantitative and qualitative factors.

From a quantitative perspective, Option 1 results in an increase in net income of $7,200, Option 2 increases net income by $5,400, and Option 3 increases net income by $1,200. However, remember that if sales increase to $140,000 in Option 2A, net income will increase by $7,200. The increase in sales predicted in Option 3 is also not known with certainty. The CEO must also assess the risk inherent in each option and the sensitivity of a decision to changes in key assumptions. For example, in Option 3, the marketing manager thinks that increased advertising could increase sales by as much as $60,000. This outcome would result in an increase in income of $6,800. Option 1 has little quantitative risk because the decrease in costs is known with certainty, no increase in sales is projected, and it is generally easier to lower costs than it is to raise sales. Based only on a quantitative analysis, Option 1 appears to be Happy Daze's best choice. However, Happy Daze must also consider the impact of the three options on the quality of its product. Of particular concern, Happy Daze should consider whether reducing labor costs in Option 1 will have a negative impact on the quality of its product. If the reduction in labor costs results from using lower-paid but inadequately skilled workers, quality may be adversely affected.

Changes in Price and Volume

Managers in almost all companies frequently make decisions using CVP analysis. One decision concerns how a price change (and the resulting change in sales volume) will impact net income. Changes in sales price can have a significant impact on sales volume. Raising the sales price may result in a decrease in sales volume. However, the impact on total sales revenue may be offset by the increase in sales price. Likewise, a decrease in sales price may result in an increase in sales volume without a corresponding increase in total sales revenue.

The change in volume is a projection based on the best information available at the time. Changes in sales price can be difficult to reverse. After a sales price is lowered, customers may react unfavorably to a later unexpected increase. Consequently, risk analysis is very important in these decisions.

Doing Business.

HOW MUCH DOES IT COST TODAY?

Dell Computer continually adjusts prices of its computer systems, offering special promotions that are available to various customer groups: business users, home users, educators, and government agencies. In addition, in order to increase sales of a particular model of computer, Dell might offer free shipping or free peripherals, such as printers, free memory upgrades, etc. By continually adjusting the prices charged for a particular system, Dell is essentially using the basics of CVP analysis to increase profit.

While differential pricing, that is, charging different prices for the same product or service has been used by Dell for several years and is common in the airline industry, it is a relatively new phenomenon in sports. In an effort to increase revenue and offset rising costs associated with high player salaries and debt payments associated with building new stadiums and arenas, a number of sports teams including the New York Mets baseball team and the Pittsburgh Penguins hockey team have begun charging fans more for weekend games and games against high-profile teams and players. The Mets increased prices for 17 of their most popular games while decreasing prices for other games. The Penguins increased their ticket revenue by over $1 million by charging an extra $5 for weekend games and games against three popular opponents. However, the policy does entail risks. Not only do teams have to figure out which opponents are going to be good and which matchups are going to be popular before the season even begins, if fans balk at the higher prices, overall profitability may decrease ("The Barry Bonds Tax: Teams Raise Prices for Good Games," *Wall Street Journal*, December 3, 2002, D1).

Changes in Cost, Price, and Volume

Changes can be made to cost, price, and volume at the same time. In fact, changes in cost, price, and volume are never made in a vacuum and almost always impact one or both of the other variables. As an example, let's look at ZIA Motors, a manufacturer of automobiles. ZIA sells only one type of automobile (the Zoomer) at the low end of the price range. The car provides good, basic transportation but has experienced a significant drop in demand (and therefore profitability) in the past year. As a result, ZIA has decided to improve the quality of the Zoomer and to market the car as a higher-quality but still economical alternative to its better-known American-made competitors. The cost of direct material and other variable costs in the redesigned model will increase by 20 percent (from $6,000 to $7,200), owing to higher labor costs and the use of higher-quality engine materials and insulation to provide a quieter ride. Fixed costs will also increase, owing to the additional machinery needed. ZIA will need to invest $100 million in new equipment and robotics, resulting in annual depreciation of $20 million. ZIA also plans a $10 million advertising and public relations campaign to let the buying public know about the enhancements to the car. ZIA also plans to increase the sales price of the redesigned Zoomer from $8,000 to $10,000. The marketing department estimates that these changes will increase demand by somewhere between 2,000 and 10,000 cars per year. (Current demand is 30,000 cars.) When pressed for its best forecast, the marketing department estimates new sales at 35,000 automobiles. Current and projected income statements for ZIA follow:

Current and Projected Income Statements for ZIA Motors

	Current	After Proposed Changes
Sales	$240,000,000	$350,000,000
Less: Variable costs	180,000,000	252,000,000
Contribution margin	$ 60,000,000	$ 98,000,000
Less: Fixed costs	75,000,000	105,000,000
Net income	$ (15,000,000)	$ (7,000,000)

As you can see, although net income increases with the proposed changes, ZIA is still losing money on the Zoomer. Even though contribution margin increases by $38 million, fixed costs increase by $30 million, resulting in an overall increase in net income of $8 million.

If sales increase by only 2,000 cars, how much will income increase (decrease)? What if sales increase by 10,000 cars? These types of what-if questions can be answered most easily by using concepts of CVP analysis already at your disposal. In the previous example, if the proposed changes are made, the sale of each car will contribute $2,800 toward fixed costs and ultimately net income. In other words, the contribution margin of each car sold is $2,800 ($10,000 sales price less $7,200 variable costs). If 32,000 cars are sold, total contribution margin will be $89,600,000 (32,000 × $2,800). Although this is an increase of $29,600,000, the change in fixed costs must also be considered. Because fixed costs increase by $30,000,000, income will actually decrease by $400,000 if only 32,000 cars are sold. On the other hand, if 40,000 cars are sold, contribution margin will be $112 million, an increase of $52 million. This more than offsets the $30 million increase in fixed costs and income will increase by $22 million.

Decisions of this nature have a very high level of uncertainty. In this case, our decision is sensitive to assumptions made concerning the demand for the remodeled car. If demand for redesigned Zoomers is only 32,000 cars, net income will actually decrease, and ZIA will choose not to make the changes. If sales increase to 35,000 or 40,000 cars, income will increase under the proposed changes.

Hitting the Bottom Line.

BETWEEN A ROCK AND A HARD PLACE

While cost-volume-profit analysis demonstrates that companies can increase profits by reducing costs, increasing volume, or increasing prices, finding the proper combination of the three is not always easy.

After the September 11, 2001 terrorist attacks as consumers cut back discretionary spending, General Motors and Ford instituted large rebates, low interest financing and other incentives in order to woo back car buyers. While such steps reduce the ultimate sales price paid by buyers, GM and Ford hoped to make up for the lower sales prices with higher volume.

After incurring large losses in 2001, and in an effort to return to profitability, Chrysler was reluctant to match the incentives. However, as buyers flocked to GM and Ford, Chrysler's share of the U.S. market shrank. Faced with sharply reduced sales, in early 2002 Chrysler increased its rebates and incentives on a variety of models. The result? Chrysler was able to increase sales and break even for the year and return to profitability in the third and fourth quarters of 2002.

Break-Even Analysis

In addition to what-if analysis, it is useful for a company to know how many units or the dollar amount of sales that are necessary for it to break even. The **break-even point** is the level of sales at which contribution margin just covers fixed costs and consequently net income is equal to zero. Break-even analysis is really just a variation of CVP analysis in which volume is increased or decreased in an effort to find the point at which net income is equal to zero.

Break-even analysis is facilitated through the use of a mathematical equation derived directly from the contribution margin income statement. Another way to look at these relationships is to put the income statement into equation form:

$$\text{Sales} - \text{Variable Costs} - \text{Fixed Costs} = \text{Net Income}$$
$$SP(x) - VC(x) - FC = NI$$

where

$$SP = \text{Sales price per unit}$$
$$VC = \text{Variable costs per unit}$$
$$FC = \text{Total fixed costs}$$
$$NI = \text{Net income}$$
$$x = \text{Number of units sold}$$

> **Objective 4**
>
> Compute a company's break-even point in a single and a multiproduct environment

At the break-even point, net income is equal to zero, so:

$$SP(x) - VC(x) - FC = 0$$

Rearranging and dividing each side by the contribution margin $(SP - VC)$, the number of units (x) that must be sold to reach the break-even point is found by dividing the total fixed costs by the contribution margin (CM) per unit:

$$(SP - VC)(x) = FC$$
$$\text{and } x = FC/CM$$

By dividing the contribution margin of each product into the fixed cost, we are calculating the number of units that must be sold to cover the fixed costs. At that point, the total contribution margin will be equal to fixed costs, and net income will be zero.

$$\text{Break-even (units)} = \frac{\text{Fixed costs}}{\text{Contribution margin per unit}}$$

For example, if Happy Daze has fixed costs of $35,000 and the contribution margin per unit is $3.50, as shown earlier, the break-even point is computed as follows:

$$\text{Break-even (units)} = \frac{\text{Fixed costs}}{\text{Contribution margin per unit}}$$
$$= \$35,000 / \$3.50$$
$$= 10,000 \text{ units}$$

We can use a similar formula to compute the amount of sales dollars needed to break even:

$$\text{Break-even (\$)} = \frac{\text{Fixed costs}}{\text{Contribution margin ratio}}$$

Using the amounts from the previous example,

$$\text{Break-even (\$)} = \frac{\$35,000}{28\% \text{ (see page 179)}}$$
$$= \$125,000$$

Graphically, the break-even point can be found by comparing a company's total revenue with its total costs (both fixed and variable). As seen in Exhibit 6-3, the break-even point is the volume at which total revenue is equal to total cost.

EXHIBIT 6-3   Break-Even Graph

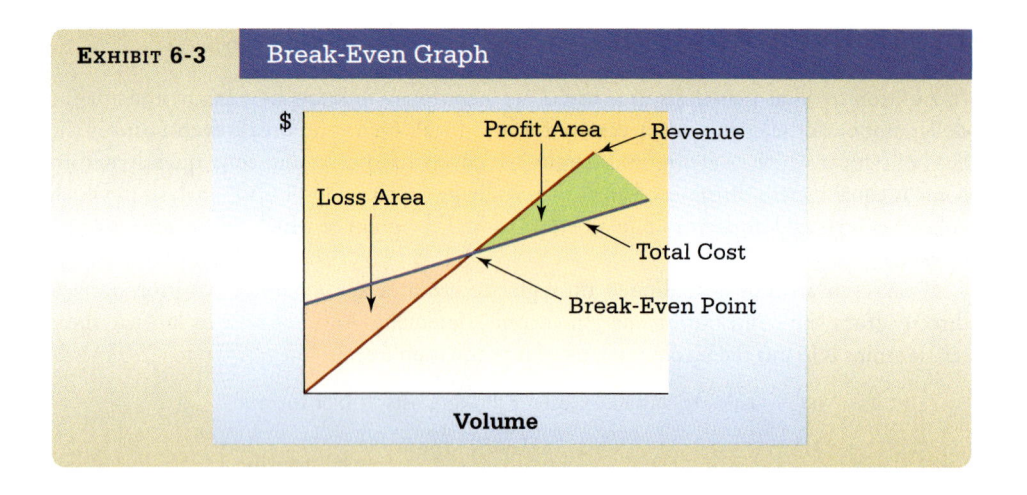

Break-Even Calculations with Multiple Products

Break-even calculations become more difficult when more than one product is produced and sold. In a multiproduct environment, a manager calculating the break-even point is concerned not so much with the unit sales or the dollar sales of a single product but with the amount of total sales necessary to break even. This requires the calculation of an "average" contribution margin for all the products produced and sold. This in turn requires an estimate of the sales mix—the relative percentage of total units or total sales dollars expected from each product.[1] However, customers (and sales volume) will not always behave in the manner that we predict. For example, although the expected sales product mix may be 600 units of Product A and 400 units of Product B, we can estimate our customers' buying habits only from past experience. If the sales product mix ends up being 700 units of A and 300 units of B, the break-even analysis will change accordingly.

Assume that Happy Daze adds another game to its product line. The company estimates that the new game will achieve sales of approximately 4,500 units. The expected sales product mix (in units) is therefore 64 percent $\left(\frac{8,000}{12,500}\right)$ old game and 36 percent $\left(\frac{4,500}{12,500}\right)$ new game. The new game will be priced at $15 per unit and requires $11 of variable production, selling, and administrative costs, so the contribution margin per unit is $4. The game will also require an investment of $15,000 in additional fixed costs. A summary of the price and cost of the old and new games follows:

Happy Daze Game Company

	Old Game (8,000 units)	Per Unit	New Game (4,500 units)	Per Unit
Sales	$100,000	$12.50	$67,500	$15.00
Less: Variable costs	72,000	9.00	49,500	11.00
Contribution margin	$ 28,000	$ 3.50	$18,000	$ 4.00
Less: Fixed costs	35,000		15,000	
Net income (loss)	$ (7,000)		$ 3,000	

---

[1] Calculating the optimum mix of products to produce given limited resources and demand constraints is addressed in Chapter 7. The optimum mix will result in the highest overall contribution margin and also the highest overall profit for a company.

The calculation of "average" contribution margin is *really* a weighted average. Although the simple-average contribution margin of the old game ($3.50) and the new game ($4.00) is $3.75, the weighted average is $3.68. This can be seen most easily by examining the income statement below:

Happy Daze Game Company

	Old Game (8,000)	Per Unit	New Game (4,500)	Per Unit	Total (12,500)	Per Unit
Sales	$100,000	$12.50	$67,500	$15.00	$167,500	$13.40
Less: Variable costs	72,000	9.00	49,500	11.00	121,500	9.72
Contribution margin	$ 28,000	$ 3.50	$18,000	$ 4.00	$ 46,000	$ 3.68
Less: Fixed costs	35,000		15,000		50,000	
Net income (loss)	$ (7,000)		$ 3,000		$ (4,000)	

Dividing the total contribution margin of $46,000 by 12,500 units sold gives us a total contribution margin of $3.68 per unit. The weighted-average contribution margin can be calculated more directly by multiplying the unit contribution margin for each game by the proportion of each game in the sales mix and adding the resulting numbers. This effectively weights each product's contribution margin by the relative sales mix for that product.

$$\text{Old game} = .64 \times \$3.50 = \$2.24$$
$$\text{New game} = .36 \times \$4.00 = \$1.44$$

The weighted-average contribution margin for Happy Daze Game Company is therefore $3.68 per game ($2.24 + $1.44). The break-even formula for a company with multiple products is as follows:

$$\text{Break-even (units)} = \frac{\text{Fixed costs}}{\text{Weighted-average contribution margin per unit}}$$

Happy Daze's break-even point is therefore: $\left(\frac{\$50,000}{3.68}\right)$, or 13,587 units (rounded). How is this number interpreted? Remember that the weighted-average contribution margin is dependent on the sales mix. Likewise, the break-even point is dependent on the sales mix. Assuming a sales mix of 64 percent old games and 36 percent new games, Happy Daze must sell 8,696 old games and 4,891 new games (rounded) to break even.

$$\text{Old game: } 13,587 \times .64 = 8,696$$
$$\text{New game: } 13,587 \times .36 = 4,891$$

If the sales mix changes to 50 percent old games and 50 percent new games, what will be the impact on the break-even point? What if the sales mix changes to 40 percent old games and 60 percent new games? With the sales mix at 50 percent old and 50 percent new, the weighted-average contribution margin becomes $3.75 ((0.50 × $3.50) + (0.50 × $4.00)). When the mix changes to 40 percent old and 60 percent new, the weighted-average contribution margin changes to $3.80 ((0.40 × $3.50) + (0.60 × $4.00)). Notice that when the volume shifts toward selling more of the product with the highest contribution margin, the weighted-average contribution margin increases. As the weighted-average contribution margin increases, the break-even point will decrease.

The break-even point calculated using a weighted-average contribution margin for multiple products is valid only for the sales mix used in the calculation. If the sales mix changes, the break-even point will also change. Obviously, the more products involved in the sales mix, the more sensitive the calculation becomes to changes in sales mix.

Doing Business.

AN OLYMPIC BREAK-EVEN POINT

In addition to issuing coinage for the U.S. government, the U.S. mint produces commemorative coins for special events like the 1996 Summer Olympic Games in Atlanta, Georgia. In 1992, Congress authorized the mint to manufacture and sell Olympic gold, silver, and clad (a mix of nickel and copper over copper) coins in 1995 and 1996 and mandated that the price must be sufficient to cover all material, manufacturing, packaging, selling, and general and administrative costs; provide support in the form of a surcharge that goes to the sponsoring organization (in this case the U.S. Olympic Committee); and provide a profit for the U.S. government.

In determining the break-even point of 1.2 million coin sets, the mint estimated a sales mix of 30 percent clad coins, 60 percent silver coins and 10 percent gold coins and defined variable costs to include material costs for gold and silver, fabrication costs, labor, dies and collars used to make ridges at the end of coins, packaging material, product delivery, the surcharge and 50 percent of overhead costs, and general and administrative costs. Fixed costs included the other 50 percent of overhead and general and administrative costs as well as product promotion costs (Michael E. Kess, "The Development of Cost Estimates for the Pricing of Commemorative Coins at the U.S. Mint," *Cost Engineering*, Volume 37, Issue 9, September 1995).

Break-Even Calculations Using Activity-Based Costing

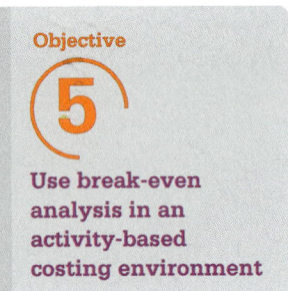

Objective 5

Use break-even analysis in an activity-based costing environment

Computing break-even when using activity-based costing (ABC) requires some slight modifications to the general formulas presented thus far. Conventional CVP analysis assumes that all costs are either variable or fixed. In ABC, costs are classified as unit-, batch-, product-, or facility-level, and CVP analysis must be modified accordingly. Whereas unit-level costs behave like true variable costs and vary directly with volume, and facility-level costs behave like fixed costs, batch- and product-level costs are likely to vary with drivers related to the complexity of a product or product diversity. Along with fixed costs, batch- and product-level costs are included in the numerator of the break-even formula. However, unlike traditional break-even analysis, they are allowed to vary with changes in their appropriate cost drivers. Although it may appear that the value of CVP would diminish when using ABC, in fact CVP analysis may be even more useful in decision making because the cost behavior information in an ABC system is more accurate.

The break-even equation when using ABC is modified as follows:

$$\text{Break-even (units)} = \frac{(\text{Fixed costs} + \text{Batch-level costs} + \text{Product-level costs})}{\text{Contribution margin per unit}}$$

In the formula, batch-level costs are equal to the cost per unit multiplied by the appropriate batch-level driver(s), and product-level costs are equal to the cost per unit multiplied by the appropriate product-level driver(s). The contribution margin per unit is calculated by subtracting unit-level variable costs from the sales price. The main differences between the two calculations are as follows:

1. The fixed costs differ. Some costs that were previously identified as being fixed may actually vary with nonunit cost drivers (batch- and product-level costs).

2. These nonunit-level variable costs are included in the numerator along with fixed costs.

Sales price	$ 12.50 per unit
Variable costs:	
Direct material	$ 3.00 per unit
Direct labor	2.00 per unit
Variable overhead	4.00 per unit
Total variable costs	$ 9.00 per unit
Setup costs (batch)	$10,000 (10 setups @ $1,000 per setup)
Testing costs (product)	$ 5,000 (200 testing hours @ $25 per testing hour)
Facility-level fixed costs	$20,000

Putting these numbers into the ABC break-even formula results in the following:

$$\text{Break-even (units)} = \frac{(\$20{,}000 + \$10{,}000 + \$5{,}000)}{\$3.50}$$
$$= 10{,}000 \text{ units}$$

As you can see, using the ABC formula, the numerator of $35,000 consists of true fixed costs as well as nonunit-level variable costs associated with setups and testing. Under conventional break-even analysis, each of these costs would have been considered fixed. Consequently, as long as the number of setups and inspection hours remain constant, the break-even will be the same under conventional break-even analysis and ABC. However, if setups or the number of inspection or testing hours change, break-even will be different. Conventional break-even calculations ignore the changes in batch- and product-level costs. (Remember that they are treated as fixed under a conventional break-even analysis.) But these activity levels can change. For example, if Happy Daze discovers that it can reduce the direct labor involved with production of games from $2.00 to $1.85 per unit, its contribution margin will increase to $3.65, and the conventional break-even point will decrease to 9,589 units ($35,000/$3.65). Using the conventional break-even formula would lead one to believe that the reduction in direct labor does in fact reduce the break-even point. However, what if Happy Daze has to increase the amount of time spent inspecting or testing the product as a result of the reduction in direct labor? Because the ABC system treats inspection or testing time as a nonunit-level variable cost, the additional hours of inspection time will impact the break-even point. If the reduction in direct labor adds 70 inspection hours, total costs will increase to $6,750 (270 hours × $25 per hour), and the break-even point will be as follows:

$$\text{Break-even (units)} = \frac{(\$20{,}000 + \$10{,}000 + \$6{,}750)}{\$3.65}$$
$$= 10{,}069 \text{ units (rounded)}$$

As can be seen from this computation of the break-even point using the ABC formula, the break-even point actually is higher than before the reduction in direct labor. Why is that? At a sales volume of 10,000 units (the old break-even point), the reduction in direct labor is $1,500 (10,000 × 0.15), but the increased inspection expense is $1,750 (70 hours × $25). So what appears to be a cost reduction really isn't. Break-even analysis using ABC allows managers to more clearly see these tradeoffs, often leading to better decisions.

Target Profit Analysis (Before and After Tax)

The goal of most businesses is not to break even but to earn a profit. Luckily, we can easily modify the break-even formula to compute the amount of sales needed to earn a target profit (before tax). Instead of solving for the sales necessary to earn a net income of zero, we simply solve for the sales necessary to reach a target profit.

$$\text{Sales} - \text{Variable Costs} - \text{Fixed Costs} = \text{Target Profit (Before Tax)}$$
$$SP(x) - VC(x) - FC = TP$$

Objective 6

Analyze target profit before and after the impact of income tax

where

$$SP = \text{Sales price per unit}$$
$$VC = \text{Variable costs per unit}$$
$$FC = \text{Total fixed costs}$$
$$TP = \text{Target profit (before tax)}$$
$$x = \text{Number of units sold}$$

$$SP(x) - VC(x) - FC = TP \text{ (before tax)}$$

Rearranging and dividing each side by the contribution margin $(SP - VC)$, the number of units (x) that must be sold to earn a before-tax target profit is found by dividing the sum of the fixed costs and the target profit by the contribution margin (CM) per unit:

$$(SP - VC)(x) = (FC + TP)$$

$$\text{and } x = \frac{(FC + TP \text{ (before tax)})}{CM}$$

Consequently,

$$\text{Sales volume (to reach a target profit before tax)} = \frac{(FC + TP \text{ (before tax)})}{CM}$$

Happy Daze has decided that it must earn a target profit of $100,000 or the owners will not want to continue their investment in the business. The question is how many games does the company have to sell to earn that amount of profit?

$$\text{Sales volume (to reach a target profit before tax)} = \frac{(\$35,000 + \$100,000)}{\$3.50}$$
$$= 38,572 \text{ units (rounded)}$$

Although Happy Daze must sell only 10,000 games to break even, the company must sell 38,572 games to reach a before-tax target profit of $100,000. In fact, once we know that Happy Daze's break-even point is 10,000 units, we can directly calculate the sales necessary to reach a target profit of $100,000, using the CM per unit. Because each additional unit sold (above the break-even point) will contribute $3.50 toward net income, Happy Daze must sell an additional 28,572 units $\left(\frac{\$100,000}{3.50}\right)$ to earn a profit of $100,000.

The multiple-product break-even and ABC break-even formulas can be modified in a similar fashion to solve for the sales necessary to reach a target profit. In a multiple-product environment:

$$\text{Sales volume (to reach target profit)} = \frac{(\text{Fixed costs} + \text{Target profit})}{\text{Weighted-average contribution margin per unit}}$$

Using ABC, we modify the formula as follows:

$$\text{Sales volume (to reach target profit)} = \frac{(\text{Fixed costs} + \text{Batch-level costs} + \text{Product-level costs} + \text{Target profit})}{\text{Weighted-average contribution margin per unit}}$$

The Impact of Taxes

The payment of income taxes also needs to be considered in the target profit formula. If Happy Daze sells 38,572 games and earns the projected $100,000 in target profit, the company still won't have $100,000 cash flow to distribute to the owners as dividends, because it must pay income tax on the profit. If we assume that the income tax rate for Happy Daze is 35 percent, the company will have to pay $35,000 in income tax ($100,000 × 35%) and will be left with after-tax profit of $65,000. The after-tax profit can be found by multiplying the before-tax profit by (1 − tax rate). Correspondingly, the before-tax profit equals the after-tax profit divided by (1 − tax rate):

$$\text{Before-tax profit} = \text{After-tax profit}/(1 - \text{tax rate})$$

If Happy Daze desires to earn an after-tax profit of $100,000, the company must earn a before-tax profit of $153,846 (rounded).

$$\text{Before-tax profit} = \$100,000/(1 - .35) = \$153,846$$

Modifying the before-tax target profit equation accordingly, we have

$$\text{Sales volume (to reach an after-tax target profit)} = \frac{(FC + \text{After-tax profit}/(1 - \text{tax rate}))}{CM}$$

Consequently, Happy Daze must sell 53,956 units in order to reach a before-tax profit of $153,846 and an after-tax profit of $100,000.

$$\text{Sales volume (to reach an after-tax target profit)} = \frac{(\$35,000 + \$153,846)}{\$3.50}$$
$$= 53,956 \text{ units}$$

This is confirmed in the following income statement for Happy Daze:

Sales (53,956 units)	$674,450
Less: Variable costs	485,604
Contribution margin	$188,846
Less: Fixed costs	35,000
Income before taxes	$153,846
Less: Income tax @ 35%	53,846
Net income after tax	$100,000

KEY CONCEPT

The payment of income taxes is an important variable in target profit and other CVP decisions.

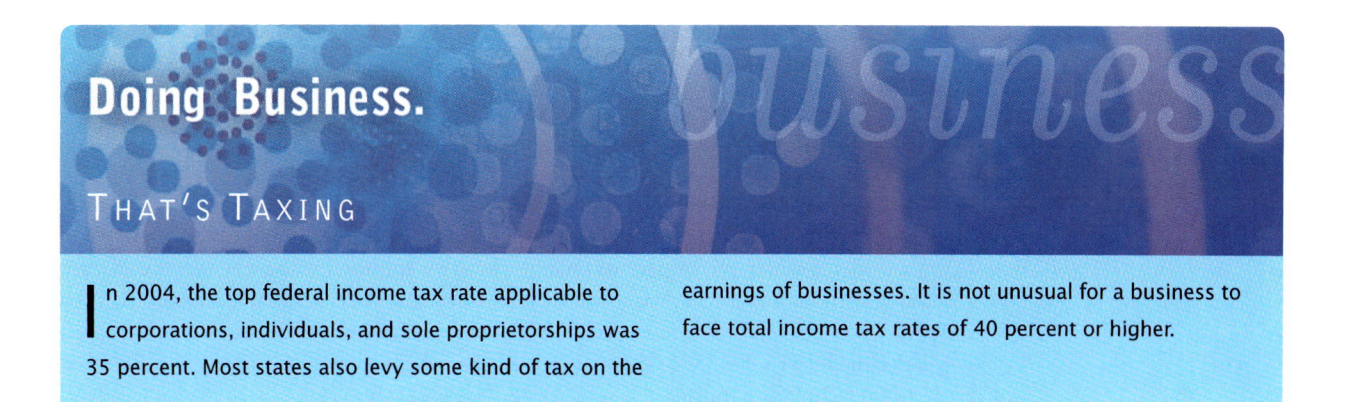

Doing Business.

THAT'S TAXING

In 2004, the top federal income tax rate applicable to corporations, individuals, and sole proprietorships was 35 percent. Most states also levy some kind of tax on the earnings of businesses. It is not unusual for a business to face total income tax rates of 40 percent or higher.

Assumptions of CVP Analysis

As in any form of analysis involving projections of the future, certain assumptions must be considered. The major assumptions are as follows:

1. The selling price is constant throughout the entire relevant range. In other words, we assume that the sales price of the product will not change as volume changes.

2. Costs are linear throughout the relevant range. As discussed in Chapter 5, although costs may behave in a curvilinear fashion, they can often be approximated by a linear relationship between cost and volume within the relevant range.

3. The sales mix used to calculate the weighted-average contribution margin is constant.

4. The amount of inventory is constant. In other words, the number of units produced is equal to the number of units sold.

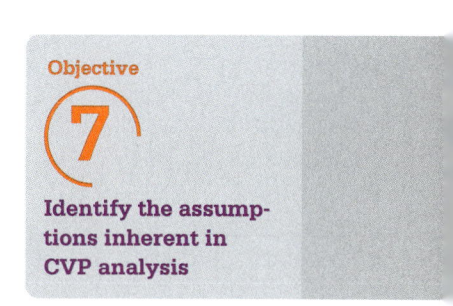

Objective 7

Identify the assumptions inherent in CVP analysis

Although some of these assumptions appear to be violated often in real business settings, the violations are usually minor and have little or no impact on management decisions. CVP analysis can still be considered valid and very useful in decision making.

Cost Structure and Operating Leverage

As mentioned in Chapter 5, cost structure refers to the relative proportion of fixed and variable costs in a company. Highly automated manufacturing companies with large investments in property, plant, and equipment are likely to have cost structures dominated by fixed costs. On the other hand, labor-intensive companies, such as home builders, are likely to have cost structures dominated by variable costs. Even companies in the same industry can have very different cost structures. A company's cost structure is important because it directly affects the sensitivity of a company's profits to changes in sales volume. Consider, for example, two companies that make the same product (furniture), with the same sales and same income. Company A is highly automated and uses state-of-the-art machinery to design, cut, and assemble its products. On the other hand, Company B is highly labor intensive and uses skilled craftspeople to cut and assemble its products. Contribution margin income statements for both companies are provided in Exhibit 6-4.

EXHIBIT 6-4 — Contribution Margin Ratio and Operating Leverage

	Company A	Company B
Sales	$200,000	$200,000
Less: Variable costs	40,000	80,000
Contribution margin	$160,000	$120,000
Less: Fixed costs	80,000	40,000
Net income	$ 80,000	$ 80,000
Contribution margin ratio	80%	60%
Operating leverage	2.0	1.5

Which company would you prefer to be? Although you might opt for Company A with its high level of automation and correspondingly higher contribution margin ratio relative to Company B, consider the impact of changes in sales volume on the net income of each company. Although *increasing* sales will benefit Company A more than Company B, what happens when sales *decline*? If sales decline by 10 percent ($20,000), the income of Company A will decline by $16,000 ($20,000 × 80%), whereas the income of Company B will decline by $12,000 ($20,000 × 60%).

A company with a cost structure characterized by a large proportion of fixed costs relative to variable costs will see wider fluctuations in income as sales increase and decrease than a company with more variable costs in its cost structure.

Operating Leverage

Operating leverage is a measure of the proportion of fixed costs in a company's cost structure and is used as an indicator of how sensitive profit is to changes in sales volume. A company with high fixed costs in relation to variable costs will have a high level of operating leverage. In this case, net income will be very sensitive to changes in sales volume. In other words, a small percentage increase in sales dollars will result in a large percentage increase in net income. On the other hand, a company with high variable costs in relation to fixed costs will have a low level of operating leverage, and income will not be as sensitive to changes in sales volume. Operating leverage is computed using the following formula:

$$\text{Operating leverage} = \frac{\text{Contribution margin}}{\text{Net income}}$$

In Exhibit 6-4, Company A has an operating leverage of 2.0 ($160,000/$80,000), whereas Company B has an operating leverage of 1.5 ($120,000/$80,000). What does this mean? When sales increase (decrease) by a given percentage, the income of Company A will increase (decrease) by 2 times that percentage increase (decrease), whereas the income of Company B will increase (decrease) by 1.5 times the percentage change in sales. When sales increase by 10 percent, the income of Company A will increase by 20 percent, or $16,000 ($80,000 × 20%). In other words, when sales of Company A increase to $220,000, income will increase to $96,000. The income of Company B will increase by 15 percent, or $12,000 ($80,000 × 15%), to a new income of $92,000. Likewise, when sales decrease by 10 percent, the income of Company A will decrease by 20 percent, whereas the income of Company B will decrease by 15 percent.

As summarized in Exhibit 6-5, when operating leverage is high, a change in sales results in large changes in profit. On the other hand, when operating leverage is low, a change in sales results in small changes in profits.

EXHIBIT 6-5 Operating Leverage and the Impact on Profit

	Operating Leverage	
	High	Low
Percent increase in profit with increase in sales	Large	Small
Percent increase in loss with decrease in sales	Large	Small

Unlike measures of contribution margin, operating leverage changes as sales change (see Exhibit 6-6).

EXHIBIT 6-6 Company B—Operating Leverage at Various Levels of Sales

	500 Units	1,000 Units	2,000 Units
Sales	$100,000	$200,000	$400,000
Less: Variable costs	40,000	80,000	160,000
Contribution margin	$60,000	$120,000	$240,000
Less: Fixed costs	40,000	40,000	40,000
Net income	$20,000	$80,000	$200,000
Operating leverage	$\dfrac{\$60,000}{\$20,000} = 3.0$	$\dfrac{\$120,000}{\$80,000} = 1.5$	$\dfrac{\$240,000}{\$200,000} = 1.2$

At a sales level of 1,000 units ($200,000), Company B's operating leverage is 1.5. A 10 percent increase in sales increases net income by 15 percent. At a sales level of 500 units, operating leverage increases to 3.0, and a 10 percent increase in sales will increase net income by 30 percent (3 × 10%). At a sales level of 2,000 units, operating leverage is reduced to 1.2, and a 10 percent increase in sales will increase income by 12 percent.

As a company gets closer and closer to the break-even point, operating leverage will continue to increase, and income will be very sensitive to changes in sales. For example, when Company B sells 334 units (see Exhibit 6-7), contribution margin is equal to $40,080, income is equal to $80, and operating leverage is equal to 501 ($40,080/$80). A 10 percent increase in sales at this point will increase net income by 5,010 percent!

KEY CONCEPT

A company operating near the break-even point will have a high level of operating leverage, and income will be very sensitive to changes in sales volume.

EXHIBIT 6-7 — Company B—Operating near the Break-even Point

Sales (334 units)	$66,800
Less: Variable costs	26,720
Contribution margin	$40,080
Less: Fixed costs	40,000
Net income	$ 80
Operating leverage	$\frac{\$40,080}{\$80} = 501$

Understanding the concepts of contribution margin and operating leverage and how they are used in CVP analysis are very important in managerial decision making. Using these tools, managers can quickly estimate the impact on net income of changes in cost, sales volume, and price.

Variable Costing for Decision Making

Objective 8

Identify the differences between variable costing and absorption costing and recognize the benefits of using variable costing for decision making

In Chapter 2, a system of product costing was introduced in which all manufacturing costs, fixed and variable, were treated as product costs. Product costs included direct materials, direct labor, and all manufacturing overhead (both fixed and variable). You will recall that product costs attach to the product and are expensed only when the product is sold. On the other hand, selling and administrative costs (period costs) are expensed immediately in the period in which they are incurred. Commonly called **absorption costing,** or **full costing,** this method is required for both external financial statements prepared under generally accepted accounting principles (GAAP) and for income tax reporting.

On the other hand, **variable costing,** or **direct costing,** treats only variable production costs (direct material, direct labor, and variable manufacturing overhead) as product costs, whereas fixed manufacturing overhead is treated as a period cost (along with selling, general and administrative costs). Variable costing is more consistent with CVP's focus on differentiating fixed from variable costs and provides useful information for internal decision making that is often not apparent when using absorption costing.

Exhibit 6-8 provides a summary of the two costing methods. As you can see, *the only difference between absorption and variable costing is the treatment of fixed overhead.* Under absorption costing, fixed overhead is treated as a product cost, added to the cost of the product and expensed only when the product is sold (as cost of goods sold). Under variable costing, fixed

EXHIBIT 6-8 — Absorption and Variable Costing

Absorption Costing		Variable Costing	
Product Costs	**Period Costs**	**Product Costs**	**Period Costs**
Direct materials		Direct materials	
Direct labor	Selling, general and administrative costs	Direct labor	Selling, general and administrative costs
Variable overhead		Variable overhead	
Fixed overhead			Fixed overhead

overhead is treated as a period cost and is expensed as incurred. The impact of this difference on reported income becomes evident when a company's production and sales are different (units produced are greater than units sold or units sold are greater than units produced).

Because absorption costing treats fixed overhead as a product cost, if units of production remain unsold at year-end, fixed overhead remains attached to those units and is included on the balance sheet as an asset (the cost of inventory). Using variable costing, all fixed manufacturing overhead is expensed each period, regardless of the level of production or sales. Consequently, when production is greater than sales and inventories increase, absorption costing will result in higher net income than will variable costing.

Let's look at a simple example in which a company produces 100,000 units each year. The cost of each unit includes direct material of $0.30, direct labor of $0.35, and variable overhead of $0.10 per unit. In addition, fixed manufacturing overhead costs of $30,000 are incurred. Variable selling and administrative costs are $0.05 per unit sold, and fixed selling and administrative costs are equal to $10,000. The selling price of one unit is $2. The cost of one unit of product under absorption and variable costing is calculated as follows:

Product Costs

Absorption Costing		Variable Costing	
Direct material	$0.30	Direct material	$0.30
Direct labor	0.35	Direct labor	0.35
Variable overhead	0.10	Variable overhead	0.10
Fixed overhead	0.30		
Total per unit	$1.05	Total per unit	$0.75

The only difference between the two methods is $0.30 of fixed overhead $\left(\frac{\$30,000}{\$100,000 \text{ units}}\right)$, which is treated as a product cost under absorption costing and a period cost under variable costing. If all 100,000 units are sold in year 1, how much income is reported under each method?

Under absorption costing, fixed manufacturing costs are expensed as part of cost of goods sold. Under variable costing, fixed manufacturing overhead costs are deducted as a fixed period cost. Regardless, when all units produced are sold, the net income reported under each method would be the same.

Year 1 Comparison of Absorption and Variable Costing

Absorption Costing		Variable Costing	
Sales	$200,000	Sales	$200,000
Less: Cost of goods sold	105,000	Less: Variable costs	80,000
Gross profit	$ 95,000	Contribution margin	$120,000
Less: S&A costs	15,000	Less: Fixed costs	40,000
Net income	$ 80,000	Net income	$ 80,000

Assume that in year 2, 100,000 units are produced but only 80,000 units are sold. In this case, the variable-costing method would expense the entire $30,000 of fixed manufacturing overhead as a period cost, whereas the absorption method would expense only $24,000 (80,000 units sold × $0.30 per unit). When production exceeds sales, absorption costing will report higher net income than will variable costing. Part of the $30,000 of fixed overhead (20,000 units × $0.30 per unit, or $6,000) remains in inventory until those units are sold.

Year 2 (80,000 units sold)

Absorption Costing		Variable Costing	
Sales	$160,000	Sales	$160,000
Less: Cost of goods sold*	84,000	Less: Variable costs	64,000
Gross profit	$ 76,000	Contribution margin	$ 96,000
Less: S&A costs	14,000	Less: Fixed costs†	40,000
Net income	$ 62,000	Net income	$ 56,000

*Cost of goods sold includes $24,000 (80,000 × $0.30) of fixed manufacturing overhead.
†Fixed costs include $30,000 of fixed manufacturing overhead.

Assume that in year 3, 100,000 units are produced and 120,000 units are sold. (The 20,000 remaining units from year 2 are sold.) In this case, under variable costing, $30,000 of fixed manufacturing overhead would continue to be expensed as a period cost. Under absorption costing, the $30,000 would get expensed plus an extra $6,000 related to the 20,000 units produced last year and sold this year (20,000 units × $0.30 per unit = $6,000). When units sold exceed units produced, variable costing will report higher net income than will absorption costing.

Year 3 (120,000 units sold)

Absorption Costing		Variable Costing	
Sales	$240,000	Sales	$240,000
Less: Cost of goods sold*	126,000	Less: Variable costs	96,000
Gross profit	$114,000	Contribution margin	$144,000
Less: S&A costs	16,000	Less: Fixed costs†	40,000
Net income	$ 98,000	Net income	$104,000

*Cost of goods sold includes $36,000 (120,000 × $0.30) of fixed manufacturing overhead.
†Fixed costs include $30,000 of fixed manufacturing overhead.

To summarize the three rules:

1. When units sold equal units produced, net income is the same under both costing methods.

2. When units produced exceed units sold, absorption costing will report higher net income than will variable costing.

3. When units sold exceed units produced, variable costing will report higher net income than will absorption costing.

The use of absorption costing for internal decision making can result in less than optimal decisions. For example, consider the case of the unemployed executive who offered his services to a manufacturing company for only $1 per year in salary and a bonus equal to 50 percent of any increase in net income generated for the year. Reviewing the absorption costing income statement for the previous year, he learned that although 10,000 units of product were produced and sold, the company had the capacity to produce 20,000 units. In addition, variable production costs were $40 per unit, variable selling and administrative costs were $10 per unit sold, fixed manufacturing overhead costs were equal to $300,000 ($30 per unit produced), and fixed selling and administrative costs were equal to $100,000. As shown here, last year's net income was $100,000.

Absorption Costing Income (10,000 units produced)

Sales (10,000 units)	$1,000,000
Less: Cost of goods sold*	700,000
Gross profit	$ 300,000
Less: S&A costs	200,000
Net income	$ 100,000

*Includes $300,000 (10,000 units × $30) of fixed manufacturing overhead.

By increasing production to 20,000 units, the per unit allocation of fixed manufacturing overhead is reduced to $15 $\left(\frac{\$300,000}{20,000 \text{ units}} = \$15\right)$. Remember that under absorption costing, fixed overhead is a product cost and is expensed only when the product is sold. Therefore, only $150,000 of fixed overhead costs will be expensed. The remaining $150,000 of fixed manufacturing overhead costs is included in inventory and is reported as an asset on the balance sheet. The cost of goods sold is reduced to $550,000, and net income is increased by $150,000, to $250,000. The manager is entitled to a bonus of $75,000, whereas the company is saddled with 10,000 units of unsold inventory and the attendant costs of storing and insuring it.

Absorption Costing Income (20,000 units produced)

Sales (10,000 units)	$1,000,000
Less: Cost of goods sold*	550,000
Gross profit	$ 450,000
Less: S&A costs	200,000
Net income	$ 250,000

*Includes $150,000 (10,000 units × $15) of fixed costs.

KEY CONCEPT

Variable costing is consistent with CVP's focus on differentiating fixed from variable costs and provides useful decision-making information that is often not apparent when using absorption costing.

If income had been measured using a variable-costing approach, net income would be the same each year, and the manager would not be able to pull off this scheme. Problems like these are minimized in a just-in-time (JIT) environment, in which inventory levels are minimized and companies strive to produce only enough product to meet demand.

THE ETHICS OF BUSINESS
How to Make a Profit!

Most people believe that companies make profit by selling products at prices that exceed the costs to produce those products. Without a doubt, that is the only viable long-term strategy. However, that is not the way Gillette made some of its profits from 1996 to 1999. During those years the company's finished goods inventory swelled by more than 40 percent to almost $1.3 billion, while its sales remained virtually flat at $6.9 billion per year. So, what was the trick and how did this enable the company to "earn" profits? By following generally accepted accounting principles and using absorption costing to accumulate and report inventory costs the company was able to make "paper profits." This peculiar result occurs when a company's production exceeds its sales. In essence, a company is able to defer the costs associated with fixed manufacturing overhead by recording the costs as part of finished goods inventory on the balance sheet. Only when those products are ultimately sold will those costs be shown on the income statement. And, that is exactly what Gillette admitted would happen after it announced plans to cut its inventory. The bottom line was simple: Gillette produced more product than it needed to meet current customer orders to create paper profits. All the while, the company knew there would be a day of reckoning when that extra inventory would be sold and all of those fixed manufacturing overhead costs would be deducted from income.

It's Your Choice—Think about the decisions that Gillette made from 1996 to 1999 and consider how those decisions resulted in what some investors may have believed to be profits. Had production exceeded sales for a year, there probably would not be much of a story here, but the fact that production exceeded sales for three years and by such a large amount suggests a conscious decision to inflate profits. Did Gillette act unethically by deciding to produce more product than it could sell? Did the company's decisions harm anyone? If so, how?

Summary of Key Concepts

- *The contribution margin income statement is structured to emphasize cost behavior as opposed to cost function. (p. 176)*
- *For every unit change in sales, contribution margin will increase or decrease by the contribution margin per unit multiplied by the increase or decrease in sales volume. (p. 178)*
- *The contribution margin per unit and the contribution margin ratio will remain constant as long as sales vary in direct proportion to volume. (p. 179)*
- *For every dollar change in sales, contribution margin will increase or decrease by the contribution margin ratio multiplied by the increase or decrease in sales dollars. (p. 179)*
- *The payment of income taxes is an important variable in target profit and other CVP decisions. (p. 191)*
- *A company operating near the break-even point will have a high level of operating leverage, and income will be very sensitive to changes in sales volume. (p. 194)*
- *Variable costing is consistent with CVP's focus on differentiating fixed from variable costs and provides useful decision-making information that is often not apparent when using absorption costing. (p. 197)*

Key Definitions

Cost-volume-profit (CVP) analysis A tool that focuses on the relationship between a company's profits and (1) the prices of products or services, (2) the volume of products or services, (3) the per unit variable costs, (4) the total fixed costs, and (5) the mix of products or services produced (p. 176)

Gross profit The difference between sales and cost of goods sold (p. 176)

Contribution margin per unit The sales price per unit of product less all variable costs to produce and to sell the unit of product; used to calculate the change in contribution margin resulting from a change in unit sales (p. 177)

Contribution margin ratio The contribution margin divided by sales; used to calculate the change in contribution margin resulting from a dollar change in sales (p. 179)

Break-even point The level of sales at which contribution margin just covers fixed costs and net income is equal to zero (p. 185)

Operating leverage The contribution margin divided by net income; used as an indicator of how sensitive net income is to the change in sales (p. 192)

Absorption (full) costing A method of costing in which product costs include direct material, direct labor, and fixed and variable overhead; required for external financial statements and for income tax reporting (p. 194)

Variable (direct) costing A method of costing in which product costs include direct material, direct labor, and variable overhead; fixed overhead is treated as a period cost; consistent with CVP's focus on cost behavior (p. 194)

Multiple Choice

1. Sales of Quickie Computers are down, and management has planned to increase salespersons' commissions on sales by 10 percent in hopes of raising sales volume by 10 percent. What effect should this change have?
   a. Sales price will increase.
   b. Sales price will decrease.
   c. Variable costs will increase.
   d. Variable costs will decrease.

2. Which of the following items is not subtracted from sales revenue to arrive at contribution margin on a contribution margin income statement?
   a. Variable manufacturing costs
   b. Sales commissions paid only on items that are sold
   c. Variable sales and administrative expenses
   d. Fixed manufacturing overhead

3. The contribution margin income statement is structured in such a way as to emphasize:
   a. cost functionality.
   b. cost behavior.
   c. organizational efficiency.
   d. cost drivers.

4. If a company has a positive contribution margin but net income is low or negative, what are some ways of increasing net income?
   a. Increase sales price.
   b. Increase sales volume.
   c. Decrease variable costs.
   d. All of the above are ways to increase net income.

5. What impact will selling a product with a sales price of $25 and a contribution margin of $17 have on a company's net income? Ignore income taxes.
   a. Net income will increase by $8.
   b. Net income will increase by $25.
   c. Net income will increase by $17.
   d. Net income will increase by an amount that cannot be determined from the information given.

6. The following data relate to a small specialty lightbulb sold by Walt Zarnoch's Lighting, Inc.:

Sales price	$ 4.50 per unit
Variable costs	$ 3.25 per unit
Fixed costs	$ 5,000
Units sold	20,000

   If one more unit is sold, net income will:
   a. increase by $4.50.
   b. increase by $1.25.
   c. decrease by $3.25.
   d. decrease by $3.50.

7. Which of the following factors is not directly relevant to a company that is evaluating "what-if" scenarios to examine the impact of options on the company's financial statements?
   a. Changes in a product's sales price
   b. Advertising expenses that will not change
   c. Increases in a product's variable manufacturing costs
   d. The quantity of product that is expected to sell

8. Which of the following statements is correct as it relates to a company that sells multiple products?
   a. CVP analysis cannot be used.
   b. Contribution margin is based on sales mix.
   c. CVP analysis is much easier to use.
   d. The break-even point remains the same even if sales mix changes.

9. Hoagland Company has the following product information:

Sales price	$ 6.00 per unit
Variable costs	$ 2.00 per unit
Fixed costs	$ 12,000
Units sold	20,000

   What is the break-even point in sales dollars?
   a. $12,000
   b. $15,000
   c. $18,000
   d. $21,000

10. Greer Corp. has the following product information:

Sales price	$ 6.00 per unit
Contribution margin ratio	35%
Fixed costs	$ 42,000

What is the break-even point in units?
a. 7,000
b. 2,471
c. 20,000
d. 18,850

11. Scuffy Company has the following product information:

Sales price	$ 7.25 per unit
Variable costs	$ 2.25 per unit
Fixed costs	$ 10,000

What is the break-even point in units?
a. 1,380
b. 2,000
c. 4,445
d. 5,000

12. Which of the following is a correct form of the break-even equation when using activity-based costing?
a. Break-even ($) = (Fixed costs + Batch-level costs)/Contribution margin per unit
b. Break-even (units) = (Fixed costs + Facility-level costs)/Contribution margin per unit
c. Break-even ($) = (Fixed costs + Batch-level costs + Product-level costs)/Contribution margin per unit
d. Break-even (units) = (Fixed costs + Batch-level costs + Product-level costs)/Contribution margin per unit

13. John Abner Enterprises has a contribution margin ratio of 80 percent and fixed costs of $20,000. What would sales have to be for an after-tax net income of $60,000? The company is in the 40 percent tax bracket.
a. $80,000
b. $100,000
c. $120,000
d. $150,000

14. Which of the following is not an assumption of cost-volume-profit analysis?
a. Selling prices change only at the end of the month.
b. Costs can be thought of as fitting a linear function within the relevant range.
c. Sales mix is constant.
d. Inventory levels do not change.

15. Emily Sand Corp. has the following information available regarding last year's operations:

Sales (150,000 units)	$300,000
Variable costs	100,000
Contribution margin	$200,000
Fixed costs	100,000
Net income	$100,000

The company's operating leverage was:
a. 1.25
b. 1.67
c. 2.00
d. 2.25

16. Murdock's Munchies has the following cost information:

Variable S&A costs	$ 2.00 per unit
Direct materials	$ 7.50 per unit
Variable overhead	$ 2.25 per unit
Direct labor	$ 1.25 per unit
Fixed S&A costs	$ 50,000
Fixed overhead	$ 75,000

If 25,000 units are produced and sold at a price of $20, what is the net income under variable costing and absorption costing, respectively?
a. $0; $0
b. $125,000; $50,000
c. $50,000; $50,000
d. $125,000; $125,000

17. Which of the following statements is correct?
a. When an equal number of units are produced and sold, net income is significantly higher under absorption costing than variable costing.
b. When an equal number of units are produced and sold, net income is higher under variable costing than absorption costing.
c. When an equal number of units are produced and sold, net income is marginally higher under absorption costing than variable costing.
d. When an equal number of units are produced and sold, net income under absorption costing is the same as net income under variable costing.

Concept Questions

18. *(Objective 1)* Describe the primary difference between traditional income statements and contribution margin income statements.
19. *(Objective 1)* What happens to the contribution margin when fixed expenses decrease and variable costs per unit remain constant?
20. *(Objective 2)* Define the term *contribution margin*.
21. *(Objective 3)* If the total contribution margin decreases by a given amount, what will be the effect on income?
22. *(Objective 4)* Describe the formula for computing the break-even point in sales dollars and units.
23. *(Objective 4)* How might a company decrease its break-even point?
24. *(Objective 5)* What additional costs must be considered in computing the break-even point for a company that uses activity-based costing?
25. *(Objective 6)* How do income taxes affect CVP computations?
26. *(Objective 8)* What is the primary difference between absorption costing and variable costing?
27. *(Objective 8)* If a company uses absorption costing to prepare its financial statements, is it possible to increase net income without increasing sales or decreasing expenses? How?

Exercises

28. Companies who wish to distribute their income statements to outside parties such as banks must prepare those statements using the traditional income statement format. These same companies may also prepare contribution margin income statements to more fully understand their costs. The following terms are commonly used in describing contribution margin income statements and related topics.

Gross profit	Decrease
Contribution margin	Fixed costs
Net income	Contribution margin ratio
Variable costs	Increase

Required

Choose the term from the list above that most appropriately completes the following statements.
  a. Once a company has paid all of its fixed costs, net income increases in an amount equal to _____ for each unit sold to customers.
  b. When production and sales are equal, whether a company prepares a traditional income statement or a contribution margin income statement, two numbers do not change. One of these is sales and the other is _____.
  c. _____, the difference between sales and cost of goods sold, is not reported on the contribution margin income statement.
  d. For every unit sold, contribution margin will _____ in total.
  e. The _____ is computed by dividing the contribution margin by sales dollars.
  f. Of these two cost categories, only _____ increases and decreases contribution margin.
  g. If a company is unable to increase sales or _____ variable costs, the company can increase net income by reducing _____.

29. Eric Ziegler started a lawn mowing service in high school. He currently prices his lawn mowing service at $35 per yard. He estimates that variable expenses related to gasoline, supplies, and depreciation on his equipment total $21 per yard.

Required

If Eric wants to increase his price by 40 percent, how many fewer yards can he mow before his net income decreases?

30. Last year, Mayes Company had a contribution margin of 30 percent. This year, fixed expenses are expected to remain at $120,000, and sales are expected to be $550,000, which is 10 percent higher than last year.

Required

What must the contribution margin ratio be if the company wants to increase net income by $15,000 this year?

31. Katie and Holly founded Hokies Plumbing Company after graduating from college. They wanted to be competitive so they set their rate for house calls at a modest $100. After paying the company's gas and other variable costs of $60, the women thought there would be enough profit. Because they were ready to live life a bit, they set their salaries at $100,000 each. There were no other fixed costs at all.

Required

Calculate the number of house calls that Hokies Plumbing must make to break even.

32. Callahan's Calabash Seafood Restaurant is a family-owned business started by Marc Callahan over 10 years ago. Callahan's is only open Thursday through Saturday and only serves dinner. In the last several months, Marc has seen a drop off in business. Just last month the restaurant broke even. Marc looked over the records and saw that the restaurant served 1,000 meals (variable cost is $10 per meal) and paid other bills totaling $25,000. He looked over the bills and realized that they all represented fixed costs. The restaurant currently breaks even at 1,000 meals.

Required

Calculate Callahan's average selling price for a meal.

33. Lincoln Company sells logs for an average of $18 per log. The company's president, Abraham, estimates the variable manufacturing and selling costs total $6 per log. Logging operations require substantial investments in equipment so fixed costs are quite high and total $108,000 per month. Abraham is considering making an investment in a new piece of logging equipment that will increase monthly fixed costs by $12,000.

Required

Assist Abraham by calculating the number of additional logs that must be sold to break even after considering the new equipment.

✓ Logs that must be sold to break even before the new equipment is purchased: 9,000

34. Kim Johnson's company produces two well-known products, Glide Magic and Slide Magic. Glide Magic accounts for 60 percent of her sales and Slide Magic accounts for the rest. Glide currently sells for $16 per tube and has variable manufacturing and selling costs of $8. Slide sells for just $12 and has variable costs of $9 per tube. Kim's company has total fixed costs of $36,000.

Required

Calculate the total number of tubes that must be sold for Kim's company to break even.

✓ Weighted average CM for one unit of Glide Magic: $4.80

35. Donald Tweedt started a company to produce and distribute natural fertilizers. Donald's company sells two fertilizers that are wildly popular: green fertilizer and compost fertilizer. Green fertilizer, the most popular among environmentally minded consumers, commands the highest price and sells for $16 per 30-pound bag. Green fertilizer also requires additional processing and includes environmentally friendly ingredients that increase its variable costs to $10 per bag. Compost fertilizer sells for $12 and has easily acquired ingredients that require no special processing. It has variable costs of $8 per bag. Tweedt's total fixed costs are $35,000. After some aggressive marketing efforts, Tweedt has been able to drive consumer demand to be equal for each fertilizer.

Required

Calculate the bags of green fertilizer that will be sold at break-even.

✓ Weighted average CM for one bag of green fertilizer: $3.00

36. Hatteras Hatters produces a variety of hats for beachgoers. Hatteras produces hats in batches and currently produces six batches per year. The company's controller recently implemented an activity-based costing system and would like to calculate break-even sales for the owner under this new costing system. She has prepared the following representative data:

Average hat sales price	$	10.00
Direct materials	$	2.50
Direct labor	$	1.75
Variable overhead	$	0.75
Setup cost (per batch)	$	1,000
Fixed costs	$	29,000

Required

Calculate the number of hats Hatteras Hatters must sell to break even.

37. Lockwood Company currently sells its deadbolt locks for $30 each. The locks have a variable cost of $10, and the company's annual fixed costs are $150,000. The company's tax rate is 40 percent.

Required

Calculate the number of locks that must be sold to earn an after-tax profit of $24,000.

38. Kingman Corp. has long been concerned with maintaining a solid annual profit. The company sells a line of fire extinguishers that are perfect for homeowners for an average of $10 each. The company has perfected its production process and now produces extinguishers with a variable cost of $4 per extinguisher. Kingman's annual fixed costs are $105,000.

Required

Calculate the number of extinguishers Kingman must sell to earn a 10 percent return on sales.

39. Like many forms of analysis, cost-volume-profit (CVP) analysis must make assumptions so that calculations can be made. The following statements *inaccurately* describe the basic assumptions of CVP analysis.
    a. The selling price varies throughout most of the relevant range. In other words, we assume that the sales price of the product changes somewhat as volume changes.
    b. Costs are curvilinear. Although costs may behave in a linear fashion, they can be approximated by a curvilinear or quadratic relationship between cost and volume within the relevant range.
    c. The sales mix used to calculate the contribution margin is proportional to the product mix.
    d. The amount of inventory varies as sales occur. In other words, the number of units produced does not equal the numbers of units sold.

Required

Review these statements and then rewrite them in their correct form.

40. Yankee Doodle Dandy Candy Company manufactures a single product, an awesome chocolate bar. Last year, the company produced 4,000 bars and sold 3,500 of them. They had no candy bars at the beginning of the year. The company has the following costs:

Variable costs per unit:		
Production	$	4.00
Selling and administrative	$	1.00
Fixed costs in total:		
Production	$	12,000
Selling and administrative	$	8,000

Required

Calculate the unit product cost assuming that the company uses variable costing.

41. Refer to exercise 40.

Required

Calculate the unit product cost assuming that the company uses absorption costing.

LO 8

✓ Net income: $2,000

42. Kristi Bostock started Bostock Boutique three years ago. Her business has grown handsomely and she now produces and sells thousands of items each year. Selected operational and financial data are shown below.

Units in beginning inventory	0
Units produced	20,000
Units sold	19,000
Selling price per unit	$ 100
Variable costs per unit:	
Direct materials	$ 12.00
Direct labor	25.00
Manufacturing overhead	3.00
Selling and administrative	2.00
Fixed costs in total:	
Manufacturing overhead	$ 500,000
Selling and administrative	$ 600,000

Required

Calculate Bostock Boutique's net income assuming that the company uses variable costing.

Problems

LO 2 4

EXCEL

43. Don Waller and Company sells canisters of three mosquito repellant products: Citronella, DEET, and Mean Green. The company has annual fixed costs of $260,000. Last year, the company sold 5,000 canisters of its mosquito repellant in the ratio of 1:2:2. Waller's accounting department has compiled the following data related to the three mosquito repellants:

	Citronella	DEET	Mean Green
Price per canister	$ 11.00	$ 15.00	$ 17.00
Variable costs per canister	6.00	12.00	16.00

Required

A. Calculate the total number of canisters that must be sold for the company to break even.
B. Calculate the number of canisters of Citronella, DEET, and Mean Green that must be sold to break even.
C. How might Don Waller and Company reduce its break-even point?

LO 2 3 4 6

44. ZIA Motors is a small automobile manufacturer. Chris Rickard, the company's president, is currently evaluating the company's performance and is considering options that might be effective at increasing ZIA's profitability. The company's controller, Holly Smith, has

prepared the following cost and expense estimates for next year based on a sales forecast of $3,000,000.

Direct materials	$ 800,000
Direct labor	700,000
Factory overhead	750,000
Selling expenses	300,000
Other administrative expenses	100,000
	$ 2,650,000

After Chris received and reviewed the cost and expense estimates, he realized that Holly had given him all the data without breaking it out into its fixed and variable components. He called her and she told him the following: "Factory overhead and selling expenses are 40 percent variable, but other administrative expenses are 30 percent variable."

Required

A. How much revenue must ZIA generate to break even?
B. Chris Rickard has set a target profit of $700,000 for next year. How much revenue must ZIA generate to achieve Chris's goal?

45. Gigi LeBlanc founded a company to produce a special bicycle suspension system several years ago after her son, who worked for a bicycle delivery service, was hurt in a riding accident. The market's response has been surprisingly favorable to the company's new suspension system. Riders report feeling as though they experience fewer "unpredictable" bumps than with traditional suspension systems. Gigi made an initial investment of $100,000 and has set a target of earning a 30 percent return on her investment. Gigi expects her company to sell approximately 10,000 suspension systems in the coming year. Based on this level of activity, variable manufacturing costs will be $5 for each suspension system. Fixed selling and administrative expenses will be $2 per system and other fixed costs will be $1 per system.

Required

A. Calculate the sales price that Gigi LeBlanc's company must charge for a suspension system if she is to earn a 30 percent return on her investment.
B. Calculate the company's break-even point.
C. Assuming Gigi's company maintains the current activity level, how can she increase her return on investment to 35 percent?

✓ Break-even: 5,000

46. Hacker Aggregates mines and distributes various types of rocks. Most of the company's rock is sold to contractors who use the product in highway construction projects. Treva Hacker, company president, believes that the company needs to advertise to increase sales. She has proposed a plan to the other managers that Hacker Aggregates spend $100,000 on a targeted advertising campaign. The company currently sells 25,000 tons of aggregate for total revenue of $5,000,000. Other data related to the company's production and operational costs are shown below.

✓ CM ratio: 65%

Direct labor	$1,500,000
Variable production overhead	200,000
Fixed production overhead	350,000
Selling and administrative expenses:	
Variable	50,000
Fixed	300,000

Required

A. Compute the break-even point in units (i.e., tons) for Hacker Aggregates.
B. Compute the contribution margin ratio for Hacker Aggregates.
C. If Treva decides to spend $100,000 on advertising and the company expects the advertising to increase sales by $200,000, should the company increase the advertising? Why?

47. Lauren Tarson and Michele Progransky opened Top Drawer Optical seven years ago with the goal of producing fashionable and affordable eyewear. Tarson and Progransky have been very pleased with their revenue growth. One particular design, available in plastic and metal, has become one of the company's best sellers. The following data relate to this design:

	Plastic Frames	Metal Frames
Sales price	$ 60.00	$ 80.00
Direct materials	20.00	18.00
Direct labor	13.50	13.50
Variable overhead	6.50	8.50
Budgeted unit sales	10,000	30,000

Currently, the company produces exactly as many frames as it can sell. Therefore, it has no opportunity to substitute a more expensive frame for a less expensive one. Top Drawer Optical's annual fixed costs are currently $1,225,000.

Required

Each of the following questions relates to an *independent* situation.
A. Calculate the total number of frames that Top Drawer Optical needs to produce and to sell to break even.
B. Calculate the total number of frames that Top Drawer Optical needs to produce and sell to break even if budgeted direct material costs for plastic frames decrease by $10 and annual fixed costs increase by $12,500 for depreciation of a new production machine.
C. Tarson and Progransky have been able to reduce the company's fixed costs by eliminating certain unnecessary expenditures and downsizing supervisory personnel. Now, the company's fixed costs are $1,122,000. Calculate the number of frames that Top Drawer Optical needs to produce and sell to break even if the company sales mix changes to 35 percent plastic frames and 65 percent metal frames.

48. Matthew Hagen started his company, The Sign of Things to Come, three years ago after graduating from Upper State University. While earning his engineering degree, Matthew became intrigued by all of the neon signs he saw at bars and taverns around the university. Few of his friends were surprised to see him start a neon sign company after leaving school. Matthew is currently considering the introduction of a new custom neon signage product that he believes will sell like hotcakes. In fact, he is estimating that the company will sell 7,000 of the signs. The signs are expected to sell for $75 and require variable costs of $25. The Sign of Things to Come has annual fixed costs of $300,000.

Required

A. How many signs must be sold to break even?
B. How many signs must be sold to earn a profit of $15,000?
C. If 7,000 signs are sold, how much profit will The Sign of Things to Come earn?
D. What would be the break-even point if the sales price decreased by 20 percent? Round your answer to the next highest number.
E. What would be the break-even point if variable costs per sign decreased by 40 percent?
F. What would be the break-even point if fixed costs increased by $50,000?

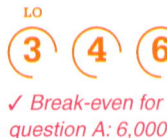

49. Happy Daze Game Co. produces a wildly popular board game called Stump Me! The company is known for both its progressive and interesting board games and its willingness to embrace nontraditional business techniques. Recently, the company's controller, Renee McKim, suggested to the president that she accumulate data based on an activity-based costing system in addition to the costs that are currently accumulated based on the company's traditional costing system. The president gave her the go ahead and she has accumulated the following data related to Stump Me!

LO 5

✓ Break-even for question A: 10,500

Sales price	$	13.50
Variable costs per unit:		
Direct material		3.50
Direct labor		2.50
Variable overhead		3.50
Fixed costs:		
Setup costs		11,000
Testing costs		6,000
Other fixed costs		25,000

The company's production manager told Renee that the game requires a machine setup each time the plant produces a batch of the games. Currently, the company produces 10 batches each year. Also, he told her that the games are tested and verified before new editions are released to the public. This year he expects that Stump Me! will require 200 testing hours. He also told her that this testing is unique and distinct to Stump Me! Other games require different types of testing.

Required
  A. Compute break-even, using the conventional break-even formula.
  B. Compute break-even, using the ABC break-even formula.
  C. Explain the difference between the break-even analysis from questions A and B.

50. HD Inc. produces a variety of products for the computing industry. CD burners are among its most popular products. The company's controller, Katie Jergens, spoke to the company's president at a meeting last week and told her that the company was doing well, but that the financial picture depended on how product costs and net income were calculated. The president did not realize that the company had an option on how to calculate either of these numbers, so she asked Katie to prepare some information and be ready to meet with her to talk more about this. In preparing for the meeting, Katie accumulated the following data:

LO 8

✓ Absorption cost per unit: $98

Units produced	100,000
Units sold	95,000
Fixed manufacturing overhead	$ 300,000
Direct material per unit	55.00
Direct labor per unit	25.00
Variable manufacturing overhead per unit	15.00

Required

A. Compute the cost per unit using absorption costing.
B. Compute the cost per unit using variable costing.
C. Compute the difference in net income between the two methods. Which costing method results in a higher net income?
D. Assume that production was 80,000 units and sales were 100,000 units. What would be the difference in net income between the two methods? Which costing method shows the greater net income?
E. Assume that production was 100,000 units and sales were 100,000 units. What would be the difference in net income between the two methods?
F. Which method is required by GAAP?

51. Oliver Inc. produces an oak rocking chair that is designed to ease back problems. The chairs sell for $200 each. Results from last year's operations are as follows:

✓ Variable cost per unit: $105

Inventory and production data:	
Units in beginning inventory	0
Units produced during the year	20,000
Units sold during the year	18,000
Variable costs (unit):	
Direct materials	$ 70.00
Direct labor	20.00
Variable manufacturing overhead	15.00
Variable selling and administrative	10.00
Fixed costs:	
Fixed manufacturing overhead	$ 500,000
Fixed selling and administrative	530,000

Required

A. Compute the unit product cost for one rocking chair assuming the company uses variable costing.
B. Prepare an income statement based on variable costing.
C. Compute the unit product cost for one rocking chair assuming the company uses absorption costing.
D. Prepare an income statement based on absorption costing.
E. Compare the two income statements. What causes the net incomes to differ?
F. If the company produced 18,000 chairs and sold 20,000 chairs (assume that the additional 2,000 chairs were in beginning inventory), what would be the impact on the two income statements? In other words, which method provides the higher net income?

52. Jaclyn Rourke is the president and chief executive officer of Parker Company. Parker is a family-owned business that is one of the oldest watch producers in the United States. The last several years have been very difficult for Parker primarily because of the increasing price pressures brought to bear by foreign competition. At this point, Parker hopes to stay in business, but the company's 120-year history does not ensure current competitiveness. Jaclyn asked the company's accounting manager to accumulate certain operational and financial data from last year. These data are shown below:

Beginning inventory (units)	25,000
Units produced	90,000
Units sold	95,000
Direct material per unit	$ 15.00
Direct labor per unit	5.00
Variable manufacturing overhead per unit	10.00
Fixed manufacturing overhead	100,000

Required

A. Jaclyn is going to the company's primary bank to negotiate a line of credit and wants to show the maximum amount of income without actually changing last year's results. What costing method of inventory (variable or absorption) should she choose? Why?
B. If the bank requires GAAP financial statements, what method would Jaclyn choose?
C. The bank sends her off with the comment, "We need more net income for a couple of months before we can grant you the line of credit." Because Jaclyn projects no increase in demand for the company's watches in the next few months, what options are available to her?
D. Which option should she choose and why? Do you think the options are legal? Are they ethical?

Cases

53. Moore, Inc. invented a secret process to double the growth rate of hatchery trout and manufactures a variety of products related to this process. Each product is independent of the others and is treated as a separate division. Product managers have a great deal of freedom to manage their divisions as they think best. Failure to produce target division income is dealt with severely; however, rewards for exceeding one's profit objective are, as one division manager described them, lavish.

    The Morey Division sells an additive that is added to pond water. Morey has had a new manager in each of the three previous years because each manager failed to reach Moore's target profit. Bryan Endreson has just been promoted to manager and is studying ways to meet the current target profit for Morey.

    The target profit for Morey for the coming year is $800,000 (20 percent return on the investment in the annual fixed costs of the division). Other constraints on division operations are as follows:

    - Production cannot exceed sales, because Moore's corporate advertising stresses completely new additives each year, even though the "newness" of the models may be only cosmetic.
    - The Morey selling price may not vary above the current selling price of $200 per gallon, but it may vary as much as 10 percent below $200 (i.e., $180).

    Endreson is now examining data gathered by his staff to determine whether Morey can achieve its target profit of $800,000.

    - Last year's sales were 30,000 units at $200 per gallon.
    - The present capacity of Morey's manufacturing facility is 40,000 gallons per year, but capacity can be increased to 80,000 gallons per year with an additional investment of $1,000,000 per year in fixed costs.

✓ Annual fixed costs: $4,000,000

- Present variable costs amount to $80 per unit, but if commitments are made for more than 60,000 gallons, Morey's vendors are willing to offer raw material discounts amounting to $20 per gallon, beginning with gallon 60,001.

Endreson believes that these projections are reliable, and he is now trying to determine what Morey must do to meet the profit objectives assigned by Moore's board of directors.

Required

A. Calculate the dollar value of Morey's current annual fixed costs.
B. Determine the number of gallons that Morey must sell at $200 per gallon to achieve the profit objective. Be sure to consider any relevant constraints. What if the selling price is $180?
C. Without prejudice to your previous answers, assume that Bryan Endreson decides to sell 40,000 gallons at $200 per gallon and 24,000 gallons at $180 per gallon. Prepare a pro forma income statement for Morey, showing whether Endreson's decision will achieve Morey's profit objectives.

54. McDonnell Douglas Aircraft Corporation manufactures the C-17, the newest jet transport used by the U.S. Air Force. The company sells the C-17 for a "flyaway cost" of $175,000,000 per jet. The variable production cost of each C-17 was estimated to be approximately $165,000,000. When the C-17 was first proposed, the Air Force expected to eventually purchase 400 jets. However, following the collapse of the former Soviet Union, the projected total purchase volume dropped to just 300 jets, then 200, then 150, and finally 120 jets.

Production began, and at one point the company was faced with the following situation. With 20 jets finished, a block of 20 more in production, and funding approved for purchase of a third block of 20 jets, the U.S. Congress began indicating that it would approve funding for the order and purchase of only 20 more jets (for a total of 80). This was a problem for the company because company officials had indicated previously that the break-even point for the C-17 project was around 100 aircraft.

Because the company is headquartered in St. Louis, all the members of Congress from Missouri rushed to the company's aid and now at least 120 C-17s will be ordered.

✓ Break-even for question A: 100 jets

Required

A. Assume that McDonnell Douglas must cover its fixed costs of $1 billion. Compute the actual break-even point for the C-17.
B. What would the income or loss be if the company only sold 80 C-17s?
C. Assume that McDonnell Douglas had been told up front that the Air Force would buy only 80 jets. Calculate the selling price per jet that the company would have to charge to achieve a target profit (before tax) of $10,000,000 per jet.
D. Because McDonnell Douglas must provide its stockholders an acceptable return on their investment, how should the company manage the risks of projects such as the C-17 becoming a very big and expensive mistake?

Group Exercises

55. Ryan Rees, cost accountant for Southeast Construction, has just finished his break-even analysis for the company. His analysis reveals a deficiency with three product lines: Townhouses, Standard houses, and Custom houses. A different division constructs each of these houses. Based on current sales forecasts, the company as a whole will not reach the sales volume needed to break even. However, if two of the three product lines (Townhouses, Standard houses, and Custom houses) are dropped, the company will remain profitable. Ryan recommended that Townhouses and Custom houses be dropped.

When Ryan started with the company, he worked for the division that manufactures Standard houses. In fact, his wife, Mary, still works for that division. Discuss the ethical issues associated with Ryan's decision within your group. What does your group see as the ethical issues in this decision? How should Ryan handle this apparent conflict of interest?

56. Hedrick Tours operates a tour bus company in the southeastern United States. Although Hedrick operates tours throughout the continental United States, most of the company's clients are interested in trips to certain popular destinations including Florida, Washington, D.C., and New Orleans. Recently, the company's president, Jerry Hedrick, agreed to take 80 high school students on a four-day trip to Washington, D.C. Because the company's buses were not reserved and because business has been a bit slow, Jerry discounted the tour price by almost 20 percent. Shortly after verbally agreeing on this trip, the company was contacted by a local retirement community about a trip to Florida. The retirement community representative explained to Jerry that she would need all of Jerry's buses and that if the service were acceptable, she felt confident that the two of them would be able to arrange a multi-year contract. When Jerry told her of the agreement to take the students to Washington, D.C., she was unconcerned and simply said that her contract was more valuable to his company and she knew he would make the smart business decision.

Within your group discuss the choice that Jerry must make. What are Jerry's alternatives? Is there an "easy" answer? What is the "smart business decision?"

Chapter 7: Short-Term Tactical Decision Making

In Chapter 5, we emphasized that relevant costs and factors should be considered by managers when making decisions. Following the decision-making framework developed in Chapter 1 and building on what we know about the behavior and relevancy of costs from Chapter 5, in Chapter 7 we analyze a variety of short-term decisions affecting managers. These decisions include the pricing of special orders; whether to outsource labor; whether to make or buy a component used to manufacture a product; whether to add or drop a product, product line, or service; and how to utilize limited resources to maximize profit. We also consider the impact of activity-based costing on these decisions.

Learning Objectives

After studying the material in this chapter, you should be able to:

1. Analyze the pricing of a special order

2. Analyze a decision involving the outsourcing of labor or making or buying a component

3. Analyze a decision dealing with adding or dropping a product, product line, or service

4. Analyze a decision dealing with scarce or limited resources

5. Describe the theory of constraints and explain the importance of identifying bottlenecks in the production process

6. Analyze a decision dealing with selling a product or processing it further

Introduction

As we discussed in Chapter 1, operating activities include a wide range of decisions that managers make on a day-to-day basis. The manager of a company that makes t-shirts must determine the price for a special one-time order. The manager of a restaurant must continually assess the status of its menu items, just as managers of a large manufacturer of stereo components must consider whether to add new products or to drop unprofitable ones. Managers of a company that makes bicycles must decide whether to buy tires from another manufacturer or to make them internally. Colleges and universities must decide whether to provide janitorial services in dorms and food service (cafeterias, etc.) to students, using their own employees, or to outsource those services to someone else. The manager of a hardware store must determine which products to put on the shelves, and a book publisher must determine which books to publish. All these decisions require relevant, timely accounting information to aid in the decision-making process. As discussed earlier in the book, relevant costs are costs that differ among alternatives. Another way to view relevant costs is to identify the costs that are avoidable or can be eliminated by choosing one alternative over another. Because sunk costs have already been incurred and cannot be avoided, they are not relevant in decisions. Likewise, future costs that do not differ among alternatives are not relevant because they cannot be eliminated by choosing one alternative over another. On the other hand, opportunity costs are relevant in decision making. In this chapter, we discuss the tools that managers use to make these short-term tactical decisions.

Special Orders

Objective 1: Analyze the pricing of a special order

Deciding whether to accept a special order is really just a pricing decision. However, **special-order decisions** are short-run decisions. Management must decide what sales price is appropriate when customers place orders that are different from those placed in the regular course of business (one-time sale to a foreign customer, etc.).[1] These decisions are affected by whether the company has excess production capacity and can produce additional units with existing machinery, labor, and facilities. A special order would almost never be accepted if a company does not have excess capacity. If a company does not have excess capacity, it will have to turn away current customers in order to fill a special order. These current customers may very well turn to other companies to fill their needs. Filling a special order under these circumstances may permanently damage the relationship with these customers. Even if a special order is profitable from a quantitative perspective, the impact on customer relations should be considered before deciding whether to accept or reject the order. If customers find other suppliers due to delivery delays, the overall profit of the company might decrease.

Even when a company has excess capacity, qualitative factors must be considered before deciding to accept a special order, particularly if the special order price is below the price offered to regular customers. In these situations, care must be taken so that regular customers do not feel like they have been treated unfairly.

Consider the case of Sunset Airlines. A major corporation has asked the company to provide 150 seats to San Diego for corporate executives attending a convention. The corporation offers the airline $125 per ticket, although the normal fare for this route is $275. The tickets can be used on only one day, but the executives need to be able to fly one of the five flights offered that day. The aircraft that Sunset Airlines flies on this route carries 180 passengers, and Sunset has five scheduled flights each day, resulting in a seat capacity of 900 seats. The normal passenger load on the day requested is between 77 percent and 78 percent of available capacity (700 passengers), so Sunset should have plenty of excess capacity (40 seats per plane, or 200 seats total). However, should Sunset accept the special order at the discounted price of $125 per ticket? That depends on the company's objectives.

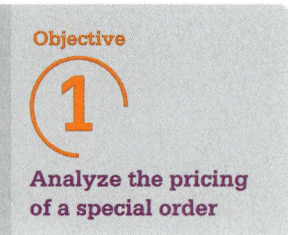

---

[1] Although rush orders and orders requiring special handling, packaging, or different manufacturing specifications might be considered "special orders," these types of decisions are not discussed here.

The objective of Sunset Airlines is to maximize income in the short run without reducing income in the long run. The options in this case include selling the tickets for $125 (accepting the special order), letting the marketplace determine the level of sales at a predetermined price of $275, or selling the tickets at another price. The risk in this situation is that the airline will have to turn away full-fare passengers if it accepts the special order. An analysis of the options requires that the relevant costs and other factors be identified. The accounting department of Sunset Airlines has provided the following information:

	Per Passenger	Per Round-trip
Cost of meals and drinks	$ 6.50	$ 1,170
Cost of fuel	88.89	16,000
Cost of cabin crew (four flight attendants)	6.11	1,100
Cost of flight crew	11.11	2,000
Depreciation of aircraft	16.67	3,000
Aircraft maintenance	8.33	1,500
Total	$137.61	$24,770

This decision appears to be an easy one, as the special-order price of $125 is less than the total cost per passenger of $137.61. Based on the full cost reported by the accounting department, Sunset Airlines would be losing $12.61 on each passenger purchasing a ticket for $125. But would it? To analyze the options in this decision problem correctly, only the relevant costs should be considered. In this decision, the only costs that are relevant are those that will differ depending on whether the special order is accepted. Another way to look at the problem is by determining which costs can be avoided by choosing one alternative over the other.

In this case, almost all the costs are fixed with respect to the number of passengers on the plane. In fact, owing to the unique nature of the airline business, most operating costs are fixed. For example, the aircraft will require the same maintenance and flight crew costs regardless of how many passengers are on board. Although the costs of the cabin crew may vary, let us assume that in this situation, regulations require four flight attendants for any flight with more than 125 passengers. In this case, four flight attendants are required regardless of whether the plane carries 125 passengers or 180 passengers, and acceptance of the special order will not change the cost of the cabin crew. In essence, the cost of the flight crew is fixed. Likewise, depreciation is a fixed cost. Even fuel costs would not be expected to vary much with the addition of 30 to 40 passengers. In fact, the only cost that would vary with the number of passengers on the plane is likely to be the small additional cost of meals and drinks. Because Sunset Airlines appears to have plenty of excess capacity (empty seats), any sales price above the variable costs of providing the seats will increase the income of the company. If the cost of meals and drinks is the only variable cost, Sunset should be willing to accept the special order at any price over $6.50. In situations in which excess capacity exists, the general rule is that in order to maximize income, the special-order price must simply be higher than the additional variable costs incurred in accepting the special order.

What if Sunset does not have any excess capacity? If the airline expects to sell out all its tickets at the regular price of $275, accepting the special order involves an opportunity cost. Remember from Chapter 1 that an opportunity cost is the benefit forgone from choosing one alternative over another. If Sunset Airlines accepts the special order, it will forgo the receipt of $268.50 of contribution margin on each ticket ($275 selling price less the $6.50 variable cost of meals and drinks). Therefore, it would not be willing to accept a special order for any price below the $275 market price. The relevant costs in this case are the variable costs of $6.50 and the opportunity cost of $268.50. As demonstrated in Exhibit 7-1, when Sunset Airlines has excess capacity, accepting the special order will result in a profit of $118.50 for each ticket sold. However when there is not sufficient capacity, Sunset Airlines can only meet the special order by turning away full-paying customers and incurring an opportunity cost. As a result, the company would lose $150.00 for each ticket sold.

Exhibit 7-1   The Special Order Decision

	Excess Capacity	No Excess Capacity
Relevant costs:		
Meals	$ 6.50	$ 6.50
Opportunity costs from lost ticket revenue (Contribution margin lost)	0	$ 268.50
Total relevant costs	$ 6.50	$ 275.00
Special order ticket price	125.00	125.00
Profit (loss) from accepting special order	$118.50	$(150.00)

Fixed costs can be relevant to a special-order decision when they change depending on the option chosen. For example, let's consider the case of flight attendants again. Instead of requiring four flight attendants for any flight with more than 125 passengers, let's assume that regulations require one flight attendant for every 35 passengers. Whereas four attendants are sufficient for a flight of 140 passengers, adding 30 additional passengers will require the addition of an extra flight attendant at a cost of $275, or $9.17 per additional passenger. Assuming that excess capacity exists, the special-order price would need to exceed $15.67 to be acceptable to Sunset Airlines.

Instead of 150 extra passengers flying on the five regularly scheduled flights, assume that Sunset Airlines has an additional airplane that is currently idle but can be chartered for the flight. In this case, fuel costs, salaries of the flight and cabin crews, and maintenance are likely to be relevant but depreciation is still not relevant. It is important to note that determining what is relevant and what is not depends on the specific situation.

A number of qualitative factors must also be considered in special-order decisions. First, if it accepts the special order and its passenger-load predictions are wrong, Sunset Airlines may have to turn away passengers that would otherwise pay full fare. If that happens and these passengers turn to competing airlines, Sunset Airlines faces the potential of losing long-term customers. Second, the impact of selling seats at a discount on those customers paying regular fares must be considered.

KEY CONCEPT

The price of a special order must be higher than the additional variable costs incurred in accepting the special order plus any opportunity costs incurred.

Objective 2

Analyze a decision involving the outsourcing of labor or making or buying a component

Outsourcing and Other Make-or-Buy Decisions

The decision to outsource labor or to purchase components used in manufacturing from another company rather than to provide the services or to produce the components internally affects a wide range of manufacturing, merchandising, and service organizations. For example, a university can contract with an outside company to provide janitorial and repair services for on-campus dormitories, or it can provide those services by using university employees. A local florist can provide payroll processing internally, or it can hire a CPA to provide those services. Hewlett-Packard can make carrying cases for its calculators internally, or it can buy them from an outside supplier.

Strategic Aspects of Outsourcing and Make-or-Buy Decisions

An analysis of outsourcing and **make-or-buy decisions** requires an in-depth analysis of relevant quantitative and qualitative factors and a consideration of the costs and benefits of outsourcing and vertical integration. For example, Sunset Airlines might consider outsourcing the maintenance function on their airplanes to an outside organization. Sunset Airlines now pays all maintenance personnel $20 per hour plus 30 percent for fringe benefits. Total labor costs are $26 per hour. The outside agency offers to perform the maintenance for $22 per hour plus the cost of parts and supplies. From a quantitative perspective this is a money-saving move. Let's assume that Sunset Airlines has 100 maintenance personnel who all work 40 hours per week. The savings from outsourcing would be $16,000 per week or $832,000 per year. However, Sunset Airlines needs to consider a number of qualitative factors before making this decision. Is the quality of work the same? What are the risks associated with outsourcing maintenance if poor quality work results in an airplane accident? How will outsourcing maintenance impact other employees of the airline including ticket agents and ground service personnel? Other employees may become demoralized and worry about losing their own jobs. They may be less motivated to do the best job possible, leading to quality problems, operational slowdowns, and even employee strikes. They may very well leave the company if and when a better opportunity presents itself.

There are other potential risks to outsourcing. When medical claims processing and brokerage transaction processing are outsourced, companies risk revealing confidential information about their clients. Unforeseen costs may be incurred associated with providing severance pay for workers that lose their jobs and training new workers. Increasingly, U.S. companies are coming under fire from the government, employee rights groups, and the general public for outsourcing jobs to foreign companies—computer programming jobs to China, manufacturing jobs to Mexico and Asia, call centers to India. Outsourcing to foreign workers entails additional risks including communication and language breakdowns and problems resulting from cultural differences.

Hitting the Bottom Line.
OUTSOURCING CAN SAVE BIG BUCKS!

According to IBM, a computer programmer in China with three to five years of experience would cost the company about $12.50 per hour, including salary and benefits, compared to about $56 per hour for a comparable U.S. employee. As a result, in early 2004, the company announced plans to shift several thousand programming jobs to China. Even though the company expects to incur severance costs of $30 million in 2004 and $47 million in 2005 related to laying off the U.S. employees, the outsourcing is expected to result in overall cost savings of $40 million in 2005 and $168 million per year starting in 2006.

Vertical integration is accomplished when a company is involved in multiple steps of the value chain. In an extreme example, the same company might own a gold mine, a manufacturing facility to produce gold jewelry, and a retail jewelry store. Most companies operate with some form of vertical integration (they market the products they produce, or they develop the products that they manufacture), but the extent of integration varies greatly from company to company and indeed from product to product within a company. All elements of the value chain—from initial research and development through design, manufacture of the product, marketing, distribution, and customer service—must be considered for making or buying components needed for production of the final product.

THE ETHICS OF BUSINESS
Cut Your Price or Else!

The Big Three U.S. automakers (Ford, GM, and DaimlerChrysler) have been under tremendous competition from foreign manufacturers for the last decade. Unable to cut labor costs because of collective bargaining agreements with employee labor unions, the companies have turned their attention to their suppliers. For example, Ford and GM contacted Superior Industries International, a supplier of wheels for the companies, and requested that Superior match the price offered by a potential new supplier located in China. The only way that Superior Industries can meet the price is by outsourcing some of their own labor. Essentially, while GM and Ford cannot outsource their labor and reduce that component of product cost, they have forced their suppliers to cut costs for them.

It's Your Choice—Imagine you are the owner of a company that supplies components to Ford and GM and you are approached with the above dilemma. What would you do? What are your ethical obligations to your company, family, employees, community, and customers? What do you think is the ultimate impact of this type of forced outsourcing?

There are advantages to making components internally instead of buying them from an outside supplier. Vertically integrated companies are not dependent on suppliers for timely delivery of services or components needed in the production process or for the quality of those services and components. However, vertically integrated companies have disadvantages as well.

There are disadvantages to making parts internally. The supplier may be able to provide a higher-quality part for less cost. For this reason, computer manufacturers do not produce their own computer chips. The producers of those chips produce in such large quantities that they can provide the chips more cheaply than the company could produce them internally. Chip manufacturers also spend billions of dollars on research and development to ensure high-quality and high-performance chips.

Doing Business.
SOMETIMES SUPPLIERS ARE NOT THE PROBLEM

In the summer of 1998, General Motors (GM) found it difficult to restart production in its vehicle plants because of strikes in two of its *own* plants that supplied body stampings and other parts used in GM cars. In this case, the lack of alternative suppliers forced GM to shut down plants that were not directly affected by the strike (*Wall Street Journal*, July 8, 1998, A3).

The Make-or-Buy Decision

Birdie Maker Golf Company produces custom sets of golf clubs that are advertised to be far superior to other golf clubs on the market. These golf clubs sell for $1,000 per set, and Birdie currently sells about 1,000 sets each year. Birdie Maker currently manufactures all the golf clubs in the set but is considering acquiring the putter from Ace Putters, Inc., a manufacturer of custom putters. The purchased putter would be customized for Birdie and matched to the other clubs, so customers should not be able to distinguish it from the rest of the clubs in the set. The costs incurred in the manufacture of the putter are as follows:

	Total (1,000 putters)	Per Unit
Direct materials	$ 5,000	$ 5.00
Direct labor	9,000	9.00
Variable manufacturing overhead	3,000	3.00
Fixed manufacturing overhead	9,500	9.50
Total cost	$26,500	$26.50

The expected production for the year is 1,000 putters, so the full cost of each putter is $26.50 ($26,500/1,000). Ace Putters is offering to sell the putters to Birdie Maker for $25 per putter. Although this decision seems to be a very easy one ($25 is less than $26.50), the decision is more complex than it appears.

Although Birdie Maker would like to maximize income by producing or buying the putter at the lowest possible cost, the company is also very concerned about the quality of the putter and the potential impact of the putter on sales of other clubs.

As we discussed in Chapter 5, relevant costs are those that can be avoided by choosing one alternative over another. The key, then, is to analyze the costs of manufacturing the putter with an eye toward identifying those costs that can be *avoided* or eliminated if the putter is purchased from Ace Putters. If Birdie Maker continues to manufacture the putter internally, it will incur costs of $26,500. If Birdie Maker decides to purchase the putters from Ace Putters, it will incur costs of $25,000 ($25 × 1,000 putters) *plus* any manufacturing costs that are not avoidable. Although the costs related to direct material, direct labor, and variable manufacturing overhead are variable (and thus avoidable), fixed manufacturing overhead is not.

So although it appears on the surface that Birdie Maker can save $1,500 ($26,500 − $25,000) by buying the putters from Ace Putters, as you can see in Exhibit 7-2, it will in reality cost Birdie an additional $8 per club, or $8,000. Note that the fixed overhead of $9.50 per unit is incurred regardless of the decision to make or buy. We could have come to the same conclusion by comparing the $17 variable costs of making putters ($5.00 of direct materials + $9.00 of direct labor + $3.00 of variable overhead) to the outside purchase price of $25. What is the best solution? From a purely quantitative perspective, Birdie Maker would maximize its income by choosing to continue making putters. However, before making this decision, the company must be convinced that it can manufacture a putter of acceptable quality and that it will be able to keep up with any technological changes affecting the manufacture of the putter in the future.

EXHIBIT 7-2 The Make-or-Buy Decision

	Cost to Make (per unit)	Cost to Buy (per unit)
Direct materials	$ 5.00	
Direct labor	9.00	
Variable manufacturing overhead	3.00	
Fixed manufacturing overhead	9.50	$ 9.50
Purchase price from Ace Putters		25.00
	$26.50	$34.50

Sometimes, fixed costs are relevant to the analysis. For example, assume that $5,500 of the fixed manufacturing cost is for specialized machinery that is currently being leased under a month-to-month contract. If the putters are purchased from Ace Putters, the equipment will be returned to the lessor. That means that $5.50 of the fixed manufacturing costs ($5,500/1,000 putters) is avoidable if the putter is bought from Ace Putters and that only $4.00 of fixed overhead will be incurred if the putter is purchased. The resulting analysis is shown in Exhibit 7-3.

EXHIBIT 7-3 The Make-or-Buy Decision with Relevant Fixed Costs

	Cost to Make	Cost to Buy
Direct materials	$ 5.00	
Direct labor	9.00	
Variable manufacturing overhead	3.00	
Fixed manufacturing overhead	9.50	$ 4.00
Purchase price from Ace Putters		25.00
	$26.50	$29.00

Although it still remains preferable to make the putters internally, the cost difference shrinks to $2.50 per putter instead of $8.00. In this situation, Birdie Maker must carefully consider the qualitative factors relevant to the decision, including the quality of the putters, the importance of keeping up with changing technology, and the dependability of the supplier.

Another way to look at this analysis is to compare the total avoidable costs to the purchase price. In this case, if the putter is purchased, the avoidable costs include direct materials ($5.00), direct labor ($9.00), variable manufacturing overhead ($3.00), and $5.50 per putter for fixed manufacturing overhead. The $22.50 of total avoidable costs should then be compared to the $25.00 purchase price. Regardless of how you choose to look at the problem, Birdie Maker is better off by $2.50 per putter if it continues making the putter.

Opportunity costs should also be considered in make-or-buy decisions. Using the same facts as Exhibit 7-3, consider the impact of renting out for $10,000 the factory space that is now used to manufacture putters.

By effectively reducing the cost to purchase the putters by $10,000, or $10 per putter, Exhibit 7-4 shows that the effective cost to purchase the putter is reduced to $24.50, so Birdie Maker would be better off by $2.00 per putter by purchasing the putters.

KEY CONCEPT

A product should continue to be made internally and labor incurred internally if the avoidable costs are less than the additional costs that will be incurred by buying or outsourcing.

EXHIBIT 7-4 The Make-or-Buy Decision with Relevant Opportunity Costs

	Cost to Make	Cost to Buy
Direct materials	$ 5.00	
Direct labor	9.00	
Variable manufacturing overhead	3.00	
Fixed manufacturing overhead	9.50	$ 9.50
Purchase price from Ace Putters		25.00
Rental of unused factory space		(10.00)
	$26.50	$24.50

Once again, as an alternative, we could treat the $10 opportunity cost as a relevant cost of making the putter internally. In that case, the total relevant costs of making the putter increase to $36.50 compared to the purchase price of $34.50. In addition to quality and reliability considerations, other factors to consider in this case include the long-term potential for renting out the unused space, potential other uses of the space, and so on.

The Decision to Drop a Product or a Service

The decision to drop a product or a service is among the most difficult that a manager can make. Like other decisions discussed in this chapter, deciding whether to drop an old product or product line hinges on an analysis of the relevant costs and qualitative factors affecting the decision. Qualitative factors are sometimes more important than focusing solely on income.

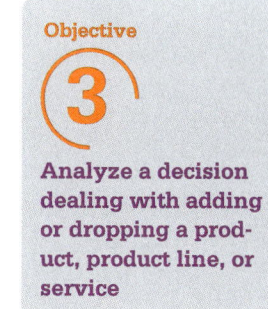

Objective 3

Analyze a decision dealing with adding or dropping a product, product line, or service

Hitting the Bottom Line.
MAKING THE TOUGH DECISIONS

Fierce competition is part of the reality of today's business environment. Faced with increasing competition from the likes of Wal-Mart, Winn-Dixie (a grocery store primarily located in the southeast) announced plans to close or sell more than 150 stores and lay off 10,000 employees. These reductions amount to a 14 percent decrease in the company's stores and a 10 percent decrease in number of employees. Why did the company make these decisions? In short, the company believed that it had no choice if it is to remain a viable business. Winn-Dixie believes that the key to its future success lies in shedding underperforming stores. During the quarter ended March 31, 2004, the company reported net income of only $610,000 compared to almost $51 million a year earlier. While the company estimates that the store closings will create one-time losses of between $275 million and $400 million in the next year, in the long run, Winn-Dixie has said that the closings will generate annual cash savings of approximately $70 million.

Clayton Herring Tire Company is considering dropping one of the 10 models of tires that it manufactures and sells. Sales of a special mud and snow tire have been disappointing, and based on the latest financial information (shown in the following table), the tires appear to be losing money.

	Mud and Snow	All Other Tires	Total
Sales	$25,500	$150,000	$175,500
Less: Direct material	12,000	50,600	62,600
Direct labor	5,000	30,000	35,000
Variable overhead	2,000	12,000	14,000
Contribution margin	$ 6,500	$ 57,400	$ 63,900
Less: Fixed overhead	7,000	21,000	28,000
Net income	$ (500)	$ 36,400	$ 35,900

Chris (the CEO of Clayton Herring Tire) asked Karen (the controller) why the mud and snow tires were losing money. Karen explained that the tires required more machine time than other tires. Consequently, they were allocated a greater portion of fixed overhead. Chris then asked Karen whether she would recommend that production of the mud and snow tires be discontinued. Karen explained that although it appears that net income for the company would increase to $36,400 if the mud and snow tires were dropped from the product line, further analysis revealed that a large portion of the fixed overhead allocated to the tires resulted from the rental of machines used to make the tires. On further inspection, Karen determined that these machines were used to make several models of tires and could not be disposed of if the mud and snow tires were dropped. Consequently, $5,000 of the fixed costs allocated to mud and snow tires would have to be reallocated to other product lines. These costs would remain even if the mud and snow tires were discontinued. Based on this new information, Karen prepared another report for Chris, showing the effect of dropping the mud and snow tires (see Exhibit 7-5).

EXHIBIT 7-5   The Decision to Drop a Product

	With Snow Tires	Without Snow Tires	Difference
Tire sales	$175,500	$150,000	
Less: Direct material	62,600	50,600	
Direct labor	35,000	30,000	
Variable overhead	14,000	12,000	
Contribution margin	$ 63,900	$ 57,400	$(6,500)
Less: Fixed overhead	28,000	26,000	2,000
Net income	$ 35,900	$ 31,400	$(4,500)

Why did the net income for the company decrease by $4,500 (from $35,900 to $31,400) when the mud and snow tires were dropped, even though they appeared to be losing money? The answer is that contribution margin decreased by $6,500, whereas fixed costs decreased by only $2,000 when the tires were dropped. Only $2,000 of the fixed costs were avoidable and relevant to this decision. The other $5,000 of fixed costs originally allocated to the mud and snow tires would simply be reallocated to one or more of the other models of tires. A simple way to analyze this problem is to compare the contribution margin lost when the product line is dropped to the fixed costs that are avoided. In this case, Clayton Herring Tire Company loses $6,500 of contribution margin while saving (avoiding) only $2,000 of fixed overhead (see Exhibit 7-6).

If the machine used to produce the tires was unique and could be disposed of, resulting in a savings of $5,000, how much would income increase (decrease) if the mud and snow tires were discontinued? (Assume that the other $2,000 of fixed overhead could still be avoided.) Although contribution margin would still be reduced by $6,500, the entire $7,000 of fixed costs would be avoided, resulting in an overall increase in net income of $500. But what about qualitative factors in this decision? As we discussed earlier, qualitative factors are sometimes more important than quantitative factors in these decisions. For example, what impact will discontinuing the sale of mud and snow tires have on sales of the remaining product lines? Tire retailers are likely to prefer purchasing tires from a company offering a full line of tires. Retailers that cannot offer mud and snow tires may have difficulty selling tires to individuals in the winter.

KEY CONCEPT

A product should be dropped when the fixed costs avoided are greater than the contribution margin lost.

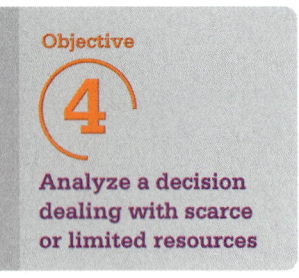

Objective 4

Analyze a decision dealing with scarce or limited resources

Resource Utilization Decisions

A company faces a **constraint** when the capacity to manufacture a product or to provide a service is limited in some manner. A **resource utilization decision** requires an analysis of how best to use a resource that is available in limited supply. The limited resource may be a rare material or component used in manufacturing a product but more likely is related to the time required to make a product or to provide a service or the space required to store a product. For example, building custom furniture requires skilled craftspeople, who may be in short supply. Deciding how best to utilize the limited labor time available is a resource utilization decision. The manufacture of golf clubs requires special machinery. If a company has only one machine that can be used to manufacture shafts for putters and other clubs, machine time may be a limited resource.

What is likely to be a limited resource in a grocery store? Grocery stores and other retail stores have limited shelf space. The resource utilization decision involves an analysis of how best to use this limited resource. Which products should be carried? How many? Although it may seem easy to conclude that stores should carry those products that are most profitable, decisions like this are complicated by the fact that the multitudes of products carried in large stores require different amounts of shelf space. Multipacks of paper towels take up several times the shelf space required for a box of macaroni and cheese. Although the multipack of paper towels may be more profitable per unit, this information has to be balanced with the requirement of more shelf space. A decision concerning how much of each product to have on hand must also consider the impact of qualitative factors, such as customer reaction if a product is not carried, the impact on sales of other products, and so on.

Resource utilization decisions are typically short-term decisions. In the short run, such resources as machine time, labor hours, and shelf space are fixed and cannot be increased. However, in the long run, new machines can be purchased, additional skilled laborers can be hired, and stores can be expanded. When faced with short-run constraints, managers must focus on the contribution margin provided by each product per unit of limited resource rather than on the profitability of each product.[2]

Birdie Maker produces two types of golf balls: the pro model and the tour model. The balls are sold to retailers in cartons containing 360 balls (30 boxes containing 4 sleeves per box, with each sleeve holding 3 balls). Both models are made using the same machines. The constraint, or limited resource, is the number of hours that the machines can run. The pro model golf ball takes 30 minutes of machine time to produce 360 balls, whereas the tour ball takes 45 minutes to produce the same number. The difference in production time results mainly from the different materials used in construction. Although weekend golfers purchase both models, professionals on the PGA Tour use the tour model. The relevant data concerning the two models follows:

	Pro Model	Tour Model
Sales price (per carton)	$450	$540
Less: Direct material	200	265
Direct labor	50	50
Variable overhead	50	75
Contribution margin	$150	$150

In this case, the contribution margin per carton is the same for both the pro model and the tour model. Other things being equal, each model is equally profitable. However, if we compute contribution margin per unit of the constrained, or limited, resource, we see that each carton of pro-model balls has a contribution margin of $300 per hour of machine time, whereas each carton of tour-model balls has a contribution margin of $200 per hour of machine time (see Exhibit 7-6).

---

[2]Decisions involving limited resources or constraints often include multiple constraints, such as storage space, machine time, labor hours, and even dollars available to invest. When we have more than one constraining factor, the decision-making process becomes more complicated and is facilitated by the use of computerized linear programming models. A discussion of linear programming is beyond the scope of this textbook.

Exhibit 7-6: The Resource Utilization Decision

	Pro Model	Tour Model
Sales price (per carton)	$450	$540
Less: Direct material	200	265
Direct labor	50	50
Variable overhead	50	75
Contribution margin	$150	$150
Required machine time	÷ 0.50 hours	÷ 0.75 hours
Contribution margin per machine hour	$300	$200

If demand is not a factor and qualitative considerations are not important, Birdie Maker will maximize profit by producing and selling only pro model golf balls. However, if demand for either product is limited, the company must decide on the optimal product mix. For example, if machine time is limited to 300 hours per month, the demand for the pro model is 400 cartons per month, and the demand for the tour model is 150 cartons, how much of each product should Birdie Maker produce? Although Birdie Maker has the capacity to produce 600 cartons (300 hours/0.5 hours) of pro model balls, it can sell only 400 cartons. Producing 400 cartons requires 200 machine hours, leaving 100 additional machine hours per month for the production of tour balls. Birdie Maker can maximize income by producing 400 cartons of pro balls and 133 cartons of tour balls each month.

Qualitative factors, including the impact of discontinuing the sale of the tour ball, must also be considered. Visibility of the tour ball on the professional tour may be a valuable source of advertising, contributing to sales of the pro model.

Other options include adding machines to increase the amount of available machine hours or reducing the machine time needed to produce a carton of balls. Maximizing profits by focusing on the constraint itself in order to loosen the constraint is the focus of the theory of constraints.

KEY CONCEPT

Resource utilization decisions hinge on an analysis of the contribution margin earned per unit of the limited resource.

Objective 5

Describe the theory of constraints and explain the importance of identifying bottlenecks in the production process

The Theory of Constraints

The **theory of constraints** is a management tool for dealing with constraints. The theory of constraints identifies **bottlenecks** in the production process. Bottlenecks limit throughput, which can be thought of as the amount of finished goods that result from the production process. In the previous example, machine time is a bottleneck that limits the amount of throughput. In the airline industry, certain tasks performed while the aircraft is on the ground may delay departure and increase the turnaround time for the plane.

The key to the theory of constraints is identifying and managing bottlenecks. Once a bottleneck is identified, management must focus its time and resources on relieving the bottleneck. Utilizing resources to increase the efficiency of a non-bottleneck operation will rarely increase throughput. For example, increasing the efficiency of machines with excess capacity in a factory or reducing flight time for an airline will result in very limited increases in throughput (if any) until bottlenecks are relieved.

In Exhibit 7-7, Birdie Maker has discovered that delays in delivery of golf clubs to customers result from the extra time it takes to order and receive putters from Ace Putters. Options for relieving this bottleneck include requiring Ace Putters to reduce its delivery time. If Ace cannot speed up delivery, Birdie Maker might consider using another supplier or perhaps making the putters in-house instead of outsourcing. Reducing the time spent manufacturing irons or woods would not reduce overall delivery time until the bottleneck with the putters is relieved.

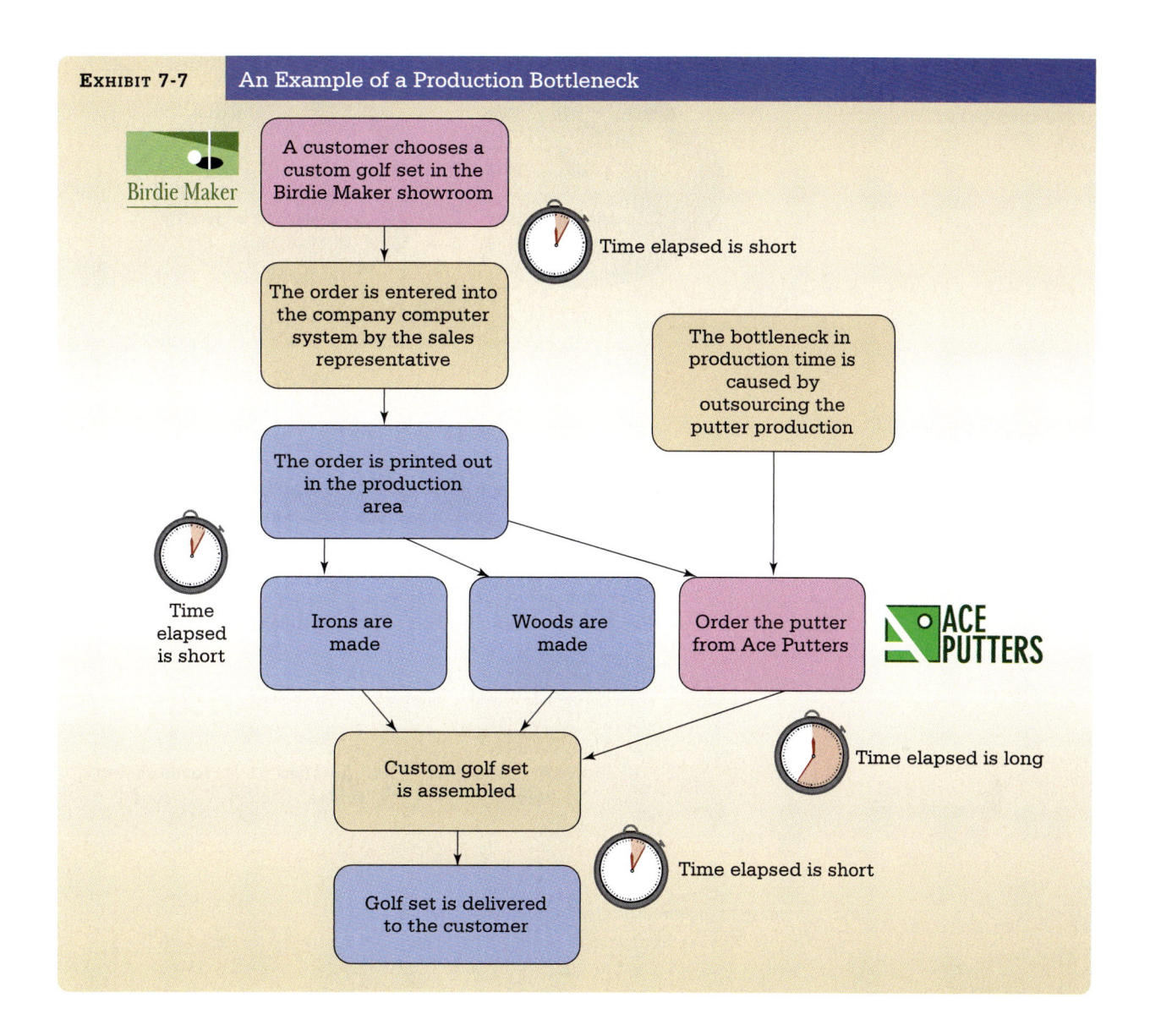

EXHIBIT 7-7 An Example of a Production Bottleneck

- Birdie Maker
- A customer chooses a custom golf set in the Birdie Maker showroom
- Time elapsed is short
- The order is entered into the company computer system by the sales representative
- The bottleneck in production time is caused by outsourcing the putter production
- The order is printed out in the production area
- Time elapsed is short
- Irons are made
- Woods are made
- Order the putter from Ace Putters
- ACE PUTTERS
- Time elapsed is long
- Custom golf set is assembled
- Time elapsed is short
- Golf set is delivered to the customer

Decisions to Sell or Process Further

The decision to sell a product as is or to process it further to generate additional revenue is another common management decision. For example, furniture manufacturers may sell furniture unassembled and unfinished, assembled and unfinished, or assembled and finished (see Exhibit 7-8). The key in deciding to sell or process further is that all costs that are incurred up to the point where the decision is made are sunk costs and therefore not relevant.

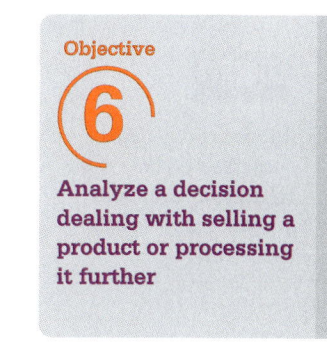

Objective 6

Analyze a decision dealing with selling a product or processing it further

Exhibit 7-8 The Sell or Process Further Decision

Unassembled and unfinished furniture → Assembled but unfinished furniture → Assembled and finished furniture

Compare costs to assemble with additional revenue from selling assembled furniture

Compare costs to finish with additional revenue from selling assembled and finished furniture

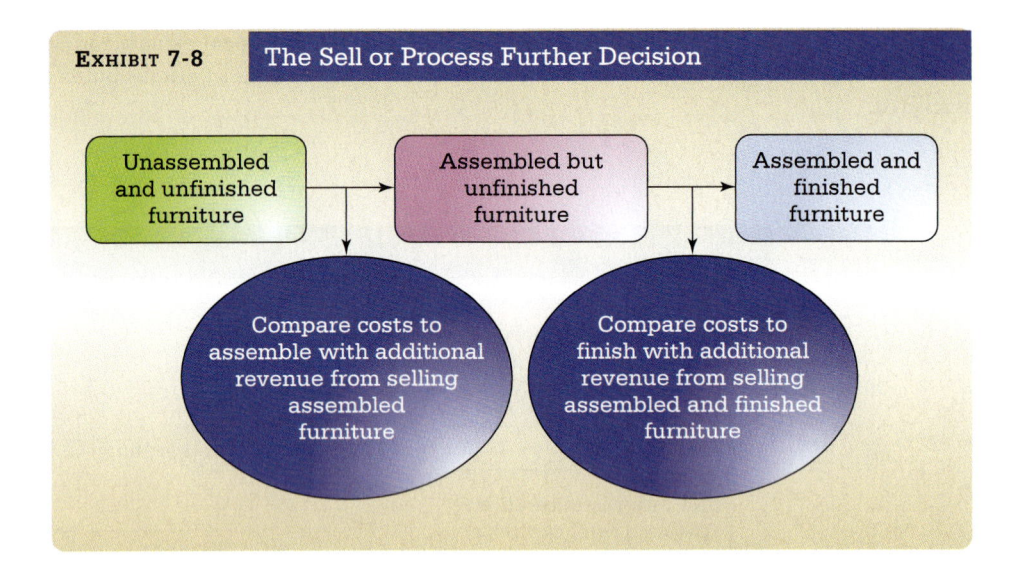

The relevant costs are the incremental or additional processing costs. Managers should compare the additional sales revenue that can be earned from processing the product further to the additional processing costs. If the additional revenue is greater than the additional costs, the product should be processed further. If the additional costs exceed the revenues, the product should be sold as is.

For example, assume that unassembled and unfinished tables cost $100 to produce and can be sold for $150. The company is considering selling assembled and finished tables for $225 each. Additional assembly and finishing costs of $45 per table would be required.

	Unassembled and unfinished tables	Assembled and finished tables	Incremental revenue and cost
Sales price	$150	$225	$75
Cost to produce	100	145	45
Increase in income from further processing			$30

KEY CONCEPT

A product should be processed further if the additional revenue is greater than the additional cost.

As shown above, the additional (incremental) revenue from selling assembled and finished furniture is $75 per table. As long as the additional (incremental) costs of assembly and finishing are less than $75, the company will maximize profits by further processing of the tables. Assuming that it has sufficient demand for the assembled and finished tables, the company will make an additional $30 per table ($75 incremental revenue less $45 incremental costs) by selling assembled, finished tables. You should note that the $100 cost of producing the unassembled and unfinished table is not relevant in the analysis because it is a sunk cost. It is incurred regardless of the decision to sell unassembled and unfinished tables or to process further.

Doing Business.

TURNING SMOKE INTO FERTILIZER

Sometimes, further processing of an undesirable by-product can even be profitable. Since 1970, electric utilities have been scrubbing the smoke emitted from their smokestacks to remove sulfur and ash from the atmosphere. They do this by spraying a mixture of water and ground limestone into the smoke. Until recently, the utilities collected the toothpastelike mixture that accumulated at the bottom of the stacks and buried it in landfills. However, adding oxygen turns the mixture into calcium sulfate, which has the same chemical composition as gypsum. The gypsum can be sold to farmers as a soil enhancer or to wallboard manufacturers as a raw material (*Wall Street Journal,* October 5, 1998, B1).

ABC and Relevant-Cost Analysis

As described in Chapter 4, activity-based costing uses multiple cost drivers to trace overhead costs directly to products. ABC's focus on activities that cause costs to be incurred sheds new light on the concept of relevant costs. Whereas traditional cost analysis focuses on changes in costs associated with volume, ABC focuses on changes in costs associated with a variety of activities, including material handling, inspection, purchasing, and machine setups. Although fixed costs may appear to be unavoidable (and therefore not relevant) under traditional costing because they do not vary with changes in volume, these same costs may be avoidable when the amount of material, inspections, purchase orders, or setups is changed. ABC helps managers to identify what costs are really avoidable in a relevant-cost analysis.

However, it is important to remember that not all traceable costs are relevant costs. For example, ABC may trace depreciation of a machine directly to a product. However, if the depreciation relates to an existing piece of equipment, the depreciation is a sunk cost and is still not relevant.

Summary of Key Concepts

- *The price of a special order must be higher than the additional variable costs incurred in accepting the special order plus any opportunity costs incurred. (p. 218)*

- *A product should continue to be made internally and labor incurred internally if the avoidable costs are less than the additional costs that will be incurred by buying or outsourcing. (p. 222)*

- *A product should be dropped when the fixed costs avoided are greater than the contribution margin lost. (p. 224)*

- *Resource utilization decisions hinge on an analysis of the contribution margin earned per unit of the limited resource. (p. 226)*

- *A product should be processed further if the additional revenue is greater than the additional cost. (p. 228)*

Key Definitions

Special-order decisions Short-run pricing decisions in which management must decide what sales price is appropriate when customers place orders that are different from those placed in the regular course of business (one-time sale to a foreign customer, etc.) (p. 216)

Make-or-buy decision A short-term decision to outsource labor or purchase components used in manufacturing from another company rather than to provide services or to produce components internally (p. 219)

Vertical integration Accomplished when a company is involved in multiple steps of the value chain (p. 219)

Constraint A restriction that occurs when the capacity to manufacture a product or to provide a service is limited in some manner (p. 224)

Resource utilization decision A decision requiring an analysis of how best to use a resource that is available in limited supply (p. 224)

Theory of constraints A management tool for dealing with constraints; identifies and focuses on bottlenecks in the production process (p. 226)

Bottlenecks Production-process steps that limit throughput or the number of finished products that go through the production process (p. 226)

Multiple Choice

1. The Beach Hut sells hotdogs for $2 each. The costs associated with each hotdog are estimated to be $1.00 of variable costs and $0.35 of fixed overhead costs. A summer camp, whose campers will be visiting the beach once during the summer, wishes to buy 100 hotdogs for $1.25 each. If the special order were accepted, net income would:
   a. increase by $125.
   b. increase by $25.
   c. decrease by $75.
   d. decrease by $10.

2. Shoeworks produces and sells athletic shoes for children. The costs associated with each pair of shoes are estimated to be $12 of variable costs and $4 of fixed overhead costs. The shoes typically sell for $20 per pair. A local children's football league has contacted Shoeworks with an offer to purchase 50 pairs of sneakers for $15 each. Which of the following factors should be considered before making this special-order decision?
   a. Does Shoeworks have the available capacity to produce these 50 pairs of shoes in addition to its usual sales?
   b. Will regular customers become angry if they learn that the football players have paid less for their shoes?
   c. Will the relevant costs of providing these 50 pairs of shoes be covered?
   d. Each of the above should be considered.

3. Which of the following costs is least likely to be relevant in deciding whether to accept a special order?
   a. Variable direct labor costs
   b. Variable selling costs
   c. Fixed manufacturing overhead
   d. Variable packaging and shipping costs

4. Book Manufacturer, Inc., operates a bookbinding division. Management is considering whether the binding should be done internally or outsourced at a cost of $25 per book. The current internal binding costs average $26.50, including fixed costs of $4,000 for

the 1,000 books bound annually; however, 75 percent of the fixed costs can be avoided if the binding is outsourced. What would you recommend Book Manufacturer do in this situation, and what is the effect on net income?
   a. Make internally; increases net income by $500
   b. Make internally; increases net income by $1,500
   c. Outsource; increases net income by $500
   d. Outsource; increases net income by $1,500

5. Which of the following statements most accurately describes vertical integration?
   a. Vertical integration is achieved when a company saturates one critical aspect of the value chain.
   b. Vertical integration is achieved when a company saturates one non-critical aspect of the value chain.
   c. Vertical integration is achieved when a company is involved in multiple steps of the value chain.
   d. Vertical integration is achieved when a company is not involved in any critical aspects of the value chain.

6. Make-or-buy decisions are often complicated by a number of strategic factors. Which of the following factors is least likely to be a strategic disadvantage associated with outsourcing?
   a. Perceived lack of stability in the company
   b. Reduced product cost
   c. Reduced employee morale
   d. Lack of loyalty in the workforce

7. Bubblemania has three product lines: A, B, and C.

	A	B	C	Total
Sales	$10,000	$ 9,000	$12,000	$ 31,000
Variable costs	4,500	7,000	6,000	17,500
Contribution margin	$ 5,500	$ 2,000	$ 6,000	$ 13,500
Fixed costs	3,500	6,000	3,000	12,500
Net income	$ 2,000	$ (4,000)	$ 3,000	$ 1,000

Product line B appears unprofitable, and management is considering discontinuing the line. If it is discontinued, $1,000 of the line's fixed costs can be avoided. The discontinuation of product line B would:
   a. increase net income by $3,000.
   b. decrease net income by $3,000.
   c. increase net income by $1,000.
   d. decrease net income by $1,000.

8. Which of the following statements is true with respect to when a product should be dropped?
   a. A product should be dropped when fixed costs avoided are less than the contribution margin lost.
   b. A product should be dropped when variable costs and contribution margin are equivalent.
   c. A product should be dropped when fixed costs avoided are greater than the contribution margin lost.
   d. A product should be dropped when fixed costs are less than variable costs.

9. Soft Mattress, Inc. produces both a queen- and king-size soft bed. Selected data related to each product follow:

	Queen	King
Sales price	$525	$635
Direct material	$350	$365
Direct labor	$ 75	$ 85
Variable Overhead	$ 25	$ 35
Stuffing hours	1	3

The two employees who are trained to stuff the secret soft ingredient into the mattresses have a maximum of 4,000 stuffing hours per year. If demand were strong for both beds and the company could sell an unlimited number of units produced for either style, which beds should be produced?
   a. 4,000 queen-size beds
   b. 4,000 king-size beds
   c. 1,333 king-size beds
   d. 2,000 queen-size beds and 667 king-size beds

10. Resource utilization decisions:
    a. are typically long-term in nature.
    b. typically involve significant and irreversible commitments of resources.
    c. are typically short-term decisions.
    d. are not sufficiently described by any of the above statements.

11. Novakoske Electronics produces Standard and Deluxe model televisions. Selected data related to each product follow:

	Standard	Deluxe
Sales price	$725	$935
Direct material	$325	$400
Direct labor	$200	$210
Variable overhead	$ 75	$125
Tuning hours	2	4

Television tuning is performed on one of four expensive tuning machines that can operate a maximum of 8,000 tuning hours per year. What is the contribution margin per limited resource for each type of television?
   a. $125 for Standard and $200 for Deluxe
   b. $200 for Standard and $125 for Deluxe
   c. $62.50 for Standard and $50 for Deluxe
   d. $50 for Standard and $62.50 for Deluxe

12. Resource utilization decisions require managers to maximize:
    a. gross profit per unit produced.
    b. contribution margin per unit produced.
    c. contribution margin per unit of scarce resource.
    d. gross profit per unit of scarce resource.

13. Which of the following is most likely to represent a bottleneck?
    a. A production machine that is underutilized.
    b. A workstation that requires significant supervision.
    c. A production machine that has limited capacity.
    d. An employee who has one hour of idle time each day.

14. Canned Foods Unlimited is deciding whether to sell its canned corn in whole kernels or to process it further into creamed corn. The cost of producing whole kernel corn is $0.20 per can, and the can sells for $0.40. Additional processing costs to produce creamed corn are $0.06 per can, and each can sells for $0.45. Which of the following costs are relevant in this decision to sell or process further?
    a. $0.20 production cost
    b. $0.06 additional processing cost
    c. Both a and b are relevant.
    d. Neither a nor b is relevant.

15. Bakery Creations has three pastries that can be sold after baking or being decorated and then sold. All pastries sell whether presented as baked or as decorated. The following sales and cost information is provided:

	Pastry A	Pastry B	Pastry C
Initial sales price	$1.25	$1.50	$1.75
Initial cost	$0.75	$0.75	$0.75
Sales price after decorating	$1.60	$2.00	$2.25
Cost of decorating	$0.30	$0.60	$0.40
Number sold per day	100	50	30

    What is the maximum amount that net income could increase with further processing?
    a. $85
    b. $8
    c. $3
    d. No increase is possible as all pastries will be sold either way.

Concept Questions

16. *(Objective 1)* Production of a special order will increase income when the additional revenue from the special order is greater than what?
17. *(Objective 1)* In considering a special order that will enable a company to make use of presently idle capacity, list the costs that would more than likely be relevant in the decision-making process.
18. *(Objective 2)* What costs are usually relevant in a make-or-buy decision?
19. *(Objective 2)* Name some qualitative factors that would cause a decision maker to favor the buy choice in a make-or-buy decision.
20. *(Objective 2)* What are some of the disadvantages of outsourcing the production of a component part?
21. *(Objective 2)* In deciding whether to manufacture a part or to buy it from an outside supplier, name a cost that would not be relevant to that short-run decision.
22. *(Objective 3)* The decision to drop a product line should be based on what factors?

23. *(Objective 4)* What should be the goal of a manager who is faced with a limited resource decision?

24. *(Objective 5)* What steps should be taken when dealing with a production bottleneck?

25. *(Objective 6)* What is the general rule of thumb that should be followed when making a decision to sell as is or process a particular product further?

Exercises

LO 1

✓ Minimum profit per chair: $10

26. Bob Johnson, Inc. sells a lounging chair for $25 per unit. It incurs the following costs for the product: direct materials, $11; direct labor, $7; variable overhead, $2; and fixed overhead, $1. The company received a special order for 50 chairs. The order would require rental of a special tool that rents for $300. Bob Johnson, Inc. has sufficient idle capacity to produce the chairs for this order.

Required

Calculate the minimum price per chair that the company could charge for this special order if management requires a $500 minimum profit on any special order.

LO 1

27. Rick Nicotera sells special terra cotta trays that are perfect for planting in dry climates. The trays have per unit variable production costs of $15 and fixed costs of $4 (based on 8,000 units). Rick's company has excess capacity to accept a special order up to 500 units.

Required

What is the minimum price that could be charged for this special order?

LO 1

28. Husky Sports manufactures footballs. The forecasted income statement for the year before any special orders is as follows:

	Total	Per Unit
Sales	$ 4,000,000	$10.00
Manufacturing cost of goods sold	3,200,000	8.00
Gross profit	$ 800,000	$ 2.00
Selling expenses	300,000	0.75
Net income	$ 500,000	$ 1.25

Fixed costs included in the preceding forecasted income statement are $1,200,000 in manufacturing cost of goods sold and $100,000 in selling expenses. Husky Sports received a special order for 50,000 footballs at $7.50 each. Assume that Husky Sports has sufficient capacity to manufacture 50,000 more footballs.

Required

Calculate the relevant unit cost that Husky Sports should consider in evaluating this special order.

LO 1

29. Great Falls Brewery's regular selling price for a case of beer is $15. Variable costs are $8 per case and fixed costs total $2 per case based on production of 250,000 cases. The fixed costs remain unchanged within a relevant range of 50,000 to 300,000 cases. After sales of 180,000 cases were projected for the year, a special order was received for an additional 30,000 cases.

Required

Calculate Great Falls Brewery's minimum acceptable selling price for the special order of 30,000 cases.

30. Suckert Company manufactures lacrosse sticks. The company's capacity is 4,500 sticks per month; however, it currently sells only 3,000 sticks per month. Long Meadow Sports has offered to buy 700 lacrosse sticks for $50 each from Suckert. Normally, the company sells its sticks for $65. Suckert's accounting records report the cost of each stick to be $40, including fixed costs of $20 each.

Required

If Suckert were to accept Long Meadow's offer, what would be the impact on Suckert's income?

31. Engstrom, Inc. uses 10,000 pounds of a specific raw material in the production of life preservers each year. Presently, the material is purchased from an outside supplier for $11 per pound. For some time now, the factory has had idle capacity that could be utilized to make the material. Engstrom's costs associated with manufacturing the material are as follows:

Direct materials per lb.	$3
Direct labor per lb.	$3
Variable overhead per lb.	$2
Fixed overhead per unit (based on annual production of 10,000 lbs.)	$2
Annual salary of new supervisor	$32,000

Required

If Engstrom chooses to make the product instead of buying it from the outside supplier, what would be the change, if any, in the company's income?

32. Switzer Corporation makes motorcycle engines. The company's records show the following unit costs to manufacture part #61645:

✓ *Relevant costs of making the part: $47*

Direct materials	$12
Direct labor	$15
Variable overhead	$20
Fixed overhead	$10

Another manufacturer has offered to supply Switzer Corporation with part #61645 for a cost of $50 per unit. Switzer uses 1,000 units annually.

Required

If Switzer accepts the offer, what will be the short-run impact on income?

33. Humphrey Sports is considering outsourcing its maintenance work. The total labor cost for the maintenance department is $150,000 and the company has an offer from Robyn Maintenance to provide the service for $125,000. The maintenance equipment currently used cannot be sold and has annual depreciation of $10,000. The overhead allocated to the maintenance department is $20,000 per year and would not be avoidable.

Required

Based on the information given, what should Humphrey Sports do with respect to outsourcing its maintenance work?

34. Langer Company has three products (A, B, and C) that use common facilities. The relevant data concerning these three products follow:

	A	B	C	Total
Sales	$10,000	$30,000	$ 40,000	$ 80,000
Variable costs	5,000	20,000	25,000	50,000
Contribution margin	$ 5,000	$10,000	$ 15,000	$ 30,000
Fixed costs	5,000	15,000	30,000	50,000
Operating loss	$ 0	$ (5,000)	$(15,000)	$(20,000)

Required

If fixed costs allocated to product line C are not avoidable and if product line C is dropped, what will be the impact on income?

35. Woodruff Ltd. sells three rockers (Unfinished, Stained, and Painted) that use common facilities. The relevant data concerning these three products follow:

	Unfinished	Stained	Painted	Total
Sales	$10,000	$30,000	$ 40,000	$ 80,000
Variable costs	5,000	20,000	25,000	50,000
Contribution margin	$ 5,000	$10,000	$ 15,000	$ 30,000
Fixed costs	5,000	15,000	30,000	50,000
Operating loss	$ 0	$ (5,000)	$(15,000)	$(20,000)

Required

If $15,000 of the fixed costs allocated to the Painted rockers are avoidable and the company drops Painted rockers from its product line, what will be the impact on income?

36. Finlay Grace Sullivan & Company has two sales offices: one located in Portland and one in Portsmouth. Management is considering dropping the Portland office. The company's records report the following information:

	Portland	Portsmouth
Sales	$40,000	$50,000
Direct costs:		
Variable	15,000	25,000
Fixed	10,000	10,000

Required

What will be the effect on income if Portland is eliminated and half of its fixed costs are avoided?

37. Kerrie Velinsky Productions produces music videos in two lengths on separate compact discs. The company can sell its entire production of either product. The relevant data for these two products follow:

	Compact Disc 1	Compact Disc 2
Machine time per CD (hours)	2	5
Selling price per CD	$10	$20
Variable costs per CD	$ 2	$ 4

Total fixed overhead is $240,000. The company has only 100,000 machine hours available for production. Because of the constraint on the maximum number of machine hours, Kerrie must decide which CD to produce to maximize the company's income.

Required

Which product should the company select to maximize operating profits?

✓ Contribution margin per unit of CD1: $8

38. Ryan Miller Toys manufactured 500 stuffed lobsters that were defective. The manufacturing costs of the lobsters were:

Direct materials	$30
Direct labor	24
Variable overhead	10
Fixed overhead	12

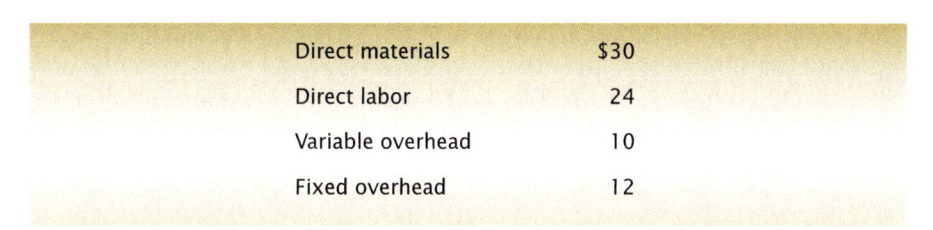

The lobsters normally sell for $100. The company can rework the lobsters, which will cost $20 for direct materials, $20 for direct labor, and $2 for variable overhead. In addition, fixed overhead will be applied at the rate of 75 percent of direct labor cost. Alternatively, the company could sell the lobsters "as is" for a selling price of $70.

Required

What should management do to maximize profits?

39. Swine Enterprises produces hams from locally raised pigs. The cost of getting the meat ready for market is $1 per pound. Hams weigh an average of 12 pounds and sell for $1.50 per pound. The company can smoke the hams for an additional $0.50 per pound. The smoked hams would sell for $2.25 per pound.

Required

Should the company smoke the hams? What if the selling price were $1.75 per pound?

40. DePaulis Furniture Manufacturers makes unfinished furniture for sale to customers from its own stores. Recently, the company has been considering taking production one additional step and finishing some of the furniture to sell as finished furniture. To analyze the problem, DePaulis is going to look at only one product, a very popular dining room chair. The chair can be produced now for $65 and sells for $85 unfinished. If DePaulis were to finish the chair, the cost would increase to $90, but the company could sell the finished chairs for $125.

Required

Should DePaulis finish the chairs or continue to sell them unfinished? Show computations to support your decision.

Problems

41. Lindsey Smith, Inc. has the following cost structure for the upcoming year:

Sales (20,000 units @ $25)	$ 500,000
Manufacturing costs:	
Variable	$ 10 per unit
Fixed	$ 180,000
Marketing and administrative costs:	
Variable	$ 5 per unit
Fixed	$ 20,000

Required

A. What is the expected level of profit?
B. Should the company accept a special order for 1,000 units at a selling price of $20 if variable marketing expenses associated with the special order were $2 per unit? What is the incremental profit if the order is accepted?
C. Suppose that the company received a special order for 3,000 units at a selling price of $19 with no variable marketing expenses. What is the impact on profit?
D. Assume that if the special order is accepted, all the regular customers would be aware of the price paid for the special order. Would that influence your decision? Why?

✓ *Incremental profits for question B: $8,000*

42. The Belik Company has the capacity to produce 5,000 units per year. Its predicted operations for the year are as follows:

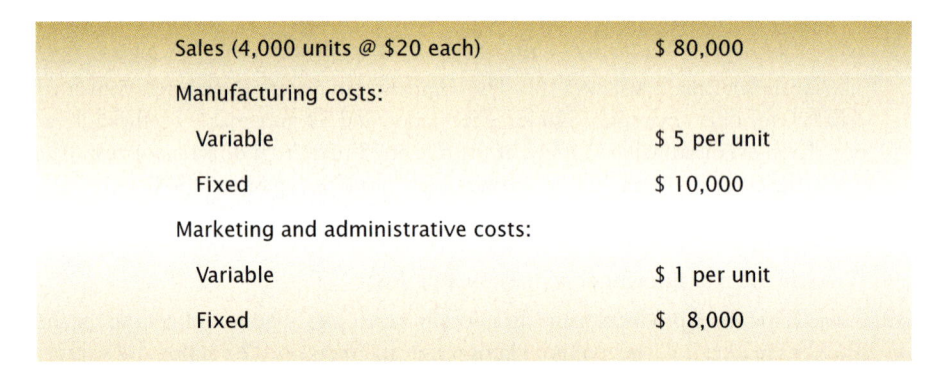

Sales (4,000 units @ $20 each)	$ 80,000
Manufacturing costs:	
Variable	$ 5 per unit
Fixed	$ 10,000
Marketing and administrative costs:	
Variable	$ 1 per unit
Fixed	$ 8,000

✓ *Incremental profits for question A: $1,500*

The accounting department has prepared the following projected income statement for the coming year for your use in making decisions:

Sales		$ 80,000
Variable costs:		
Manufacturing ($5 × 4,000)	$ 20,000	
Marketing ($1 × 4,000)	4,000	24,000
Contribution margin		$ 56,000
Fixed costs:		
Manufacturing	$ 10,000	
Marketing	8,000	18,000
Operating profit		$ 38,000

Required

A. Should the company accept a special order for 500 units at a selling price of $8? Assuming that there are no variable marketing and administrative costs for this order and that regular sales will not be affected, what is the impact of this decision on company profits?
B. Suppose that the preceding order has a one-time setup fee of $1,000. Should the special order be accepted? Why or why not?
C. What other factors should be considered, and how would they impact your decision to accept the special order?
D. Disregarding questions A through C, suppose that regular sales would be reduced by 200 units if the special order were accepted. What impact would this have on the company's decision?

43. Jain Simmons Company needs 10,000 units of a certain part to be used in production. If Jain Simmons Company buys the part from Sullivan Company instead of making it themselves, Jain Simmons Company could not use the present facilities for another manufacturing activity. Sixty percent of the fixed overhead applied will continue regardless of what decision is made. The following quantitative information is available regarding the situation presented:

Cost to make the part:	
Direct materials	$ 6
Direct labor	24
Variable overhead	12
Fixed overhead applied	15
	$57
Cost to buy the part:	$ 53

✓ Total relevant costs: $48

Required

A. In deciding whether to make or buy the part, what are Simmons' total relevant costs to make the part?
B. Which alternative (make or buy) is more desirable for Simmons and by what amount?
C. Suppose that Simmons Company is in an area of the country with high unemployment and that it is unlikely that displaced employees will find other employment. How might that impact your decision?

44. The Hemp Division of West Company produces rope. One-third of the Hemp Division's output is sold to the Hammock Products Division of West; the remainder is sold to outside customers. The Hemp Division's estimated sales and cost data for the fiscal year ending September 30 are as follows:

	Hammock Products	Outsiders
Sales	$15,000	$40,000
Variable costs	10,000	20,000
Fixed costs	3,000	6,000
Gross margin	$ 2,000	$14,000
Unit sales	10,000	20,000

✓ Net benefit of producing the rope (question B): $7,500

The Hemp Division has an opportunity to purchase 10,000 feet of identical-quality rope from an outside supplier at a cost of $1.25 per unit on a continuing basis. Assume that the Hemp Division cannot sell any additional product to outside customers.

Required

A. Should West allow its Hemp Division to purchase the rope from the outside supplier? Why or why not?
B. Assume that the Hemp Division is now at full capacity and that sufficient demand exists to sell all production to outsiders at present prices. What is the differential cost (benefit) of producing the rope internally?
C. Assume that the quality of the rope is found to be of a lesser, but still satisfactory, quality. What factors should be considered?
D. Assume that the quality of the rope is found to be of questionable quality but that the price is $1.00 per unit. What factors should be considered in the decision?

45. The James Manufacturing Co. manufactures part #81199 for use in producing a mountain bike. The costs per unit for 20,000 units of part #81199 are as follows:

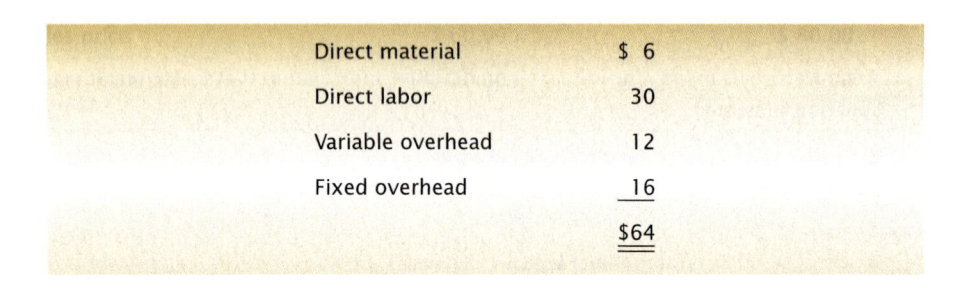

Direct material	$ 6
Direct labor	30
Variable overhead	12
Fixed overhead	16
	$64

Kelley Manufacturing has offered to sell James 20,000 units of part #81199 for $60 per unit. The company will buy the part from Kelley if the savings total $250,000. If the part is purchased from the outside supplier, James will realize savings of $9 per part for fixed overhead. Furthermore, the released facilities could be leased for additional revenue.

Required

What amount of lease payment must be charged to reach the required $250,000 savings? What qualitative factors should be considered before making a final decision? Why?

46. Smoluk Mining Company currently is operating at less than 50 percent of capacity. The management of the company expects sales to drop below the present level of 10,000 tons of ore per month very soon. The sales price per ton is $3 and the variable cost per ton is $2. Fixed costs per month total $10,000.
    Management is concerned that a further drop in sales volume will generate a loss and, accordingly, is considering the temporary suspension of operations until demand in the metals markets rebounds and prices once again rise. Over the past year, management has implemented a cost-reduction program that has been successful in reducing costs to the point that suspending operations appears to be the only viable alternative. Management estimates that suspending operations would reduce fixed costs by $6,000 per month.

✓ *Suspension of operations is desirable when volume is less than 6,000 tons*

Required

A. Why does management estimate that the fixed costs will persist at $4,000 even though the mine is temporarily closed?
B. At what sales volume will the loss be greater or less than the shutdown cost of $4,000 per month?
C. List any qualitative factors that you think management should consider in this decision, and discuss the potential impact of each factor on the decision.

47. Casagrande Company is currently operating at 80 percent capacity. Worried about the company's performance, Mike, the general manager, reviewed the company's operating performance.

	Segment			
	North	South	East	West
Sales	$30	$40	$ 20	$ 10
Less variable costs	12	8	21	8
Contribution margin	$18	$32	$ (1)	$ 2
Less fixed costs	9	12	6	3
Operating profit (loss)	$ 9	$20	$ (7)	$ (1)

✓ Current profits for company as a whole: $21

Required
- A. What is the current operating profit for the company as a whole?
- B. Assuming that all fixed costs are unavoidable, if Mike eliminated the unprofitable segments, what would be the new operating profit for the company as a whole?
- C. What options does management have to maximize profits?
- D. What qualitative factors do you think management should consider before making this decision? What impact could these qualitative factors have on the decision?

48. Robinson's Grocery Store is a small corner grocery store in rural Montana, and shelf space is very limited. Management must decide how to allocate shelf space for salsa. Robinson's has been given an opportunity to sell a very popular brand of salsa produced by Bobby Tutor, a popular rock star. The unique bottle is taller and thinner than the other popular brands on the market, increasing its visibility on the shelf. The sales and cost data for the new salsa and the three other brands presently sold are shown below:

	Salsa #1	Salsa #2	Salsa #3	New Salsa
Sales price per jar	$2.50	$2.75	$3.00	$4.00
Cost to purchase	1.25	1.35	1.50	3.20
Contribution margin	$1.25	$1.40	$1.50	$0.80
Bottles per foot of shelf space	10	9	7	12

✓ Salsa #1 generates revenue of $250

Required
- A. Rank the salsas based on expected revenue if each is given 10 feet of shelf space and all bottles are expected to be sold.
- B. Based on the information given, which salsa should get the most shelf space? Why?
- C. What qualitative factors should be considered in this decision? How would these factors impact the decision?

49. Sun Devil Golf Balls produces two types of golf balls: the pro model and the tour model. The balls are sold to retailers in cartons containing 360 balls (30 boxes containing 4 sleeves per box, with each sleeve holding 3 balls). Both models are made using the same machines. It takes 15 minutes of machine time to produce 360 pro-model golf balls, whereas it takes 30 minutes to produce the same number of the tour-model balls. The difference in production time results mainly from the different materials used in construction. The relevant data concerning the two models are as follows:

	Pro Model	Tour Model
Sales price (per carton)	$500	$590
Less: Direct material	200	265
Direct labor	50	50
Variable overhead	50	75
Contribution margin	$200	$200
Required machine time	1/4 hour	1/2 hour

✓ Contribution margin per hour for Tour Model: $400

Required

A. If the amount of machine time available to Sun Devil Golf Balls is limited, which golf ball should be produced in the larger quantity?
B. If the total machine time available is 110 hours per month and the demand for each model of golf ball is 108,000 balls per month, how many of each model should be produced to maximize profit? (Round your answer to the nearest carton.)
C. What other factors should be considered in this decision, and how would they impact the decision?

50. DeBaca's Fish House buys fish from local fishermen and sells the fish to the public from its booth at the public market. Lately, the fish house has had a number of requests for smoked salmon and has decided to investigate whether that would be a profitable item. The salmon DeBaca's buys now costs the company $2 per pound. DeBaca's would have to take the new salmon to a smoke house to have it smoked, which would increase the total cost to $3.25 for each pound of salmon. The salmon currently sells for $5.50 per pound, but would sell for $6.50 per pound if it were smoked.

Required

A. Based on the facts given, would it be profitable to smoke the salmon? Why or why not?
B. If the cost of the smoking process could be reduced by $0.50 per pound, would it be profitable to smoke the salmon?
C. What qualitative factors should be considered before making a final decision?

Cases

51. Foggy Mountain Company manufactures several styles of banjos. Management estimates that during the second quarter of the current year, the company will be operating at 80 percent of normal capacity. Because Foggy Mountain wants to increase utilization of the plant, the company has decided to consider special orders for its products.

Foggy Mountain has just received inquiries from a number of companies concerning the possibility of a special order and has narrowed the decision to two companies. The

✓ Excess capacity in 2nd quarter: 45,000 hours

first inquiry is from CCR Company, which would like to market a banjo very similar to one of Foggy Mountain's. The CCR banjo would be marketed under CCR's own label. CCR has offered Foggy Mountain $57.50 per banjo for 20,000 banjos to be shipped by June 1. The cost data for the Foggy Mountain banjo are as follows:

Regular selling price per banjo	$ 90.00
Costs per unit:	
Raw material	$ 25.00
Direct labor (5 hours @ $6)	30.00
Overhead (2.5 machine hours @ $4)	10.00
Total costs	$ 65.00

According to the specifications provided by CCR, the banjo that the company wants requires less expensive raw material. Consequently, the raw material would cost only $22 per banjo. Foggy Mountain has estimated that all remaining costs would not change.

The second special order was submitted by Seager & Buffet Company for 7,500 banjos at $75 per banjo. These banjos would be marketed under the Seager & Buffet label and also would be shipped by June 1. However, the Seager & Buffet model is different from any banjo in the Foggy Mountain product line. The estimated per unit costs are as follows:

Raw material	$32.50
Direct labor (5 hours @ $6)	30.00
Overhead (5 machine hours @ $4)	20.00
Total costs	$82.50

In addition, Foggy Mountain will incur $15,000 in additional setup costs and will have to purchase a $22,500 special machine to manufacture these banjos; this machine will be discarded once the special order is completed.

The Foggy Mountain manufacturing capabilities are limited in the total machine hours available. The plant capacity under normal operations is 900,000 machine hours per year, or 75,000 machine hours per month. The budgeted fixed overhead for the year is $2,160,000. All manufacturing overhead costs are applied to production on the basis of machine hours at $4 per hour.

Foggy Mountain will have the entire second quarter to work on the special orders. Management does not expect any repeat sales to be generated from either special order. Company practice precludes Foggy Mountain from subcontracting any portion of an order when special orders are not expected to generate repeat sales.

Required

A. What is the excess capacity of machine hours available in the second quarter?
B. What is the variable overhead rate per machine hour?
C. Based on the preceding information and your analysis, would you accept CCR's offer?
D. What is the unit contribution margin per banjo for the Seager & Buffet order?
E. What is the actual gain (loss) incurred by accepting Seager & Buffet's offer?

LO 2, 4

Activity Making Decision A

✓ Contribution margin per DLH for skateboards: $39

52. Avery, Inc. is a wholesale distributor supplying a wide range of moderately priced sporting equipment to large chain stores. About 60 percent of Avery's products are purchased from other companies, and the remainder of the products are manufactured by Avery. The company has a plastics department that is currently manufacturing molded fishing tackle boxes. Avery is able to manufacture and sell 8,000 tackle boxes annually, making full use of its direct labor capacity at available workstations. The following table presents the selling price and costs associated with Avery's tackle boxes:

Selling price		$86.00
Costs per box:		
Molded plastic	$ 8.00	
Hinges, latches, handle	9.00	
Direct labor ($15/hour)	18.75	
Manufacturing overhead	12.50	
Selling and administrative cost	*17.00	65.25
Profit per box		$20.75

*Includes $6 per unit of fixed distribution costs.

Because Avery believes that it could sell 12,000 tackle boxes, the company has looked into the possibility of purchasing the tackle boxes from another manufacturer. Craig Products, a supplier of quality products, could provide up to 9,000 tackle boxes per year at a per unit price of $68. Variable selling and administrative costs of $4 per unit will be incurred if the tackle boxes are purchased from Craig Products.

Bart Johnson, Avery's product manager, has suggested that the company could make better use of its plastics department by purchasing the tackle boxes and manufacturing skateboards. To support his position, Johnson has a market study that indicates an expanding market for skateboards and a need for additional suppliers. Johnson believes that Avery could expect to sell 17,500 skateboards annually at a price of $45.00 per skateboard. Johnson's estimate of the costs to manufacture the skateboards follows:

Selling price per skateboard		$45.00
Costs per skateboard:		
Molded plastic	$ 5.50	
Wheels, plastic	7.00	
Direct labor ($15/hour)	7.50	
Manufacturing overhead	5.00	
Selling and administrative cost	*9.00	34.00
Profit per skateboard		$11.00

*Includes $6 per unit of fixed distribution costs.

In the plastics department, Avery uses direct labor hours as the application base for manufacturing overhead. Included in the manufacturing overhead for the current year is $50,000 factory-wide, fixed manufacturing overhead that has been allocated to the plastics department.

Required

A. Define the problem faced by Avery based on the facts as presented.
B. What are the relevant objectives in this problem?
C. What options are available to Avery in solving the problem?
D. Rank the options in order of preference.
E. What qualitative factors should Avery consider in the decision?
F. Should Avery consider the potential liability that comes with selling skateboards? It has been shown that skateboards are responsible for 25 deaths per year and more than 500 serious accidents. Would that change your decision to make skateboards?

Group and Internet Exercises

53. Outsourcing has received increasing attention as more jobs are shipped overseas. Companies routinely point to the significant cost savings that are achieved through the use of outsourcing. Within your group conduct an Internet search to locate an article about a company that has chosen to outsource a function to another country. Prepare a memo that describes the company's decision and discuss the ethical implications of the decision.

54. Many companies have made decisions to reduce their workforces, close stores, and otherwise contract their businesses. Within your group conduct an Internet search to locate an article about a company that has recently announced significant layoffs, store closings, or other business contractions. Prepare a memo that explains the company's reasons for the announced action. Does the article discuss how the company will assist displaced employees? What obligations, if any, do companies have to employees and communities that are impacted by their actions?

Chapter 8

Long-Term (Capital Investment) Decisions

Chapter 8 Long-Term (Capital Investment) Decisions

Long-term decisions require a consideration of the time value of money in addition to cost behavior and the relevance of costs. In this chapter, we develop tools that aid managers in making long-term decisions to purchase new property, plant, and equipment (capital investment decisions). These tools help managers quantify the impact of paying or receiving cash flows in different time periods.

Net present value and internal rate of return are two methods that allow for the explicit consideration of the time value of money. The use of these tools in both screening decisions and preference decisions is discussed, as is the impact of income taxes on the analysis. The impact of new manufacturing techniques on capital investment decisions and the importance of qualitative factors in the analysis are also discussed. An approach to long-term purchasing decisions that does not consider the time value of money, the payback method, is also mentioned.

Learning Objectives

After studying the material in this chapter, you should be able to:

1. Discuss the importance of focusing on cash flow in capital investment decisions

2. Discuss key assumptions of the net present value (NPV) and internal rate of return (IRR) methods

3. Evaluate capital investment decisions using the NPV method

4. Evaluate capital investment decisions using the IRR method

5. Distinguish between screening and preference decisions and use the profitability index to evaluate preference decisions

6. Evaluate the impact of taxes on capital investment decisions

7. Evaluate capital investment decisions using the payback method and discuss the limitations of the method

Introduction

Capital investment decisions are made by all types and sizes of organizations and involve the purchase (or lease) of new machinery and equipment and the acquisition or expansion of facilities used in a business. A decision by a local florist to purchase or to lease a new delivery van is a capital investment decision, as is the decision to upgrade the computer system at a law firm. A decision by Wal-Mart to build and open a new store and a decision by Ford to invest in new automated production equipment are capital investment decisions. Long-term purchasing decisions such as these often involve large sums of money and considerable risk because they commit companies to a chosen course of action for many years.

One of the key factors to be considered in a long-term purchasing decision is the return of the investment and also the return on the investment—in other words, whether the benefits of the investment exceed its cost. The costs and benefits include both qualitative and quantitative factors. Qualitative costs and benefits include employee, customer, and community reaction to changes in location, the impact of automation on displaced employees, quality improvements that result from new equipment, and so forth. Quantitative costs and benefits include large initial outlays of cash and the need for future repairs and maintenance, the potential for increased sales, and reductions in production and other costs.

Hitting the Bottom Line.
INVESTING FOR THE FUTURE

Someone at General Electric has heard the old saying that "it takes money to make money" because the company has been investing heavily in its aircraft engine division in recent years even as the overall economy has been shrinking. The division's Durham, North Carolina, plant has been one of the biggest beneficiaries of GE's investment. The state-of-the-art manufacturing plant utilizes highly skilled labor and, wherever possible, automation to produce some of the most widely used jet engines in the world. Therein lies one of the plant's greatest strengths—flexibility. Employees can produce engines for the venerable Boeing 747 or small regional jets that seat just 70 passengers. Partly due to this flexibility, GE's Aircraft Engine division won part of a $40 billion contract to produce engines for Boeing's new 7E7 Dreamliner jet. Although the first new engine will be completed in 2008, GE estimates that it will not earn profits until 2023, or 15 years into production. Clearly, the company has decided that investing in the future is good business! ("Durham Plant is GE's 'Go-To'," *The News & Observer*, April 22, 2004, 1D.)

Objective 1

Discuss the importance of focusing on cash flow in capital investment decisions

Focus on Cash Flow

Because capital investments involve large sums of money and last for many years, a quantitative analysis of the costs and benefits of capital investment decisions must consider the **time value of money**. In addition, the focus of the time value of money is on cash flow, not accounting net income. Accounting net income and cash flow are often not the same. Accounting net income is calculated based on the accrual of income and expenses rather than on the receipt and payment of cash. Whereas measurements of both income and cash flow are useful to managers, investors, and creditors, time-value-of-money calculations are based on the concept that a dollar received (paid) today is worth more (less) than a dollar received (paid) in the future and thus focus on the cash flow of an organization.

Doing Business.

PAY ATTENTION TO THE CASH

Although stock analysts and investors have traditionally focused on current and expected earnings of a company in assessing its potential as an investment, analysts increasingly favor the use of cash flow. Analysts like focusing on cash flow because, they say, it "ignores accounting tricks and shows the true economic health of companies" ("Analysts Increasingly Favor Using Cash Flows over Reported Earnings in Stock Valuations," *Wall Street Journal,* April 1, 1999, C2).

Typical cash outflows include the original investment in the project, any additional working capital needed during the life of the investment, repairs and maintenance needed for machinery and equipment, and additional operating costs that may be incurred. Typical cash inflows include projected incremental revenues from the project, cost reductions in operating expenses, the salvage value (if any) of the investment at the end of its useful life, and the release of working capital at the end of a project's useful life.

With the exception of the initial cash outflow associated with the investment, other cash inflows and outflows are likely to be estimates. The extended time period involved in long-term purchasing decisions makes the projection of these cash inflows and outflows difficult at best. The impact of uncertainty on capital investment decisions and the use of sensitivity analysis are discussed in more detail later in the chapter.

> **KEY CONCEPT**
>
> Long-term investment decisions require a consideration of the time value of money. The time value of money is based on the concept that a dollar received today is worth more than a dollar received in the future.

Discounted Cash Flow Analysis

The time value of money is considered in capital investment decisions by using one of two techniques: the net present value method or the internal rate of return method.[1] In both methods, two simplifying assumptions are made when discounting cash flows to their present value. The first is that all cash flows are assumed to occur at the end of each period (typically at the end of a year). Although most cost reductions and cash inflows resulting from increased sales are likely to occur uniformly throughout the year, this assumption greatly simplifies present-value calculations. The second is that all cash inflows are immediately reinvested in another project or investment. This assumption is analogous to the immediate reinvesting of dividends in a stock investment. The rate of return assumed earned on the reinvested amounts depends on whether the net present value or the internal rate of return method is used. Under the NPV method, cash inflows are assumed to be reinvested at the discount rate used in the analysis. Under the IRR method, cash inflows are assumed to be reinvested at the internal rate of return of the original investment.

> **Objective 2**
>
> Discuss key assumptions of the net present value (NPV) and internal rate of return (IRR) methods

> **KEY CONCEPT**
>
> The time value of money is considered in capital investment decisions by using one of two techniques: the net present value (NPV) method or the internal rate of return (IRR) method.

---

[1] The following discussion assumes that readers are already familiar with the basic concepts of discounting and the calculation of present value for single sums and annuities. If not, you should study the appendix at the end of this chapter.

Objective 3

Evaluate capital investment decisions using the NPV method

Bud and Rose's Flower Shop

KEY CONCEPT

If the present value of cash inflows is greater than or equal to the present value of cash outflows (the NPV is greater than or equal to zero), the investment provides a return at least equal to the discount rate (the minimum required rate of return), and the investment is acceptable.

Net Present Value

The **net present value (NPV)** method requires the choice of a discount rate to be used in the analysis. Many companies choose to use the **cost of capital**. The cost of capital represents what the firm would have to pay to borrow (issue bonds) or to raise funds through equity (issue stock) in the financial marketplace. In NPV analysis, the **discount rate** serves as a minimum required rate of return, or a hurdle rate—the return that the company feels must be earned in order for any potential investment to be profitable. For purposes of Chapter 8, we will refer to this discount rate as a minimum required rate of return although in practice it is commonplace to use both terms. The discount rate is often adjusted to reflect the risk and the uncertainty of cash flows expected to occur many years in the future. Adjusting the rate for uncertainty is discussed in more detail later in the chapter.

Computing net present value requires comparing the present value of all cash inflows associated with a project with the present value of all cash outflows. If the present value of the inflows is greater than or equal to the present value of the outflows (the NPV is greater than or equal to zero), the investment provides a return at least equal to the discount rate (the minimum required rate of return), and the investment is acceptable. If the present value of the outflows is greater than the present value of the inflows, the NPV will be negative, and the investment will not be acceptable, because it provides a return less than the discount rate.

To illustrate NPV decisions, let's discuss Bud and Rose's Flower Shop, which is considering the purchase of a new refrigerated delivery van that will cost $50,000. It will allow the company to accept large flower orders for weddings, receptions, and so on and is expected to increase cash income from sales (net of increased expenses) by $14,000 per year for six years. The van is not expected to have any salvage value at the end of the six years. Bud and Rose have a minimum required rate of return of 12 percent and use that as their discount rate.

The only cash outflow in this case is the initial purchase price of $50,000. The annual cash inflow of $14,000 can most easily be viewed as an ordinary annuity for purposes of calculating present value. NPV calculations using present-value factors are as follows:[2]

Transaction	Cash Flow	Year	Amount	12% Factor	Present Value
Purchase of refrigerated van	Initial investment	Now	$(50,000)	1.0000	$(50,000.00)
Sales of flowers	Annual cash income (net of increased expenses)	1–6	14,000	4.1114	57,559.60
Net present value					$ 7,559.60

Using the built-in function in Microsoft Excel, =PV(12%,6,−14000) returns a present value for the cash inflows equal to $57,559.70 (see Exhibit 8-1). The $0.10 difference results from rounding.

---

[2] Extended present-value tables can be found on the endsheets in the back of your textbook

Exhibit 8-1 Finding the Present Value Using the PV Function in Excel

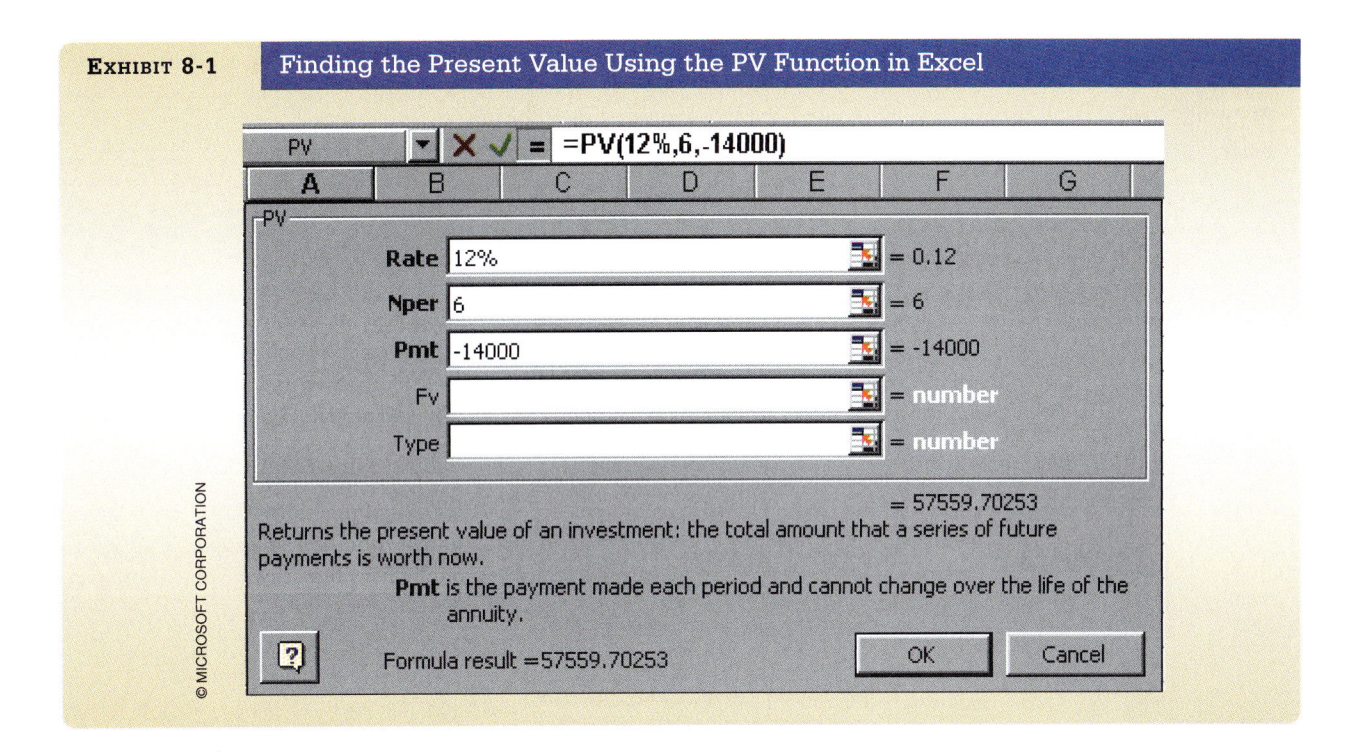

[Excel PV function dialog box: =PV(12%,6,-14000); Rate = 12% = 0.12; Nper = 6 = 6; Pmt = -14000 = -14000; Fv = number; Type = number; = 57559.70253; Formula result = 57559.70253]

Because the NPV is positive, the delivery van should be purchased. Although the positive NPV tells us that the return on the investment is at least 12 percent, it does not tell us exactly what the return is. Is it 14 percent, 16 percent, or an even higher number? We could find the actual return by trial and error. Remember, an NPV of zero means that an investment is earning exactly the discount rate used in the analysis. Increasing the discount rate to 14 percent reduces the NPV to $4,442. Going up to 16 percent reduces the NPV to $1,586, but going up to 18 percent results in a negative NPV of $1,034. The true yield of the investment must be somewhere between 16 percent and 18 percent and would be close to 17 percent. The present value of an annuity table can also be used to find the true rate of return for the delivery van.

As discussed in the appendix, the present value of an annuity (PVA) can be found using the following formula:

$$PVA = R(DFA_{n,r})$$

In this case, we know the *PVA*, the annual cash inflow (*R*), and the number of periods (*n*) and can solve indirectly for the interest rate (*r*).

$$PVA_{6,??} = \$14,000(DFA_{6,??})$$
$$\$50,000 = \$14,000(DFA_{6,?})$$
$$DFA_{6,?} = 3.5714$$

Using the present value of annuity table in the back of your textbook and looking at the row for an *n* of 6, we see that a *DFA* of 3.5714 is about halfway between an *r* of 16 percent and an *r* of 18 percent.

Internal Rate of Return

The **internal rate of return (IRR)** is the actual yield, or return, earned by an investment. We can find the yield of an investment in a number of ways. One way of looking at the IRR is that it is the discount rate that equates the present value of all cash inflows to the present value of all cash outflows. In other words, IRR is the discount rate that makes the NPV = 0.

Objective 4

Evaluate capital investment decisions using the IRR method

KEY CONCEPT

The internal rate of return (IRR) is the actual yield, or return, earned by an investment.

Although a present value table *can* be used to calculate IRR, it is inconvenient in this case because the true yield lies between the rates provided on the table. However, IRR can easily be calculated using a financial calculator or Microsoft Excel (see appendix). In Excel, =RATE (6,−14000,50000,0,0) generates an annual yield of 17.191 percent (see Exhibit 8-2).

EXHIBIT 8-2 Finding the Internal Rate of Return Using the RATE Function in Excel

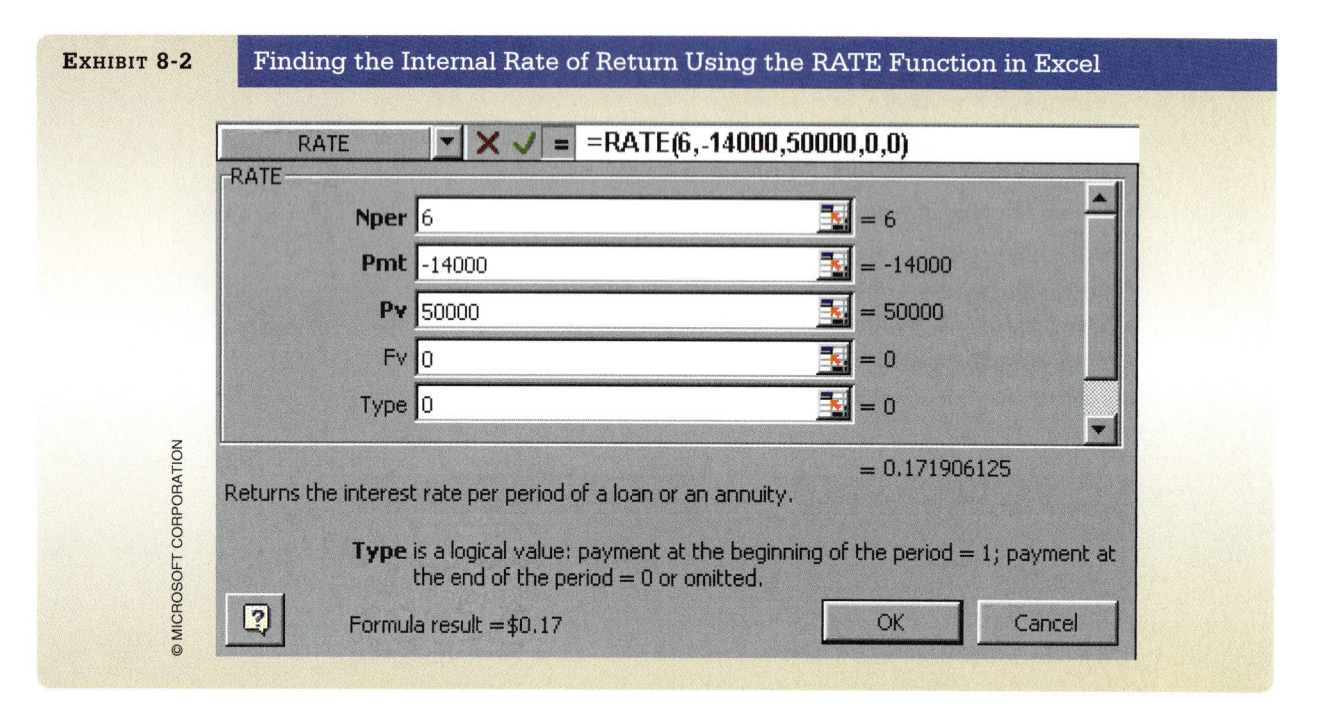

[Excel RATE dialog box showing:
- Nper: 6
- Pmt: -14000
- Pv: 50000
- Fv: 0
- Type: 0
- = 0.171906125
- Formula result = $0.17]

The Problem of Uneven Cash Flows

Harbourside Hospital

Calculations of net present value and internal rate of return get significantly more difficult when cash inflows and outflows are more numerous and when the cash flows are uneven. Consider an example in which Harbourside Hospital is considering the purchase of a new X-ray machine for cardiac care patients. Harbourside is a nonprofit hospital and has a minimum required rate of return of 10 percent. In addition, one of the hospital's objectives is to improve the quality of care provided to cardiac patients in the area. Currently, patients have to travel as far as 100 miles to a hospital equipped with this type of X-ray machine. The machine will cost $1,200,000 plus installation costs of another $50,000 and will have a useful life of approximately six years. Owing to frequent changes in technology, the machine would have little salvage value at the end of its useful life. Harbourside expects that it can sell the machine to a hospital in a developing country for $20,000. It is expected to increase revenues by $400,000 per year but will require the hiring of two new technicians at $40,000 per year for each technician, and it will require maintenance and repairs averaging $20,000 per year, which results in a net annual cash flow of $300,000 ($400,000 − $80,000 − $20,000). In addition, it is expected to require the installation of a new X-ray tube at the end of years 3 and 5 at a cost of $50,000 each. The detailed NPV analysis follows.

Transaction	Cash Flow	Year	Amount	10% Factor	Present Value
Purchase of new machine	Initial investment	Now	$(1,250,000)	1.0000	$(1,250,000)
Increased patient revenue less related expenses	Net annual cash inflows	1–6	300,000	4.3553	1,306,590
Repairs and maintenance	Cash outflow	3	(50,000)	0.7513	(37,565)
Repairs and maintenance	Cash outflow	5	(50,000)	0.6209	(31,045)
Sale of machine	Cash inflow	6	20,000	0.5645	11,290
Net present value					$ (730)

In this case, the NPV is negative, indicating that this investment would earn Harbourside less than its minimum required rate of return of 10 percent. Using Microsoft Excel's IRR function, the internal rate of return of the X-ray machine is calculated as 9.9796 percent (see Exhibit 8-3).

EXHIBIT 8-3 Finding the Internal Rate of Return Using the IRR Function in Excel

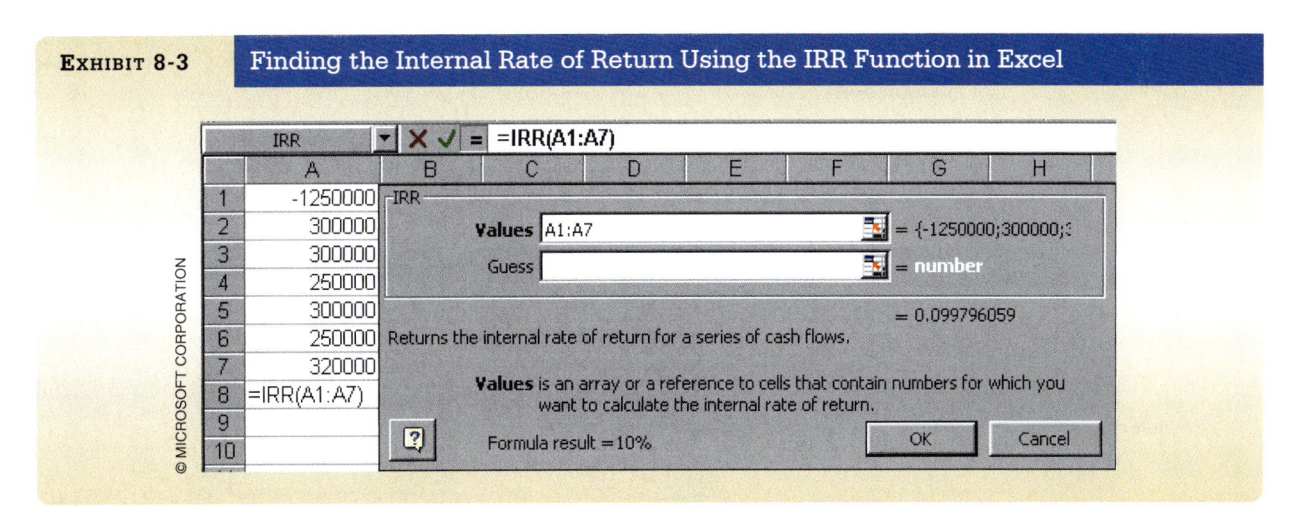

Although the quantitative analysis indicates that the investment is not acceptable, Harbourside should also consider qualitative factors in its decision. In this case, because improving the quality of patient care is very important to Harbourside, it may very well approve the investment even though its IRR is slightly below the normal acceptable level. Harbourside must also consider the impact of uncertainty on the decision. In this case, the only cash flow known with certainty is likely to be the initial purchase price. Changes in assumptions about future revenue and costs are likely to affect the decision. Adjusting the discounted cash flow analysis for the impact of uncertainty is discussed in more depth later in the chapter.

Screening and Preference Decisions

Capital investment decisions typically fall into one of two categories: screening decisions or preference decisions. **Screening decisions** involve deciding whether an investment meets a predetermined company standard, that is, whether it is acceptable, whereas **preference decisions** involve choosing between alternatives.

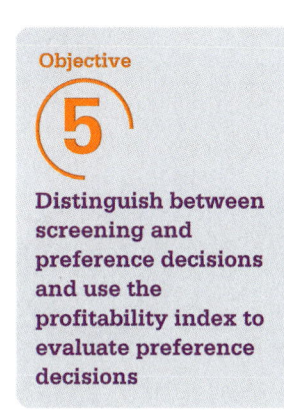

Objective 5

Distinguish between screening and preference decisions and use the profitability index to evaluate preference decisions

Typical problems addressed in capital investment decisions are as follows:

1. Should old equipment be replaced with new equipment that promises to be more cost efficient?
2. Should a new delivery vehicle be purchased or leased?
3. Should a manufacturing plant be expanded?
4. Should a new retail store be opened?

Once the problem is defined, the next step is to identify objectives. Objectives include both quantitative factors (increase production, increase sales, reduce costs) and qualitative factors (make a higher-quality product, provide better customer service). Analyzing the options involves both a quantitative analysis of the options, using tools that recognize the time value of money, and a qualitative analysis. Once the potential investments are screened and analyzed, the best option is chosen.

Both NPV and IRR can be used as a screening tool. They allow a manager to identify and to eliminate undesirable projects. Although the methods accomplish the same objective, it is important to remember that they are used in different ways. With net present value, the cost of capital is typically used as the discount rate to compute the net present value of each proposed investment. Any project that has a negative net present value should be rejected unless qualitative reasons exist for considering the project further.

With the internal rate of return, the cost of capital or other measure of a company's minimum required rate of return is compared to the computed internal rate of return. If the internal rate of return is equal to or greater than the minimum required rate of return, the investment is acceptable unless qualitative reasons exist for rejecting the project (see Exhibit 8-4).

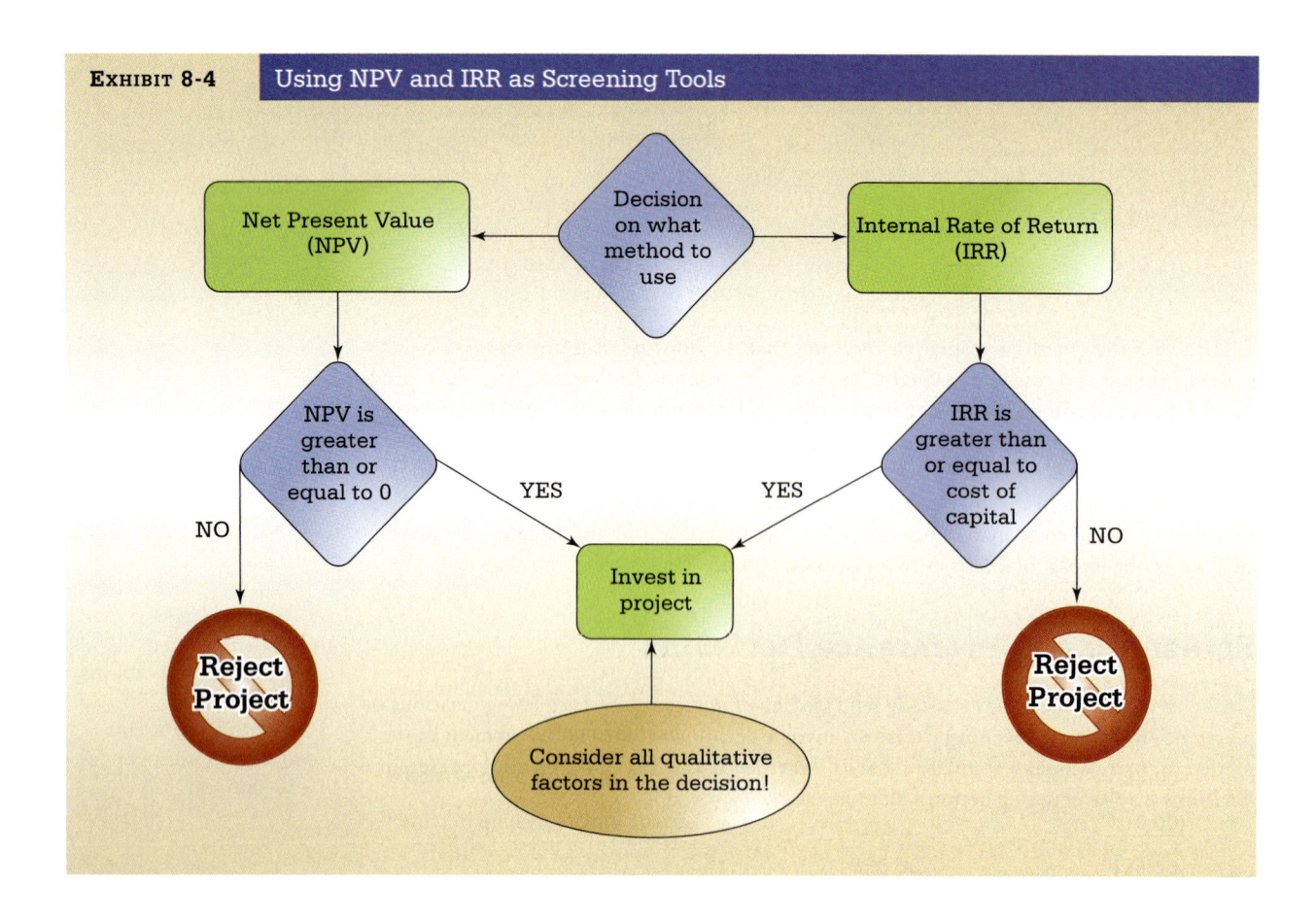

EXHIBIT 8-4 Using NPV and IRR as Screening Tools

The NPV method does have some advantages over the IRR method for making screening decisions. Adjusting the discount rate to take into account the increased risk and the uncertainty of cash flows expected to occur many years in the future is possible using net present value. When using the IRR method, users would have to adjust cash flows directly to adjust for risk.

However, NPV (without adjustment) cannot be used to compare investments (make preference decisions) unless the competing investments are of similar magnitude. Consider, for example, two competing investments, each with a five-year useful life. The first requires an investment of $10,000 and generates cash savings with a present value of $12,000 (cash inflows of $3,165.56 per year for five years discounted at 10 percent). Its NPV is therefore $2,000. The second requires an initial investment of $20,000 and generates cash inflows with a present value of $22,000 (cash inflows of $5,803.52 per year for five years). As you can see, both investments have the same NPV of $2,000.

	Investment 1	Investment 2
Initial investment	$(10,000)	$(20,000)
Present value of cash inflows	12,000	22,000
Net present value	$ 2,000	$ 2,000

Which is preferred? Intuitively, the $10,000 investment should be preferred to the $20,000 investment. Think of it this way. You could invest in two $10,000 projects and generate cash inflows of $6,331.12 per year instead of the $5,803.52 generated from one $20,000 investment. The NPV analysis can be modified slightly through the calculation of a profitability index to better allow the comparison of investments of different size. The **profitability index (PI)** is calculated by dividing the present value of the cash inflows (netted with the present value of any cash outflows occurring after the project starts) by the initial investment (netted with any other cash flows occurring on the project start date). A profitability index greater than 1.0 means that the NPV is positive (the PV of the inflows is greater than the initial investment), and the project is acceptable. When comparing the profitability index of competing projects, the project with the highest PI is preferred. The PI of investments 1 and 2 is calculated as follows:

	Investment 1	Investment 2
Present value of cash inflows	$12,000	$22,000
Initial investment	÷ $10,000	÷ $20,000
Profitability index	1.20	1.10

The $10,000 investment has a higher PI of 1.20 and is preferred over the $20,000 investment with a PI of 1.10. We can confirm this by calculating the IRR of both investments.

Using Microsoft Excel's RATE function, the IRR of investment 1 is 17.55 percent (=RATE (5, 3165.56, −10000,0,0) = 17.55%), whereas the IRR of investment 2 is only 13.84 percent (=RATE (5, 5803.52, −20000,0,0) = 13.84%).

In cases like this, in which the investment lives are equal and the cash flows follow similar patterns (annual cash flows for five years), IRR can be used to make preference decisions. However, when asset lives are unequal and cash flows follow different patterns, the use of IRR can result in incorrect decisions even when the initial investment is the same.

Consider the following example, in which two $20,000 projects are being considered. Project A reduces cash operating costs (increases cash flow) by $12,500 per year for the next two years, whereas project B reduces operating costs by $5,000 per year for six years.

Assuming a discount rate of 10 percent, the NPV, PI, and IRR of each investment are calculated as follows:

	Project A	Project B
Initial investment	$(20,000.00)	$(20,000.00)
PV of cash inflows	21,693.75	21,776.50
NPV	$ 1,693.75	$ 1,776.50
PI	1.085	1.089
IRR	16.26%	12.98%

Although IRR would indicate that project A is preferable to project B, NPV and PI indicate that project B is better. Which is right? Well, it depends. As we discussed earlier in the chapter, the IRR method assumes that cash inflows are immediately reinvested at the IRR earned on the original investment—in this case, over 16 percent. In contrast, the NPV method assumes that cash inflows are reinvested at the cost of capital or other discount rate used in the analysis—10 percent in our analysis. If you can reinvest the large cash inflows received in project A at the end of years 1 and 2 at a high rate of return, project A would indeed be preferred. If not, project B, offering a return of almost 13 percent for six years, would be preferred. The use of IRR generally favors short-term investments with high yields, whereas NPV favors longer-term investments even if the return is lower.

The Impact of Taxes on Capital Investment Decisions

Objective 6

Evaluate the impact of taxes on capital investment decisions

Nonprofit organizations, such as Harbourside Hospital, don't pay income taxes and don't need to consider the impact of income taxes on capital investment decisions (or other decisions, for that matter).[3] However, profit-making companies must pay income taxes on any taxable income earned (just like individuals must) and must therefore consider the impact of income taxes on capital investment and other management decisions. With federal income tax rates on corporations ranging from 15 percent to 35 percent of taxable income (and state income taxes typically adding another 5 to 10 percent), taxes are a major source of cash outflows for many companies and must be taken into consideration for any long-term investment decision.

As demonstrated in Chapter 5, the after-tax benefit or cost of a taxable cash inflow or a tax-deductible cash outflow is found by multiplying the before-tax cash inflow or before-tax cash outflow by (1 − tax rate). For a company with a combined federal and state income tax rate of 40 percent, a taxable cash inflow of $100,000 results in a $60,000 after-tax cash inflow ($100,000 × (1 − 0.40)). Likewise, a $20,000 tax-deductible cash outflow for repairs results in an after-tax outflow of only $12,000.

The disposal of assets may also have tax consequences. When an asset is sold or otherwise disposed of, gain or loss is calculated on the difference between the sales price and book value. Because current tax law rules do not consider salvage value in the computation of depreciation (assets are depreciated to zero even if they have a salvage value), the book value of an asset at the end of its useful life will be zero, and any salvage value realized will be taxed as gain. The

---

[3]Hospitals, museums, churches, and a multitude of other organizations are often structured as organizations exempt from federal and state income taxes. In order to qualify, they must meet certain requirements as specified by Congress and the Internal Revenue Service. These organizations may also be exempt from local property taxes.

after-tax cash flow associated with the sale of an asset for its salvage value is therefore found by multiplying the salvage value by (1 − tax rate).[4] For simplicity, we will assume that a gain on disposal of an asset is taxed at the same rate as the operating income of a company. In practice, the tax calculation on the sale of depreciable assets can be quite complicated.

Not all tax-deductible expenses involve cash outflows. Depreciation is a tax-deductible expense that does not involve a direct payment of cash. Although depreciation does not result in a direct cash outflow, it does result in an indirect cash *inflow* owing to the impact of depreciation on income taxes paid. Depreciation expense reduces a company's taxable income and thus its income tax, resulting in an increase in cash flow.

For example, in Exhibit 8-5, the revenue and expenses of Company A and Company B are identical except for $10,000 of depreciation expense incurred by Company B. This depreciation reduces Company B's taxable income by $10,000 and reduces its income tax by $4,000. As a result, Company B's cash flow *increases* by $4,000. (Remember that the depreciation expense itself does not result in a cash outflow.)

EXHIBIT 8-5 Tax Savings from Depreciation

	Company A Income	Company A Cash Flow	Company B Income	Company B Cash Flow
Cash revenue	$100,000	$100,000	$100,000	$100,000
Cash expense	60,000	60,000	60,000	60,000
Depreciation	0	0	10,000	0
Income (before tax)	$ 40,000		$ 30,000	
Income tax (40% rate)	16,000	16,000	12,000	12,000
Net income	$ 24,000		$ 18,000	
Cash flow		$ 24,000		$ 28,000

The tax savings from depreciation (called the **depreciation tax shield**) can easily be found by multiplying the depreciation expense by the tax rate. In this case, Company B's $10,000 of depreciation expense multiplied by the 40 percent tax rate results in $4,000 of tax savings.

As an example, consider a company contemplating the purchase of a new piece of manufacturing equipment. The equipment will cost $50,000 and will generate cost savings of $13,000 per year for six years. The company has a cost of capital of 10 percent.

Let's assume that the equipment will be depreciated using the straight-line method over six years for federal income tax purposes.[5] Depreciation expense is equal to $5,000 for years 1 and 6 and $10,000 for years 2 through 5. Assuming an income tax rate of 40 percent, the depreciation deduction results in tax savings of $2,000 for years 1 and 6 ($5,000 × 40%) and $4,000 for years 2 through 5 ($10,000 × 40%), as shown in the following table.

> **KEY CONCEPT**
>
> Taxes are a major source of cash outflows for many companies and must be taken into consideration in calculations of the time value of money.

---

[4]When assets are sold during their useful life, it is possible to generate tax-deductible losses as well as taxable gains. When assets are sold at a loss, their after-tax cash flow is more difficult to compute. It consists of the cash received from the sale *plus* the tax savings generated from the deductible loss.

[5]Although the equipment would be depreciated over a useful life of five years, tax law generally requires the use of a convention whereby a half year of depreciation is deducted in the year of acquisition (regardless of when the asset is purchased) and a half year's depreciation is deducted in the sixth year. In addition, the tax law currently allows the use of an accelerated method of depreciation for machinery and equipment. The intricacies of tax depreciation rules are beyond the scope of this book.

The Impact of Depreciation on Cash Flow

Year	Depreciation Expense Calculation	Non-cash depreciation expense	Tax Savings from Depreciation — Depreciation expense × tax rate	Cash Inflow
1	$50,000/5 × 1/2	$ 5,000	$ 5,000 × .40	$ 2,000
2	$50,000/5	$10,000	$10,000 × .40	$ 4,000
3	$50,000/5	$10,000	$10,000 × .40	$ 4,000
4	$50,000/5	$10,000	$10,000 × .40	$ 4,000
5	$50,000/5	$10,000	$10,000 × .40	$ 4,000
6	$50,000/5 × 1/2	$ 5,000	$ 5,000 × .40	$ 2,000

Now let's calculate the after-tax NPV. In the following table, the annual cash inflow of $13,000 has been adjusted to the equivalent after-tax amount ($13,000 × 0.6 = $7,800). In addition, the discount rate has been changed to its equivalent after-tax rate (10% × 0.6 = 6%).

Cash Flow	Year	After-Tax Amount	6% Factor	Present Value
Initial investment	Now	($50,000)	1.0000	($50,000.00)
Annual cash income	1–6	7,800	4.9173	38,354.94
Tax savings from depreciation	1	2,000	0.9434	1,866.80
	2	4,000	0.8900	3,560.00
	3	4,000	0.8396	3,358.40
	4	4,000	0.7921	3,168.40
	5	4,000	0.7473	2,989.20
	6	2,000	0.7050	1,410.00
Net present value				$ 4,707.74

The NPV of the new equipment is positive, indicating that it will provide a return greater than the company's 6 percent after-tax cost of capital. Using Excel's IRR function, the after-tax return of the investment is 8.938 percent (see Exhibit 8-6).

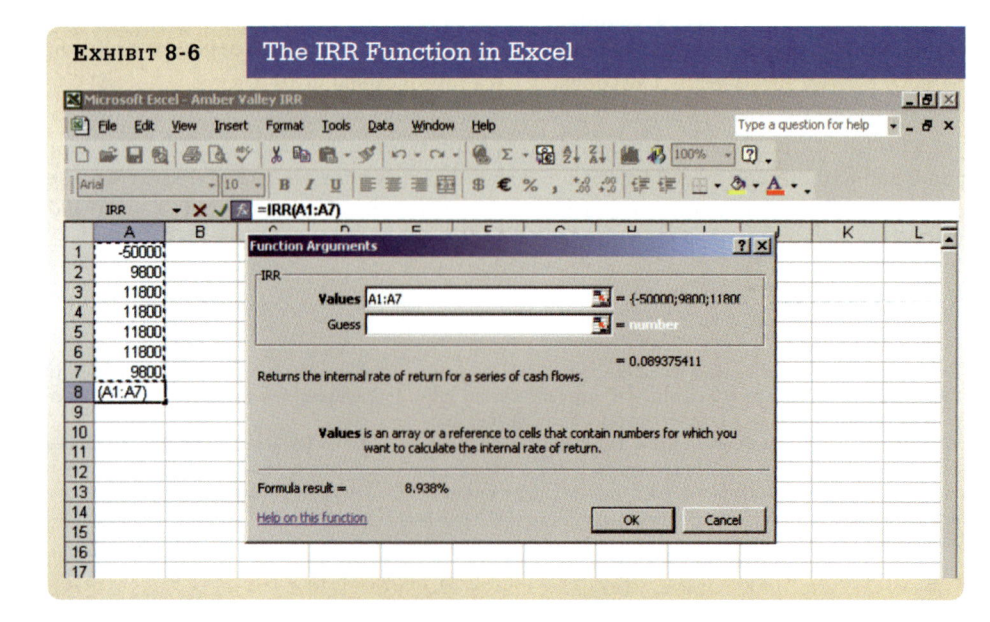

EXHIBIT 8-6   The IRR Function in Excel

Hitting the Bottom Line.

Speed Means Money

In order to boost attendance and reduce the time that skiers wait in lift lines, ski resorts across the country have spent hundreds of millions of dollars over the last few years replacing or upgrading their ski lifts. New high-speed quad lifts and aerial trams can travel as fast as 22 miles per hour and move as many as 125 skiers up a mountain at one time. Less wait time means more skiers, and with lift tickets costing over $60 per day in some locations, that means more revenue ("Ski Lifts: The Uphill Battle," *Wall Street Journal*, January 11, 2002, p. W4).

An Extended Example

Amber Valley Ski Resort is considering installing a chair lift for a new undeveloped area that would expand the area available for skiing. The options are to install a double, triple, or quadruple chair lift to carry two, three, or four skiers on each chair (a preference decision). The costs of the chair lifts are $3,000,000, $5,000,000, and $7,000,000, respectively. The chair lifts all have a 25-year life and will be depreciated using the straight-line method. The operating costs (including routine maintenance) of the new lifts are $250,000, $300,000, and $350,000 per year. In addition, the chair lifts require major repairs every five years (at the end of years 5, 10, 15, and 20) of $100,000, $125,000, and $150,000, respectively. The lifts are difficult to resell and are assumed to have no salvage value at the end of their 25-year useful life.

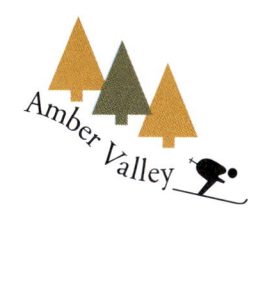

Lift tickets are $49 per day and allow the skiers to ride any of the lifts at the resort. Any increase in revenue from the new chair lift will have to come from increasing the number of skiers who visit the resort. The management of Amber Valley believes that with the addition of a new lift and the new slopes, they can attract more skiers to the resort. Right now, the lift lines at the existing chair lifts are considered too long by most skiers. The overall use of the resort is down, and part of the blame is attributed to the crowded conditions. Amber Valley averages 5,000 skiers per day at the present time. The projections used for the new lifts assume that the average number of skiers per day will increase by 100, 200, and 260 skiers, respectively. Assuming 120 ski days per year, this will increase revenue by $588,000, $1,176,000, and $1,528,800, respectively.

The managers of Amber Valley are confident that the new lift will increase the number of skiers sufficiently to justify its addition. However, they have asked the controller to analyze the proposed acquisition and to provide a recommendation concerning the purchase of the double, triple, or quadruple lift. Amber Valley's combined federal and state income tax rate is 40 percent, and it has an after-tax cost of capital of 8 percent.

Before-tax cash inflows and outflows associated with the purchase of each chair lift are summarized as follows:

Before-Tax Cash Inflows and Outflows

Cash Flows	Double Chair Lift	Triple Chair Lift	Quad. Chair Lift
Purchase price	$3,000,000	$5,000,000	$7,000,000
Additional revenue	588,000	1,176,000	1,528,800
Annual operating costs	(250,000)	(300,000)	(350,000)
Major repairs (every five years)	(100,000)	(125,000)	(150,000)

After-tax cash flows as adjusted are shown as follows:

After-Tax Cash Inflows and Outflows

Cash Flows	Double Chair Lift	Triple Chair Lift	Quad. Chair Lift
Purchase price	$3,000,000	$5,000,000	$7,000,000
Additional revenue	352,800	705,600	917,280
Annual operating costs	(150,000)	(180,000)	(210,000)
Major repairs (every 5 years)	(60,000)	(75,000)	(90,000)
Annual tax savings from depreciation*	80,000	133,333	186,667

*Although the lifts have a useful life of 25 years, they would likely be depreciated over 15 years for tax purposes. To simplify calculations, depreciation was calculated using the straight-line method, ignoring the half-year convention (a full year's depreciation was assumed for each of the 15 years). Once again, the intricacies of the tax rules for depreciation are beyond the scope of this book.

Should the decision be evaluated using NPV, IRR, PI, or some combination of the three methods? Because it involves investments of different sizes, NPV should not be used without calculating a profitability index. Because the investments have similar useful lives and patterns of cash flow, IRR can also be used to provide the quantitative analysis for the problem.

As you can see in Exhibit 8-7, the NPV of the double lift is negative (and the PI is less than 1.0), indicating that the investment is not acceptable. The IRR of 6.93 percent confirms the fact that the project provides a return below the minimum acceptable rate of return of 8 percent. Both the triple lift and the quadruple lift are acceptable investments with positive NPVs, PIs greater than 1.0, and IRRs exceeding the cost of capital. Note, however, when comparing the triple lift with the quadruple lift, that the quadruple lift has the higher NPV but the triple lift has the higher PI and IRR. Given the different-size investments required, management should focus on the PI or the IRR and choose to purchase the triple lift.

Exhibit 8-7 NPV, PI, and the IRR

Double Lift

	Years	Cash Flow	Present Value
Cost to purchase	Now	$(3,000,000.00)	$(3,000,000.00)
After-tax cash flow	1 through 25	202,800.00	2,164,844.61
Tax savings from depreciation	1 through 15	80,000.00	684,758.30
Major repairs	5, 10, 15, 20	(60,000.00)	(100,414.00)
Discount rate	8%		
Net present value			$ (250,811.09)
Profitability index			0.916
Internal rate of return			6.93%

Triple Lift

	Years	Cash Flow	Present Value
Cost to purchase	Now	$(5,000,000.00)	$(5,000,000.00)
After-tax cash flow	1 through 25	525,600.00	5,610,662.36
Tax savings from depreciation	1 through 15	133,333.00	1,141,260.97
Major repairs	5, 10, 15, 20	(75,000.00)	(125,517.49)
Discount rate	8%		
Net present value			$ 1,626,405.84
Profitability index			1.325
Internal rate of return			11.83%

Quadruple Lift

	Years	Cash Flow	Present Value
Cost to purchase	Now	$(7,000,000.00)	$(7,000,000.00)
After-tax cash flow	1 through 25	707,280.00	7,550,055.70
Tax savings from depreciation	1 through 15	186,667.00	1,597,772.21
Major repairs	5, 10, 15, 20	(90,000.00)	(150,620.99)
Discount rate	8%		
Net present value			$ 1,997,206.92
Profitability index			1.285
Internal rate of return			11.38%

The Impact of Uncertainty on Capital Investment Decisions

As discussed previously, all long-term purchasing decisions involve some uncertainty. Whenever decisions involve long periods of time, there is uncertainty. In fact, the longer the projected time frame of the project, the more the uncertainty. As has been discussed, one way to adjust for risk is to increase the cost of capital used in the NPV calculation. Raising the discount rate has the effect of reducing the present value of future cash inflows, thus reducing the NPV of an investment.

For example, if Amber Valley increases the discount rate used in its NPV and PI analyses to 10 percent, is the triple lift still an acceptable investment? Exhibit 8-7 is provided as an Excel template accessible from the textbook website (http://jackson-managerial.swlearning.com). Using the template, compute the NPV and PI for each lift if the discount rate is 10 percent instead of 8 percent.

After computing the NPV and PI for each alternative, we can see that the triple lift is still acceptable and the best choice. Its NPV is positive, and it has the highest PI of the three lifts. In fact, had we simply focused on the IRR of the triple and quadruple lifts in Exhibit 8-7, we could have surmised that both the triple and the quadruple lifts would be acceptable at a discount rate of 10 percent because the internal rate of return of both exceeded 10 percent.

Sensitivity Analysis

Amber Valley estimates an increase in skiers of 100, 200, or 260 per day for each of the lifts. What if the number of skiers increases by only 150 per day for the triple lift? Will the acquisition of the new lift still result in a sufficient return of and on investment? **Sensitivity analysis** is used to highlight decisions that may be affected by changes in expected cash flows. We can use what-if analysis to determine how sensitive capital investment decisions are to these changes.

Using the template provided on the textbook website (http://jackson-managerial.swlearning.com), compute the NPV, PI, and IRR for the triple lift if the number of skiers increases by only 150 per day. The after-tax cash flow (additional revenues less annual operating costs) will be $349,200. With an increase of only 150 skiers, the NPV of the triple lift will be negative, and the PI will be slightly less than 1.0. The IRR of 7.35 percent is a little less than the cost of capital of 8 percent. Based on a quantitative analysis, the triple lift will not be an acceptable investment with an increase of 150 skiers per day.

How many more skiers would be required in order for the triple lift to be acceptable? Hint: Using the template, compute the number of skiers necessary in order to provide a PI of 1.0 or an IRR of 8 percent. Increasing the number of skiers to 157 per day would result in additional after-tax cash flows of $373,896. This would result in a PI of 1.001 and an IRR of 8.02 percent.

All decisions should be evaluated after they are implemented in order to see whether they accomplished their objectives. However, in this example, as in most long-term purchasing decisions, the project is very difficult to reverse. Once a ski lift is installed, it must be used even if the projected skier volume is not reached. At that point, other decisions would be made regarding how to increase the numbers of skiers. Thus, short-term decisions may become critical in making long-term capital investment decisions successful.

The Impact of the New Manufacturing Environment on Capital Investment Decisions

Investments in automated and computerized design and manufacturing equipment and robotics tend to be very large, although many of the benefits may be indirect and intangible or at the very least difficult to quantify (increased quality resulting in fewer warranty expenses). These types of investments may be difficult to evaluate using purely quantitative data. For this reason, it is critically important to consider the impact of qualitative factors in these decisions.

Automating a process in a manufacturing environment is much more extensive and expensive than just purchasing a piece of equipment. The total cost of automating a process can be as much as 30 or 40 times that of installing a single machine, owing to additional software needs, additional training of personnel, and the development of new processes. The benefits of automating production processes include the following:

1. Decreased labor costs
2. An increase in the quality of the finished product or a reduction in defects, resulting in fewer inspections, less waste in the production process, less rework of defective goods, and less warranty work on defective goods
3. Increased speed of the production process

4. Increased reliability of the finished product
5. An overall reduction in the amount of inventory

These improvements will not only save costs but may also allow the company to increase market share. When the competition has automated production systems, companies must often follow suit or risk loss of business. Although some of the preceding benefits are difficult to measure, they must nevertheless be considered when making capital investment decisions in the new manufacturing environment.

KEY CONCEPT

Analyzing the costs and benefits of investments in automated and computerized design and manufacturing equipment and robotics requires careful consideration of both quantitative and qualitative factors.

THE ETHICS OF BUSINESS
Man vs. Machine

Throughout much of the 20th century, manufacturing was accomplished mostly with manual labor. While laborers used machines to help perform many routine tasks, necessary knowledge and skill resided within the mind of the human laborer. During the last decade there has been a trend toward manufacturing automation that has changed this long-standing relationship between man and machine. Some companies have come to view automation as a means to reduce labor costs, improve efficiency, and improve product quality. Still others see it as a means of eliminating a chronic shortage of skilled labor. This latter view is held by many in Sweden, one of the world's leading users of manufacturing automation. By the early 1990s more than 25,000 robots were being used for industrial production in Sweden, more than three times the number used in the United States. Many Swedish companies and employees view automation as a positive step that is consistent with their customer orientation and their emphasis on employee motivation and satisfaction. On the other hand, many U.S. employees feel threatened by automation, fearing they may lose their jobs.

It's Your Choice—Does the trend towards automation threaten jobs? To what extent do companies owe their employees opportunities to work when automation offers cost savings? To what extent should companies use automation? And, how can these companies and the government create opportunities for workers who are displaced because of automation?

The Payback Method

Capital investment tools that recognize the time value of money and use discounted cash flow techniques are preferred by most decision makers when dealing with capital investment decisions. In practice, however, some managers still use nondiscounting methods. Although these methods are declining in popularity, the payback method can still be useful in some cases as a fast, easy approximation of the more complicated, discounted cash flow methods.

The **payback period** is defined as the length of time needed for a long-term project to recapture, or pay back, the initial investment. In other words, how long does it take for a project to pay for itself? Obviously, the quicker the payback, the more desirable the investment. The formula used to compute the payback period is as follows:

Payback period = Original investment / Net annual cash inflows

For example, using our earlier example of Bud and Rose's purchase of a delivery van (see pages 250 and 251), the delivery van's payback period would be 3.57 years.

$$\frac{\$50,000 \text{ original investment}}{\$14,000 \text{ net annual cash inflow}} = 3.57 \text{ years}$$

Objective 7

Evaluate capital investment decisions using the payback method and discuss the limitations of the method

Because the payback method ignores the time value of money, it must be used with caution. Consider an example in which we consider investing in project A or project B, each requiring an initial investment of $20,000. (This is the same example as used earlier, on page 000.) Project A promises cash inflows of $12,500 per year for two years, whereas project B promises cash inflows of $5,000 per year for six years.

	Project A	Project B
Initial investment	$(20,000.00)	$(20,000.00)
Annual cash inflows	12,500.00	5,000.00
PV of cash inflows	21,693.75	21,776.50
NPV	$ 1,693.75	$ 1,776.50
PI	1.085	1.089
Payback	1.6 years ($20,000/$12,500)	4 years ($20,000/$5,000)

Although a manager using the payback method would prefer project A, the method ignores the time value of money and ignores any cash flow received after the initial investment is paid for. While NPV and PI signal that project B should be chosen, project A has the shortest payback period.

Payback calculations are slightly more complicated with uneven cash flows. Using Amber Valley Ski Resort as an example, we can calculate the payback period for the three chair lifts being considered. In Exhibit 8-8, the first column for each ski lift shows the cash flow each year. The second column shows the amount of original investment that still must be recovered at the end of each year. For the double lift, the investment is almost fully recovered after the eleventh year. At the end of year 11, only $9,200 of the original $3,000,000 investment has not been paid back. In year 12, another $282,800 of cash inflows are received. Thus, it takes an additional 0.033 of a year (9,200/282,800) to fully recover the investment. The calculations for the triple and quadruple lifts are similar.

Exhibit 8-8 The Payback Period

	Double Lift		Triple Lift		Quadruple Lift	
Year	Cash Flow	Unrecovered	Cash Flow	Unrecovered	Cash Flow	Unrecovered
0	$(3,000,000.00)		$(5,000,000.00)		$(7,000,000.00)	
1	282,800.00	$(2,717,200.00)	658,933.00	$(4,341,067.00)	893,947.00	$(6,106,053.00)
2	282,800.00	(2,434,400.00)	658,933.00	(3,682,134.00)	893,947.00	(5,212,106.00)
3	282,800.00	(2,151,600.00)	658,933.00	(3,023,201.00)	893,947.00	(4,318,159.00)
4	282,800.00	(1,868,800.00)	658,933.00	(2,364,268.00)	893,947.00	(3,424,212.00)
5	222,800.00	(1,646,000.00)	583,933.00	(1,780,335.00)	803,947.00	(2,620,265.00)
6	282,800.00	(1,363,200.00)	658,933.00	(1,121,402.00)	893,947.00	(1,726,318.00)
7	282,800.00	(1,080,400.00)	658,933.00	(462,469.00)	893,947.00	(832,371.00)
8	282,800.00	(797,600.00)	658,933.00		893,947.00	
9	282,800.00	(514,800.00)				
10	222,800.00	(292,000.00)				
11	282,800.00	(9,200.00)				
12	282,800.00					
Payback		11.033 years		7.702 years		7.931 years

If we use the payback period to evaluate the desirability of these options, the triple lift is preferable. It has a payback of 7.7 years versus a payback of 7.9 years for the quadruple lift and slightly more than 11 years for the double lift. In this case, this is the same preference ordering that we got using the profitability index and IRR to evaluate the lifts. The payback method can be useful as a quick approximation of the discounted cash flow methods when the cash flows follow similar patterns. It can also be useful in screening decisions if cash flow is a serious concern and management wants to eliminate projects that would have adverse cash flow consequences. For example, smaller businesses, such as Bud and Rose's Flower Shop, may be very concerned about cash flow in the short run even if the long-term profitability of a project is lower than with alternative projects. In these situations, the amount of time needed to recover cash outlays may be a very important criterion when evaluating capital investment decisions.

> **KEY CONCEPT**
>
> *The payback method can be useful as a quick approximation of the discounted-cash-flow methods when the cash flows follow similar patterns.*

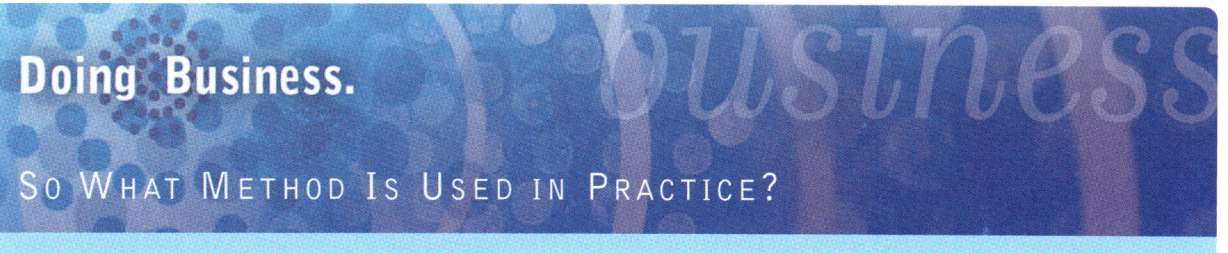

Doing Business.

SO WHAT METHOD IS USED IN PRACTICE?

In a survey of chief financial officers (CFOs), about 75 percent said that they always or almost always use IRR or NPV techniques to evaluate potential long-term investments, while 56 percent routinely use the payback method. Older CFOs and CFOs in small companies relied more heavily on the payback method than their counterparts in larger companies ("How do CFOs make Capital Budgeting and Capital Structure Decisions?", *The Journal of Applied Corporate Finance*, Volume 15, Number 1, pp. 8–22).

APPENDIX: Time Value of Money and Decision Making

When decisions are affected by cash flows that are paid or received in different time periods, it is necessary to adjust those cash flows for the time value of money (TVM). Because of our ability to earn interest on money invested, we would prefer to receive $1 today rather than a year from now. Likewise, we would prefer to pay $1 a year from now rather than today. A common technique used to adjust cash flows received or paid in different time periods is to discount those cash flows by finding their present value. The **present value (PV)** of cash flows is the amount of future cash flows discounted to their equivalent worth today. To fully understand the calculations involved in finding the present value of future cash flows, it is necessary to step back and examine the nature of interest and the calculation of interest received and paid. Interest is simply a payment made to use someone else's money. When you invest money in a bank account, the bank pays you interest for the use of your money for a period of time. If you invest $100 and the bank pays you $106 at the end of the year, it is clear that you earned $6 of interest on your money (and 6 percent interest for the year).

Future Value

Mathematically, the relationship between your initial investment (present value), the amount in the bank at the end of the year (future value), and the interest rate (r) is as follows:

$$FV_{(\text{year 1})} = PV(1 + r)$$

In our example, $FV_{(\text{year 1})} = 100(1 + 0.06) = \$106$. If you leave your money in the bank for a second year, what happens? Will you earn an additional $6 of interest? It depends on whether the bank pays you simple interest or compound interest. **Simple interest** is interest on the invested amount only, whereas **compound interest** is interest on the invested amount plus interest on previous interest earned but not withdrawn. Simple interest is sometimes computed on short-term investments and debts (that is, those that are shorter than six months to a year). Compound interest is typically computed for financial arrangements longer than one year. We will assume that interest is compounded in all examples in this book. Extending the future-value formula to find the amount we have in the bank in two years gives us the following formula:

$$FV_{(year\ 2)} = PV(1 + r)(1 + r)$$

or

$$FV_{(year\ 2)} = PV(1 + r)^2$$

In our example, $FV_{(year\ 2)} = 100(1 + 0.06)^2$, or $112.36. We earned $6.36 of interest in year 2—$6 on our original $100 investment and $0.36 on the $6 of interest earned but not withdrawn in year 1 ($6 × 0.06).

In this example, we have assumed that compounding is on an annual basis. Compounding can also be calculated semiannually, quarterly, monthly, daily, or even continually. Go back to our original $100 investment in the bank. If the bank pays 6 percent interest compounded semiannually instead of annually, we would have $106.09 after one year. Note that the interest rate is typically expressed as a percentage rate per year. We are really earning 3 percent for each semiannual period, not 6 percent. It is usually easier to visualize the concept of interest rate compounding graphically, with the help of time lines. Exhibit 8A-1 graphically demonstrates the impact of annual, semiannual, and monthly compounding of the 6 percent annual rate on our original $100 investment.

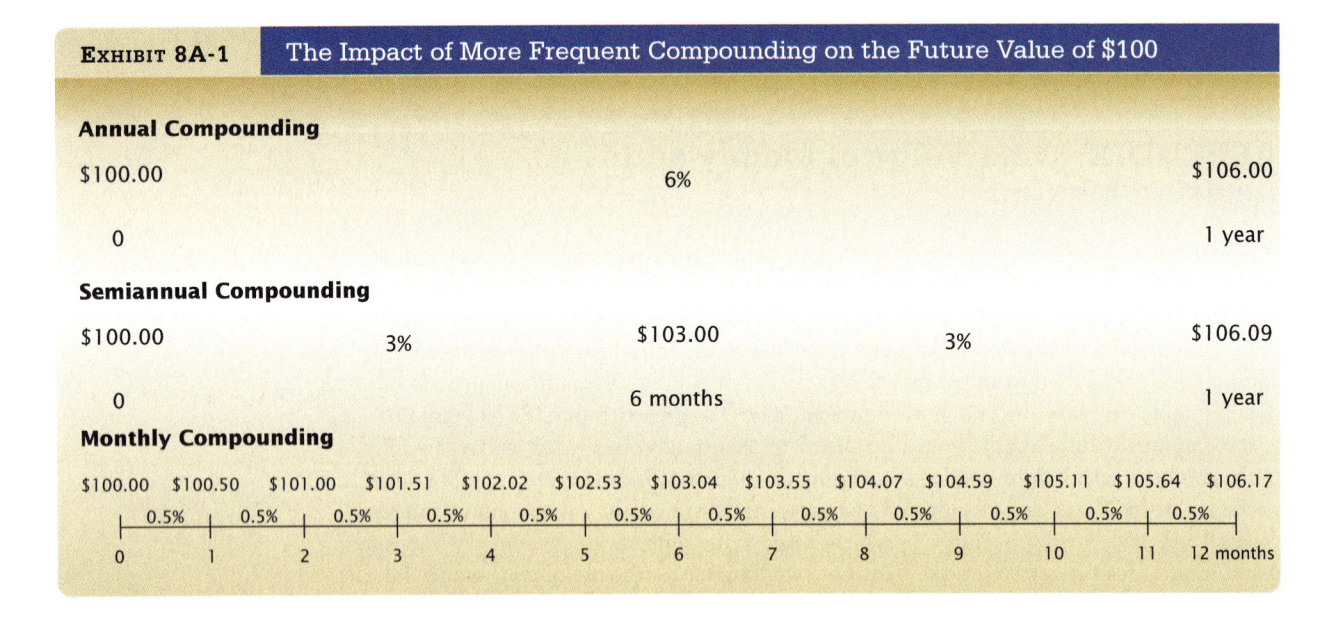

EXHIBIT 8A-1 The Impact of More Frequent Compounding on the Future Value of $100

Annual Compounding

$100.00 ———————————— 6% ———————————— $106.00

0 ———————————————————————————————— 1 year

Semiannual Compounding

$100.00 ———— 3% ———— $103.00 ———— 3% ———— $106.09

0 ———————————— 6 months ———————————— 1 year

Monthly Compounding

$100.00 $100.50 $101.00 $101.51 $102.02 $102.53 $103.04 $103.55 $104.07 $104.59 $105.11 $105.64 $106.17
   0.5%   0.5%   0.5%   0.5%   0.5%   0.5%   0.5%   0.5%   0.5%   0.5%   0.5%   0.5%

0   1   2   3   4   5   6   7   8   9   10   11   12 months

Mathematically, our formula for future value can once again be modified slightly to account for interest rates compounded at different intervals. $FV_{(n\ periods\ in\ the\ future)} = PV(1 + r)^n$, where n is the number of compounding periods per year multiplied by the number of years, and r is the annual interest rate divided by the number of compounding periods per year. Before the advent of handheld calculators and computers, tables were developed to simplify the calculation of FV by providing values for $(1 + r)^n$ for several combinations of n and r. These tables are still commonly used, and an example is provided in Exhibit 8A-2. The factors in Exhibit 8A-2 are commonly referred to as cumulative factors (CF) and are simply calculations of $(1 + r)^n$ for various values of n and r.

Exhibit 8A-2 Future Value of $1

n/r	0.5%	1%	2%	3%	4%	5%	6%	7%	8%	10%	12%
1	1.0050	1.0100	1.0200	1.0300	1.0400	1.0500	1.0600	1.0700	1.0800	1.1000	1.1200
2	1.0100	1.0201	1.0404	1.0609	1.0816	1.1025	1.1236	1.1449	1.1664	1.2100	1.2544
3	1.0151	1.0303	1.0612	1.0927	1.1249	1.1576	1.1910	1.2250	1.2597	1.3310	1.4049
4	1.0202	1.0406	1.0824	1.1255	1.1699	1.2155	1.2625	1.3108	1.3605	1.4641	1.5735
5	1.0253	1.0510	1.1041	1.1593	1.2167	1.2763	1.3382	1.4026	1.4693	1.6105	1.7623
6	1.0304	1.0615	1.1262	1.1941	1.2653	1.3401	1.4185	1.5007	1.5869	1.7716	1.9738
7	1.0355	1.0721	1.1487	1.2299	1.3159	1.4071	1.5036	1.6058	1.7138	1.9487	2.2107
8	1.0407	1.0829	1.1717	1.2668	1.3686	1.4775	1.5938	1.7182	1.8509	2.1436	2.4760
9	1.0459	1.0937	1.1951	1.3048	1.4233	1.5513	1.6895	1.8385	1.9990	2.3579	2.7731
10	1.0511	1.1046	1.2190	1.3439	1.4802	1.6289	1.7908	1.9672	2.1589	2.5937	3.1058
11	1.0564	1.1157	1.2434	1.3842	1.5395	1.7103	1.8983	2.1049	2.3316	2.8531	3.4785
12	1.0617	1.1268	1.2682	1.4258	1.6010	1.7959	2.0122	2.2522	2.5182	3.1384	3.8960
24	1.1272	1.2697	1.6084	2.0328	2.5633	3.2251	4.0489	5.0724	6.3412	9.8497	15.1786
36	1.1967	1.4308	2.0399	2.8983	4.1039	5.7918	8.1473	11.4239	15.9682	30.9127	59.1356
48	1.2705	1.6122	2.5871	4.1323	6.5705	10.4013	16.3939	25.7289	40.2106	97.0172	230.3908

Using this new terminology, the future value formula is simply

$$FV_{(n \text{ periods in the future})} = PV(CF_{n,r})$$

With 6 percent annual compounding, our $100 investment grows to

$$\$100(CF_{1, 6\%}) = \$100(1.060) = \$106.00$$

With 6 percent semiannual compounding,

$$\$100(CF_{2, 3\%}) = \$100(1.0609) = \$106.09$$

With 6 percent monthly compounding,

$$\$100(CF_{12, .5\%}) = \$100(1.0617) = \$106.17$$

Most financial calculators will compute future value after the user inputs data for present value, the annual interest rate, the number of compounding periods per year, and the number of years. For example, using a business calculator to compute the future value of $100.00 with 6 percent annual compounding requires the following steps:

Keys	Display	Description
1 [P/YR]	1.00	Sets compounding periods per year to 1 because interest is compounded annually
100 [±] [PV]	−100.00	Stores the present value as a negative number
6.0 [I/YR]	6.0	Stores the annual interest rate
1 [N]	1	Sets the number of years or compounding periods to 1
[FV]	106.00	Calculates the future value

Calculating the future value of $100 with 6 percent monthly compounding simply requires changing both the compounding periods per year (P/YR) and number of compounding periods (N) to 12.

Keys	Display	Description
12 P/YR	12	Sets compounding periods per year to 12
12 N	12	Sets the number of compounding periods to 12
FV	106.17	Calculates the future value

Likewise, many spreadsheet programs (Microsoft Excel, Lotus 1-2-3, etc.) have built-in functions (formulas) that calculate future value. The Excel function called FV simply requires input of an interest rate (Rate), number of compounding periods (Nper), and present value (Pv) in the following format =FV(Rate, Nper, Pmt, Pv, Type).[6] Entries for Pmt and Type are not applicable to simple future-value problems. To calculate the future value of $100 in one year at 6 percent interest compounded monthly, enter =FV(.5%, 12, −100). Excel returns a value of $106.17 (see Exhibit 8A-3).

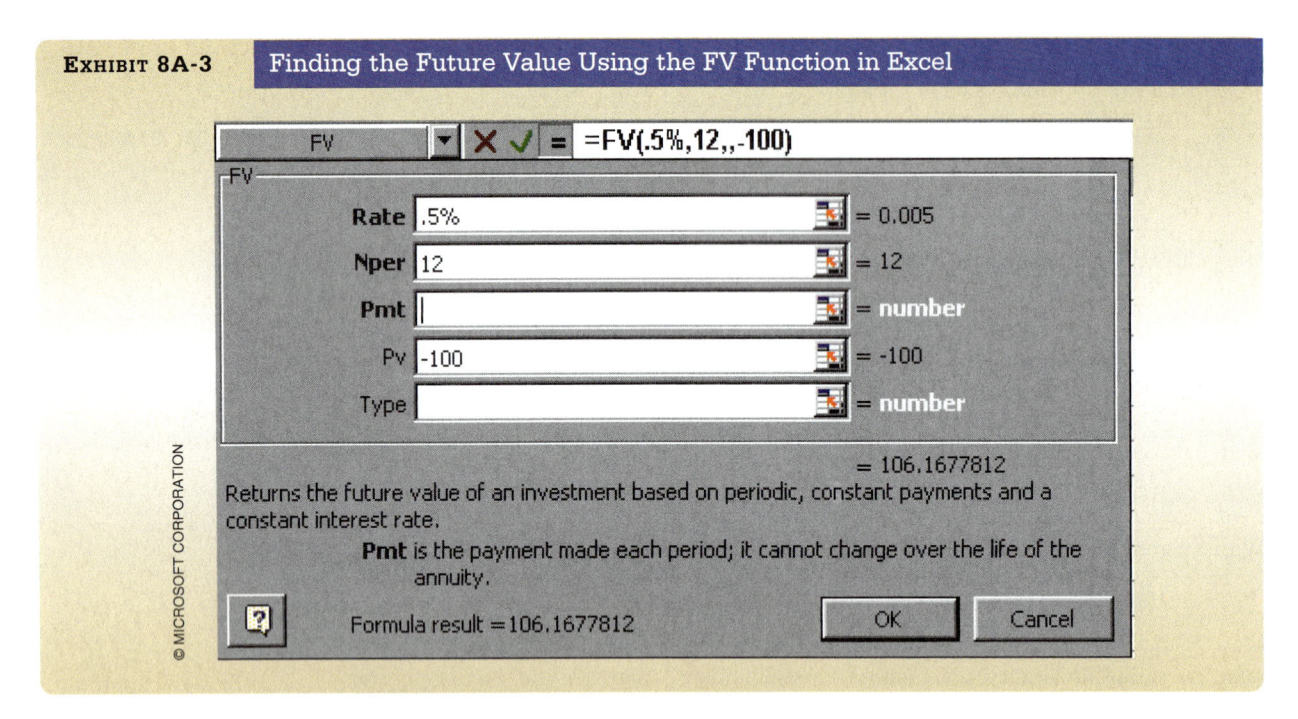

EXHIBIT 8A-3 Finding the Future Value Using the FV Function in Excel

Present Value

A present value formula can be derived directly from the future value formula. If

$$FV_{(n \text{ periods in the future})} = PV(1+r)^n$$

then

$$PV = FV \div (1 + r)^n \text{ or } PV = FV(1 \div (1 + r)^n)$$

---

[6]Built-in functions can be accessed in Microsoft Excel by clicking on the paste function icon, clicking on financial, and then scrolling down to the desired function.

Just as a cumulative factor table was developed to calculate $(1 + r)^n$, present value tables calculate $1 \div (1 + r)^n$ for various combinations of n and r. These factors are called discount factors, or DFs. An example of a DF table is provided in Exhibit 8A-4. Our PV formula can now be rewritten as follows:

$$PV = FV(DF_{n,r})$$

Exhibit 8A-4 Present Value of $1

n/r	0.5%	1%	2%	3%	4%	5%	6%	7%	8%	10%	12%
1	0.9950	0.9901	0.9804	0.9709	0.9615	0.9524	0.9434	0.9346	0.9259	0.9091	0.8929
2	0.9901	0.9803	0.9612	0.9426	0.9246	0.9070	0.8900	0.8734	0.8573	0.8264	0.7972
3	0.9851	0.9706	0.9423	0.9151	0.8890	0.8638	0.8396	0.8163	0.7938	0.7513	0.7118
4	0.9802	0.9610	0.9238	0.8885	0.8548	0.8227	0.7921	0.7629	0.7350	0.6830	0.6355
5	0.9754	0.9515	0.9057	0.8626	0.8219	0.7835	0.7473	0.7130	0.6806	0.6209	0.5674
6	0.9705	0.9420	0.8880	0.8375	0.7903	0.7462	0.7050	0.6663	0.6302	0.5645	0.5066
7	0.9657	0.9327	0.8706	0.8131	0.7599	0.7107	0.6651	0.6227	0.5835	0.5132	0.4523
8	0.9609	0.9235	0.8535	0.7894	0.7307	0.6768	0.6274	0.5820	0.5403	0.4665	0.4039
9	0.9561	0.9143	0.8368	0.7664	0.7026	0.6446	0.5919	0.5439	0.5002	0.4241	0.3606
10	0.9513	0.9053	0.8203	0.7441	0.6756	0.6139	0.5584	0.5083	0.4632	0.3855	0.3220
11	0.9466	0.8963	0.8043	0.7224	0.6496	0.5847	0.5268	0.4751	0.4289	0.3505	0.2875
12	0.9419	0.8874	0.7885	0.7014	0.6246	0.5568	0.4970	0.4440	0.3971	0.3186	0.2567
24	0.8872	0.7876	0.6217	0.4919	0.3901	0.3101	0.2470	0.1971	0.1577	0.1015	0.0659
36	0.8356	0.6989	0.4902	0.3450	0.2437	0.1727	0.1227	0.0875	0.0626	0.0323	0.0169
48	0.7871	0.6203	0.3865	0.2420	0.1522	0.0961	0.0610	0.0389	0.0249	0.0103	0.0043

Now we are ready to calculate the present value of a future cash flow. For example, how much must be invested today at 8 percent compounded annually to have $1,000 in two years? Mathematically,

$$PV = \$1{,}000(1 \div (1 + 0.08)^2) = \$857.34$$

or using the DF table,

$$PV = \$1{,}000(DF_{2,.08}) = \$1{,}000(0.8573) = \$857.30 \text{ (rounded)}$$

Once again, the frequency of compounding affects our calculation. Just as more frequent compounding *increases* future values, increasing the frequency of compounding decreases present values. This is demonstrated in Exhibit 8A-5 for annual, semiannual, and quarterly compounding.

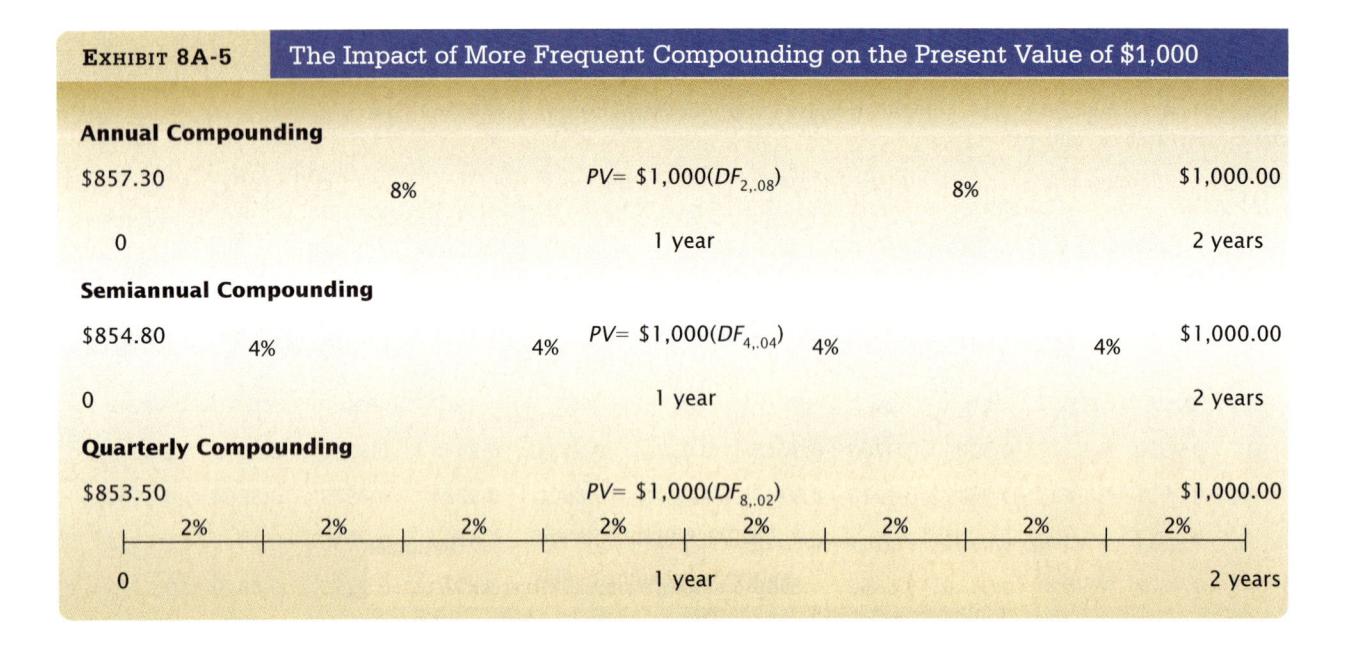

Exhibit 8A-5: The Impact of More Frequent Compounding on the Present Value of $1,000

Annual Compounding

$857.30	8%	$PV = \$1,000(DF_{2,.08})$	8%	$1,000.00
0		1 year		2 years

Semiannual Compounding

$854.80	4%	4%	$PV = \$1,000(DF_{4,.04})$	4%	4%	$1,000.00
0			1 year			2 years

Quarterly Compounding

$853.50	2%	2%	2%	2%	$PV = \$1,000(DF_{8,.02})$ 2%	2%	2%	2%	$1,000.00
0					1 year				2 years

Using a business calculator to compute present value is similar to computing future value. For example, the present value of $1,000 received or paid in two years at 8 percent compounded quarterly requires the following steps:

Keys	Display	Description
4 [P/YR]	4.00	Sets the compounding periods per year to 4
1,000 [FV]	1000.00	Stores the future value as a positive number
8.0 [I/YR]	8.0	Stores the annual interest rate
8 [N]	8.0	Sets the number of compounding periods to 8
[PV]	−853.49	Calculates the present value

In Microsoft Excel, the built-in function is called PV and requires input of the applicable interest rate (Rate), number of compounding periods (Nper), and future value (Fv) in the following format (=PV(Rate, Nper, Pmt, Fv, Type)). In the previous example, entering =PV(2%, 8, −1000) returns a value of $853.49. Note once again that Pmt and Type are left blank in simple present value problems, as they were in future value calculations (see Exhibit 8A-6).

When *FV* and *PV* are known, either formula can be used to calculate one of the other variables in the equations (*n* or *r*). For example, if you know that your $100 bank deposit is worth $200 in six years, what rate of interest compounded annually did you earn? Using the mathematical present value formula,

$$PV = FV(1 \div (1 + r)^n)$$

or

$$\$100 = \$200(1 \div (1 + r)^6)$$

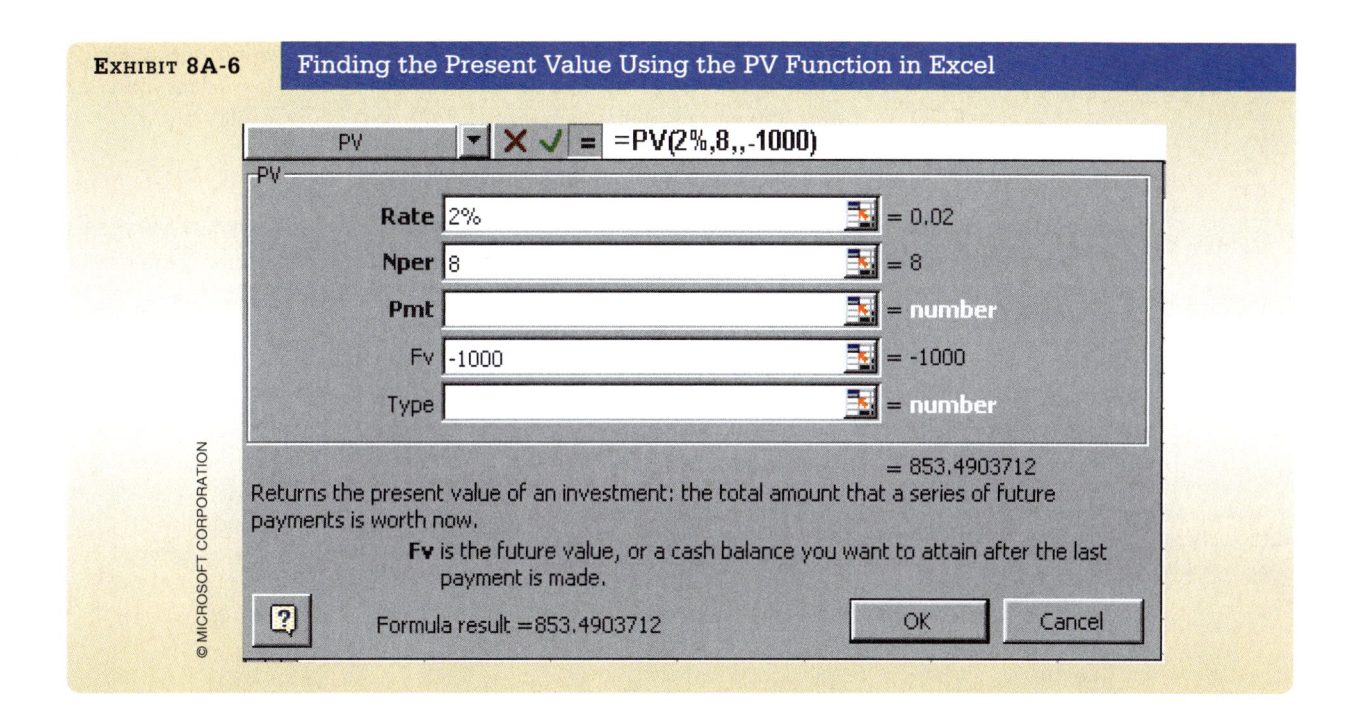

EXHIBIT 8A-6 — Finding the Present Value Using the PV Function in Excel

PV = =PV(2%,8,,-1000)

- Rate: 2% = 0.02
- Nper: 8 = 8
- Pmt: = number
- Fv: -1000 = -1000
- Type: = number

= 853.4903712

Returns the present value of an investment: the total amount that a series of future payments is worth now.

Fv is the future value, or a cash balance you want to attain after the last payment is made.

Formula result =853.4903712

© MICROSOFT CORPORATION

Simplifying by dividing each side by $100, $1 = 2 \div (1 + r)^6$ and multiplying each side by $(1 + r)^6$, the equation is simplified to $(1 + r)^6 = 2$. The value of r can be calculated by using a financial calculator or mathematically by using logarithmic functions.[7] When using a business calculator, the following steps are typical:

Keys	Display	Description
1 P/YR	1.00	Sets compounding periods per year to 1
200 FV	200	Stores the future value
100 ± PV	−100	Stores the present value as a negative number
2 N	2.0	Sets the number of compounding periods to 2
I/YR	0.122462	Calculates the annual interest rate

The tables can also be used to solve for n and r. Using our table formula, $PV = FV(DF_{n,r})$, if $PV = 100$ and $FV = 200$, DF must be equal to 0.5. If we know that n is equal to 6, we can simply move across the table until we find a factor close to 0.5. The factor at 12 percent is 0.5066. If we examine the factors at both 10 percent (0.5645) and 14 percent (0.456), we can infer that the actual interest rate will be slightly higher than 12 percent. Our logarithmic calculation is 12.2462 percent. In Microsoft Excel, the RATE function requires input of Nper, Pv, and Fv in the following format: =RATE(Nper, Pmt, Pv, Fv, Type, Guess). Because Excel

---

[7]In logarithmic form, $(1+r)^6 = 2$ can be rewritten as $\log(1+r)^6 = \log 2$, or $6 \log(1+r) = \log 2$. Therefore, $\log(1+r) = \log 2 \div 6$, which simplifies to $\log(1+r) = 0.1155245$. Switching back to the equivalent exponential form, $e^{0.1155245} = (1+r)$, $(1+r) = 1.122462$, and $r = 0.122462$ (12.2462%).

uses an iterative trial-and-error method to calculate the interest rate, Guess provides a starting point. It is generally not necessary but may be required in complicated problems. Entering =RATE(6, −100, 200) returns an interest rate of 12.2462 percent (see Exhibit 8A-7).

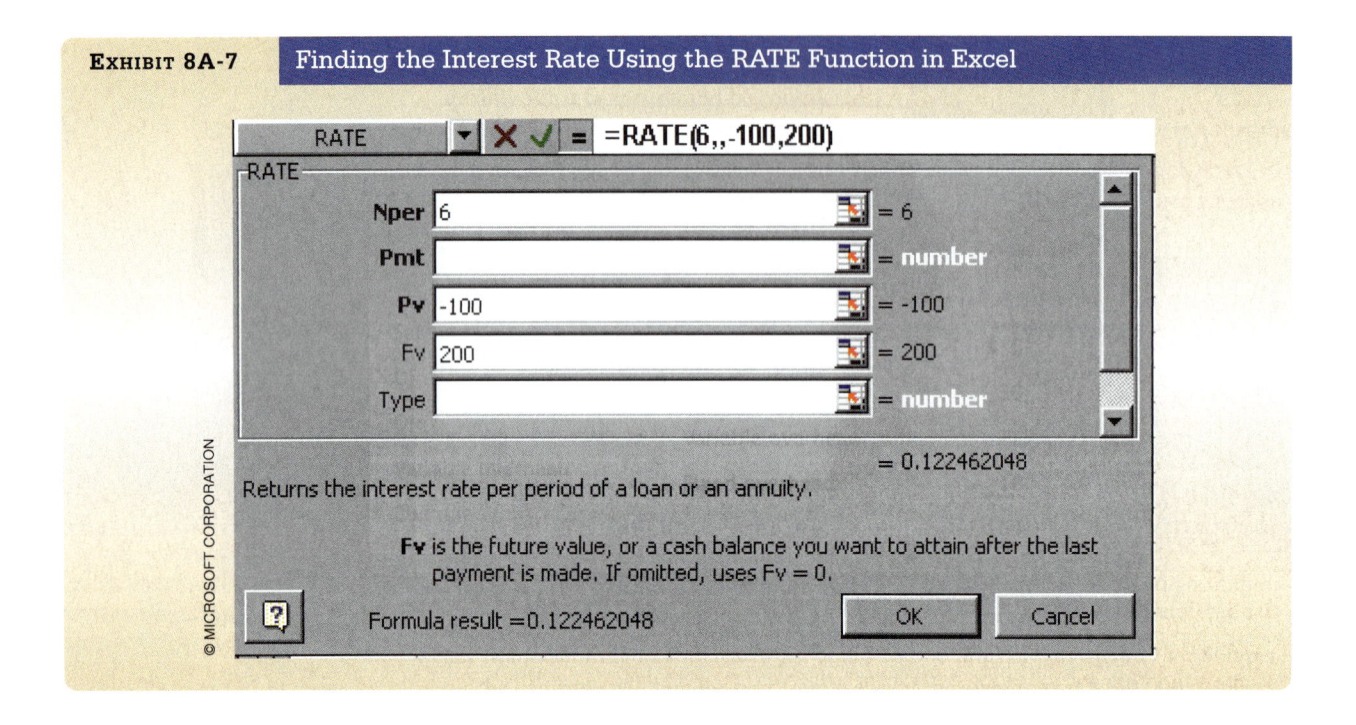

EXHIBIT 8A-7 Finding the Interest Rate Using the RATE Function in Excel

The calculation of n is done in a similar fashion. If we know that our investment earns 12 percent but do not know how long it will take for our $100 to grow to $200, mathematically, we have the following:

$$PV = FV(1 \div (1 + r)^n)$$

or

$$\$100 = \$200(1 \div (1 + 0.12)^n)$$

Solving the equation by using logarithms or a financial calculator gives us an n of 6.116 years.[8] Using the DF formula, DF must again be equal to 0.5. If r is known to be 12 percent, we simply move down the 12 percent column until we find a DF close to 0.5. Not surprisingly, we find a factor of 0.5066 for an n of 6. Examining the factors for an n of 5(0.5674) and 7(0.4523), we can infer that the actual time will be something slightly greater than 6 years. The NPER function in Microsoft Excel requires input of Rate, Pmt, Pv, Fv, and Type in the following format: (=NPER(12%, −100, 200)) and returns a value of 6.116 years. Note that Pv is entered as a negative amount and that Pmt and Type are not necessary, as this is essentially a present value problem (see Exhibit 8A-8).

---

[8] Using a business calculator, simply input 1 P/YR, 200 FV, 100 PV, and 12 I/YR and solve for n. In logarithmic form, $(1+0.12)^n = 2$ can be rewritten as $\log(1+0.12)^n = \log 2$, or $n \log 1.12 = \log 2$. Therefore, $n = (\log 2)/(\log 1.12) = 6.116$.

EXHIBIT 8A-8 Finding the Number of Periods Using the NPER Function in Excel

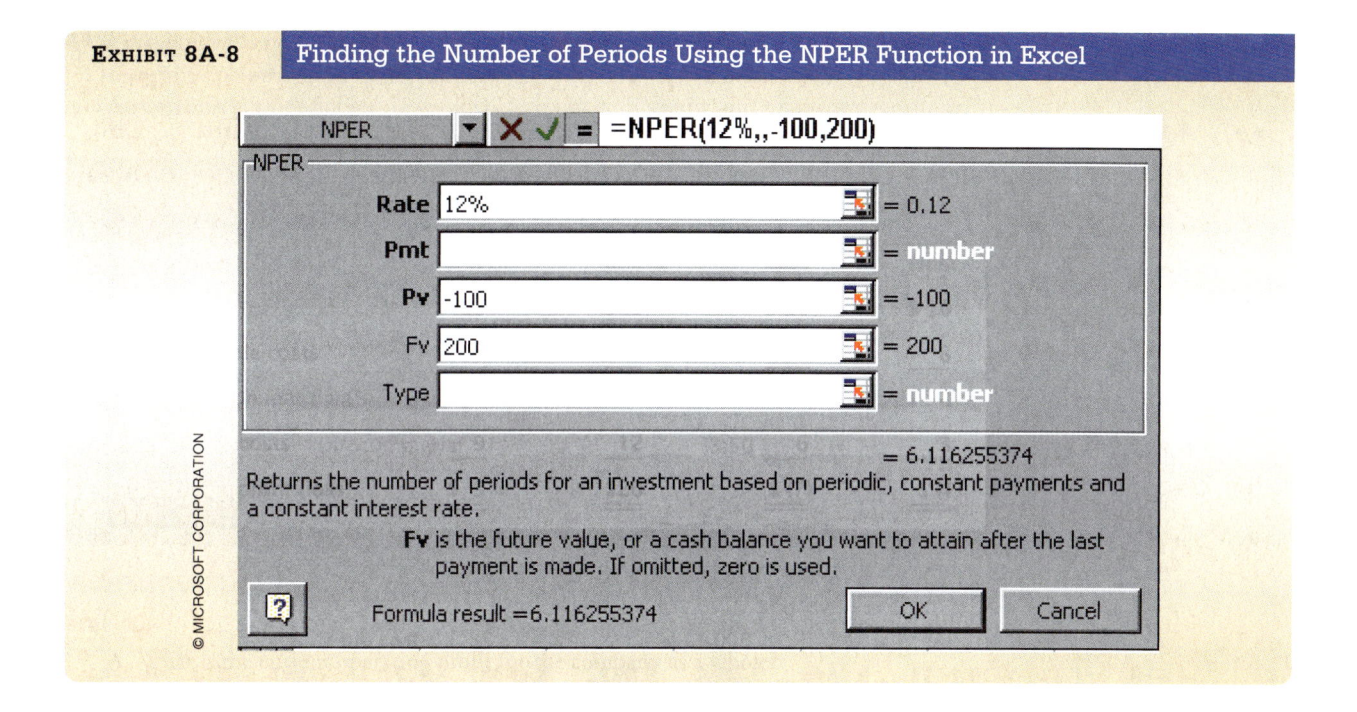

Annuities

An **annuity** is a series of cash flows of equal amount paid or received at regular intervals.[9] Common examples include mortgage and loan payments. The present value of an ordinary annuity (PVA) is the amount invested or borrowed today that will provide for a series of withdrawals or payments of equal amount for a set number of periods. Conceptually, the present value of an annuity is simply the sum of the present values of each withdrawal or payment. For example, the present value of an annuity of $100 paid at the end of each of the next four years at an interest rate of 10 percent looks like this:

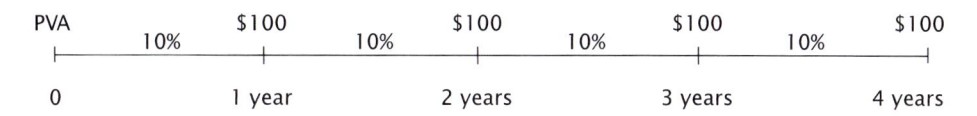

```
PVA        $100      $100      $100      $100      $100
     10%        10%       10%       10%       10%
├──────────┼─────────┼─────────┼─────────┼─────────┤
0         1 year    2 years   3 years   4 years
```

Although cumbersome, the present value of an annuity can be calculated by finding the present value of each $100 payment, using the present value table on page 269 (see Exhibit 8A-4).

$$PVA = \$100(DF_{1,.10}) + \$100(DF_{2,.10}) + \$100(DF_{3,.10}) + \$100(DF_{4,.10})$$
$$= \$100(0.9091) + \$100(0.8264) + \$100(0.7513) + \$100(0.6830)$$
$$= \$316.98$$

The mathematical formula for PVA can be derived from the formula for PV and is equal to:

$$PVAn, r = R\left(\frac{1 - \frac{1}{(1+r)^n}}{r}\right)$$

where R refers to the periodic payment or withdrawal (commonly called a rent). Calculated values for various combinations of n and r are provided in Exhibit 8A-9.

---

[9]An ordinary annuity is paid or received at the end of each period, whereas an annuity due is paid or received at the beginning of each period. In examples throughout this book, we will assume the annuity is ordinary.

Exhibit 8A-9 Present Value of an Ordinary Annuity

n/r	0.50%	1%	2%	3%	4%	5%	6%	7%	8%	10%	12%
1	0.9950	0.9901	0.9804	0.9709	0.9615	0.9524	0.9434	0.9346	0.9259	0.9091	0.8929
2	1.9851	1.9704	1.9416	1.9135	1.8861	1.8594	1.8334	1.8080	1.7833	1.7355	1.6901
3	2.9702	2.9410	2.8839	2.8286	2.7751	2.7232	2.6730	2.6243	2.5771	2.4869	2.4018
4	3.9505	3.9020	3.8077	3.7171	3.6299	3.5460	3.4651	3.3872	3.3121	3.1699	3.0373
5	4.9259	4.8534	4.7135	4.5797	4.4518	4.3295	4.2124	4.1002	3.9927	3.7908	3.6048
6	5.8964	5.7955	5.6014	5.4172	5.2421	5.0757	4.9173	4.7665	4.6229	4.3553	4.1114
7	6.8621	6.7282	6.4720	6.2303	6.0021	5.7864	5.5824	5.3893	5.2064	4.8684	4.5638
8	7.8230	7.6517	7.3255	7.0197	6.7327	6.4632	6.2098	5.9713	5.7466	5.3349	4.9676
9	8.7791	8.5660	8.1622	7.7861	7.4353	7.1078	6.8017	6.5152	6.2469	5.7590	5.3282
10	9.7304	9.4713	8.9826	8.5302	8.1109	7.7217	7.3601	7.0236	6.7101	6.1446	5.6502
11	10.6770	10.3676	9.7868	9.2526	8.7605	8.3064	7.8869	7.4987	7.1390	6.4951	5.9377
12	11.6189	11.2551	10.5753	9.9540	9.3851	8.8633	8.3838	7.9427	7.5361	6.8137	6.1944
24	22.5629	21.2434	18.9139	16.9355	15.2470	13.7986	12.5504	11.4693	10.5288	8.9847	7.7843
36	32.8710	30.1075	25.4888	21.8323	18.9083	16.5469	14.6210	13.0352	11.7172	9.6765	8.1924
48	42.5803	37.9740	30.6731	25.2667	21.1951	18.0772	15.6500	13.7305	12.1891	9.8969	8.2972

The PVA formula can therefore be rewritten as follows:

$$PVA = R(DFA_{n,r})$$

As previously discussed, common examples of annuities are mortgages and loans. For example, say you are thinking about buying a new car. Your bank offers to loan you money at a special 6 percent rate compounded monthly for a 24-month term. If the maximum monthly payment you can afford is $399, how large a car loan can you get? In other words, what is the present value of a $399 annuity paid at the end of each of the next 24 months, assuming an interest rate of 6 percent compounded monthly? Using a time line, the problem looks like this:

PVA $399 $399 $399 $399 $399 $399 $399 $399 $399 $399 $399 $399 $399 $399 $399 $399 $399 $399 $399 $399 $399 $399 $399 $399

0.5% 0.5% 0.5% 0.5% 0.5% 0.5% 0.5% 0.5% 0.5% 0.5% 0.5% 0.5% 0.5% 0.5% 0.5% 0.5% 0.5% 0.5% 0.5% 0.5% 0.5% 0.5% 0.5% 0.5%

0   24 months

Mathematically,

$$PVA_{24,.005} = 399\,(1 - 1/(1 + 0.005)^{24}/0.005)$$

$$PVA_{24,.005} = 399\left(\frac{1 - \frac{1}{(1 + 0.5)^{24}}}{0.005}\right)$$

Using the DFA table,

$$PVA_{24,.005} = \$399(DFA_{24,.005}) = \$399(22.5629) = \$9{,}002.60 \text{ (rounded)}$$

The following steps are common when using a business calculator:

Keys	Display	Description
12 [P/YR]	12.00	Set periods per year
2×12 [N]	24.00	Stores number of periods in loan
0 [PV]	0	Stores the amount left to pay after 2 years
6 [I/YR]	6	Stores interest rate
399 [±] [PMT]	−399.00	Stores desired payment as a negative number
12 [P/YR]	12.00	Set periods per year
[PV]	9,002.58	Calculates the loan you can afford with a $399 per month payment

In Microsoft Excel, the PV function is used to calculate the present value of an annuity, with additional entries for the payment amount (Pmt) and type of annuity (Type). The payment is entered as a negative number, and the annuity type is 0 for ordinary and 1 for an annuity due. The format is therefore PV(Rate, Nper, Pmt, Fv, Type). Entering =PV(.5%, 24, −399, 0, 0) returns a value of $9,002.58 (see Exhibit 8A-10).

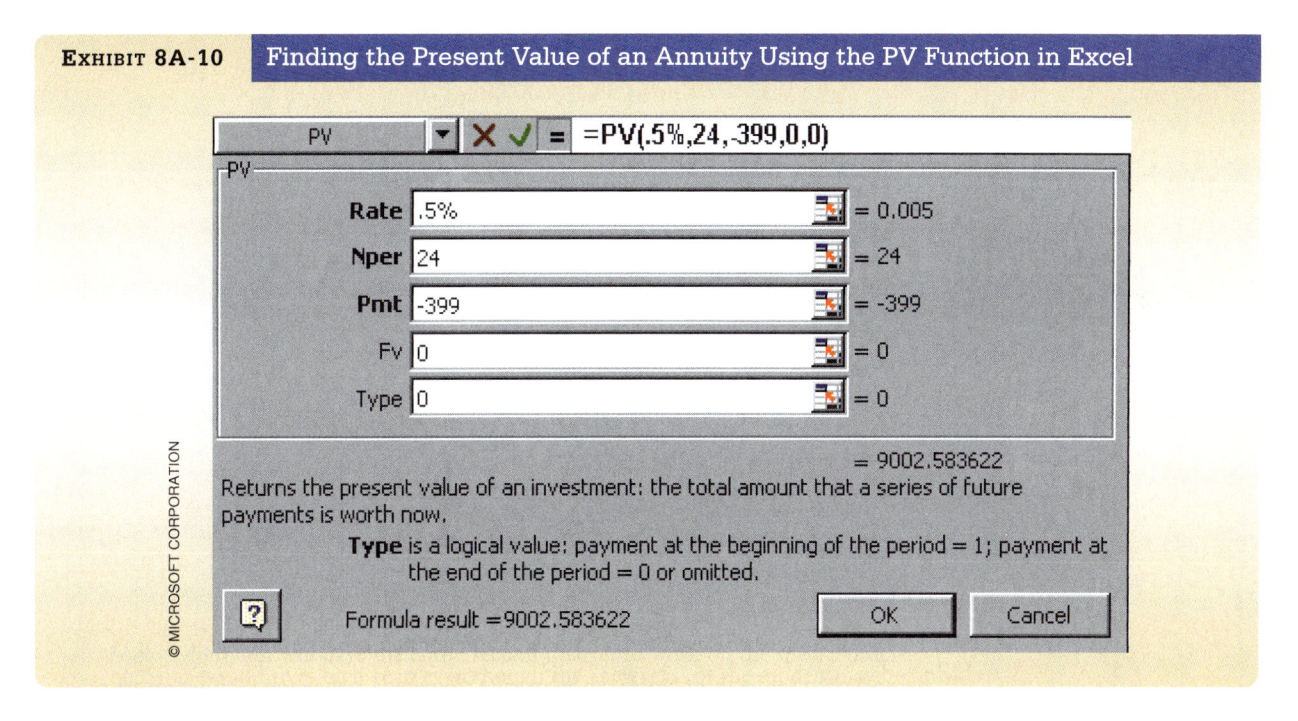

EXHIBIT 8A-10 Finding the Present Value of an Annuity Using the PV Function in Excel

The PVA formula can also be used to calculate R, r, and n if the other variables are known. This is most easily accomplished using the DFA table or using a financial calculator. If the car you want to buy costs $20,000 and you can afford a $3,000 down payment (your loan balance is $17,000), how much will your 36 monthly payments be, assuming that the bank charges you 6 percent interest compounded monthly?

Using the DFA table,

$$PVA_{36,.005} = R(DFA_{36,.005})$$

$$\$17{,}000 = R(32.871)$$

$$R = \$517.17$$

The following steps are common when using a business calculator:

Keys	Display	Description
12 [P/YR]	12.00	Set periods per year
3×12 [N]	36.00	Stores number of periods in loan
0 [PV]	0	Stores the amount left to pay after 3 years
12 [P/YR]	12.00	Set periods per year
6 [I/YR]	6	Stores interest rate
17,000 [PV]	17,000	Stores amount borrowed
[PMT]	−517.17	Calculates the monthly payment

In Microsoft Excel, the calculation is simply =PMT (.005, 36, −17000, 0, 0) (see Exhibit 8A-11).

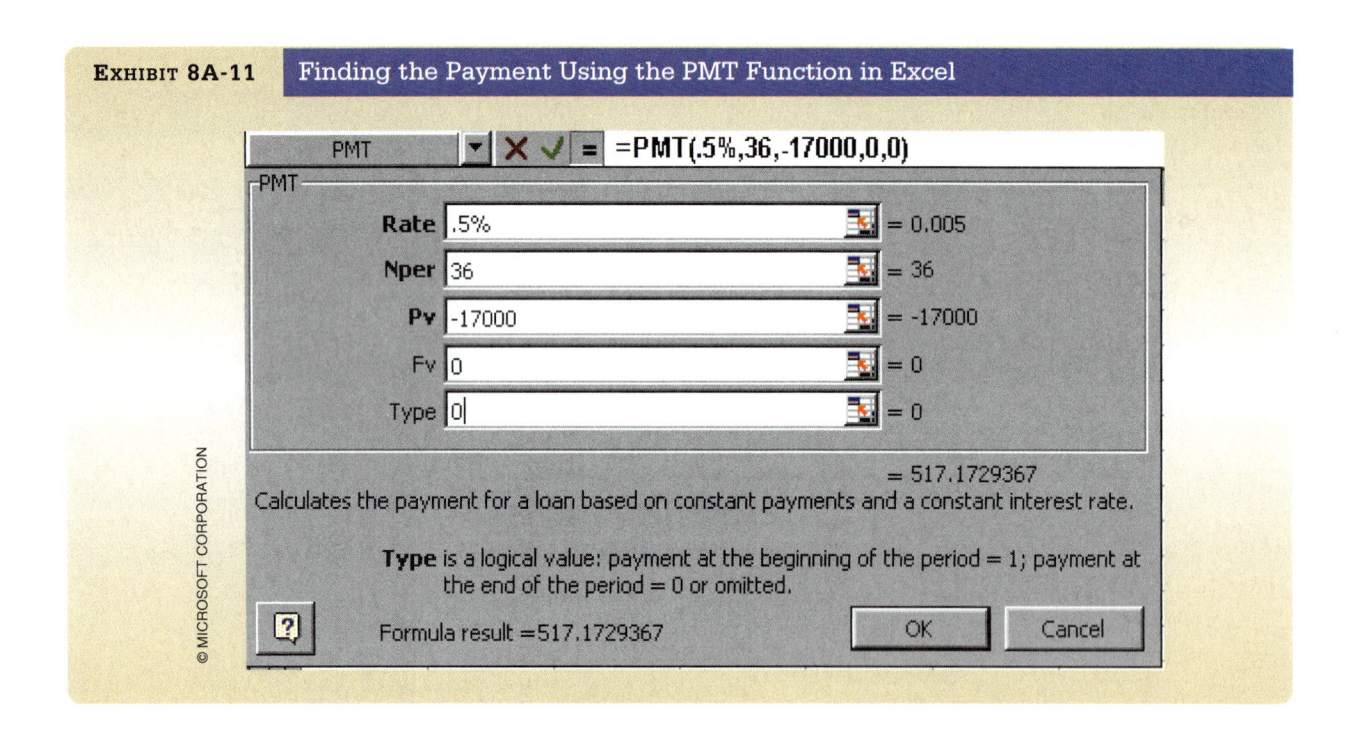

EXHIBIT 8A-11 Finding the Payment Using the PMT Function in Excel

In a similar fashion, assume that a used-car dealer offers you a "special deal" in which you can borrow $12,000 with low monthly payments of $350 per month for 48 months. What rate of interest are you being charged in this case? Using the DFA table,

$$PVA_{48,.??} = \$350(DFA_{48,.??})$$
$$\$12,000 = 350(DFA_{48,.??})$$
$$DFA_{48,.??} = 34.2857$$

Looking at the row for an n of 48, we see that a DFA of 34.2857 is about halfway between an r of 1 percent and r of 2 percent (closer to 1 percent), which means that you are being charged an annual rate of almost 18 percent (1.5% × 12)—not such a good deal after all! Using a business calculator, observe the following:

Keys	Display	Description
12 [P/YR]	12.00	Set periods per year
4×12 [N]	48.00	Stores number of periods in loan
0 [PV]	0	Stores the amount left to pay after 4 years
12,000 [PV]	12,000	Stores amount borrowed
350 [±] [PMT]	−350	Stores the monthly payment
[I/YR]	17.60	Calculates the annual interest rate

In Excel, =RATE(48, −350, 12,000, 0) generates a monthly rate of 1.4667 percent and an annual rate of 17.60 percent. The use of the RATE function requires that the payments are the same each period. Excel's IRR function is more flexible, allowing different payments. However, each payment has to be entered separately. For example, if the car is purchased for $17,000 with annual payments of $4,000, $5,000, $6,000, and $7,000 at the end of each of the next four years, the interest rate charged on the car loan can be calculated by using the IRR function (see Exhibit 8A-12).

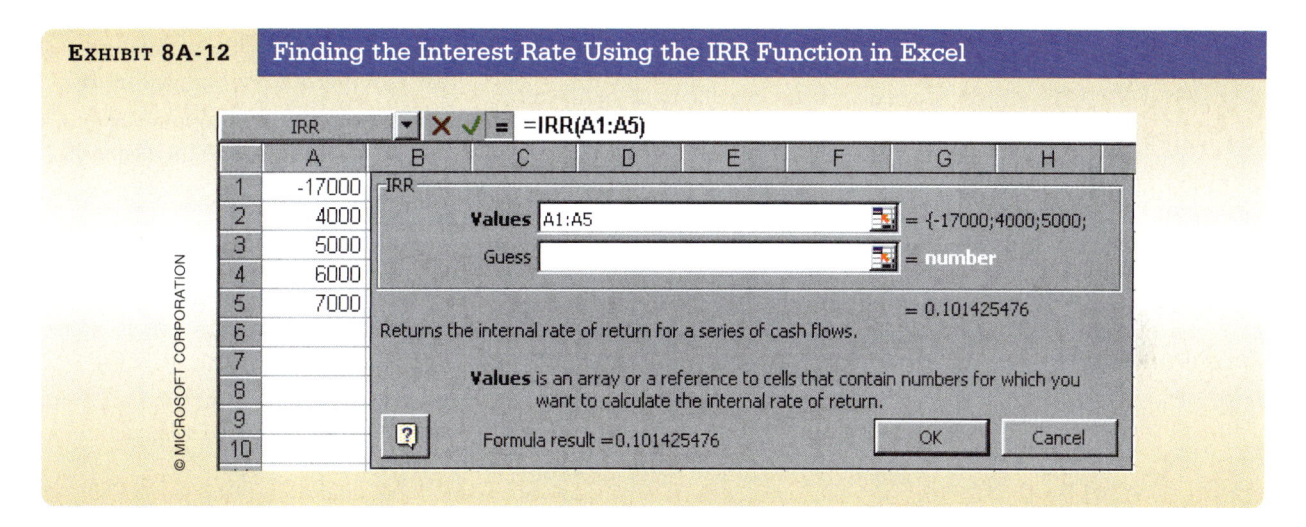

EXHIBIT 8A-12 Finding the Interest Rate Using the IRR Function in Excel

Summary of Key Concepts

- Long-term investment decisions require a consideration of the time value of money. The time value of money is based on the concept that a dollar received today is worth more than a dollar received in the future. (p. 249)

- The time value of money is considered in capital investment decisions by using one of two techniques: the net present value (NPV) method or the internal rate of return (IRR) method. (p. 249)

- If the present value of cash inflows is greater than or equal to the present value of cash outflows (the NPV is greater than or equal to zero), the investment provides a return at least equal to the discount rate (the minimum required rate of return), and the investment is acceptable. (p. 250)

- The internal rate of return (IRR) is the actual yield, or return, earned by an investment. (p. 252)

- *Taxes are a major source of cash outflows for many companies and must be taken into consideration in calculations of the time value of money. (p. 257)*
- *Analyzing the costs and benefits of investments in automated and computerized design and manufacturing equipment and robotics requires careful consideration of both quantitative and qualitative factors. (p. 263)*
- *The payback method can be useful as a quick approximation of the discounted cash flow methods when the cash flows follow similar patterns. (p. 265)*

Key Definitions

Capital investment decisions Long-term decisions involving the purchase (or lease) of new machinery and equipment and the acquisition or expansion of facilities used in a business (p. 248)

Time value of money The concept that a dollar received (paid) today is worth more (less) than a dollar received (paid) in the future (p. 248)

Net present value (NPV) A technique for considering the time value of money whereby the present value of all cash inflows associated with a project is compared with the present value of all cash outflows (p. 250)

Cost of capital What the firm would have to pay to borrow (issue bonds) or raise funds through equity (issue stock) in the financial marketplace (p. 250)

Discount rate Used as a hurdle rate, or minimum rate of return in calculations of the time value of money; adjusted to reflect risk and uncertainty (p. 250)

Internal rate of return (IRR) The actual yield, or return, earned by an investment (p. 251)

Screening decisions Decisions about whether an investment meets a predetermined company standard (p. 253)

Preference decisions Decisions that involve choosing between alternatives (p. 253)

Profitability index (PI) Calculated by dividing the present value of cash inflows by the initial investment (p. 255)

Depreciation tax shield The tax savings from depreciation (p. 257)

Sensitivity analysis Used to highlight decisions that may be affected by changes in expected cash flows (p. 262)

Payback period The length of time needed for a long-term project to recapture, or pay back, the initial investment (p. 263)

Present value (PV) The amount of future cash flows discounted to their equivalent worth today (p. 265)

Simple interest Interest on the invested amount only (p. 265)

Compound interest Interest on the invested amount plus interest on previous interest earned but not withdrawn (p. 266)

Annuity A series of cash flows of equal amount paid or received at regular intervals (p. 273)

Multiple Choice

1. Calculations of the time value of money are based on the premise that:
    a. a dollar received today is worth more than a dollar received in the future.
    b. a dollar received today is worth less than a dollar received in the future.
    c. a dollar of net income in the future is equal to cash flows paid today.
    d. large cash outlays require cash flow projections to be successful.
2. Which of the following is not a typical cash outflow associated with a capital investment?
    a. Repairs and maintenance needed for purchased equipment
    b. Additional operating costs resulting from the capital investment
    c. Salvage value received when the newly purchased equipment is sold
    d. Purchase price of new equipment

3. NPV calculations generally require which of the following simplifying assumptions?
   a. All cash flows occur in the middle of the period.
   b. All cash flows occur evenly during the period.
   c. Cash flows occur equally at the beginning and end of the period.
   d. All cash flows occur at the end of the period.

4. Under the IRR method, cash inflows are assumed to be reinvested at:
   a. the average cost of capital.
   b. the company's discount rate.
   c. the original internal rate of return.
   d. the prevailing market interest rate.

5. The Unique Bookshelf Company is considering the purchase of a custom delivery van costing approximately $50,000. Using a discount rate of 20 percent, you estimate the present value of future cost savings at $51,200. To yield the 20 percent return, the actual cost of the van should not exceed the $50,000 estimate by more than:
   a. $50,000.
   b. $51,200.
   c. $1,200.
   d. $48,800.

6. Which of the following cash flows does not have to be "discounted" for use in NPV calculations?
   a. Salvage value of newly purchased equipment to be received in 7 years
   b. Additional investments of operating capital required in 3 years
   c. Estimated additional cost savings over the 5 years of a project's life
   d. Cost of the initial investment in a project

7. Shumate Company is considering an investment with a cost of $55,000. Annual cash savings of $10,000, with a present value at 12 percent of $53,282, are expected for the next nine years. Given this information, which of the following statements is true?
   a. This investment offers a 12 percent rate of return.
   b. This investment offers more than a 12 percent rate of return.
   c. This investment offers less than a 12 percent rate of return.
   d. Not enough information is available to answer this question.

8. Each of the following statements describes the relationship between IRR and NPV. Identify the correctly worded statement.
   a. The IRR is the discount rate that results in a zero NPV.
   b. The IRR is the discount rate that results in a positive NPV.
   c. The IRR is equal to the company's cost of capital used in NPV calculations.
   d. None of the above statements is correctly worded.

9. Screening decisions involve:
   a. choosing between alternatives.
   b. identifying objectives.
   c. defining a problem.
   d. deciding whether an investment meets a predetermined criterion.

10. You are considering the following two projects:

	Project A	Project B
Initial investment	$(2,000)	$(4,000)
PV of cash inflows	2,600	3,400
Net present value	$ 600	$ (600)

    Calculate a profitability index for each project and determine which is/are acceptable?
    a. A only
    b. B only
    c. A and B
    d. Neither A nor B

11. Preference decisions involve:
    a. choosing between alternatives.
    b. identifying objectives.
    c. defining a problem.
    d. deciding whether an investment meets a predetermined criterion.

12. Which of the following has/have tax consequences that should be considered when making capital investment decisions?
    a. Positive net income
    b. Disposal of an asset
    c. Depreciation
    d. Each of the above

13. If Warner Enterprises is in the 40 percent tax bracket and has a 10 percent rate of return, its after-tax benefit should be calculated by using a rate of return of:
    a. 6 percent.
    b. 10 percent.
    c. 40 percent.
    d. 60 percent.

14. Your company has a policy of accepting projects with a payback period of seven years or less. Which of the following projects would be acceptable?

	Project A	Project B
Initial investment	$40,000	$50,000
Annual cash flows	7,000	5,000

    a. A only
    b. B only
    c. A and B
    d. Neither A nor B

15. Which of the following capital investment evaluation techniques does not require the use of discounted cash flows?
    a. IRR
    b. NPV
    c. Payback period
    d. Each of the above requires discounted cash flows.

Concept Questions

16. *(Objective 1)* Define the term *time value of money*.

17. *(Objective 2)* Compare net present value (NPV) with internal rate of return (IRR). What are the principal differences in the two methods?

18. *(Objective 2)* For the internal rate of return to rank projects the same as net present value, which conditions must exist?

19. *(Objective 3)* Define the term *cost of capital*. How would cost of capital be used in an investment decision?

20. *(Objective 3, 4)* If the net present value of a proposed project is negative, then the actual rate of return is what?

21. *(Objective 4)* Describe the process by which projects are accepted using the internal rate of return.

22. *(Objective 5)* Define profitability index and discuss how it is used in capital investment decisions.

23. *(Objective 5)* Compare screening decisions with preference decisions.
24. *(Objective 7)* Which method of project selection ignores the time value of money?
25. *(Objective 7)* Define payback period.

Exercises

26. Capital investments require significant amounts of money frequently over an extended period of time. The following are examples of typical cash flows associated with capital investments.
    a. Reductions in operating expenses
    b. Original investment in a project
    c. Additional operating costs that are required
    d. Incremental revenue received from a project
    e. Cost of repairs and maintenance needed for equipment
    f. Salvage value of an investment at the end of its useful life
    g. Release of working capital at the end of a project

    Required

    Classify each of the above cash flows as either an "inflow" or an "outflow."

    LO 1

27. Discounted cash flow analysis techniques are used by managers to understand the impact of investment decisions in terms of "today's dollars." Two common techniques that use discounted cash flows are net present value (NPV) and internal rate of return (IRR). Like most analysis techniques, each of these methods requires us to make certain assumptions.

    Required

    Describe the assumptions underlying NPV and IRR.

    LO 2

28. Wilson, Inc. has a project with an expected cash inflow of $1 million at the end of year 5. Wilson has a second project with an expected cash inflow of $200,000 to be received at the end of each year for the next five years.

    Required

    If both projects have the same expected cash outflows, what can be said of the net present value of the first project compared to the second project?

    LO 3

29. Kim Johnson purchased an asset for $80,000. Annual operating cash inflows are expected to be $30,000 each year for four years. At the end of the asset life, Kim will not be able to sell the asset because it will have no salvage value.

    Required

    What is the net present value if the cost of capital is 12 percent (ignore income taxes)?

    LO 3

30. Schaefer Organic Farms purchased a new tractor at a cost of $80,000. Annual operating cash inflows are expected to be $30,000 each year for four years. At the end of the tractor's useful life, the salvage value of the tractor is expected to be $5,000.

    Required

    What is the net present value if the cost of capital is 12 percent (ignore income taxes)?

    LO 3

    ✓ NPV: $14,297

31. Carrie Rushing is considering the purchase of a new production machine that costs $120,000. She has been told to expect decreased annual operating expenses of $40,000 for four years. At the end of the fourth year the machine will have no salvage value and will be scrapped.

    Required

    What is the net present value of the machine if Carrie's cost of capital is 9 percent (ignore income taxes)?

    LO 3

32. A planned factory expansion project has an estimated initial cost of $800,000. Based on a discount rate of 20 percent, the present value of the future cost savings from the expansion is $843,000.

Required

To yield exactly a 20 percent return on investment, the actual investment expenditure should not exceed the $800,000 estimated cost by more than what amount?

33. Powers, Inc. has a project that requires an initial investment of $43,000 and has the following expected stream of cash flows:

Year 1	$20,000
Year 2	30,000

Required

Use Excel to calculate the project's internal rate of return.

34. The Pearce Club, Inc. is considering investing in an exercise machine that costs $5,000 and would increase revenues by $1,500 a year for five years.

Required

Use Excel to calculate the equipment's internal rate of return (ignore income taxes). Round your answer to two decimals.

35. The Pearce Club, Inc. is considering investing in an exercise machine that costs $5,000 and would increase revenues by $1,500 a year for five years. The machine would be depreciated using the straight-line method over its useful life and have no salvage value.

Required

Use Excel to calculate the equipment's internal rate of return. Assume that the tax rate is 30 percent. Round your answer to two decimals.

36. The Golden Golf Club is considering an investment in golf carts that requires $21,000 and promises to return $29,000 in three year's time. The company will depreciate the golf carts over the three years and will be unable to sell them for any amount at the end of that time. The company's income tax rate is 40 percent.

Required

Use Excel to calculate the equipment's internal rate of return. Round your answer to two decimals.

37. An investment manager is currently evaluating a project that requires an initial investment of $10,000 and will provide future cash flows that have a present value of $17,000.

Required

Calculate the project's profitability index.

38. Kuntz Company has a project that requires an initial investment of $35,000 and has the following expected stream of cash flows:

Year 1	$25,000
Year 2	20,000
Year 3	10,000

Required

Assuming the company's cost of capital is 12 percent, what is the profitability index for the project?

39. A particular project requires an initial investment of $10,000 and is expected to generate future cash flows of $4,000 for year 1 and $3,000 for years 2 through 5.

Required

Calculate the project's payback period in years.

40. The Happy Day Care Center is considering an investment that will require an initial cash outlay of $300,000 to purchase nondepreciable assets that have a 10-year life. The organization requires a minimum four-year payback.

Required

Assuming the investment generates equivalent annual cash flows, what minimum amount of annual cash flows must be generated by the project for the company to make the investment?

Problems

41. Harriman Enterprises has three possible projects. Each project requires the same initial investment of $1,000,000. Harriman's chief financial officer has prepared the following cash flow projections for each project:

Year	Project X	Project Y	Project Z
1	$ 1,250,000	$ 0	$ 500,000
2	1,250,000	0	2,000,000
3	1,250,000	0	2,000,000
4	1,250,000	5,000,000	500,000

✓ NPV for Project X: $2,568,750

Jim Harriman, the company's president, is unsure of which project to pursue. Each holds promise for the company, but he is confused about what to do because each project generates the same amount of cash flow over the four-year period.

Required

Ignoring taxes, compute the net present value of each project at a 15 percent cost of capital. Which project should be chosen? Why?

42. Tate Enterprises is a nonprofit organization that has a cost of capital of 10 percent. The organization is considering the replacement of its computer system. The old system has a net book value of $3,000 and a remaining useful life of five years, with no expected salvage value at the end of the five years. The company estimates the system's current salvage value to be $1,500. A new computer system will cost $10,000 and is expected to have a useful life of five years, with no salvage value. Annual cash operating costs are $4,000 for the old computer and $2,000 for the new computer.

✓ PV of cash flows for old machine: $15,163

Required

A. What is the present value of the operating cash outflows for the old machine?
B. What is the present value of the operating cash outflows for the new machine?
C. What is the present value of the salvage value of the old machine if it is replaced now?
D. Would you advise the organization to replace the machine? Show calculations to support your recommendation.

43. Stephens Industries is contemplating four projects: Project P, Project Q, Project R, and Project S. The capital costs and estimated after-tax net cash flows of each mutually exclusive project are shown in the table below. Stephens' after-tax cost of capital is 12 percent, and the company has a capital budget of $450,000 for the year. Excess funds cannot be reinvested at greater than 12 percent.

	Project P	Project Q	Project R	Project S
Initial cost	$200,000	$235,000	$190,000	$210,000
Annual cash flows:				
Year 1	93,000	90,000	45,000	40,000
Year 2	93,000	85,000	55,000	50,000
Year 3	93,000	75,000	65,000	60,000
Year 4	0	55,000	70,000	65,000
Year 5	0	50,000	75,000	75,000
Net present value	23,370	29,827	27,233	(7,854)
Internal rate of return	18.7%	17.6%	17.2%	10.6%
Profitability index	1.12	1.13	1.14	0.95

Required

A. Which project will the company choose? Why?

B. If only one project can be accepted, which one should the company choose?

44. Winona Miller, president of CLJ Products, is considering the purchase of a computer-aided manufacturing system that requires an initial investment of $4,000,000 and is estimated to have a useful life of 10 years. CLJ Products' cost of capital is currently 12 percent. The annual after-tax cash benefits/savings associated with the system are as follows:

Decrease in defective products	$ 100,000
Revenue increase due to improved quality	150,000
Decrease in operating costs	300,000

✓ Payback: 7.27 years

Required

A. Calculate the payback period for the system. Assume that the company has a policy of accepting only projects with a payback of five years or less. Should the system be purchased?

B. Calculate the NPV and the IRR (use Excel to calculate the IRR) for the project. Should the system be purchased? What if the system purchase does not meet the payback criterion?

C. The project manager reviewed the projected cash flows and pointed out that two items had been missed. First, the system would have a salvage value, net of any tax effects, of $500,000 at the end of 10 years. Second, the increased quality would allow the company to increase its market share by 30 percent leading to an additional annual after-tax benefit of $180,000. Given this new information, recalculate the payback period, NPV, and IRR. Would your recommendation change? Why?

45. Greer Law Associates is evaluating a capital investment proposal for new office equipment for the current year. The initial investment would require the firm to spend $50,000. The equipment would be depreciated on a straight-line basis over five years with no salvage value. The firm's accountant has estimated the before-tax annual cash inflow from the investment to be $15,000. The income tax rate is 40 percent and all taxes are paid in the year that the related cash flows occur. The desired after-tax rate of return is 15 percent. All cash flows occur at year-end.

Required

What is the net present value of the capital investment proposal? Should the proposal be accepted? Why or why not?

46. Sullivan Company plans to acquire a new asset that costs $400,000 and is anticipated to have a salvage value of $30,000 at the end of four years. Sullivan's policy is to depreciate all assets using straight-line depreciation with no half-year convention. The new asset will replace an old asset that currently has a tax basis of $80,000 and can be sold for $60,000 now. Sullivan will continue to earn the same revenues as with the old asset of $200,000 per year. However, savings in operating costs will be experienced as follows: a total of $120,000 in each of the first three years and $90,000 in the fourth year. Sullivan is subject to a 40 percent tax rate and has an after-tax cost of capital of 10 percent.

✓ NPV: $23,029

Required

A. What is the present value of the depreciation tax shield for the new asset for year 1?
B. What are the cash flows (net of tax) associated with the disposal of the old asset?
C. What is the investment's net present value (after tax)?

47. Bit and Byte sells computer services to its clients. The firm is contemplating the acquisition of a computer but is undecided whether it should be leased or purchased. Information regarding the computer follows:

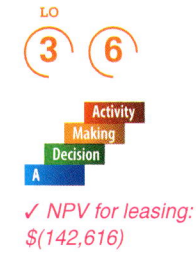

✓ NPV for leasing: $(142,616)

Equipment Purchase Information

Cash purchase price	$275,000
Annual maintenance	25,000
Salvage value at the end of three years	120,000

Equipment Leasing Information

Annual rental fee (includes maintenance)	$75,000 plus 10 percent of billings

Other Information

Estimated billings:	
Year 1	$230,000
Year 2	250,000
Year 3	240,000
Annual operating expenses	75,000
Equipment setup	20,000
Income tax rate	40%
Depreciation method	Straight-line
Minimum desired after-tax rate of return	12%

Required

Prepare a net present value analysis that compares the purchase and leasing options. Which alternative is best for Bit and Byte?

LO 3 5 7

Activity Making Decision A

✓ Payback for Project 2: 2.167 years

48. Alfred Stein is about to invest $1,000. Alfred is a very cautious man and would like to have some expert advice on which of two projects is best for him. He has not told you of his exact cost of capital because he likes to keep such information private, but he has told you to consider 8 percent, 10 percent, and 12 percent in your calculations. He also told you that the salesperson from whom he expects to purchase his equipment has given him the following expected cost savings patterns:

Year	Project 1	Project 2
1	$600	$300
2	600	600
3	600	800
4	600	700

Required

A. Calculate the present value of each project at each of Alfred's potential costs of capital and indicate which project is acceptable at each.
B. Calculate the payback period for each project. Does your recommendation to Alfred change?
C. Calculate the profitability index for each project, using a cost of capital of 10 percent. Which project would you recommend Alfred pursue?

LO 3 7

49. Stewart Corporation is reviewing an investment proposal. The initial cost and related data for each year of the project's life are presented in the schedule below. Stewart assumes that the cash flows take place at the end of the year. Stewart further assumes that the investment's salvage value at the end of each year is equal to its then net book value, but Stewart does not expect there to be a salvage value at the end of the investment's useful life.

Year	Initial Cost and Book Value	Annual Net After-Tax Cash Flows	Annual Net Income
0	$105,000	$ 0	$ 0
1	70,000	50,000	15,000
2	42,000	45,000	17,000
3	21,000	40,000	19,000
4	7,000	35,000	21,000
5	0	30,000	23,000

Stewart uses a 24 percent after-tax target rate of return for new investment proposals.

Required

A. Calculate the payback period for the project.
B. Calculate the project's net present value.

LO 6 7

50. Stembridge Medical Associates is planning to acquire a $250,000 X-ray machine that promises to provide increased efficiencies and higher resolution X-rays. The medical group expects a reduction in annual operating costs of $80,000. The machine will be depreciated by the straight-line method over five years (no half-year convention), with no salvage value at the end of five years.

Required

Compute the X-ray machine's payback period assuming a 40 percent income tax rate.

Cases

51. Armstrong Company manufactures three models of paper shredders, including the waste container, which serves as the base. Whereas the shredder heads are different for all three models, the waste container is the same. The number of waste containers that Armstrong will need during the next five years is estimated as follows:

Year	Number of Containers
2005	50,000
2006	50,000
2007	52,000
2008	55,000
2009	55,000

LO 3 6

Activity Making Decision A

✓ NPV of purchasing the equipment: $51,676

The equipment used to manufacture the waste container must be replaced because it is broken and cannot be repaired. The new equipment has a purchase price of $945,000 and is expected to have a salvage value of $12,000 at the end of its economic life in 2009. The new equipment would be more efficient than the old equipment, resulting in a 25 percent reduction in direct material and a one-time decrease in working capital requirements of $2,500 resulting from a reduction in direct material inventories. This working capital reduction would be recognized at the time of equipment acquisition.

The old equipment is fully depreciated and is not included in the fixed overhead. The old equipment can be sold for a salvage amount of $1,500. Armstrong has no alternative use for the manufacturing space at this time, so if the waste containers were purchased from an outside supplier, the old equipment would be left in place.

Rather than replace the equipment, one of Armstrong's production managers has suggested that the waste containers be purchased. One supplier has quoted a price of $27 per container. This price is $8 less than the current manufacturing cost, which is comprised of the following:

Direct materials	$10.00	
Direct labor	8.00	
Variable overhead	6.00	$24.00
Fixed overhead:		
Supervision	$ 2.00	
Facilities	5.00	
General	4.00	11.00
Total manufacturing cost per unit		$35.00

Armstrong employs a plantwide fixed overhead rate in its operations. If the waste containers were purchased outside, the salary and benefits of one supervisor, included in the fixed overhead at $45,000, would be eliminated. There would be no other changes in the other cash and noncash items included in fixed overhead.

Armstrong is subject to a 40 percent income tax rate. Management assumes that all annual cash flows and tax payments occur at the end of the year and uses a 12 percent after-tax discount rate.

Required

A. Define the problem that Armstrong faces.
B. Calculate the net present value of the estimated after-tax cash flows for each option you identify.
C. What is your recommendation? Support your recommendation by explaining the logic behind it.

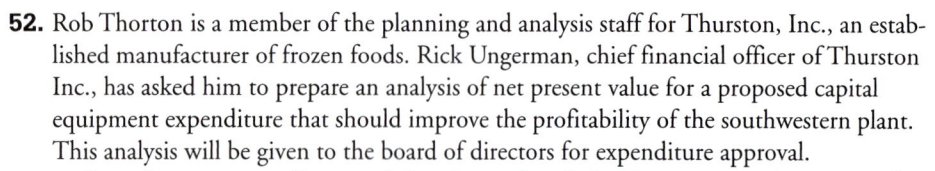

52. Rob Thorton is a member of the planning and analysis staff for Thurston, Inc., an established manufacturer of frozen foods. Rick Ungerman, chief financial officer of Thurston Inc., has asked him to prepare an analysis of net present value for a proposed capital equipment expenditure that should improve the profitability of the southwestern plant. This analysis will be given to the board of directors for expenditure approval.

    Several years ago, as director of planning and analysis, Ungerman was instrumental in convincing the board to open the southwestern plant. However, recent competitive pressures have forced each of Thurston's manufacturing divisions to consider alternatives to improve their market position. To Ungerman's dismay, the southwestern plant may be sold in the near future unless significant improvements in cost control and production efficiency are achieved.

    The southwestern plant's production manager, an old friend of Ungerman's, has submitted a proposal for the acquisition of an automated materials-movement system. Ungerman is eager to have this proposal approved, as it will ensure the continuance of the southwestern plant and preserve his friend's position. The plan calls for the replacement of a number of forklift trucks and operators with a computer-controlled conveyor belt system that feeds directly into the refrigeration units. This automation would eliminate the need for a number of materials handlers and increase the output capacity of the plant.

    Ungerman has given this proposal to Thorton and instructed him to use the following information to prepare his analysis:

Projected useful life	10 years
Purchase/installation of equipment	$4,500,000
Increased working capital needed*	1,000,000
Increased annual operating costs (exclusive of depreciation)	200,000
Equipment repairs to maintain production efficiency (end of year 5)	800,000
Increase in annual sales revenue	700,000
Reduction in annual manufacturing costs	500,000
Reduction in annual maintenance costs	300,000
Estimated salvage value of conveyor belt system	850,000

*The working capital will be released at the end of the 10-year useful life of the conveyor belt system.

The forklift trucks have been fully depreciated and have a zero net book value. If the conveyor belt system is purchased now, these trucks will be sold for $100,000. Thurston has a 40 percent effective tax rate, has chosen the straight-line depreciation method, and uses a 12 percent after-tax discount rate. For the purpose of analysis, all tax effects and cash flows from the equipment acquisition and disposal are considered to occur at the time of the transactions, whereas those from operations are considered to occur at the end of each year.

When Thorton completed his initial analysis, the proposed project appeared quite healthy. However, after investigating equipment similar to that proposed, he discovered that the estimated residual value of $850,000 was very optimistic; information several

✓ NPV based on revised estimates: $(291,780)

vendors previously provided estimates this value to be $100,000. He also discovered that industry trade publications considered eight years to be the maximum life of similar conveyor belt systems. As a result, he prepared a second analysis, based on this new information. When Ungerman saw the second analysis, he told Thorton to discard this revised material, warned him not to discuss the new estimates with anyone, and ordered him not to present any of this information to the board of directors.

Required

    A. Prepare an analysis of the net present value of the purchase and installation of the materials-movement system, using the revised estimates obtained by Thorton. Be sure to present supporting calculations.
    B. Accurately describe the decision problem facing Thorton.
    C. What alternatives does he have?
    D. What is the best alternative from a quantitative analysis?
    E. What other qualitative factors should be considered and why?

Group and Internet Exercises

53. An increasing number of companies and industries are embracing automation. Despite the tremendous capital investments required, many companies determine that automation is preferable to reliance on manual labor. Often automation is seen as a method to reduce defects, increase efficiency, reduce reliance on manual laborers, decrease production costs, and increase production capacity. Conduct an Internet search to find a story about a company that has automated its processes. Prepare a memo that describes the company's rationale for investing in automation, the impact on the company's cash flow, the challenges encountered due to the automation, unexpected benefits of automation, the reaction of company employees, and whether the company's management believes the automation has been successful.

54. Companies must make capital investments for a variety of reasons, not the least of which is to efficiently produce products. Often because of their shear size, companies stake their financial futures on the success of these investments. Conduct an Internet search to find a story about a company that recently made a large capital investment in manufacturing equipment or other facilities. Prepare a brief memo that describes to the extent possible the following: the nature of the investment, why the company chose to make the investment, how the company paid for the investment, the method (that is, NPV, IRR, payback, etc.) used to evaluate the investment, and whether the company is satisfied with the outcome of the investment.

Big Al's Pizza, Inc.

Part Two: Costs and Decision Making Summary Problem

Section A

During the first two years of operations, Big Al's overhead costs have fluctuated from month to month. Although overhead appears to go up and down according to the number of pizzas produced each month, the accounting manager has noticed that this is not always the case. For example, in the fourteenth month of operations, the manufacturing facility was closed for almost 10 days because of severe weather, and production for the month was very low. However, overhead costs were only about 25 percent lower than those incurred in the previous month. In an effort to estimate overhead costs in year 3, the manager has collected the following information for the past 24 months of operation and has asked for your assistance in analyzing the data.

Month	Pizzas Produced	Total Overhead Costs
1	25,784	$17,200
2	25,897	17,300
3	25,750	17,450
4	26,352	17,600
5	27,567	17,950
6	28,492	18,125
7	27,398	17,900
8	28,112	17,955
9	29,499	18,507
10	28,879	18,295
11	29,344	18,325
12	29,399	18,550
13	30,879	19,825
14	15,167	14,800
15	28,379	18,732
16	29,765	19,832
17	30,334	19,965
18	30,761	19,786
19	31,300	20,359
20	31,804	20,149
21	31,795	20,508
22	32,016	20,489
23	32,379	21,166
24	32,675	20,852

Required:

A. Do the data present any special problems that might impact the accuracy of using either the high/low method or regression analysis to predict overhead costs? What suggestions would you make to the company accountant before analyzing the data?
B. Analyze the data (both with and without month 14) using the high/low method. Estimate the fixed and variable components of total overhead costs.
C. Analyze the data (both with and without month 14) using regression analysis. Estimate the fixed and variable components of total overhead costs.
D. Should the accounting manager consider using an independent variable other than the number of pizzas produced to predict overhead costs? What suggestions do you have?
E. During year 3, Big Al's estimates January production of 33,000 pizzas. Based on the expected production of 33,000 pizzas and the results in parts B and C, how much overhead would you estimate that Big Al's will incur in January?

Section B

During the third year of operations, Big Al's estimates that 415,000 pizzas (385,000 meat and 30,000 veggie) will be produced. Direct material costs per unit are $.74 per meat pizza and $.62 per veggie pizza. Direct labor costs are $2.51 per meat pizza and $2.78 per veggie pizza. Monthly fixed selling and administrative costs are $15,300 while monthly fixed manufacturing overhead is $2,851. The variable overhead cost is $.55 per pizza. The sales price for veggie pizzas is $5.25 per pizza and the sales price for meat pizzas is $5.00.

Required:

A. Compute the break-even point in year 3 for Big Al's pizzas. How many veggie and meat pizzas must be sold in order to break even?
B. What options does Big Al's have to reduce the break-even point? Discuss both the quantitative and the qualitative factors that must be considered with each option.
C. How many meat and veggie pizzas, respectively, would Big Al's need to sell in year 3 to earn a before-tax profit of $150,000?
D. If its tax rate is 30 percent, how many pizzas does Big Al's need to sell in year 3 to earn an after-tax profit of $150,000?
E. How will the break-even point change if the sales mix changes to 80 percent meat pizzas and 20 percent veggie pizzas?
F. What would happen to the break-even point if labor costs increased by 10 percent?
G. What would happen to the break-even point if Big Al's increases the sales price of veggie pizzas to $5.50 and meat pizzas to $5.25?

Section C

In March of year 3, Big Al's receives a special order from an athletic arena to purchase 5,000 meat pizzas and 3,000 veggie pizzas for a special charity event.

Required:

A. Assuming that Big Al's has sufficient excess capacity, what is the minimum price that Big Al's would be willing to accept for this special order? Assuming that Big Al's does not have sufficient excess capacity, what minimum price would be acceptable? What qualitative factors should Big Al's consider before agreeing to accept the special order?
B. Big Al's is nearing its manufacturing capacity and needs to consider ways to increase throughput. What options does Big Al's have to increase capacity? What bottlenecks does it face? What recommendations would you make?

Section D

Big Al's currently leases its equipment from Pizza Products for $2,500 per month. Two years of the five-year lease term remain. Big Al's can terminate the lease at any time by paying a penalty of $10,000. Big Al's is considering purchasing equipment to replace the leased equipment. Big Al's must purchase 10 units of each piece of equipment. Big Al's can purchase equipment at the following prices:

Equipment	Price (per unit)
Dough ball press	$5,450
Assembly table	2,100
Cardboard cutter	4,100
Plastic sealer	2,695
Label installer	1,000

Required:

A. Using NPV analysis, compare the present value of the lease payments with the cost of buying the equipment. Assuming a discount rate of 10 percent (before tax), which option is preferable?
B. Big Al's has the option of purchasing equipment from another supplier at a cost of $190,000. The supplier promises that the new equipment will reduce operating costs by $1,000 per month over the life of the equipment. Assuming a 10 percent discount rate (before tax), which option is preferable?
C. Calculate the after-tax NPV for each option discussed previously. If purchased, all equipment will be depreciated over five years, using straight-line depreciation, and will have no salvage value. Big Al's tax rate is 30 percent. Is your decision still the same?
D. What factors other than cost savings should Big Al's consider in these decision problems?

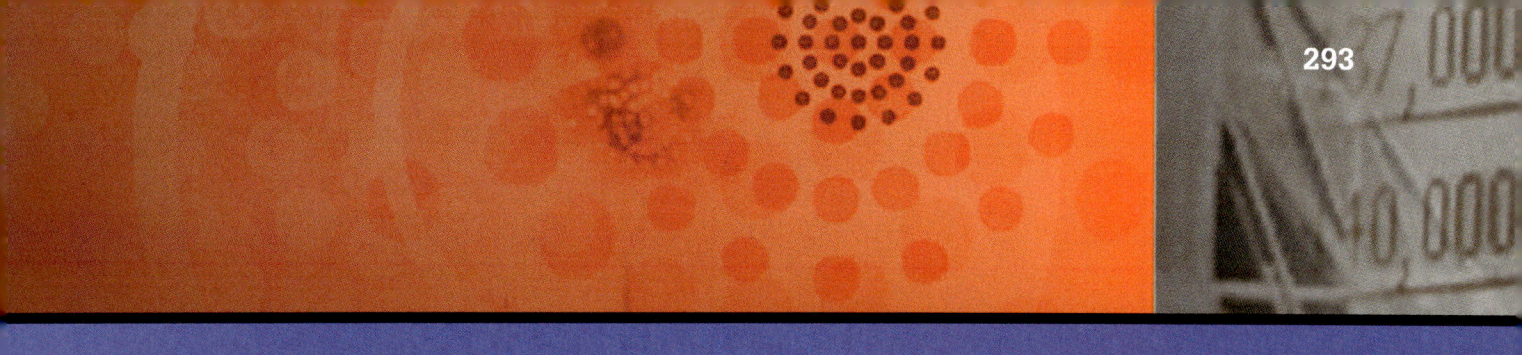

Part III: Planning, Performance Evaluation, and Control

Chapter 9   The Use of Budgets in Planning and Decision Making

Chapter 10   The Use of Budgets for Cost Control and Performance Evaluation

Chapter 11   Other Tools for Cost Control and Performance Evaluation

Chapter 12   Nonfinancial Measures of Performance

Chapter 9: The Use of Budgets in Planning and Decision Making

Chapter 9 The Use of Budgets in Planning and Decision Making

In this chapter, we introduce the concept of budgeting and discuss how budgets assist managers in planning and decision making. As discussed in Chapter 1, planning involves the development of both short-term (operational) and long-term (strategic) goals and objectives. Budgeting helps managers determine the resources needed to meet their goals and objectives and thus is a key ingredient in good decision making. In this chapter, we discuss and demonstrate the preparation of operational budgets for a traditional manufacturing company with inventory, as well as for a company operating in a JIT environment. We also discuss the use of operational budgets in merchandising and service companies.

The focus of budgeting is planning—planning for production requirements, planning for purchases of raw materials, planning for the use of direct labor and other resources, and, most important, planning for cash needs. In this chapter, we pay special attention to the preparation and use of the cash budget for managerial decision making and tie it into the preparation of the statement of cash flows used extensively by external users.

In the last section of the chapter, static and flexible budgets are discussed, with particular emphasis on the impact of ABC on flexible budgets. Nonfinancial budgets are also introduced.

Learning Objectives

After studying the material in this chapter, you should be able to:

1. Describe the budget development process, the use of budgets in planning, and the advantages of budgeting

2. Demonstrate the preparation of a sales budget and explain how managers develop a sales forecast

3. Prepare a production budget and recognize how it relates to the material purchases, direct labor and manufacturing overhead budgets

4. Prepare budgets for material purchases, direct labor, manufacturing overhead and selling and administrative expenses

5. Explain the importance of budgeting for cash and prepare a cash receipts budget, a cash disbursements budget and a summary cash budget

6. Prepare budgeted income statements and balance sheets and evaluate the importance of budgeted financial statements for decision making

7. Contrast budgeting in a manufacturing company with budgeting in a merchandising company and service company, describe the use of nonfinancial budgets and discuss issues that must be considered in budgeting in an international environment

8. Differentiate static budgets from flexible budgets and describe how flexible budgets are used in activity-based costing

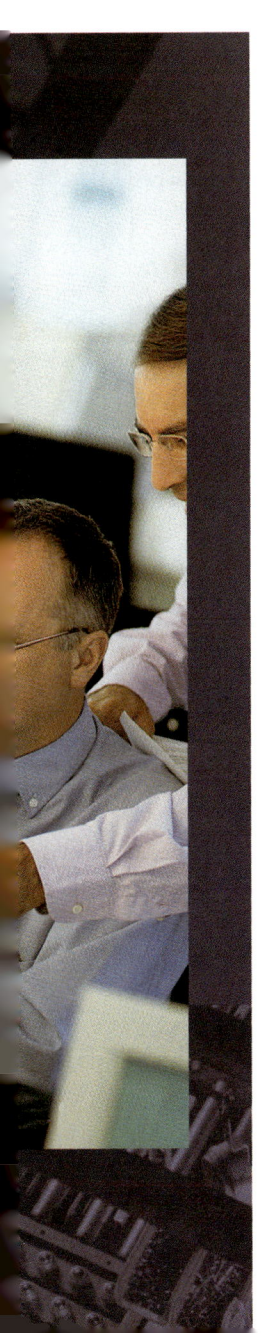

Introduction

Budgets are plans dealing with the acquisition and use of resources over a specified time period. Everyone budgets, from the college student to the large multinational corporation. Although budgets are often thought of in terms of dollars (monetary or financial budgets), budgets are used for other purposes as well. For example, a college student carrying 15 credit hours, working 20 hours a week in a part-time job, and volunteering 10 hours per week at the local hospital might need to prepare a time budget to plan his or her use of time throughout the week. A monetary budget for a college student can be as simple as jotting down expected cash inflows from loans, parents, and maybe a part-time job and expected outflows for school and living expenses.

At the other end of the budgeting spectrum, multinational companies may have very sophisticated budgets, used to plan for the acquisition and use of thousands of different materials, the manufacture of hundreds of products, and the sale of those products.

The Budget Development Process

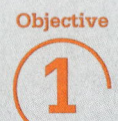

Objective 1
Describe the budget development process, the use of budgets in planning, and the advantages of budgeting

Traditionally, budgeting is a bottom-up process dependent on departmental managers providing a detailed plan for the upcoming month, quarter, or year. Some companies start their budget process based on last year's numbers, whereas others employ **zero-based budgeting.** Zero-based budgets require managers to build budgets from the ground up each year rather than just add a percentage increase to last year's numbers.

Although we typically think of budgets as being prepared annually, many state governments prepare budgets biannually (every two years). This can cause major problems when unexpected costs are incurred because of natural disasters or when tax revenue falls because of unexpected downturns in the economy.

Regardless of the specific process used, budgets must start with a top-down strategic plan that guides and integrates the whole company and its individual budgets. In addition, in order to motivate managers and other employees to meet the objectives and goals provided in budgets, companies must structure bonuses, merit pay, and other tangible and intangible rewards in ways that link these rewards to measurable goals outlined in the budgets. These concepts are discussed more fully in Chapter 13.

> **KEY CONCEPT**
> *Budgets must start with a top-down strategic plan that guides and integrates the whole company and its individual budgets.*

One of the misconceptions about budgeting is that the budgeting process is just a mechanical number-crunching task for bookkeepers. While budgeting can be tedious, the use of spreadsheets, such as Microsoft Excel, make their preparation much simpler. In recent years, more and more companies are using enterprise resource planning (ERP) systems as a key budgeting tool. As discussed in Chapter 1, ERP systems link data from across all areas of a business—a key for effective budgeting and planning. In reality, budgeting is a management task, not a bookkeeping task, and it requires a great deal of planning and thoughtful input from a broad range of managers in a company. This concept of budgeting as a management task will focus our discussion of the budgeting process in this chapter.

> **KEY CONCEPT**
> *Budgeting is a management task, not a bookkeeping task.*

Budgets for Planning, Operating, and Control

Managers use budgeting as they go about their **planning, operating,** and **control** activities (see Exhibit 9-1). Planning is the cornerstone of good management. Planning requires developing objectives and goals for the organization, as well as the actual preparation of budgets. Operating activities entail day-to-day decision making by managers, which is facilitated by budgets. Control activities include ensuring that the objectives and goals developed by the organization are being attained. Control often involves a comparison of budgets to actual performance and the use of budgets for performance evaluation purposes. The use of budgets for cost control and performance evaluation is discussed in more depth in Chapter 10.

> **KEY CONCEPT**
> *Budgets are used throughout managers' planning, operating, and control activities.*

In this chapter, we emphasize the use of budgets in planning and operating activities, including decisions concerning how much of a product to produce, how much material to

EXHIBIT 9-1 Budgeting Is an Integral Part of Managers' Planning, Operating, and Control Activities

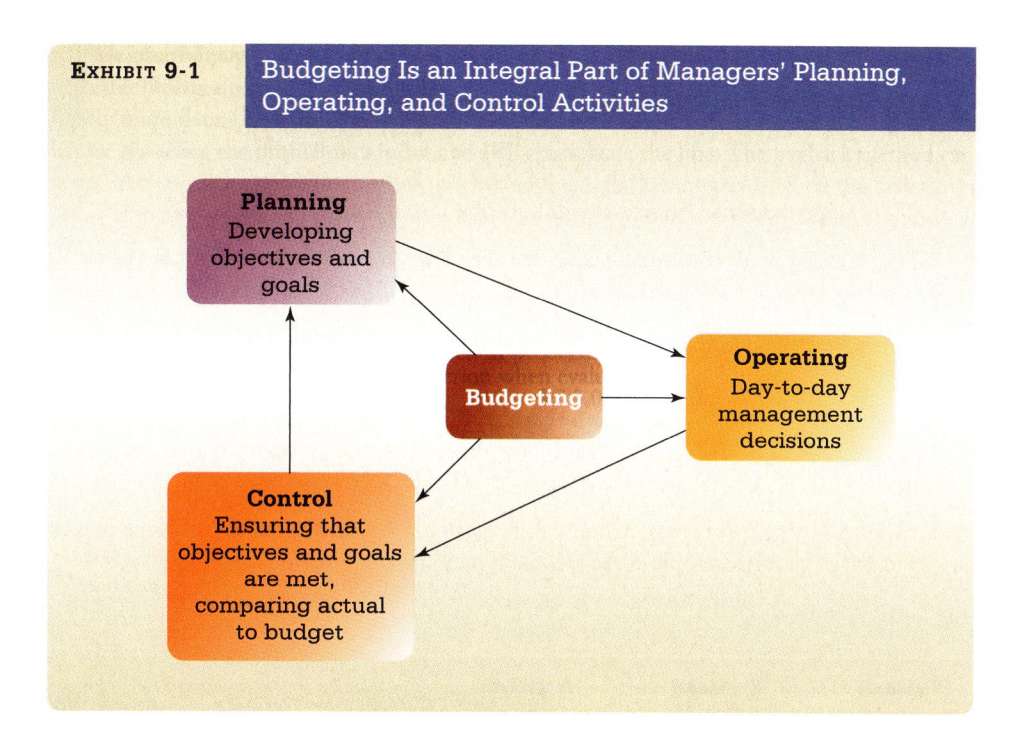

- **Planning**: Developing objectives and goals
- **Operating**: Day-to-day management decisions
- **Control**: Ensuring that objectives and goals are met, comparing actual to budget
- **Budgeting** (central)

buy, how much labor to hire, and the borrowing and investment of cash. The concept of budgeting for cash is tied back to the operating cycle. The operating cycle focuses on cash flow, beginning with the investment of cash in inventory or the use of cash to manufacture products, continuing with the sale of those products to customers, and ending with the collection of cash from those customers (see Exhibit 9-2).

EXHIBIT 9-2 The Operating Cycle

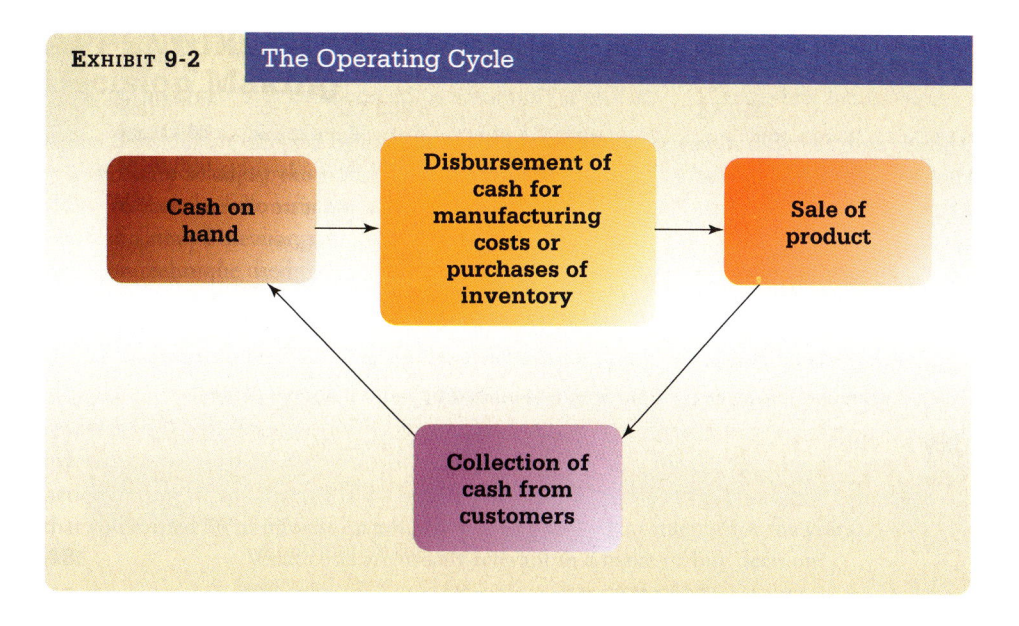

Cash on hand → Disbursement of cash for manufacturing costs or purchases of inventory → Sale of product → Collection of cash from customers → (back to Cash on hand)

One of the main reasons small businesses fail is the lack of adequate planning for cash needs. A small business that views budgeting for cash as too time consuming or expensive is destined for failure. With the availability and affordability of computers in today's business environment, even the smallest business can very easily perform the analysis necessary to successfully plan and budget for the future.

Advantages of Budgeting

Although the previous introduction pointed out the clear need for budgeting as a planning, operating, and control tool requiring managers to think about organizational goals and objectives, budgeting has other advantages as well.

1. The budgeting process forces communication throughout the organization.
2. The budgeting process forces management to focus on the future and not be distracted by daily crisis in the organization.
3. The budgeting process can help management identify and deal with potential bottlenecks or constraints before they become major problems.
4. The budgeting process can increase the coordination of organizational activities and help facilitate goal congruence. Goal congruence refers to making sure that the personal goals of the managers are closely aligned with the goals of the organization.
5. The budgeting process can define specific goals and objectives that can become benchmarks, or standards of performance, for evaluating future performance.

Hitting the Bottom Line.
"Managing Expectations"

The budgeting process serves many useful purposes such as identifying bottlenecks, creating benchmarks against which actual performance can be judged, and communicating management's expectations and plans. This last purpose extends beyond a company's walls to influence the expectations of outside parties such as investors, bankers, and financial analysts. In fact, financial analysts may base investment recommendations about buying and selling a company's stock on management's ability to meet its budgeted sales and income. Because of their potential significance to the stock market, management must carefully consider factors used in establishing budgets. Factors that management might consider include general economic conditions, competitive forces, new products, and planned advertising campaigns. Failure to deliver performance at the budgeted level can have significant negative effects. The recent experience of Amazon provides an example of how failing to meet budget by a small amount can negatively impact a company and its owners. In July 2004, Amazon reported net income of $76.5 million. While a significant improvement from the previous year's $43 million net loss, the amount of income failed to meet analysts' expectations and the company's stock price declined by more than five percent.

Source: *The New York Times*, July 23, 2004.

The Master Budget

The **master budget** consists of an interrelated set of budgets prepared by a business. A master budget for a manufacturing company is shown in Exhibit 9-3 with a corresponding master budget for a merchandising company shown in Exhibit 9-4. The starting point in both is forecasting sales and preparing a sales budget.

EXHIBIT 9-3 The Master Budget for a Manufacturing Company

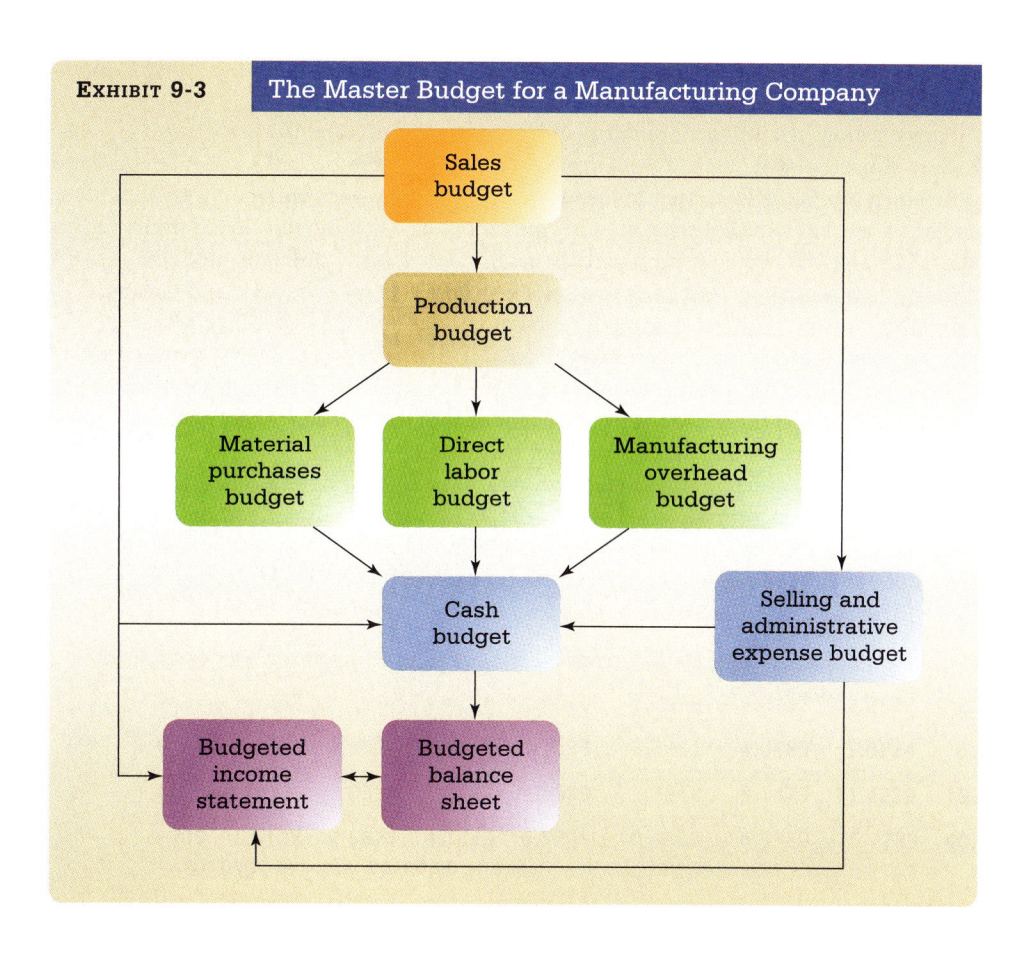

```
                    Sales
                   budget
                      ↓
                  Production
                   budget
            ↙         ↓         ↘
    Material      Direct      Manufacturing
    purchases    labor         overhead
    budget       budget        budget
            ↘       ↓       ↙
                  Cash              ←    Selling and
                 budget                   administrative
                   ↓                      expense budget
        ↙                  ↘
    Budgeted            Budgeted
    income      ↔       balance
    statement           sheet
```

EXHIBIT 9-4 The Master Budget for a Merchandising Company

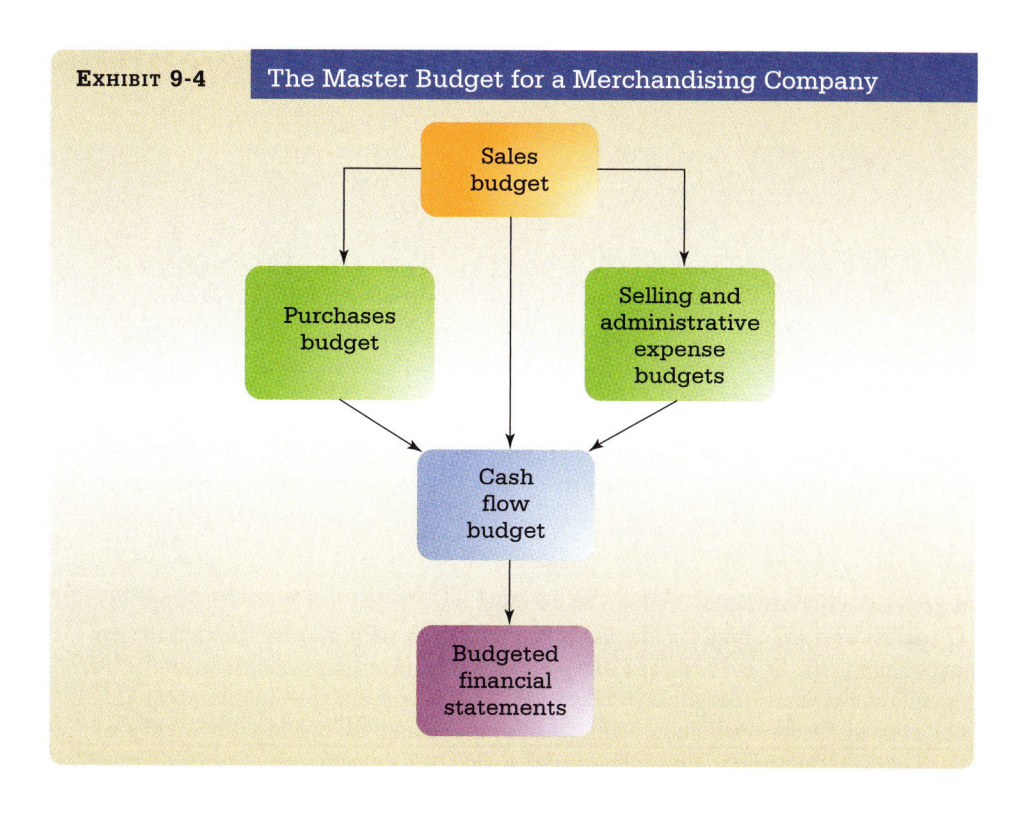

```
                   Sales
                  budget
             ↙              ↘
      Purchases         Selling and
      budget            administrative
                        expense
                        budgets
             ↘              ↙
                  Cash
                  flow
                 budget
                    ↓
                Budgeted
                financial
                statements
```

Objective 2

Demonstrate the preparation of a sales budget and explain how managers develop a sales forecast

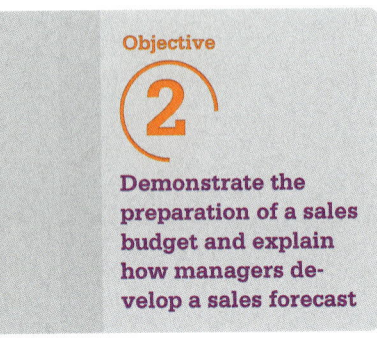

Budgeting for Sales

All organizations require the forecasting of future sales volume and the preparation of a sales budget. A professional baseball team needs to forecast the number of fans that attend home games each season. Airlines need to forecast the number of passengers who fly on each route, and hotels need to forecast occupancy rates for various days and months. Retail stores, such as Wal-Mart and J. C. Penney, must forecast retail sales of many different products at many different locations. Manufacturing firms, such as Ford, DaimlerChrysler, and General Motors, must forecast consumer demand for each model of car or truck that they sell.

The **sales forecast** and **sales budget** are the starting points in the preparation of production budgets for manufacturing companies and purchases budgets for merchandising companies. The sales budget is a key component used in the overall strategic planning process and is also used in planning the cash needs of businesses.

There are many different ways to forecast sales. Most forecasting will combine information from many different sources either informally or through the use of computer programs. Regardless of the size of the company or the sophistication of the forecasting methods used, the usual starting point in sales forecasting is last year's level of sales. Other factors and information sources typically used in sales forecasting are as follows:

1. Historical data, such as sales trends for the company, competitors, and the industry (if available).
2. General economic trends or factors, such as inflation rates, interest rates, population growth, and personal spending.
3. Regional and local factors expected to affect sales.
4. Anticipated price changes in both purchasing costs and sales prices.
5. Anticipated marketing or advertising plans.
6. The impact of new products or changes in product mix on the entire product line.
7. Other factors, such as political and legal events.

Every organization will have unique factors that it needs to consider and each organization will also attach a different level of importance to each factor.

Doing Business.

HOW'S THE WEATHER?

For some businesses, forecasting sales can be as difficult as forecasting the weather! For example, forecasting sales revenue (and the number of skiers) for a major ski resort requires not only the consideration of general economic conditions, the impact of new resorts and the potential impact of advertising but a consideration of the weather. While snow-making equipment has reduced the dependence of resorts on natural snow, weather can sometimes affect your business in ways that cannot be easily predicted. In a recent winter, New England ski areas had plenty of snow, but the communities at lower elevations (from which most of their customers came) did not. Even though the ski resorts used extensive advertising to promote the good ski conditions, skiers stayed away from the slopes because of the warm weather and lack of snow at home.

The size and complexity of the organization will often determine the complexity of the sales forecasting system. In large companies, preparation of the sales forecast is usually accomplished by the marketing department and requires significant effort in the area of market research to arrive at an accurate forecast of expected sales. In smaller companies, the sales forecast may be made by an individual or a small group of managers. Some companies will use elaborate econometric planning models and regression analysis to forecast sales volume. Others may use very informal models and rely heavily on the intuition and opinions of managers. Regardless of the level of sophistication used in forecasting models, it is important to remember that sales forecasting is still just that—a forecast.

As you will see in the rest of this chapter, all the remaining budgets and the decisions that are made based on their forecasts are dependent on this estimate of sales. For that reason, it is important to estimate sales with as much accuracy as possible. A small error in a sales forecast can cause larger errors in other budgets that depend on the sales forecast.

KEY CONCEPT

Budgets are future oriented and make extensive use of estimates and forecasts.

Operating Budgets—An Example

Operating budgets are used by companies to plan for the short term—usually one year or less. As an example of the budgeting process, let's consider the case of Tina's Fine Juices, a bottler of orange juice located in the Northeast. Tina's produces bottled orange juice from fruit concentrate purchased from suppliers in Florida, Arizona, and California. The only ingredients in the juice are water and concentrate. The juice is blended, pasteurized, and bottled for sale in 12-ounce plastic bottles. The process is heavily automated and is centered on five machines that control the mixing and bottling of the juice. Each machine is run by one employee and can process 10 bottles of juice per minute, or 600 bottles per hour.

The juice is sold by a number of grocery stores under their store brand name and in smaller restaurants, delis, and bagel shops under the name of Tina's Fine Juices. Tina's has been in business for several years and uses a sophisticated sales forecasting model based on prior sales, expected changes in demand, and economic factors affecting the industry. Sales of juice are highly seasonal, peaking in the first quarter of the year. Forecasted sales for the first quarter of 2005 are as follows:

Sales Forecast

	January	250,000 bottles
	February	325,000 bottles
	March	450,000 bottles

Tina's sells the juice for $1.05 per 12-ounce bottle, in cartons of 50 bottles. A sales budget is the projected volume of product to be sold times the expected sales price per unit (see Exhibit 9-5).

Objective 3

Prepare a production budget and recognize how it relates to the material purchases, direct labor, and manufacturing overhead budgets

Production Budget

For manufacturing companies, the next step in the budgeting process is to complete the **production budget**. Once the sales volume has been projected, companies must forecast how many units of product to produce in order to meet the sales projections. Although this might seem to be an easy task—just manufacture what you plan to sell—traditional manufacturing companies, as you will recall from Chapter 2, often choose to hold a minimum level of finished goods inventory (as well as direct material inventory) to serve as buffers in case of unexpected demand for products or unexpected problems in production.

Exhibit 9-5 Sales Budget

Tina's Fine Juices
Sales Budget

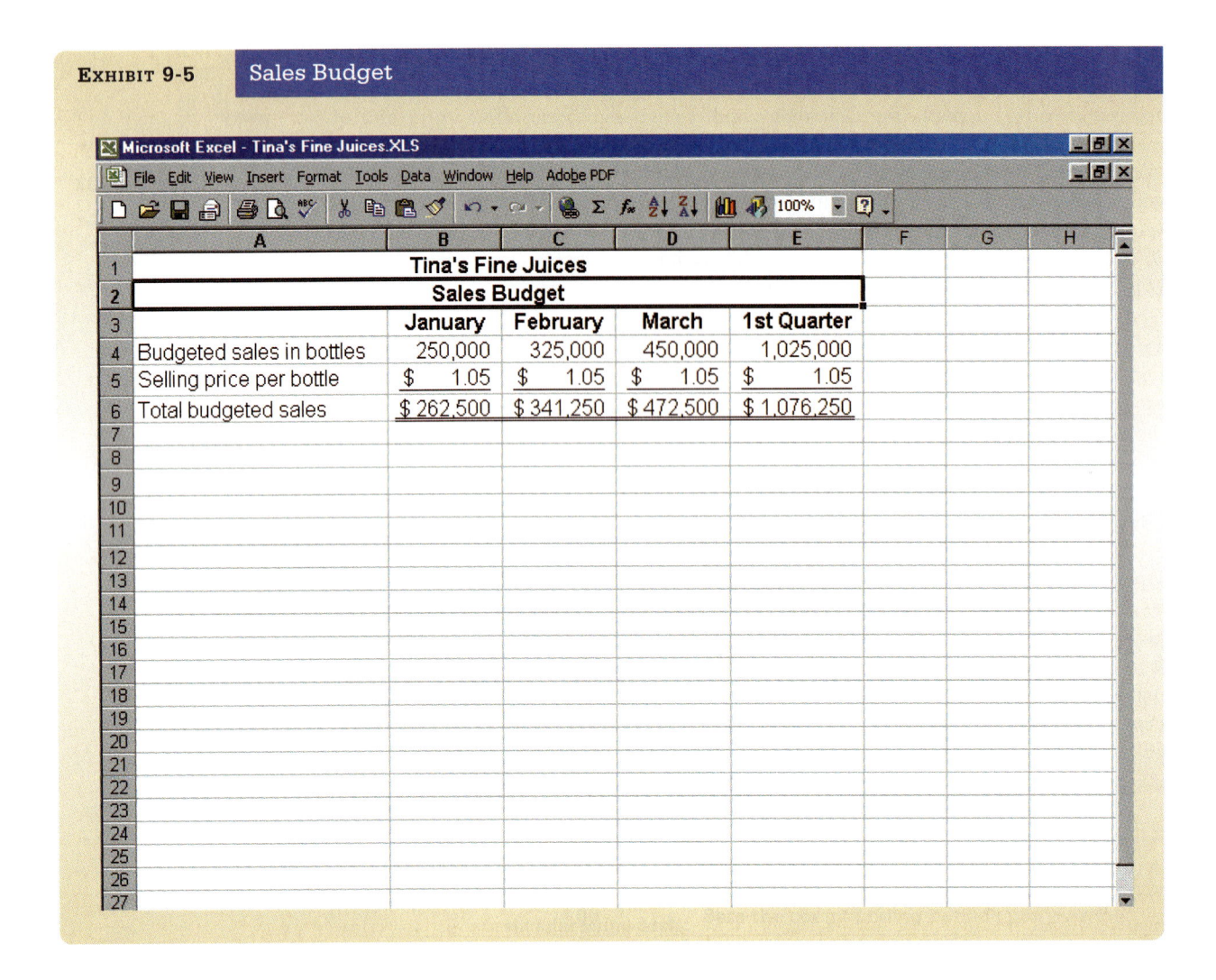

	January	February	March	1st Quarter
Budgeted sales in bottles	250,000	325,000	450,000	1,025,000
Selling price per bottle	$ 1.05	$ 1.05	$ 1.05	$ 1.05
Total budgeted sales	$ 262,500	$ 341,250	$ 472,500	$ 1,076,250

In this case, the sales forecast must be adjusted to account for any expected increase or decrease in finished goods inventory. A basic production budget is as follows:

Basic Production Budget

Sales forecast (in units)
+ Desired ending inventory of finished goods
= Total budgeted production needs
− Beginning inventory of finished goods
= Required production

Tina's Fine Juices tries to maintain at least 10 percent of the next month's sales forecast in inventory at the end of each month. Because sales have been projected to increase very rapidly, the company does not want to run the risk of running out of juice to ship to customers, so Tina's Fine Juices keeps a minimum amount on hand at all times. Other problems, such as shipping delays or weather, could also affect the amount of desired ending inventory. Based on these requirements Tina's would want to have 32,500 bottles of juice on hand at the end of January (10 percent of February's forecasted sales of 325,000). A production budget for Tina's Fine Juices is shown in Exhibit 9-6.

As shown in Exhibit 9-6, the arrows demonstrate that the projected ending inventory of finished goods for one month is the projected beginning inventory for the following month.

Exhibit 9-6 Production Budget

Tina's Fine Juices
Production Budget

	January	February	March	1st Quarter
Budgeted sales (Exhibit 9-5)	250,000	325,000	450,000	1,025,000
Add desired ending inventory of finished goods[1]	32,500	45,000	50,000	50,000
Total budgeted production needs	282,500	370,000	500,000	1,075,000
Less beginning inventory of finished goods[2]	25,000	32,500	45,000	25,000
Required production	257,500	337,500	455,000	1,050,000

[1] March ending inventory is calculated as follows:
April sales are projected to be 500,000 units of finished goods.
(500,000 × .10 = 50,000 units of finished goods.

[2] January beginning inventory of 25,000 units of finished goods is given

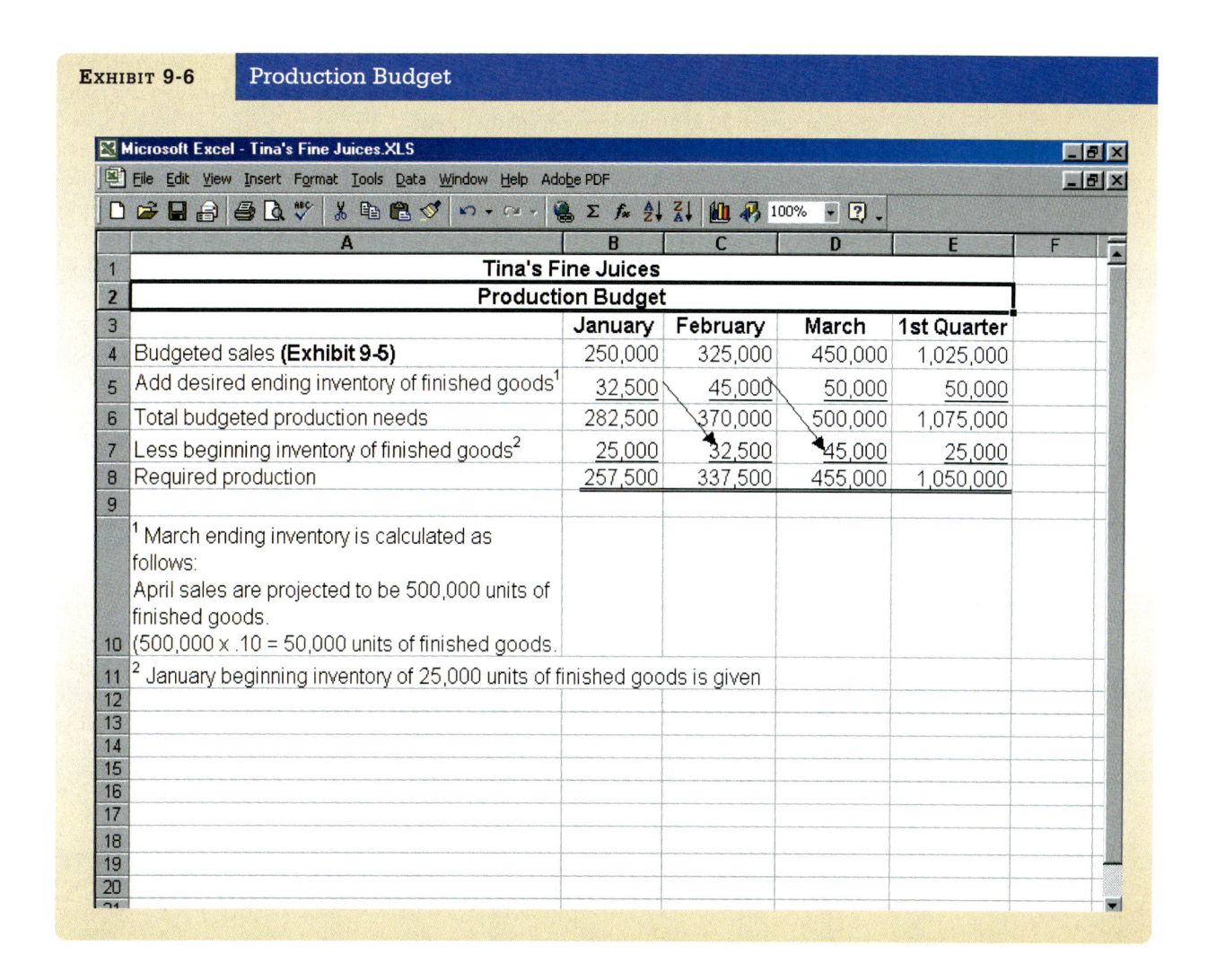

The projected ending inventory for the quarter is the ending inventory on the last day of the quarter, in this case March 31, and the projected beginning inventory for the quarter is the beginning inventory on the first day of the quarter, or January 1.

You should note that to complete the production budget for the first quarter, we need to have some additional information. We need to know the forecasted sales for April in order to determine the projected ending inventory for the end of March. April sales are projected to be 500,000 units, so the projected ending inventory is 50,000 units. The beginning inventory for January is 25,000 bottles. (This amount is also the ending inventory for December.) Closer examination of the production budget model will show that projected production needs are just the projected sales, plus or minus any projected change in inventory during the month.

Projected production = Projected sales +/− Change in finished goods inventory

In January, the projected sales are 250,000 units, and inventories are projected to increase by 7,500 units (from 25,000 to 32,500). If we add the projected inventory increase to the sales projection, we have a projected production level of 257,500 (250,000 + 7,500).

Material Purchases Budget

Once the production budget is completed, the next budget to be prepared is the **material purchases budget.** Once again, because many traditional companies desire to keep materials on hand at all times in order to plan for unforeseen changes in demand, the desired ending

Objective 4

Prepare budgets for material purchases, direct labor, manufacturing overhead and selling and administrative expenses

inventory for materials must be added to the projected production needs for materials to arrive at the total expected needs for materials. Then an adjustment is made for any raw material inventory on hand at the beginning of the month.

Tina's Fine Juices needs to prepare two purchases budgets—one for the concentrate used in its orange juice and one for the bottles that are purchased from an outside supplier. Tina's has determined that it takes one gallon of orange concentrate for every 32 bottles of finished product. Each gallon of concentrate costs $4.80. Tina's also requires 20 percent of next month's direct material needs to be on hand at the end of the budget period. Note that the starting point for this budget is the production budget. The next step in the preparation of the direct materials purchases budget is to compute the raw material needed based on the projected production. In this case, we take the number of bottles to be produced and divide by 32, which is the number of bottles that can be produced with one gallon of concentrate. The ending inventory needs are then added to that figure to arrive at the projected direct materials needed to fulfill the production and ending inventory needs. Beginning inventory is then subtracted from the projected needs to arrive at the projected purchases in gallons, and the last step is to convert that amount to dollars by multiplying the number of gallons by the price per gallon.

To calculate the projected ending inventory in March, Tina's must estimate sales for May. (April sales were already estimated to be 500,000 bottles.) If May sales are estimated at 400,000 bottles, April ending inventory will be estimated to be 40,000 bottles (0.10 × 400,000), and April production will be 490,000 bottles (April sales of 500,000 bottles + ending inventory of 40,000 bottles − beginning inventory of 50,000 bottles). The production of 490,000 bottles in April requires 15,313 gallons of concentrate (490,000 bottles/32 bottles per gallon). Accordingly, Tina's will plan on holding 3,063 gallons of concentrate in inventory at the end of March (20 percent of the material usage for April). The material purchases budget for orange concentrate is shown in Exhibit 9-7.

EXHIBIT 9-7 Material Purchases Budget—Orange Concentrate

Tina's Fine Juices
Material Purchases Budget - Orange Concentrate

	January	February	March	1st Quarter
Required production in bottles (**Exhibit 9-6**)	257,500	337,500	455,000	1,050,000
Orange concentrate needed (gallons)[1]	8,047	10,547	14,219	32,813
Add desired ending inventory of orange concentrate[2]	2,109	2,844	3,063	3,063
Total budgeted needs of orange concentrate	10,156	13,391	17,282	35,876
Less beginning inventory of orange concentrate[3]	1,609	2,109	2,844	1,609
Orange concentrate to be purchased	8,547	11,282	14,438	34,267
Cost per gallon of orange concentrate	$ 4.80	$ 4.80	$ 4.80	$ 4.80
Cost of orange concentrate to be purchased	$ 41,026	$ 54,154	$ 69,302	$ 164,482

[1] Required production divided by 32 bottles per gallon (rounded to the nearest gallon).
[2] Twenty percent of next month's materials needs
[3] January beginning inventory of 1,609 units is given.

Tina's will prepare a similar budget for bottles. The bottles are purchased from an outside supplier for $0.10 per bottle. The supplier provides labels and caps for the bottles as part of the purchase price. Tina's has the same inventory policy for bottles and orange concentrate. A material purchases budget for bottles is shown in Exhibit 9-8.

EXHIBIT 9-8 — Material Purchases Budget—Bottles

	January	February	March	1st Quarter
Required production in bottles (Exhibit 9-6)	257,500	337,500	455,000	1,050,000
Add desired ending inventory of bottles[1]	67,500	91,000	98,000	98,000
Total budgeted needs of bottles	325,000	428,500	553,000	1,148,000
Less beginning inventory of bottles[2]	51,500	67,500	91,000	51,500
Bottles to be purchased	273,500	361,000	462,000	1,096,500
Cost per bottle	$ 0.10	$ 0.10	$ 0.10	$ 0.10
Cost of bottles to be purchased	$27,350	$36,100	$46,200	$109,650

[1] March ending inventory is calculated as follows: Production for April is projected to be 490,000 bottles. Twenty percent of 490,000 bottles is 98,000.

[2] January beginning inventory of 51,500 bottles is given.

Direct Labor Budget

As with the material purchases budget, the **direct labor budget** starts with the production budget. However, since labor cannot be accumulated like raw materials, no adjustments need to be made for beginning and ending inventory.

The direct labor budget is prepared by multiplying the units to be produced by the number of direct labor hours required to produce each unit. As was discussed earlier, the production process utilizes a worker assigned to each of the five mixing and bottling machines. Each machine (and thus each worker) can process 600 bottles of orange juice per hour. At Tina's Fine Juices, factory workers are paid an average of $15 per hour, including fringe benefits and payroll taxes. If the production schedule doesn't allow for full utilization of the workers and machines, the worker is temporarily moved to another department. Dividing the labor rate of $15 by the time required per bottle shows that the amount of direct labor is $0.025 per bottle of juice ($15/600 bottles). A direct labor budget for the first quarter is shown in Exhibit 9-9.

Manufacturing Overhead Budget

Preparation of the **manufacturing overhead budget** involves estimating overhead costs. As was discussed in detail in Part I of this book, estimating overhead can be accomplished in a number of ways using plantwide or departmental predetermined overhead rates or

Exhibit 9-9 Direct Labor Budget

Tina's Fine Juices
Direct Labor Budget

	January	February	March	1st Quarter
Required production in bottles **(Exhibit 9-6)**	257,500	337,500	455,000	1,050,000
Direct labor hours per bottle	1/600	1/600	1/600	1/600
Total direct labor hours needed for production	429.17	562.50	758.33	1,750.00
Direct labor cost per hour	$ 15.00	$ 15.00	$ 15.00	$ 15.00
Total direct labor cost	$ 6,438	$ 8,437	$11,375	$ 26,250

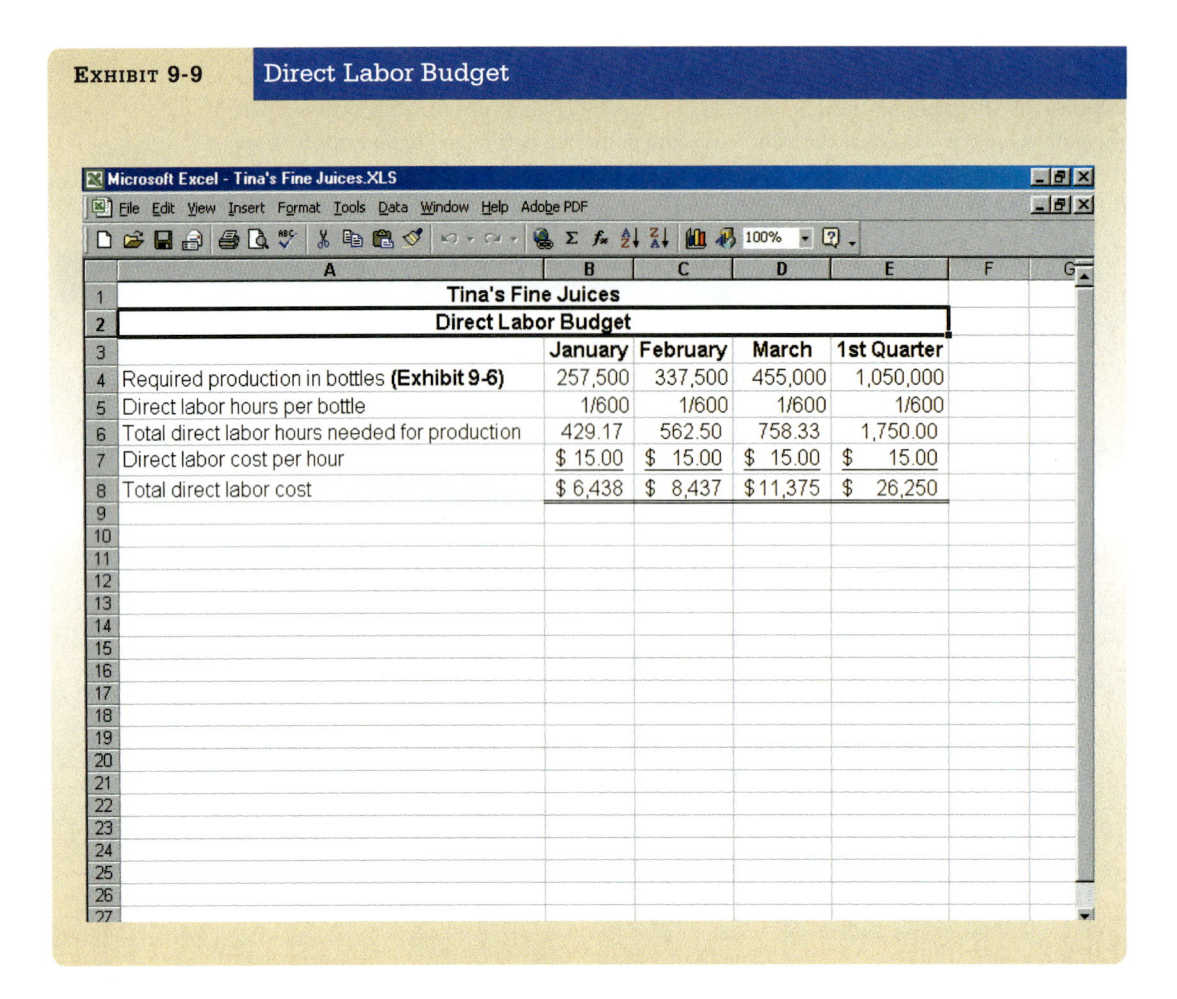

activity-based costing. At Tina's Fine Juices, most of the production process is automated, the juice is mixed by machine, and machines do the bottling and packaging. Overhead costs are incurred almost entirely in the mixing and bottling process. Consequently, Tina's has chosen to use a plantwide cost driver (machine hours) to apply manufacturing overhead to products.

However, as you will recall from Chapter 5, not all overhead is expected to behave in the same fashion, as production increases and decreases each month. Although variable overhead costs will vary in direct proportion to the number of bottles of juice produced, fixed overhead costs will remain constant regardless of production. For budgeting purposes, Tina's separates variable overhead from fixed overhead and calculates a predetermined overhead rate for variable manufacturing overhead costs.

Tina's Fine Juices has estimated that variable overhead will total $438,000 for the year and that the machines will run approximately 8,000 hours at the projected production volume for the year (4,775,000 bottles). The estimated machine hours are 80 percent of capacity for the five machines. Therefore, Tina's predetermined overhead rate for variable overhead is $54.75 per machine hour ($438,000/8,000 machine hours). Tina's has also estimated fixed overhead to be $1,480,000 per year ($123,333 per month), of which $1,240,000 per year ($103,333 per month) is depreciation on existing property, plant, and equipment.

The manufacturing overhead budget is presented Exhibit 9-10. Note that variable overhead is budgeted based on the predetermined overhead rate and varies with production each month, whereas fixed manufacturing overhead is budgeted at a constant $123,333 per month.

The material purchases budget, the direct labor budget, and the manufacturing overhead budget are summarized in a total manufacturing cost budget (see Exhibit 9-11). This budget provides Tina's Fine Juices with an estimate of the total manufacturing costs expected to be incurred in the first quarter of 2005.

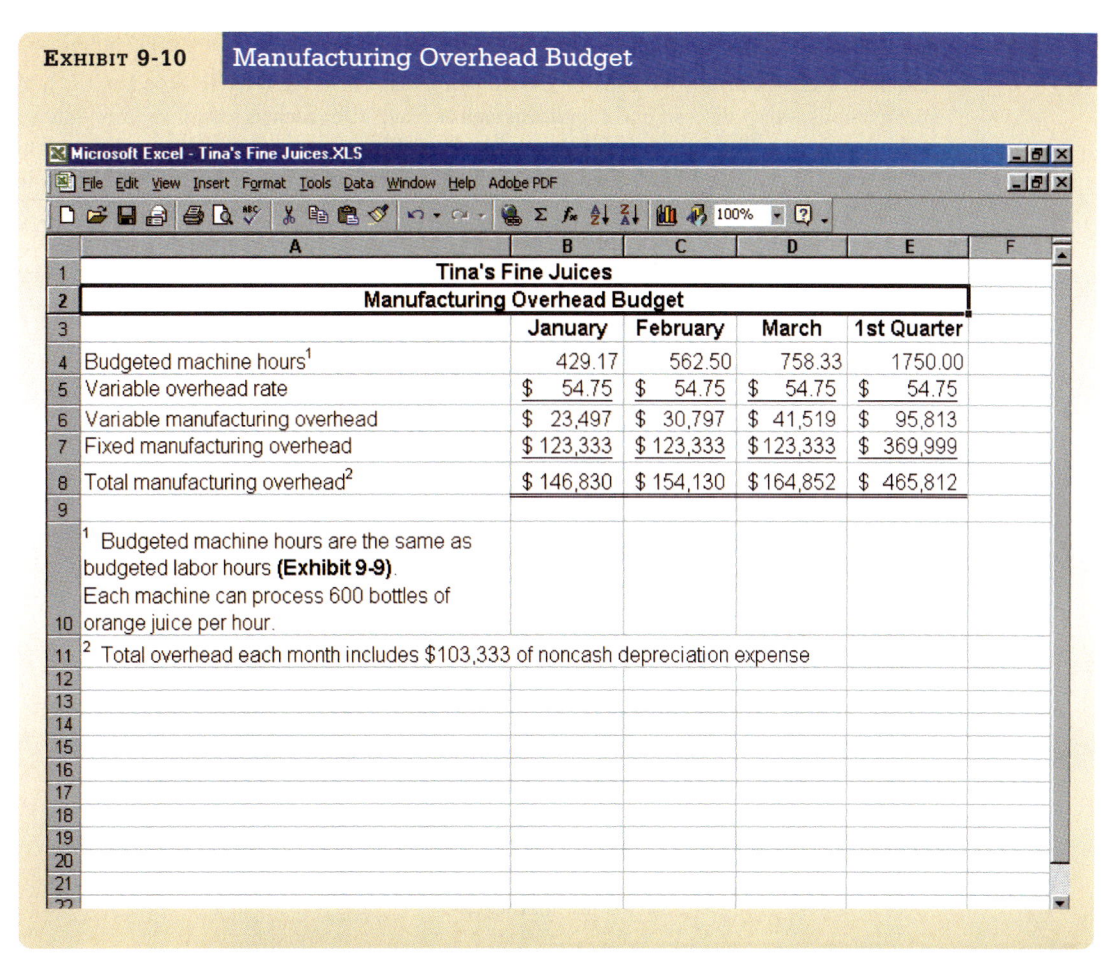

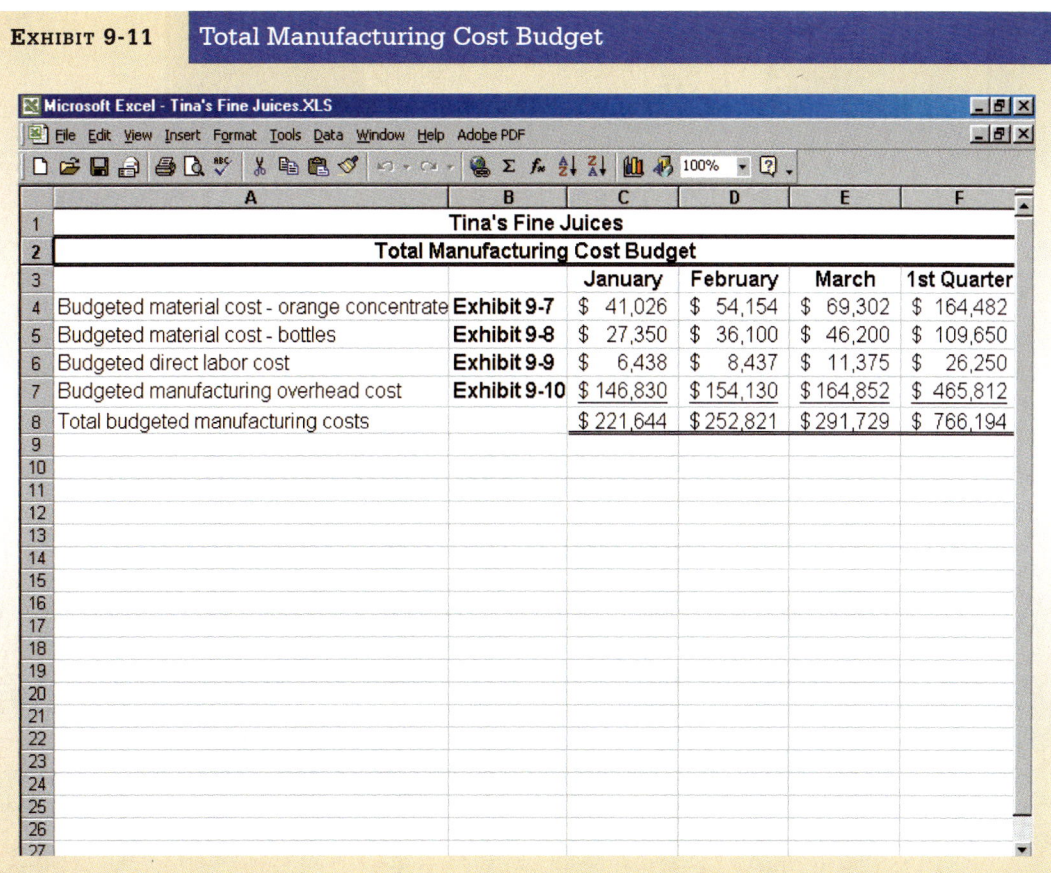

Exhibit 9-10 Manufacturing Overhead Budget

Tina's Fine Juices
Manufacturing Overhead Budget

	January	February	March	1st Quarter
Budgeted machine hours[1]	429.17	562.50	758.33	1750.00
Variable overhead rate	$ 54.75	$ 54.75	$ 54.75	$ 54.75
Variable manufacturing overhead	$ 23,497	$ 30,797	$ 41,519	$ 95,813
Fixed manufacturing overhead	$ 123,333	$ 123,333	$ 123,333	$ 369,999
Total manufacturing overhead[2]	$ 146,830	$ 154,130	$ 164,852	$ 465,812

[1] Budgeted machine hours are the same as budgeted labor hours **(Exhibit 9-9)**. Each machine can process 600 bottles of orange juice per hour.

[2] Total overhead each month includes $103,333 of noncash depreciation expense

Exhibit 9-11 Total Manufacturing Cost Budget

Tina's Fine Juices
Total Manufacturing Cost Budget

		January	February	March	1st Quarter
Budgeted material cost - orange concentrate	Exhibit 9-7	$ 41,026	$ 54,154	$ 69,302	$ 164,482
Budgeted material cost - bottles	Exhibit 9-8	$ 27,350	$ 36,100	$ 46,200	$ 109,650
Budgeted direct labor cost	Exhibit 9-9	$ 6,438	$ 8,437	$ 11,375	$ 26,250
Budgeted manufacturing overhead cost	Exhibit 9-10	$ 146,830	$ 154,130	$ 164,852	$ 465,812
Total budgeted manufacturing costs		$ 221,644	$ 252,821	$ 291,729	$ 766,194

Selling and Administrative Expense Budget

A selling and administrative expense budget for Tina's includes variable expenses, such as commissions, shipping costs and supplies as well as fixed costs, such as rent, insurance, salaries and advertising. Tina's commissions are a function of projected sales and are calculated as 10 percent of projected sales. Tina's selling and administrative expense budget is shown in Exhibit 9-12.

EXHIBIT 9-12 Selling and Administrative Expense Budget

Tina's Fine Juices
Selling and Administrative Expense Budget

	January	February	March	1st Quarter
Variable selling and administrative expenses				
Commissions[1]	$ 26,250	$ 34,125	$ 47,250	$ 107,625
Shipping costs	$ 10,500	$ 13,650	$ 18,900	$ 43,050
Supplies	$ 2,100	$ 2,720	$ 3,780	$ 8,600
Fixed selling and adminstrative expenses				
Rent	$ 20,000	$ 20,000	$ 20,000	$ 60,000
Insurance	$ 5,000	$ 5,000	$ 5,000	$ 15,000
Salaries	$ 15,000	$ 15,000	$ 15,000	$ 45,000
Advertising	$ 8,000	$ 8,000	$ 8,000	$ 24,000
Total selling and administrative expenses	$ 86,850	$ 98,495	$ 117,930	$ 303,275

[1] Commissions are based on 10% of projected sales **(Exhibit 9-5)**.

Cash Budgets

Why Focus on Cash?

Objective 5

Explain the importance of budgeting for cash and prepare a cash receipts budget, a cash disbursements budget and a summary cash budget

Many managers consider managing cash flow to be the single most important consideration in running a successful business. After all, cash, *not* income, pays the bills. Whereas income (earnings per share) is often important to external investors, cash flow often takes center stage for managers.

The timing of cash inflows and outflows is critical to the overall planning process. When cash inflows are delayed because of the extension of credit to buyers, there may not be sufficient cash to pay suppliers, creditors, and employee wages. Timely payment is necessary to maintain good business relationships with suppliers (and to keep employees happy) and to take the maximum discounts that may be available on purchases. Cash budgeting forces managers to focus on cash flow and to plan for the purchase of materials, the payment of creditors, and the payment of salaries. Sufficient cash must be available to pay dividends to stockholders and to acquire new fixed assets. As can be seen in the example in the next section, cash budgets also point out the need for borrowing cash or when excess cash can be invested or used to repay debt.

Doing Business.

"CASH IS KING"

Even in good times, cash flow is frequently a concern for small business owners. In a recent survey conducted by American Express, 62% of small business owners said managing cash flow was a priority. Of those with cash flow concerns, 35% said getting customers to pay their bills was their most significant worry, followed by 26% who worried about paying their own bills. Making sure there was enough cash on hand to fund expansion and growth was a concern for 22% of respondents. How do small business owners meet cash shortages? 30% said they would delay purchases, 24% said they would use a credit line and 18% said they would use a business credit card (Amid Growth Prospects, Cash Flow is a Concern," *Wall Street Journal,* May 18, 2004, p. B5).

The Cash Receipts Budget

The first cash budget that must be prepared is the **cash receipts budget.** The cash receipts budget shows cash receipts that are generated from operating activities—cash sales of inventory or services and customer payments on account. Other cash receipts (from the sale of property, investment income, etc.) are included in the summary cash budget.

All the sales of Tina's Fine Juices are on account. Based on experience in previous years, Tina's estimates that 50 percent of the sales each month will be paid for in the month of sale. Tina's also estimates that 35 percent of the month's sales will be collected in the month following sale and that 15 percent of each month's sales will be collected in the second month following sale.[1] As you will recall from the sales budget (Exhibit 9-5), sales for January, February, and March were projected to be $262,500, $341,250, and $472,500, respectively. Because collections lag sales by up to two months (some of November's sales will not be collected until January, and some of December's sales will not be collected until February), completing the cash receipts budget also requires that we include sales for November and December. November's sales were $200,000, whereas December's sales were $250,000.

The preparation of the cash receipts budget is straightforward once the payment scheme is set. In each month, we collect 50 percent of that month's sales (50 percent of January's sales are collected in January), 35 percent of the previous month's sales (35 percent of December's sales are collected in January), and 15 percent of the second previous month's sales (15 percent of November's sales are collected in January). And then the payment scheme is repeated for the remainder of the months in the budget. A cash receipts budget for cash received from operating activities is presented in Exhibit 9-13.

A closer look at the cash receipts budget shows that budgeted cash receipts are significantly different from budgeted sales revenue. In February and March, cash receipts are expected to be less than sales revenue. When sales are increasing, and there is a lag between sales and the collection of cash, this is usually the case. It seems ironic, but businesses that are growing rapidly will often be short of cash.

The Cash Disbursements Budget

The next component in the cash budgeting process is the **cash disbursements budget.** The cash disbursements budget includes cash outflows resulting from operating activities—payments to

---

[1] It would not be unusual for some of the sales to never be collected. If Tina's thinks that some of the accounts receivable are uncollectible, the cash receipts budget should be adjusted accordingly.

EXHIBIT 9-13 Cash Receipts Budget—Operating Activities

Tina's Fine Juices
Cash Receipts Budget - Operating Activities

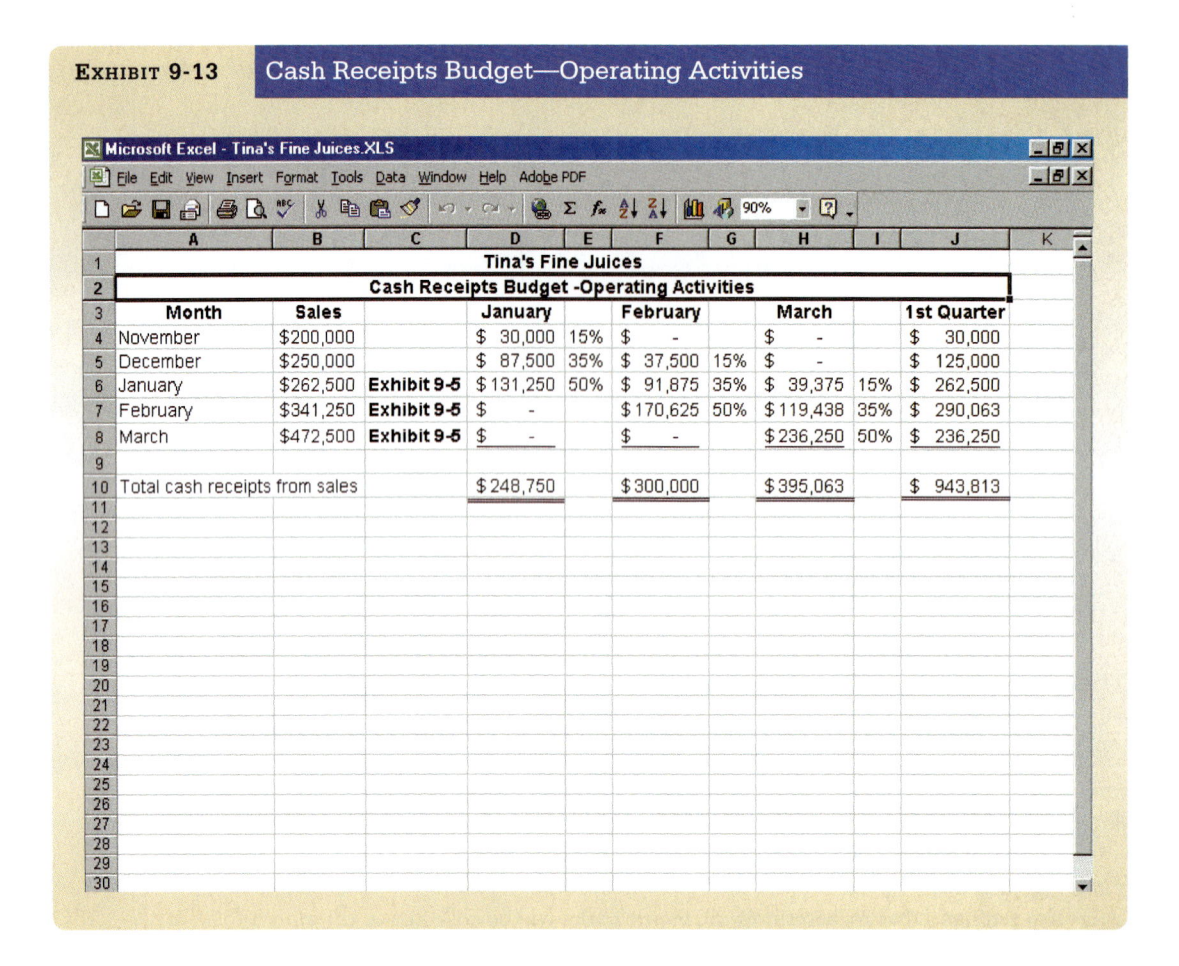

Month	Sales		January		February		March		1st Quarter
November	$200,000		$ 30,000	15%	$ -		$ -		$ 30,000
December	$250,000		$ 87,500	35%	$ 37,500	15%	$ -		$ 125,000
January	$262,500	Exhibit 9-5	$131,250	50%	$ 91,875	35%	$ 39,375	15%	$ 262,500
February	$341,250	Exhibit 9-5	$ -		$170,625	50%	$119,438	35%	$ 290,063
March	$472,500	Exhibit 9-5	$ -		$ -		$236,250	50%	$ 236,250
Total cash receipts from sales			$248,750		$300,000		$395,063		$ 943,813

suppliers for materials, cash outflows for salaries and other labor costs, and cash outflows for overhead expenditures. Cash disbursements for selling and administrative costs are also included, although other cash outflows (for equipment purchases, payment of dividends, etc.) are usually not included. These nonoperating disbursements will be included in the summary cash budget but not in the cash disbursements budget for operating activities.

Budgeting for the cash disbursements related to materials, labor, and overhead is not as easy as just looking at the material, labor, and overhead budgets. Purchases of material are often made on account, resulting in lags between the date items are purchased and the date cash actually changes hands. The manufacturing overhead budget often includes noncash items, such as depreciation, that must be adjusted as well.

A cash disbursements budget for Tina's Fine Juices is shown in Exhibit 9-14. Tina's has a policy of paying 50 percent of the direct materials purchases in the month of purchase and the balance in the month after purchase. This policy offsets to a certain extent the lag in cash receipts from sales. Purchases of direct material are taken directly off the material purchases budgets (Exhibits 9-7 and 9-8) and then cash payments are adjusted for the payment lag. For example, in January, Tina's budgeted purchases of orange concentrate total $41,026 (see Exhibit 9-7). As shown in row 6 of the cash disbursements budget (Exhibit 9-14), 50 percent of this amount or $20,513 will be paid in January, with the other 50% paid in February. Similar calculations are made for purchases of orange concentrate in February and March.

Likewise, in January, Tina's budgeted purchases of bottles total $27,350 (see Exhibit 9-8). As with purchases of orange concentrate, half of this amount or $13,675 will be paid in January and the other half in February (see row 11 of Exhibit 9-14). Similar calculations are made for purchases of bottles in February and March.

All direct labor costs are paid in the month incurred and come directly from the direct labor budget (see Exhibit 9-9).

Exhibit 9-14 Cash Disbursements Budget—Operating Activities

Tina's Fine Juices
Cash Disbursements Budget - Operating Activities

		January	February	March	1st Quarter
Purchases of concentrate	Exhibit 9-7				
December (given)		$ 18,220			$ 18,220
January		$ 20,513	$ 20,513		$ 41,026
February			$ 27,077	$ 27,077	$ 54,154
March				$ 34,651	$ 34,651
Purchases of bottles	Exhibit 9-8				
December (given)		$ 12,146			$ 12,146
January		$ 13,675	$ 13,675		$ 27,350
February			$ 18,050	$ 18,050	$ 36,100
March				$ 23,100	$ 23,100
Total disbursements for material		$ 64,554	$ 79,315	$102,878	$ 246,747
Disbursements for direct labor	Exhibit 9-9	$ 6,438	$ 8,437	$ 11,375	$ 26,250
Manufacturing overhead	Exhibit 9-10				
December (given)		$ 20,917			$ 20,917
January		$ 21,748	$ 21,749		$ 43,497
February			$ 25,398	$ 25,399	$ 50,797
March				$ 30,759	$ 30,759
Total disbursements for manufacturing overhead		$ 42,665	$ 47,147	$ 56,158	$ 145,970
Disbursements for selling & administrative expenses	Exhibit 9-12	$ 86,850	$ 98,495	$117,930	$ 303,275
Total cash disbursements		$200,507	$233,394	$288,341	$ 722,242

Like materials, manufacturing overhead costs are paid on a lag, with 50 percent paid for in the month incurred and 50 percent in the following month. However, the manufacturing overhead budget (Exhibit 9-10) must be adjusted for depreciation of property, plant, and equipment, which does not have a direct impact on cash flow.[2] While total budgeted manufacturing overhead for January is estimated to be $146,830, $103,333 of this amount pertains to noncash depreciation and will not be included in the cash disbursements budget. Of the $43,497 of cash overhead expected in January ($146,830 - $103,333), 50 percent or $21,748 will be paid in January with the remaining $21,749 paid in February (see row 20 of Exhibit 9-14). Similar calculations are made for payments of manufacturing overhead expenses in February and March.

Cash disbursements for selling and administrative costs are taken directly from Exhibit 9-12.

Summary Cash Budget

A **summary cash budget** consists of three sections: (1) cash flows from operating activities, (2) cash flows from investing activities, and (3) cash flows from financing activities. These three sections are the same as used in the cash flow statement prepared under generally accepted accounting principles. Preparation and use of the statement of cash flows is covered in detail in Chapter 16.

Cash flows from operating activities have already been discussed. Cash flows from investing activities include purchases and sales of property, plant, equipment and other investments, and interest and dividends earned on investment assets. Cash flows from financing activities include

---

[2] You will recall from Chapter 8 that depreciation can have an indirect impact on cash flow through its impact on income taxes. The impact of income tax is taken into account in the summary cash budget.

payments for the retirement of any debt issued by the company, sales or repurchases of stock, payment of dividends, and any borrowing or repayments of other long-term liabilities.

Summary cash budgets can be fairly straightforward or very complex, depending on the size and complexity of the company. Tina's summary cash budget is shown in Exhibit 9-15.

EXHIBIT 9-15   Summary Cash Budget

	A	B	C	D	E	F
1	Tina's Fine Juices					
2	Summary Cash Budget					
3			January	February	March	1st Quarter
4	Beginning cash balance		$ 50,000	$ 50,000	$ 50,000	$ 50,000
5	Cash flows from operating activities:					
6	Cash receipts	Exhibit 9-13	$ 248,750	$ 300,000	$ 395,063	$ 943,813
7	Cash disbursements	Exhibit 9-14	$(200,507)	$(233,394)	$(288,341)	$ (722,242)
8	Income taxes	Exhibit 9-18			$ (929)	$ (929)
9	Cash flows from investing activities:					
10	Equipment purchases (given)			$ (75,000)		$ (75,000)
11	Cash flows from financing activities:					
12	Payment of Dividends		$ (50,000)			$ (50,000)
13	Interest on Long-term debt[1]				$ (30,000)	$ (30,000)
14	Cash Balance before borrowing/repayment		$ 48,243	$ 41,606	$ 125,793	$ 115,642
15	Borrowing from line of credit[2]		$ 1,757	$ 8,394		$ 10,151
16	Repayments of line of credit		$ -	$ -	$ (10,151)	$ (10,151)
17	Interest on line of credit[3]		$ -	$ -	$ (184)	$ (184)
18	Ending cash balance		$ 50,000	$ 50,000	$ 115,458	$ 115,458
19	[1] Long term debt is $1,500,000 (Exhibit 9-19). Interest is paid quarterly at an annual rate of 8%. $1,500,000 × 8% × 3/12 = $30,000.					
20	[2] The minimum cash balance at the end of each month is $50,000.					
21	[3] The line of credit with interest is repaid at the end of March. The interest is calculated as $1,757 × 10% × 3/12 + $8,394 × 10% × 2/12.					

Cash receipts and disbursements from operating activities have already been summarized in the cash receipts and disbursements budgets. Tina's plans to buy some new machinery in February at a cost of $75,000 (see Exhibit 9-15, row 10). The company also plans on paying a dividend of $50,000 in January (see Exhibit 9-15, row 12). Tina's also desires to keep a cash balance of at least $50,000 on hand at the end of any month. If the projected cash balance is less than that, a line of credit at Tina's local bank will be used to make up the shortage. If Tina's draws on the line of credit, the company is charged an interest rate of 10 percent annually. If the line of credit is used, money is borrowed at the beginning of the month. Repayments are made at the end of months in which there is sufficient excess cash (over $50,000) to pay back the entire line of credit. Last, but not least, Tina's pays estimated income taxes on a quarterly basis (in March, June, September, and December) on the income earned during the respective quarter. Tina's estimates that its federal tax liability is around 15 percent of taxable income.

Objective 6
Prepare budgeted income statements and balance sheets and evaluate the importance of budgeted financial statements for decision making

Budgeted Financial Statements

Companies may also desire to prepare budgeted financial statements. These are used both for internal planning purposes and to provide information to external users. For example, a bank might want to examine a budgeted income statement and balance sheet before lending money to a company. The budgeted financial statements are often called **pro forma financial statements.**

A budgeted schedule of cost of goods manufactured and cost of goods sold is shown in Exhibits 9-16 and 9-17.

EXHIBIT 9-16 Budgeted Cost of Goods Manufactured (Absorption)

Tina's Fine Juices
Budgeted Cost of Goods Manufactured (Absorption)

	A	B	C	D
4	Beginning inventory of raw material[1]		$ 12,873	
5	Add purchases of raw material	Exhibit 9-7 and 9-8	$274,132	
6	Raw materials available for sale		$287,005	
7	Less ending inventory of raw material[2]		$ (24,502)	
8	Raw materials used in production			$262,503
9	Add direct labor	Exhibit 9-9		$ 26,250
10	Add manufacturing overhead	Exhibit 9-10		$465,812
11	Total manufacturing costs			$754,565
12	Add beginning inventory of WIP			$ -
13	Less ending inventory of WIP			$ -
14	Cost of goods manufactured			$754,565

[1] The cost of the beginning inventory is given.
[2] 3,063 gallons x $4.80 per gallon + 98,000 bottles x $.10 per bottle.

EXHIBIT 9-17 Budgeted Cost of Goods Sold (Absorption)

Tina's Fine Juices
Budgeted Cost of Goods Sold (Absorption)

	A	B	C
3	Beginning inventory of finished goods[1]		$ 17,966
4	+ Cost of goods manufactured	Exhibit 9-16	$ 754,565
5	= Cost of goods available for sale		$ 772,531
6	- Ending inventory of finished goods[2]		$ (35,932)
7	Cost of goods sold		$ 736,599

[1] Beginning inventory of finished goods is given.
[2] The cost of each of the 50,000 gallons is $.71863 per gallon. ($754,565 cost of goods manufactured / 1,050,000 bottles produced).

Note that the cost of goods manufactured and the cost of goods sold are calculated using absorption costing. Likewise, the budgeted income statement in Exhibit 9-18 is prepared using the traditional format. The budgeted balance sheet is shown in Exhibit 9-19.

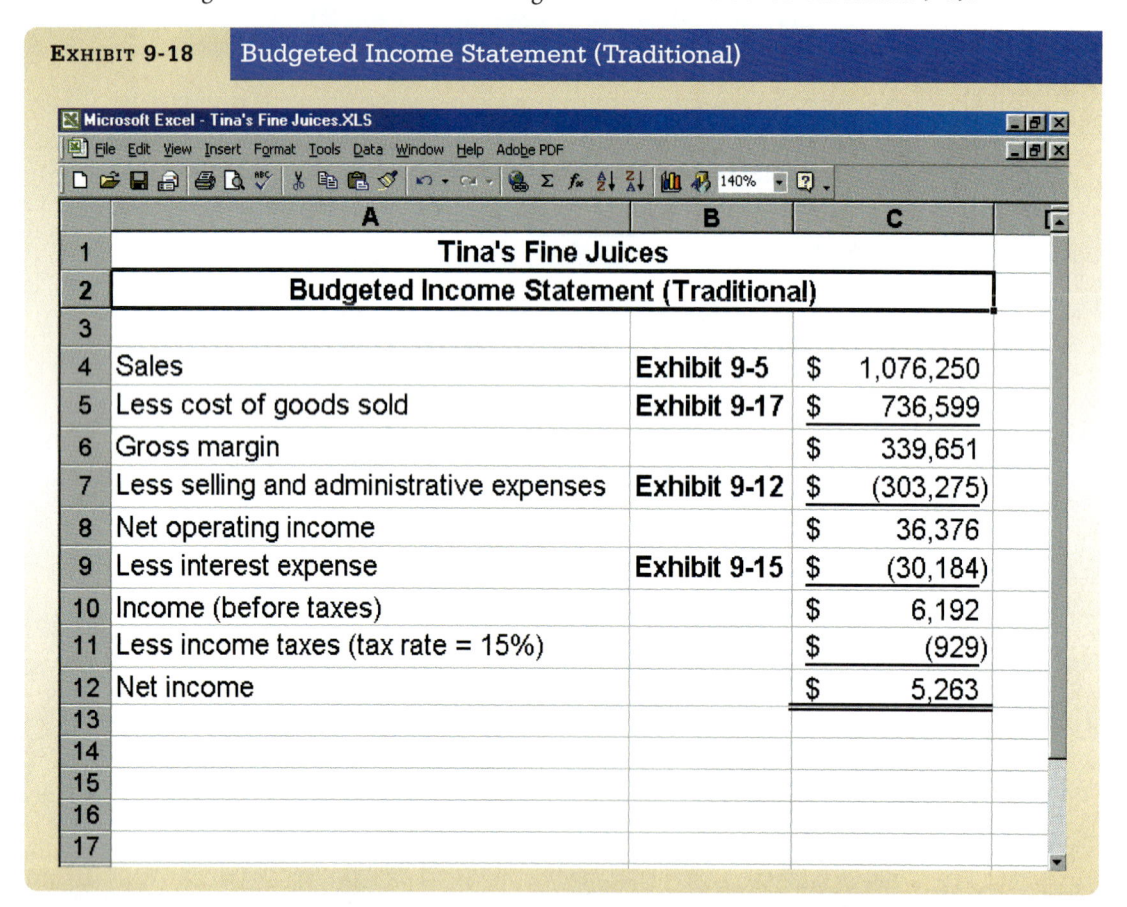

Exhibit 9-18 Budgeted Income Statement (Traditional)

Tina's Fine Juices
Budgeted Income Statement (Traditional)

	A	B	C
4	Sales	Exhibit 9-5	$ 1,076,250
5	Less cost of goods sold	Exhibit 9-17	$ 736,599
6	Gross margin		$ 339,651
7	Less selling and administrative expenses	Exhibit 9-12	$ (303,275)
8	Net operating income		$ 36,376
9	Less interest expense	Exhibit 9-15	$ (30,184)
10	Income (before taxes)		$ 6,192
11	Less income taxes (tax rate = 15%)		$ (929)
12	Net income		$ 5,263

Exhibit 9-19 Budgeted Balance Sheet

Tina's Fine Juices
Budgeted Balance Sheet

Assets
Current Assets:
- Cash $ 115,458 — Exhibit 9-15
- Accounts Receivable $ 287,437 — Exhibit 9-5 ($341,250 x .15 + $472,500 x .50)
- Inventory: Direct Materials $ 24,502 — Exhibit 9-16
- Inventory: Finished Goods $ 35,932 — Exhibit 9-17
- Inventory: WIP $ —
- Total Current Assets $ 463,329
- Fixed Assets (net of depreciation) $ 5,075,000 — $5,000,000 beginning balance (given) + $75,000 acquistions (Exhibit 9-15)
- Total Assets $ 5,538,329

Liabilities and Equity
Current Liabilities:
- Accounts Payable $ 88,511 — Exhibits 9-7, 9-8 and 9-10 ($69,302 x .5 + 46,200 x .5 + $61,519 x .5)
- Line of Credit $ —
- Income tax $ 929 — Exhibit 9-17
- Total Current Liabilities $ 89,440
- Long Term Liabilities $ 1,500,000
- Total Liabilities $ 1,589,440

Stockholders Equity:
- Common Stock $ 3,500,000 — Beginning balance (given)
- Retained Earnings $ 448,889 — Beginning balance of $493,626 (given) + income of $5,263 (Exhibit 9-18) - dividends paid of $50,000 (Exhibit 9-15)
- Total Liabilities and Stockholders Equity $ 5,538,329

As you can see, the set of operating budgets and budgeted financial statements form an interrelated set of planning tools that are vital for managers' decisions affecting the number of units to produce, the amount of materials to purchase, how many employees to schedule for a particular time period (and when to schedule training, for example), the timing of major acquisitions and sales of equipment, and the overall management of cash.

Budgets for a Manufacturing Company in a JIT Environment

As we discussed more fully in Chapter 2, the physical flow of goods is streamlined in companies adopting just-in-time (JIT) techniques. Raw materials are immediately placed into production, and all goods are typically finished and shipped out immediately to customers, resulting in little raw material, work in process, or finished goods inventory. Just as this process simplified cost flows, budgeting is simplified as well. In JIT companies, production is typically equal to sales, so the production budget and sales budget are essentially the same. Materials are purchased for current production, eliminating the need to account for beginning and ending inventories of raw materials. With no beginning or ending inventories of work in process (WIP) or finished goods, the cost of goods manufactured and the cost of goods sold are the same and are simply budgeted as the sum of raw materials used in production, direct labor costs incurred, and overhead costs incurred.

> **Objective 7**
>
> Contrast budgeting in a manufacturing company with budgeting in a merchandising company and service company, describe the use of nonfinancial budgets and discuss issues that must be considered in budgeting in an international environment

Budgets for Merchandising Companies and Service Companies

As shown in Exhibit 9-4, the budgeting process for merchandising companies is similar to that of manufacturing companies, with a few important differences. Merchandising companies are not involved in manufacturing the goods they sell. A merchandising company buys finished goods from manufacturing companies and sells them to other companies for resale (wholesalers) or to final customers (retailers). Merchandising companies will still produce a sales budget but will not prepare budgets for production, direct material purchases, direct labor, or manufacturing overhead. However, merchandising companies will prepare a purchases budget (for finished goods) based on the projections in the sales budget. In addition, many merchandising companies hold some level of finished goods inventory and will need to estimate desired inventory balances and to adjust sales projections accordingly.

The preparation of selling and administrative expense budgets, cash budgets, and budgeted financial statements in merchandising companies is similar to that in manufacturing companies. Although the budgeting process for merchandising is a little less complex than in manufacturing companies, it is just as important to effective decision making.

Service companies have the same need to budget for effective decision making, but once again, the budgets needed will differ slightly from those used in manufacturing companies. Service companies will prepare sales budgets and may prepare modified "production" budgets as well. For example, a CPA firm may budget for not only total revenues, but also the amount of revenue expected to be generated by each type of engagement (tax, audit, etc.), the number of those engagements expected (how many tax returns will be prepared), and the number of labor hours expected to be incurred in each. As a result, the main focus of budgeting for service companies will often be the labor budget. The use of time budgets by service companies is discussed in more detail in a later section on nonmonetary budgets.

Overhead is another important area of concern for service companies. A detailed budget of expected overhead expenditures (rent, utilities, insurance, etc.) is extremely useful in planning for cash outflows.

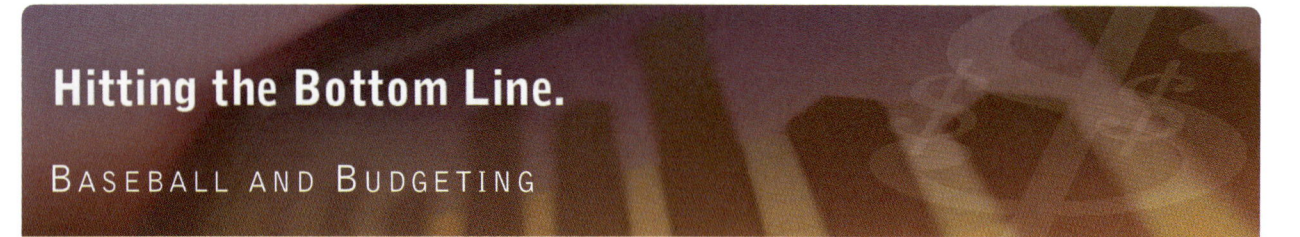

Hitting the Bottom Line.
BASEBALL AND BUDGETING

Budgeting for a professional baseball team may seem easy, but according to Tim Buzard, VP of Finance for the Chicago White Sox, "it's a challenge to predict anything." "Attendance is the greatest variable in the budget and attendance is dependent on winning. Parking, concessions and souvenir sales, and even the number of security people hired all depend on attendance. A losing season can totally change the projections of revenue. The budgeting process must be very flexible and is sometimes changed on a daily basis to account for changes in attendance." ("Budgeting for Curve Balls," *Journal of Accountancy,* Volume 186, No. 3, 89–92).

Nonfinancial Budgets

Companies may also prepare nonfinancial budgets to help in the planning, operating, and control functions of managers. These budgets are just as important and in some cases may be more important than financial budgets focusing on costs and cash flows.

Examples of nonfinancial budgets are the following:

1. *Time budgets.* In service firms, such as CPA firms and law offices, time budgets are used to plan the number of hours expected to be incurred in each engagement (tax return preparation, audit, etc.). This allows firms to better plan the timing of engagements and to utilize employees as efficiently as possible. For example, if a time budget shows that professional staff will not be fully utilized in the summer, continuing education and other training courses might be planned at that time.

2. *Customer-satisfaction measures.* Customer satisfaction is an important measure of success for many companies. Consequently, many companies prepare budgets and measure key indicators of customer satisfaction. Although businesses may have many different measures of customer satisfaction, common indicators include the number of returned or defective items, the number of customer complaints, time waiting to be served, and so on.

Budgeting in an International Environment

In today's environment, many companies operate across national borders. Companies may make sales to foreign countries, purchase supplies internationally, manufacture products in other countries, or have foreign branches and subsidiaries. In budgeting, companies with international operations must consider such things as the following:

1. Translating foreign currency into U.S. dollars (and vice versa). Because of continual fluctuations in exchange rates, this can be challenging.

2. Predicting inflation rates (and prices) in countries with unstable economies. This can add a great deal of complexity and uncertainty to the budgeting process.

3. Predicting sales in countries with different consumer preferences.
4. Dealing with different labor laws, social customs, and norms affecting wage rates and the productivity of workers.

THE ETHICS OF BUSINESS

Working Against the Clock

Few of us complain of having more time than we need; rather, many of us say there is too little time to accomplish the many important tasks in our lives. Unfortunately, the time pressure that is often felt at home is present in the workplace as well. For example, consider the typical CPA firm. Much of the work performed by staff accountants is paid for by the hour. Clients expect to pay a fair fee for an accountant's work and not a penny more. Many firms feel pressure to keep their fees low and the time spent on a client's work to an appropriate level. Sometimes a CPA firm places staff accountants under too much time pressure by establishing time budgets that are unrealistically low. Establishing unrealistic time budgets can lead to negative consequences for the staff. For example, accountants may not report all the hours they spend working on a job for a client or may shift hours to other clients in order to complete a job under budget. In addition to not being paid for the actual hours worked, under-reporting of time may result in the establishment of future time budgets that are unrealistically low. Another significant consequence is that unrealistic budgets may lead to low fee estimates being provided to new clients. The bottom line is simple - there is only so much time in a day and managers need to know how much of that time employees need to perform their work. Otherwise, employees will just begin to play a game of "working against the clock."

It's Your Choice—Is it fair to expect employees to routinely reduce the amount of time required to accomplish their tasks? Why do managers put so much pressure on their employees? Who is harmed when accountants are given an unrealistically low time budget within which to complete their work? Consider this example: If a senior member of a CPA firm told a client the preparation of a tax return would cost $200 (2 hours x $100/hour), but the junior tax accountant preparing the tax return really spent three hours completing the return, who is harmed? Should the junior tax accountant tell the senior accountant of the time difference? Should the firm charge the client for the extra hour? Why or why not?

Static versus Flexible Budgets

Static budgets are budgets that are established at the beginning of the period for one set level of activity and remain constant throughout the budget period. The budgets that are presented for Tina's Fine Juices are static budgets. Although static budgets are useful for planning and operating purposes, they can be problematic when used for control. As we discussed in Chapter 1, control involves motivating and monitoring employees and evaluating people and other resources used in

Objective 8

Differentiate static budgets from flexible budgets and describe how flexible budgets are used in activity-based costing

Doing Business.

IS THAT IN YEN OR EUROS?

Currency fluctuations and changing exchange rates create unique budgeting and cash management challenges. Exchange rates can be quite volatile and frequently change by 15 to 20 percent or more over a couple of years. Between 2002 and 2004, the U.S. dollar declined about 28 percent against the euro, 22 percent against the British pound and about 16 percent against the Canadian dollar and Japanese yen.

For example, suppose a U.S. company plans to buy a machine from a company in Japan for 200,000 yen when the exchange rate is 1 yen = .009 U.S. dollars. The U.S. company expects to pay about $1,800 for the machine (200,000 × $.009). However, if the exchange rate changes to 1 yen = .01 U.S. dollars by the time the acquisition takes place (the dollar weakens against the yen), the U.S. company will have to pay $2,000 for the machine.

Likewise, when U.S. companies sell goods to foreign buyers, the price may be set in foreign currency. For example, if a U.S. company sells a product to a German buyer for 80 euros when the exchange rate is 1 dollar = .8 euro, the U.S. company expects to receive $100 (80 euros/.8) from the German buyer. However, if the dollar weakens and is worth .75 euros by the time the German buyer makes payment, the U.S. company will receive $107 from the German buyer. Note that a weakening dollar results in the U.S. buyer paying more for the machine purchased from a foreign seller while the exporter receives more for a sale made to a foreign buyer.

What happens if the sales price is set in dollars? While revenue is not directly affected, the competitive position of the U.S. company may be impacted as the price of the product increases or decreases in terms of the foreign currency. For example, if a U.S. company sells a product in Japan for $100, when the exchange rate is $1 dollar = 110 Japanese yen, the Japanese buyer expects to pay 11,000 yen for the good. However, if the dollar weakens and is worth only 105 yen, the Japanese buyer only pays 10,500 yen for the product.

---

the operations of an organization. The purpose of control is to make sure that the goals of the organization are being attained. Control requires the comparison of actual outcomes (cost of products, sales, etc.) with desired outcomes as stated in the organization's operating and strategic plans (including budgets). The idea is to compare budgeted amounts to actual results and then to analyze any differences for likely causes. However, when static budgets are used and actual sales are different from budgeted sales, such a comparison is like comparing apples to oranges. If actual sales differ from projected sales, differences in production, material purchases, labor costs, and variable overhead should be expected. If actual sales are lower than budgeted sales, actual costs of materials, labor, and variable overhead *should* be lower than budgeted costs. The fact that a company's actual costs are lower than those budgeted under static conditions does not necessarily mean that the company (or its employees) spent less or was more efficient than budgeted.

For example, assume that Tina's Fine Juices produces 250,000 bottles of juice in January instead of the budgeted amount of 257,500 bottles. The projected direct labor cost (see Exhibit 9-9 on page 306) based on a static budget of 257,500 bottles was $6,438. At the end of January, Tina's had actual direct labor costs of $6,300. So Tina's spent $138 *less* than provided for in the static budget.

However, the comparison of actual labor costs to make 250,000 bottles with the budgeted labor costs to produce 257,500 bottles really does not make sense. Tina's ought to spend less for labor because fewer bottles were produced. The question becomes, How much less? What we would really like to know is how much the labor costs should have been had we known that production was going to be 250,000 bottles instead of 257,500.

Flexible budgets do just that. Flexible budgets take differences in cost owing to volume differences out of the analysis by budgeting for labor (and other costs) based on the *actual* number of units produced.

A flexible direct labor budget for Tina's Fine Juices would budget labor costs based on the actual January production of 250,000 bottles. Based on the labor time needed to produce 600 bottles and the direct labor rate per hour of $15, Tina's projected labor costs would be $6,250 (250,000 bottles / 600 bottles per hour = 416.666 hours; 416.666 × $15 per hour = $6,250), instead of $6,438. If we now compare the actual direct labor cost of $6,300 to the flexible budget amount of $6,250, we see that Tina's actually spent $50 *more* than expected instead of $138 *less* than expected.

> **KEY CONCEPT**
>
> Flexible budgets are based on the actual number of units produced rather than on the budgeted units of production.

	Flexible Budget	Actual	Difference
Production (bottles)	250,000	250,000	
Direct labor time per 600 bottles	1 hour		
Direct labor hours needed for production (250,000/600)	416.67		
Direct labor rate per hour	× $15		
Direct labor cost	$6,250	$6,300	$(50)

Why the turnaround? By using flexible budgeting, Tina's removes any differences in cost caused by differences in volume of production and focuses only on differences arising from other factors.

What are those other factors? Perhaps Tina's paid more than $15 per hour for labor. However, another explanation is that Tina's used more than 417 labor hours or even some combination of the two. Without further analysis, we simply don't know. In Chapter 10, the use of flexible budgets is expanded to allow managers to break down these differences into variances resulting from either spending too much (or too little) or using too much (or too little). This process is called variance analysis.

ABC and Flexible Budgets

The use of activity-based costing (ABC) makes flexible budgets even more useful (although a bit more complicated). As we discussed in Chapter 4, companies utilizing ABC to assign costs to products and services identify activities (the procedures and processes that cause work to be accomplished) and the cost drivers associated with those activities. For example, Tina's Fine Juices might identify the movement of materials (orange juice concentrate and bottles) as an activity that consumes resources, and the number of times the material is moved as the driver of the costs incurred. In preparing a flexible budget for manufacturing overhead costs, Tina's would budget costs for moving materials based on the budgeted cost per move and the actual number of moves made during the month. Likewise, Tina's would compute the per unit budget amounts for other batch-level and product-level costs and include those in the flexible budget, along with the regular variable (unit-level) costs and fixed costs. A detailed example of a flexible budget for a company utilizing ABC is provided in Chapter 10 as well.

Summary of Key Concepts

- Budgets must start with a top-down strategic plan that guides and integrates the whole company and its individual budgets. (p. 296)
- Budgeting is a management task, not a bookkeeping task. (p. 296)
- Budgets are used throughout managers' planning, operating, and control activities. (p. 296)
- Budgets are future oriented and make extensive use of estimates and forecasts. (p. 301)
- Flexible budgets are based on the actual number of units produced rather than on the budgeted units of production. (p. 319)

Key Definitions

Budgets Plans dealing with the acquisition and use of resources over a specified time period (p. 296)

Zero-based budgeting Requires managers to build budgets from the ground up each year (p. 296)

Planning The cornerstone of good management; involves developing objectives and goals for the organization, as well as the actual preparation of budgets (p. 296)

Operating Involves day-to-day decision making by managers, which is often facilitated by budgeting (p. 296)

Control Involves ensuring that the objectives and goals developed by the organization are being attained; often involves a comparison of budgets to actual performance and the use of budgets for performance-evaluation purposes (p. 296)

Master budget Consists of an interrelated set of budgets prepared by a business (p. 298)

Sales forecast Combines with the sales budget to form the starting points in the preparation of production budgets for manufacturing companies, purchases budgets for merchandising companies, and labor budgets for service companies (p. 300)

Sales budget Used in planning the cash needs for manufacturing, merchandising, and service companies (p. 300)

Operating budgets Used to plan for the short term (typically one year or less) (p. 301)

Production budget Used to forecast how many units of product to produce in order to meet the sales projections (p. 301)

Material purchases budget Used to project the dollar amount of raw material purchased for production (p. 303)

Direct labor budget Used to project the dollar amount of direct labor cost needed for production (p. 305)

Manufacturing overhead budget Used to project the dollar amount of manufacturing overhead needed for production (p. 305)

Cash receipts budget Used to project the amount of cash expected to be received from sales and cash collections from customers (p. 309)

Cash disbursements budget Used to project the amount of cash to be disbursed during the budget period (p. 309)

Summary cash budget Consists of three sections: (1) cash flows from operating activities, (2) cash flows from investing activities, and (3) cash flows from financing activities; these three sections are the same as used in the cash flow statement prepared under generally accepted accounting principles (GAAP) (p. 311)

Pro forma financial statements Budgeted financial statements that are sometimes used for internal planning purposes but more often are used by external users (p. 312)

Static budgets Budgets that are set at the beginning of the period and remain constant throughout the budget period (p. 317)

Flexible budgets Take differences in spending owing to volume differences out of the analysis by budgeting for labor (and other costs) based on the *actual* number of units produced (p. 319)

Multiple Choice

1. Budgets are:
   a. future oriented
   b. for managers only
   c. required by GAAP
   d. typically not used by small businesses

2. One advantage of the budgeting process is that it:
   a. reduces communication throughout the organization
   b. forces management to focus on the past and not be distracted by daily crisis in the organization
   c. helps management identify and manage potential bottlenecks or constraints before they become major problems
   d. can decrease the coordination of organizational activities

3. Last year, Elise Toys sold 100,000 sets of baseball cards at $1.50 each. If sales volume is expected to increase by 30 percent and the price of each deck of cards is expected to decrease 20 percent, what is the expected sales revenue for the coming year?
   a. $120,000
   b. $150,000
   c. $156,000
   d. It cannot be determined from the information provided.

4. Harrison Company produces hats for golfers. The company's projected sales for April are 15,000 hats. March sales were less than expected so the company had 1,800 hats remaining in inventory at the end of March. Harrison prefers to maintain a 5 percent inventory of the next month's sales. Expected sales for May are 14,000 hats. How many hats should the company plan to produce in April?
   a. 15,700
   b. 15,000
   c. 13,900
   d. 17,500

5. Which of the following is a correct formula for calculating projected production?
   a. Projected sales − change in work in process inventory
   b. Projected sales + change in work in process inventory
   c. Projected sales − change in finished goods inventory
   d. Projected sales + change in finished goods inventory

6. Tea Lovers produces herbal teas. The company expects to sell 125,000 boxes of tea during 2005. The company had 10,000 tea boxes on hand at the beginning of 2005. The sales budget calls for the company to sell 120,000 boxes of tea in 2006. If the company has a policy of maintaining an inventory of 10 percent of the boxes needed for next year's expected sales, how many boxes must be purchased during 2005?
   a. 125,000
   b. 127,000
   c. 137,000
   d. It cannot be determined from the information provided.

7. Refer to question 6 above. If each tea box costs $0.27, what is the total projected cost of tea boxes for 2005?
   a. $33,750
   b. $34,290
   c. $36,990
   d. It cannot be determined from the information provided.

8. The usual beginning point for a direct labor budget is the
   a. material purchases budget.
   b. sales budget.
   c. production budget.
   d. materials purchases budget or the sales budget.

9. Bell Corporation had the following purchases budgeted for the last six months of 2005:

July	$100,000
August	80,000
September	110,000
October	90,000
November	100,000
December	94,000

Historically, the company has paid one half of a month's purchases at the time of purchase and the remainder in the next month. If the company continues paying for purchases as it has in the past, what are the expected cash disbursements in November?
a. $95,000
b. $97,000
c. $100,000
d. $147,000

10. Which of the following is typically the first cash budget to be prepared?
a. Cash disbursements budget
b. Cash receipts budget
c. Summary cash budget
d. Cash usage budget

11. The cash paid as interest on long-term debt is shown in which of the following sections of a summary cash budget?
a. Operating activities section
b. Financing activities section
c. Investing activities section
d. Disbursing activities section

12. Budgeted financial statements:
a. are required by GAAP.
b. are included in the set of audited financial statements.
c. are used by both internal and external users.
d. all of the above.

13. Which of the following statements regarding budgeting by merchandisers and manufacturers is true?
a. Merchandising companies will prepare a sales budget.
b. Manufacturing companies will not prepare budgets for production, direct material purchases, direct labor, or overhead.
c. Merchandising companies will prepare a direct material purchases budget.
d. All of the above.

14. Which of the following statements regarding nonfinancial budgets is true?
a. There is no such thing as a nonfinancial budget.
b. A nonfinancial budget may be more important than a financial (monetary) budget.
c. A nonfinancial budget is useful for the control function only.
d. Even nonfinancial budgets contain some monetary items.

15. In 2005, Clarence Company budgeted sales of 45,000 units, produced 44,600 units, and sold 44,500 units. Clarence's 2005 flexible sales budget was based on _____ units.
a. 45,000
b. 44,600
c. 44,500
d. It cannot be determined from the information provided.

Concept Questions

16. *(Objective 1)* What are some of the characteristics of a typical budget?
17. *(Objective 1)* Outline, using no amounts, a budget that you might use in managing your personal finances.
18. *(Objective 2)* Why is the sales budget the most important piece of the budgeting process?
19. *(Objective 2)* List and describe some of the major factors and information sources typically used in sales forecasting.
20. *(Objective 3)* What are the essential elements of a production budget?
21. *(Objective 5)* What are several decisions that management can address using the cash receipts budget?
22. *(Objective 5)* Why is so much emphasis put on cash flow in the budgeting process?
23. *(Objective 7)* Discuss why financial budgets for merchandising companies are different from those for manufacturing companies.
24. *(Objective 7)* Give some examples of nonfinancial budgets and how management might use them.
25. *(Objective 8)* Discuss the difference between static and flexible budgets.

Exercises

26. Review the following incomplete statements regarding the advantages of budgeting.
    a. The budgeting process forces management to focus on the _____ and not be distracted by daily crisis in the organization.
    b. The budgeting process can define specific _____ and objectives that can become _____, or standards of performance, for evaluating future performance.
    c. The budgeting process forces _____ throughout the organization.
    d. The budgeting process can increase the coordination of organizational activities and help facilitate goal _____.
    e. The budgeting process can help management identify and deal with potential _____ or constraints before they become major problems.

    Required

    Complete each of the above incomplete statements with the correct term from the following list: *bottlenecks, communication, future, goals, congruence,* and *benchmarks*.

27. Harriman Entertainment produced and sold 100,000 video games for $10 each last year. Demand is strong for the company's video games and the company believes that volume will increase by 25 percent if the company increases the game price by 20 percent.

    Required

    What are Harriman's expected sales revenues for the coming year?

28. Your friend, Marcy Braeden, has been working for the last two years with a small company that produces and sells a variety of small household items. Recently, she told you how amazed she is at how the company °seems to forecast sales each year. She just does not understand how the company does it.

    Required

    Help Marcy out by describing some of the factors that her employer may consider in forecasting sales.

LO 2

29. Tim's Temple Tools sells small eyeglass repair tools for $1.25 each. Tim's marketing department prepared the following first-quarter sales forecast:

January	125,000
February	135,000
March	170,000
Total	430,000

Required

Prepare Tim's sales budget for each month of the quarter.

LO 3

✓ Projected production: 995 bikes

30. Mountain High sells specialty mountain bikes. At June 30, the company had 50 bikes in inventory. The company's policy is to maintain a bike inventory of 5 percent of next month's sales. The company expects the following sales activity for the third quarter of the year:

July	1,200 bikes
August	1,000 bikes
September	900 bikes

Required

What is the projected production for August?

LO 4

31. Lazy Day Donuts makes powdered donuts that are sold by the dozen. Each box of a dozen donuts requires 1/2 pound of flour. The company began the year with 20,000 pounds of flour on hand, but would like to have just 10,000 pounds of flour on hand at the end of the current year. Lazy Day expects to produce 200,000 boxes of donuts during the year.

Required

How many pounds of flour must be purchased during the year to have enough for production needs and the desired ending inventory?

LO 4

✓ Total chips to purchase: $1,504,600

32. Mandy's Modems estimates sales of 420,000 modems during the upcoming year. Each modem requires three internal memory chips. The company began the year with an inventory of 20,000 memory chips and no beginning inventory of modems. The company's management wants to maintain an ending inventory of modems equal to 10 percent of the current year's sales and an ending inventory of chips equal to 10 percent of the current year's projected needs.

Required

How many memory chips must Mandy's Modems purchase during the year?

LO 4

✓ Units to purchase: 1,010,000

33. Blanchard Company budgets on an annual basis for its fiscal year. The following beginning and ending inventory levels (in units) are planned for the fiscal year of July 1, 2005 through June 30, 2006:

	July 1, 2005	June 30, 2006
Raw material*	40,000	50,000
Work in process	10,000	10,000
Finished goods	80,000	50,000

*Two (2) units of raw material are needed to produce each unit of finished product.

Required

If Blanchard Company were to manufacture 500,000 finished units during the 2005–2006 fiscal year, how many units of raw material would it need to purchase?

34. The following records from Benson Inc. are provided to assist you with preparation of cash summary budgets. Benson requires a minimum cash balance of $7,000 to start each quarter. The following amounts are in thousands of dollars.

	Quarter			
	1	2	3	4
Beginning cash balance	$ 10	$?	$?	$?
Cash collections	?	?	126	80
Total cash available	$ 86	$?	$?	$?
Inventory purchases	41	59	?	33
Operating expenses	?	43	55	?
Equipment purchases	11	9	8	5
Dividends	3	3	3	3
Total disbursements	$?	$114	$?	$?
Excess (deficiency) of cash	(4)	?	30	?
Financing:				
Borrowings	?	21	—	—
Repayments*	—	—	(?)	(8)
Total	$?	$?	$?	$?
Ending cash balance	$?	$?	$?	$?

*Includes interest.

Required

Fill in the missing amounts in Benson's cash summary budget.

35. Thirst Quencher sells plastic water bottles to outdoor enthusiasts for $1.25 each. The company's marketing manager prepared the following sales forecast (in units) for the first half of 2005:

January	150,000
February	125,000
March	180,000
April	165,000
May	165,000
June	155,000
Total	940,000

✓ *Cash collected in May: $205,875*

Historically, the cash collection of sales has been as follows: 55 percent of sales collected in month of sale, 35 percent of sales collected in month following sale, and 9 percent of sales collected in second month following sale. The remaining 1 percent is never collected because customers do not pay.

Required

Prepare a cash receipts budget for each month of the second quarter (April, May, and June).

36. Cookies and Cream sells delicious chocolate chip cookies for $2.50 per box. The company's founder and lead marketing guru estimates first-quarter sales (in boxes) as follows:

January	1,500
February	1,200
March	1,600
Total	4,300

Cookies and Cream expects cash to be collected in the following manner:

55 percent of sales collected in month of sale

35 percent of sales collected in month following sale

10 percent of sales collected in second month following sale

Required

Prepare a cash receipts budget for the first quarter. How much will customers owe the company at the end of March if sales are exactly as estimated?

37. The following cash disbursements data are taken from the records of Robyn's Rocket Shop for July:

Labor costs	$14,000
Advertising expenses	1,850
Office rent	2,500
Equipment purchase	3,000
Selling expenses	5,400

Required

Prepare a cash disbursements budget for Robyn's Rocket Shop for the month of July.

38. Robyn's Rocket Shop is in the midst of negotiating a loan from First National Bank. The bank has asked Robyn to prepare a budgeted income statement for the third quarter of the year (July through September). Robyn has accumulated the following data from various budgets for this purpose:

Sales forecast	$185,000
Interest expense	2,400
Selling and administrative expenses	74,450
Cost of goods sold	56,800

Required

Prepare a budgeted income statement for Robyn's Rocket Shop for the third quarter for presentation to First National Bank. Assume the company's income tax rate is 30%.

39. Many companies now employ just-in-time (JIT) techniques to reduce inventory and costs and to streamline their business processes. A company that uses JIT will need to modify its budget process to accommodate the change in operations.

✓ Cash collected in February: $2,962.50

✓ Net income: $35,945

Required

Briefly describe the budgeting process that might be employed by a company that uses JIT.

40. Honolulu Hello produces pineapple candy. The company currently uses a static budget process. The company's controller prepared the following budget for April's production:

Estimated production	24,000 boxes
Direct labor per box	4 minutes
Direct labor required for estimated production	1,600 hours
Average direct labor rate per hour	$12.50
Estimated direct labor cost	$20,000

LO 8

✓ Difference: $(850)

Actual production during April was 26,400 boxes and actual direct labor cost was $22,850.

Required

Prepare a flexible budget for Honolulu Hello that shows the projected direct labor cost and any difference between the budget and actual labor cost.

41. The controller for Honolulu Hello is considering the use of flexible budgeting for the company. However, the company's founder, Don Hello, is uncertain of the purpose of the change. The controller has told him that the primary benefit relates to "control." Don really does not understand the controller's comment.

LO 8

Required

Explain how using flexible budgets improves a company's ability to control operations.

Problems

42. CNX Motors is preparing a sales budget for the current year for the service department that is based on last year's actual amounts. Management is interested in understanding what might happen if the service department has an increase in sales volume (i.e., the number of mechanic hours) or an increase in the average revenue per mechanic hour. They believe it is unlikely that both would increase due to economic conditions in the local market. Last year's sales amounts were as follows:

LO 1 2

EXCEL

Activity Making Decision A

✓ Average revenue per mechanic hour: $9.92

	Mechanic Hours	Total Revenues
January	1,174	$11,681
February	1,057	10,538
March	1,125	11,261
April	1,516	15,008
May	1,724	16,981
June	2,515	25,014
July	2,746	27,185
August	3,107	30,604
September	2,421	23,823
October	2,211	22,154
November	1,709	17,090
December	1,524	15,125

Required

A. Compute the average revenue per mechanic hour for the current year based on last year's actual data. You should round the average hourly rate to the nearest penny.
B. Prepare a monthly sales budget for the current year assuming that monthly sales volume (i.e., mechanic hours) will be 10 percent greater than the same month last year. Assume that the average revenue per mechanic hour is the same as you computed in question A. You should round budgeted hours to one decimal and budgeted revenues to the nearest dollar.
C. Prepare a monthly sales budget for the current year assuming that the average revenue per mechanic hour computed in question A increased by 5 percent. Assume that the number of mechanic hours stays the same as in the prior year. That is, there is no increase or decrease in the monthly sales volume. You should round the rate per mechanic hour to two decimals and budgeted revenues to the nearest dollar.
D. For the current year in total, is it more advantageous to increase sales volume by 10 percent or average revenue per hour by 5 percent? Remember the impact of variable and fixed costs on these projections.

LO 2 3 4

✓ Projected production in November: 7,440 pillows

43. Curiosity Corner sells books and various other reading-related products. One of the store's most popular reading-related products is a book pillow for hard cover and soft cover books. The pillows each sell for $8.00. Originally the pillows were handmade by a local artisan. The store's owner has been impressed with the demand for the pillow and has recently begun a small manufacturing company to produce and distribute the pillows to other stores. Estimated sales for the fourth quarter (in units) are as follows:

October	6,500
November	7,200
December	9,600
Total	23,300

Each pillow requires 1/2 yard of fabric that costs, on average, $6 per yard.

Required

A. Prepare a sales budget for the fourth quarter based on the above information.
B. Prepare a production budget for the pillow manufacturing company. The company did not have any inventory of pillows at the end of September, but the company does want to maintain a 10 percent inventory at the end of each month based on the next month's estimated sales. January's sales are expected to be low, given the post-holiday trends, and are estimated to be 4,800 units.
C. Prepare a fabric purchases budget. The company did not have any inventory of fabric at the end of September, but the company does want to maintain a fabric inventory equal to 20 percent of the next month's materials needs. January's projected production is expected to be 4,820 units.

LO 3 4

✓ Projected purchases in January: $1,737,450

44. Alvarez Company produces various component parts used in the automotive industry. The sales budget for the first eight months of 2005 shows the following projections:

Month	Units	Month	Units
January	25,000	May	31,400
February	27,000	June	34,500
March	32,000	July	36,700
April	28,500	August	35,000

Inventory at December 31 of the prior year was budgeted at 6,250 units. The desired quantity of finished goods inventory at the end of each month in 2005 is to be equal to 25 percent of the next month's budgeted unit sales. Each unit of finished product requires three pounds of raw material. The company wants to have 30 percent of next month's required raw material on hand at the end of each month.

Required

A. Prepare a production budget for January through June of 2005.
B. Prepare a materials purchases budget for the same period assuming that each pound of raw material costs $22.

45. Anderson Company produces decorative windows for residential and commercial applications. The company's marketing department has prepared a sales forecast for the first eight months of 2005 based on past sales trends and expected marketing and pricing plans. The vice president of marketing believes the sales forecast is reasonable and hopes to grow sales in the coming year based partly on the marketing and pricing changes put in place during the year. The sales forecast for 2005 is as follows:

✓ *Projected production in January: 11,050 windows*

Month	Units	Month	Units
January	10,000	May	22,100
February	17,000	June	24,300
March	13,000	July	26,200
April	18,500	August	27,000

Inventory at December 31, 2004 was budgeted at 1,500 units. The desired quantity of finished goods inventory at the end of each month in 2005 is to be equal to 15 percent of the next month's budgeted unit sales. Each completed unit of finished product requires 1.5 gallons of a special resin. The company has determined that it needs 20 percent of next month's raw material needs on hand at the end of each month.

Required

A. Prepare a production budget for January through June of 2005.
B. Prepare a materials purchases budget for the same period assuming that each gallon of the special resin costs $10.

46. Ash Company manufacturers telephone handsets under various brand names. The company has built a strong reputation based on quality telephones and has been profitable for a number of years. Harriman Lassiter, the company's president, has decided to make a significant push for labor and overhead cost controls in the coming months because of increased overseas competition. Harriman has asked the marketing and accounting departments to provide data related to labor costs and manufacturing overhead. Production budgets for the period ending June 30 are as follows:

✓ *Projected direct labor cost in January: $937,500*

Month	Units	Month	Units
January	25,000	April	28,500
February	27,000	May	31,400
March	32,000	June	34,500

Each telephone requires 2.5 hours of direct labor for assembly and testing. The company currently applies manufacturing overhead to production at the rate of $7 per direct labor hour.

Required

A. Prepare a direct labor budget for January through June. Direct labor averages $15 per hour.
B. Prepare a manufacturing overhead budget for the same period.

47. Babcock Builders is a well regarded construction company that serves as a general contractor for both residential and commercial construction projects. One of the company's signature features is its cabinetry. The company's founder and president, Bill Babcock, began manufacturing cabinets six years ago in an effort to capitalize on the company's reputation and the skills of its craftsmen. The company's production budget for the first seven months of 2005 is shown below:

Month	Units	Month	Units
January	10,000	May	22,100
February	17,000	June	24,300
March	13,000	July	26,200
April	18,500		

Babcock's most popular cabinet is a small cherry wood cabinet typically used in bathrooms. Each completed unit requires 3.5 hours of direct labor and the skilled labor costs an average of $25 per hour. The company applies overhead at the rate of $3 per direct labor hour.

Required

A. Prepare a direct labor budget for January through June.
B. Prepare a manufacturing overhead budget for the same period.

48. Barrera's Outdoor Outfitters sells many items that sporting enthusiasts find useful. The company sells shoes, pants, shirts, jackets, fly fishing equipment, hiking equipment, hunting equipment and various other products. The following sales projections were prepared by the company's sales manager and include all items for each of the first seven months of 2005:

✓ Cash received in January: $315,600

Month	Sales Volume	Month	Sales Volume
January	25,000	May	31,400
February	27,000	June	34,500
March	32,000	July	36,700
April	28,500		

The average sales price per item is $12. The company estimates that it collects 70 percent of each month's sales in the month of sale and 20 percent the following month. The remaining outstanding sales are collected in the next month. The balance of accounts receivable at December 31, 2004, was $141,600. Of the accounts receivable balance, $33,600 represents uncollected November sales.

Required

Prepare a cash receipts budget for January through June of 2005.

✓ Cash received in January: $381,100

49. Baum's is a tradition at State University. The store has served students and faculty for more than 50 years and is still regarded as the premier bookstore in the area. Baum Bookstore's sales budget shows the following projections (i.e., the number of units in each category) for the period ending May 31, 2005:

Month	Books	School Supplies	Software	Miscellaneous
January	4,000	2,700	240	1,700
February	1,400	1,450	190	1,400
March	1,000	1,310	175	1,500
April	500	1,600	100	1,650
May	1,800	1,850	145	2,125

The average sales price of each of the various items is as follows: books: $70; school supplies: $20; software: $90; and miscellaneous: $15. Because the store sells primarily to students and faculty, there are no credit sales.

Required

Prepare a cash receipts budget by item category for each month.

50. Barley Restaurant Supply sells various equipment and supplies to restaurants in the local and surrounding communities. The company's controller, Barry Barley, has requested your help in preparing a cash budget for the month of June. Barry accumulated the following information for you:
    a. The cash balance at June 1 was estimated to be $10,000.
    b. Actual sales for April and May and budgeted sales for June are as follows:

	April	May	June
Cash sales	$16,500	$15,500	$17,500
Sales on account	30,000	40,000	50,000
Total sales	$46,500	$55,500	$67,500

✓ Total cash receipts in June: $64,500

Sales on account are collected over a two-month period, with 70 percent being collected in the first month and the remainder being collected in the second month.
    c. Inventory purchases are expected to be $35,000 in June. The company pays for inventory purchases in the month following purchase. The balance of May's purchases is $22,000.
    d. Selling and administrative expenses are budgeted to be $14,000 for June. Of that amount, 50 percent is depreciation.
    e. Equipment costing $14,000 will be purchased in June for cash.
    f. Dividends in the amount of $2,500 will be paid.
    g. The company wants to maintain a minimum cash balance of $10,000 and has set up a line of credit at the local bank that can be used to cover any shortage. If the company must borrow, the loan will be made at the beginning of the month, and any repayment will be made at the end of the month of repayment.

Required

A. Prepare a cash receipts budget for June.
B. Prepare a cash disbursements budget for June.
C. Prepare a schedule that shows whether any borrowing against the line of credit is needed.

51. Hailey's Hats manufactures and distributes hats for every imaginable occasion. Henrietta Hailey started the company in her house three years ago and has been surprised at her success. She is considering an expansion of her business and needs to prepare cash budgeting information for presentation to Second National Bank to secure a loan. Henrietta is not an accountant, so she asked you to help her with preparing the necessary reports.

✓ Total cash disbursed in April: $69,275

Hailey's Hats began the month with a bank balance of $10,000. The budgeted sales for March through June are as follows:

	March	April	May	June
Cash sales	$14,000	$16,500	$15,500	$17,500
Sales on account	29,000	30,000	40,000	50,000
Total sales	$43,000	$46,500	$55,500	$67,500

Henrietta has found that she generally collects payment for credit sales over a two-month period. Typically, 70 percent is collected in the month of sale and the remainder is collected in the next month. Her policy is to purchase inventory each month equivalent to 60 percent of that month's budgeted sales. She thinks this provides her sufficient inventory levels to manage unanticipated changes in demand. Hailey's Hats pays for inventory purchases in the month following purchase. Selling and administrative expenses are budgeted to be 30 percent of each month's sales. One-half of the selling and administrative expenses is accounted for by depreciation on Henrietta's manufacturing equipment. The company purchased additional manufacturing equipment in April at a cost of $24,000. Henrietta does not receive a salary, but she does pay herself dividends as company performance allows. The first quarter of the year was very profitable, so Henrietta paid herself a dividend of $12,500 in April. Henrietta wants to maintain a minimum cash balance of $10,000 and has established a line of credit so she can borrow enough money to make up any shortfall. If the company must borrow from the line of credit, the loan will be made at the beginning of the month and any repayment will be made at the end of the month of repayment.

Required

A. Prepare a cash receipts budget for April, May, and June.
B. Prepare a cash disbursements budget for April, May, and June.
C. Prepare a summary cash budget for April, May, and June.

Case

52. Tina's Fine Juices is a bottler of orange juice located in the Northeast. The company produces bottled orange juice from fruit concentrate purchased from suppliers in Florida, Arizona, and California. The only ingredients in the juice are water and concentrate. The juice is blended, pasteurized, and bottled for sale in 12-ounce plastic bottles. The process is heavily automated and is centered on five machines that control the mixing and bottling of the juice. Each machine is operated by one employee and can process 10 bottles of juice per minute or 600 bottles per hour. The amount of labor required is very small per bottle of juice. The average worker can process 10 bottles of juice per minute or 600 bottles per hour. The juice is sold by a number of grocery stores under their store brand name and in smaller restaurants, delis, and bagel shops under the name of Tina's Fine Juices. Tina's has been in business for several years and uses a sophisticated sales forecasting model based on prior sales, expected changes in demand, and economic factors affecting the industry. Sales of juice are highly seasonal, peaking in the first quarter of the calendar year.

Forecasted sales for the last two months of 2004 and all of 2005 are as follows:

2004	Bottles
November	375,000
December	370,000
2005	
January	350,000
February	425,000
March	400,000
April	395,000
May	375,000
June	350,000
July	375,000
August	385,000
September	395,000
October	405,000
November	400,000
December	365,000

Other information that relates to Tina's Fine Juices:
a. Juice is sold for $1.05 per 12-ounce bottle, in cartons that each hold 50 bottles.
b. Tina's Fine Juices tries to maintain at least 10 percent of the next month's estimated sales in inventory at the end of each month.
c. The company needs to prepare two purchases budgets—one for the concentrate used in its orange juice and one for the bottles that are purchased from an outside supplier. Tina's has determined that it takes one gallon of orange concentrate for every 32 bottles of finished product. Each gallon of concentrate costs $4.80. Tina's also requires 20 percent of next month's direct material needs to be on hand at the end of the budget period. Bottles can be purchased from an outside supplier for $0.10 each.
d. Factory workers are paid an average of $15 per hour, including fringe benefits and payroll taxes. If the production schedule doesn't allow for full utilization of the workers and machines, the worker is temporarily moved to another department.
e. Most of the production process is automated, the juice is mixed by machine, and machines do the bottling and packaging. Overhead costs are incurred almost entirely in the mixing and bottling process. Consequently, Tina's has chosen to use a plantwide cost driver (machine hours) to apply manufacturing overhead to products.
f. Variable overhead costs will be in direct proportion to the number of bottles of juice produced, but fixed overhead costs will remain constant, regardless of production. For budgeting purposes, Tina's separates variable overhead from fixed overhead and calculates a predetermined overhead rate for variable manufacturing overhead costs.

g. Variable overhead is estimated to be $438,000 for the year and the production machines will run approximately 8,000 hours at the projected production volume for the year (4,775,000 bottles). The estimated machine hours are 80 percent of capacity for the five machines. Therefore, Tina's predetermined overhead rate for variable overhead is $54.75 per machine hour ($438,000/8,000 machine hours).

Tina's has also estimated fixed overhead to be $1,480,000 per year ($123,333 per month), of which $1,240,000 per year ($103,333 per month) is depreciation on existing property, plant, and equipment.

h. All of the company's sales are on account. Based on the company's experience in previous years, the company estimates that 50 percent of the sales each month will be paid for in the month of sale. The company also estimates that 35 percent of the month's sales will be collected in the month following sale and that 15 percent of each month's sales will be collected in the second month following sale.

i. Tina's has a policy of paying 50 percent of the direct materials purchases in the month of purchase and the balance in the month after purchase. Variable overhead costs are also paid 50 percent in the month they are incurred and 50 percent in the following month.

j. The company plans to buy some new machinery in February 2005 at a cost of $75,000. The equipment will have a useful life of 10 years and uses straight-line depreciation. The company also plans on paying a dividend of $50,000 in January 2005. Tina's also desires to maintain a cash balance of at least $50,000 at the end of any month. If the projected cash balance is less than that, a line of credit at First National Bank will be used to make up the shortage. If the company draws on the line of credit, Tina's is charged an interest rate of 10 percent annually. If the line of credit is used, money is borrowed at the beginning of the month. Repayments are made at the end of months in which there is sufficient excess cash (over $50,000) to pay back the entire line of credit. Last, but not least, Tina's pays estimated income taxes on a quarterly basis (in March, June, September, and December) on the income earned during the respective quarter. The company estimates that its total tax liability (federal and state) is around 35 percent of taxable income.

k. Selling and administrative expenses are $100,000 per month and are paid in cash as they are incurred.

Required

A. Prepare a sales budget for the first quarter of 2005.
B. Prepare a production budget for the first quarter of 2005.
C. Prepare a purchases budget for the first quarter of 2005.
D. Prepare a direct labor budget for the first quarter of 2005.
E. Prepare an overhead budget for the first quarter of 2005.
F. Prepare cash receipts and disbursements budgets for the first quarter of 2005.

Group And Internet Exercises

LO 1 5 6

53. Visit your local community's web site and find its annual financial report. Explore the annual report to identify budget information. What were the budgeted revenues for your city or county, and what were the primary sources of these revenues? What were the two largest types of expenditures in your city or county? Does anything surprise you about your city or county's budget?

LO 2 4

54. Every business must carefully monitor and manage costs and cash flows if it intends to be successful. Restaurants are among the most difficult types of businesses to operate successfully. Success often depends upon factors that are out of the owner's control such

as health trends, competition, changing tastes in foods and dining environments, and economic conditions. Within a group of three to five students, brainstorm about the challenges faced by a restaurant during the budgeting process. Imagine that your group can open the restaurant of its choice. What factors will you need to consider in budgeting for food items that you will serve in your restaurant? What factors will you need to consider in budgeting your sales? Finally, how will you determine how many employees to hire and when to have them work at your restaurant?

Chapter 10: Variance Analysis—A Tool for Cost Control and Performance Evaluation

Chapter 10 *Variance Analysis—A Tool for Cost Control and Performance Evaluation*

In Chapter 9, we discussed the use of budgets for planning and decision making. We focused on the preparation of operating budgets, beginning with the sales budget and ending with budgeted financial statements. Special emphasis was placed on the use of budgeting in cash planning and the use of operating budgets to plan production, material purchases and use, and labor requirements. We also introduced the concept of flexible budgets and their use as a mechanism for control and evaluation. In this chapter, we expand the discussion of flexible budgeting and introduce the concept of standard costs and variance analysis as tools to help managers "manage by exception" and evaluate performance in their control function. We also demonstrate the calculation of variances for direct material, direct labor, variable overhead, and fixed overhead and discuss the use of variance analysis for selling and administrative costs. The chapter ends with a discussion of variance analysis in an ABC environment, the limitations of standard costing and variance analysis, and behavioral considerations.

Learning Objectives

After studying the material in this chapter, you should be able to:

1. Describe methods of determining standard costs and discuss the use of ideal versus practical standards

2. Prepare a flexible budget using standard costs and contrast a flexible budget with a static budget

3. Compute and interpret a sales volume variance and a flexible budget variance

4. Compute and interpret a sales price variance

5. Compute and interpret price and usage variances for direct material

6. Compute and interpret rate and efficiency variances for direct labor

7. Compute and interpret spending and efficiency variances for variable overhead

8. Compute and interpret spending and volume variances for fixed overhead

9. Compute overhead spending and efficiency variances in an ABC environment

10. Analyze important considerations in using and interpreting variances, including the concept of management by exception

Introduction

As discussed in the previous chapter, budgeting is a tool that managers use to plan and make decisions. In this chapter, we expand our discussion of budgeting to include its use as a control tool. **Control** involves the motivation and monitoring of employees and the evaluation of people and other resources used in the operations of the organization. The purpose of control is to make sure that the goals of the organization are being attained. It includes the use of incentives and other rewards to motivate employees to accomplish an organization's goals as well as mechanisms to detect and correct deviations from those goals.

A control mechanism is a little like a thermostat in your house. If you desire to keep your house at 70 degrees (the budgeted temperature), the thermostat continually measures the actual temperature in the room and compares the actual temperature to the budgeted temperature. If the actual temperature deviates from 70 degrees, the thermostat will signal the heating system to come on (if the actual temperature is less than 70 degrees) or will turn on the air conditioning (if the temperature is above 70 degrees). Managers need a similar type of control system to control budgetary differences.

In business, control often involves the comparison of actual outcomes (cost of products, units sold, sales prices, etc.) with desired outcomes as stated in an organization's operating and strategic plans. Control decisions include questions of how to evaluate performance, what measures to use, and what types of incentives to use. At the end of an accounting period (month, quarter, year, etc.), managers can use the budget as a control tool by comparing budgeted sales, budgeted production, and budgeted manufacturing costs with actual sales, production, and manufacturing costs. These comparisons are typically made through a process called **variance analysis.** Variance analysis allows managers to see whether sales, production, and manufacturing costs are higher or lower than planned and, more important, *why* actual sales, production, and costs differ from those budgeted.

The key to effective variance analysis is **management by exception.** Management by exception is the process of taking action only when actual results deviate significantly from planned. The key term in this definition is *significant*. Managers typically don't have the time to investigate every deviation from budget (nor would such investigations likely add value to the organization), so they tend to focus on material, or significant, differences. This allows managers to focus their energy where they are needed and where they are likely to make a difference. The concept of materiality and its use in variance analysis is discussed in more depth later in the chapter.

Standard Costing

To facilitate the use of flexible budgeting for control purposes, it is useful to examine the budget at a micro level rather than a macro level—that is, to develop a budget for a single unit of a product or a service rather than for the company as a whole. A budget for a single unit of a product or a service is known as its **standard cost.** Just as the cost of a product consists of three components—direct material, direct labor, and manufacturing overhead—a standard cost will be developed for each component. In addition, each component consists of two separate standards—a standard quantity and a standard price. The **standard quantity** tells us the budgeted *amount* of material, labor, and overhead in a product, whereas the **standard price** tells us the budgeted *price* of the material, labor, or overhead for each unit (gallon, hour, etc.).

Standards can be determined in a couple of ways. Management can analyze historical cost and production data to determine how much material and labor was used in each unit of product and how much the material and labor cost. Likewise, management can look at historical data to determine the amount of overhead costs incurred in the past in producing a certain number of units. For companies with a long history of producing the same product, historical data can be very useful in forecasting future prices and quantities. However, historical data must be used with caution and adjusted when necessary. For example, changes in

---

KEY CONCEPT

The purpose of the control function in management is to make sure that the goals of the organization are being attained.

KEY CONCEPT

Management by exception is the key to effective variance analysis and involves taking action only when actual and planned results differ significantly.

Objective 1

Describe methods of determining standard costs and discuss the use of ideal versus practical standards

product design or manufacturing processes can dramatically change both the amounts and the prices of material, labor, and overhead.

Another method of setting standards is called **task analysis.** Task analysis examines the production process in detail, with an emphasis on determining what it *should* cost to produce a product, not what it cost last year. Task analysis typically involves the use of engineers who perform time-and-motion studies to determine how much material should be used in a product, how long it takes to perform certain labor tasks in manufacturing the product, how much electricity is consumed, and so on. Typically, some combination of task analysis and historical cost analysis will be used in determining standard costs.

Ideal versus Practical Standards

Because standard costs are used to evaluate performance, human behavior can influence how the standards are determined. Should standards be set so they are easy to attain or set so they can rarely be attained? An **ideal standard** is one that is attained only when near-perfect conditions are present. An ideal standard assumes that every aspect of the production process, from purchasing through shipment, is at peak efficiency. Some managers like ideal standards because they believe that employees will be motivated to achieve more when the goals are set very high. Others would argue that employees are discouraged by standards that are not attainable. Employees may be motivated to cut corners, use less than optimum material, or skimp on labor to achieve the standards. This type of behavior can lead to poor quality and an increase in defective units produced, which may cost the company more in the long run.

A **practical standard** should be attainable under normal, efficient operating conditions. Practical standards take into consideration that machines break down occasionally, that employees are not always perfect, that waste in materials does occur. Most managers would agree that practical standards would encourage employees to be more positive and productive.

The Ethics of Business
Is Working Hard Enough?

Competition is a fact of life for most businesses. Competitive forces result from new technologies, globalization, government regulations, and a host of other factors. While competition can be a positive force for change, managers may decide that the only response to competition is to increase output and cut costs by simply having employees work harder and harder. In these instances, companies that use standard costing create an environment in which employees are expected to continually improve their performance. Setting standards that are extraordinarily challenging, if not outright unattainable, is seen by some as the best method to truly challenge employees to be more efficient. Others view this practice as unreasonable because employees cannot realistically expect to perform at the standard's level. This, these managers would argue, demoralizes employees.

It's Your Choice—Is the use of ideal standards for motivational purposes appropriate in a work environment? How might employees react to such standards? Is it unethical to establish performance standards that managers know employees will never achieve? Does your answer to the last question change if bonuses are related to those performance standards?

Use of Standards by Nonmanufacturing Organizations

The use of standard costing applies to merchandising and service organizations as well. Just as Panasonic needs to determine how much it should cost to make a telephone, an automobile dealership needs to know how much it should cost to sell a car, the city of Atlanta needs to know how much it should cost to provide garbage pickup to a residence, and colleges and universities need to determine how much it should cost to provide an education to an incoming student. CPA firms have standards for the amount of time needed to prepare certain types of tax forms or returns, auto repair shops have standards for the time needed to make each repair, and airlines have standards for on-time departures. The use of standards is very common in all types of businesses.[1]

Doing Business.

YOU HAD BETTER WALK (AND TALK) FAST TO MEET THESE STANDARDS!

In the mid 1980s, United Parcel Service (UPS) developed standards for how fast drivers should walk to a customer's door (3 feet per second) and how long it should take to handle a customer's package. More recently, managed health care companies have developed a standard amount of time for doctors seeing patients for particular ailments. For example, an initial office visit might have a standard time of 20 minutes, whereas a full physical for a patient might have a standard time of 45 minutes.

Flexible Budgeting with Standard Costs

In Chapter 9, we introduced the concept of flexible budgeting, based on the actual volume of production rather than on the planned level of production. Flexible budgets based on standard costs are the centerpiece of effective variance analysis.

EXHIBIT 10-1 Standard Costs for Corinne's Country Rockers

	Standard Quantity	Standard Price	Standard Cost
Direct material	20 linear feet of oak	$ 2 per foot	$ 40
Direct labor	5 labor hours	12 per hour	60
Variable overhead	5 labor hours	3 per hour	15
Total variable production costs			$ 115
Variable selling and administrative costs			25
Total variable costs			$ 140
Fixed overhead ($5,000 per month, or $15,000 per quarter)			$15,000
Fixed selling and administrative costs ($6,000 per month, or $18,000 per quarter)			18,000
Total fixed costs			$33,000

---

[1]Companies also use standard costs to price products and services. For example, a CPA firm may use its budget for the time normally needed to prepare a variety of schedules on a tax return to compute the price of the tax return. Likewise, auto repair shops may use the amount of time budgeted for each type of repair to determine a price for the repair service.

To illustrate the concept of flexible budgets, consider the case of Corinne's Country Rockers. Corinne's builds a high-quality rocking chair with a reputation for lasting a lifetime and also uses a unique (and patented) rocking mechanism not found on other rockers. The chairs are sold directly by Corinne's through mail order and the Internet and have a retail price of $250 each. Corinne's produces each chair to order and has the capacity to produce 600 chairs per month. The standard quantity, standard price, and standard cost of direct material, direct labor, and variable overhead in each chair is summarized in Exhibit 10-1. Estimated variable selling and administrative costs (per unit) and total fixed overhead and fixed selling and administrative costs are also provided.

A static budget based on estimated production and sale of 1,500 chairs is provided in Exhibit 10-2. In addition, a flexible budget based on the actual production and sale of 1,600 rockers is provided.

Objective 2

Prepare a flexible budget using standard costs and contrast a flexible budget with a static budget

Exhibit 10-2 Corinne's Country Rockers

Static Budget, Flexible Budget, and Actual Results

	Static Budget	Flexible Budget	Actual Results
Units produced and sold	1,500	1,600	1,600
Sales revenue	$375,000	$400,000	$396,800
Variable manufacturing costs	− 172,500	− 184,000	− 189,200
Variable selling and administrative costs	− 37,500	− 40,000	− 40,800
Contribution margin	$165,000	$176,000	$166,800
Fixed manufacturing costs	− 15,000	− 15,000	− 16,000
Fixed selling and administrative costs	− 8,000	− 18,000	− 16,000
Operating income	$132,000	$143,000	$134,800

As you can see, the actual operating income for Corinne's is somewhere in the middle of that predicted by the static budget and the flexible budget. What does that mean? Unfortunately, not much! It means that Corinne's earned more than budgeted at the beginning of the year. But remember, the static budget was based on expected production and sales of 1,500 units. Corinne's ended up producing and selling 1,600 units. Comparing the static budget to the actual results is like comparing apples with oranges. It just does not make sense!

Sales Volume Variance

It can be useful to compare the static budget to the flexible budget. Differences in the static budget and the flexible budget are solely a result of differences in budgeted and actual production and sales. The sales volume variance is the difference between the operating income of $132,000 (based on the static budget) and the operating income of $143,000 (based on the flexible budget). Note that this $11,000 difference in operating income is the same as the $11,000 difference in contribution margin. Why is the difference between the static budget and the flexible budget contribution margin the same as the difference between the static budget and flexible budget operating income? Because budgeted fixed costs are the same in a static and a flexible budget, differences in contribution margin are directly reflected as differences in income.

The **sales volume variance** is computed by taking the difference between the actual sales volume used in the flexible budget and the budgeted sales volume and multiplying that difference by the budgeted contribution margin per unit.

Sales volume variance = (Actual − Budgeted sales volume)
× (Budgeted contribution margin per unit)

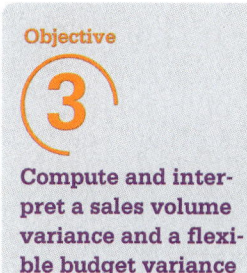

Objective 3

Compute and interpret a sales volume variance and a flexible budget variance

As discussed on page 341, the retail price of the chairs is expected to be $250 each. As shown in Exhibit 10-1, the standard variable costs for a rocker total $140 so the budgeted contribution margin is $110 per unit ($250 − $140). The sales volume variance for Corinne's is as follows:

(Actual − Budgeted sales volume) × Budgeted contribution margin per unit
(1,600 − 1,500) × $110 = $11,000

As you can see in Exhibit 10-3, Corinne's sales volume variance is a result of actual sales used for the flexible budget exceeding the static budget sales. However, beyond that it is not particularly informative. We don't know *why* actual sales were greater than budgeted. A reduction in sales price, a change in advertising strategy, or simply an increase in demand may have caused it.

EXHIBIT 10-3   Corinne's Country Rockers

The Sales Volume Variance

	Static Budget	Sales Volume Variance	Flexible Budget
Units produced and sold	1,500		1,600
Sales revenue	$375,000	$25,000	$400,000
Variable manufacturing costs	− 172,500	− 11,500	− 184,000
Variable selling and administrative costs	− 37,500	− 2,500	− 40,000
Contribution margin	$165,000	$11,000	$176,000
Fixed manufacturing costs	− 15,000		− 15,000
Fixed selling and administrative costs	− 18,000		− 18,000
Operating income	$132,000	$11,000	$143,000

Flexible Budget Variance

Comparing the flexible budget amounts with the actual results in Exhibit 10-4 is more meaningful. Remember that the flexible budget was calculated based on the actual production and sales of 1,600 units. It represents the amount of revenue and cost that Corinne's expected to incur during the first quarter for the actual number of units produced and sold. The difference between the flexible budget operating income and actual operating income is called the **flexible budget variance**. As shown in Exhibit 10-4, the flexible budget variance for Corinne's is $8,200.

EXHIBIT 10-4   Corinne's Country Rockers

The Flexible Budget Variance

	Flexible Budget	Flexible Budget Variance	Actual Results
Units produced and sold	1,600		1,600
Average sales price per unit	× $ 250		× $ 248
Sales revenue	$400,000	$3,200 under	$396,800
Variable manufacturing costs	− 184,000	5,200 over	− 189,200
Variable selling and administrative costs	− 40,000	800 over	− 40,800
Contribution margin	$176,000	9,200 under	$166,800
Fixed manufacturing costs	− 15,000	1,000 over	− 16,000
Fixed selling and administrative costs	− 18,000	2,000 under	− 16,000
Operating income	$143,000	$8,200 under	$134,800

However, we still don't have much information concerning exactly *why* operating income is $8,200 below budget. As shown in Exhibit 10-5, the unfavorable flexible budget variance of $8,200 is caused by a combination of factors—a $3,200 unfavorable sales price variance, a $5,200 unfavorable variable manufacturing overhead cost variance, a $1,000 unfavorable fixed manufacturing overhead spending variance, a $800 unfavorable variable selling and administrative cost variance and a $2,000 favorable fixed selling and administrative cost variance. These variances are discussed more fully in the following pages.

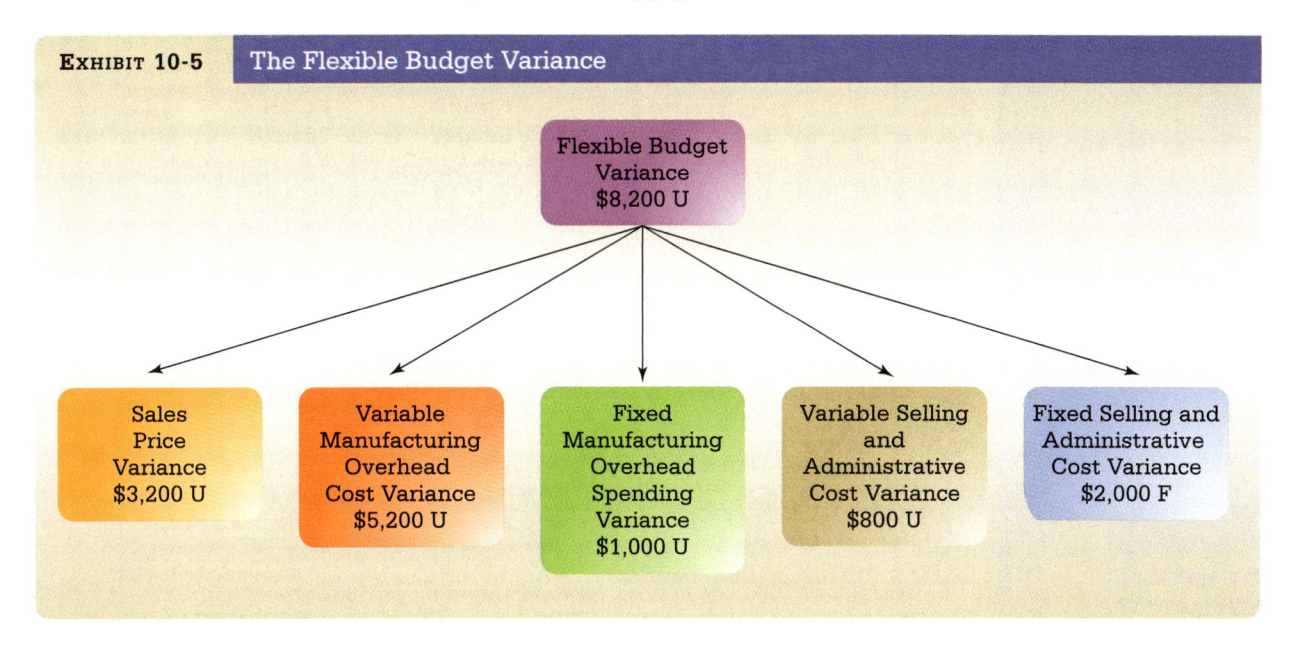

EXHIBIT 10-5　The Flexible Budget Variance

```
                    Flexible Budget
                       Variance
                       $8,200 U
         ┌──────────┬─────┴─────┬──────────┐
    Sales      Variable      Fixed      Variable Selling   Fixed Selling and
    Price      Manufacturing Manufacturing   and          Administrative
    Variance   Overhead      Overhead    Administrative   Cost Variance
    $3,200 U   Cost Variance Spending    Cost Variance    $2,000 F
               $5,200 U      Variance    $800 U
                             $1,000 U
```

Sales Price Variance

The flexible budgeting process removes any differences or variances due to variations in production and sales volume. Therefore, any differences in sales revenue between the flexible budget and actual results must be caused by differences in the sales price.

The **sales price variance** is computed by comparing the actual sales price to the flexible budget sales price and multiplying that amount by the actual sales volume.

$$\text{Sales price variance} = (\text{Actual} - \text{Expected sales price}) \times \text{Actual volume}$$

Plugging in the numbers for Corinne's, the sales price variance is as follows:

$$(\$248 - \$250) \times 1,600 = \$3,200 \text{ (under budget)}$$

The sales price variance can direct management's attention to a potential problem area. However, at this point, it is difficult to tell whether this unfavorable variance is the result of reducing the sales price of all rockers by $2 or perhaps the result of accepting a special order of 100 rockers at a price of $218 per chair. The variance simply points out that the actual sales price is different from the budgeted sales price. Management should investigate it further to determine its cause.

Objective 4

Compute and interpret a sales price variance

Variable Manufacturing Cost Variances

The flexible budget variance (see Exhibit 10-4) shows us that actual variable manufacturing costs were $5,200 higher than budgeted, but determining the true cause of that variance is a little more difficult. Did Corinne's spend too much on material or use too much? Did the company incur more labor costs than usual, owing to paying a higher wage, or did it spend more time making each chair than budgeted? Did Corinne's spend more than budgeted on electricity, supplies, and other variable overhead or use more than budgeted? We simply don't know. In fact, the real reason may be a combination of any or all of the preceding.

To analyze the variable cost variances based on a flexible budget, we must step back and examine the flexible budget in more detail. Based on the standard cost information provided in Exhibit 10-1, the flexible budget for variable manufacturing costs is as shown in Exhibit 10-6. More detail concerning the actual variable manufacturing costs of $189,200 is also provided.

Exhibit 10-6 Corinne's Country Rockers

Variable Manufacturing Costs

	Flexible Budget	Actual Costs	Flexible Budget Variance
Direct material	$ 64,000[1]	$ 63,840[4]	$ 160 F
Direct labor	96,000[2]	101,640[5]	5,640 U
Variable overhead	24,000[3]	23,720[6]	280 F
Total variable manufacturing costs	$184,000	$189,200	$5,200 U

[1] Flexible budget for direct materials = (20 feet per unit × 1,600 units) × $2 per unit = $64,000.
[2] Flexible budget for direct labor = (5 hours per unit × 1,600 units) × $12 per hour = $96,000.
[3] Flexible budget for variable overhead = (5 hours per unit × 1,600 units) × $3 per hour = $24,000.
[4] 33,600 feet × $1.90 per foot = $63,840.
[5] 8,400 hours × $12.10 per hour = $101,640.
[6] Actual variable overhead costs consist of the variable portion of utilities ($16,390), shop supplies and indirect materials ($4,140), and repairs and maintenance ($3,190).

The total variance for variable manufacturing costs is $5,200. Note that this is the same as the flexible budget variance for variable manufacturing costs shown in Exhibit 10-4. Because actual costs are greater than budgeted, this variance is called "unfavorable" (indicated by a "U" following the amount in the last column of the table). Even though Corinne's actual expenditures for total variable production costs were greater than budgeted, Corinne's spent slightly less than the amount budgeted for direct materials and variable overhead but much more for direct labor.

Because actual costs for direct materials are less than the flexible budget amount, the $160 difference is "favorable." Although it is useful to know that we spent less than budgeted for direct materials, this type of analysis still does not tell us *why* Corinne's spent less. Did the company use less lumber than budgeted or pay less for each foot? To fully utilize the available information, we need to break down the total direct material variance presented earlier into its components and calculate both price and usage (quantity) variances.

We can examine the direct labor variance in the same way. Because actual labor costs are greater than the flexible budget amount, the variance is unfavorable. However, once again we don't really know *why* Corinne's spent more than budgeted. It could be because the company used more labor hours than budgeted or paid more for each hour of labor or some combination of the two. Further analysis is necessary to break down the total labor variance into its price and usage components and to fully understand the cause of the variances.

Analyzing variable overhead is much like analyzing direct material and direct labor. Of course, direct material and direct labor are also variable costs. Although we know that Corinne's spent less on variable overhead than budgeted (the variance is favorable), we do not know whether the price paid for electricity, supplies, and other variable overhead was less than budgeted or whether Corinne's used less.

As you will recall, rather than budget each individual overhead item, we prepared the flexible budget in Chapter 9 by combining all variable overhead costs and budgeting these separately from fixed overhead costs. The flexible budget for variable overhead for Corinne's was prepared by multiplying the predetermined overhead rate of $3 per direct labor hour by the number of direct labor hours expected to be incurred in producing 1,600 units (8,000 hours).

Unfortunately, although traditional variance analysis of variable overhead can help provide answers to questions about whether a company spent more or less or used more or less in total, it does not provide us with information concerning the components of overhead. In other words, traditional analysis does not tell us whether we spent more than budgeted on electricity or supplies, just that the overall amount of spending was higher than budgeted. Companies adopting activity-based costing to allocate overhead to products can extend variance analysis to look at the overhead costs associated with each activity and its associated cost driver. This analysis provides much more detailed information than provided by traditional variance analysis. The analysis of overhead variances for companies using ABC is discussed in more detail later in the chapter.

Analyzing Variable Manufacturing Cost Variances

The next step in variance analysis is to break down the direct material, direct labor, and variable overhead variances into their components (a price variance and a usage or quantity variance), using the basic variance analysis model shown in Exhibit 10-7.

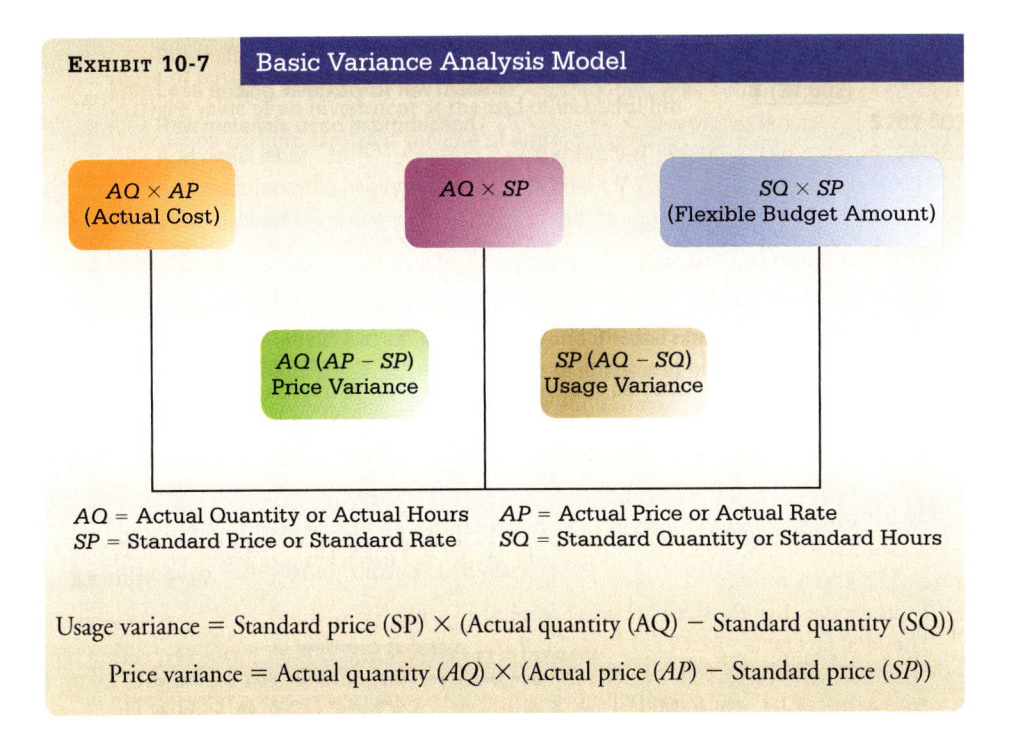

EXHIBIT 10-7 Basic Variance Analysis Model

$AQ \times AP$ (Actual Cost) $AQ \times SP$ $SQ \times SP$ (Flexible Budget Amount)

$AQ(AP - SP)$ Price Variance

$SP(AQ - SQ)$ Usage Variance

AQ = Actual Quantity or Actual Hours
SP = Standard Price or Standard Rate
AP = Actual Price or Actual Rate
SQ = Standard Quantity or Standard Hours

Usage variance = Standard price (SP) × (Actual quantity (AQ) − Standard quantity (SQ))

Price variance = Actual quantity (AQ) × (Actual price (AP) − Standard price (SP))

Whereas AQ, AP, and SP are self-explanatory, the calculation of SQ needs to be elaborated a little. In Chapter 9, the flexible budget was prepared based on the cost that should have been incurred to manufacture the actual number of units produced. SQ is a similar concept. It is the standard (budgeted) quantity of material or number of hours that should be incurred for the actual level of production.

As you can see, the material **price variance** is the difference between the actual quantity multiplied by the actual price ($AQ \times AP$) and the actual quantity multiplied by the standard price ($AQ \times SP$). Simplifying, $(AQ \times AP) - (AQ \times SP) = AQ(AP - SP)$. The price variance is simply the difference in price multiplied by the actual quantity. Likewise, the **usage variance** is the difference between the actual quantity multiplied by the standard price ($AQ \times SP$) and the standard quantity multiplied by the standard price ($SQ \times SP$). Simplifying, $(AQ \times SP) - (SQ \times SP) = SP(AQ - SQ)$. The usage variance is simply the difference in quantity multiplied by the standard price. The variance model separates the overall flexible budget variance ($AQ \times AP$) − ($SQ \times SP$) into two components—one the result of paying more or less than budgeted and the other the result of using more or less than budgeted.

Direct Material Variances

Using the standard cost data for Corinne's Country Rockers provided in Exhibit 10-1 and the breakdown of actual direct material costs shown in Exhibit 10-6, direct material variances are calculated as shown in Exhibit 10-8.

Objective 5

Compute and interpret price and usage variances for direct material

Exhibit 10-8 Analysis of Direct Material Variances

AQ × AP	AQ × SP	SQ × SP
33,600 × $1.90	33,600 × $2.00	32,000 × $2.00
= $63,840	= $67,200	(20 ft./unit × 1,600 units) × $2.00
		= $64,000

33,600 ($1.90 − $2.00)
AQ (AP − SP)
Price Variance
$3,360 F

$2.00 (33,600 − 32,000)
SP (AQ − SQ)
Usage Variance
$3,200 U

Total Direct Material Variance = $3,360 F + $3,200 U = $160 F

AQ = Actual Quantity   AP = Actual Price
SP = Standard Price   SQ = Standard Quantity

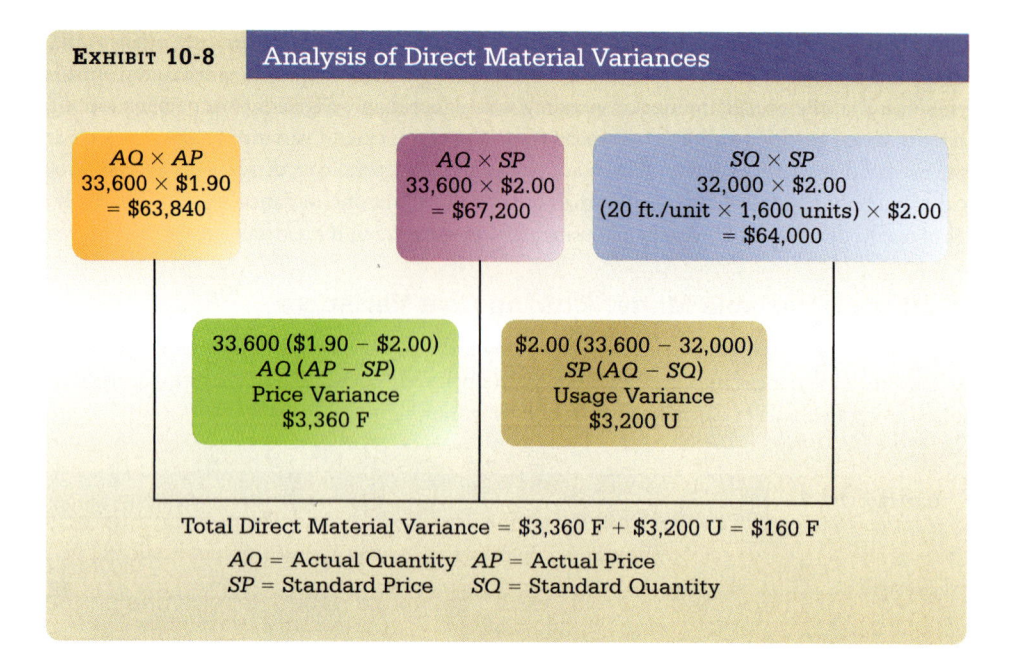

The price variance is calculated by multiplying the actual amount of material purchased (33,600 feet) by the difference in the actual price paid per foot ($1.90) and the standard, or budgeted, price per foot ($2.00). This variance of $3,360 is considered favorable because the actual price was less than the budgeted price.

The usage variance for direct materials is found by multiplying the standard price by the difference in the actual quantity used and standard quantity allowed. Remember that the standard quantity allowed is the amount of direct material that *should* have been used to produce the actual output (the flexible budget amount). In this case, the budget for materials is 20 feet of lumber per chair. Corinne's actually produced 1,600 chairs during the quarter and should have used 32,000 feet of lumber (1,600 chairs × 20 feet per chair = 32,000 feet). The variance of $3,200 is considered unfavorable because the actual quantity of material used (33,600 feet) was greater than the flexible budget amount (32,000 feet).

The total favorable variance of $160 for direct material can now be examined in more detail. It is the sum of a favorable price variance of $3,360 and an unfavorable usage variance of $3,200. Although the overall direct material variance was quite small, you can see that both the price variance and the usage variance are quite large and just happen to offset each other. Possible reasons for a favorable price variance include taking advantage of unexpected quantity discounts or negotiating reduced prices with suppliers. However, favorable direct material price variances can also result from the purchase of low-quality materials. Unfavorable material usage variances can likewise be caused by a number of reasons—poorly trained workers, machine breakdowns, or perhaps even the use of low-quality materials if they result in more defective units, machine downtime, rework, and so on.

What are some possible reasons for an unfavorable direct material price variance and a favorable material usage variance? Unfavorable material price variances might result from rush orders (requiring faster delivery and higher prices), purchasing in small lot sizes (and not taking advantage of quantity discounts), and purchasing higher-quality materials than budgeted. Favorable material usage variances are likely a result of highly efficient workers and well-maintained machinery and equipment.

Direct Material Variances When Amount Purchased Differs from Amount Used If the amount of material purchased is not the same as the amount of material used in production, the variance model for materials must be slightly modified (see Exhibit 10-9). To isolate the variances as soon as possible, the price variance should be calculated using the total amount of material purchased, whereas the usage variance should be calculated based on the amount of material actually used in production. For example, if Corinne's purchases

Exhibit 10-9: Analysis of Direct Material Variances When Quantity Purchased Differs from Quantity Used

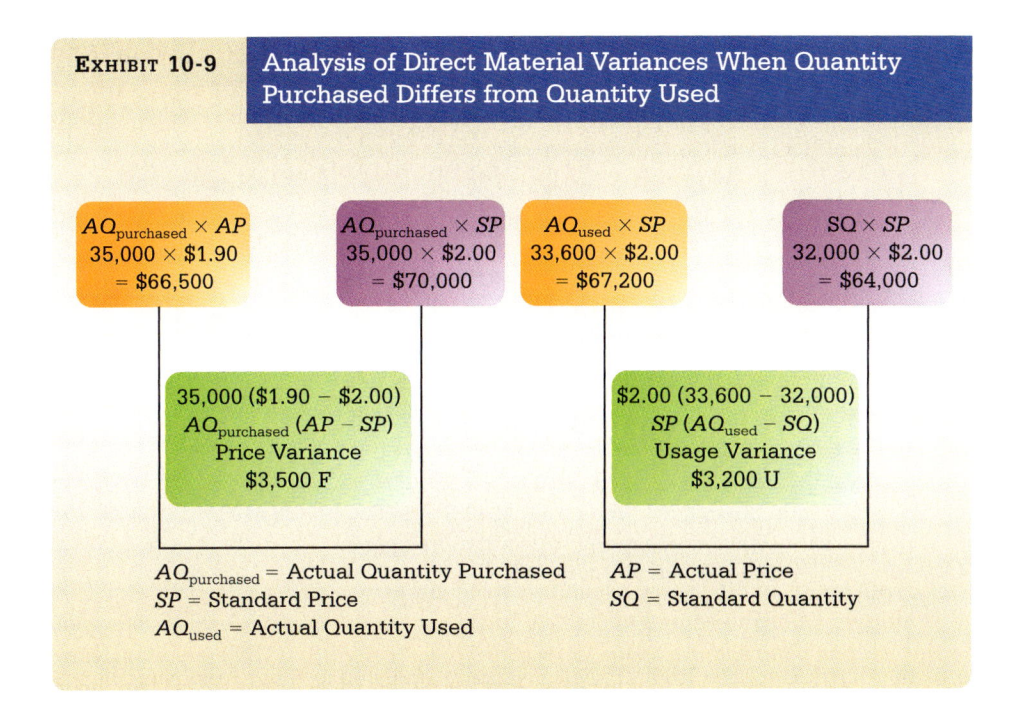

$AQ_{purchased} \times AP$
35,000 × $1.90
= $66,500

$AQ_{purchased} \times SP$
35,000 × $2.00
= $70,000

$AQ_{used} \times SP$
33,600 × $2.00
= $67,200

$SQ \times SP$
32,000 × $2.00
= $64,000

35,000 ($1.90 − $2.00)
$AQ_{purchased} (AP − SP)$
Price Variance
$3,500 F

$2.00 (33,600 − 32,000)
$SP (AQ_{used} − SQ)$
Usage Variance
$3,200 U

$AQ_{purchased}$ = Actual Quantity Purchased
SP = Standard Price
AQ_{used} = Actual Quantity Used
AP = Actual Price
SQ = Standard Quantity

35,000 feet of lumber but uses only 33,600 feet, the price variance would be calculated as follows:

$$AQ_{purchased} (AP - SP)$$
$$35,000 (\$1.90 - \$2.00) = \$3,500 \text{ F}$$

The usage variance is calculated as before, that is

$$SP (AQ_{used} - SQ)$$
$$\$2.00 (33,600 - 32,000) = \$3,200 \text{ U}$$

You should note that when the amount of material purchased is not equal to the amount of material used, the price and usage variances should not be added together to calculate the total direct material variance.

Direct Labor Variances

Direct labor variances are calculated using the same basic variance model used to calculate direct material variances. Because we are talking about labor instead of material, we substitute rates for price (*AR* and *SR* instead of *AP* and *SP*) and hours for quantity (*AH* and *SH* instead of *AQ* and *SQ*). In addition, the direct labor usage variance is often referred to as an efficiency variance. Using the standard cost data for Corinne's Country Rockers provided in Exhibit 10-1 and the breakdown of actual direct labor costs in Exhibit 10-6, direct labor variances are calculated as in Exhibit 10-10.

If we evaluate the two components of the direct labor variance, we see that most of the variance results from inefficiencies in the use of labor. Potential causes of an unfavorable direct labor efficiency variance include poorly trained workers, machine breakdowns, the use of poor-quality raw materials (resulting in more time spent in production), or just general employee inefficiencies resulting from poor supervision. In this case, the unfavorable direct labor rate variance is small but still may be important. Potential causes of unfavorable direct labor rate variances include the use of higher-paid workers than budgeted, unexpected increases in wages owing to union negotiations, and so on.

What are some possible reasons for favorable direct labor rate and efficiency variances? Hiring workers at a lower wage rate is one obvious reason for a favorable direct labor rate variance. However, that may be problematic if the workers are less skilled than required. On

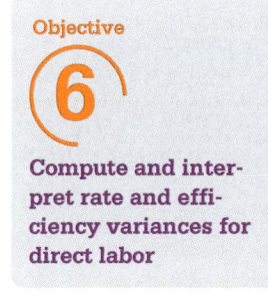

Objective 6
Compute and interpret rate and efficiency variances for direct labor

Exhibit 10-10 Direct Labor Variances

$AH \times AR$	$AH \times SR$	$SH \times SR$
$8,400 \times \$12.10$	$8,400 \times \$12.00$	$8,000 \times \$12.00$
$= \$101,640$	$= \$100,800$	$= \$96,000$

$8,400 (\$12.10 - \$12.00)$
$AH (AR - SR)$
Rate Variance
$840 U

$12 (8,400 - 8,000)$
$SR (AH - SH)$
Efficiency Variance
$4,800 U

Total Direct Labor Variance = $840 U + $4,800 U = $5,640 U

AH = Actual Hours   AR = Actual Rate
SH = Standard Hours   SR = Standard Rate

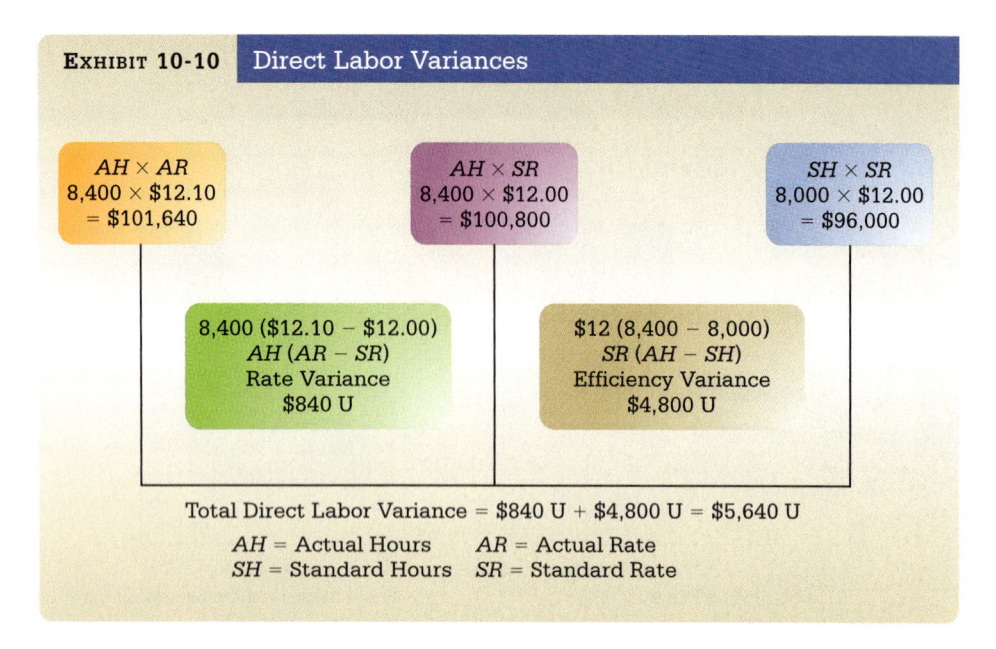

the other hand, favorable labor efficiency variances most often result from using highly skilled workers. Obviously, there are tradeoffs here. Paying higher wage rates can result in unfavorable labor rate variances and favorable labor efficiency variances, whereas paying lower wage rates can result in favorable labor rate variances and unfavorable labor efficiency variances.

Variable Overhead Variances

Objective 7: Compute and interpret spending and efficiency variances for variable overhead

With slight modifications, we can calculate variable overhead variances using the same variance model as for direct material and direct labor variances. As with direct material and direct labor, $(AQ \times AP)$ is simply the actual cost incurred—in this case, the actual variable overhead costs. SR is the variable predetermined overhead rate (sometimes called SVR). Because variable overhead was estimated using direct labor as the cost driver, AH is simply the actual number of labor hours incurred. Likewise, SH is the standard number of labor hours allowed for actual production. Consequently, $SH \times SVR$ is the amount of applied variable overhead.[2] The price variance is often called a variable overhead spending variance and like the labor usage variance, the usage variance for variable overhead is called an efficiency variance.

The variable overhead spending and efficiency variances are calculated as shown in Exhibit 10-11. What do these variances tell us? Whereas the price variance for materials and the rate variance for labor tell us whether the price of materials and the rate for labor are more or less than budgeted, the interpretation of the variable overhead spending variance is a little different. Whereas a spending variance for variable overhead indicates that the actual price of variable overhead items, such as supplies, utilities, repairs, and maintenance, was more or less than the flexible budget amount, it is also affected by excessive *usage* of overhead caused by inefficient operations or waste. For example, although the rates for electricity usage (charged by the utility) might be exactly as budgeted, excessive usage might result from poorly maintained equipment. Likewise, even if the price of supplies was lower than budgeted, excessive use of the supplies owing to waste could still result in an unfavorable variable overhead spending variance.

The variable overhead efficiency variance is also interpreted differently from the direct material and direct labor usage variances. It does not measure the efficient use of overhead at all but rather the efficient use of the cost driver, or overhead allocation base, used in the flexible budget. The efficiency variance has nothing to do with the efficient use of utilities, maintenance,

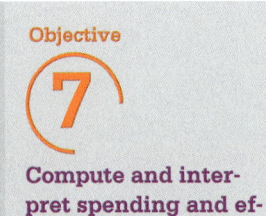

KEY CONCEPT

The variable overhead efficiency variance does not measure the efficient use of overhead but rather the efficient use of the cost driver, or overhead allocation base, used in the flexible budget.

---

[2] Of course, overhead can be applied using cost drivers other than direct labor. If overhead is applied based on machine hours, AH is simply the actual number of machine hours used, and SH is the budgeted number of machine hours allowed for actual production.

Exhibit 10-11 Variable Overhead Variances

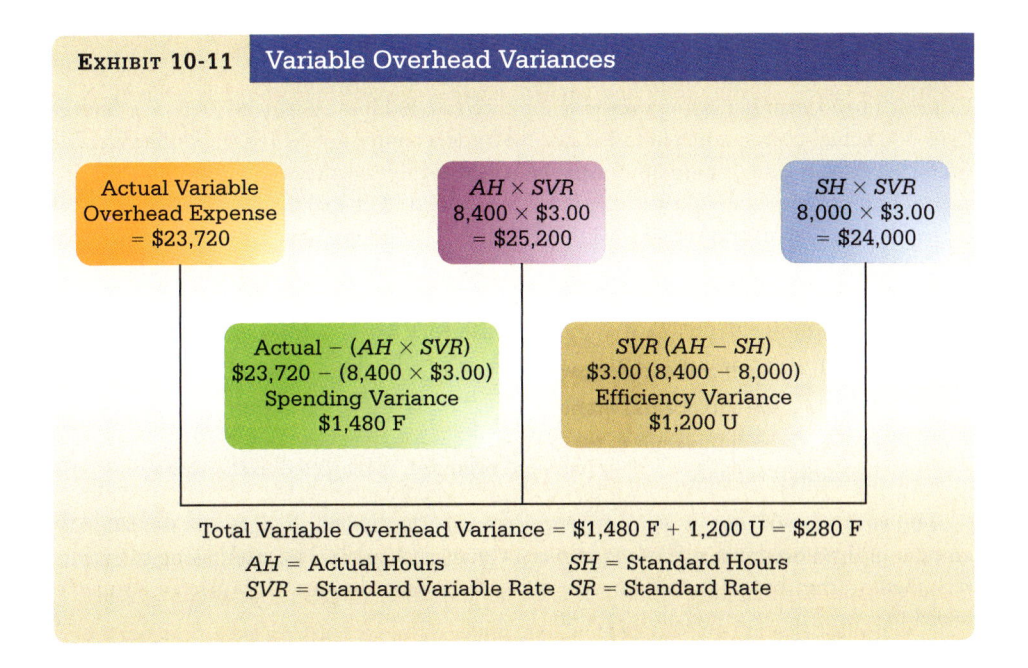

Actual Variable Overhead Expense = $23,720	AH × SVR 8,400 × $3.00 = $25,200	SH × SVR 8,000 × $3.00 = $24,000

Actual − (AH × SVR)
$23,720 − (8,400 × $3.00)
Spending Variance
$1,480 F

SVR (AH − SH)
$3.00 (8,400 − 8,000)
Efficiency Variance
$1,200 U

Total Variable Overhead Variance = $1,480 F + 1,200 U = $280 F

AH = Actual Hours   SH = Standard Hours
SVR = Standard Variable Rate   SR = Standard Rate

and supplies. The efficiency variance shows only how efficiently the organization used the base chosen to apply overhead to the cost of product produced.

In the case of Corinne's Country Rockers, the favorable variable overhead spending variance tells us that Corinne's spent less than budgeted on the items included in the variable overhead portion of its flexible budget. Although this might have resulted from paying less per kilowatt hour for electricity, it might also have resulted from using less electricity than expected. A detailed analysis of each line item would provide more information. The unfavorable variable overhead efficiency variance tells us simply that more *direct labor hours* were used than budgeted. It does not tell us anything about the efficient use of electricity, supplies, or repairs and maintenance.

The interpretation of variable overhead spending and efficiency variances is made difficult by the use of a single cost driver to apply variable overhead to products and services. The use of multiple cost drivers and ABC makes the interpretation of these variances much more useful. This is illustrated in more detail later in the chapter.

In summary, the total variable manufacturing cost variance of $5,200 that we saw in Exhibits 10-4 and 10-5 has now been broken down into six separate variances—two for direct material, two for direct labor and two for variable overhead (see Exhibit 10-12).

Exhibit 10-12 Summary of Variable Manufacturing Cost Variances

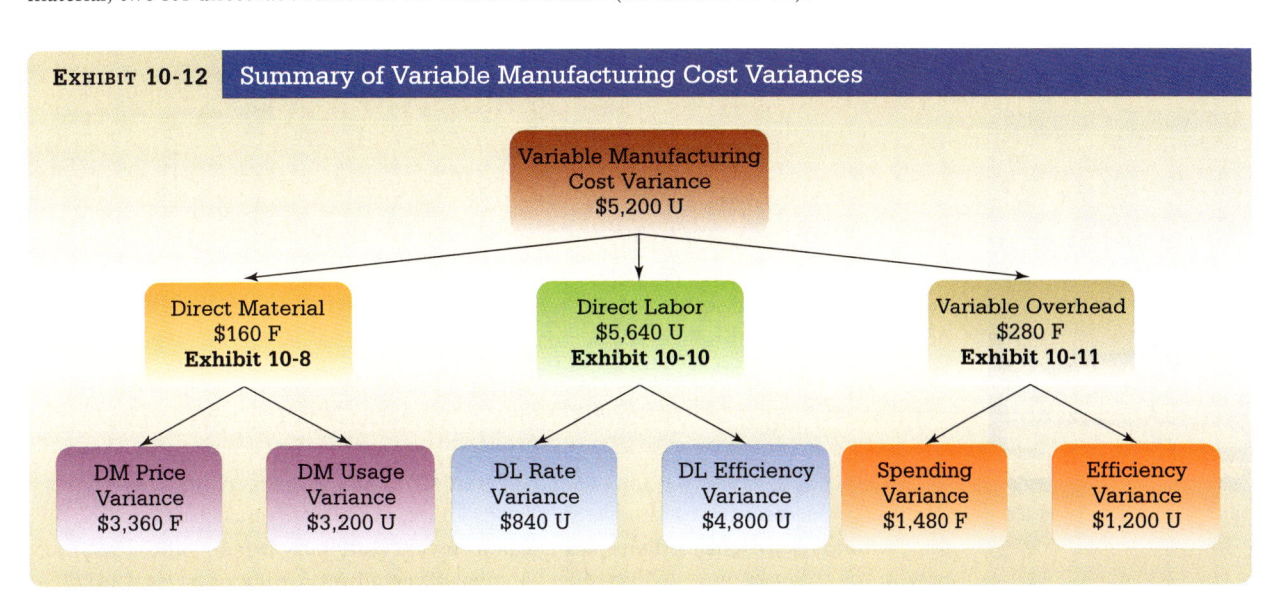

Variable Manufacturing Cost Variance $5,200 U

- **Direct Material $160 F** (Exhibit 10-8)
  - DM Price Variance $3,360 F
  - DM Usage Variance $3,200 U
- **Direct Labor $5,640 U** (Exhibit 10-10)
  - DL Rate Variance $840 U
  - DL Efficiency Variance $4,800 U
- **Variable Overhead $280 F** (Exhibit 10-11)
  - Spending Variance $1,480 F
  - Efficiency Variance $1,200 U

Objective 8

Compute and interpret spending and volume variances for fixed overhead

Fixed Overhead Variances

Corinne's fixed manufacturing overhead variance (see Exhibit 10-4) is $1,000 over budget ($16,000 actual costs compared to the flexible budget amount of $15,000). Unlike variable overhead, fixed overhead (and other fixed costs) should not be affected when production increases or decreases. Consequently, the variance model used in analyzing variable costs (direct material, direct labor, and variable overhead) is not appropriate for analyzing the fixed overhead variance.

Fixed overhead variances consist of a budget variance and a volume variance. The **budget variance** (or spending variance) is simply the difference between the amount of fixed overhead actually incurred and the flexible budget amount. Because fixed overhead does not depend on production volume, no activity levels are used in its calculation.

Fixed overhead budget (spending) variance = Actual fixed overhead − Budgeted fixed overhead

The **volume variance** is the difference between the flexible budget amount and the amount of fixed overhead *applied* to products. Overhead is applied by multiplying the predetermined overhead rate (for fixed overhead) by the standard hours (or budgeted hours) allowed to complete the actual units produced.

Fixed overhead volume variance = Budgeted fixed overhead − Applied fixed overhead

A company using variable (direct) costing rather than absorption (full) costing treats fixed overhead as a period cost and expenses it immediately (see Chapter 6). In these companies, there won't be a fixed overhead volume variance, because fixed overhead is not "applied" to products. It is simply expensed in the period incurred.

Fixed overhead variances for Corinne's Country Rockers are calculated in Exhibit 10-13. The predetermined fixed overhead rate is $2 per labor hour ($15,000 budgeted fixed overhead divided by 7,500 budgeted labor hours (1,500 budgeted units × 5 hours per unit)). Applied fixed overhead is $16,000 ($2 predetermined overhead rate × 8,000 hours (1,600 actual units × 5 hours per unit)).

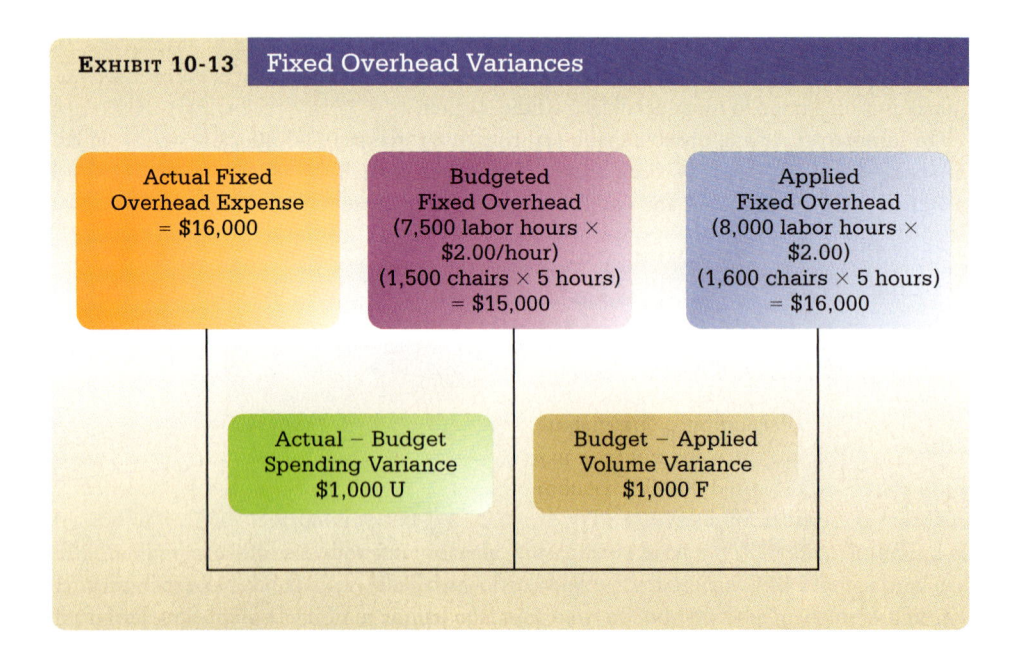

EXHIBIT 10-13 Fixed Overhead Variances

| Actual Fixed Overhead Expense = $16,000 | Budgeted Fixed Overhead (7,500 labor hours × $2.00/hour) (1,500 chairs × 5 hours) = $15,000 | Applied Fixed Overhead (8,000 labor hours × $2.00) (1,600 chairs × 5 hours) = $16,000 |

Actual − Budget
Spending Variance
$1,000 U

Budget − Applied
Volume Variance
$1,000 F

The spending variance is unfavorable because Corinne's spent more on fixed overhead items than the company had budgeted. As you can see, the volume variance is simply a result of Corinne's manufacturing more chairs than budgeted (1,600 instead of 1,500). Everything else in the comparison of budgeted and applied overhead is the same. The fixed overhead volume variance is calculated primarily as a method of reconciling the amount of overhead applied to products under an absorption costing system with the amount of overhead actually incurred—and, consequently, the over- or underapplied overhead. The total amount of the variable overhead spending variance, variable overhead efficiency variance, fixed overhead spending variance, and fixed overhead volume variance will equal the company's over- or underapplied overhead for a period.

For Corinne's, manufacturing overhead was overapplied by $280 for the quarter. Actual overhead cost was $39,720 and consisted of variable overhead of $23,720 (Exhibit 10-11) and fixed overhead of $16,000 (Exhibit 10-13). Applied overhead was $40,000 and consisted of variable overhead of $24,000 (Exhibit 10-11) and fixed overhead of $16,000 (Exhibit 10-13). The $280 difference is the sum of Corinne's $1,480 favorable variable overhead spending variance, $1,200 unfavorable variable overhead efficiency variance, $1,000 unfavorable fixed overhead spending variance, and $1,000 fixed overhead volume variance.

The fixed overhead volume variance generally should not be interpreted as favorable or unfavorable and should not be interpreted as a measure of over- or underutilization of facilities. This can be particularly problematic when the applied overhead is smaller than the budgeted amount (when a company produces fewer products than budgeted). Companies may reduce production for a number of reasons, including reduced demand for products, temporary material or labor shortages, and so on.

A summary table of the variances discussed in this chapter with references and formulas is shown in Exhibit 10-14.

> **KEY CONCEPT**
>
> *The fixed overhead volume variance should not be interpreted as favorable or unfavorable or as a measure of the efficient utilization of facilities.*

Exhibit 10-14 Summary of Variances

Variance	Reference	Formula
Sales Volume Variance	Exhibit 10-3; Page 342	(Actual - Budgeted Sales Volume) × (Budgeted Contribution Margin Per Unit)
Flexible Budget Variance	Exhibit 10-4; Page 342	Flexible Budget − Actual Results
Sales Price Variance	Page 343	(Actual - Expected Sales Price) × Actual Volume
Direct Material Price Variance	Exhibit 10-8; Page 346	Actual Quantity × (Actual Price − Standard Price)
Direct Material Usage Variance	Exhibit 10-8; Page 346	Standard Price × (Actual Quantity − Standard Quantity)
Direct Labor Rate Variance	Exhibit 10-10; Page 348	Actual Hours × (Actual Rate − Standard Rate)
Direct Labor Efficiency Variance	Exhibit 10-10; Page 348	Standard Rate × (Actual Hours − Standard Hours)
Variable Overhead Spending Variance	Exhibit 10-11; Page 349	Actual Overhead − (Actual Hours × Standard Variable Rate)
Variable Overhead Efficiency Variance	Exhibit 10-11; Page 349	Standard Variable Rate × (Actual Hours − Standard Hours)
Fixed Overhead Spending Variance	Exhibit 10-13; Page 350	Actual Fixed Overhead − Budgeted Fixed Overhead
Fixed Overhead Volume Variance	Exhibit 10-13; Page 350	Budgeted Fixed Overhead − Applied Overhead

Overhead Variance Analysis Using Activity-Based Costing

Objective 9
Compute overhead spending and efficiency variances in an ABC environment

The advantages of variance analysis for overhead costs are enhanced in companies using activity-based costing. Because ABC systems break down overhead into multiple cost pools associated with activities (with a cost driver for each), companies that employ ABC can analyze price and usage variances for each activity making up the total overhead variance. Just as the use of ABC systems enhances the quality of information available for decision making, analyzing variances by activity has a similar effect.

Corinne's flexible budget for variable overhead was $24,000, whereas the flexible budget for fixed overhead was $15,000. When Corinne's analyzes this overhead using ABC, the $39,000 of budgeted overhead is traced to six activities—material handling, setting up machinery, assembly, finishing, maintenance, and inspections. The costs associated with each activity and their respective cost drivers are shown in Exhibit 10-15.

The standard activity rate is simply the predetermined overhead rate for each activity. It is found by dividing the estimated overhead for each activity by the estimated activity level of the cost driver. Once the actual cost associated with each activity and the actual volume of cost driver associated with each activity are known (see Exhibit 10-16), a spending variance

> **KEY CONCEPT**
>
> *The advantages of variance analysis for overhead costs are enhanced in companies using activity-based costing (ABC).*

Exhibit 10-15: Corinne's Country Rockers Activity-Based Costing Flexible Budget

Activity	Flexible Budget Amount	Cost Driver	Standard Quantity	Standard Activity Rate
Material handling	$ 6,000	Number of moves	200	$ 30 per move
Setting up machinery	4,000	Number of setups	80	50 per setup
Assembly	14,000	Number of assembly (labor) hours	6,000	2.33 per assembly hour
Finishing	4,800	Number of finishing (labor) hours	2,000	2.40 per finishing hour
Maintenance	4,800	Number of maintenance hours	160	30 per maintenance hour
Inspections	5,400	Number of inspections	2,400	2.25 per inspection
Total	$39,000			

Exhibit 10-16: Corinne's Country Rockers Actual Overhead Costs

Activity	Actual Quantity	Actual Activity Rate	Actual Cost
Material handling	205 moves	$30.244 per move	$ 6,200
Setting up machinery	90 setups	$ 46.11 per setup	$ 4,150
Assembly	6,300 assembly hours	$2.2103 per assembly hour	$13,925
Finishing	2,100 finishing hours	$ 2.274 per finishing hour	$ 4,775
Maintenance	150 maintenance hours	$34.133 per maintenance hour	$ 5,120
Inspections	2,440 inspections	$2.2746 per inspection	$ 5,550

and efficiency variance can be computed. The detailed calculations of variances for each of the six activities identified at Corinne's Country Rockers are shown in Exhibit 10-17.

Although the preceding example is very simple, the ABC flexible overhead budget with variance analysis provides a wealth of information for managerial decision making. Although the total overhead variance is only $720, the detailed analysis shows us that the efficiency variances are almost all unfavorable. In all cases (except maintenance), Corinne's used more of the relevant cost driver than budgeted. On the other hand, the spending variances include an even number of favorable and unfavorable variances. Spending on machine setups, assembly, and finishing was favorable, whereas spending related to material handling, maintenance, and inspections was unfavorable. As always, Corinne's should pay special attention to any possible interactions between the variances.

Selling and Administrative Expense Variance

As shown in the flexible budget variance calculation in Exhibit 10-4, Corinne's had an $800 unfavorable variance for variable selling and administrative costs and a $2,000 favorable variance for fixed selling and administrative costs. Variable selling and administrative costs include such things as commissions on sales, advertising brochures that are sent out with each chair purchased, administrative time to process each sale, and so on. Fixed selling and administrative costs

Exhibit 10-17: Corinne's Country Rockers Spending Variances and Efficiency Variances

Activity	Actual Cost	Actual Quantity × Standard Activity Rate	Standard Quantity × Standard Activity Rate	Spending Variance	Efficiency Variance	Total Variance
Material handling	$ 6,200	205 × $ 30 = $ 6,150	200 × $ 30 = $ 6,000	$ 150 U	$ 50 U	$200 U
Setting up machinery	4,150	90 × $ 50 = $ 4,500	80 × $ 50 = $ 4,000	500 U	350 F	150 U
Assembly	13,925	6,300 × $2.33 = $14,679	6,000 × $2.33 = $14,000	679 U	754 F	75 F
Finishing	4,775	2,100 × $2.40 = $ 5,040	2,000 × $2.40 = $ 4,800	240 U	265 F	25 F
Maintenance	5,120	150 × $ 30 = $ 4,500	160 × $ 30 = $ 4,800	300 F	620 U	320 U
Inspections	5,550	2,440 × $2.25 = $ 5,490	2,400 × $2.25 = $ 5,400	90 U	60 U	150 U
Totals	$39,720	$40,359	$39,000	$1,359 U	$639 F	$720 U

include the salaries of the sales manager and personnel manager and such facility costs as rent and insurance. Like overhead variances, selling and administrative variances are difficult to analyze and to interpret. However, companies utilizing ABC systems may have sufficient detail to analyze portions of this variance in more detail. For example, Corinne's is interested in reducing the costs associated with processing mail-order sales made by telephone and has established a quantity standard for the time spent to process each call (6 minutes). Likewise, it has established a price standard for this activity, consisting of the salary costs incurred by sales representatives handling the call ($1 per call based on a salary of $10 per hour) plus the direct costs of the toll-free line ($0.60 at $0.10 per minute). The actual costs incurred in handling sales calls can then be compared to the flexible budget amount, and price and usage variances can be calculated.

Interpreting and Using Variance Analysis

Objective 10
Analyze important considerations in using and interpreting variances, including the concept of management by exception

Although standard costs and variance analysis can be useful to managers attempting to diagnose organizational performance, they are most effective in stable companies with mature production environments characterized by a heavy reliance on direct labor. On the other hand, they may not be much help in rapidly changing companies, companies with flexible manufacturing systems (in which more than one product is manufactured on an assembly line), companies with heavily automated manufacturing processes, or companies that emphasize continuous improvement and reducing non-value-added activities in the production process. Although variance analysis may still be of value as a summary report for top management, it has a number of drawbacks when used in many modern manufacturing environments:

1. The information from variance analysis is likely to be too aggregated for operating managers to use. To be useful, material variances may need to be broken down into detail by specific product lines and even batches of product, whereas labor variances may need to be calculated for specific manufacturing cells.

2. The information from variance analysis is not timely enough to be useful to managers. As product life cycles are reduced, timely reporting is even more critical than in the past.

3. Traditional variance analysis of variable and fixed overhead provides little useful information for managers.

> **KEY CONCEPT**
>
> *Variance analysis is most effective in stable companies with mature production environments and has a number of drawbacks when used in many modern manufacturing environments.*

4. Traditional variance analysis focuses on cost control instead of product quality, customer service, delivery time, and other nonfinancial measures of performance. These measures are discussed in more detail in Chapter 12.

Even in traditional and stable manufacturing environments, the effective use of variance analysis for control and performance purposes requires the proper application of "management by exception" and careful interpretation of variances (including understanding their causes).

Management by Exception

The proper application of "management by exception" requires an understanding that it is neither necessary nor desirable to investigate all variances. If you think about it, it is likely that actual costs will always deviate from budgeted costs to some extent. Utility prices are affected by the weather, and prices of raw materials can change suddenly owing to shortages, surpluses, and new sources of competing products. Unexpected machine breakdowns affect the amount of time workers spend manufacturing products. Even fixed costs can differ from budgeted costs when rent is unexpectedly increased, new equipment is purchased, or insurance rates go up. Because of these random fluctuations, managers should generally investigate variances (favorable or unfavorable) that are material in amount and outside a normal acceptable range. Traditionally, materiality thresholds were often based on absolute size (investigate everything over $1,000) or relative size (investigate everything over 10 percent of the budgeted amount) or some combination of the two. Today, companies are more likely to use statistical techniques and to investigate variances that fall outside a "normal" range of fluctuations. For example, companies may investigate variances that are more than two standard deviations from the mean. Regardless of materiality, trends in variances might also warrant investigation. For example, continually occurring and increasing material price variances might be vitally important to a restaurant regardless of their absolute size.

Interpreting Favorable and Unfavorable Variances

> **KEY CONCEPT**
>
> *Favorable and unfavorable variances should not necessarily be interpreted as good or bad.*

Although we have referred to variances as favorable or unfavorable, these designations should not necessarily be interpreted as good or bad. In order to interpret variances, the underlying cause must be determined. The decision-making model, introduced in Chapter 1, aids in the proper use and interpretation of variances and their causes. The first step in making good decisions requires an accurate definition of the problem. This definition requires input from managers across all functional areas of a company.

For example, consider a manager who is investigating an unfavorable direct labor efficiency variance. Although on the surface, the unfavorable variance would seem to indicate a problem in worker efficiency, the real problem may be the combination of a workforce that is fixed in the short run and a lack of sufficient orders to keep workers busy. Companies may be reluctant to lay off workers for short periods of time when demand is unexpectedly reduced or other production problems make it difficult to keep them fully employed. It may be costly to rehire workers or they may find other jobs. As discussed elsewhere, this often makes direct labor a fixed cost in the short run.

Likewise, an unfavorable direct material usage variance generally points to a problem in production. However, further analysis might reveal that usage was high because of an unusual number of defective parts and that the large number of defective parts was a result of the purchasing manager buying materials of inferior quality. This problem becomes one of the purchasing manager buying inferior materials, not the production manager using excessive amounts of material. Note that in this case, even though the purchasing manager caused the problem, the material price variance would likely be favorable.

Identifying management's objectives is vitally important in deciding how to use and interpret variances. If the problem is one of insufficient orders and management is truly concerned about controlling costs, management must be careful not to use the direct labor efficiency variance for purposes of motivating and controlling the production supervisor. Although this conclusion may seem counterintuitive, put yourself in the shoes of the production supervisor. The production supervisor really has two options—either continue producing products to keep workers busy or have an unfavorable labor efficiency variance. But keeping workers busy has definite drawbacks. For example, building inventory levels is costly. Holding high levels of inventory results in additional costs of storage and insurance and can result in increased waste from theft and obsolescence.

In other situations, understanding whether the primary objective of management is cost control or producing a high-quality product is important. If cost control is paramount, an unfavorable direct material price variance might well be considered "bad"; however, if management's objective is to provide a high-quality product, an unfavorable material price variance might be acceptable if the higher price is necessary to obtain high quality materials.

Once managers are sure of the root cause(s) of a variance and have considered their own objectives in utilizing variance analysis, they can intelligently consider options available to deal with the problem. For example, if management finds that an unfavorable direct labor efficiency variance is caused by a lack of customer orders and a workforce that is "fixed" in the short run, options may include accepting special orders, utilizing the workers in other areas, utilizing the time to train workers or to repair machinery, and so on.

Hitting the Bottom Line.

HOW DOES THAT COKE TASTE?

For Coca-Cola, controlling the amount and mix of ingredients into bottles and cans of Coca-Cola products is of critical importance. In the past, bottling facilities routinely performed quality tests every 20 minutes, but technology has now made it possible to monitor the levels of ingredients and temperature every 10 seconds. This type of testing allows the company to perform real-time variance analysis that can then be used to resolve problems or temporarily halt production. The company reports that the new technology resulted in syrup savings averaging .2 percent and that the expected savings would pay for the investment in the new equipment within 15 months (*Beverage World*, Volume 118, 75).

Behavioral Considerations

As you have seen throughout this chapter, the use of standard costs and variance analysis, although useful for control and performance evaluation, can also cause dysfunctional behavior among employees and management. The use of ideal standards can cause resentment among managers when continually faced with "unfavorable" variances. Some companies tie compensation to performance that is at least partly measured by variances. Even though this is likely to make managers aware of costs, it may have undesirable side effects. Too much emphasis on the direct material usage variance can cause production managers to increase production so as to appear efficient, causing inventories to rise above acceptable levels. By focusing on variances, a purchasing manager may be encouraged to purchase inferior products to make his or her performance appear better, even though the manager knows that the poor-quality material will cause problems in the production area. It is important to understand the root causes of variances and to assign responsibility accordingly. It is also important to remember that variance analysis provides just one measure of performance. The uses of other financial and nonfinancial measures of performance are discussed in Chapters 11 and 12.

Summary of Key Concepts

- The purpose of the control function in management is to make sure that the goals of the organization are being attained. (p. 338)

- Management by exception is the key to effective variance analysis and involves taking action only when actual and planned results differ significantly. (p. 338)

- The variable overhead efficiency variance does not measure the efficient use of overhead but rather the efficient use of the cost driver, or overhead allocation base, used in the flexible budget. (p. 348)

- The fixed overhead volume variance should not be interpreted as favorable or unfavorable or as a measure of the efficient utilization of facilities. (p. 351)

- The advantages of variance analysis for overhead costs are enhanced in companies using activity-based costing (ABC). (p. 351)

- Variance analysis is most effective in stable companies with mature production environments and has a number of drawbacks when used in many modern manufacturing environments. (p. 354)

- "Favorable" and "unfavorable" designations for variances do not always refer to "good" and "bad." (p. 354)

Key Definitions

Control Involves the motivation and monitoring of employees and the evaluation of people and other resources used in the operations of the organization (p. 338)

Variance analysis Allows managers to see whether sales, production, and manufacturing costs are higher or lower than planned and, more important, *why* actual sales, production, and costs differ from budget (p. 338)

Management by exception The process of taking action only when actual results deviate significantly from planned results (p. 338)

Standard cost A budget for a single unit of product or service (p. 338)

Standard quantity The budgeted amount of material, labor, or overhead for each product (p. 338)

Standard price The budgeted price of the material, labor, or overhead for each unit (p. 338)

Task analysis A method of setting standards that also examines the production process in detail to determine what it should cost to produce a product (p. 339)

Ideal standard A standard that is attained only when near-perfect conditions are present (p. 339)

Practical standard A standard that should be attained under normal, efficient operating conditions (p. 339)

Sales volume variance The difference between the actual sales volume and the budgeted sales volume times the budgeted contribution margin (p. 341)

Flexible budget variance The difference between the flexible budget operating income and actual operating income (p. 342)

Sales price variance Computed by comparing the actual sales price to the flexible budget sales price times the actual sales volume (p. 343)

Price variance The difference between the actual price and the standard price times the actual volume purchased (p. 345)

Usage variance The difference between the actual quantity and the standard quantity times the standard price (p. 345)

Budget variance The difference between the amount of fixed overhead actually incurred and the flexible budget amount; also known as the spending variance (p. 350)

Volume variance The difference between the flexible budget and the fixed overhead applied to a product (p. 350)

Multiple Choice

1. A standard cost is:
   a. not determinable in most manufacturing environments.
   b. equivalent to the budget for a single unit of a product or service.
   c. equivalent to the budget for total production of a batch of products.
   d. none of the above.

2. What causes differences between flexible and static budgets?
   a. Differences in budgeted and actual sales
   b. Difference in budgeted and actual production
   c. Both A and B
   d. Neither A nor B

3. Last year, Taquita Corporation estimated harvesting (i.e., production) and sales of 7,000 banana treats. The company actually produced and sold 6,000 treats. Each treat has a standard stipulating 1.4 pounds of ingredients at a budgeted cost of $1.50 per pound and 3 hours of mixing time at a cost of $10.50 per hour. The treats sell for $30 each. Actual costs for the production of 6,000 treats were $12,900 for ingredients (8,600 pounds at $1.50 per pound) and $178,350 for labor (17,400 hours at $10.25 per hour). What is Taquita's income/(loss) based on a flexible budget?
   a. ($11,250)
   b. $11,250
   c. $21,600
   d. ($21,600)

4. Refer to the information in question 3 above. What is Taquita's flexible budget variance?
   a. $10,350 U
   b. $10,950 F
   c. $10,350 F
   d. $10,950 U

5. Last year, Bandana Corporation budgeted for production and sales of 11,000 bandanas. The company produced and sold 10,500 bandanas. Each bandana has a standard requiring 2 feet of material at a budgeted cost of $1.50 per foot and 30 minutes of sewing time at a cost of $0.30 per minute. The bandanas sell for $14.75. Actual costs for the production of 10,500 bandanas were $33,880 for materials (22,000 feet at $1.54 per foot) and $92,800 for labor (320,000 minutes at $0.29 per minute). What was Bandana's sales volume variance?
   a. $1,695
   b. $1,345
   c. $1,375
   d. $1,595

6. Refer to the information in question 5 above. Bandana's actual revenue from bandana sales was $154,875. What was Bandana's sales price variance?
   a. $1,950 F
   b. $1,950 U
   c. $ 0
   d. It cannot be determined from the information provided.

7. Refer to the information in question 5 above. What was Bandana's direct material price variance?
   a. $1,500 F
   b. $1,500 U
   c. $880 F
   d. $880 U

8. Refer to the information in question 5 above. What was Bandana's direct material usage variance?
   a. $1,500 F
   b. $1,500 U
   c. $880 F
   d. $880 U

9. Refer to the information in question 5 above. What was Bandana's direct labor rate variance?
   a. $1,500 F
   b. $1,500 U
   c. $3,200 F
   d. $3,200 U

10. Refer to the information in question 5 above. What was Bandana's direct labor efficiency variance?
    a. $1,500 F
    b. $1,500 U
    c. $3,200 F
    d. $3,200 U

11. Hedrick Corporation incurred actual variable overhead expenses of $33,750 last year for production of 6,000 units. Variable overhead is applied at a rate of $3.00 per direct labor hour and 2 direct labor hours are budgeted for each unit. The company used 11,990 direct labor hours for production. What was Hedrick's variable overhead spending variance?
    a. $2,250 F
    b. $2,220 F
    c. $2,250 U
    d. $2,220 U

12. Refer to the information in question 11 above. What was Hedrick's variable overhead efficiency variance?
    a. $250 F
    b. $250 U
    c. $30 U
    d. $30 F

13. Fixed overhead variances consist of:
    a. a spending variance and an efficiency variance.
    b. a spending variance and a standard variance.
    c. a spending variance and a volume variance.
    d. an efficiency variance and a standard variance.

14. Which of the following statements about activity-based costing (ABC) and variance analysis is true?
    a. Advantages of variance analysis for overhead costs are enhanced in companies using ABC.
    b. Because ABC systems break down overhead into multiple cost pools associated with activities (with a cost driver for each), companies that use ABC can analyze price and usage variances for each activity making up the total overhead variance.
    c. Just as the use of ABC systems enhances the quality of information available for decision making, analyzing variances by activity has a similar effect.
    d. All of the above.

15. The proper application of "management by exception":
    a. requires managers to investigate all variances.
    b. suggests that managers should generally investigate only those variances that are material in amount and outside a normal acceptable range.
    c. prohibits the use of materiality thresholds to trigger investigations of variances.
    d. is effective only for direct material and labor variances.

Concept Questions

16. *(Objective 1)* Discuss ideal versus practical standards and how they might affect employee behavior.
17. *(Objective 2)* What is the primary difference between a static budget and a flexible budget?
18. *(Objective 2)* Discuss the value of a flexible budget to management decision making.
19. *(Objective 3)* What are some of the possible causes of a sales volume variance?
20. *(Objective 4)* Which area of management would normally be responsible for sales price variances? Why?
21. *(Objective 5, 6, 7)* What is the focus of a usage variance?
22. *(Objective 6)* What are some possible causes for an unfavorable direct labor efficiency variance?
23. *(Objective 7)* What does a variable overhead efficiency variance tell management?
24. *(Objective 8)* The predetermined fixed overhead application rate is a function of a predetermined "normal" activity level. If standard hours allowed for good output are equal to this predetermined activity level for a given period, what will the volume variance be?
25. *(Objective 10)* Discuss the advantages and disadvantages of using "management by exception" techniques.

Exercises

26. Review the following incomplete statements about standard costing and related issues.
    a. A(n) _____ standard allows for normal and efficient operations and takes into consideration typical production problems.
    b. A budget for a single unit of a product is referred to as a _____.
    c. Managers must compare actual and budgeted results to control operations. This comparison process is generally called _____.
    d. The _____ indicates how much a company should generally pay for the material, labor, or overhead for a single unit of product.
    e. _____ is often the key to effective variance analysis.

    Required

    Complete the above incomplete statements with the correct term from the list of terms provided (note that not all terms will be used): *variance analysis, ideal standard, practical standard, standard cost, standard price, management by exception,* and *task analysis*.

27. A direct marketing company expects to incur fixed expenses of $50,000 per month and variable costs of $4 per sales call and $2 per telephone call in generating sales of $75,000. During the month, the sales force made 100 sales calls and 500 telephone calls and generated sales of $70,000. Actual costs incurred included $52,000 for fixed costs and $1,200 for variable costs.

    Required

    Prepare a flexible budget for the direct marketing company.

    ✓ Flexible budget income: $23,600

28. Refer to the information in question 27 above.

    Required

    Compute the flexible budget variance for the direct marketing company.

    ✓ Actual income: $16,800

LO 2 ✓ Sales revenue: $1,250

29. Gordon knits wool caps for sale at the local ski resorts. He prepared the following budget for the production and sale of 150 wool caps. Unfortunately, Gordon fell ill with a bad case of the flu and was able to make and sell only 125 wool caps.

Sales revenue	$1,500.00
Variable costs:	
Direct material (yarn)	375.00
Direct labor	750.00
Commission to resort	112.50
Fixed costs	75.00
Net income	$ 187.50

Required

Prepare a flexible budget for Gordon based on the production and sale of 125 wool caps.

LO 4

30. The Quick Brick Shop had an unfavorable sales price variance of $150. The budgeted selling price was $10 per unit and 50 bricks were sold.

Required

What was the actual selling price of Quick Brick's bricks?

LO 5 ✓ Material price variance: $49.50 F

31. Wheeler Corporation produces and sells special eyeglass straps for sporting enthusiasts. In 2005, the company budgeted for production and sales of 1,200 straps. However, the company produced and sold just 1,100 straps. Each strap has a standard requiring 1 foot of material at a budgeted cost of $1.50 per foot and 2 hours of assembly time at a cost of $12 per hour. Actual costs for the production of 1,100 items were $1,435.50 for materials (990 feet at $1.45 per foot) and $29,161 for labor (2,420 hours at $12.05 per hour).

Required

A. Calculate the direct materials price variance.
B. Calculate the direct materials usage variance.

LO 6

32. Refer to the information in question 31 above.

Required

A. Calculate the direct labor rate variance.
B. Calculate the direct labor efficiency variance.

LO 5 ✓ Material usage variance: $500 U

33. The Woods Enterprises prepared the following standard costs for the production of one stuffed pooh:

Direct materials	1.5 pounds of stuffing @ $2 per lb
Direct labor	2 hours of assembly @ $15 per hr

Actual production costs for the production of 1,000 stuffed poohs required 1,750 pounds of stuffing at a cost of $1.95 per pound and 1,950 labor hours at $15.25 per hour.

Required

A. Calculate the direct materials price variance.
B. Calculate the direct materials usage variance.

LO 6 ✓ Labor rate variance: $487.50 U

34. Refer to the information in question 33 above.

Required

A. Calculate the direct labor rate variance.
B. Calculate the direct labor efficiency variance.

35. Bittermen Company, which uses standard costing, reported the following overhead information for the last quarter of the year:

Actual overhead incurred:	
Fixed	$ 10,500
Variable	66,810
Budgeted fixed overhead	11,000
Variable-overhead rate per direct labor hour	5.00
Standard hours allowed for actual production	13,100
Actual labor hours used	13,000

Required

A. What is the variable overhead spending variance?
B. What is the variable overhead efficiency variance?

✓ Spending variance: $1,810 U

36. Simon Enterprises applies variable overhead at a rate of $1.50 per direct labor hour and fixed overhead at a rate of $1.75 per direct labor hour. The company budgets two direct labor hours for each of the 5,900 units that are scheduled for production. Simon incurred actual variable overhead totaling $18,750 and actual fixed overhead totaling $21,500 last year for the production of 6,000 units. In addition, 11,800 direct labor hours were actually incurred.

Required

A. Calculate the variable overhead efficiency variance.
B. Calculate the variable overhead spending variance.

✓ Efficiency variance: $300 F

37. Refer to the information in question 36 above.

Required

A. Calculate the fixed overhead volume variance.
B. Calculate the fixed overhead spending variance.

38. Hennings Travel Company specializes in the production of travel items (e.g., clocks, personal care kits, etc.). The following data were prepared so that a variance analysis could be performed.

Forecast Data (expected capacity)

Direct labor hours	40,000
Estimated overhead:	
Fixed	$16,000
Variable	$30,000

Actual Results

Direct labor hours	37,200
Overhead:	
Fixed	$16,120
Variable	$28,060

The number of standard hours allowed for actual production was 37,000 hours.

✓ Spending variance: $160 U

Required

A. Calculate the variable overhead spending variance.
B. Calculate the variable overhead efficiency variance.

39. Refer to the information in question 38 above.

Required

A. Calculate the fixed overhead volume variance.
B. Calculate the fixed overhead spending variance.

40. Variance analysis allows managers to compare budgeted and actual performance so that necessary corrective steps can be taken. Frequently, the analysis helps managers identify operational inefficiencies and other areas that can be improved. Nonetheless, variance analysis does have several potential drawbacks.

Required

Describe the various drawbacks of variance analysis.

Problems

41. Petty Petroleum, Inc. uses various chemicals to manufacture its products. Variance data for last month for the three primary chemicals used in production are shown below (F indicates a favorable variance; U indicates an unfavorable variance):

	X42	AY8	9BZ
Material price variance	$ 84,000 F	$ 50,000 F	$ 42,000 U
Material usage variance	80,000 U	60,000 U	96,000 U
Total materials variance (net)	$ 4,000 F	$ 10,000 U	$138,000 U
Products requiring this chemical	200,000	220,000	250,000

The standard required one pound of chemical for each product requiring the specific chemical. Because of falling prices in the chemical industry, Petty Petroleum generally paid less for chemicals last month than in previous months. Specifically, the average price paid was $0.40 per pound less than standard for chemical X42; it was $0.20 less for chemical AY8; and it was $0.14 greater for chemical 9BZ. All of the chemicals purchased last month were also used during the month.

Required

A. For chemical X42, calculate the number of pounds of material purchased, the standard cost per pound of material, and the total standard material cost.
B. For chemical AY8, calculate the number of pounds of material purchased, the standard cost per pound of material, and the total standard material cost.
C. For chemical 9BZ, calculate the number of pounds of material purchased, the standard cost per pound of material, and the total standard material cost.

42. Fort Worth Company is a printer and bindery of specialized booklets and pamphlets. Last year the company's sales manager estimated sales to be 10,000 combined booklets and pamphlets. The sales manager also estimated that the items would retail for approximately $10 each. Various production costs including direct and indirect material, direct and indirect labor, and variable overhead were estimated to total $50,000, while fixed costs were estimated to be $20,000.

During the year, Fort Worth's unit sales equaled its production of 12,000 units. Because of changing market conditions, competition specifically, the average selling price fell to just $9.50 per unit. There were increased variable costs as well that resulted in average per unit variable costs of $6. At the end of the year, the company's controller accumulated fixed costs and found them to be $21,000.

Required

Prepare a report to show the difference between the actual contribution margin and the budgeted contribution margin per the static budget. Then, compare the actual contribution margin and the budgeted contribution margin per the flexible budget.

43. Byrd Company is a manufacturer affiliated with the furniture industry. The company produces a wide variety of "hardware" component parts. Product examples include drawer slides, hinges, door pulls and handles, springs, and locks. Dent Tripoli is the company's new chief financial officer. Dent is very concerned with providing the company's president and board of directors with accurate financial reports. He is concerned that the company's use of static budgeting does not convey a fair presentation of the company's performance. The following contribution margin format income statement reports the results of Byrd Company's operations for the last quarter of 2005.

LO 2 3 4

✓ Sales price variance: $40,000 F

Sales Revenues (400,000 units)		$2,440,000
Variable Costs		
Manufacturing	$1,060,000	
Marketing and administrative	748,000	1,808,000
Contribution margin		$ 632,000
Fixed Costs		
Manufacturing	$ 400,000	
Marketing and administrative	200,000	600,000
Operating profit		$ 32,000

Byrd's 2005 budgets were based on production and sales of 375,000 units at an average selling price of $6. At that volume, variable manufacturing costs were budgeted to be $2.50 per unit, and variable marketing and administrative costs were budgeted to be $2.00 each. Had the company's actual performance equaled the budgeted performance, Byrd would have reported operating profit of $62,500.

Required

A. Based on the information provided in the problem, recreate Byrd's 2005 static budget. Be sure to include a comparison between the static budget and the actual results for the year.
B. Based on the information provided in the problem, prepare a flexible budget for Byrd for 2005. Be sure to include a comparison between the flexible budget and the actual results that reports the flexible budget variance.
C. Calculate Byrd's sales price variance for 2005. Is the variance favorable or unfavorable?
D. Calculate Byrd's sales volume variance for 2005.

44. Timmer Bachman founded the Bachman Corporation over 25 years ago. The company's genesis was the unique climbing apparatus developed by Timmer, an avid mountaineer. Bachman Corporation has continued to produce that first product, but it has now diversified into other outdoor activity equipment as well. In fact, the vast majority of the company's revenues are now accounted for by non-climbing product sales. Timmer is considering whether his company should continue producing and selling some of its oldest products, all of which relate to mountain climbing.

LO 3 4 5 6

✓ Sales volume variance: $4,720 F

To begin his decision-making process, Timmer asked the company's controller, Marin Hennesy, to accumulate data on the original locking carabiner that set the company on its way. Accordingly, Marin accumulated the following data for last year:

Budgeted production and sales: 5,000 carabiners.

Actual production and sales: 6,000 carabiners.

The standard for a carabiner requires 1.5 ounces of material at a budgeted cost of $1.52 per ounce and 2 hours of assembly and testing time at a cost of $12.50 per hour.

The carabiner sells for $32 each.

Actual production costs for the 6,000 carabiners totaled $12,900 for 8,600 ounces of materials and $161,700 for 13,200 labor hours.

Required

A. What was the budgeted contribution margin per carabiner?
B. What was the actual contribution margin per carabiner?
C. What was Bachman's sales volume variance for the year?
D. What was Bachman's flexible budget variance?
E. What was Bachman's direct material price variance?
F. What was Bachman's direct material usage variance?
G. What was Bachman's direct labor rate variance?
H. What was Bachman's direct labor efficiency variance?
I. What would the sales price variance be if each carabiner sold for $33?
J. Based on the available information, should Bachman continue making the carabiner?

45. Turner Corporation produces overdrive transmission parts for several small specialty automobile companies. Prior to founding the company, Benson Turner, the company's president, had an illustrious stock car racing career. After several serious injuries, Benson's family convinced him that it was time to retire from the sport and pursue a calmer and safer line of work.

The company has been operating for just over 5 years and is beginning to show signs of significant growth. Benson is a planner and he wants to get a handle on his manufacturing operations before the company's growth becomes his primary preoccupation. The company's plant manager and controller met last week to pull together information that they could present to Benson. While the company produces over 150 different parts, the two of them thought that accumulating detailed data on one single typical part would be sufficient for the quickly called meeting. As a consequence, the following data were captured for the last 12 months:

Budgeted production and sales: 12,000 parts.

Actual production and sales: 11,000 parts.

Each part has a standard requiring 1 pound of material at a budgeted cost of $1.50 per pound.

Each part has a standard requiring 20 minutes of assembly time at a cost of $0.25 per minute.

Average wholesale price for each part is $8.

Actual costs for the production of 11,000 parts were $17,094 for 11,100 pounds of material.

Actual labor costs were $58,080 for 242,000 minutes of labor time.

Required

A. What was the budgeted contribution margin per part?
B. What was the actual contribution margin per part?
C. What was Turner's sales volume variance?
D. What was Turner's flexible budget variance?
E. What was Turner's direct material price variance?
F. What was Turner's direct material usage variance?
G. What was Turner's labor rate variance?
H. What was Turner's labor efficiency variance?

LO 3 5 6

✓ Actual contribution margin: $1.166 per part

46. Sparky Electric produces a special type of grounded outlet. The outlets are used in areas where water is likely to be present such as kitchens, bathrooms, outdoor work areas, porches, pool sides, workshops, and so forth. Sparky Electric has a policy that it maintains as little inventory of Materials A and B as possible. For the quarter included in this analysis, there was no beginning or ending inventory of either material. Selected standard cost information is provided below:

✓ Units produced: 3,200

Cost Standards

Material A	2 pounds at $6.00 per pound	$12.00
Material B	3 gallons at $3.00 per gallon	9.00
Labor	4 hours at $3.20 per hour	12.80
Total standard unit cost		$33.80

The performance report for the third quarter of 2005 appears as follows (F indicates a favorable variance; U indicates an unfavorable variance):

Comparison of Actual and Standard

	Actual	Standard	Total Variance
Material A	$ 37,515	$38,400	$ 885 F
Material B	30,195	28,800	1,395 U
Labor	39,525	40,960	1,435 F

Analysis of Variance

	Usage	Price/Rate	Total Variance
Material A	$ 1,500 F	$ 615 U	$ 885 F
Material B	900 U	495 U	1,395 U
Labor	160 F	1,275 F	1,435 F

Required

A. How many units were produced during the quarter?
B. How many pounds of Material A were used during the quarter?
C. What was the actual price paid per pound for Material A during the quarter?
D. How many gallons of Material B were purchased during the quarter?
E. What was the actual price paid per gallon for Material B during the quarter?
F. How many actual labor hours were used during the quarter?
G. What was the actual wage rate per hour during the quarter?

47. Small Tykes World Company mass produces chairs for children. The chairs can be purchased in a variety of colors, but only one basic design. The chairs are wildly popular, especially with young, highly educated parents. The design is the key to the company's success and there seems to be no end to the demand for Small Tykes' products. The following data were extracted from the company's standard cost sheet:

✓ Material price variance: $9,250 F

Plastic	10 pounds at $4.50 per pound
Molding	3 feet at $3.00 per foot
Direct labor	4 hours at $6.00 per hour
Variable overhead	$3 per direct labor hour
Fixed overhead	$55,000 per period

Transactions during the month of June were:

Small Tykes purchased plastic at $4.45 per pound and issued 185,000 pounds to production.

Small Tykes purchased molding at $3.10 per foot and issued 50,000 feet to production.

The direct labor payroll totaled $435,000 for 72,500 hours.

Total overhead costs were $275,000, including $221,125 of variable overhead.

Small Tykes produced 18,000 chairs during the month.

Required

A. Calculate all material, labor, variable overhead, and fixed overhead variances.
B. Interpret the material and labor variances. What do they indicate about the company's performance?
C. Based on your response to question B, what areas need to be investigated?
D. How could the company control or better manage its operations?
E. In your opinion, what are the best options? Why?

LO 7 8

✓ Volume variance: $600

48. Surfs Up manufactures surf boards on the Big Island in Hawaii. The company's founder and world famous surfer, Danny Kehono, has an accounting degree from Upper Island State University. He understands the importance of standards for production control and planning. The following standard costing data are available for the current period:

Actual fixed overhead	$ 10,500
Actual variable overhead	66,810
Budgeted fixed overhead	11,000
Variable overhead rate per labor hour	5.00
Fixed overhead rate per labor hour	0.80
Standard hours allowed for actual production	13,100
Actual labor hours used	13,000

Required

A. Calculate the variable overhead spending variance.
B. Calculate the variable overhead efficiency variance.
C. Calculate the fixed overhead spending variance.
D. Calculate the fixed overhead volume variance.

LO 1 7 8

✓ VOH Spending variance: $22,000 U

49. Franklin Glass Works' production budget for the year ended November 30, 2005, was based on 200,000 units. Each unit requires two standard hours of labor for completion. Total overhead was budgeted at $900,000 for the year, and the fixed overhead rate was estimated to be $3 per unit. Both fixed and variable overhead are assigned to the product on the basis of direct labor hours. The actual data for the year ended November 30, 2005, are as follows:

Production in units	198,000
Labor hours	440,000
Variable overhead	$ 352,000
Fixed overhead	$ 575,000

Required

A. What are the total standard hours allowed for actual production for the year ended November 30, 2005?
B. What is Franklin's variable overhead efficiency variance?
C. What is Franklin's variable overhead spending variance?
D. What is Franklin's fixed overhead spending variance?
E. What is Franklin's fixed overhead volume variance?

50. Corinne's Country Rockers uses flexible budgeting. The company's budget for variable overhead is $24,000 and for fixed overhead is $15,000. When Corinne's analyzes this overhead using activity-based costing, the budgeted overhead of $39,000 is traced to six activities: material handling, machinery setup, assembly, finishing, maintenance, and inspections. The costs associated with each activity and their respective cost drivers are as follows:

✓ Assembly efficiency variance: $699 U

Activity	Flexible Budget Amount	Cost Driver	Budgeted Volume
Material handling	$ 6,000	Number of moves	200
Setting up machinery	4,000	Number of setups	80
Assembly	14,000	Number of labor hours	6,000
Finishing	4,800	Number of labor hours	2,000
Maintenance	4,800	Number of maintenance hours	160
Inspections	5,400	Number of inspections	2,400

The actual cost and total volume for each activity are as follows:

Activity	Cost	Volume
Material handling	$ 7,400	205 moves
Setting up machinery	4,375	90 setups
Assembly	14,500	6,300 labor hours
Finishing	6,010	2,100 labor hours
Maintenance	5,700	150 maintenance hours
Inspections	5,900	2,440 inspections

Required

A. Compute the overhead application rate for each activity. Put your answer in the format of an activity-based costing flexible budget.
B. Using the actual volume and cost, compute the spending variance, the efficiency variance, and the total variance for each activity.

Cases

51. Jan Dan, Inc. (JDI) is a specialty frozen food processor located in the southeastern United States. Since its founding in 1992, JDI has enjoyed a loyal local clientele that is willing to pay premium prices for the high-quality frozen foods it prepares from specialized recipes. In the past 2 years, the company has experienced rapid sales growth in its operating region and has had many inquiries about supplying its products on a national basis. To meet this growth, JDI expanded its processing capabilities,

which resulted in increased production and distribution costs. Moving on to the national scene has also caused JDI to encounter pricing pressure from competitors outside its region.

Because JDI wants to continue expanding, Nick Guice, the company's chief executive officer, has engaged a consulting firm to assist in determining its best course of action. The consulting firm concluded that premium pricing is sustainable in some areas, but if sales growth is to be achieved, JDI must make price concessions in some other areas. Also, to maintain profit margins, costs must be reduced and more tightly controlled. The consulting firm recommended the implementation of a standard cost system that would facilitate a flexible budgeting system to better accommodate the changes in demand that can be expected when serving an expanding market area.

Guice met with his management team and explained the consulting firm's recommendations. He then assigned the task of setting standards to his management team. After discussing the situation with their respective staffs, the management team met to review the matter.

Janie Morgan, purchasing manager, advised that meeting expanded production would necessitate obtaining basic food supplies from companies other than JDI's traditional sources. This would entail increased raw material and shipping costs and might result in lower-quality supplies. Consequently, these increased costs would need to be counterbalanced by reduced costs in the processing department if current cost levels are to be maintained or reduced.

Dan Walters, processing manager, suggested that the need to accelerate processing cycles to increase production, coupled with the possibility of receiving lower-grade supplies, can be expected to result in a poorer quality and a greater product rejection rate. Under these circumstances, per unit labor utilization cannot be maintained or increased, and forecasting future unit labor content becomes very difficult.

Corinne Kelly, production engineer, advised that if the equipment is not properly maintained and thoroughly cleaned at prescribed daily intervals, it can be anticipated that the quality and unique taste of the frozen food product will be affected. Kent Jackson, vice president of sales, stated that if quality cannot be maintained, JDI cannot expect to increase sales to the levels projected.

When Guice was apprised of the problems encountered by his management team, he advised them that if agreement could not be reached on appropriate standards he would arrange to have them set by the consulting firm, and everyone would have to live with the results.

Required

A. List the major advantages of using a standard cost system.
B. List disadvantages that can result from using a standard cost system.
C. Identify those who should participate in setting standards, and describe the benefits of their participation in the standard-setting process.
D. Explain the general features and characteristics associated with the introduction and operation of a standard cost system that make it an effective tool for cost control.
E. What could be the consequences if Nick Guice has the standards set by the consulting firm?
F. Explain what is meant by variance and variance analysis.
G. Discuss material variances and why they might occur at JDI.
H. Explain overhead variances in the context of this case. Include a discussion of variable and fixed overhead variances.

52. Ben Fun, Inc. manufactures video games. Market saturation and technological innovations have caused pricing pressures, which have resulted in declining profits. To stem the slide in profits until new products can be introduced, top management has turned its attention to both manufacturing economics and increased production. To realize these objectives, an incentive program has been developed to reward production managers who contribute to an increase in the number of units produced and effect cost reductions.

The production managers have responded to the pressure of improving manufacturing in several ways that have resulted in increased completed units over normal production levels. The video game machines are put together by the programming group (PG) and the graphics group (GG). To attain increased production levels, PG and GG groups commenced rejecting games that previously would have been tested and modified to meet manufacturing standards. Preventive maintenance on machines used in the production of these games has been postponed, with only emergency repair work being performed to keep production lines moving. This decision has been disconcerting to maintenance personnel who are concerned that this could result in serious breakdowns and unsafe operating conditions.

The more aggressive assembly group production supervisors have pressured maintenance personnel to attend to their machines at the expense of other groups. This has resulted in machine downtime in the PG and GG groups, which, when coupled with demands for accelerated delivery by the assembly group, has led to more frequent rejections and increased friction among departments.

Ben Fun operates under a standard cost system. The standard costs for video games are as follows:

✓ Material quantity variance: $0

Cost Item	Quantity	Cost	Total
Direct Materials			
CD	1	$ 20.00	$ 20.00
Package	1	15.00	15.00
Labels	2	1.00	2.00
Direct Labor			
Assembly group	2 hours	8.00	16.00
PG group	1 hour	9.00	9.00
GG group	1.5 hours	10.00	15.00
Variable overhead	4.5 hours	2.00	9.00
Total standard cost per unit			$ 86.00

Ben Fun prepares monthly performance reports based on standard costs. Presented in the following table is the contribution report for May, when production and sales both reached 2,200 units:

Ben Fun, Inc. Contribution Report for May

	Budget	Actual	Variance
Units	2,000	2,200	200 F
Revenue	$ 200,000	$ 220,000	$ 20,000 F
Variable Costs			
Direct material	$ 74,000	$ 85,600	$ 11,600 U
Direct labor	80,000	93,460	13,460 U
Variable overhead	18,000	18,800	800 U
Total variable costs	$ 172,000	$ 197,860	$ 25,860 U
Contribution margin	$ 28,000	$ 22,140	$ 5,860 U

Ben Fun's top management was surprised by the unfavorable contribution margin given the increased sales in May. Al Miller, the cost accountant, was assigned to identify and report on the reasons for the unfavorable contribution margin results as well as the individuals or groups responsible. After completing his review, Miller prepared the following usage report:

Ben Fun, Inc. Usage Report for May

	Quantity	Actual Cost
Direct Materials		
CDs	2,200 units	$ 44,000
Package	2,200 units	35,000
Labels	4,400 units	6,600
Direct Labor		
Assembly	3,900 hours	31,200
CDs	2,400 hours	23,760
Packages/labels	3,500 hours	38,500
Variable overhead	9,800 hours	18,800
Total variable cost		$197,860

Miller reported that the PG and GG groups supported the increased production levels, but experienced abnormal machine downtime, causing idle labor, which required the use of overtime to keep up with the accelerated demand for parts. The idle time was charged to direct labor. Miller also reported that the production managers of these two groups resorted to parts rejection as opposed to testing and modification procedures as used in the past. Miller determined that the assembly group met management's objectives by increasing production while using lower than standard hours.

Required

A. For May, Ben Fun's labor rate variance was $5,660 unfavorable, and the labor efficiency variance was $200 favorable. By using these two variances and calculating the following five variances, prepare an explanation of the $5,860 unfavorable variance between budgeted and actual contribution margin during May.
  1. Material price variance
  2. Material quantity variance
  3. Variable overhead efficiency variance
  4. Variable overhead spending variance
  5. Sales volume variance
B. Tell the story of the variances.
C. Identify and briefly explain the behavioral factors that may promote friction among the production managers and between the production managers and the maintenance manager.
D. Evaluate Al Miller's analysis of the unfavorable contribution results in terms of its completeness and its effect on the behavior of the production groups. What decisions need to be made about increasing the contribution margin?

Group Exercises

53. Imagine that you are the vice president of production for an international manufacturer of a variety of home electronics. The company is one of the most well-respected in the industry and more often than not your company has no difficulty in finding employees. Recently the company has faced growing pressure to improve productivity and reduce production costs. The pressure is the result of attempts to improve the company's financial performance so that the stock price will, in turn, increase. You have been catching a lot of heat in the past few weeks to implement new production standards within the company. The president does not believe that current standards are sufficient and that they are not properly motivating employees. She suggests that you consider standards that are closer to so-called ideal standards. With this background in mind, form small groups and discuss the advantages and disadvantages of using ideal and practical standards to motivate employees. How should you respond to the president's request to implement standards that are more similar to ideal standards?

54. Management by exception is a technique used to effectively identify and investigate variances in the operating environment. There are no firm guidelines that direct managers as to which variances they should investigate. Instead, managers are expected to identify variances that are significant and in need of explanation. Within your group discuss the "rules of thumb" that managers might follow to decide on which variances to investigate.

Chapter 11: Decentralization and Performance Evaluation

In this chapter, we discuss cost control and performance evaluation in a decentralized environment and the impact of responsibility accounting and segment reporting on decision making in decentralized organizations. We discuss performance evaluation in cost, profit, and investment centers utilizing variance analysis and other financial measures of performance, including the segmented income statement, return on investment (ROI), residual income, and economic value added (EVA). We also discuss the use of cash, stock, and other forms of compensation to motivate and reward individual managers in an organization. We conclude the chapter with a discussion of transfer pricing issues with respect to cost control and performance evaluation.

Learning Objectives

After studying the material in this chapter, you should be able to:

1 Describe the structure and management of decentralized organizations and evaluate the benefits and drawbacks of decentralization

2 Evaluate how responsibility accounting is used to help manage in a decentralized organization

3 Define cost, revenue, profit, and investment centers and explain why managers of each must be evaluated differently

4 Compute and interpret segment margin in an organization

5 Compute and interpret return on investment (ROI), residual income, and economic value added (EVA) as measures of financial performance for investment centers

6 Compare and contrast the use of ROI and residual income and discuss potential problems with their use

7 Recognize the importance of using incentives to motivate managers and discuss the advantages and disadvantages of using cash-based, stock-based and other forms of managerial compensation

8 Establish minimum and maximum transfer prices using the general model and discuss the use of market prices, cost-based prices, and negotiated prices in establishing a transfer price

Introduction

As the CEO of a chain of local retail shoe stores, you would be responsible for all aspects of your company's performance—from purchasing shoes to setting prices to investing in new fixtures or even to expanding operations by opening new stores. Consequently, your performance should be evaluated based on all these factors—the costs incurred, the revenue generated, and the investment made in the company. Contrast the responsibilities of the CEO of the company to the responsibilities of a manager of a specific store. As the store manager, you are likely to have some authority over setting prices of shoes, but purchasing decisions are made for the entire chain. Likewise, although you are likely to have some responsibility over making improvements to your store, major renovations and expansions can be made only with the approval of the CEO. Obviously, it would not be fair to the store manager to evaluate his or her performance based on the profit earned by the entire chain. In addition, it would probably not be appropriate to evaluate the store manager's performance based on the profit of his or her store, as a major component of the costs (the costs of shoes sold) is out of the store manager's control. In general, managers should be held responsible for only those things over which they have control. The dilemma for companies is to find tools that allow the evaluation of managers at all levels in the organization—from a plant manager in a factory to the manager of a retail store to the regional sales manager to the CEO.

Management of Decentralized Organizations

Objective 1

Describe the structure and management of decentralized organizations and evaluate the benefits and drawbacks of decentralization

A **decentralized organization** is one in which decision-making authority is spread throughout the organization as opposed to being confined to top-level management. When a few individuals at the top of an organization retain decision-making authority, the organization is referred to as centralized. In a decentralized environment, managers at various levels throughout the organization make key decisions about operations relating to their specific areas of responsibility. These areas are called segments. Segments can be branches, divisions, departments or individual products. Any activity or part of the business for which a manager needs cost, revenue, or profit data can be considered a segment. Reporting financial and other information by segments is called segment reporting. This chapter discusses segment reporting and cost control and performance evaluation issues in segments of decentralized organizations.

Decentralization varies from organization to organization. Most organizations are decentralized to some degree. At one end of the spectrum, managers are given complete authority to make decisions at their level of operations. At the other extreme, managers have little, if any, authority to make decisions. Most firms will fall somewhere in the middle. However, the tendency is to move toward more, rather than less, decentralization.

Doing Business.

DECENTRALIZATION AT FORD

In the late 1990s, Ford Motor Company reorganized its senior management by shifting authority to its regional operations in an effort to react more quickly to changing market conditions and to boost sales. Under the new structure, Ford's regional and brand executives have more authority in deciding what kinds of cars and trucks to make and how to market them. Ford's decentralization was designed in part to help develop new talent by giving more executives responsibilities for entire businesses ("Ford's Wallace Gets Top Financial Post, and Some Management Is Decentralized," *Wall Street Journal,* October 18, 1999, B4).

There are several benefits to decentralization:

- Generally, those closest to a problem are most familiar with the problem and its root causes. By pushing decision-making authority down to lower levels, managers most familiar with a problem have the opportunity to solve it.

- At the same time, top management is left with more time to devote to long-range strategic planning, as decentralization removes the responsibility for much of the day-to-day decision making.

- Studies have shown that managers allowed to make decisions in a decentralized environment have higher job satisfaction than do managers in centralized organizations.

- Managers who are given increased responsibility for decision making early in their careers generally become better managers because of the on-the-job training they receive. In other words, experience is the best teacher.

- Decisions are often made in a more timely fashion.

However, there can be drawbacks as well:

- When decision-making authority is spread among too many managers, a lack of company focus can occur. Managers may become so concerned with their own areas of responsibility that they lose sight of the big picture. Because of this lack of focus on the company as a whole, managers may tend to make decisions benefiting their own segments, which may not always be in the best interest of the company.

- Managers may not be adequately trained in decision making at the early stages of their careers. The costs of training managers can be high, and the potential costs of bad decisions while new managers are being trained should be considered.

- There may be a lack of coordination and communication between segments.

- Decentralization may make it difficult to share unique and innovative ideas.

- Decentralization may result in duplicative efforts and duplicative costs.

Hitting the Bottom Line.

CENTRALIZATION OR DECENTRALIZATION?

General Motors has been a decentralized company since the early 1920s. Over the years, Buick, Cadillac, Chevrolet, GMC, Oldsmobile, Pontiac and more recently Hummer and Saturn have operated as separate entities with their own manufacturing plants and distinct management syles and product development philosophies. However, in 2004, GM began to move towards a more centralized strategy. The reason? To reduce duplication of costs related to design and manufacturing of GM cars. Rather than allowing brand managers to develop and design new cars in isolation, the goal is to develop cars that share parts and can be sold anywhere in the world. As an example, GM currently uses 270 different types of radios in its cars. By reducing that number to 50, the company can save 40 percent in related costs ("Reversing 80 Years of History, GM is Reining in Global Fiefs," *Wall Street Journal,* October 6, 2004, A1).

Decentralized organizations require well-developed and well-integrated information systems. The flow of information and open communication between divisions and upper and lower management is critical. This can be a problem for companies whose systems simply don't provide the kind of quantitative and qualitative information needed at the segment level. For this reason, the use of enterprise resource planning (ERP) systems has been particularly helpful in decentralized organizations. As discussed in Chapter 1, ERP systems integrate and provide information to managers throughout an organization. Information on individual segments and business lines is more readily available than ever before.

Responsibility Accounting and Segment Reporting

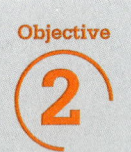

Objective 2

Evaluate how responsibility accounting is used to help manage in a decentralized organization

The key to effective decision making in a decentralized organization is **responsibility accounting**—holding managers responsible for only those things under their control. In reality, the amount of control a manager has can vary greatly from situation to situation. For example, 75 percent of the shoes offered for sale at the shoe department of a store may be purchased by a regional purchasing manager in order to obtain quantity-purchase discounts from suppliers. Only 25 percent are purchased at the discretion of the individual store manager. In this case, since the local manager does not control how many shoes, what styles of shoes, and how much is paid for most of the shoes sold in his store, the manager should not be held responsible for the cost of shoes purchased and the profit earned on shoe sales in his store.

In the previous chapter, variance analysis was used to help evaluate the performance of managers by focusing on who had responsibility for a variance. Usage variances were typically the responsibility of production managers, and price variances were typically the responsibility of purchasing managers. However, as you will recall, general rules like this must be used with caution. For example, the purchasing manager might be responsible for a usage variance if low-quality materials contributed to excessive waste.

In decentralized organizations, detailed information is needed to evaluate the effectiveness of managerial decision making. Companywide budgets, cost standards, income statements, and so on are not sufficient to evaluate the performance of each of a company's segments. For example, overall financial statements generated for external reporting purposes would be of limited use in evaluating the performance of the numerous managers at General Motors. The manager of the Buick car division would be evaluated just on the results of that division, while the manager of the Saturn division would be evaluated just on the results of that division. Going down a step further, a production manager dealing only with the manufacture of the Saturn ION and a production manager who works only with the Saturn VUE would be evaluated using different information. Even within a product line, managers should be held responsible only for those things under their control. A manager on an engine assembly line should not be evaluated and held responsible for a production problem dealing with the vehicle body. Plant managers would be evaluated based on activities in their plant, regional sales managers would be held responsible for sales in their region, and so on.

KEY CONCEPT

The key to effective decision making in a decentralized organization is responsibility accounting—holding managers responsible for only those things under their control.

Cost, Revenue, Profit, and Investment Centers

To enhance the use of responsibility accounting for decision making, organizations typically identify the different segments, or levels of responsibility, as cost, revenue, profit, or investment centers and attach different levels of responsibility to each segment (see Exhibit 11-1).

EXHIBIT 11-1 Responsibility Levels at Cost, Revenue, Profit and Investment Centers

Cost Center	Revenue Center	Profit Center	Investment Center
Responsible for costs only	Responsible for revenue only	Responsible for costs and revenues	Responsible for profit and investments in property, plant & equipment

A **cost center** manager has control over costs but not over revenue or capital investment (long-term purchasing) decisions. The purchasing manager of a store, the production manager for a particular type of DVD player, the maintenance manager in a hotel, and the human resources manager of a CPA firm would likely be considered managers of cost centers. The manager of a cost center should be evaluated on how well he or she controls costs in the respective segment. Consequently, performance reports typically focus on differences between budgeted and actual costs using variance analysis. **A performance report** provides key financial and nonfinancial measures of performance appropriate for a particular segment.

A **revenue center** manager has control over the generation of revenue but not costs. Examples include the sales manager of a retail store, the sales department of a production facility, and the reservation department of an airline. Performance reports of a revenue center often focus on sales volume and sales price variances (discussed in Chapter 10).

A **profit center** manager has control over both cost and revenue but not capital investment decisions. While the purchasing manager of a retail store was a cost center manager, the overall manager of the store would probably be a profit center manager. Likewise, the manager of an entire product line in a factory, the manager of a particular location of a hotel chain, and the partner in charge of the tax department at a CPA firm would be considered profit center managers. It is important to understand that profit center managers still don't have control over decisions to invest in and purchase new property, plant and equipment. For example, the profit center managers described here could not make decisions to remodel a store, buy new manufacturing equipment, add a swimming pool to a hotel, or open a new office.

The manager of a profit center should be evaluated on both revenue generation and cost control. Consequently, performance reports typically focus on income measures, such as the overall flexible budget variance (discussed in Chapter 10). The flexible budget variance is the difference between the actual and budgeted operating income. However, this can be a problem when uncontrollable fixed costs are included in the analysis. Segment managers should be held responsible for only those costs under their control. Consequently, other measures of profit center performance, such as segment margin, are also commonly used.

Objective 3

Define cost, revenue, profit, and investment centers and explain why managers of each must be evaluated differently

Hitting the Bottom Line.

PRISON AS A PROFIT CENTER

In Oregon, voters amended the state constitution and approved a measure requiring that work programs in state prisons achieve a net profit. In a typical program, inmates work with a local business and earn normal hourly wages. However, employers are not required to provide medical insurance, health, or other benefits and are not liable for Social Security, Medicare, or workers' compensation, reducing their payroll costs by up to 35 percent. Prisons are paid a royalty averaging about $.95 per hour of labor for providing the cheap labor. The Oregon Department of Corrections estimates that the prison system will make $10 million a year from its inmates by 2006 ("Prison as a Profit Center," *Wall Street Journal*, March 15, 2000, B1).

In addition to being responsible for a segment's revenue and expenses, an **investment center** manager is responsible for the amount of cash and other assets invested in generating its income. An investment center is in essence a separate business with its own value chain. Consequently, investment centers are frequently referred to as **strategic business units** or SBUs. An investment center manager is involved in decisions ranging from research and development to production to marketing and sales and customer service.

Although the manager of an investment center can be evaluated using some of the same tools as profit centers, the amount of assets or investment under the manager's control must also be considered. Measures of performance for investment centers are discussed later in the chapter.

Doing Business.

INVESTMENT CENTERS AT DAIMLERCHRYSLER

Large international companies may have several core businesses operating as investment centers or strategic business units. For example, DaimlerChrysler has four major divisions—the Mercedes car group, the Chrysler group, the commercial vehicles group, and the services group (which includes fleet management services and DaimlerChrysler Bank). The revenue generated from the SBUs ranges from $17 billion annually in the services group to more than $60 billion in both the Mercedes car group and the Chrysler group.

Profit Center Performance and Segmented Income Statements

Segmented income statements calculate income for each major segment of an organization in addition to the company as a whole. Although it is usually easy to keep records of sales by segment, tracing costs to a particular segment and deciding how to treat costs that benefit more than one segment can be very difficult.

Variable costs (unit-level costs) are generally traced directly to a segment. Remember, variable costs vary in direct proportion to sales volume. Therefore, they can be allocated to a segment based on sales volume.

Deciding which fixed costs to assign, or allocate, to a segment requires an analysis of the overall company and the individual areas of responsibility (segments) within an organization. **Segment costs** should include *all* costs attributable to that segment but *only* those costs that are actually caused by the segment. Fixed costs that can be easily and conveniently traced to a segment should obviously be assigned to that segment. The problem is that many fixed costs are indirect in nature. Should indirect fixed costs be allocated to segments? A good test for deciding whether to allocate indirect fixed costs is to determine whether the cost would be reduced or eliminated if the segment were eliminated. If the cost cannot be reduced or eliminated, it is referred to as a common cost. **Common costs** are indirect costs that are incurred to benefit more than one segment and cannot be directly traced to a particular segment or allocated in a reasonable manner based on what causes the cost to be incurred. In general, common costs should not be allocated to segments for purposes of performance evaluation.

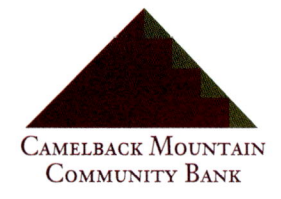

For example, Camelback Mountain Community Bank (headquartered in Phoenix, Arizona) has six branches located in and around the Phoenix metropolitan area. One of those branches is located in Tempe. The Tempe branch incurs fixed lease expense to rent the building in which the bank is located. Obviously, this lease expense is directly traceable to the individual branch (a segment) and should be allocated to that segment. However, if the lease expense is for the corporate headquarters building in Phoenix, the cost is an indirect one and probably should not be allocated to the Tempe branch. In this case, it is doubtful that the lease expense for the headquarters building would be reduced or eliminated if the Tempe branch were eliminated. Therefore, it is probably best treated as a common cost and not allocated to the segment. In practice, companies sometimes allocate common costs from headquarters to segments without using them for evaluation purposes. This practice has the advantage of making the segment manager aware that the cost is being incurred and that the cost must ultimately be paid for by revenue generated by the segment.

Other indirect costs can be allocated to segments if there is a sufficient causal relationship between the cost and the segment. For example, all loan processing for Camelback Mountain Community Bank is done in the headquarters building in Phoenix. Although these costs (for credit checks, loan processing, staff salaries, etc.) may be difficult to directly trace to the Tempe branch, they can be allocated in a manner that reflects the cause of the costs (the number of loans processed, the dollar amount of loans processed, etc.). In addition, it is reasonable to assume that at least some of the loan processing costs would be reduced or eliminated if the branch were closed.

To allocate indirect costs, there should be a causal relationship between the allocation base and a segment's use of the common cost. Allocating costs using an arbitrary allocation base is inappropriate. Although Camelback Mountain Community Bank could allocate the lease cost of the headquarters building to its branches based on an allocation base, such as square footage or total deposits, such a base would be completely arbitrary. There is no causal relationship between the square footage or total deposits in a branch and the lease expense in the headquarters building. Arbitrary allocations like this may result in a profitable segment appearing unprofitable and may lead to less than optimal decisions concerning that segment.

The Segmented Income Statement

Garcia and Buffett is a full-service local CPA firm offering services in three departments: tax, audit, and consulting. The tax department is further broken down into individual and business divisions. Garcia and Buffett has annual client billings of $1,000,000, with 50 percent generated from the tax department, 40 percent from the audit department, and the remaining 10 percent from the consulting department. The following table shows a segmented income statement broken down into three segments based on the three practice departments:

	Segmented Income Statement Using Contribution Format Segments Defined as Departments			
	Total Firm	**Tax Department**	**Audit Department**	**Consulting Department**
Client billings	$1,000,000	$500,000	$400,000	$100,000
Less: Variable expenses	400,000	200,000	160,000	40,000
Contribution margin	$ 600,000	$300,000	$240,000	$ 60,000
Less: Traceable fixed expenses	200,000	100,000	75,000	25,000
Segment margin	$ 400,000	$200,000	$165,000	$ 35,000
Less: Common fixed expenses	200,000			
Net income	$ 200,000			

The $100,000 of fixed costs traceable to the tax department include advertising specifically geared to the tax department, the salary of the tax manager, the costs of research material used in the tax library, and computer software used for tax preparation. Common fixed costs (for the firm as a whole) include salaries of the managing partner of the firm, the human resources manager, and the receptionist and depreciation of the office building.

In the following table, Garcia and Buffett goes a step further and provides a segmented income statement for the two divisions within the tax department. Note that the statements are based on the contribution margin format introduced in Chapter 6. The primary difference is the separation of fixed costs into traceable fixed costs and common fixed costs and the interim calculation of segment margin.

	Segmented Income Statement Using Contribution Format Segments Defined as Departments		
	Tax Department	Individual Tax Division	Business Tax Division
Client billings	$500,000	$100,000	$400,000
Less: Variable expenses	200,000	80,000	120,000
Contribution margin	$300,000	$ 20,000	$280,000
Less: Traceable fixed expenses	80,000	30,000	50,000
Divisional segment margin	$220,000	$ (10,000)	$230,000
Less: Common fixed expenses	20,000		
Departmental segment margin	$200,000		

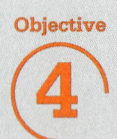

Objective 4

Compute and interpret segment margin in an organization

Note that although $100,000 of fixed costs were traced to the tax department in the first table (when segments were defined as departments), only $80,000 are subsequently traced to the individual and business divisions; $20,000 of traceable costs have become common costs. In this case, the advertising costs for the tax division and the cost of research materials in the tax library cannot be traced directly to either the individual or the business division.

As discussed in Chapter 6, contribution margin is primarily a measure of short-run profitability, as it ignores fixed costs. It is used extensively in short-run decisions, such as CVP analysis and evaluation of special orders. On the other hand, **segment margin** is a measure of long-term profitability and is more appropriate in addressing long-term decisions, such as whether to drop product lines. When segment margin is used to evaluate performance and to make such decisions as whether a segment should be discontinued, it is important to remember that costs are incurred throughout the value chain, not just in the manufacturing process. The value chain includes costs associated with research and development, product design, manufacturing, marketing, distribution, and customer service (see Exhibit 11-2).

EXHIBIT 11-2 The Value Chain

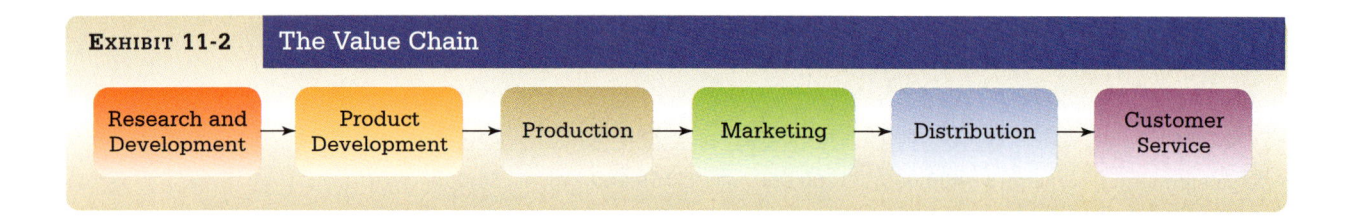

Research and Development → Product Development → Production → Marketing → Distribution → Customer Service

In the case of Garcia and Buffett, the segment margin of the tax department is positive, but the segment margin of the individual tax division is negative. In the long run, the individual tax division is not profitable. However, before the firm decides to eliminate the individual tax division, it should consider other factors (both quantitative and qualitative), including the impact on its highly profitable business tax division.

For example, it may be important for the firm to be perceived as a full-service firm where owners of small businesses can come for help with all their tax and business problems. In addition, planning for a small business must often be integrated with planning for the individual owner of the business. For these reasons, the firm may decide to retain the division even if it has not been profitable. Instead of eliminating the division, Garcia and Buffett may decide to focus on ways to make the division profitable through expanding the array of services offered to clients. For example, the firm may begin offering personal financial planning services to its clients to help them meet their overall financial goals.

Doing Business.

WHAT DRIVES COSTS IN A CPA FIRM?

CPA firms incur a variety of costs related to auditing and providing other services to large clients that are publicly held (have stock owned by the general public). These costs (additional training for employees, peer reviews, and other quality reviews mandated by regulators, etc.) might traditionally be considered fixed because they don't vary with revenue or other measures of volume. However, they are in fact driven by the size of clients serviced. If a firm has only a few large publicly held clients, it may choose to stop servicing those clients in order to eliminate a variety of these product-level costs.

Segment Performance and Activity-Based Costing

The use of activity-based costing (ABC) can affect the classification of costs as traceable or common. As you will recall from the discussion in Chapter 4, when ABC is used, many costs that were previously considered "fixed" are found to vary with respect to batch- or product-level cost drivers. In manufacturing firms, batch-level and product-level activities and costs are often driven by such factors as the number of setups, the number of parts, the number of customer orders, the number of supervision hours, and so on. In service-oriented companies, these costs may vary with the number of customers serviced, the size of the client, or the number of hours spent reviewing files. For example, the "fixed" costs of a research aid in the tax research library at Garcia and Buffett might be driven by the number of research hours provided to each division.

Investment Centers and Measures of Performance

In addition to being responsible for a segment's revenue and expenses, an investment center manager is responsible for the amount of capital invested in generating its income. Investment center managers can make capital purchasing decisions, including decisions to remodel facilities, purchase new equipment, expand facilities, or add new locations. Investment centers are typically major divisions or branch operations of a company involved in all aspects of the value chain. In addition to being evaluated using the approaches discussed earlier for cost and profit centers, evaluating investment centers requires focusing on the level of investment required in generating a segment's profit. For this reason, performance reports focus on measures specifically developed for this purpose—return on investment, residual income, and economic value added.

Managers of investment centers are given complete control over all activities in their respective segments. Managers want to be associated with well-run, profitable divisions. Competition between investment center managers within an organization is sometimes intense. Because of compensation issues, such as year-end bonuses based on performance, managers of investment centers must also be evaluated. Although all the financial measures of performance used in evaluating the managers of cost, revenue, and profit centers apply to investment center managers, they are not sufficient.

To some extent, controlling costs and generating revenue is a function of the amount of assets under a manager's control. For example, if a manager had unlimited assets and resources, production costs could be reduced by buying the most efficient manufacturing equipment available. Likewise, sales might be maximized by additional spending on advertising. Very large companies typically have higher revenue and higher income than very small companies. However, the manager of an investment center should not be evaluated with respect to the amount of costs, revenue and income generated without reference to the size of the investment center being managed and the assets under the manager's control.

KEY CONCEPT

Evaluating investment centers requires focusing on the level of investment required in generating a segment's profit.

Objective 5

Compute and interpret return on investment (ROI), residual income, and economic value added (EVA) as measures of financial performance for investment centers

Return on Investment

DuPont was the first major company in the United States to recognize that the performance of an investment center must consider the level of investment along with the income generated from that investment. **Return on investment (ROI)** measures the rate of return generated by an investment center's assets.

ROI can be a very simple concept. For example, if you invest $1,000 in a bank certificate of deposit for one year and receive $50 at the end of the year, your return on that investment is 5 percent ($50/$1,000). However, the calculation of return gets a little more complicated when the income is reinvested in another certificate, the amount of assets change, and costs are incurred to manage the money.

In business, the calculation of ROI is generally broken down into two components—a measure of operating performance (called margin) and a measure of how effectively assets are used during a period (called asset turnover). **Margin** is found by dividing an investment center's net operating income by its sales. As such, it can be viewed as the profit that is earned on each dollar of sales. A margin of 10 percent indicates that 10 cents of every sales dollar is profit. **Asset turnover** is calculated by dividing an investment center's sales by its average operating assets during a period. It measures the sales that are generated for a given level of assets.

The formula for return on investment (ROI) is as follows:

$$\text{ROI} = \text{Margin} \times \text{Turnover}$$
$$\text{Margin} = \text{Net operating income/Sales}$$
$$\text{Turnover} = \text{Sales/Average operating assets}$$

$$\text{ROI} = \frac{\text{Net operating income}}{\text{Sales}} \times \frac{\text{Sales}}{\text{Average operating assets}}$$

or

$$\text{ROI} = \frac{\text{Net operating income}}{\text{Averaging operating assets}}$$

The elements comprising ROI are shown in graphical form in Exhibit 11-3.

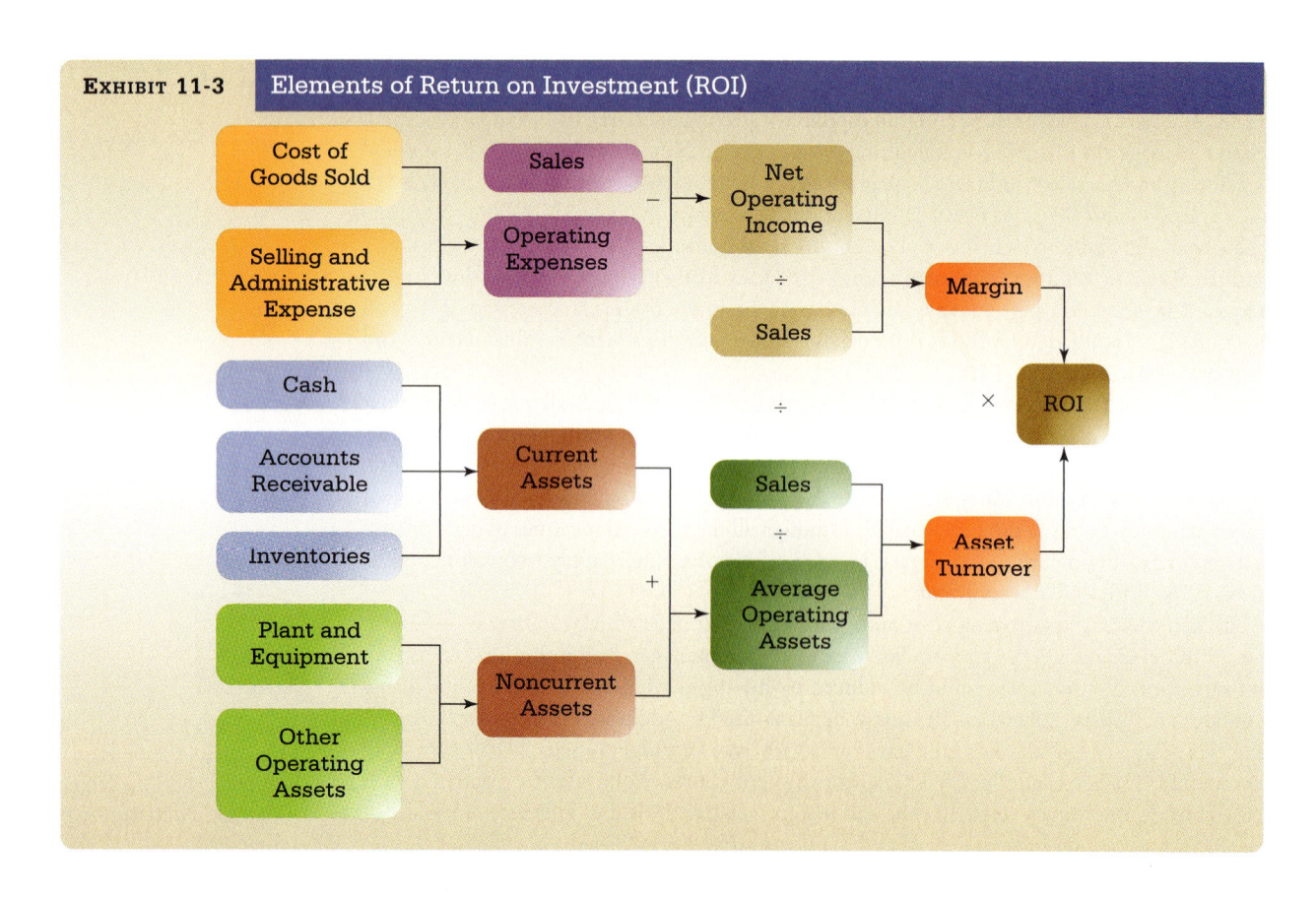

EXHIBIT 11-3 Elements of Return on Investment (ROI)

Although various investment centers (including companies) may have similar ROIs, their margin and turnover may be very different. For example, a grocery store and a furniture store both have an ROI of 20 percent. However, the grocery store's ROI may be made up of a profit margin of $0.02 per dollar of product sold and a turnover of 10, whereas the furniture store may have a margin of $0.10 per dollar of product sold and a turnover of 2. In this case, the grocery store does not make much from each dollar of sales but generates a lot of sales for the amount of its assets. On the other hand, the furniture store makes more from each sale but does not generate as many sales for the amount of assets under its control.

Net operating income is most frequently used as the measure of income in the ROI formula. **Net operating income** is a measure of operating performance and is defined as income before interest and taxes. Interest and taxes are typically omitted from the measure of income in the ROI calculation because they may not be controllable by the manager of the segment being evaluated.

Likewise, the most common measure of investment is average operating assets. **Operating assets** typically include cash, accounts receivable, inventory, and property, plant, and equipment needed to operate a business. Land and other assets held for resale or assets that are idle (a plant that is not being used) are typically not included in operating assets. Because income is measured over time, assets are also generally measured as an average of beginning and end-of-period numbers. By focusing on operating income and average operating assets, ROI attempts to isolate the financial performance of a company's core operations.

Whereas cash, accounts receivable, and inventory are generally easy to measure, the measurement of depreciable property, plant, and equipment for purposes of determining ROI poses some interesting questions. The use of net book value (the cost of the assets less accumulated depreciation) is consistent with the calculation of operating income (which includes depreciation expense) but can have some undesirable consequences. For example, as an asset ages, the net book value of the asset decreases. Using net book value can cause ROI to increase over time simply because of the reduction in book value of assets used in the calculation. Choice of depreciation method can also affect ROI calculations. By choosing an accelerated method over straight-line, the book value of the asset decreases more rapidly, increasing ROI. Both of these factors may discourage managers from replacing old assets, such as manufacturing equipment. If managers are evaluated based on ROI, they may be very reluctant to replace aging machinery with a very low book value with an expensive but more efficient piece of equipment.

The use of gross book value to measure operating assets eliminates age of an asset as a factor in the ROI calculation and any distortions that can be caused by the depreciation method chosen.

To illustrate the use of ROI, consider the financial results of Big Al's Pizza Emporium (see Exhibit 11-4). During 2004, Big Al's had average operating assets of $100,000, consisting of cash, accounts receivable, inventory, and furniture and equipment at book value. Big Al's sales for the year were $350,000 (consisting of $275,000 for 23,000 pizzas and

Inventory turnover in a grocery store is likely to be much higher than turnover in a furniture store.

$75,000 for drinks and other side orders). The ROI for Big Al's, using the net book value method, would be 17.5 percent, consisting of margin of .05 ($17,500/$350,000) and asset turnover of 3.5 ($350,000/$100,000).

EXHIBIT 11-4 ROI with Operating Assets of $100,000 and Sales of $350,000

Sales revenue	$350,000
Variable costs	250,000
Contribution margin	$100,000
Fixed costs	82,500
Net operating income	$ 17,500
Average operating assets	$100,000
ROI	$17,500/$100,000 = 17.5%

If Al would like to increase ROI, what are his options? In general, sales can be increased, operating expenses can be reduced, or the investment in operating assets can be reduced. The first two alternatives increase operating income, and the last option decreases net operating assets.

Increase Sales Volume or Sales Price Sales revenue can be raised by either increasing sales volume without changing the sales price or by increasing the sales price without affecting volume. Remember that when sales volume increases, variable costs increase by the same proportional amount because variable costs stay the same per unit but increase in total as more units are sold. In addition, fixed costs remain the same. Thus, if sales volume increases by 5 percent (resulting in sales revenue of $367,500), income will increase by $5,000 to $22,500. As shown in Exhibit 11-5, ROI will correspondingly increase to 22.5 percent.

EXHIBIT 11-5 ROI when Sales Increases to $367,500

Sales revenue	$367,500
Variable costs	262,500
Contribution margin	$105,000
Fixed costs	82,500
Net operating income	$ 22,500
Average operating assets	$100,000
ROI	$22,500/$100,000 = 22.5%

If Al just changes the price of his products, the analysis is a little different. Increasing sales prices (without a corresponding change in volume) does not affect variable costs or fixed costs. Thus, if revenue were increased by $17,500 because of a 5 percent increase in sales price, income would increase by the same $17,500. ROI would increase to 35 percent ($35,000/$100,000).

Decrease Operating Costs ROI can also be increased by decreasing operating costs. The decrease in costs can be concentrated in variable or fixed costs or both. The key is that any decrease in operating costs will increase operating income and have a positive impact on ROI. In Exhibit 11-6, variable costs are reduced to $241,250 by using a different supplier for direct materials. Income increases by $8,750, resulting in an ROI of 26.25 percent.

EXHIBIT 11-6 ROI when Variable Costs Are Reduced to $241,250

Sales revenue	$350,000
Variable costs	241,250
Contribution margin	$108,750
Fixed costs	82,500
Net operating income	$ 26,250
Average operating assets	$100,000
ROI	$26,250/$100,000 = 26.25%

Decrease the Amount of Operating Assets The third way to increase ROI is to decrease the amount invested in operating assets. Although this may be difficult to do in the short run with property, plant, and equipment, average operating assets can be decreased through better management of inventory. For example, let's assume that Big Al's reduces operating assets by 10 percent by reducing the amount of materials kept in inventory. As shown in Exhibit 11-7, reducing average operating assets to $90,000 will increase ROI to 19.44 percent.

EXHIBIT 11-7 ROI when Operating Assets Are Reduced to $90,000

Sales revenue	$350,000
Variable costs	250,000
Contribution margin	$100,000
Fixed costs	82,500
Net operating income	$ 17,500
Average operating assets	$ 90,000
ROI	$17,500/$90,000 = 19.44%

Residual Income

As an alternative to ROI, the manager of an investment center can be evaluated based on the residual income generated by the investment center. **Residual income** is the amount of income earned in excess of a predetermined minimum rate of return on assets. All other things being equal, the higher the residual income of an investment center, the better.

$$\text{Residual Income} = \text{Net operating income} - \left(\text{Average operating assets} \times \text{Minimum required rate of return} \right)$$

Referring back to the original scenario in Exhibit 11-4 (average operating assets of $100,000 and net operating income of $17,500), and assuming that Big Al's has a minimum required rate of return of 15 percent, the residual income would be calculated as follows:

$$\$17,500 - (\$100,000 \times 15\%) = \$2,500$$

When Big Al's increases sales to $367,500, net operating income increased to $22,500 and ROI increased to 22.5 percent (see Exhibit 11-5). Likewise, residual income will increase to $7,500:

$$\$22,500 - (\$100,000 \times 15\%) = \$7,500$$

When Big Al's decreased variable costs to $241,250, net operating income increased to $26,250 and ROI increased to 26.25 percent (see Exhibit 11-6). Under the new scenario, residual income would be $11,250:

$$\$26,250 - (\$100,000 \times 15\%) = \$11,250$$

Objective 6

Compare and contrast the use of ROI and residual income and discuss potential problems with their use

ROI vs. Residual Income

In some cases, evaluating the performance of an investment center and its manager using ROI can cause problems. For example, Al is thinking about opening a second location and bringing in a new manager to run the business at the existing location. Because the new location will be substantially larger than the existing location, he wants to devote his full attention to the successful start-up of the new location.

Currently, ROI at the existing location is 25 percent. ($25,000 net operating income and average operating assets of $100,000). Big Al's goal and minimum acceptable return for both locations is to maintain an ROI of 15 percent. However, if the new manager is evaluated based on the location's ROI, he may reject potential projects or investments that are profitable (and earn a return greater than 15 percent) but would lower the location's overall ROI.

As an example, the new manager is considering purchasing a new automated pizza oven that will reduce the time it takes to make a pizza and the electricity consumed. The equipment costs $15,000 and is expected to result in increased income of $3,200. Although the return on investment for this particular piece of equipment is over 21 percent ($3,200/$15,000), the manager is likely to reject the purchase because it will reduce his overall ROI from 25 percent ($25,000/$100,000) to 24.5 percent ($28,200/$115,000).

Note that using residual income avoids this problem. If the new manager has the opportunity to purchase a new pizza oven at a cost of $15,000 and expects that profits will increase by $3,200, evaluating the new manager using residual income will result in the manager's purchasing the new oven. The residual income of the existing location will increase from $10,000 ($25,000 − ($100,000 × 15%)) to $10,950 ($28,200 − ($115,000 × 15%)).

However residual income is not without its own problems. Since it is an absolute measure, it should not be used to compare the performance of investment centers of different sizes. For example, Big Al's new location will be considerably larger than the existing location. As shown in Exhibit 11-8, average operating assets in the new location total $300,000, compared to $100,000 in the existing location.

EXHIBIT 11-8 Return on Investment and Residual Income

	Existing Location	New Location
Average operating assets	$100,000	$300,000
Minimum required return	15%	15%
Net operating income	$ 25,000	$ 70,000
Residual income	$ 10,000	$ 25,000
ROI	25%	23.3%

As demonstrated in Exhibit 11-8, the residual income of the new location (run by Al) is higher than the residual income of the existing location (run by the new manager). However, Al did not necessarily manage the new location better; it's just bigger. As you can see, the ROI of the new division is actually lower than the ROI of the existing location. Which measure is better? Both are useful but often for different purposes. Residual income is more useful as a performance measure for a single investment center. On the other hand, since ROI is independent of size, it is better suited as a comparative measure.

Economic Value Added (EVA®)

The most contemporary measure of investment center performance is **economic value added (EVA)**.[1] In a nutshell, by focusing on whether after-tax profits are greater than the cost of capital, EVA tells management whether shareholder wealth is being created. Although EVA is

---

[1] EVA is a registered trademark used with permission of Stern Stewart & Company.

primarily a measure of shareholder wealth, companies may use it internally as part of incentive compensation plans or to encourage managers to undertake desired behavior.

The calculation of EVA is similar to that of residual income. However, EVA does have several important differences.

$$\begin{matrix} \text{Economic} \\ \text{value} \\ \text{added} \end{matrix} = \begin{matrix} \text{After-tax} \\ \text{operating} \\ \text{profit} \end{matrix} - \left(\left(\begin{matrix} \text{Total} \\ \text{assets} \end{matrix} - \begin{matrix} \text{Current} \\ \text{liabilities} \end{matrix} \right) \times \begin{matrix} \text{Weighted} \\ \text{average cost} \\ \text{of capital)} \end{matrix} \right)$$

EVA is based on after-tax operating profit rather than before-tax operating profit. In the EVA calculation, assets are often shown net of current liabilities. Reducing assets by current liabilities focuses attention on assets financed from long-term sources of capital rather than short-term borrowing that will require repayment in the near future. In addition, companies may modify income and asset measurements based on generally accepted accounting principles (GAAP) to better reflect the changing nature of business today. For example, to encourage investments in research and development, employee training, and customer development, expenditures in these areas may be capitalized as an asset for EVA purposes rather than expensed against income. Inventories may be restated to their replacement cost, and the value of assets may be restated to reflect their true economic value.

The weighted average cost of capital considers the cost of both debt and equity financing as compared to a minimum required rate of return that is frequently used in residual income calculations. The calculation of the cost of debt is straightforward and is equal to the after-tax cost of interest paid on that debt. However, the cost of equity is more complex and is basically assumed to be the amount that an investor could earn on an investment with similar risk.

As an example, assume that a division operating as an investment center has the following results:

Operating income (before tax) per GAAP financial statements	$1,000,000
Total assets per GAAP financial statements	4,000,000
Expenditures related to employee training, research and development, and customer development*	1,000,000
Fair market value of property, plant, and equipment†	2,500,000
Current liabilities	500,000
Tax rate	40%
Weighted average cost of capital	10%

*These expenditures were expensed on the GAAP financial statements. Management chooses to capitalize them for purposes of calculating EVA.
†Included on the balance sheet at cost of $2,000,000. Management chooses to use the fair market value of assets in calculating EVA.

After adjusting for the impact of capitalizing expenditures related to employee training, research and development, and customer development, operating income is equal to $2,000,000, and after-tax operating income is $1,200,000 (($2,000,000 × (1 − 0.40)). Total assets of $4,000,000 (per GAAP) are increased by $1,500,000 to reflect the impact of the capitalized expenses of $1,000,000 and to increase property, plant, and equipment to fair market value. After adjusting for current liabilities, assets used in the EVA calculation are equal to $5,000,000.

$$\begin{matrix} \text{Economic} \\ \text{value} \\ \text{added} \end{matrix} = \begin{matrix} \text{After-tax} \\ \text{operating} \\ \text{profit} \end{matrix} - \left(\left(\begin{matrix} \text{Total} \\ \text{assets} \end{matrix} - \begin{matrix} \text{Current} \\ \text{liabilities} \end{matrix} \right) \times \begin{matrix} \text{Weighted} \\ \text{average cost} \\ \text{of capital} \end{matrix} \right)$$

EVA = $1,200,000 − (($5,500,000 − $500,000) × 10%) = $700,000

Doing Business.
EVA AT SPRINT

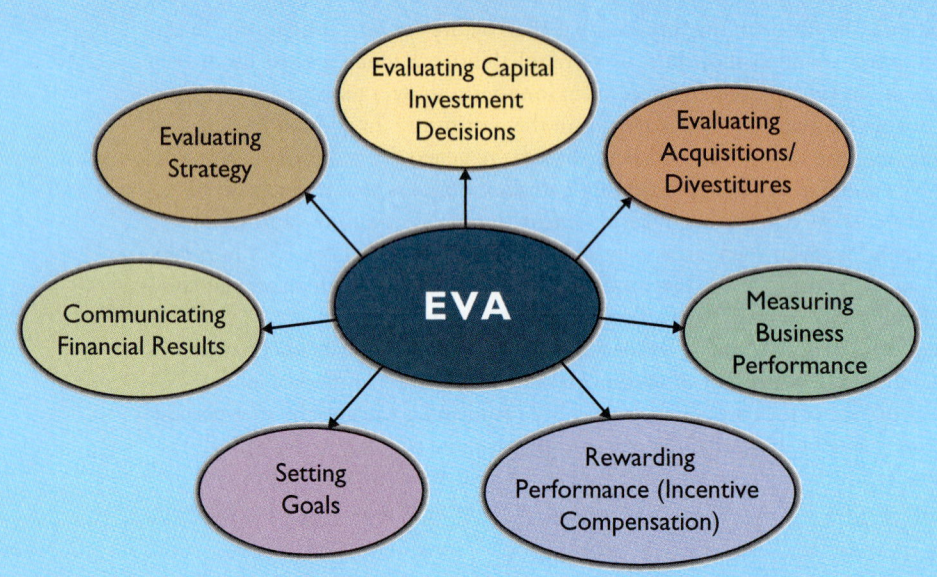

Diagram: EVA at center, connected to: Evaluating Capital Investment Decisions, Evaluating Acquisitions/Divestitures, Measuring Business Performance, Rewarding Performance (Incentive Compensation), Setting Goals, Communicating Financial Results, Evaluating Strategy.

At Sprint, managers are given recommendations on how to incorporate EVA into their everyday decisions.

Commit new capital to value-creating projects. For example:

- What equipment should we buy to provide new and better products and services to our customers?
- What new marketing efforts will improve customer satisfaction and result in increased sales and profits?
- What new business opportunities should we pursue?

Increase profits without using additional capital. For example:

- How can we reduce customer turnover or sell more products without spending more?
- What costs can be reduced through Business Process Improvement efforts?
- How can we change government regulation to make our business operate more efficiently?

Withdraw capital from activities that produce inadequate returns compared to other uses for that capital. For example:

- What products and customers are not as profitable as we expect?
- How can accounts receivable or inventories be reduced to free up cash?
- What assets should be sold or redeployed?

EVA is used in a variety of business management processes to align our actions with creating value.

Hitting the Bottom Line.

CREATING WEALTH?

There is little debate over the profound effect that Microsoft has had on the global economy. The company's operating system and software are pervasive. Since its founding in 1975, the company has grown to a behemoth with annual sales of over $32 billion, net income of almost $10 billion, and cash and other short-term investments of almost $50 billion as of June 30, 2003.

However, according to an article by Paul Strassmann in *ComputerWorld*, Microsoft's EVA for the last several years has declined from a positive $1.2 billion in 1999 to a negative $1.8 billion in 2000, negative $2.8 billion in 2001, negative $176 million in 2002, and negative $998 million in 2003. While positive EVA suggests that the company is innovating and creating wealth in excess of the company's cost of capital, negative EVA suggests that the company is not innovating.

According to Strassmann, the fact that Microsoft has had a negative EVA for the last four years suggests that the company is struggling to find meaningful opportunities to create wealth for its shareholders. This may be why the company has recently decided to unload $32 billion of its cash in the form of a $3 per share special dividend to shareholders. Unable to reinvest its cash hoard in new projects and opportunities to benefit shareholders, Microsoft decided to return the cash directly to shareholders instead (*ComputerWorld*, "Depend on Microsoft?" August 2, 2004, Volume 38, Issue 31, 27).

Decentralization and Performance Evaluation in a Multinational Company

Segments or divisions in a multinational company are often created along geographic lines. Frequently, U.S. companies have subsidiaries that operate in other countries. Sometimes these subsidiaries are involved in manufacturing, but in other cases may be responsible for marketing or distributing products and services in foreign countries. These foreign divisions may operate as cost, profit, revenue, or investment centers.

When responsibility centers are located in more than one country, the management style and decision-making structures used by the companies and the methods of performance evaluation employed by the companies must take into account differences in economic, legal and political, educational, and cultural factors in the business environment.

Economic factors include things like the stability of the economy, whether the country is experiencing high inflation, the strength of underlying capital markets and the strength of the local currency. As discussed in Chapter 9, variations in currency exchange rates can wreak havoc on budgeting but can also cause problems when trying to evaluate performance from period to period. Legal and political factors include the degree of governmental control and regulation of business and the political stability of the country. Educational factors include the availability of an educated, adequately trained work force. Cultural factors may include things like attitudes toward authority, work ethic, and loyalty and commitment to employers by employees and to employees by employers. Due to the unique challenges facing multinational companies as a result of these factors, there are often clear advantages to decentralizing operations in a multinational company, including improving the quality and timeliness of decision making when made at the local level, and the minimization of social, cultural, political, and language barriers.

Performance and Management Compensation Decisions

Objective 7

Recognize the importance of using incentives to motivate managers and discuss the advantages and disadvantages of using cash-based, stock-based, and other forms of managerial compensation

Measuring the performance of a segment is not always the same as measuring the performance of the manager of that segment. For example, certain types of advertising might be specifically traced to a segment representing a geographic sales district (the midwest or southeast) or for a particular product. However, if advertising decisions and the advertising budget are controlled at the national level instead of by the segment manager, the cost of advertising should not be included in evaluating the performance of the segment manager. Likewise, while the segment manager's own salary or the property taxes paid by a segment are traceable to the segment, they are either controllable by others or not controllable at all. Measuring the performance of a manager should be based on variables that the manager controls. This approach, as mentioned earlier, is the goal of responsibility accounting.

In small companies that are owned and managed by the same person, motivating the owner/manager to do his or her best is usually not an issue. If the owner/manager works hard and the company is successful, the owner/manager directly reaps the benefits of the company's success and is rewarded through the receipt of salary or other forms of compensation from the company. Likewise, if the owner does not manage the company well and the company fails, the owner/manager runs the risk of losing his entire investment in the company.

However, in most companies, owners hire managers to run the company for them. It is the owner's job to motivate managers in such a way that the managers make decisions and work to improve the performance of the company as a whole, and hence maximize the owner's wealth, not just the individual manager's salary or other compensation. As such, management compensation plans typically include incentives tied to company performance. The objective is to encourage goal congruence between the individual manager and the company and its owners.

The choice of the specific incentive structure is very important for both parties involved and can include cash compensation in the form of salary and bonuses, stock-based compensation in the form of stock options and restricted stock, and other noncash benefits and perquisites (often called perks).

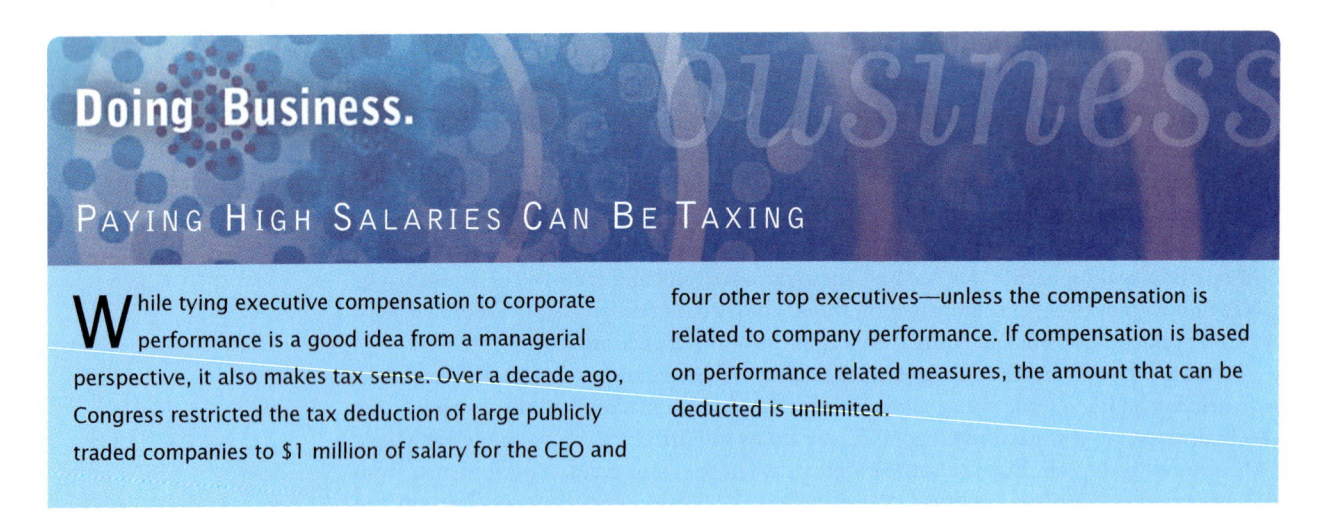

Doing Business.

PAYING HIGH SALARIES CAN BE TAXING

While tying executive compensation to corporate performance is a good idea from a managerial perspective, it also makes tax sense. Over a decade ago, Congress restricted the tax deduction of large publicly traded companies to $1 million of salary for the CEO and four other top executives—unless the compensation is related to company performance. If compensation is based on performance related measures, the amount that can be deducted is unlimited.

Cash Compensation

Cash compensation can be paid in the form of salary or end-of-period bonuses. Many companies use a combination of the two in which a base salary is paid without regard to meeting individual or company performance criteria and bonuses are paid if managers meet or exceed established goals. For example, a manager may earn a base annual salary of $150,000 and a yearly bonus of $30,000 if the individual (or company) meets certain preestablished goals. Goals vary from company to company but might include individual measures such as meeting individual sales quotas, success in attracting and retaining key employees, attracting new customers, and so on. Bonuses may also be tied to companywide measures of performance such as ROI, residual income and EVA, increasing sales, or increasing net income by a certain dollar amount or percentage.

Tying bonuses to single measures of performance like income can be problematic. For example, a manager may increase income by putting off needed repairs and maintenance or may postpone the acquisition of new equipment (in order to keep depreciation low). As discussed in Chapter 6, if a company uses absorption costing to cost products, a manager may be able to increase income (at least in the short run) by increasing production.

THE ETHICS OF BUSINESS
Pressure to Deliver

Every company wants to motivate employees and managers to perform at a high level. Often companies use compensation plans to achieve this motivation. The idea is really rather simple—link performance to pay and employees will work harder to achieve a particular goal or objective. In theory this may sound like a good idea. However, employees might be driven to act unethically, or even illegally, if they feel as though the potential rewards are sufficient to do so.

Take Enron as an example. Enron used a system referred to as "rank and yank" in which only the very top performers were promoted and highly compensated, while other employees were evaluated poorly and labeled as underperformers. Such a system can have a negative effect on employee morale and can create an environment in which employees are willing to "do anything" in order to increase their compensation and be recognized for their achievements.

It's Your Choice—Would you like to work for a company that primarily linked compensation to your performance? What do you see as the pros and cons of such an approach? Are there potential conflicts of interest when managers are compensated based on a company's financial performance?

Stock-Based Compensation

To encourage managers to take a longer term view, many companies provide compensation to top managers and executives in the form of stock-based compensation. The inclusion of stock in the management compensation package is designed to encourage goal congruence between the owners and management by making managers owners. One method of stock-based compensation used frequently in the late 1990s was to grant stock options to key employees.

A **stock option** is the right to buy a share of stock at a set price (called the option price or strike price) at some point in the future. For example, a company may give a manager an option to buy 1,000 shares of stock at a strike price of $15 per share. If the stock is currently selling for $10, the options are worthless. (A rational person would not pay $15 to exercise the option when he could go out and buy the stock for $10). However, if the stock price increases to $25 per share, the manager has the right to exercise the option and purchase 1,000 shares for $15 per share. The value of the options increases as the stock price increases. This policy should encourage management to work hard to enhance the value of the stock over the long run. However, the use of stock options as compensation can result in short-term dysfunctional behavior if managers focus on increasing the share price in the short-term rather than focus on the longer term success of the business. Stock options may have other disadvantages as well. From an individual manager's perspective, the stock price can vary due to other factors not subject to his or her control. As such, a manager may not be rewarded even if his or her individual performance is very good.

> **KEY CONCEPT**
>
> In order to motivate managers and ensure goal congruence, the compensation of managers should be linked to performance and based on a combination of short-term and long-term measures.

A related method of stock-based compensation involves the use of **restricted stock**. With restricted stock compensation plans, a company makes outright transfers of company stock instead of stock options. However, the shares of stock come with restrictions. Frequently, in order to ultimately receive the stock, the manager has to stay with the company for a set period of time or meet established performance measures.

Noncash Benefits and Perks

Most management compensation plans include a variety of noncash benefits and perquisites. These may include club memberships, company cars, a corner office, and so on depending on the desires of the particular manager. Benefits and perks such as these can be used to motivate managers to strive to attain the goals of the organization.

Measuring and Rewarding Performance in a Multinational Environment

Like all organizations, companies that do business in more than one country must develop and use performance measures that provide incentives for managers to work towards the goals of the overall organization. However, what works in one country may not work in another. Cultural differences may impact the desires and needs of managers in different countries. Attitudes toward work and leisure time vary in different countries. For example, German and French workers typically enjoy shorter work weeks than their American counterparts in addition to having more vacation time and more holidays. The average worker in France gets 30 days of paid vacation. In Germany, the average worker gets 24 days off. In contrast, workers in Japan average 18 days and workers in the U.S. average only 10 vacation days per year. Some explain the U.S. dominance in global markets to the American work ethic, which encourages and rewards hard work and risk taking.

As another example, in Japan, employees are often evaluated as part of teams. Because many management control systems in the United States are designed around individual responsibility centers, developing and implementing measures evaluating team performance may be difficult for U.S. companies with operations in Japan.

As a final example, managers' sense of commitment and loyalty to their employers may vary from country to country. In Japan, companies have typically viewed their workers as permanent employees with opportunities for lifetime employment. This commitment on the part of the employer may result in a greater sense of loyalty by employees who clearly have a vested interest in the long-run success of the company.

Doing Business.
EXECUTIVE COMPENSATION

The National Association of Corporate Directors' Commission on Executive Compensation recommends the following in determining executive compensation:

- The individuals who make decisions with respect to the compensation of top executives (compensation committees) should be independent of the company
- Compensation committees should evaluate the fairness of the CEO's pay compared to the pay of other senior managers
- Executives should be rewarded for meeting short-term targets as well as for achieving key goals over a longer period of time
- Executive pay should be linked to performance as reported and goals should not be changed in mid-year
- Every component of compensation should be clearly disclosed to investors and other stakeholders—even if the company is not required to do so

("What's Next in Corporate Pay Practices," *Journal of Accountancy*, July 2004, 59).

Segment Performance and Transfer Pricing

When segments within the same company sell products or services to one another, special problems arise when evaluating performance of the segments. For example, when an automobile manufacturer also manufactures car batteries, what price does the battery division charge the auto division for the battery? This may seem like an unimportant question because the transfer is made within the same company. After all, if I am the owner of the company, what comes out of one pocket simply goes in the other. However, when the managers of the separate divisions are evaluated based on profit or other performance measures, such as ROI or EVA, the transfer price becomes very important. When the buying division and selling division are located in the same country, the goal of transfer pricing is to establish prices that motivate managers of both the selling division and the buying division, allow for performance evaluation, encourage goal congruence and most importantly, benefit the company as a whole.

Objective 8

Establish minimum and maximum transfer prices using the general model and discuss the use of market prices, cost-based prices, and negotiated prices in establishing a transfer price

General Model for Computing Transfer Prices

A general formula for computing **transfer prices** can be developed in which the maximum transfer price is established as the market price of the product (if available) and the minimum transfer price is the variable cost of making and selling the product plus any contribution margin that may be lost to the selling division as a result of giving up sales to outside customers.

$$\text{Maximum price} = \text{Market price}$$

$$\text{Minimum transfer price} = \text{Variable costs of producing and selling} + \text{Contribution margin lost on outside sales}$$

The contribution margin lost on outside sales is an opportunity cost—the benefit the selling division would forgo by not selling to an outside buyer.

Another way to view minimum and maximum transfer prices is that the maximum transfer price is the price at which the buying division is no worse off buying internally than buying from an outside party. Likewise, you can view the minimum transfer price as the price at which the selling division is no worse off selling internally than selling to an outside party.

Within this general framework, there are three basic approaches to establishing transfer prices. The first is to use the market price. As you will see, when a reliable market price exists, the general model will establish both a minimum transfer price and a maximum transfer price equal to the market price. The second is to base the transfer price on the cost of the product transferred. When no outside market exists or when the selling division has excess capacity, transfer prices are often established based on the cost of the product being transferred. The third is to let the buyer and the seller negotiate the price. Negotiated prices work best when there is no reliable market price or in situations in which the general transfer pricing formula provides different minimum and maximum transfer prices.

Let's refer back to Chapter 7 and use Birdie-Maker Golf, Inc. as an example. As you will recall, Birdie-Maker manufactures and sells golf clubs. Birdie-Maker is organized into two divisions—a club division that manufactures the shafts and heads for its clubs and a grip division that manufactures grips for its clubs. Because Birdie-Maker evaluates division managers based on the profit generated in their respective profit centers, the manager of the grip division will want to charge the highest possible price for its product, and the manager of the club division will want to buy grips at the lowest possible price. Birdie-Maker's grip division manufactures grips for $6, which consists of $4 of direct material, direct labor, and variable overhead and $40,000 of fixed manufacturing costs (based on a capacity of 20,000 grips). Administrative costs include $1 of variable costs and $20,000 of fixed costs. When an outside market exists for the grips (Birdie-Maker can sell grips to other club manufacturers), the transfer price hinges on whether the manufacturing facility has excess capacity.

Full Capacity with Reliable Market Price If the grip division is at full capacity (that is they cannot make any additional grips), can sell all its grips to an outside buyer for $10, and the buying division can purchase grips from outsider suppliers for $10, the maximum transfer price should be the $10 market price. At that price, the buying division is no worse off buying internally than buying externally. The minimum transfer price will also be $10 consisting of $5 of variable costs and $5 of lost contribution margin. For every grip that is sold internally, the grip division will lose $5 of contribution margin on outside sales. Note that at the $10 price, the selling division will be no worse off selling internally than selling externally.

In reality, few transfers take place at exactly the market price. For example, while the grip division of Birdie-Maker can sell grips to another club manufacturer for $10 per grip, if it sells internally to the Birdie-Maker club division, it will realize some cost savings from reduced storage and shipping costs. This may lead to negotiations between the manager of the grip division and the manager of the club division and a transfer at a price under $10. If the selling division is not at full capacity, the transfer price will often be adjusted as well.

Outside Market and Excess Capacity If the grip division is not at full capacity but still has an outside market for its product, the pricing gets more interesting. For example, if the grip division has the capacity to make 20,000 grips but can sell only 8,000 to outside buyers, it is likely that the two divisions will set transfer prices based on cost or negotiate a transfer price below the full market price of the grips. If the club division needs all 20,000 grips, the transfer price on the first 8,000 should be set at the market price of $10. The other 12,000 can be sold at any price greater than the $5 of variable costs. If all 20,000 grips are transferred internally, the general pricing formula gives us a minimum price of $7.00. The variable costs of making the grips equal $5, whereas the contribution margin lost on outside sales equals $2.00 per grip (8,000 grips sold at market price of $10 − variable costs of $5 = a lost contribution margin of $40,000; spread over the entire 20,000 grips, the lost contribution margin per grip is $2.00). Note that if all 20,000 grips are transferred at an internal price of $7.00, the total revenue to the grip division is equal to $140,000. This is the same as the revenue earned if the grip division sells 8,000 grips at $10 each to outside buyers while selling 12,000 grips internally at the minimum transfer price of $5. Thus the selling divison is no worse off selling all the grips internally at a transfer price of $7.00 or selling 8,000 grips externally at $10 and 12,000 grips internally at $5.00 per grip. If the club division needs 12,000 grips or less, the minimum transfer price would be $5 (there would be no lost contribution margin in this case) and a transfer price could be negotiated between the $5 minimum and the $10 maximum price.

No Outside Market Let's assume that Birdie-Maker's grip is unique and therefore cannot be sold to other club manufacturers. If Birdie-Maker chooses to set the transfer price using product cost as the basis, the question becomes, at what cost? Variable manufacturing costs are $4 per grip, and total variable costs are $5 per grip, whereas the full absorption cost of making a grip is $6. Total costs, including the fixed administrative costs, are $7. In order for the grip division to truly operate as a profit center (and to be evaluated as such), it must be able to earn a profit. However, the club division may be reluctant to "buy" at whatever price is established by the grip division. What price is fair? The objective of the company is to set a price that does not adversely affect either manager or the firm and to maximize Birdie-Maker's overall profit.

Based on our general transfer pricing model, the minimum transfer price will be the total variable costs of $5. Because there is no outside market, there is no lost contribution margin. As long as the buying division cannot purchase grips from an outside supplier, there is no maximum price under our general formula. Instead, it is likely that the actual transfer price would be negotiated up from the $5 minimum. Note that unless the transfer price is negotiated up to a minimum of $7, the grip division cannot be evaluated as a profit center. Rather, it should be evaluated as a cost center and be held responsible only for the costs incurred in manufacturing grips. Transfers based on costs also can result in some problems from the buying division's perspective. If the selling division is simply allowed to pass along all costs to the buying division, inefficiencies in cost control in the selling division will be passed along to the buying division in the form of a higher "price."

A key concept in transfer pricing is that no matter what the desires of the division managers, the transfer price that provides the most benefit to the company as a whole is the one that should be chosen. Forcing a transfer when the best course of action for the company is to buy outside or preventing a transfer when the best choice is to transfer the product internally results in inefficient use of a company's resources.

KEY CONCEPT

The transfer price that provides the most benefit to the company as a whole is the one that should be chosen.

International Aspects of Transfer Pricing

When an organization has international divisions, the same type of problems arise, but the goals and objectives of transfer pricing change. The focus of transfer pricing when international divisions are involved centers on minimizing taxes, duties, and tariffs and reducing foreign exchange risks. Issues of international competition and government relations are also important components of international transfer pricing decisions. Managers must be aware and sensitive to geographic, political, and economic circumstances in the environment in which they operate.

If the selling division is in a high-tax country, companies have incentives to set transfer prices "low" in order to reduce the income of the selling division in the high-tax country and to increase the income of the buying division in the low-tax country. On the other hand, if the selling division is in a low-tax country, companies have incentives to set transfer prices "high", in order to increase the income of the selling division in the low-tax country while correspondingly reducing the income of the buying division located in the high-tax country.

For example, suppose that a U.S. company has a division that manufactures computer components in a low-tax country. The actual cost of producing the computer component in the low-tax foreign country is $30 per unit. Ultimately, the components will be purchased by the U.S buying division and sold to U.S. consumers for $70 per unit. If the company establishes a transfer price using a "normal" markup on cost of 50 percent, the transfer price would be $45 and the selling division would earn a profit of $15 on each unit sold (taxed in the low-tax country) and the buying division would earn a profit of $25 on each unit sold (taxed in the U.S. at higher rates). However, what if the selling division uses a markup of 100 percent and sets the transfer price at $60? Now the selling division earns a profit of $30 per unit and the buying division earns a profit of only $10. Note that the total before-tax profit ($40) earned by the company is the same regardless of the transfer price used. However, as seen in Exhibit 11-9, if the buying division in the U.S. pays a tax rate of 30 percent while the selling division in the foreign country pays a tax rate of only 10 percent, the after-tax profit is $31 if the transfer price is set at $45 and the after-tax profit is $34 if the transfer price is set at $60.

Selling and shipping goods internationally introduces many opportunities for manipulating transfer prices.

Exhibit 11-9: The Impact of Transfer Pricing on After-tax Profit

	Transfer price of $45		Transfer price of $60	
	Before-tax profit	After-tax profit	Before-tax profit	After-tax profit
Selling division in low-tax country	$15.00	$13.50	$30.00	$27.00
Buying division in U.S.	25.00	17.50	10.00	7.00
Total profit	$40.00	$31.00	$40.00	$34.00

Doing Business.

Transfer Prices and Taxes

A recent study estimates that multinational companies avoided paying $53.1 billion in U.S. income taxes in 2001 by artificially manipulating transfer prices between divisions located in different countries. Trade with Japan accounted for over $12 billion of the lost revenue. Examples of abnormally low exported items include aluminum ladders exported to Japan at $4.40 each, car seats exported to Belgium at $1.66 each, automatic teller machines exported to France at $97 each and missile and rocket launchers exported to Israel at $52 each. By lowering the price, the U.S. operations show no profit and pay no or little taxes in the United States. U.S. companies also buy products from related companies at artificially high prices, including lawn mower blades from Australia for $2,327 each, battery powered smoke detectors from Germany for $3,500 each, and plastic buckets from the Czech Republic for $973 each ("An Estimate of 2001 Lost U.S. Federal Income Tax Revenues Due to Over-Invoiced Imports and Under-Invoiced Exports," Trade Research Institute, Inc., Miami, Florida, October 31, 2002).

Summary of Key Concepts

- The key to effective decision making in a decentralized organization is responsibility accounting—holding managers responsible for only those things under their control. (p. 376)

- Evaluating investment centers requires focusing on the level of investment required in generating a segment's profit. (p. 381)

- In order to motivate managers and ensure goal congruence, the compensation of managers should be linked to performance and based on a combination of short-term and long-term measures. (p. 392)

- The transfer price that provides the most benefit to the company as a whole is the one that should be chosen. (p. 394)

Key Definitions

Decentralized organization An organization in which decision-making authority is spread throughout the organization (p. 374)

Responsibility accounting An accounting system that assigns responsibility to a manager for those areas that are under that manager's control (p. 376)

Cost center An organizational segment, or division, in which the manager has control over costs but not over revenue or investment decisions (p. 377)

Performance report Provides key financial and nonfinancial measures of performance for a particular segment (p. 377)

Revenue center An organizational segment, or division, in which the manager has control over revenue but not costs or investment decisions (p. 377)

Profit center An organizational segment, or division, in which the manager has control over both costs and revenue but not investment decisions (p. 377)

Investment center An organizational segment, or division, in which the manager has control over costs, revenue, and investment decisions (p. 377)

Strategic business unit (SBU) Another term for investment center (p. 377)

Segmented income statements Reports income for each major segment of an organization in addition to the company as a whole (p. 378)

Segment costs All costs attributable to a particular segment of an organization but only those costs that are actually caused by the segment (p. 378)

Common costs Indirect costs that are incurred to benefit more than one segment and cannot be directly traced to a particular segment or allocated in a reasonable manner (p. 378)

Segment margin The profit margin of a particular segment of an organization, typically the best measure of long-run profitability (p. 380)

Return on investment (ROI) Measures the rate of return generated by an investment center's assets (p. 382)

Margin For each sales dollar, the percentage that is recognized as net profit (p. 382)

Asset turnover The measure of activity used in the ROI calculation; it measures the sales that are generated for a given level of assets (p. 382)

Net operating income Net income from operations before interest and taxes (p. 383)

Operating assets Typically include cash, accounts receivable, inventory, and property, plant, and equipment needed to operate a business (p. 383)

Residual income The amount of income earned in excess of a predetermined minimum level of return on assets (p. 385)

Economic value added (EVA) A contemporary measure of performance focusing on shareholder wealth (p. 386)

Stock option The right to buy a share of stock at a set price (called the option price or strike price) at some point in the future (p. 391)

Restricted stock A form of management compensation in which employees receive shares of stock with restrictions such as requirements to stay with the company for a set period of time or requirements to meet established performance measures (p. 392)

Transfer price The price charged by one segment, or division, to another segment, or division, within the same organization for the transfer of goods or services (p. 393)

Multiple Choice

1. When a few individuals at the top of an organization retain decision-making authority, the organization is referred to as a(n):
    a. centralized organization.
    b. decentralized organization.
    c. profit center.
    d. investment center.

2. Which of the following is not a drawback of a decentralized organization?
   a. Decentralization increases opportunities for managers to gain in experience.
   b. Decentralized organizations can lose focus if decision makers are unaware of a central strategy.
   c. Managers often become too focused on their own division or area of the organization.
   d. Managers may not receive the necessary training for making business decisions in the early parts of their careers.

3. Which of the following statements about responsibility accounting is true?
   a. With responsibility accounting, managers are held responsible for both usage and price variances.
   b. Companywide budgets and cost standards are useful in evaluating the performance of company segments.
   c. The theme of responsibility accounting is that managers are held responsible for only those activities under their control.
   d. All of the above.

4. A revenue center manager will most likely be held accountable for:
   a. sales volume variances.
   b. sales price variances.
   c. variable overhead variances.
   d. a and b, but not c.

5. In order of increasing responsibility, which of the following is most likely to be a manager's progression through the various components of an organization?
   a. Investment center, cost center, revenue center, profit center
   b. Revenue center, cost center, profit center, investment center
   c. Cost center, profit center, investment center, revenue center
   d. Cost center, revenue center, profit center, investment center

6. Which of the following statements about segment costs is not true?
   a. Common costs are indirect costs that are incurred to benefit more than one segment and cannot be directly traced to a particular segment.
   b. Segment costs should include all costs attributable to that segment but only those costs that are actually caused by the segment.
   c. A good test for deciding whether to allocate indirect fixed costs is to determine whether the cost would be reduced or eliminated if the segment were eliminated.
   d. In general, all common costs should be allocated to segments.

7. If the segment margin of a division is positive, but the segment margin of an individual branch within the division is negative:
   a. the individual branch should be closed immediately.
   b. in the long run, the individual branch is not profitable.
   c. before deciding to eliminate the individual division, the firm should consider a number of quantitative and qualitative factors.
   d. Both b and c.

8. Kids Place offers day care for two-, three-, and four-year-old children. Monthly data for each division within the facility are as follows:

	Two-Year Olds	Three-Year Olds	Four-Year Olds
Revenues	$15,000	$15,000	$20,000
Variable costs	12,000	10,000	8,000
Contribution margin	$ 3,000	$ 5,000	$12,000
Traceable fixed costs	2,000	2,000	8,000

Common fixed costs of $6,000 are divided equally among the divisions. Segment margin for four-year olds is:
a. $4,000
b. $2,000
c. $ 0
d. ($2,000)

9. Candy Creations had sales of $950,000 and net operating income of $575,000. Operating assets during the year averaged $450,000. The manager of Candy Creations is considering the acquisition of a new machine, which would increase average operating assets by 10 percent. The new ROI would be:
a. 60.5%
b. 116.2%
c. 127.7%
d. 211.1%

10. Residual income:
a. is an alternative to ROI for manager performance evaluation.
b. is the amount of income earned in excess of a predetermined minimum level of return on assets.
c. is equal to ROI − (Average operating assets × Minimum required rate of return).
d. Both a and b.

11. Economic value added is equal to:
a. Before-tax operating profit − ((Total Assets − Current liabilities) × Weighted-average cost of capital)
b. After-tax operating profit − ((Total Assets − Current liabilities) × Weighted-average cost of capital)
c. Before-tax operating profit − ((Current Assets − Current liabilities) × Weighted-average cost of capital)
d. After-tax operating profit − ((Current Assets − Current liabilities) × Weighted-average cost of capital)

12. Which of the following statements comparing ROI and residual income is correct?
a. ROI is more useful as a performance measure for a single investment center.
b. Residual income is a better comparative measure than ROI.
c. ROI and residual income are equally good performance measures for a single investment center.
d. Residual income is more useful as a performance measure for a single investment center.

13. Managers may not perform at a desired level for a number of reasons. Which of the following is not one of those reasons?
a. Managers may lack the skills and abilities.
b. Managers may not be motivated enough to put forth the required effort.
c. a but not b.
d. Neither a nor b.

14. Creative Child Learning Company manufactures and sells children's CD-ROMs. The costs per unit for "Kid Fun" CD-ROMs are as follows:

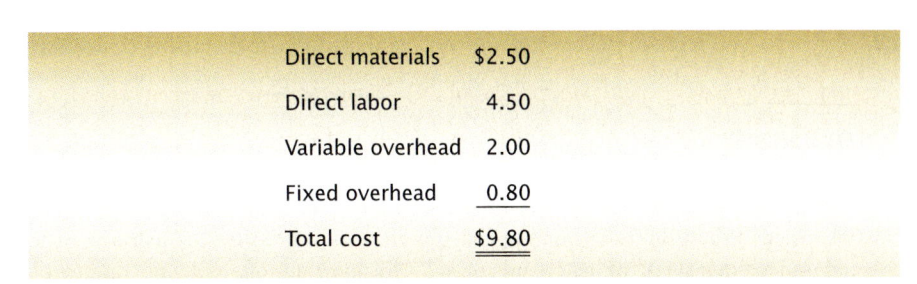

Direct materials	$2.50
Direct labor	4.50
Variable overhead	2.00
Fixed overhead	0.80
Total cost	$9.80

The company sells CD-ROMs to retail outlets for full cost plus a 25 percent markup. Each "Kid Fun" CD can also be sold to another corporate division to be upgraded and packaged with other CD-ROMs. The minimum transfer price for "Kid Fun" CD-ROMs, assuming that no contribution margin loss on outside sales exists, is:
a. $7.00
b. $9.00
c. $9.80
d. less than $7.00

15. Silly Slippers Company manufactures and sells children's slippers. The costs for each pair of infant slippers are as follows:

Direct materials	$0.75
Direct labor	1.00
Variable overhead	1.00
Fixed overhead	0.75
Total cost	$3.00

The company sells slippers to retail outlets for full cost plus a 20 percent markup. Slippers can also be sold to another corporate division to be packaged with a bib and a rattle as a gift set. Because an outside market exists for the product, the appropriate transfer price would be:
a. $2.25
b. $3.00
c. $3.60
d. It cannot be determined from the information provided.

Concept Questions

16. *(Objective 1)* Identify the advantages and disadvantages of decentralization.
17. *(Objective 1)* Discuss the impact of accounting information systems (AIS) on decentralization.
18. *(Objective 2)* What is responsibility accounting, and what is its impact on decision making?
19. *(Objective 3)* Define an investment center and explain how investment center managers might be evaluated.
20. *(Objective 4)* Describe segment costs and compare them to common costs.
21. *(Objective 5)* Define residual income and discuss how it compares to ROI.
22. *(Objective 6)* What is EVA?
23. *(Objective 6)* When is ROI a more useful performance measure than residual income?
24. *(Objective 7)* Why is noncash compensation important?
25. *(Objective 8)* Explain the term *transfer pricing* and why transfer pricing is necessary.

Exercises

26. Organizations use a variety of performance measures to evaluate managers. Central to the idea of responsibility accounting is that performance measures are reflective of activities under a manager's influence and control. Organizations often identify different levels of responsibility and refer to these levels as segments. The following performance measures and reports are used to evaluate managers of various segments.

a. Return on investment
b. Cost budgets
c. Labor usage variance
d. Sales budget
e. Segment margin
f. Sales volume variance
g. Residual income
h. Overall flexible budget variance
i. Sales price variance

Required

For each performance measure and report listed above, indicate which segment (e.g., cost center, revenue center, profit center, investment center) they would most likely be used to evaluate.

27. BTO, Inc. produces and sells two products—X-100 and X-200. Revenue and cost information for the two products are as follows:

	X-100	X-200
Selling price per unit	$ 10.00	$ 27.00
Variable expenses per unit	4.30	19.00
Traceable fixed expenses per year	$142,000	$54,000

✓ Segment margin for X-100: $100,250

BTO's common fixed expenses total $125,000 per year. Last year, the company produced and sold 42,500 units of X-100 and 19,000 units of X-200.

Required

Prepare a segmented income statement using the contribution format for BTO.

28. Paradise Burger Company makes two burgers, each in a separate division: cheeseburgers and chiliburgers. Segmented income statements for the most recent year follow:

	Cheeseburgers	Chiliburgers
Sales	$ 250,000	$ 600,000
Variable expenses	185,000	360,000
Contribution margin	$ 65,000	$ 240,000
Traceable fixed expenses	45,000	100,000
Segment margin	$ 20,000	$ 140,000

✓ Contribution margin ratio for cheeseburgers: 26%

Paradise Burger's management is considering a special advertising campaign during broadcast coverage of a major sporting event. Management has determined that based on the expense of the advertising campaign, $28,000, only one division can be featured. In-house marketing studies suggest that the campaign could increase sales of the Cheeseburgers division by $100,000 or increase sales of the Chiliburgers division by $75,000.

Required

Which product should be featured in the campaign? Why? Show computations to support your recommendation.

29. Henrietta Ltd. produces fine clothing for women. There are two primary divisions within the company: professional wear and formal wear. The following income statements were prepared for the divisions.

✓ Income for professional wear: $145,000

	Professional	Formal
Sales	$ 1,200,000	$ 1,750,000
Variable expenses	955,000	1,360,000
Contribution margin	$ 245,000	$ 390,000
Fixed expenses	115,000	175,000
Income	$ 130,000	$ 215,000

The above income statements were prepared by an inexperienced staff accountant. Common fixed expenses of $50,000 were allocated to the two divisions as follows: 30 percent to professional wear and 70 percent to formal wear.

Required

Prepare new segment income statements for Henrietta Ltd. after removing the common fixed expenses.

30. Dinning Corporation has two divisions. In the most recent year the Sintering Division reported sales of $150,000 and an asset turnover ratio of 3.0. The division's controller reported to headquarters that the rate of return on average invested assets was 18.0 percent.

Required

Calculate the percentage of net income to sales (i.e., margin).

31. Advanced Electronics has two separate, but related divisions: digital video and analog video. The digital video division has sales of $800,000, net operating income of $80,000, and average operating assets of $1,000,000.

Required

What is the ROI for the digital division?

32. Brew-Me-A-Cup is a new and growing chain of coffee shops. The company operates its business using segments to control and manage operations. The most profitable division is the Specialty Drinks division. In the Hillsborough Avenue location, the division has sales of $600,000, net operating income of $15,000, and average operating assets of $1,200,000.

Required

What is the asset turnover for the Specialty Drinks division?

33. Watson Investments generates sales of $2,500,000 and net operating income of $75,000 on $1,500,000 of assets under the company's control.

Required

What is Watson's margin?

34. Allied Electronics has a particular division that generates $3,000,000 in sales and operating income of $250,000 on average operating assets of $1,250,000. The company's management team has made it clear that division managers are expected to generate sufficient income to guarantee a minimum return of 10 percent.

Required

What is the division's residual income?

35. Garringer Glove is an old, family operated business. Current management is concerned that the company is beginning to lose its competitive advantage and fears that the company may encounter significant business challenges in the future. The company's controller has prepared the following data for use in the calculation of the economic value added (EVA) measure for presentation to the company's owners:

Before-tax profit	$ 100,000
Total assets	$2,500,000
Current liabilities	$1,200,000
Average interest rate on debt	7 %
Average tax rate	28 %

✓ EVA®: $(19,000)

Required

Calculate Garringer Glove's EVA. Is the company creating wealth for its owners?

36. Williamson Group operates a chain of bookstores. A recent business expansion plan resulted in the opening of more than 25 new stores. The Upland store has one additional feature that the Stowe store does not have—a small coffee shop. Early indications are that the coffee shop has driven up the location's revenues and profits. Operating data for two of these stores is provided below:

✓ Residual income for Stowe: $(1,500)

	Upland	Stowe
ROI	18.75 %	14.0 %
Net operating income	?	?
Minimum required return	15 %	15 %
Average operating assets	$200,000	$150,000
Residual income	?	?

Required

A. Calculate net operating income and residual income for each division.

B. Compare the two divisions and discuss the usefulness of ROI and residual income for the purpose of comparing the divisions.

37. The Upstart Shoe Company has two divisions: Stitching and Soles. The Soles division has a total cost of $15 per unit for its product, rubber soles, of which $10 is fixed. The Soles division also has idle capacity for up to 25,000 units per month. The Stitching division would like to purchase 20,000 units from the Soles division but feels that the $15 price is too high.

Required

Determine the lowest price the Soles division can sell at without incurring additional losses.

38. The Newton Company has two divisions: Hamilton and Jasper. The Hamilton division has a total cost of $30 per unit for its product, of which $20 is fixed. The Hamilton division is at full capacity. The Jasper division would like to purchase 20,000 units from Hamilton but thinks that the $35 price Hamilton typically charges outside customers is too high.

Required

Calculate the price at which the Hamilton division should sell the units to the Jasper division such that Hamilton will not incur additional losses.

39. The Robson division can sell its products externally for $60 per unit. The division's variable manufacturing costs are $26 per unit, and fixed manufacturing costs per unit are $10.

Required

Calculate the opportunity cost of transferring units internally if the division is operating at capacity.

40. Miller Company has two divisions, each of which is operated as a profit center. The Wheel Division charges the Molding Division $35 per unit for each unit transferred to them. Other data for the Wheel Division are as follows:

Variable cost per unit	$30.00
Total fixed costs	$10,000
Annual sales to Molding	5,000 units
Annual sales to outside customers	50,000 units

The Wheel Division is planning to raise its transfer price to $50 per unit. The Molding Division can purchase units at $40 each from outside vendors, but doing so would idle the Wheel Division's facilities that are now committed to producing units for the Molding Division. The Wheel Division cannot increase its sales to outside customers because there is not sufficient demand.

Required

From the perspective of the company as a whole, from whom should the Molding Division acquire the units, assuming the Molding Division's market is unaffected?

41. TerraTec, Inc. is a distributor of gardening supplies. The company is currently exploring manufacturing facilities in a foreign country that has a tax rate of 20% where it will produce a popular gardening tool that it sells in the U.S. for $50. TerraTec estimates the actual cost of producing the tool at $20 per unit. The company's U.S. tax rate is 30%.

Required

  A. Calculate the total after-tax profits that TerraTec would earn if the company sets a transfer price based on a 40% markup on cost.
  B. Calculate the total after-tax profits that TerraTec would earn if the company sets a transfer price based on a 70% markup on cost.

Problems

42. Simon Hinson Company operates two divisions: Gordon and Ronin. A segmented income statement for the company's most recent year is as follows:

	Total Company	Gordon Division	Ronin Division
Sales	$850,000	$250,000	$600,000
Less variable expenses	505,000	145,000	360,000
Contribution margin	$345,000	$105,000	$240,000
Less traceable fixed costs	145,000	45,000	100,000
Division segment margin	$200,000	$ 60,000	$140,000
Less common fixed costs	130,000		
Net income	$ 70,000		

LO 4

✓ Increase in income for question A: $35,700

Required

A. If the Gordon division increased its sales by $85,000 per year, how much would the company's net income change? Assume that all cost behavior patterns remained constant.
B. Assume that the Ronin division increased sales by $100,000, the Gordon division sales remained the same, and there was no change in fixed costs.
  (1) Calculate the net income amounts for each division and the total company.
  (2) Calculate the segment margin ratios before and after these changes and comment on the results. Explain the changes.
C. How do the sales increases and decreases impact divisional contribution margin and segment margin?

43. Top management is trying to determine a consistent but fair valuation system to use to evaluate each of its four divisions. This year's performance data is summarized as follows:

LO 5 6

✓ ROI for division 1 in question A: 25%

	Division			
	1	2	3	4
Operating income	$1,000	$1,200	$ 1,600	$1,600
Operating assets	4,000	6,000	15,000	8,000
Current liabilities	400	2,000	2,400	200

Required

A. Which division would earn a bonus if top management used ROI based on operating assets?
B. Which division would earn a bonus if top management used ROI based on operating assets minus current liabilities?
C. Which division would earn a bonus if top management calculated residual income based on operating assets with a minimum return of 12%?
D. Which division would earn a bonus if top management calculated residual income based on operating assets minus current liabilities with a minimum return of 12%?

✓ ROI if machine is not purchased: 37.5%

44. You are the manager of a franchise operating division of the Kwik-Copies Company. Your company evaluates your division using ROI, computed with end-of-year gross asset balances, and calculates manager bonuses based on the percentage increase in ROI over the prior year. Your division has $9,000,000 in assets. Your budgeted income statement for the fiscal year is as follows:

Sales	$16,500,000
Variable expenses	3,000,000
Contribution margin	$13,500,000
Fixed expenses	7,750,000
Depreciation expense	2,375,000
Division profit	$ 3,375,000

During the year, you consider buying a new copy machine for $4,000,000, which will enable you to expand the output of your division and reduce operating costs. The copy machine would have no salvage value and would be depreciated over five years using straight-line depreciation. It will increase output by 10 percent while reducing fixed costs by $4,000,000. If you decide to purchase the copy machine, it will be installed in late December but will not be ready for use until the following year. As a result, no depreciation will be taken on it this year.

If you do buy the copy machine, you will have to dispose of the copy machine you are now using, which you just purchased during the current year. The old copy machine cost you $4,000,000 but has no salvage value. Of the depreciation in the income statement, $1,000,000 is for this machine. In the ROI calculations, the company includes any gains or losses from copy equipment disposal as part of the company's operating income.

Required

A. What is your division's ROI this year if you do not acquire the new machine?
B. What is your division's ROI this year if you do acquire the new copy machine?
C. What is your division's expected ROI for next year if the copy machine is acquired and meets expectations? Assume that unit costs and prices do not change.
D. As the manager, what action will you take and why?

✓ ROI for the scrubber: 8.57%

45. Jim McLean, manager of the Airflow division of Beal Manufacturing, is contemplating two investment alternatives. Because Beal does not have excess cash to make the necessary investment, the company will borrow $1,400,000. The company will pay interest at the rate of 8 percent. Without either investment included, his division has after-tax income of $3,500,000 and average operating assets of $29,000,000. The company's tax rate is 30 percent. Information related to the two investment alternatives follows:

	Scrubber	Cooling System
After-tax operating income	$ 60,000	$ 90,000
Investment expenditure	$700,000	$700,000

Required

A. Calculate the ROI for each investment. Round your answer to two decimals.
B. If Beal borrows the entire $1,400,000 for the two investments, what is the combined EVA for the two investments? Will the investments create wealth for Beal Manufacturing?

46. Raddington Industries produces tool and die machinery for various manufacturers. The company expanded vertically in 2003 by acquiring Regis Steel Company, one of its suppliers of alloy steel plates. In order to manage the two separate businesses, the operations of Regis Steel are reported separately as an investment center.

Raddington monitors its divisions on the basis of both unit contribution and return on average investment (ROI), with the investment defined as average operating assets used. Raddington has a policy of basing all employee bonuses on divisional ROI. All investments in operating assets are expected to earn a minimum return of 11 percent before income taxes.

Regis's cost of goods sold is considered to be entirely variable, whereas the division's administrative expenses are not dependent on volume. Selling expenses are a mixed cost with 40 percent attributed to sales volume. Regis's ROI has ranged from 11.8 percent to 14.7 percent since 2003. During the fiscal year ended November 30, 2005, Regis contemplated a capital acquisition with an estimated ROI of 11.5 percent; however, division management decided against the investment because it believed that the investment would decrease Regis's overall ROI

The 2005 income statement for Regis is presented below. The division's operating assets were $15,750,000 at November 30, 2005, a 5 percent increase over the 2004 year-end balance.

LO 5 6

✓ ROI for 2005: 12%

Regis Steel Division
Operating Statement
For the Year Ended November 30, 2005
($000 omitted)

Sales revenue	$25,000
Cost of goods sold	16,500
Gross profit	$ 8,500
Administrative expenses	3,955
Selling expenses	2,700
Income from operations before income taxes	$ 1,845

Required

A. Calculate the unit contribution for Regis Steel Division if 1,484,000 units were produced and sold during the year ended November 30, 2005.
B. Calculate the return on investment (ROI) for Regis Steel Division for 2005.
C. Calculate the residual income using the average operating assets employed for 2005 for the Regis Steel Division.
D. Explain why the management of Regis Steel Division would have been more likely to accept the contemplated acquisition if residual income rather than ROI were used as a performance measure.
E. The Regis Steel Division is a separate investment center within Raddington Industries. Identify several items that Regis Steel should control if it is to be evaluated fairly by either the ROI or residual income performance measure.

47. Eat More Food Company began business in January 2005. It produces various food products that pass through two divisions. The Lansing Division processes the food, and the Simeon Division packages it. During 2005, the Lansing Division processed 100,000 pounds of food for a total production cost of $250,000. Its selling and administrative expenses amounted to $50,000. The Simeon Division incurred $100,000 of additional production costs in completing the 100,000 pounds. The Simeon Division sold the 100,000 pounds of completed units for $450,000 and incurred selling and administrative expenses for the year of $30,000.

LO 8

EXCEL

Activity Making Decision A

✓ Net income for the Simeon Division in question A: $20,000

Required

A. Prepare divisional income statements for 2005 for each of these two divisions, assuming that the transfer price is equal to Lansing Division's total costs (i.e., production costs and selling and administrative expenses).
B. Prepare divisional income statements for 2005 for each of these two divisions, assuming that the transfer price is based on the external market price of $3.50 per pound that Lansing would charge outside customers.
C. Which statement presents a better measure of each division's performance? Why?

48. Adler Industries is a vertically integrated firm with several divisions that operate as decentralized profit centers. Adler's Systems Division manufactures scientific instruments and uses the products of two other Adler divisions. The Board Division manufactures printed circuit boards (PCBs). One PCB model is made exclusively for the Systems Division, using proprietary designs, whereas less complex models are sold to outside customers. The products of the Transistor Division are sold in a well-developed competitive market; however, one transistor model is also used by the Systems Division.

The costs per unit of the products used by the Systems Division are as follows:

	PCB	Transistor
Direct materials	$ 2.50	$ 0.80
Direct labor	4.50	1.00
Variable overhead	2.00	0.50
Fixed overhead	0.80	0.75
Total cost	$ 9.80	$ 3.05

The Board Division sells its commercial products at full cost plus a 25 percent markup and believes that the proprietary board made for the Systems Division would sell for $12.25 per unit on the open market. The market price of the transistor used by the Systems Division is $3.70 per unit.

Required

A. What would be the impact on the Transistor Division if the per unit transfer price from the Transistor Division to the Systems Division were the full cost of $3.05?
B. Assume that the Systems Division is able to purchase a large quantity of transistors from an outside source at $2.90 per unit. The Transistor Division, having excess capacity, agrees to lower its transfer price to $2.90 per unit. Would this benefit the company as a whole?
C. The Board and Systems Divisions have negotiated a transfer price of $11.00 per printed circuit board. What is the likely response from each division if this negotiated price is used?

Cases

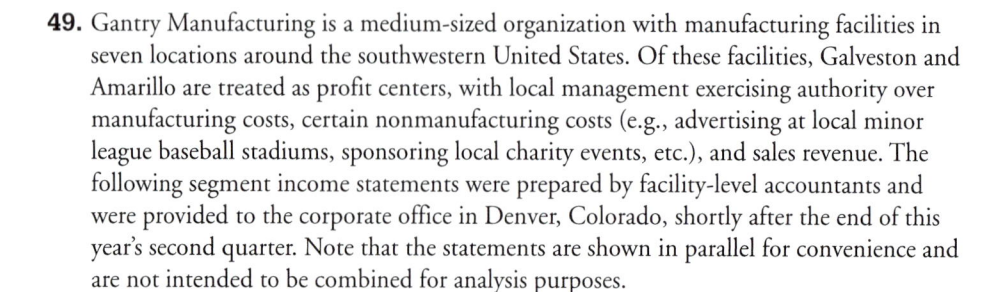

49. Gantry Manufacturing is a medium-sized organization with manufacturing facilities in seven locations around the southwestern United States. Of these facilities, Galveston and Amarillo are treated as profit centers, with local management exercising authority over manufacturing costs, certain nonmanufacturing costs (e.g., advertising at local minor league baseball stadiums, sponsoring local charity events, etc.), and sales revenue. The following segment income statements were prepared by facility-level accountants and were provided to the corporate office in Denver, Colorado, shortly after the end of this year's second quarter. Note that the statements are shown in parallel for convenience and are not intended to be combined for analysis purposes.

Segmented Income Statements Galveston and Amarillo Facilities
For the quarter ending June 30, 2005

	Galveston	Amarillo
Sales	$22,500,000	$18,450,000
Variable expenses	19,850,000	17,640,000
Contribution margin	$ 2,650,000	$ 810,000
Divisional fixed expenses	1,400,000	1,030,000
Segment margin	$ 1,250,000	$ (220,000)

The managers of these two facilities are former classmates at the University of Texas at Austin and routinely stay in touch with each other. Shortly after receiving the quarterly results from his accountant the Amarillo manager, Jim Lowell, called his friend in Galveston to talk about the surprising loss shown on his facility's income statement. After a short conversation with the Galveston manager, Jim met with his accountant. He learned the following:

- A recent memo sent from the corporate controller to all facility controllers indicated that new manufacturing overhead rates should be used beginning May 1, 2005. The old rate was $2.80 per direct labor hour and the new rate is $3.25 per direct labor hour. The memo had a new policy statement attached to it that stated individual manufacturing facilities could no longer establish individual overhead rates.

- An average of 210 employees worked 40 hours per week during the quarter. There were 13 weeks during the second quarter.

- Each division was required to record a one-time expense associated with ethics training for all new and current employees. The Amarillo facility received an expense allocation of $58,000. Sixty-five percent of the allocation is related to manufacturing employees and the remainder is related to administrative employees.

- The corporate office also implemented a new policy related to certain divisional employees' retirement, insurance, and other benefits. In prior years, all benefits were paid by the corporate office and were not allocated to local facilities. However, the company's new president believes that those costs are more properly reflected in the expenses of the individual facilities because they are incurred by local employees. In total, additional retirement and insurance expenses of $46,500 were incurred for each month during the quarter ended June 30, 2005. Thirty percent of the monthly expenses are related to manufacturing employees and the remainder is related to administrative employees.

Jim was immediately frustrated by all that he learned from the accountant. Because his and other managers' bonuses depend on quarterly financial performance, he feels that the corporate memos unfairly reduce his division's profits. He asked his controller to prepare a revised income statement without the changes implemented by the corporate office during the quarter. Amarillo's revised income statement appeared as follows:

Segmented Income Statement Amarillo Facility
For the quarter ending June 30, 2005
(Revised)

Sales	$18,450,000
Variable expenses	17,511,310
Contribution margin	$ 938,690
Divisional fixed expenses	912,050
Segment margin	$ 26,640

Jim is not particularly pleased with the financial performance of his facility, but prefers to report a small profit as opposed to a more significant loss. He now must decide how to communicate with the corporate office about this revised income statement. You should bear in mind that the corporate office only provides administrative services and does not manufacture goods; however, sales activities for five of the company's facilities are handled in the corporate office.

Required

    A. Assist Jim by identifying reasons that support his desire to not require the Amarillo facility to implement the changes made by the corporate office.

    B. What are the implications of having the corporate office issue memos requiring the facilities to record certain expenses given the company's bonus structure? How will the corporate office's new policy affect the facility management's motivation?

    C. What are some of the possible bases that Gantry Manufacturing could use to allocate fixed expenses?

50. Elaine Shumate has been working for GSM, a pharmaceutical research company, for more than seven years. It is her first job since finishing her graduate work in molecular biology and her performance evaluations have been exemplary. She has received increasing responsibility as opportunities have become available at GSM. Unfortunately, her knowledge and experience have not prepared her for the situation she currently faces. GSM has invested heavily in a molecular identification process (MIP) that the company's top management believes holds tremendous promise for the future. If all goes well, the company plans to patent the process and license the process to large pharmaceutical companies for their use in medication production. Elaine is the lead manager on MIP and she is worried that the latest research results do not look as promising as earlier results. The vice president of research, Blake Walton, has asked Elaine to meet with him to discuss the results. After a brief discussion in the hallway, Blake suggests that Elaine take another look at the latest results. He doesn't believe that her interpretation of the data is correct.

    In preparing for their meeting, she looked over the company's earlier cost estimates and operating income projections for the project. Records indicate that the estimated research and development costs were $140 million and annual operating income was expected to be approximately $25 million. Given the latest results, MIP may have fewer applications in the pharmaceutical industry than originally believed.

    Elaine spoke with Richard Lawrence, vice president of sales, to get an updated estimate of the potential market value for MIP. Richard suggested that MIP would likely generate operating income of just $17.5 million per year if the recent results hold up after further testing. Elaine knows that Blake is not going to be happy with this news. Blake is scheduled to meet with the company's board of directors next week to discuss the need for additional investment capital from venture capitalists in the next year and the company's plans for a public stock offering in the next several years. Elaine stands to benefit substantially from stock options if the company goes public. GSM's future may ride on the outcome of that meeting.

Required

    A. What is the ROI for MIP based on original estimates? What is the ROI if Richard Lawrence's new revenue projections are used?

    B. Elaine feels pressure to deliver "good news" to Blake. What advice would you give to her? Given the possible personal financial rewards that Elaine may enjoy if GSM goes public, would your advice change?

    C. What responsibilities does Elaine have to other GSM employees, the board of directors, and the venture capitalists?

Group and Internet Exercises

51. Visit Stern Stewart & Co.'s website to learn more about the economic value added framework. The company describes four primary uses of the economic value added framework, referred to as the "Four M's." Prepare a memo that explains the four primary uses of the economic value added framework.

52. Executive compensation has received a great deal of attention in light of the many corporate scandals that have occurred in the last several years. Some observers believe that management often makes decisions that are good for management, but not so good for shareholders and other stakeholders. Many proponents of change suggest that upper management should be compensated such that they have a long-term focus as opposed to a short-term one. Conduct a search on the Internet or in your school's library to locate articles in the financial press (e.g., *Wall Street Journal*, *Business Week*, *Fortune*, etc.) that discuss some of the suggested changes to executive compensation. Prepare a brief memo that describes these changes. Do you think the suggestions will be successful at encouraging management to adopt a long-term focus on business?

Chapter 12 Performance Evaluation Using the Balanced Scorecard

In the previous two chapters, we discussed cost control and performance evaluation in responsibility centers, using such financial measures as variance analysis, segmented income statements, return on investment, residual income, and economic value added. In this chapter, we expand that analysis to include a variety of nonfinancial and qualitative measures used in a "balanced scorecard" approach to measuring performance. Because of changing technology, global competition, and an increased awareness of the need to focus on customer needs, these nonfinancial and qualitative performance measures have become an integral component of effective managerial decision making.

The balanced scorecard looks at performance from four unique but related perspectives: financial, customer, internal business, and learning and growth. The chapter concludes with a discussion of key measures of quality, environmental impact, productivity, efficiency and timeliness, and marketing effectiveness within the four perspectives of the balanced scorecard.

Learning Objectives

After studying the material in this chapter, you should be able to:

1 Describe the balanced scorecard approach to performance measurement

2 Describe key dimensions of the financial, customer, internal business, and learning and growth perspectives of the balanced scorecard

3 Define quality costs and explain the tradeoffs among prevention costs, appraisal costs, internal failure costs, and external failure costs

4 Define environmental costs and explain the tradeoffs among prevention costs, appraisal costs, internal failure costs, and external failure costs

5 Compute key measures of efficiency and timeliness including customer response time, manufacturing cycle time, and throughput

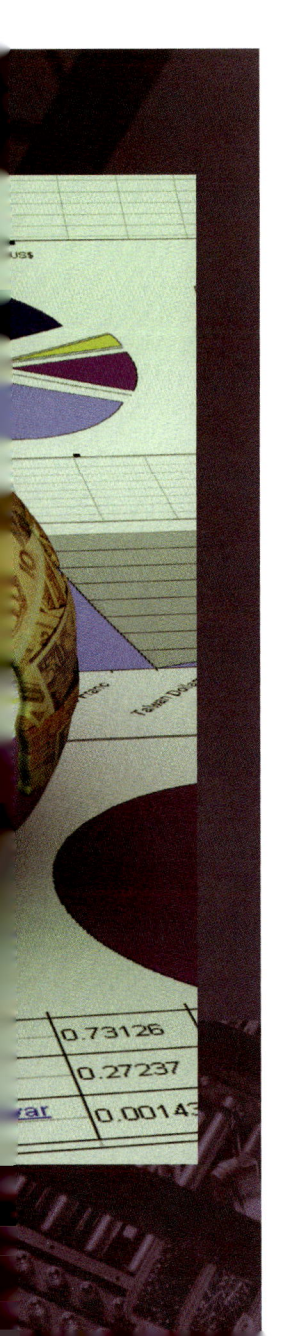

Introduction

When customers choose a restaurant for a meal, they are probably *not* concerned with how well the restaurant meets its cost goals, whether its segment margin is positive, or the level of its return on investment (ROI). Customers probably *are* concerned with the price of the meal, how long they have to wait to be seated and waited on, and the quality of the food that is served. These factors are all critically important to the success of the restaurant.

Customers who have a bad experience may choose to not return to the restaurant. Those customers also have a tendency to inform friends or relatives about the bad experience. While financial measures of performance would eventually capture customer service problems (a decrease in customer satisfaction will eventually lead to reduced sales, which will reduce income and have a negative impact on ROI), these measures are not captured quickly enough and are not detailed enough to help management correct customer service problems in a timely manner.

In today's competitive business environment, characterized by rapidly changing technology, global competition, and a focus on meeting and exceeding customer's expectations, managers, in order to be successful, must focus on factors other than financial performance. Traditional measures of financial performance are simply not adequate to fully assess the performance of companies and their segments in this environment. Quality may be more important than cost, timeliness more important than meeting budget, and customer service more important than ROI.

The Balanced Scorecard

Traditional accounting measures of performance dealing with historical financial data are of little use in making decisions concerning customer satisfaction, quality issues, productivity, efficiency, and employee satisfaction. Managers also need information concerning the success or failure of new products or marketing campaigns and the success of programs designed to enhance customer value. The **balanced scorecard** approach to performance measurement uses a set of financial and nonfinancial measures that relate to the overall strategy of the organization. By integrating financial and nonfinancial performance measures, the balanced scorecard helps to keep management focused on all of a company's critical success factors, not just its financial ones. The balanced scorecard also helps to keep short-term operating performance in line with long-term strategy.

As shown in Exhibit 12-1, utilizing a balanced scorecard approach requires looking at performance from four different but related perspectives: financial, customer, internal business, and learning and growth.

Objective 1
Describe the balanced scorecard approach to performance measurement

KEY CONCEPT
The balanced scorecard approach integrates financial and nonfinancial performance measures.

EXHIBIT 12-1 The Balanced Scorecard Approach to Performance Measurement

- **Financial Perspective**: How do we create value for our stakeholders?
- **Customer Perspective**: How do customers view us?
- **Internal Business Perspective**: At what business processes must we excel?
- **Learning and Growth Perspective**: How do we continue to improve, learn and grow?
- **Strategy** (center)

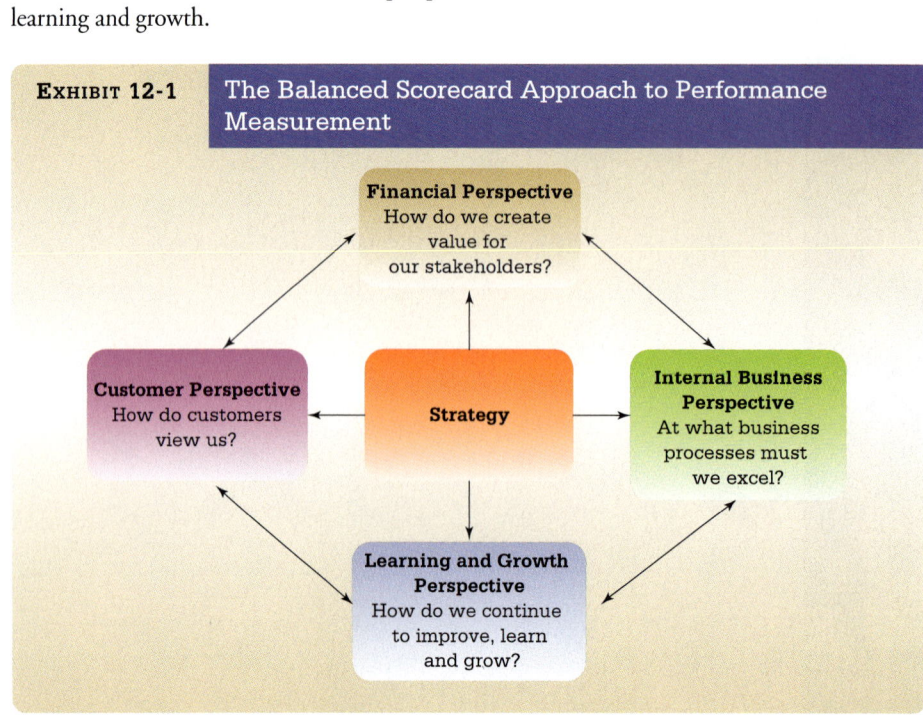

Financial Perspective

The primary goal of every profit-making enterprise is to show a profit. Profit allows the enterprise to provide a return on investment to investors, to repay creditors, and to adequately compensate management and employees. Critical success factors under this perspective include sales, costs, measures of profit such as operating income and segment margin, and measures of investment center performance such as ROI, residual income and EVA. However, under the balanced scorecard approach, financial performance is seen in the larger context of the company's overall goals and objectives relating to its customers and suppliers, internal processes, and employees.

> **Objective 2**
>
> Describe key dimensions of the financial, customer, internal business, and learning and growth perspectives of the balanced scorecard

Customer Perspective

Many successful businesses have found that focusing on customers and meeting or exceeding their needs is more important in the long run than simply focusing on financial measures of performance. After all, it is the customer who ultimately incurs the costs of producing products and contributes to a company's profits. Considering the customer perspective is therefore critical in attaining the financial goals of a company. Critical success factors under this perspective are likely to include increasing the quality of products and services, reducing delivery time, and increasing customer satisfaction. Measures of performance appropriate under this perspective include the number of warranty claims and returned products (for quality), customer response time and the percentage of on-time deliveries (for reducing delivery time), and customer complaints and repeat business (for customer satisfaction).

A second dimension of the customer perspective focuses on the critical success factors of increasing market share and penetrating new markets. Measures of performance appropriate for this dimension include market share, market saturation, customer loyalty, and new products introduced into the marketplace. Focusing on the customer perspective can result in impressive financial returns. For example, at Ford, a one percentage point increase in customer loyalty represents a $100 million increase in profits.

Internal Business Perspective

The internal business process perspective deals with objectives across the company's entire value chain: from research and development to post-sale customer service. It is linked to the financial perspective through its emphasis on improving the efficiency of manufacturing processes and with the customer perspective through its focus on improving processes and products to better meet customer needs. Every company will approach this perspective differently, as the processes that add value to products and services are likely to differ by company. However, critical success factors include productivity, manufacturing cycle time and throughput, and manufacturing cycle efficiency (MCE).

Learning and Growth Perspective

The learning and growth perspective links the critical success factors in the other perspectives and ensures an environment that supports and allows the objectives of the other three perspectives to be achieved. If learning improves, internal business processes will improve, leading to increased customer value and satisfaction and ultimately to better financial performance. Critical success factors center on three areas. The first is the efficient and effective use of employees (employee empowerment). Measures include improving employee morale, increasing skill development, increasing employee satisfaction, reducing employee turnover, and increasing the participation of employees in the decision process. The second critical success factor is increasing information systems capabilities through improving the availability and timeliness of information. The third critical success factor involves measures of product innovation, such as increasing the number of new products, new patents, and so on. Exhibit 12-2 provides a summary of critical success factors within each of these perspectives.

> **KEY CONCEPT**
>
> The balanced scorecard approach requires looking at performance from four different but related perspectives: financial, customer, internal business, and learning and growth.

EXHIBIT 12-2 Critical Success Factors Related to the Four Perspectives of the Balanced Scorecard

Critical Success Factors	Financial	Customer	Internal Business	Learning and Growth
Sales, costs, measures of profit (operating income, segment margin, etc.), ROI, residual income, EVA	X			
Quality		X	X	
Delivery time (customer response time)		X		
Customer satisfaction		X		
Market share		X		
New markets		X		
Environmental management		X		
Productivity			X	
Manufacturing cycle time and throughput				X
Manufacturing cycle efficiency (MCE)		X	X	
Employee empowerment				X
Information systems capabilities				X
Product innovation		X		X

Measuring and Controlling Quality Costs

Over the past 20 years or so, the demand by customers for quality products and services at an affordable price has drastically changed the way companies do business. As a result, one of the critical success factors under the customer perspective of the balanced scorecard is increasing the quality of products and services. Quality is no longer just a buzzword but a way of life. Managers have come to realize that improving quality increases sales through higher customer satisfaction and demand, reduces costs, and increases the long-term profitability of companies.

However, before we go any further, just what is meant by quality? Although you may "know it when you see it," most businesses describe **quality** as "meeting or exceeding customers' expectations." Of course, this requires that a product perform as it is intended but also requires that a product be reliable and durable and that these features be provided at a competitive price.

Companies have focused on improving the quality of the products or services they sell through a variety of initiatives, such as total quality management (TQM), market-driven quality, and strategic quality management. Although the details of these methods may differ, all focus on meeting or exceeding customer expectations, continuous improvement, and employee empowerment. Continuous improvement, an idea pioneered by Toyota in Japan, refers to a system of improvement based on a series of gradual and often small improvements rather than major changes requiring very large investments. Called **kaizen** in Japan, it requires active participation by all of a company's employees—from the CEO to the worker on the assembly line. Kaizen takes the view that everyone is responsible for continuous improvement.[1] Employee empowerment refers to companies' providing appropriate opportunities for training, skill development, and advancement so those employees can become active participants and active decision makers in an organization. As discussed earlier, empowering employees is a key dimension of the learning and growth perspective of the balanced scorecard.

Along with their quality improvement initiatives, many companies seek ISO 9000 certification. **ISO 9000** is a set of guidelines for quality management focusing on the design, production, inspection, testing, installing, and servicing of products, processes, and services. Although originally developed by the International Standards Organization (ISO) to control the quality of products sold in Europe, it has been widely adopted in the United States and in other countries worldwide. U.S. companies may also compete for the Malcolm Baldrige National Quality Award. This award was created in 1987 to recognize quality excellence in manufacturing, small business, service, education, and health care.

Improving the quality of products and services is an important component in both the customer perspective and the internal business perspective of the balanced scorecard. From a customer perspective, one of the most important measures of quality is customer satisfaction and the number of customer complaints. If the number of meals returned to the kitchen is increasing, management should probably infer that customers are unhappy with the quality of the meal. The number of warranty claims can also serve as a measure of quality. The increase in warranty work performed on a certain model of automobile indicates a potential problem with the production process and the quality of the car produced. If customer complaints and warranty claims are increasing, they provide a signal to management that quality may be a problem. However, poor quality is not the only explanation for increasing customer complaints. In addition, these measures are not perfect in that customers do not always complain or return products when quality problems are evident. For example, restaurant patrons may not complain about subpar meals, and customers may simply discard defective merchandise instead of returning it. Therefore, management must be careful to provide a mechanism to make it easy for customers to complain, easy to return defective products, and so on.

From the internal business perspective, quality measures center on improving output yields, reducing defects in raw materials and finished products, and reducing downtime owing to quality problems. Ideally, defects are detected before they leave the factory and the manufacturing process adapted accordingly. The amount of scrap can also indicate potential quality problems in the production process. Although a certain amount of scrap is acceptable and even necessary in most manufacturing environments, an excessive amount should raise a red flag indicating possible problems that are causing an increase in the number of defective units in the process.

Doing Business.

HOW DO THEY DO IT?

For years, automobiles built by Toyota have been ranked at the top with respect to most measures of quality and reliability. Although American automakers have been trying to close the quality gap between their cars and those produced by Toyota, it has been a struggle. What is the key to Toyota's ability to produce high quality automobiles year after year? While Toyota strives for *kaizen* or continuous improvement in its manufacturing processes, at the same time, it strives for *hejunka* or standardization. How does standardization increase quality? In a stable manufacturing environment, the "noise" created by a sudden defect caused by a malfunctioning machine, low quality materials, or other problems stands out to such an extent that it is easy for managers to identify and fix ("Why Toyota Wins Such High Marks on Quality Surveys," *Wall Street Journal*, March 15, 2001, A11).

---

[1] In addition to quality improvements, kaizen techniques are used to continually reduce the cost of products and services in target costing (see Chapter 13).

The Costs of Quality

Objective 3

Define quality costs and explain the tradeoffs among prevention costs, appraisal costs, internal failure costs, and external failure costs

Improving quality can be costly. On average, U.S. companies spend 20 to 30 percent of every sales dollar on quality costs.[2] The results of a study published in *Business Week* found that companies that had received quality awards enjoyed higher growth in sales, assets, and operating income compared with a control group and that the stock price of the quality award winners showed higher appreciation than the stock price of other companies.[3]

In evaluating managers based on quality concerns, it is useful to have a framework for comparing the benefits of providing a high-quality product or service with the costs that result from poor quality. To facilitate this comparison, quality costs are typically classified into four general categories: (1) prevention costs, (2) appraisal costs, (3) internal failure costs, and (4) external failure costs. Examples of specific types of prevention, appraisal, internal failure and external failure costs are shown in Exhibit 12-3.

EXHIBIT 12-3 Quality Costs

Prevention Costs	Appraisal (Detection) Costs	Internal Failure Costs	External Failure Costs
Design and engineering costs	Inspecting raw materials	Material, labor and other manufacturing costs incurred in rework	Cost of repairs made under warranty
Quality training	Testing goods in the manufacturing process	Cost of scrap	Replacement of defective parts
Supervision	Final product testing	Cost of spoilage	Product recalls
Quality improvement projects		Cost of downtime	Liability costs from defective products
Training and technical support provided to suppliers		Cost of design changes	Lost sales
		Cost of reinspections	
		Disposal of defective products	

Prevention costs are incurred to prevent product failure from occurring. These costs are typically incurred early in the value chain and include design and engineering costs, as well as training, supervision, and the costs of quality improvement projects. If parts are purchased from an outside supplier, these costs may include providing training and technical support to the supplier in order to increase the quality of purchased materials. Prevention costs are incurred to eliminate quality problems before they occur. Most companies find that incurring prevention costs up front is less expensive in the long run than product failure costs.

Appraisal (detection) costs are incurred in inspecting, identifying, and isolating defective products and services before they reach the customer. These include the costs of inspecting raw materials, testing goods throughout the manufacturing process, and final product testing and inspection. In practice, it is very difficult to ensure quality through inspection. It is time consuming and costly to inspect every unit of product. Therefore, sampling is usually used to identify the problems with the production process. However, sampling is certainly not foolproof and is not likely to catch all quality problems. In general, it is more effective to design quality into a product through prevention activities rather than to inspect quality into a product using appraisal activities.

If a product or a service is defective in any way or does not meet customer expectations, failure costs are incurred. **Internal failure costs** are incurred once the product is produced and then determined to be defective (through the appraisal process) but before it is sold to

---
[2]Michael R. Ostrega, "Return on Investment Through the Costs of Quality," *Journal of Cost Management* (Summer 1991): 37.
[3]"Rewards of Quality Awards," *Business Week*, September 21, 1998, 26.

customers. Internal failure costs include the material, labor, and other manufacturing costs incurred in reworking defective products and the costs of scrap and spoilage. Internal failure costs also include downtime caused by quality problems, design changes, and the costs of reinspections and retesting. If no defects exist, internal failure costs will be zero. On the other hand, a high level of internal failure costs should be an indication to management that more attention needs to be spent in preventing quality problems to eliminate or to reduce the number of defective products during the production process.

External failure costs are incurred after a defective product is delivered to a customer. External failure costs include the cost of repairs made under warranty or the replacement of defective parts, product recalls (such as in the automobile industry), liability costs arising from legal actions against the seller, and eventually lost sales. Although the cost of potential lawsuits and lost sales may be difficult to measure, the cost of external failures is likely to exceed other quality costs. Failure costs, both internal and external, are like bandages—they address only symptoms rather than fix the underlying problem. When unhappy customers decide not to purchase products from a company because of quality problems, the domino effect can be devastating—particularly when safety is a concern.

Hitting the Bottom Line.

THE REAL COST OF QUALITY

In the summer of 1999, Coca-Cola faced one of the most serious crises in its history. The problem? A Coke bottling plant in Antwerp, Belgium, failed to follow crucial quality control procedures, including receiving quality assurances from its suppliers and simply making sure that the carbon dioxide used to give Coke its fizz tasted and smelled fresh. As a result, contaminated carbon dioxide was pumped into the holding tanks at the bottling plant, resulting in bad-smelling Coca-Cola and hundreds of sick consumers. In the aftermath, Coke products were recalled all over Europe. Coca-Cola Enterprises, Inc. (the bottling company owned 40 percent by Coca-Cola) estimates that the problems resulted in a charge against earnings of more than $100 million. More recently, Mitsubishi, the maker of popular SUVs and automobiles such as the Diamante, Eclipse, Outlander, and Galant admitted to more than 10 years of covering up potentially deadly defects and hiding them from government regulators. Since June 2004, the company has issued recalls affecting more than 26 different models and 225,000 vehicles. The impact on the company has been severe—a 40 percent decline in sales during the 2004 fiscal year. To give this impact even more context, consider that the company had annual sales of more than $32 billion in 2003. There is little doubt that the real cost of quality for Mitsubishi has been in the form of external failure costs—lost sales of approximately $13 billion ("Anatomy of a Recall: How Coke's Controls Fizzled Out in Europe," *Wall Street Journal*, June 29, 1999, "Coca Cola Enterprises Raises Estimate of Cost of Big Recall in Europe," *Wall Street Journal*, July 13, 1999, "Mitsubishi Motors Asks Rescuers for More Money," *Wall Street Journal*, June 30, 2004, and Mitsubishi Motors Corp.'s website).

Minimizing Quality Costs

Although quality costs in many U.S. companies may reach 20 to 30 percent of sales, experts suggest that the total costs of quality should not exceed 2 to 4 percent of sales. The problem faced by management is to reduce the costs of quality while maintaining a high-quality product or service. The goal, of course, is to minimize all the quality costs. However, it may be prudent to increase expenditures in one or more areas in order to decrease other costs. For example, as you have seen, external failure costs are serious and potentially devastating to companies. Both external and internal failure costs can be reduced (theoretically to zero) by paying more attention to quality issues early in the value chain. Products can be designed to emphasize quality and durability, suppliers can be certified, employees can be trained, and the manufacturing process can be improved to increase quality throughout the value chain. Increasing expenditures related to prevention and appraisal can result in significant overall cost savings in the long run. As you can see in Exhibit 12-4, the traditional view of managing total quality costs suggests that increasing prevention and appraisal costs will reduce defective units (and failure costs) but that there are tradeoffs in doing so. The traditional view suggests that total quality costs are minimized at a level of product quality below 100 percent.

Exhibit 12-4 implies that total quality costs are minimized at a point less than that associated with zero defects. However, additional prevention and appraisal activities are likely to reduce defects even further. Should companies continue to incur prevention and appraisal costs beyond this point?

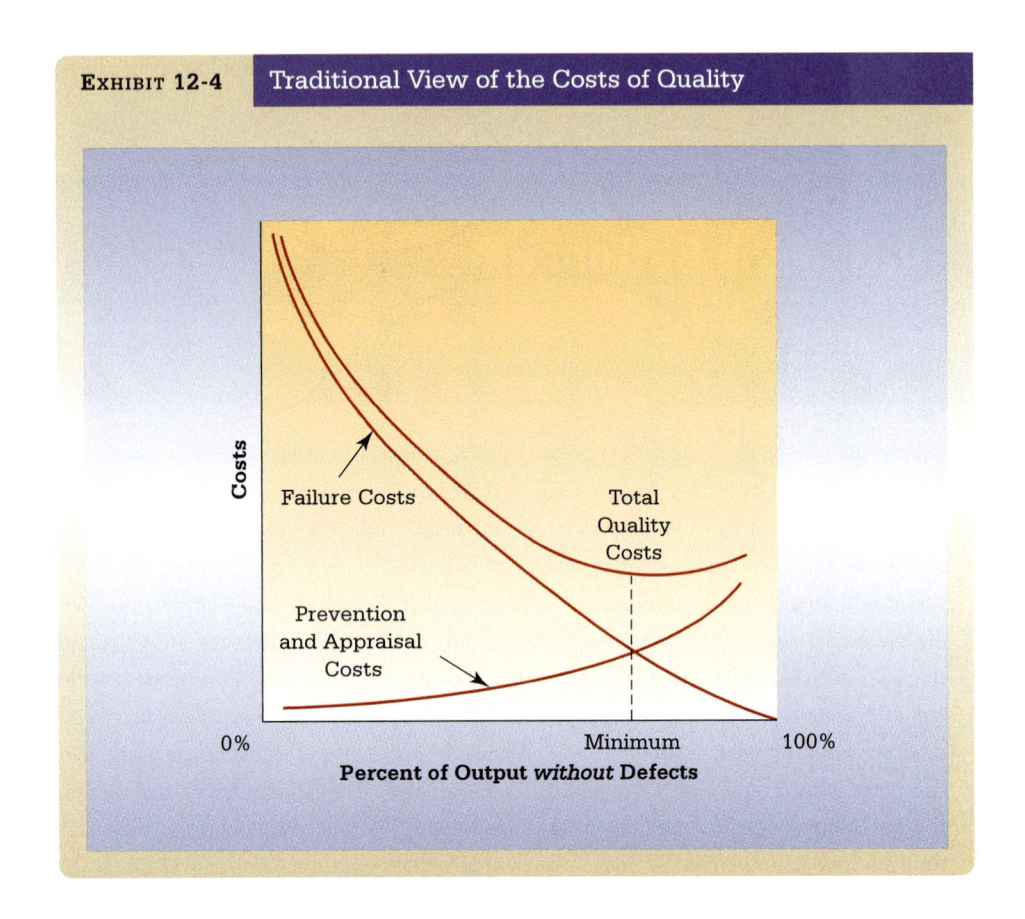

EXHIBIT 12-4 Traditional View of the Costs of Quality

A more contemporary view of quality costs recognizes that a number of failure costs are difficult to measure. For example, poor quality can lead to lost sales. This outcome tends to increase the costs of external failures as the percentage of defective units increases. In addition, rather than continually increasing as quality improves (as in Exhibit 12-4), prevention and appraisal costs may actually decrease as a company nears a level of zero defects. As you can see in Exhibit 12-5, this implies that total quality costs are minimized at a level of zero defects.

To illustrate how different measures of quality might be used in a variety of companies, let's go back and look at some of the companies featured throughout the book. As previously discussed, Northern Lights Custom Cabinets manufactures custom kitchen and bathroom cabinets. Although Big Al's Pizza Emporium and Garcia & Buffett CPAs are not manufacturing companies, they too may want to measure quality as a critical success factor. For all three, quality measures might center on factors such as customer satisfaction, the number of defective or "bad" products, and the percentage of external failures. Specific measures of quality for each of the three companies is shown in Exhibit 12-6.

Exhibit 12-5 Contemporary View of the Costs of Quality

(Graph: Costs vs. Percent of Output with Defects, from 0% to 100%. Shows Total Quality Costs curve, Failure Costs curve rising steeply, and Prevention and Appraisal Costs curve declining. Minimum marked near left side.)

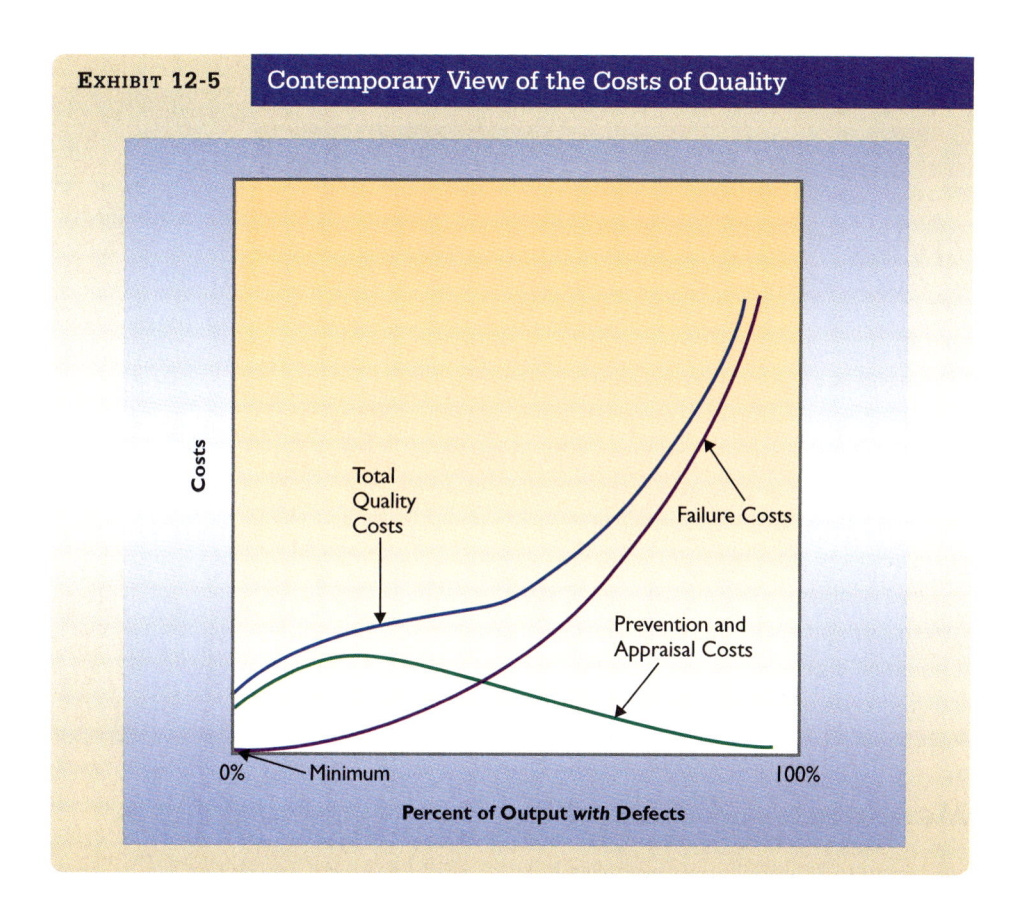

Exhibit 12-6 Quality Measures

Northern Lights Custom Cabinets
Customer complaints

Warranty claims and returns

Hours of time to rework defective cabinets

Pounds of scrap lumber compared to raw material put into production

Big Al's Pizza Emporium
Customer complaints

Returned meals

Amount of leftover food

Amount of food not meeting quality criteria

Food discarded in kitchen

Garcia & Buffett CPAs
Client complaints

Number of lost clients

Number of new clients referred by current clients

Number of IRS audits

Mistakes on client financial statements

THE ETHICS OF BUSINESS
Hiding the Truth

Mitsubishi has admitted to more than 10 years of covering up potentially deadly defects and hiding them from government regulators. As a result of the cover-up, Mitsubishi's president and five other executives were arrested and charged with a variety of offenses. In addition, the Japanese government has responded to Mitsubishi's dishonesty by banning the company from bidding on any government contracts and announcing that it would no longer certify the company's trucks, making it impossible to sell them in Japan ("Mitsubishi Motors Corp.: Former Executives are Arrested on Charges of Hiding Defects," *Hoover's Company Information* and *Wall Street Journal*, June 11, 2004).

It's Your Choice—Why would company officials knowingly cover up defects that could lead to injury or death? What steps should a company's management take to ensure that all employees properly report instances of suspected and known defects in the company's products? Do you think that the Japanese government acted appropriately by arresting the company's executives and banning the sale of some vehicles in Japan?

Measuring and Controlling Environmental Costs

Objective 4
Define environmental costs and explain the tradeoffs among prevention costs, appraisal costs, internal failure costs, and external failure costs

Measuring and controlling environmental costs is a critical success factor under the customer perspective of the balanced scorecard. Environmental management has become a major issue for many companies as state, local and national governments have enacted more stringent regulations and penalties for environmental contamination and as environmental friendliness has become a key competitive issue.

Environmental costs are defined as the costs of producing, marketing, and delivering products and services—including any post-purchase costs caused by the use and disposal of products—that may have an adverse effect on the environment.

Hitting the Bottom Line.
SAVING THE ENVIRONMENT CAN BE COSTLY

Over the last 20 years, government regulators have forced manufacturers to improve the energy efficiency of many household appliances including refrigerators, washing machines, and room air conditioners. Central air conditioners currently account for almost 10 percent of the country's residential electricity use—significantly more during times of peak demand in the summer. In an effort to reduce electricity consumption and avoid brownouts and blackouts in the summer months, the U.S. government has mandated that manufacturers make residential central air conditioners 30 percent more energy efficient by January 2006. While the Department of Energy estimates that the cost of an air conditioner will increase by about $335 as a result of these measures, consumers should also save about $42 per year in electricity costs, a payback period of about eight years ("Air Conditioners Get New Rules on Energy Use," *Wall Street Journal*, March 18, 2004).

Environmental Costing

Another way to look at environmental costs is that they are incurred because poor environmental quality exists. Like quality costs, environmental costs can be classified into four broad categories: prevention costs, detection costs, internal failure costs, and external failure costs.

Environmental prevention costs are the costs of activities carried out to prevent the production of contaminants and/or waste that could cause damage to the environment and include:

- Evaluating and selecting suppliers
- Evaluating and selecting pollution control equipment
- Designing processes and products
- Conducting environmental impact studies

Environmental detection costs are the costs of activities executed to determine whether products, processes, and other activities within the firm are in compliance with appropriate environmental standards. Environmental detection costs include:

- Auditing environmental activities
- Inspecting products and processes
- Developing environmental performance measures
- Testing for contamination
- Verifying supplier environmental performance
- Measuring contamination levels

Environmental internal failure costs are the costs of activities performed to eliminate and manage contaminants and waste that have been produced but not discharged into the environment. Examples of environmental internal failure costs include:

- Operating and maintaining pollution control equipment
- Treating and disposing of toxic waste
- Recycling scrap

Environmental external failure costs are the costs of activities performed after discharging contaminants and waste into the environment. Examples of environmental external failure costs include:

- Cleaning up contaminated water, soil, and air
- Medical costs for employees and local community related to environmental contamination
- Losing sales due to poor environmental reputation
- Losing employees due to concerns about working in a contaminated work environment, breathing contaminated air, etc.
- Losing natural resources (forests, lakes, etc.) for recreational use

Measuring environmental costs may reveal opportunities to control those costs throughout a product's environmental life cycle including resource extraction, product manufacture, product use, and product recycling and disposal.

Just as ISO 9000 provides companies with a set of guidelines for quality management, ISO 14000 provides companies with guidelines with respect to improving environmental management, such as reducing the consumption of natural resources, minimizing the harmful effects on the environment caused by the company's activities, and continuous improvement of a company's environmental performance.

These objectives may be met in a variety of ways including improvement in extraction methods for raw materials, reducing the use of natural resources by changing a product's design or how a product is manufactured, and recycling of parts and components used in manufacturing in order to reduce the impact on the environment.

Benefits of measuring and controlling environmental costs often include improving a company's public image and relations with the local community, improving the health of employees (and the related insurance premiums and overall medical costs), and developing new market opportunities. With effective environmental management, organizations can produce goods and services while simultaneously reducing negative environmental impacts, resource consumption, and environmental costs. This means producing more goods and services using less materials, energy, water, and land, while minimizing air emissions, water discharges, waste disposal, and the dispersion of toxic substances.

For Northern Lights Custom Cabinets and Big Al's Pizza Emporium, environmental measures will likely focus on minimizing the use of energy and water, minimizing the use of raw materials, reducing waste and increasing the amount of recycled materials. Specific examples of environmental management measures for Northern Lights Custom Cabinets and Big Al's Pizza Emporium are shown in Exhibit 12-7.

Exhibit 12-7 Environmental Measures

Northern Lights Custom Cabinets

Types and quantities of hazardous materials used including paints, stains, strippers and glue

Amount of water and electricity used

Amount of waste-water discharged

Physical measures of waste including board feet of lumber disposed of

Pounds of wood scrap recycled

Board feet of "old" lumber salvaged and reused

Big Al's Pizza Emporium

Amount of water and electricity used

Physical measures of waste including pounds of garbage

The amount of materials used that are not biodegradable

Percentage reduction of packaging materials

Amount of leftover food donated to food banks, food pantries, etc.

Doing Business.

EVA AND THE ENVIRONMENT

Georgia-Pacific manufactures tissue, packaging, paper, building products, pulp, and related chemicals. The company evaluates its environmental projects related to reducing pollution and waste using a variety of measures including economic value added (EVA).

While environmental projects can have quantifiable benefits including increased revenue, lower selling costs, and reduced fines and penalties, an advantage of using EVA is that it allows a broad definition of benefits including those that are difficult to measure like the impact on reputation, the impact on employee health, and the impact on the local community (Marc J. Epstein and S. David Young, "Greening with EVA," *Management Accounting*, Volume 80, Issue 7, 45).

Productivity

Productivity is simply a measure of the relationship between outputs and inputs. How many cars are produced per labor hour, how many loaves of bread are baked per bag of flour, how many calculators are produced per machine hour, how many customers are serviced per shift, and how many sales dollars are generated per full-time sales clerk are all measures of productivity. As such, productivity is typically viewed as a critical success factor under the internal business perspective of the balanced scorecard. Measures of output per unit of input, such as labor or machine hours, can be very important when evaluating the efficiency of a production process. These measures are similar to the traditional financial measures used in variance analysis (direct material and direct labor efficiency variances). However, the focus when using productivity measures is on continually improving productivity rather than simply using less material or incurring fewer labor hours than budgeted.

In service organizations, productivity measures are important when evaluating the efficiency of personnel. For example, in a doctor's office, the number of patients seen per physician in a given time period can be an important measure of profitability. Likewise, advertising agencies and CPA and law firms are very concerned with the revenue generated per partner.

To be useful, productivity measures must be used in conjunction with quality measures. A company that uses fewer workers, machines, materials, and other resources to generate the same amount of goods and services as its competitors will realize a competitive advantage only if the quality of products and services is not compromised in the process.

As with all companies, productivity measures for Northern Lights Custom Cabinets, Big Al's Pizza Emporium, and Garcia & Buffett CPAs will focus on measures of output per unit of input. Specific examples for each company are shown in Exhibit 12-8.

EXHIBIT 12-8 Productivity Measures

Northern Lights Custom Cabinets

Output per hour of labor

Output per machine hour

The number of finished jobs per board foot of lumber

Big Al's Pizza Emporium

Finished meals per measure of key ingredients

Meals per table per hour (table turns)

Sales dollars per table

The number of pizzas per hour of pizza oven use

Garcia & Buffett CPAs

Revenue per dollar of payroll

Revenue per partner

Billable hours per professional staff member

Hitting the Bottom Line.

How Many Hours Does It Take to Make a Car?

The average labor hours needed to build a car as it travels through an automaker's stamping, engine, and assembly plants is an important measure of performance for automakers. The average labor hours per vehicle for Ford, DaimlerChrysler, and GM is higher than for Honda, Toyota, and Nissan. In 2003, the amount of labor time per vehicle at Ford was almost 38 percent more than the labor time per vehicle at Nissan (Harbor Report North America, 2004). As you can see in the following table, factory productivity is directly related to profitability as well.

Automaker	Hours per Vehicle	Profit (loss) per Vehicle
Ford	38.60	$ (48)
DaimlerChrysler	37.42	$ (498)
GM	35.20	$ 178
Honda	32.09	$1,488
Toyota	30.01	$1,742
Nissan	28.09	$2,402

Efficiency and Timeliness

Objective 5

Compute key measures of efficiency and timeliness including customer response time, manufacturing cycle time, and throughput

Although quality is certainly a primary focus of the customer perspective, products and services must also be provided on a timely basis. Customer response time is another critical success factor related to the customer perspective of the balanced scorecard. **Customer response time** is the time it takes to deliver a product or a service after an order is placed. As shown in Exhibit 12-9, it includes such non-value-added time as order receipt time (time from when the order is placed to when the order is ready for setup) and order wait time (time from when the order is ready for setup to when the setup is complete). Order receipt time can occur when orders are mailed or when there is a delay between the placing of an order and its production. This can occur when products are made in batches or when an order is too small to initiate a production run. Total customer response time also includes the time that the order spends in the actual manufacturing process and any delivery time required to get the product into the customer's hands.

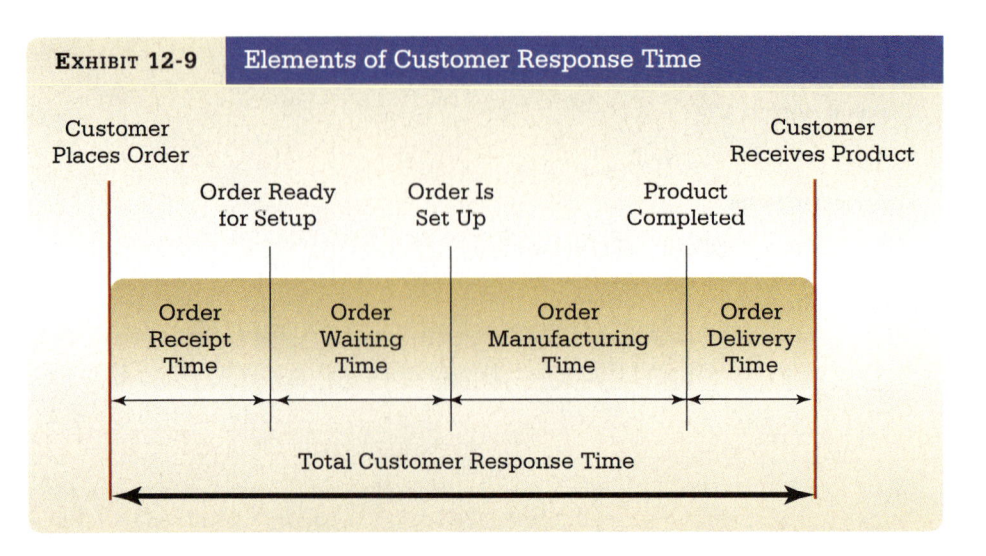

Exhibit 12-9 Elements of Customer Response Time

Obviously, the standard customer response time will vary with the type of product or service provided. In a restaurant, the response time should be relatively short. On the other hand, when ordering an automobile with special options or a custom piece of furniture, the customer response time can be considerably longer.

From an internal business perspective, efficiency and timeliness are often measured using manufacturing cycle time, velocity, throughput, and manufacturing cycle efficiency. **Manufacturing cycle time** is the amount of time it takes to produce a good unit of product from the time raw material is received until the product is ready to deliver to customers. As such, it is one element in the customer response time (see Exhibit 12-10). In addition to actual processing time, cycle time includes time spent moving materials and products from one place to the next, time spent waiting for machine availability, and time spent inspecting materials and finished goods. The concept of manufacturing cycle time is directly related to velocity, or throughput. Whereas manufacturing cycle time is the time required to produce a unit of product, **throughput** refers to the number of good units that can be made in a given period of time. The shorter the manufacturing cycle time, the greater the throughput. Because manufacturing cycle time and throughput focus on the production of good units, they are directly influenced by quality (see Exhibit 12-10). As such, you can view throughput and manufacturing cycle time as directly related to quality and productivity measures.

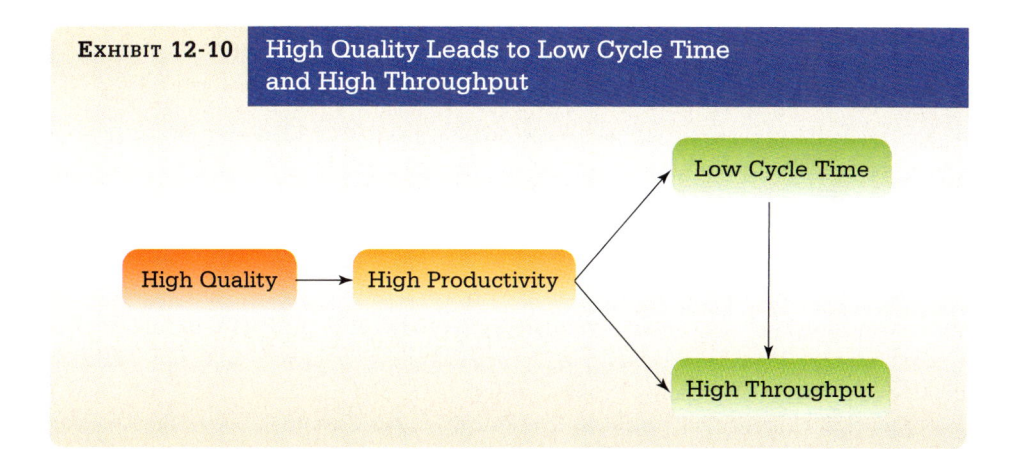

EXHIBIT 12-10 High Quality Leads to Low Cycle Time and High Throughput

High Quality → High Productivity → Low Cycle Time
High Productivity → High Throughput
Low Cycle Time → High Throughput

Manufacturing cycle efficiency (MCE) is the value-added time in the production process divided by the total manufacturing cycle time:

$$\text{MCE} = \text{Value-added time} / \text{Manufacturing cycle time}$$

Value-added time includes time spent in the actual manufacturing of a product (machining, assembly, painting, etc.). Non-value-added time includes the time a product is waiting to move to the next step in the production process or time spent moving the product to the next step. Manufacturing cycle efficiency is a key measure of performance directly related to the customer service perspective as well as to the internal operations perspective. By increasing MCE, customer response time is reduced, and non-value-added activities are reduced.

As an example, consider Northern Lights Custom Cabinets. Northern Lights manufactures approximately 30 custom cabinets each year. The cabinets are shipped to the job site as soon as they are complete. Northern Lights maintains records related to wait time, inspection time, processing time, and move time of its cabinets as follows:

Wait time	12 hours
Inspection time	2 hours
Processing time	48 hours
Move time	2 hours

Northern Lights used these amounts to compute the values shown in Exhibit 12-11.

> **EXHIBIT 12-11** | **Northern Lights' Efficiency Measures**
>
> **Manufacturing Cycle Time**
> Wait time + Processing time + Inspection time + Move time
> 12 + 48 + 2 + 2 = 64 hours, or 8 days
>
> **Throughput**
> Workdays per year/Manufacturing cycle time
> 250 work days per year/8 days = 31.25 units
>
> **Value-Added Time**
> Processing time
> 48 hours, or 6 days
>
> **Non-Value-Added Time**
> Wait time + Inspection time + Move time
> 12 hours + 2 hours + 2 hours = 16 hours, or 2 days
>
> **Manufacturing Cycle Efficiency (MCE)**
> Value-added time/Manufacturing cycle time
> 6 days/8 days = 75 percent

So what do these values mean? Once raw materials are received by Northern Lights, it takes an average of eight days to manufacture a set of custom cabinets. With 250 work days each year, throughput (the number of cabinets that can be manufactured each year) is 31.25 units. Seventy-five percent of the manufacturing cycle time is value added (related to actual processing of the cabinets), whereas only 25 percent is non-value-added, resulting in an MCE of 75 percent.

Although an MCE of 75 percent would likely be considered very good, these numbers can really be analyzed only by comparison to previous months or to industry standards for this type of business. Regardless, the MCE of 75 percent highlights the non-value-added waiting time, which Northern Lights may be able to reduce.

Measures of efficiency and timeliness for Northern Lights Custom Cabinets, Big Al's Pizza Emporium, and Garcia & Buffett CPAs are likely to focus on measures of customer response time, delivery performance and manufacturing cycle efficiency. Specific measures for the three companies are shown in Exhibit 12-12.

> **EXHIBIT 12-12** | **Measures of Efficiency and Timeliness**
>
> **Northern Lights Custom Cabinets**
> Time between customer order and delivery
> Time spent servicing cabinets already installed
> Time from completion to installation of cabinets
> Manufacturing cycle time (total production time)
> Manufacturing cycle efficiency (value-added time divided by cycle time)
>
> **Big Al's Pizza Emporium**
> Time from customer order to delivery of food
> Manufacturing cycle time (meals served per hour)
>
> **Garcia & Buffett CPAs**
> Total time between client's delivering tax information and completion of return
> Number of tax returns filed by April 15th

Marketing Effectiveness

Marketing measures are linked to the financial, customer, and learning and growth perspectives of the balanced scorecard. Market share is directly associated with financial performance and is indirectly linked to customer satisfaction. As an example, a large supermarket chain in the Northeast started giving customers double credit for manufacturer coupons in order to increase market share by enticing customers away from competing stores. The chain stated that each 1 percent increase in market share in New England was worth $50 million dollars in annual sales.

Other measures of marketing effectiveness include the success of new products. The number of new products introduced by a toy company, the number of new patents applied for by a drug company, and the number of new services offered and used by customers of a bank are market measures linked to both the customer service and innovation and growth perspectives of a business.

Measures of marketing effectiveness for Northern Lights Custom Cabinets, Big Al's Pizza Emporium, and Garcia & Buffett CPAs are likely to focus on growth in market share, product innovation and new market saturation. Specific examples of measures are shown in Exhibit 12-13.

EXHIBIT 12-13 Measures of Marketing Effectiveness

Northern Lights Custom Cabinets
Percentage of remodeling jobs and new homes installing Northern Lights cabinets
The number of new features and designs offered

Big Al's Pizza Emporium
Percentage change in sales compared to industry standards
Sales of new menu items

Garcia & Buffett CPAs
Percentage change in sales compared to industry standards
Sales of new services to existing clients
Percentage of new businesses that become clients

A Summary of Key Nonfinancial Measures of the Balanced Scorecard

Although specific measures used in companies will differ, virtually every organization has a need to measure performance using nonfinancial measures of quality, environmental management, productivity, efficiency and timeliness, and marketing effectivenss. Combined with traditional financial measures of performance, such as cost variances, segment margin, ROI, and EVA, these measures allow companies to integrate the financial, customer, internal business, and learning and growth perspectives of the balanced scorecard.

> **KEY CONCEPT**
> *The four perspectives of the balanced scorecard revolve around measures of quality, environmental management, productivity, efficiency and timeliness, and marketing effectiveness.*

Summary of Key Concepts

- *The balanced scorecard approach integrates financial and nonfinancial performance measures. (p. 414)*

- *The balanced scorecard approach requires looking at performance from four different but related perspectives: financial, customer, internal business, and learning and growth. (p. 415)*

- *The four perspectives of the balanced scorecard revolve around measures of quality, environmental management, productivity, efficiency and timeliness, and marketing effectiveness. (p. 429)*

Key Definitions

Balanced scorecard An approach to performance measurement that uses a set of financial and nonfinancial measures that relate to the overall strategy of the organization (p. 414)

Quality Usually defined as meeting or exceeding customers' expectations (p. 416)

Kaizen A system of improvement based on a series of gradual and often small improvements (p. 416)

ISO 9000 A set of guidelines for quality management focusing on the design, production, inspection, testing, installing, and servicing of products, processes, and services (p. 417)

Prevention costs Costs incurred to prevent product failures from occurring, typically related to design and engineering (p. 418)

Appraisal (detection) costs Costs incurred to inspect finished products or products in the process of production (p. 418)

Internal failure costs Costs incurred once the product is produced and then determined to be defective (p. 418)

External failure costs Costs incurred when a defective product is delivered to a customer (p. 419)

Environmental costs The costs of producing, marketing, and delivering products and services—including any post-purchase costs caused by the use and disposal of products—that may have an adverse effect on the environment (p. 422)

Productivity A measure of the relationship between outputs and inputs (p. 425)

Customer response time The time it takes to deliver the product or service after the order is received (p. 426)

Manufacturing cycle time The total time a product is in production, which includes process time, inspection time, wait time, and move time; cycle time will include both value-added and non-value-added time (p. 427)

Throughput The amount of product produced in a given amount of time, such as a day, week, or month (p. 427)

Manufacturing cycle efficiency (MCE) The value-added time in the production process divided by the throughput, or cycle time (p. 427)

Multiple Choice

1. Which of the following statements about the balanced scorecard is true?
    a. The four perspectives of the balanced scorecard revolve around measures of quality, productivity, efficiency and timeliness, and marketing success.
    b. The balanced scorecard approach requires looking at performance from four different but related perspectives: financial, customer, internal business, and learning and growth.
    c. The balanced scorecard approach integrates financial and nonfinancial performance measures.
    d. All of the above.

2. Which of the following is least likely to be a benefit of the balanced scorecard?
    a. The approach helps balance short-term and long-term performance perspectives.
    b. The approach combines financial and nonfinancial measures in a manner that provides a more balanced view of a company.
    c. The approach combines financial and nonfinancial measures, but weighs the nonfinancial measures most heavily.
    d. The approach often requires companies to design information systems that capture nonfinancial measures.

3. The efficient and effective use of employees is a measure of performance under which perspective of the balanced scorecard?
   a. Financial
   b. Customer
   c. Internal business
   d. Learning and growth

4. The number of warranty claims and returned products are measures of performance under which perspective of the balanced scorecard?
   a. Financial
   b. Customer
   c. Internal business
   d. Learning and growth

5. Which of the following is least likely to be a critical success factor within the internal business perspective of the balanced scorecard?
   a. Increasing productivity
   b. Decreasing productivity
   c. Improving quality throughout the production process
   d. Increasing efficiency and timeliness

6. Which balanced scorecard perspective addresses objectives across the company's entire value chain: from research and development to post-sale customer service?
   a. Financial
   b. Customer
   c. Internal business
   d. Learning and growth

7. Which of the following statements about quality costs is true?
   a. Both external and internal failure costs can be reduced (theoretically to zero) by paying more attention to quality issues early in the value chain.
   b. Increasing expenditures related to prevention and appraisal can result in significant overall cost savings in the long run.
   c. It may be prudent to increase expenditures in one or more areas in order to decrease other costs.
   d. All of the above.

8. External failure costs include:
   a. lost sales.
   b. costs associated with product repairs made under warranty.
   c. product recall costs.
   d. all of the above.

9. Which of the following statements about prevention costs is true?
   a. Prevention costs are generally incurred after problems occur.
   b. Design and engineering costs are not properly considered prevention costs.
   c. Generally, companies find that the incurrence of prevention costs reduces long-run product failure costs.
   d. None of the above is true.

10. Which of the following statements regarding quality is true?
    a. Over the past 20 years or so, the demand by customers for quality products and services at an affordable price has drastically changed the way companies do business.
    b. Improving quality increases sales through higher customer satisfaction and demand, reduces costs, and increases the long-term profitability of companies.
    c. Companies have focused on improving the quality of the products or the services they sell through a variety of initiatives, such as total quality management (TQM), market-driven quality, and strategic quality management.
    d. All of the above.

11. Which of the following is not a likely environmental cost?
    a. Cleaning contaminated water and soil
    b. Costs related to recycling products
    c. Contamination testing costs
    d. Each of the above is an environmental cost.

12. Which of the following is not an appropriate category of environmental costs?
    a. Prevention costs
    b. Internal failure costs
    c. Period costs
    d. Detection costs

13. Which of the following statements about productivity measures is true?
    a. In order to be useful, productivity measures must be used in conjunction with activity-based costing.
    b. In service organizations, productivity measures are important when evaluating the efficiency of personnel.
    c. When using productivity measures, the focus is on reducing manufacturing cycle efficiency.
    d. All of the above.

14. Productivity is a measure of:
    a. the effectiveness of the relationships between a company and its customers.
    b. the leverage needed to generate efficient employees.
    c. the relationship between outputs and inputs.
    d. the return earned on the investment in production equipment.

15. Which of the following is not a common metric used to measure efficiency and timeliness?
    a. Manufacturing cycle time
    b. Customer response time
    c. Internal failure rate
    d. Manufacturing cycle efficiency

Concept Questions

16. *(Objective 1)* Describe a balanced scorecard, and explain how it helps an organization meet its goals.

17. *(Objective 2)* Discuss the financial perspective of the balanced scorecard. How does this perspective differ from financial measures of performance discussed earlier in this textbook? How does this perspective relate to the other balanced scorecard perspectives?

18. *(Objective 2)* Explain why a company might seek ISO 9000 certification.

19. *(Objective 3)* Discuss what is meant by quality in today's manufacturing environment.

20. *(Objective 3)* Describe the two costs of controlling quality and the two costs of failing to control quality.

21. *(Objective 4)* Describe several benefits of measuring and controlling environmental costs.

22. *(Objective 4)* Describe each of the four broad categories related to environmental costs.

23. *(Objective 5)* Discuss the use of throughput. What does it measure?

24. *(Objective 5)* Describe value-added time and give several examples.

25. *(Objective 5)* Describe non-value-added time and give several examples.

Exercises

26. The balanced scorecard integrates financial and nonfinancial measures that relate to four perspectives: financial, customer, internal business, and learning and growth. This view of a company places emphasis on both financial and nonfinancial measures as each contributes to the understanding of a company's performance.

Required

List two possible performance measures for each of the four perspectives included in the balanced scorecard.

27. Improving the quality of products and services is an important component in both the customer perspective and the internal business perspective of the balanced scorecard.

Required

Discuss how quality can be assessed (i.e., measured) for the customer perspective and the internal business perspective. Use short and concise statements.

28. No company can simply wish quality into being; rather, quality comes at a cost. Quality costs are often classified into four general categories: prevention costs, appraisal costs, internal failure costs, and external failure costs.

Required

Briefly describe each of the four general categories of quality costs and provide several examples of costs that may be included in each category.

29. The following are partially completed statements that relate to quality and the costs of quality. Read each of the statements carefully.
   a. _____ include the cost of repairs made under warranty or the replacement of defective parts.
   b. Costs incurred in reworking defective products and the costs of scrap and spoilage are referred to as _____.
   c. Costs of inspecting, identifying, and isolating defective products before they reach the customer are called _____.
   d. _____ are incurred to prevent product failures from occurring.
   e. The _____ developed ISO 9000 as a set of guidelines for quality management.
   f. Kaizen, also called _____, refers to a system of improvement based on a series of gradual and often small improvements.

Required

Complete each of the above partially completed statements by using one of the following terms: appraisal costs, prevention costs, external failure costs, International Standards Organization, continuous improvement, and internal failure costs.

30. Like quality costs, environmental costs can be classified into four broad categories: prevention costs, detection costs, internal failure costs, and external failure costs.

Required

Give several examples of activities that may create costs under each of the above categories.

31. Jerri's Jackets produces an item that gives rise to the following activities:

Activity	Hours
Processing (two departments)	45.0
Inspecting	3.0
Rework	7.5
Moving (three moves)	12.0
Waiting (for the second process)	36.0
Storage (before delivery to the customer)	46.5

Required

A. Calculate the manufacturing cycle time for the item.
B. Calculate the manufacturing cycle efficiency for the item.

32. Hanna's Bananna Shack is a distributor of tropical fruit candies. The following activities occur in Hanna's manufacturing facility for a batch of a particular type of candy:

Activity	Hours
Fruit cleaning (three departments)	25.0
Pectin inspection	10.0
Fruit grading (for quality of candy)	15.0
Moving fruit (two moves)	10.0
Waiting (for the second and third processes)	20.0
Storage (before delivery to the customer)	40.0

Required

A. Calculate the manufacturing cycle time for the item.
B. Calculate the manufacturing cycle efficiency for the item.
C. What is the company's throughput in batches of the candy if the company has 255 work days available during the year?

Problems

33. Tiffany Lamp Company produces stained glass lamps appropriate for home and office use. The company expects sales to total approximately $50 million for the current year. Tiffany's management team has become increasingly concerned about a perception among some customers that quality is not particularly important to the company. Consequently, management recently implemented a quality improvement program and after several months accumulated the following data:

✓ Prevention costs: $305,000

Warranty claims	$ 60,000
Rework costs	200,000
Quality training	305,000
Inspection of incoming materials	900,000
Statistical process control	400,000
Scrap costs	100,000
Product quality audits	250,000

Required

A. What are total prevention costs?
B. What are total appraisal costs?
C. What are total internal failure costs?
D. What are total external failure costs?
E. Based on your calculations, is there a basis for the perception that quality is not important to Tiffany Lamp Company?

34. Timmer Meats is a large meat processor in the southeastern United States. The company's most recent year's sales totaled $50,000,000. Over the last several years, the company has had an unfortunate number of quality problems that threaten the company's existence. Webb Timmer, the company's president, asked the company's controller and quality control manager to accumulate data related to product quality. These two individuals prepared the following data for Webb:

Warranty claims	$ 120,000
Food poisoning liability lawsuits	200,000
Remaking entrees	600,000
Quality training	305,000
Inspection of incoming ingredients	900,000
Statistical process control	650,000
Spoilage and waste	300,000
Product quality audits	475,000

✓ External failure costs: $320,000

Required

A. Compute total prevention costs.
B. Compute total appraisal costs.
C. Compute total internal failure costs.
D. Compute total external failure costs.
E. Webb is considering spending more on inspections. What is the likely impact on other failure costs? What do you recommend?

35. Wailai Macadamia Confectioners is a maker of fine candies and chocolates. The company's founder believes that production has become less well controlled in recent months, resulting in a decrease in overall quality and a growing tide of customer dissatisfaction. Nimi Naoro, quality control manager, is also concerned but she believes that the company is being sufficiently proactive to combat most quality concerns. She asked the controller to accumulate any data that might relate to the company's current quality control efforts. The following data were provided to Nimi:

Product refunds due to quality guarantee claims	$ 60,000
Product liability claim (one lawsuit that was settled)	100,000
Rework costs	300,000
Quality training	152,500
Inspection of incoming ingredients	450,000
Statistical process control	325,000
Spoilage of chocolates, candies, and ingredients	150,000
Product quality audits	237,500
Total annual sales	25,000,000

✓ Appraisal costs: $687,500

Required

Prepare a report that shows total prevention, appraisal, internal failure, and external failure costs. Based on the report, what recommendations would you make to the company? Be sure to consider the relation between quality costs and annual sales.

36. Tanner Leathers implemented a quality control and improvement program in 2001. The quality control manager, a daughter of the company's president, developed the following table that shows the components of quality cost as a percentage of the company's sales for the last five years.

Year	Prevention	Detection	Internal Failure	External Failure
2001	3%	4%	9%	13%
2002	4	5	8	11
2003	5	6	6	8
2004	6	5	4	6
2005	7	2	1	2

Required

A. Prepare a graph (i.e., a trend graph) that shows the trend for each quality cost category. To complete the graph in Excel, use the chart wizard and select the "XY (scatter) graph with data points connected by lines" as the chart type. You should have one graph with four separate lines. Show the percentage of sales on the vertical axis and the year on the horizontal axis.

B. What does the graph tell you about the success of Tanner Leathers' quality program?

37. Rebecca's Pottery Loft makes a variety of handmade pottery items. She has asked for your advice on one of the items manufactured—a clay pelican. The following information is provided:

Number of defective pelicans	1,100
Number of pelicans returned	150
Number of pelicans reworked	200
Profit per good pelican	$ 10.00
Processing cost of a returned pelican	$ 20.00
Profit per defective pelican	$ 5.00
Cost to rework defective pelican	$ 4.00
Total appraisal costs	$ 3,400
Total prevention costs	$ 6,000

✓ Profits lost: $4,500

Required

A. Calculate the total profits lost because Rebecca sold defective pelicans.
B. Calculate the rework cost.
C. Calculate the cost of processing customer returns.
D. Calculate total failure cost.
E. Calculate total quality cost.

38. Cheryl's Country Creations is a chain of craft stores. The company evaluates its managers on the basis of both financial and nonfinancial performance measures. One of the nonfinancial measures used is throughput to measure performance in the manufacturing

division. The following data pertain to the company's branch in Biloxi, Mississippi. The unit of measurement is units.

✓ Manufacturing cycle efficiency: 75%

Units started into production	180,000
Total good units completed	135,000
Total hours of value-added production time	90,000
Total production hours	120,000

Required

A. Compute the manufacturing cycle efficiency.
B. What was the total throughput per hour? Round your answer to two decimal places.

39. Dan Foley's Pubs is a chain of brewpubs in the Pacific Northwest. The company evaluates its managers on the basis of both financial and nonfinancial performance measures. One of the nonfinancial measures used is throughput to measure performance in the brewing division. The following data pertain to the company's brewpub in Federal Way, Washington:

LO 5

✓ Throughput: 52.8 gallons / hour

Defective product rate	4.00%
Total hours of value-added production time	475,000
Total units produced during the period	27,500,000 gallons

Required

A. If manufacturing cycle efficiency were 95 percent, how many total production hours were used by Dan Foley's Pubs?
B. What was the total throughput per hour?

40. Lifeboat Yacht Company has always measured divisional performance based solely on financial measures. Top management has started to question this approach and is evaluating alternative measures. The managers are specifically interested in focusing on activities that generate value for their customers; so they are considering the use of throughput as a measure. They have gathered the following data and have asked for your opinion.

LO 5

✓ Manufacturing cycle efficiency: 78%

Units started into production	300
Total good units completed	294
Total hours of value-added production time	191,100
Total hours of division production time	245,000

Required

A. What is Lifeboat's manufacturing cycle efficiency?
B. What is the total throughput per hour?
C. Is there evidence of potentially poor quality in the production process as measured by the number of defective units? (Remember the type of business.)

Case

41. Jernigan Ltd. is a textile manufacturer with annual sales of $15,000,000 located in the southeastern United States. Jernigan is a weaver of high-end upholstery fabric. Until just a few years ago, the U.S. textiles industry had remained the leading producer of such high-end fabrics, but recent improvements in technology and growing investment in nations around the world have changed the industry. The president of Jernigan Ltd., Mary Jernigan, is committed to remaining competitive in the increasingly challenging market. Mary believes that her company cannot effectively compete on price alone. Instead, she believes that quality control is the most likely strategy for ensuring the company's competitiveness. After a recent meeting of the industry trade group, Mary has decided that it is time for an expanded emphasis on quality. She just instructed her quality control manager and the company's controller to accumulate data related to existing quality control processes, so she can assess whether the company is doing all it can in this area. They prepared the following bulleted list of data for Mary's consideration:

- Customer returns during the most recent year totaled 16,000 yards of fabric. Each yard of fabric required repairs costing an average of $6 per yard.
- Jernigan employs five fabric quality inspectors who perform inspections after the production process is completed. Each individual is paid an annual salary of $27,000.
- The final inspection generally results in a rejection of 30,000 yards each year. Approximately 70 percent of this fabric can be reworked at an average cost of $3.00 per yard.
- The quality inspectors use special equipment that requires periodic maintenance by the equipment manufacturer's technicians. This maintenance and related operating costs total $200,000.
- An average of 40,000 yards is scrapped annually. The fabric generally has an average cost of $12.50 per yard.
- The company's quality control program requires all new employees to complete a one-day training program. In addition, current employees are required to complete a one-half day refresher program each year. The training program costs $80,000 annually.
- An additional "roaming" supervisor was hired this year at a salary of $55,000. Her job is targeted to address quality problems before fabric is through the production process.
- The quality control manager estimates the company has lost sales of $750,000 due to quality concerns. She based this on several customers' complaints about past orders and their decisions to purchase their fabric from other suppliers.
- Annual sales allowances issued to customers due to quality problems are approximately $195,000.

Required

A. Prepare a report that shows quality costs by category and in total. What comments do you have related to the relative proportion of the various costs to total annual sales?
B. Discuss the distribution of quality costs among the four categories. For example, what is the relative proportion of total quality costs devoted to prevention, detection, and so forth? Are they distributed in an appropriate manner? Explain your answer.
C. Mary Jernigan is considering the implementation of a quality control program that promises to reduce quality costs to 3 percent of sales and limiting failure costs (i.e., internal and external failure costs) to just 20 percent of the total quality costs. By how much will profit increase if sales remain at $15,000,000?

Group and Internet Exercises

42. Each of us receives services from government agencies on a daily basis. And, we expect that those services will be efficient and effective when we need them. Many government agencies have begun using the balanced scorecard approach to managing their

organizations. Visit The Balanced Scorecard Institute's website to answer the following questions about how the balanced scorecard can be used in a governmental setting:

- What are some of the reasons given by the Balanced Scorecard Institute for implementing a balanced scorecard performance measurement system?
- What are appropriate metrics (i.e., measures) of performance for government?
- What are the three basic categories of governmental agency's functions or activities?

43. The Malcolm Baldrige National Quality Award was created in 1987 to recognize excellence in quality in manufacturing, small business, education, healthcare, and service businesses. It is a highly coveted award because its recipients generally exemplify hard work and a commitment to excellence. Search the Internet to learn more about this award. Prepare a short memo that describes the award. Be sure to explain why the award was established and the Baldrige criteria.

Big Al's Pizza, Inc.

Part Three: Planning, Performance Evaluation, and Control Summary Problem

Section A

Big Al's Pizza, Inc. needs a cash budget for year 3 and has provided you with the following information. Sales are all on account and are estimated to be collected over a three-month period, with 70 percent collected in the month of sale, 25 percent collected in the next month and 4 percent collected in the third month. The remaining 1 percent is estimated to be uncollectible. December and November sales from the previous year were $201,638 and $185,000 respectively.

Because of the lag in collecting cash from sales on account, Big Al's delays payment on some of its purchases of materials. Big Al's estimates that 60 percent of each month's material purchases are paid in the month of purchase and 40 percent in the following month. The accounts payable balance for materials at the end of the previous year was $20,000.

Big Al's also requires a minimum balance of $40,000 in cash at the end of each month. The company will use its line of credit when needed to bring the balance up to that minimum level. For any money borrowed, the interest rate is 6 percent compounded annually. For simplicity, you can assume that cash is borrowed on the first day of the month and that loan repayments are made at the end of the month.

Big Al's plans to exercise the option on the leased production equipment in March (as described in Part Two, Section B). The purchase price on the equipment will be $153,450, with payments of $3,260.36 per month. Big Al's also plans on expanding the existing production space in May at a cost of $200,000. Big Al's would like to finance the expansion out of current earnings and so will use the line of credit, if necessary, in May. The expansion will cause fixed manufacturing overhead to increase by $10,000 per month, starting in May.

Required

A. Prepare a cash receipts budget for year 3, assuming estimated sales of 385,000 meat pizzas and 30,000 veggie pizzas and the following monthly distribution of sales.

January	8.3%	July	8.5%
February	9.2	August	9.8
March	10.3	September	7.5
April	7.6	October	9.1
May	8.0	November	7.2
June	6.9	December	7.6

Direct material costs per unit are $.74 per meat pizza and $.62 per veggie pizza. Direct labor costs are $2.51 per meat pizza and $2.78 per veggie pizza. Monthly fixed selling and administrative costs are $15,300, while monthly fixed manufacturing overhead is $2,851. The variable overhead cost is $.55 per pizza. The sales price for veggie pizzas is $5.25 per pizza and the sales price for meat pizzas is $5.00.

B. Prepare a cash disbursements budget for the year.
C. Prepare a summary cash budget for the year, showing any borrowing and repayment of debt with interest. Discuss Big Al's ability to repay the expansion loan. Include a discussion of the feasibility of the project. Include qualitative factors to be considered.
D. What if the sales forecast was increased by 50 percent? What impact does that have on the budget, and what is the potential impact on the company?

Section B

In December (month 24) of year 2 of operations, Big Al's produced and sold 32,675 pizzas, consisting of 30,570 meat pizzas and 2,105 veggie pizzas. The budgeted sales price for meat pizzas was $5.00, and for veggie pizzas, $5.25. The estimated production and sales during December was 31,678 meat pizzas and 2,595 veggie pizzas.

Required

A. Compute the price and volume variances for sales, assuming that Big Al's sold all pizzas produced for $137,565 (meat) and $9,051 (veggie). What might explain these variances?
B. Compute the price and quantity variances for direct materials for each type of pizza, assuming that Big Al's paid $29,093 for 32,325 units of raw material for meat pizzas and $1,453 for 2,401 units of raw material for veggie pizzas. (A unit consists of dough shell, sauce, cheese, meat or veggies, and assembly materials.) In addition, 30,995 units were used to produce meat pizzas, and 2,149 units were used to produce veggie pizzas. How would these variances be interpreted? What might explain these variances? Would you consider them to be large enough to be important?
C. Compute the labor rate and efficiency variances, assuming that Big Al's paid $71,350 in labor costs for 7,150 hours of labor for meat pizzas and $6,425 in labor costs for 650 hours of labor for veggie pizzas. How would these variances be interpreted? What might explain them? Would you consider them to be large enough to be important?
D. Using the predetermined overhead rate from Part One: Section C (with direct labor hours as the cost driver), compute the variable overhead rate and efficiency variances. Assume that Big Al's paid $20,852 in total overhead costs, consisting of $17,002 of variable overhead and $3,850 of fixed overhead. How would these variances be interpreted? What might explain these variances? Would you consider them to be large enough to be important?
E. How might Big Al's extend its variance analysis to be compatible with its use of activity-based costing as discussed in Part One: Section C?

Section C

Big Al's Pizza Emporium, a subsidiary of Big Al's Pizza, Inc., has decided to sell frozen pizzas in its restaurants. Restaurant customers will take these pizzas home and cook them. The restaurants will sell frozen meat pizzas for $10 and frozen veggie pizzas for $11.50.

Although the restaurants would like to purchase the pizzas from Big Al's Pizza, Inc., Big Al's Pizza Emporium has found an unrelated supplier that will provide the meat pizzas for $4.55 and veggie pizzas for $5.75. Assume that Big Al's Pizza, Inc. has excess capacity and can supply the frozen pizzas to Big Al's Pizza Emporium without impacting current sales.

Required

A. Using estimated cost data for year 3, given in Section A (question A), at what minimum price should Big Al's Pizza, Inc. agree to transfer meat and veggie pizzas to Big Al's Pizza Emporium?
B. What is the maximum price that Big Al's Pizza Emporium should pay Big Al's Pizza, Inc. for the pizzas?
C. If Big Al's Pizza Emporium purchases pizzas from Big Al's Pizza, Inc., what is the ideal transfer price? Why?
D. Should Big Al's Pizza Emporium buy pizzas from Big Al's Pizza, Inc.? What qualitative factors should be considered in making this decision?
E. What should the transfer price be if Big Al's Pizza, Inc. is at full capacity?

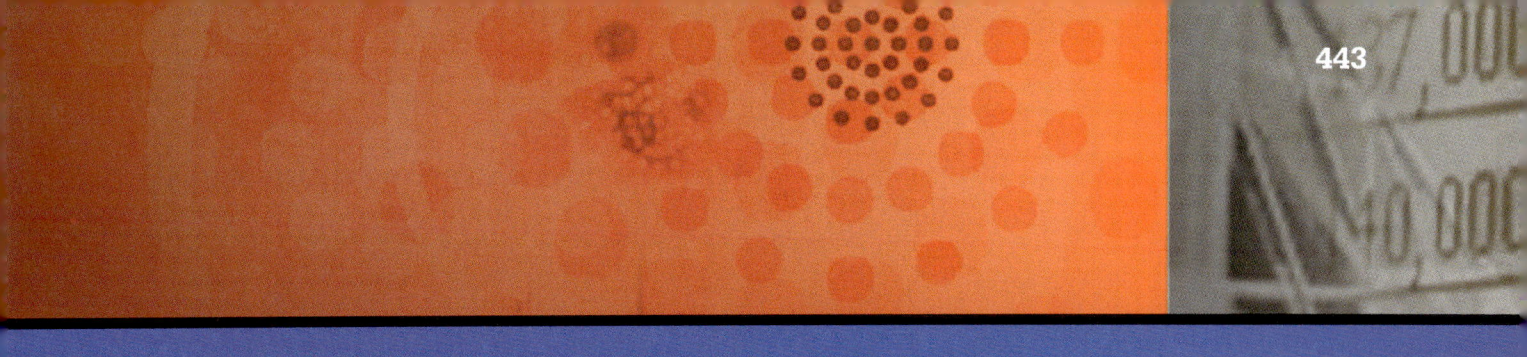

Part 4: The Impact of Management Decisions

Chapter 13   The Strategic Use of Managerial Accounting Information

Chapter 14   Internal Control, Corporate Governance, and Ethics

Chapter 13 The Strategic Use of Managerial Accounting Information

Chapter 13: The Strategic Use of Managerial Accounting Information

In this chapter, we examine the strategic use of managerial accounting information, that is, how companies use managerial accounting information in developing, monitoring, and maintaining a long-term competitive strategy. In the first section of the chapter, we discuss the general strategies companies use in creating a competitive advantage. In the second section, we discuss pricing and strategy including the use of cost-plus pricing and target pricing. In the third section, we discuss the influence of cost management on strategy including such topics as value-chain analysis, supply-chain management, customer relationship management, and activity-based management.

Learning Objectives

After studying the material in this chapter, you should be able to:

1. Explain the three primary strategies for obtaining a competitive advantage
2. Identify and discuss factors affecting the pricing of goods and services
3. Determine prices of products and services using target pricing, cost-plus pricing, and time and material pricing
4. Explain the importance of value-chain analysis in identifying internal and external linkages
5. Differentiate structural, organizational, and operational activities and give examples of each
6. Define and give examples of supply-chain management
7. Define and give examples of customer relationship management
8. Describe and contrast the two dimensions of activity-based management
9. Describe the role of activity-based management in identifying and eliminating non-value-added activities

Introduction

Strategy refers to a set of policies, procedures, and approaches to business that relate to the long-term success of a business. Strategy starts with an organization's mission, or basic purpose for doing business. Mission statements are typically very broad. For example, IBM's mission statement is "to be the most successful information technology company in the world." Mission statements are supported by goals and objectives that are sometimes a part of the mission statement itself. As an example, the mission statement of Sara Lee includes a statement of primary purpose—"to create long-term shareholder value" and more specific goals of "building leadership brands in three highly focused global businesses: Food and Beverage, Intimates and Underwear, and Household Products." Likewise, Ford Motor Company's mission statement includes an objective "to be a low-cost producer of the highest quality products and services that provide the best customer value." A strategy can be defined as a specific course of action that is undertaken to accomplish an objective or goal. For example, at Ford, strategies for being a low-cost producer of high quality products might include establishing relationships with a select group of highly reliable and efficient suppliers, investing in state of the art manufacturing equipment, and maintaining a highly trained and flexible workforce.

The balanced scorecard (as discussed in Chapter 12) helps companies operationalize their mission statements into specific objectives, strategies, and performance measures for each of the four different perspectives: the financial perspective, the customer perspective, the internal business perspective, and the learning and growth perspective.

Strategy and Creating a Competitive Advantage

Objective 1
Explain the three primary strategies for obtaining a competitive advantage

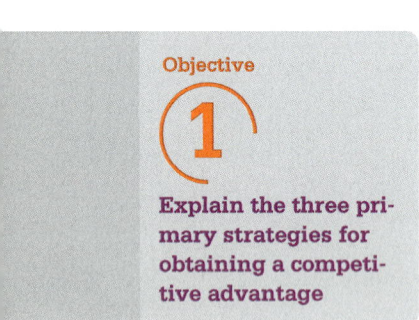

KEY CONCEPT

The key to achieving long-term growth and success is to gain a competitive advantage.

In competitive business environments, companies must make fundamental decisions with respect to how they will position their products or services in the marketplace to ensure their long-term growth and survival. The key to achieving long-term growth and success is to gain a competitive advantage.

Three general strategies for obtaining a competitive advantage are:

1. Cost leadership
2. Differentiation of products and services
3. Focusing by identifying market niches

A company pursues a **cost leadership strategy** when its goal is to provide the same or better value to customers at a lower cost than its competitors. Cost leadership frequently results from productivity increases and the aggressive pursuit of cost reduction throughout the development, production, marketing, and distribution processes. Achieving cost leadership allows a company to earn higher profits than its competitors while selling products and services at the same or lower prices. As a result, cost leadership is often accompanied by large market share. Examples of companies that follow a cost leadership strategy include Wal-Mart, Dell Computer, and Southwest Airlines.

A **product differentiation strategy** focuses on distinguishing a product or service a company offers from those of its competitors. Product differentiation can result from unique design features, technological leadership, unique uses of products, and attributes like quality, environmental impact, and customer service. The combination of features and attributes are often described as a product's functionality. Examples of differentiation strategies include L.L. Bean's focus on quality and customer service, Apple Computer's focus on unique features and user friendliness, and Maytag's focus on quality.

A **focusing strategy** involves selecting or emphasizing a market or customer segment in which to compete. Companies adopting a focusing strategy may choose only to compete in a certain geographic area or may target a product or service to a particular group based on age, gender, or income level. This strategy takes into consideration that some segments and customers are more profitable than others. Examples include local microbreweries that target certain regions of the country, and clothing manufacturers that target teenage girls.

In practice, many companies use a combination of strategies to create a competitive advantage and must compete on the basis of both cost and functionality. However, it can be dangerous to try to be all things to all customers. Reducing costs by lowering quality or deleting key features can backfire as can being stuck in the middle with no distinguishing strategy.

Pricing of Products and Services

In a competitive marketplace, consumers will seek out the best product at the most favorable price. Determining the selling price of products is one of the most important decisions that management will be required to make. If the price of the product is too high, market demand for that product may be less than is needed to earn a fair profit. On the other hand, if the price of the product is too low, the demand may be very high but the product may produce minimal profit or even show a negative contribution margin.

Objective 2

Identify and discuss factors affecting the pricing of goods and services

Economic Concepts and Pricing

Because price affects demand, producers want to know just how much a price change will affect quantity. **Elastic demand** for a good means that a price increase (decrease) of a certain percent lowers (raises) the quantity demanded by more than that percentage. Luxury goods are often price elastic. Necessities can also be price elastic if there are many substitutes for a product. For example, the price of orange juice might increase due to a reduction of the orange crop in Florida. However, if consumers view apple juice, grape juice, and milk as substitutes for orange juice, any attempt to increase prices may be met with a significant reduction in demand.

In contrast, when demand is **inelastic**, demand is not greatly affected by an increase or decrease in price. Goods that are inelastic typically have few substitutes and are often necessities. For example, gasoline is relatively price inelastic (at least in the United States). Although the price of gasoline has increased significantly over the last several years, demand has not been affected.

Costs and Pricing

In some business situations, the cost of the product or the service does not affect the sales price. In these circumstances, the market determines the selling price, and the company will produce the product as efficiently as possible and sell it for a predetermined market price. Many agricultural products fall into this category.

However, in most instances, the cost of a product or a service is very important in establishing price. Consider, for example, the manufacture of furniture or automobiles. In these situations, higher-cost items are typically priced higher than are lower-cost items. In other words, if the car costs more to produce, the price to the consumer will be higher because the extra costs usually mean higher quality or more options. Even when cost is used to help establish the price of products or services, other factors may be equally or more important. For example, although the price of lumber has risen over the past couple of years, furniture manufacturers have been reluctant to pass on those price increases to retailers. In some cases, manufacturers may try to help retailers maintain key "price points," knowing that consumers may be reluctant to spend above a threshold dollar amount on a product.

In the long run, the selling price of a product or service must be sufficient to cover the "cost" of the product plus provide a profit. The question then becomes what is the cost of the product? As we have discussed throughout the book, there are a number of ways to compute the cost of a product. In Chapter 6, we learned that absorption, or full costing, includes fixed manufacturing overhead as a product cost, whereas variable costing includes only direct material, direct labor, and variable manufacturing costs. Chapters 3 and 4 stated that some companies assign overhead to products by using traditional volume-based cost drivers, whereas other companies use activity-based costing (ABC). In Chapter 4, we saw that the use of ABC can have a tremendous impact on the calculation of cost. The use of multiple cost drivers in ABC generally results in more accurate product costs.

> **KEY CONCEPT**
>
> The price of a product must be sufficient to cover all the costs of the product and to provide a profit.

> **Objective 3**
>
> Determine prices of products and services using target pricing, cost-plus pricing, and time and material pricing

Regardless of the way companies compute the cost of their product or service, in the long run, the price of a product must be sufficient to cover all the costs incurred in developing, designing, manufacturing, marketing, distributing, and servicing the product—in other words, all costs in the value chain. In practice, companies use a variety of approaches to determine prices.

Target Pricing

Target pricing is used when a price is preset by market conditions or when a company wishes to set a price in order to capture a predetermined market share or to meet other marketing goals. In situations in which the price is preset by market conditions (as with agricultural products), the product manufacturer or service provider has little control over sales price. In these cases, the decision is really not one of establishing a price at all but rather deciding whether a product can be developed and manufactured at a cost low enough to provide an acceptable profit. In other situations, a company has control over setting prices but sets a price based on the marketing goals (to enter a new market, establish a predetermined market share, etc.) rather than the cost of the product or service. Surveys indicate that almost 20 percent of U.S. companies routinely use some sort of market-based target pricing.

Target pricing is used to determine the maximum cost that can be incurred in order to earn a desired profit (the target profit). This maximum cost is often called the target cost and is calculated by subtracting the target profit from the target selling price:

$$\text{Target cost} = \text{Target price} - \text{Target profit}$$

For example, Birdie Maker Golf Clubs has determined that a set of new clubs should have a target price of $1,300. If Birdie Maker has a target profit equal to 30 percent of the set's cost, the target cost (TC) of the new set of clubs can be solved as follows:

$$TC = \$1{,}300 - (30\% \times TC)$$
$$1.3\ TC = \$1{,}300$$
$$TC = \$1{,}000$$

Target pricing (and target costing) is common in the computer industry, in which the goal may be to produce a laptop computer that can be priced at $1,700 or less. After determining an acceptable profit on the computer ($300, for example), the goal is to determine how to design, develop, manufacture, sell, and service the computer for a cost no higher than $1,400.[1] If the target cost is within the range of acceptable estimates, the computer can be manufactured. On the other hand, if the target cost is lower than a product's current (or projected) cost, a company must consider options for reducing costs in order to reach the target. Companies may reduce costs in a variety of ways including:

1. Investing in new manufacturing technologies to increase productivity

2. Reducing material costs and labor costs by working with suppliers and employee unions

3. Redesigning products

As discussed on page 447, companies frequently must compete on both cost and functionality. Value engineering is used in target costing to analyze the tradeoffs between product cost and product functionality. Value engineering includes the identification of key product attributes and features and customer preferences for those features, followed by an analysis of the cost of providing each of the important product attributes. Value engineering may also include the development of multiple product designs, each with different features and different costs. Most production costs are determined during the research and development and design stages of the value chain, and very little can be done to control these costs once the product is

---

[1] Determining a target cost is more difficult when the target price is not known with certainty. For example, in the agricultural market, coffee bean prices are set by auction and are not known until after the beans are grown and harvested.

in production. This means that estimating costs accurately and at an early stage is crucial in deciding whether a product can ultimately be sold at a profit.

Kaizen (see Chapter 12) is also used in target costing. The process of kaizen or continuous improvement focuses management's attention on continually improving a product while simultaneously reducing the costs of manufacturing a product through improving the productivity of manufacturing processes, implementing just-in-time manufacturing systems, implementing total quality management initiatives, identifying and reducing non-value-added activities, and so on.

Cost-Plus Pricing

When the market allows some flexibility in setting prices, companies often use some sort of cost-plus pricing to determine the selling price of products or services. With **cost-plus pricing,** a desired markup is generally added to the product's cost (called the base cost). The markup is typically expressed as a percentage and must be sufficient to cover costs not included in the base cost plus a desired profit. Common markups can be calculated as follows:

$$\text{Markup on cost of goods sold} = \frac{\text{Selling and administrative expenses} + \text{Desired profit}}{\text{Cost of goods sold}}$$

$$\text{Markup on direct materials} = \frac{\text{Direct labor} + \text{Overhead} + \text{Selling and administrative expenses} + \text{Desired profit}}{\text{Direct materials}}$$

For example, Northern Lights Custom Cabinets is preparing a bid on a kitchen remodeling job for a client. Northern Lights expects that the job will require $2,500 of direct materials, $4,000 of direct labor, and $3,000 of overhead costs. Selling and administrative expenses for the job are expected to be $700. On average, Northern Lights has a target profit of $5,000 on a job this size. Northern Lights applies a markup on cost of goods sold to arrive at a cost-plus price. In this case, the cost of goods sold is $9,500, consisting of $2,500 of direct materials, $4,000 of direct labor, and $3,000 of overhead costs. Accordingly, the markup is calculated as follows:

$$\text{Markup on cost of goods sold} = (\$700 + \$5,000)/\$9,500 = 60\%$$

Once the markup percentage is determined, the formula for determining a target selling price using a cost-plus approach is:

$$\text{Target selling price} = \text{Base cost} + (\text{Markup \%} \times \text{Base cost})$$

In this case, the target selling price is $15,200. The base cost is the $9,500 cost of goods sold and the markup is $5,700 (calculated as 60% × $9,500).

As you can see in Exhibit 13-1, the target selling price covers the cost of goods sold of $9,500 and the selling and administrative costs of $700 and provides a profit of $5,000.

EXHIBIT 13-1 Cost-Plus Pricing with a Markup on Cost of Goods Sold

Direct materials	$ 2,500
Direct labor	4,000
Manufacturing overhead	3,000
Cost of goods sold	$ 9,500
Selling and administrative expenses	+ 700
Profit	+ 5,000
Cost-plus price	$15,200

Some companies only consider variable costs in their base cost; other companies use absorption or full costs. Using variable costs is consistent with the economic model of maximizing profit by setting prices in which marginal cost is equal to marginal revenue. However, it can be misleading to managers focusing on long-run decisions. Using full costs has the benefit of motivating managers to control fixed costs. In practice, full costs are used to cost products by almost 70 percent of U.S. companies, whereas variable costs are used by only 12 percent ("How Manufacturers Price Products," *Management Accounting*, Volume 76, Issue 8, 37).

For a company using total variable costs (both variable manufacturing and variable selling and administrative costs) as the base cost, the markup must cover fixed manufacturing costs, fixed selling and administrative costs, and a desired profit. For a company using variable manufacturing costs as the base, the markup must also cover variable selling and administrative costs. On the other hand, for a company using full costs (both variable and fixed manufacturing and selling and administrative costs) as the cost base, the markup must only cover the desired profit.

In some cases, costs are estimated and selling prices are set based on those estimates. In other cases, companies can wait until they know their actual costs before setting the selling price in a cost-plus contract. For example, a builder of custom houses would probably use cost-plus pricing. In Chapter 4, TopSail Construction used full costing and ABC to determine the total manufacturing costs of a custom house to be $239,107 (see page 112). The selling price of $299,000 was determined by adding a predetermined markup of 25 percent on the total manufacturing costs (and rounding up to the nearest thousand). If TopSail uses estimated costs to determine a selling price (and enters a contract to build a house for a predetermined price), it becomes critically important for TopSail to accurately estimate those costs. If costs are estimated too high and the selling price is too high, TopSail will not be awarded the construction job; if costs are estimated too low (and the price is too low), the company may lose money or make less profit than desired.

Doing Business.

PRICING AT PARKER BROTHERS

Some companies use a combination of target pricing and cost-plus pricing. For example, Parker Brothers (a division of Hasbro) manufactures and sells board games, such as Monopoly and Scrabble. The company's approach to pricing is to first have the marketing department estimate the probable retail-selling price of a prototype game—the target price. Parker Brothers then backs into the maximum cost (the target cost) that can be incurred in manufacturing the game by applying predetermined profit margins at the retail and wholesale levels. If the target cost is too low (the company cannot manufacture the game at or below the target cost), Parker Brothers then takes a cost-plus approach to pricing and goes back to the marketing department with a higher suggested wholesale price. It is then up to the marketing department to decide whether the game can be successfully marketed at this higher price.

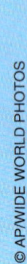

Time and Material Pricing

Time and material pricing is often used in service industries in which labor is the primary cost incurred. For example, CPA firms that provide audit services must provide a client with an estimate of an audit fee prior to starting the work. This fee usually will not vary unless additional work is needed that was unanticipated before the engagement began. Also, extreme problems can arise that cause the firm to spend much more time on the engagement, which could cause the fee to increase. The price is based on the estimated number of hours needed to complete the audit and the level of the staff members providing the services. For example, the services of a staff accountant with three years of experience might be billed at a rate of $100 per hour while the services of an experienced manager might be billed at a rate of $200 per hour and a partner might be billed at a rate of $300 per hour or more. Obviously, more complex audit engagements require more time and more skilled employees and will be priced at higher rates than simple engagements. As another example of time and material pricing, auto repair shops frequently charge customers based on mechanic labor hours plus any parts used in the repair. The mechanic's time is usually charged at a standard rate, say of $45 per hour. In some cases, the repair shop bases the bill on the actual time spent in fixing the car. In other situations, the repair shop bases the bill on a standard time. So if an engine repair normally takes four hours of time, the shop will charge the customer $180 plus parts, regardless of whether the actual repair takes three hours or five hours.

Value Pricing

In special circumstances, the price of services is based on the perceived or actual value of the service provided to a customer. A good example of **value pricing** occurs in the consulting business. Consulting firms may charge clients based on a percentage of cost savings that result from an engagement. Large CPA firms often enter into these types of arrangements. For example, a CPA firm may contract with a client to evaluate its property tax assessments and to negotiate reductions in those taxes based on faulty valuations of property. Rather than establishing a fixed price for the services (or working on a cost-plus contract), the firm may set a price equal to 30 percent of the cost savings.

Other Pricing Policies

Penetration pricing is the pricing of a new product at a low initial price to build market share quickly or to establish a customer base. **Price skimming** involves charging a higher price when a product or service is first introduced. Companies do this in order to recoup the expenses of research and development through high initial pricing.

Legal and Ethical Issues in Pricing

A variety of laws at the local, state, and national levels prevent companies from using predatory pricing to prevent or eliminate competition. Many types of price discrimination are illegal unless the differences in price are based on cost differences in servicing and selling to different customers.

Predatory pricing is the practice of setting prices very low (frequently below cost) for the purpose of injuring competitors and eliminating competition. Predatory pricing on the international market is sometimes referred to as dumping. Although penetration pricing is legal, dumping is prohibited by the General Agreement on Tariffs and Trade (GATT) overseen by the World Trade Organization. The problem with price dumping is that once the competition is eliminated, consumers may see an increase in price as companies attempt to recover their losses.

Price discrimination refers to the charging of different prices to different customers for essentially the same product. The Robinson-Patman Act was passed in 1936 as a means of outlawing price discrimination by manufacturers and suppliers. In general, price discrimination is allowed only if the competitive situation demands it, and if costs can justify the difference in price. This second condition allows price discrimination on the basis of identifiable cost savings. However, the burden of proof for companies accused of violating this act is on the company.

Price gouging, or setting the price higher for unusual situations, such as doubling the price of plywood when a hurricane is approaching, may also be illegal in some cases. In addition to the legal implications of pricing decisions, companies must consider the ethical issues involved in pricing products and services. For example, pharmaceutical companies may choose to sell a drug below cost and doctors may treat some patients at little or no cost. However, examples also abound of companies' taking advantage of customers by increasing the prices of products and services that are in high demand.

The Ethics of Business
Fair Prices to Farmers?

There is a growing campaign in the United States and Europe to pay farmers in poor countries more than market prices for products like coffee, bananas, and nuts. Although such fair-trade practices can provide aid to struggling farmers, in some cases most of the benefits go to the retailer, not the farmer. For example, a retail store sells fair-trade coffee to consumers for $8.50 per pound. Of this $8.50, $1.40 goes to the coffee grower (about 40 cents per pound more than the market rate), another $3.60 goes to the wholesaler (including a profit of $.20 per pound), and the remaining $3.50 is the retail store's markup ("At Some Retailers, Fair Trade Carries a Very High Cost," *Wall Street Journal*, June 8, 2004).

It's Your Choice—Is it ethical for a company to charge customers a premium for fair-trade products? How much? Should the price paid to farmers be disclosed to customers?

Cost Management and Strategy

Organizations use cost management to help support their missions, objectives, and strategies. As discussed in Chapter 1, the role of the managerial accountant in an organization is to develop cost and other information to support the management of the firm and the achievement of its strategic goals.

Objective 4
Explain the importance of value-chain analysis in identifying internal and external linkages

The Value Chain

Long-term success through the attainment of a competitive advantage requires that managers understand the organization's value chain. As shown in Exhibit 13-2, the **value chain** is the set of activities that increase the value of an organization's products and services. The value chain includes activities that are performed both within an organization and outside an organization and include activities such as research and development, product development, the acquisition of raw materials, production, marketing and distribution, and customer service (including post-sale customer service and the ultimate disposal of the product by customers).

Exhibit 13-2 The Value Chain

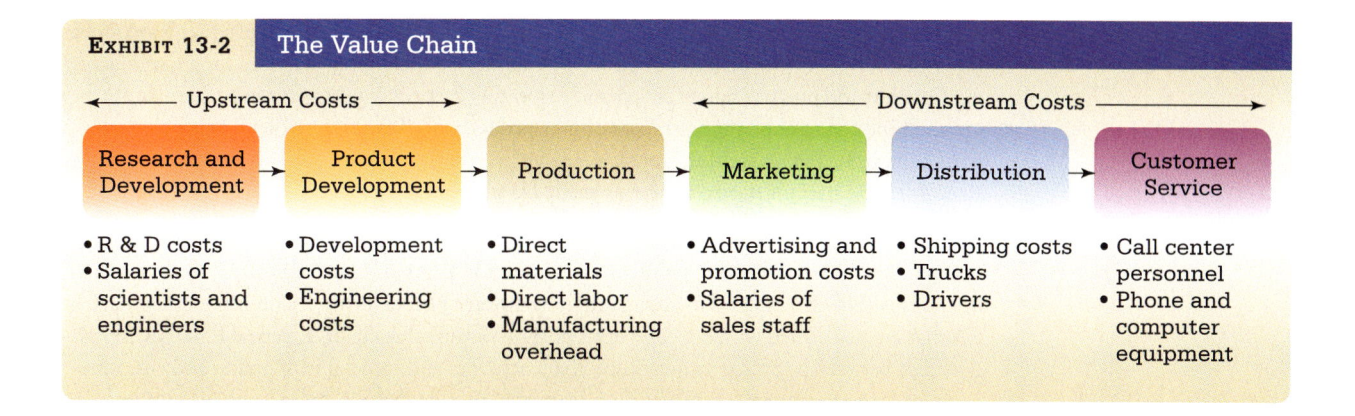

Upstream Costs

- **Research and Development**
  - R & D costs
  - Salaries of scientists and engineers
- **Product Development**
  - Development costs
  - Engineering costs
- **Production**
  - Direct materials
  - Direct labor
  - Manufacturing overhead

Downstream Costs

- **Marketing**
  - Advertising and promotion costs
  - Salaries of sales staff
- **Distribution**
  - Shipping costs
  - Trucks
  - Drivers
- **Customer Service**
  - Call center personnel
  - Phone and computer equipment

Companies typically are involved in only some parts of the value chain. For example, a furniture manufacturer usually is not involved in the growing, harvesting, and cutting of timber into usable lumber. The choice of which part of the value chain to be involved in is a strategic decision that involves an analysis of the competition and whether the company can establish a competitive advantage. In some cases, companies that compete directly in the marketplace may be involved in different aspects of the value chain. For example, Reebok and Nike compete directly in the highly competitive market for sport shoes. However, while Reebok designs and manufactures its shoes, Nike focuses on design and marketing elements of the value chain and leaves the actual manufacturing element of the value chain to other companies.

Value-chain analysis requires an understanding of the differences between a company's structural, organizational, and operational activities. As defined in Chapter 4, activities are procedures or processes that cause work to be accomplished. Activities consume resources and products ultimately consume activities.

KEY CONCEPT

Long-term success through the attainment of a competitive advantage requires that managers understand and manage the organization's value chain.

Structural, Organizational, and Operational Activities **Structural activities** involve fundamental decisions concerning a company related to the basic size and scope of an organization's operations. For a manufacturing company, structural activities include such decisions as where to locate a factory, how big the factory should be, what types of technologies will be used to make products (heavily automated or labor based), and other related decisions. In addition to decisions about location and size, structural activities for a retail organization might include decisions about the type and variety of products to carry, and whether to use manual or bar code scanning at cash registers. Structural activities directly impact costs incurred by an organization and affect organizational activities.

Objective 5

Differentiate structural, organizational, and operational activities and give examples of each

Organizational activities have to do with decisions about how a company is organized and how decisions are made within the company. Examples include making decisions with respect to adopting a JIT or traditional manufacturing system, the number of employees that will be hired, and how employees will be trained, organized, and utilized within a company (teams, departments, etc). Organizational activities also include decisions with respect to how many and which suppliers to use and how equipment is organized in the factory. In a retail setting, organizational activities would include decisions about which employees have the authority to place orders for merchandise, how a store is laid out, and what brands of merchandise will be sold.

Note that organizational decisions and activities are frequently influenced by structural decisions and activities. For example, the location of a factory is likely to influence the number and choice of suppliers. Organizational activities also include the degree of decentralization within a firm and how decision-making authority is shared within a company.

Operational activities involve the day-to-day activities undertaken as a product is manufactured or a service is provided. As discussed in Chapter 4, operational activities for a manufacturing firm include purchasing, receiving and inspecting incoming parts, moving materials, setting up machines, assembly, processing customer orders, and shipping products to customers. As with organizational activities, operational decisions and activities are influenced by earlier structural and organizational decisions made by an organization's managers.

Internal Linkages, External Linkages, and the Value Chain Understanding and managing the value chain requires a recognition of the complex linkages and interrelationships among activities both within and external to an organization. **Internal linkages** are relationships among activities that are performed within a company's portion of the value chain. **External linkages** are relationships between a company's own value-chain activities and those of its suppliers and customers.

In order to maintain a competitive advantage, an organization must be able to understand the relationship between these internal and external linkages and the costs that the company incurs, and must take advantage of opportunities to utilize internal and external linkages in furthering the organization's strategy and maintaining a competitive advantage. **Value-chain analysis** involves identifying and taking advantage of internal and external linkages with the objective of strengthening a firm's strategic position.

Taking advantage of internal linkages often involves the redesign of products. For example, a company might identify the number of parts handled as a cost driver for several activities including material handling, receiving and inspecting, moving materials, and assembly. In this case, redesigning the product using fewer parts or perhaps parts that are used in other products might substantially reduce costs related to multiple activities.

JIT manufacturing systems can also be used to exploit internal linkages. In many companies, the time and distance raw materials and finished products move in a factory are significant cost drivers. As discussed in Chapter 2, a manufacturing cell structure is often used in a JIT system to reduce the handling and moving of products. In a manufacturing cell, each cell is essentially a mini-factory and workers are able to perform all of the production tasks associated with the cell, increasing the speed and efficiency of the process. Taking advantage of external linkages typically involves two primary strategies—supply-chain management and customer relationship management.

Doing Business.

SUPPLY-CHAIN MANAGEMENT AT L.L. BEAN

The vice president of product acquisition for L.L. Bean selects the factories that supply the company with the multitude of products available in its catalogs. Rather than focusing solely on the price charged by a supplier, the first criterion in choosing a supplier is product quality, the second is delivery reliability, and the third is the price of the merchandise. All these factors are captured in L.L. Bean's view of "cost" as a concept that includes the entire spectrum of value—price, quality, reliability, and the ultimate success of the product in the marketplace (*Wall Street Journal*, April 16, 1999, B1).

Supply-Chain Management

Supply-chain management includes a variety of activities centered on building long-term relationships between buyers and sellers with the goal of making the relationship profitable for both parties. Rather than simply focusing on suppliers that can meet a company's requirements at the lowest cost, supply-chain management looks at suppliers as partners and involves them in multiple aspects of the company's operations.

As discussed in Chapter 1, the evolution of enterprise resource planning systems and electronic data interchange allows a company to place a great deal of the burden of inventory management and raw materials ordering in the hands of its suppliers, resulting in an evolution of supply-chain management from "loosely coupled relationships into virtual organizations."[2] In vendor-managed inventory systems, suppliers monitor sales in real time (and sometimes on-site) and determine order quantities and order times for buyers.

Objective 6

Define and give examples of supply-chain management

Doing Business.

MORE THAN A MANUFACTURER

TAL Apparel Ltd, a closely held Hong Kong clothing manufacturer, makes one in eight dress shirts sold in the United States and supplies clothes to a number of U.S. companies including Land's End and J. C. Penney. But TAL is much more than just a manufacturer. TAL collects point-of-sale data for Penney's shirts directly from its stores, decides how many and what styles, colors, and sizes of shirts to make, and then ships the shirts directly to individual stores, all without the direct involvement of Penney. The benefit to Penney? Before working with TAL, Penney would hold up to six months of inventory in its warehouses and three months of inventory in its stores. Today, it holds virtually no inventory for some lines of clothing ("Invisible Supplier Has Penney's Shirts All Buttoned Up," *Wall Street Journal*, September 11, 2003).

As another example, consider a manufacturer that incurs substantial assembly costs due to the large number of parts used in its products. Active involvement of the supplier might lead to the supplier providing pre-assembled components to the buyer, redesigning the components purchased by the buyer to make assembly faster and more efficient, or developing components that can be used in more than one product.

In a company employing a JIT manufacturing system, external linkages may be exploited by negotiating long-term contracts with a small number of suppliers, choosing suppliers located close to the production facility, and by involving suppliers directly in the inventory management process. Establishing relationships with suppliers so that they deliver quality products in a timely manner is vital to the success of a JIT system. However, the relationship has to benefit both the buyer and the supplier. As such, contracts must be negotiated so that suppliers understand that their success is tied to the success of the buyer.

The key in supply-chain management is that suppliers and buyers work together to develop opportunities for their mutual benefit. How does supply-chain management benefit the supplier? A buyer may be willing to reduce the number of suppliers used and to establish long-term contracts with these suppliers. This partnership may provide suppliers with a growing and predictable source of sales. Active monitoring and management of inventory for buyers allows suppliers to reduce their own costs of storing and holding inventory and to be more efficient. Buyers may even be willing to pay more to suppliers if the supplier cooperates with the buyer by making more frequent deliveries of parts, and by taking over the inventory monitoring and ordering process.

KEY CONCEPT

The key in supply-chain management is that suppliers and buyers work together to develop opportunities for their mutual benefit.

---

[2] O'Leary, "Supply Chain Processes and Relationships for Electronic Commerce," *Handbook of Electronic Commerce*, Springer Verlag, 2000, 431–444.

Objective 7: Define and give examples of customer relationship management

Customer Relationship Management

The goal of **customer relationship management** (CRM) is to bring a company closer to its customers in order to serve them better. In *The One to One Manager*, Peppers and Rogers (1999) describe CRM as a four-step process:

1. Identify your customers
2. Differentiate your customers
3. Interact with your customers
4. Customize your business to your customers

Regardless of manufacturing, merchandising, or service, a company must identify its customers in order to differentiate them. Although this step might seem easy for a business-to-business company (a company that sells to other businesses), in practice this step requires not only knowing the companies that purchase your products or services, but also learning the names of the individuals within a customer's organization who have the authority to authorize and make purchases. Differentiating your customers requires recognizing that customers have different needs, customers present different opportunities, and that some customers are more valuable than others. Interaction with your customers allows you to identify their unique needs and ultimately capitalize on their unique opportunities. However, interactions must not only be effective, they must also be efficient. The last step in customer relationship management is to customize your business or some aspect of your business to your customers. This step might involve providing special services to a customer, customizing the ordering process, or even developing a new product specifically to meet a customer's needs.

Doing Business.
SUPPLY-CHAIN CITIES

One of the latest innovations in supply-chain management is the creation of supply-chain cities. As an example, Luen Thai Holdings, Ltd. (a clothing maker that supplies products to Liz Claiborne and Ralph Lauren) is building a huge complex in China in which fashion designers from Liz Claiborne, technicians from fabric suppliers, and engineers from button and garment manufacturers can come together in one location, drastically reducing the time it takes for new clothes to go from the concept stage to delivery to retail outlets. The new supply chain will also reduce costs by reducing the number of employees spread between the United States and Asia and by reducing shipping costs ("Making Labels for Less," *Wall Street Journal*, August 13, 2004).

The use of CRM creates an interactive feedback "loop" from customers to companies, making it possible to more accurately and consistently forecast, manage, and meet customer expectations. Through CRM an organization can manage the entire life cycle of its customer relationships, including marketing analysis and planning, customer acquisition and retention, order management, and customer service and support.

CRM can also point out opportunities to take advantage of internal and external linkages. For example, customer surveys may indicate that customers are incurring significant costs (and inconvenience) related to disposing of a product due to the use of a hazardous material. The company might react by providing recycling opportunities to its customers or by redesigning the product to eliminate the use of the particular material. Such options may benefit the seller by attracting new customers and may allow the seller to charge a higher price if customers are willing to pay extra for the convenience of easy recycling.

The use of ERP systems facilitates CRM by allowing customer information to be gathered, stored, and most important, easily accessed and shared. CRM allows organizations to focus sales efforts on what the customer values and to anticipate and react to customer needs.

> **KEY CONCEPT**
>
> The goal of customer relationship management (CRM) is to bring a company closer to its customers in order to serve them better.

Doing Business.
CRM AT SAS

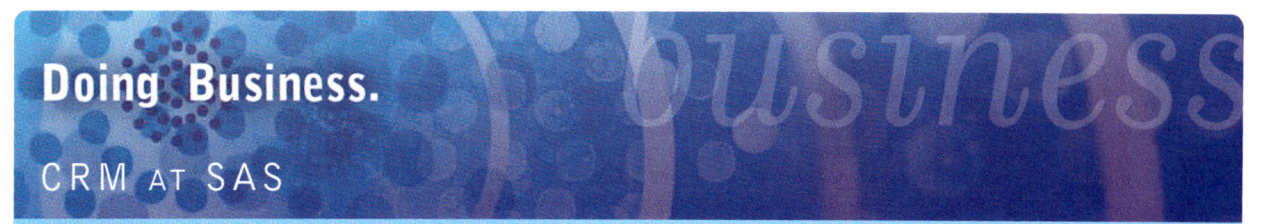

SAS Institute is the world's largest privately held software company. SAS uses a variety of tools including customer surveys to get a detailed picture of customer needs—suggestions for new software features, options, add-ons, and capabilities. Results of the surveys are provided to the company's research and development division, which implements over 85 percent of the suggestions. Most of SAS's new products are developed with direct involvement of one or more of its customers (Don Peppers and Martha Rogers, *The One to One Manager*, Doubleday, a division of Random House, Inc., 1999).

Activity-Based Management and the Value Chain

Although activity-based costing focuses on allocating costs to products based on activities, **activity-based management (ABM)** focuses on managing activities to reduce costs and make better decisions. As such it is critical in helping companies create and maintain a competitive advantage.

As shown in Exhibit 13-3, ABM has two dimensions: a cost dimension and a process dimension. The cost dimension (ABC) provides cost information about resources, activities, and cost objects of interest. The objective of the cost dimension is improving the accuracy of costing products, services, and other cost objects. The process dimension provides information about what activities are performed, why they are performed, and how well they are performed.

Objective 8

Describe and contrast the two dimensions of activity-based management

KEY CONCEPT

Activity-based management is critical in helping companies create and maintain a competitive advantage.

EXHIBIT 13-3 The Cost and Process Dimensions of Activity-Based Management

Cost Dimension (ABC): Resources → Activities → Cost Objects

Process Dimension (ABM): Cost Drivers → Activities → Performance Measures

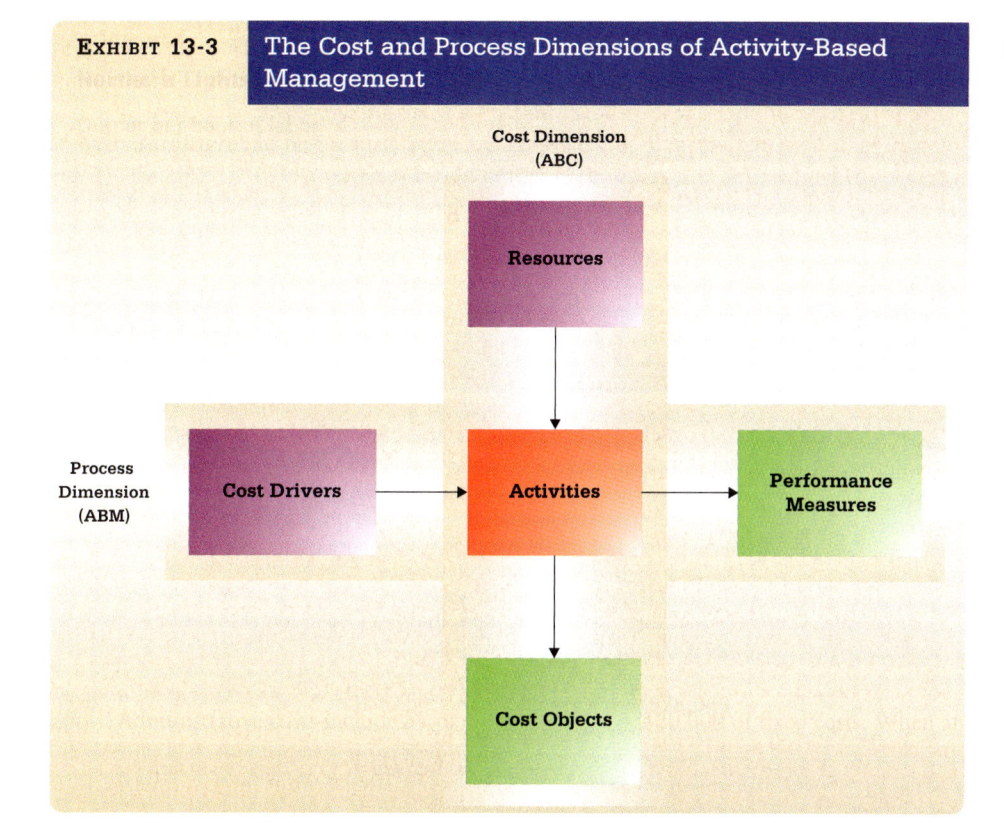

As discussed in Chapter 4, one of the benefits of ABC is that it makes managers aware of exactly what causes costs to be incurred. For example, the number of different parts and supplies used might drive costs incurred in ordering parts and supplies. Understanding this internal linkage

allows managers to take steps to reduce those costs by redesigning products to use similar or fewer parts. This can result in huge cost savings. In the first 10 or so years after implementing ABC, Chrysler estimates that it saved hundreds of million of dollars by simplifying product designs.[3]

Value-Added and Non-Value-Added Activities One of the goals of ABM is to identify and to eliminate activities and costs that don't add value to goods and services. In today's competitive business environment, customers demand high-quality products and services, and organizations that supply these products and services must strive to make sure that each step in the value chain adds value to the product or service in the mind of the customer.

However, not all activities create value. **Non-value-added activities** are those that can be eliminated without affecting the quality or performance of a product and are not necessary to meet the overall needs of the organization. Examples of non-value-added activities include storage of materials, work in process, and finished goods; moving of materials and parts from storage to the factory in a manufacturing company; idle time of employees while waiting for work; and so on. Likewise, packaging products (unless done for health/safety reasons or to make a product more appealing to a consumer) might be considered a non-value-added activity. Companies that have successfully implemented quality improvement programs resulting in extremely low numbers of defective products may consider quality inspections as a non-value-added activity. These companies would argue that if products are designed correctly and production processes are monitored and controlled effectively, quality of products will be ensured throughout the process. Consequently, inspections of finished products are redundant and don't add value to the product.

On the other hand, value-added activities contribute to customer value or help meet an organization's needs. In order to be value-added, activities must generally produce an observable, identifiable, or measurable change of state that is not achievable by preceding activities.

To be competitive, companies must strive to eliminate or to minimize non-value-added activities. Remember that activities cause costs. So reducing or eliminating non-value-added activities would correspondingly reduce costs. The use of JIT production techniques can eliminate (or at least minimize) non-value-added costs associated with inventory storage, product movements, and other activities involved with ordering, receiving, and handling inventory. Likewise, the implementation of total quality management (TQM) programs can significantly reduce non-value-added costs associated with quality inspections, resolving customer complaints owing to defective or poor-quality products and services, recalls, warranties, and so on.

Although the elimination of non-value-added activities is a goal of ABM, it can also be used to reduce the time and resources required by value-added activities through activity selection (choosing among various activities) and increasing the efficiency of activities.

> **Objective 9**
>
> Describe the role of activity-based management in identifying and eliminating non-value-added activities

THE ETHICS OF BUSINESS

Putting "Values" in Value-Added Activities

In the 1990s Marks & Spencer, a retailer based in the United Kingdom, was accused of selling clothing produced by underage workers in foreign factories. The company became concerned about the potential impact of this accusation on its business and reputation and adopted a "strategy for ethical global sourcing" to make sure that values remain a part of its value chain.

It's Your Choice—Over the last several years, there has been increasing emphasis on corporate social responsibility. Do you believe that this emphasis is merely a trend or a shift in the way in which business is conducted? Does Marks & Spencer's commitment to its strategy for ethical global sourcing benefit the company's shareholders? Or, is it just another expense that reduces shareholder value? (*Journal of Organizational Excellence*, Spring 2004.)

---

[3]Ness and Cucuzza, "Tapping the Full Potential of ABC," *Harvard Business Review*, Volume 73, Issue 4.

Successful Implementation of ABC and ABM Utilizing activity-based costing information to reduce costs, eliminate non-value-added activities, and manage more effectively requires the cooperation of all functional areas of a business organization and top management. Without active involvement in the process, marketing managers may balk when price changes are thrust on them, production managers may be hesitant to change a production process used successfully for many years, and human resource managers may criticize the motivational and behavioral implications of suggested changes. Successful implementation also requires a strong commitment from upper management in terms of vocal support, resources provided, and prioritization among the company's other initiatives, such as TQM and JIT.

The full benefits of ABC and ABM require a long-term commitment by management. The benefits of ABC and ABM are simply not realized overnight, and management must be willing to focus on the long-term benefits that are possible through their implementation.

> **KEY CONCEPT**
>
> *The successful implementation of ABC and ABM requires a long-term commitment by top management and the cooperation of all functional areas of a business organization.*

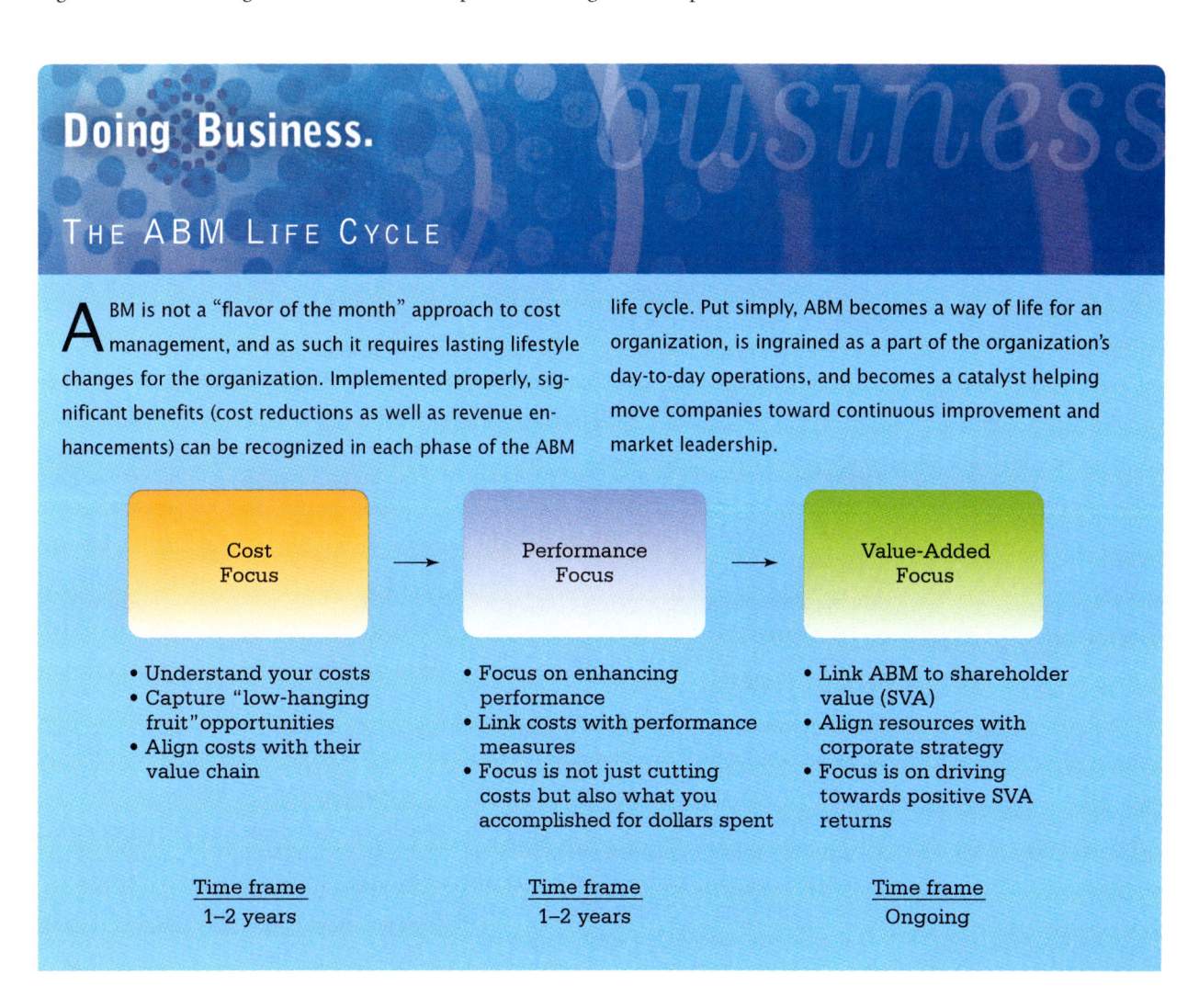

Doing Business.

THE ABM LIFE CYCLE

ABM is not a "flavor of the month" approach to cost management, and as such it requires lasting lifestyle changes for the organization. Implemented properly, significant benefits (cost reductions as well as revenue enhancements) can be recognized in each phase of the ABM life cycle. Put simply, ABM becomes a way of life for an organization, is ingrained as a part of the organization's day-to-day operations, and becomes a catalyst helping move companies toward continuous improvement and market leadership.

Cost Focus	→	Performance Focus	→	Value-Added Focus
• Understand your costs • Capture "low-hanging fruit" opportunities • Align costs with their value chain		• Focus on enhancing performance • Link costs with performance measures • Focus is not just cutting costs but also what you accomplished for dollars spent		• Link ABM to shareholder value (SVA) • Align resources with corporate strategy • Focus is on driving towards positive SVA returns
Time frame 1–2 years		Time frame 1–2 years		Time frame Ongoing

---

Summary of Key Concepts

- The key to achieving long-term growth and success is to gain a competitive advantage. (p. 446)

- The price of a product must be sufficient to cover all the costs of the product and to provide a profit. (p. 448)

- Long-term success through the attainment of a competitive advantage requires that managers understand and manage the organization's value chain. (p. 453)

- *The key in supply-chain management is that suppliers and buyers work together to develop opportunities for their mutual benefit. (p. 455)*
- *The goal of customer relationship management (CRM) is to bring a company closer to its customers in order to serve them better. (p. 456)*
- *Activity-based management is critical in helping companies create and maintain a competitive advantage. (p. 457)*
- *The successful implementation of ABC and ABM requires a long-term commitment by top management and the cooperation of all functional areas of a business organization. (p. 459)*

Key Definitions

Strategy The set of policies, procedures and approaches to business that relate to the long-term success of a business (p. 446)

Cost leadership strategy A strategy used when a company's goal is to provide the same or better value to customers at a lower cost than its competitors (p. 446)

Product differentiation strategy A strategy used when a company's goal is to distinguish the product or service offered by a company from those of its competitors (p. 446)

Focusing strategy A strategy involving selecting or emphasizing a market or customer segment in which to compete (p. 446)

Elastic demand A price increase (decrease) of a certain percent lowers (raises) the quantity demanded by more than that percentage (p. 447)

Inelastic demand Demand is not greatly affected by an increase or decrease in price (p. 447)

Target pricing A pricing method used when a price is preset by market conditions or when a company wishes to set a price in order to capture a predetermined market share or to meet other marketing goals (p. 448)

Cost-plus pricing A method of pricing in which managers determine the cost of the product or service and then add a markup percentage to that cost to arrive at the sales price (p. 449)

Time and material pricing A pricing method often used in service industries, in which labor is the primary cost incurred (p. 451)

Value pricing A pricing method that bases the price of services on the perceived or actual value of the service provided to a customer (p. 451)

Penetration pricing The pricing of a new product at a low initial price to build market share quickly or to establish a customer base (p. 451)

Price skimming Charging a higher price when a product or service is first introduced (p. 451)

Predatory pricing Setting prices below cost for the purpose of injuring competitors and eliminating competition (p. 451)

Price discrimination Charging different prices to different customers with no justification based on the competitive situation or identifiable cost savings (p. 451)

Price gouging Setting prices higher for unusual situations (p. 452)

Value chain The set of activities that increase the value of an organization's products and services (p. 452)

Structural activities Involve fundamental decisions concerning a company's size and scope of operations (p. 453)

Organizational activities Involve decisions concerning how a company is organized and how decisions are made within the company (p. 453)

Operational activities Involve the day-to-day activities undertaken as a product is manufactured or a service is provided (p. 454)

Internal linkages Relationships among activities that are performed within a company's portion of the value chain (p. 454)

External linkages Relationships between a company's own value-chain activities and those of its suppliers and customers (p. 454)

Value-chain analysis Involves identifying and taking advantage of internal and external linkages with the objective of strengthening a firm's strategic position (p. 454)

Supply-chain management Includes a variety of activities centered on building long-term relationships between buyers and sellers with the goal of making the relationship profitable for both parties (p. 454)

Customer relationship management A four-step process involving identification of customers, differentiating of customers, interacting with customers, and customizing business to customers (p. 456)

Activity-based management (ABM) Focuses on managing activities to reduce costs, improve customer value, and make better decisions (p. 457)

Non-value-added activities Activities that can be eliminated without affecting the quality or performance of a product and that are not necessary to meet the overall needs of the organization (p. 458)

Multiple Choice

1. Strand's Hardware Store is a locally owned and operated hardware store located in Richmond, Virginia. The store is known for its great customer service and knowledgeable salespeople. The store's primary competition includes a large national chain hardware and lumber store. Strand's strategy for obtaining a competitive advantage is probably:
   a. a cost leadership strategy.
   b. a differentiation strategy.
   c. a focusing strategy.
   d. a combination strategy.

2. If the demand for a product does not vary with price, the product is described as:
   a. competitive.
   b. profitable.
   c. inelastic.
   d. price sensitive.

3. In cost-plus pricing, the markup percentage:
   a. is determined by market conditions.
   b. is typically calculated as a percentage of a base cost such as cost of goods sold or direct materials.
   c. is usually set by the board of directors and stated in the company's articles of incorporation.
   d. is all of the above.

4. When the price of a product is established by market conditions and firms determine the desired cost of the product that must be met in order to reach a target profit, the company is using:
   a. penetration pricing.
   b. market pricing.
   c. target pricing.
   d. cost-plus pricing.

5. When foreign companies sell products in the U.S. below cost in order to drive out competition, the practice is called:
   a. predatory pricing or dumping.
   b. price skimming.
   c. penetration pricing.
   d. price gouging.

6. An automobile manufacturer is developing a new hybrid gas/electric car with a target price of $22,000. In order to maintain a target profit equal to 25 percent of the new model's cost, the target cost must be:
   a. $5,500.
   b. $17,600.
   c. $19,500.
   d. $27,500.

7. Taking advantage of external linkages may include:
   a. involving suppliers in the inventory management process.
   b. asking suppliers to redesign parts.
   c. developing long-term relationships with suppliers.
   d. working with customers to reduce the costs of disposing of a product.
   e. all of the above.

8. Structural activities would include all of the following except:
   a. organizing the workforce into teams.
   b. deciding to build a new manufacturing facility.
   c. deciding where to locate a new retail store.
   d. All of the above are structural activities.

9. Organizational activities would include all of the following except:
   a. deciding how many suppliers to use.
   b. processing purchase orders.
   c. the degree of decentralization in a company.
   d. deciding how employees will be trained, organized, and utilized.

10. An example of an operational activity is:
    a. organizing equipment in manufacturing cells in a JIT environment.
    b. deciding on the size of an inventory warehouse.
    c. inspecting parts as they are received.
    d. deciding how many employees to hire.

11. The primary goal of supply-chain management is best described as:
    a. to reduce the costs of components and parts purchased from suppliers.
    b. to require suppliers to share a greater burden for managing inventory.
    c. to improve the quality of components and parts purchased from suppliers.
    d. to build long-term relationships that increase the profitability of both buyers and sellers.

12. Customer relationship management (CRM) can be used to:
    a. determine the needs of customers.
    b. identify customers that are not profitable.
    c. develop new products.
    d. identify cost savings.
    e. all of the above.

13. The process dimension of activity-based management focuses on:
    a. what, why, and how activities are performed.
    b. tracing resources to activities.
    c. identifying activities.
    d. tracing costs to cost objects.

14. Which of the following statements regarding value-added and non-value-added activities is false?
    a. To be competitive, companies must strive to eliminate non-value-added activities.
    b. Companies that have successfully implemented just-in-time programs are able to minimize or control non-value-added costs.
    c. Companies that have successfully implemented total quality management programs often can significantly reduce non-value-added costs by increasing quality inspections.
    d. Each of the above statements is correct.

15. Of the following processes, which is not commonly found in the "performance focus" stage of the activity-based management life cycle?
    a. Connecting costs with performance measures.
    b. Emphasizing performance improvement.
    c. Evaluating the value received from company investments.
    d. Developing a detailed understanding of costs.

Concept Questions

16. *(Objective 1)* Define a cost leadership strategy and give three examples of companies that successfully use a cost leadership strategy.
17. *(Objective 1)* Define a product differentiation strategy and give three examples of companies that successfully use a product differentiation strategy.
18. *(Objective 1)* What is meant by a focusing strategy? Give three examples of companies that successfully use a focusing strategy.
19. *(Objective 2)* Discuss some of the key factors affecting the pricing of goods and services.
20. *(Objective 3)* What is the definition of "cost" in cost-plus pricing?
21. *(Objective 3)* What is target pricing, and when would it be appropriate to use it?
22. *(Objective 3)* Distinguish between predatory pricing and penetration pricing. Are they the same thing?
23. *(Objective 3)* Explain the link between kaizen and target costing.
24. *(Objective 4)* Define and give an example of value-chain analysis.
25. *(Objective 5)* Explain the relationship among structural, organizational, and operational activities.
26. *(Objective 6)* Give examples of supply-chain management in a company utilizing just-in-time manufacturing techniques.
27. *(Objective 7)* Describe the four-step process of customer relationship management.
28. *(Objective 8)* Explain the difference between activity-based costing and activity-based management.
29. *(Objective 9)* How can ABM be used to help eliminate non-value-added activities?
30. *(Objective 9)* Is inspecting materials a value-added or non-value-added activity?
31. *(Objective 9)* Why is it important for management to distinguish between value-added and non-value-added activities? Give several examples of common non-value-added activities.

Exercises

32. As the manager of a new bike shop in town, you must find a way to create a competitive advantage and to distinguish the company from large discount stores like Wal-Mart, sporting goods stores that sell bikes, and online bike sellers.

Required

What strategic position might you employ that would allow you to successfully compete in this situation?

33. The Lukawitz Construction Company builds custom homes and uses cost-plus pricing. The company just finished a house with a base cost of $256,000. The company establishes selling price based on a markup of 25 percent.

Required

What is the selling price of the new house?

34. Based on marketing data, Birdie Maker Golf Company has set a target price of $700 for a set of new golf clubs. The company's target profit is 30 percent of cost.

Required

What is the target cost for a set of golf clubs?

35. The Old Balance Company has developed a new lacrosse stick that uses high-tech composite materials that provide better performance and durability. The primary cost of the new stick is direct materials with a cost of $40. Direct labor cost is estimated to be $10 per unit, overhead is estimated to be $15 per unit, and selling and administrative expenses are estimated to be $5 per unit.

Required

If Old Balance desires a profit of $30 per unit, what is the required markup on direct materials?

36. Performance Cycles sells high performance racing motorcycles. Currently, the company purchases motorcycles from Harley-Davidson and other manufacturers and heavily customizes the frames and engines for racing applications. The company is contemplating designing and manufacturing their own frames from scratch, using engines and other components available in the secondary market.

Required

From a value-chain perspective, comment on Performance Cycles' new strategy. What segment(s) of the value chain does Performance currently occupy? What segment(s) of the value chain will the company occupy if it pursues its new strategy?

37. A value chain for an airline such as Delta or American would typically include marketing and promotion, ticketing and reservations, airport operations, and aircraft operations.

Required

Outline the specific activities that are performed in each of these broad areas. Does an airline necessarily perform all of these activities or are some of them contracted out to other companies? Identify segments of the value chain and specific activities that an airline might modify in order to add value for a customer.

38. How might an airline such as Delta use the concepts of supply-chain management in negotiations with airplane manufacturers like Boeing and Airbus? How might they use the concepts of customer relationship management in order to improve service to customers?

39. Classify each of the following as a structural, organizational, or operational activity:
   a. Reorganizing the manufacturing equipment into a cell layout as part of a switch to JIT manufacturing
   b. Deciding to organize employees into teams
   c. Deciding to build a new manufacturing facility in the midwestern United States
   d. Packing an order for shipment
   e. Deciding to automate a new factory instead of relying on manual labor
   f. Deciding how many employees to hire
   g. Deciding to expand operations to a neighboring state
   h. Moving materials within the factory
   i. Developing relations with one or two key suppliers
   j. Processing purchase orders

40. Morgret Manufacturing Company makes electric heaters for residential use and purchases a variety of electrical components from Marquis Electronics. Due to safety issues and potential liability concerns, Morgret inspects all of the purchased components.

Required

   A. Is inspection of the components a value-added or non-value-added activity?
   B. How can supply-chain management be used to reduce the costs of inspecting the components purchased from Marquis?

41. One of the problems facing college bookstores is managing the inventory of textbooks. If a bookstore orders too many textbooks, it incurs costs in repacking and shipping the books back to the textbook publisher. On the other hand, if the bookstore has too little inventory, the store may lose sales (if students go elsewhere to buy their books) or the store may incur costs related to expediting shipments from the publisher.

Required

How might the campus bookstore at your college or university use supply-chain management concepts to improve its management of inventory?

42. In an effort to develop more accurate product costs, Bell Corporation decided to adopt an activity-based costing (ABC) system. However, much to management's surprise, the product costs determined under ABC were not significantly different from the old product costs. The accounting manager wants to switch back to the old method, which was much easier and less costly.

Required

Should Bell Corporation abandon the ABC system? Why or why not?

43. Companies in every industry must strive to reduce or, if possible, eliminate non-value-added activities. Often the process of identifying and managing these types of activities requires companies to critically evaluate every process to ensure that either internal or external constituents receive benefits.

Required

For a company of your own choosing, identify several value-added activities and several non-value-added activities. Identify possible techniques the company could use to reduce or eliminate these activities.

44. Table Tops, a manufacturer of occasional tables for the home, operates in a just-in-time environment. The company is currently evaluating its operations to find areas where the company is incurring costs without creating corresponding value in its products. The following activities were identified:
   a. Completed tables receive a final inspection before being shipped to the buyer. (Note: Each employee is responsible for inspecting his or her own work.)
   b. Unstained tables are carefully sanded to ensure a smooth surface.

c. Maintenance workers replace air filters in the facility's heating and cooling system monthly.
d. Inventory warehouse personnel unload supplier trucks and arrange raw materials in the warehouse.
e. Production employees assemble the tables.
f. Shipping department personnel wrap each table to ensure that it arrives at the buyer's home in excellent condition.
g. Partially completed tables (that is, work in process inventory) are moved by employees from one work station to the next as needed.
h. Tables that are found to be defective on final inspection must be returned to various work stations to be repaired before being shipped to the buyer.
i. Raw materials are delivered to various work stations by inventory warehouse personnel.
j. Tables are painted or stained to the buyer's specification in a special painting booth.

Required

Identify each of the above activities as either a non-value-added or a value-added activity.

45. Fitzpatrick and Ramamurthy MDs operate a general practitioner medical practice. The company is currently evaluating its operations to find areas where the company is incurring costs without creating corresponding value in its services. The following activities were identified:
    a. Scheduling of appointments by receptionist
    b. Patient arrives and sits in waiting room
    c. Patient moves to examination room
    d. Patient waits for nurse
    e. Nurse checks patient's blood pressure, heart rate, and other vital signs
    f. Physician reviews patient's file
    g. Physician examines and advises patient
    h. Physician dictates notes to be added to patient's file by secretary
    i. Patient is "checked out" by receptionist and schedules appointment for additional diagnostic tests
    j. Receptionist files billing information with patient's insurance company
    k. Receptionist sends patient a bill for amounts that were not paid by insurance company

Required

Identify each of the above activities as either a non-value-added or a value-added activity.

Problems

46. Robin Thomas, the owner of Thomas' Custom Cabinets, is preparing a bid on a kitchen remodeling job for Matt and Heather. Robin expects that the job will require $1,700 of direct materials, $2,800 of direct labor, and $2,200 of overhead costs. Selling and administrative expenses for the job are expected to be $600. On average, last year Robin earned about $3,000 profit on a job this size and would like to increase the profit by 5 percent on new contracts. Robin normally applies a markup on cost of goods sold to arrive at an initial bid price and then adjusts the price if necessary in order to meet competitor's prices. Matt and Heather already have one bid from a national home improvement chain to do the job for $8,000.

✓ Robin's initial bid: $10,450

Required

A. Calculate the markup percentage on the new job.
B. What is Robin's initial bid?
C. In light of the competitor's price of $8,000, what would you recommend as a bid price for Robin?

Chapter 13 The Strategic Use of Managerial Accounting Information

47. Remmele and Little CPAs has decided to bid on the audit of Tanner, Inc., a local manufacturing firm. After learning all they can about the potential new client, the partners have estimated the following:

All staff, managers, and partners are paid on average 30 percent of the desired client billing rate ($75, $125, $250). Fringe benefits average 30 percent of the pay rate. Other out-of-pocket costs include supplies, travel, and clerical costs and are usually fairly accurate.

Staff accountant hours	1,500
Manager hours	200
Partner hours	100
Other out-of-pocket costs (estimate)	$10,000

Required

A. If the firm normally marks up nonlabor costs by 20 percent to arrive at the client fee, what should the bid price be?
B. Using the information available to you, compute the actual out-of-pocket cost to the CPA firm to complete this audit. Out-of-pocket costs do not include any profit built into the client billing rate.
C. Using your answer in B, what is the lowest price the CPA firm could charge and not lose money?
D. If Tanner, Inc. rejects the bid and states that it will pay no more than $100,000 for the audit, what are the options open to the CPA firm?

48. Montana Fishing Equipment Company (MFEC) manufactures a variety of fly-fishing equipment including fly-fishing rods and reels. The company would like to develop a unified approach to pricing its product line for next year using cost-plus pricing but does not know what cost base should be used.

✓ *Recommended sale price: $324*

Last year, MFEC earned $140,000 of profit from sales of its products and would like to earn $200,000 next year. Last year, the company incurred the following costs:

Manufacturing Costs	
Variable	$250,000
Fixed	150,000
Selling and Administrative Costs	
Variable	$100,000
Fixed	200,000

Required

A. Calculate the markup percentage for each of the following cost bases.
   1. Full costs including all manufacturing and selling and administrative costs
   2. Cost of goods sold
   3. Total variable costs
   4. Variable manufacturing costs
B. Explain why the markup percentage calculated in question A is lower when using full costs as the base than when using variable manufacturing costs as the base.

C. MFEC's best fly rod (the Trout Catcher model) costs $150 to manufacture and includes $90 of variable manufacturing costs and $60 of fixed overhead costs. Assuming the company uses a markup on variable manufacturing costs, what is the recommended sales price of the rod?
D. Competitors sell comparable fly rods for $299. Based on this information, should MFEC price the Trout Catcher model by using a cost-plus approach or a different approach?

Case

49. Your lifelong dream has been to run a successful business. As a coffee aficionado, you have decided to use your inheritance to open up a new coffee shop in your local community. After a visit to Hawaii last year, you have decided to serve only Kona coffee in your new business. Your current competition includes a national coffee chain as well as a locally owned coffee shop.

Required:

A. What strategy will you use in order to successfully compete with area coffee shops?
B. Based on your response to question A, how do you plan to determine the price of your products?
C. Identify two structural activities.
D. Identify two organizational activities.
E. How might your company strengthen its strategic position using supply-chain management?
F. How might your company strengthen its strategic position using customer relationship management?

Group and Internet Exercises

50. In the summer of 2004, several major hurricanes struck Florida, causing tens of billions of dollars of damage and resulting in dozens of deaths. In the aftermath of the hurricanes, several companies came under fire for increasing the price of electric generators and other supplies that were in high demand. The companies defended their price increases arguing that they had incurred higher costs from their own suppliers, had paid more to expedite shipping of the generators from other states, etc. Is this an example of price gouging, or are the companies justified in increasing their prices to maintain the same profit margin on their products?

51. As discussed in the chapter, Nike and Reebok occupy different parts of the value chain. While Reebok designs and manufactures its own shoes, Nike focuses on design and marketing and leaves the actual manufacturing to other companies. Look at the Nike and Reebok websites and other sources for information about the companies' choice of strategy. Who makes Nike shoes? Where are the shoes made? Where are Reebok's shoes made? Prepare a one- to two-page summary that briefly describes each organization's strategy with respect to manufacturing. What advantages and disadvantages do you see?

52. A good source of information on activity-based management and customer relationship management and how they are successfully used by companies can be found at the SAS website by clicking on the "Success Stories" link. Using the SAS site or other sources on the Internet, conduct a search for stories about companies or organizations that have successfully implemented activity-based management and customer relationship management. Prepare a one-page summary that briefly describes the organization's experience. Based on your reading of the article, was the implementation successful? What were the factors that resulted in the success or lack of success?

Chapter 14: Internal Control, Corporate Governance, and Ethics

This chapter describes fraud and several methods by which organizations combat fraudulent activities. The two types of fraud, fraudulent financial reporting and misappropriation of assets, are discussed as are common methods of perpetrating fraud. Next, we discuss internal control, corporate governance, and ethics in the business environment. The elements of internal control are explained and examples of common control activities are discussed. Corporate governance is then described along with selected current best practices. Finally, the chapter discusses how establishing an ethical environment is critical to an organization's long-term success. Matters related to establishing and writing codes of ethics and addressing ethics violations are explained.

Learning Objectives

After studying the material in this chapter, you should be able to:

1. Describe and explain the two types of fraud: fraudulent financial reporting and misappropriation of assets

2. Describe the fraud triangle and typical causes of fraud

3. Describe methods of combating fraud

4. Define internal control and describe the five elements of internal control

5. Describe the impact of information technology on internal control

6. Describe corporate governance and forces that shape governance systems

7. Explain the need to establish an ethical business environment and an ethics program

8. Describe the types and purposes of codes of ethics

9. Describe appropriate organizational responses to ethics violations

Introduction

Recent corporate scandals have rocked Wall Street and Main Street. Although frauds at companies such as Enron, WorldCom, Adelphia, Tyco, and others have caused many to lose faith in corporate America, there are some encouraging signs. Each of the major stock exchanges in the United States including the American Stock Exchange, NASDAQ, and the New York Stock Exchange has announced significant corporate governance reforms affecting companies whose securities are traded on the exchanges. Enactment of the Sarbanes-Oxley Act in 2002 ushered in what some have hailed as the most sweeping corporate reform legislation in more than 75 years. In addition, the Securities and Exchange Commission (SEC) has issued a variety of rules and regulations aimed at improving financial reporting, strengthening corporate boards, and holding management more accountable for their actions. Although the matters involved in these reform efforts are often complex, this chapter aims to describe some of the most fundamental issues related to them.

No study of accounting is complete without some understanding of the types and causes of fraud. Similarly, such a study necessitates an exploration of methods used to detect and prevent fraud. Accordingly, this chapter provides an overview of fraud and discusses the elements of a three-pronged approach to combating fraud.

Fraud

In late 2001, the once high-flying company Enron filed for bankruptcy protection. Revelations that followed the company's bankruptcy revealed a series of questionable transactions that were designed by Enron's chief financial officer, Andrew Fastow, to enrich himself and his associates while simultaneously bilking Enron's shareholders. Though the cost of Enron's collapse is still not known, early estimates are that shareholders and creditors lost more than $60 billion.

WorldCom filed for bankruptcy in June 2002 after revelations of a massive accounting fraud. Bernie Ebbers, former chief executive officer, and Scott Sullivan, former chief financial officer, have been charged along with other former members of top management for reporting fraudulent profits of more than $10 billion.

Another recent fraud involved HealthSouth, the largest provider of healthcare services in the United States. A special investigation by the company found more than $3.3 billion in either false or questionable transactions. Often the false transactions involved reclassifying operating expenses as assets, in direct violation of generally accepted accounting principles, and overstating patient revenues. Apparently the company's senior management colluded to hide their misdeeds by recording the fraudulent transactions in amounts of less than $5,000 each because they knew the company's external auditors would not likely examine such "immaterial" transactions.

A final example involves Tyco, a corporate conglomerate whose products include fire suppression systems, surgical equipment, electrical tape, garbage bags, and pain medication. Although the company restated its financial statements to the tune of more than $1 billion for 1998 to 2001, much of the attention paid to the company has centered on its former chief executive officer, Dennis Kozlowski, and former chief financial officer, Mark Swartz. Together, Kozlowski and Swartz have been accused of looting the company of more than $600 million through unauthorized compensation and loans.

KEY CONCEPT

Fraud costs businesses and consumers billions of dollars each year. Accordingly, its prevention is of paramount importance.

Sarbanes-Oxley Act of 2002

As a response to the rash of corporate scandals and frauds that began with the implosion of Enron in late 2001, the U.S. Congress held hearings that eventually led to the passage of the Sarbanes-Oxley Act. Many of the hearings devoted significant time to the role played by Arthur Andersen, Enron's external financial statement auditor. When the Enron scandal broke, Andersen was also performing the audits of WorldCom and Waste Management, two companies that also experienced scandals of their own. Eventually, the Securities and Exchange

Commission prohibited Arthur Andersen from accepting new audit clients and then prohibited the firm from performing audits of any public company. Just as Arthur Andersen was dissolved in the summer of 2002, President Bush signed the Sarbanes-Oxley Act into law.

Sarbanes-Oxley includes a number of significant provisions. For example, the law requires management to provide certifications about internal controls over financial reporting. In addition, management is required to make its own assessment of the effectiveness of those controls and to have them attested to by the company's external financial statement auditor. Management's assessment and the auditor's assessment become part of the so-called Section 404 report. Because Congress wanted to include a significant deterrent in the law, Sarbanes-Oxley also increases the criminal penalties associated with financial statement fraud to a maximum fine of $5,000,000 and imprisonment of 20 years. Another provision of the law requires companies to establish procedures to allow employees to make complaints about accounting and auditing matters directly to members of the audit committee. And, companies must ensure that employees who make such complaints are not harassed or otherwise discriminated against by others within the organization.

In sum, Sarbanes-Oxley has increased the level of scrutiny of public companies' financial statements. Many observers believe that the law will significantly improve the quality of financial reporting in the United States and rebuild the public's trust in the nation's financial markets.

Types of Fraud

Fraud is generally defined as a *knowingly* false representation of a material fact made by a party with the *intent* to deceive and induce another party to justifiably rely on the representation, to his or her detriment. You should note the two critical elements of this definition—knowledge and intent. Because most business decisions are risky and can have unintended consequences, the law defines fraud in this way. Otherwise, stockholders could claim that managers had defrauded them every time a business decision turned out to be "bad." Imagine the economic consequences if every "bad" business decision were questioned in this way. One likely consequence would be a chilling effect on managers' willingness to take on certain risks such as investing in research and development of new medicines, purchasing new cutting-edge technologies, and expanding their businesses into new regions of the world. Few of us would think that curtailing managers' activities in these ways is desirable. So, the law has

Objective 1

Describe and explain the two types of fraud: fraudulent financial reporting and misappropriation of assets

KEY CONCEPT

Frauds may be perpetrated by either management (fraudulent financial reporting) or employees (misappropriation of assets).

taken great care in defining fraud. There are two general types of fraud: fraudulent financial reporting and misappropriation of assets.

Fraudulent Financial Reporting

Fraudulent financial reporting is the intentional misstatement of or omission of material, very significant information from a company's financial statements. This type of fraud is often called management fraud because it generally requires management's active involvement. Many cases of fraudulent financial reporting involve misstated amounts, but some relate to inadequate or missing disclosures. For example, Enron engaged in thousands of transactions with so-called special-purpose entities (SPEs) that were, in numerous instances, established and managed by the company's chief financial officer. Although these transactions were not entirely illegitimate, many of them were detrimental to the company and beneficial to the chief financial officer. Enron committed fraud when it decided to record and report these transactions incorrectly and to not disclose them accurately.

THE ETHICS OF BUSINESS
Turning Trash into Treasure

Waste Management is one of the largest and most recognizable waste collection companies in the United States. Headquartered in Houston, Texas, the company has more than 400 collection operations and almost 300 landfill sites around the country. During the mid- to late 1990s, the company's most senior members of management including the chairman of the board, president, chief financial officer, corporate controller, and general counsel engaged in a massive earnings management scheme. Because the company's growth was not keeping pace with expectations, management used a number of techniques to manage earnings including:

- The manipulation of depreciation expense on the company's garbage trucks
- The failure to record expenses related to the company's landfills
- The intentional decision to not record expenses related to abandoned landfill development projects
- The improper reporting of expenditures as assets rather than expenses

In the words of the former chief financial officer, the company managed earnings to "make the financial statements look the way we want to show them." Essentially, these individuals failed in their responsibilities to stockholders, employees, and many others by ignoring reality and manipulating the accounting records to suit their ends.

It's Your Choice—It is hard to imagine that individuals involved in the earnings management fraud at Waste Management began their careers by making a conscious decision to commit fraud. Why would managers commit this type of crime? What are the implications of ignoring reality as these managers did when preparing a company's financial statements? Can you imagine circumstances in which you might be tempted to participate in a fraudulent scheme such as the one described above?

The most common types of fraudulent financial reporting involve overstating revenues and assets and understating liabilities. Frequently, management commits frauds such as these because they feel pressure to meet the expectations of investors and creditors. This pressure may come from stockholders to meet earnings expectations but may also be a result of unrealistic sales goals or other budgets set internally or compensation plans that are tied directly to the financial results of the organization. For example, a company receives a large sales order on January 2, 2005, but management is under pressure to meet its profit forecast for 2004. Management may decide to fraudulently "book" the sale early and record the transaction in 2004. However, you should note that while this fraud has the effect of increasing revenue and profit for 2004, it will correspondingly reduce revenue and profit in 2005. As a result, it may lead to further fraudulent activity as management will have to generate additional sales in 2005 to make up for those sales that were fraudulently recorded in 2004. Fraudsters who have been caught often speak of the ever mounting pressure to cover up their past frauds with current ones. This is just one reason that we rarely hear of a one-time fraud.

Occasionally, companies resort to creating fictitious assets. One of the earliest and most famous cases of this type of fraud involved the pharmaceutical company McKesson-Robbins. In the late 1930s, the company reported inventory and accounts receivable that simply did not exist. The company supported the fictitious accounts with forged invoices, customer statements, and other business documents. There is one lingering lesson from the McKesson-Robbins case—a carefully perpetrated fraud involving upper management is very difficult, if not impossible to detect.

Generally accepted accounting principles (GAAP) are the principles that guide the preparation of financial statements for external users. However, the very same financial statements may be used by internal decision makers for a variety of purposes, including promotion decisions, compensation levels, and year-end bonuses to management. In addition, GAAP leaves considerable leeway for managers to make choices that can impact earnings. For example, management has control over depreciation methods and determining the useful lives of assets. Management also has control over when to write off obsolete or damaged inventory or bad debts. These and other choices provide management with opportunities to manage earnings. Earnings management may be used to "smooth" earnings from quarter to quarter or to otherwise manipulate financial results for a variety of reasons.

KEY CONCEPT

Fraud involving upper management can be very difficult, if not impossible to detect.

Doing Business.
Channel Stuffing

Bristol-Myers Squibb, a pharmaceutical company, agreed to pay $150 million to the Securities and Exchange Commission to settle charges that the company engaged in channel stuffing during 2000 and 2001. Channel stuffing is a practice in which a company ships more products to customers than they order or can expect to sell in the normal course of business. In Bristol-Myers' case, the company offered discounts and other incentives to customers so they would stock up on drugs they did not actually need. The company also agreed to pay $300 million to settle a class-action lawsuit related to the same matter (Securities and Exchange Commission, Litigation Release No. 18822, August 6, 2004).

Misappropriation of Assets

Misappropriation of assets involves the theft of a company's assets. Usually these frauds are committed by lower-level employees and involve small amounts that do not have a significant impact on a company's financial statements. And very frequently, employees who commit fraud have never committed other criminal activities. However, misappropriation of assets may involve upper management. For example, in the case of Tyco discussed earlier, the company's chief executive officer and chief financial officer allegedly stole $600 million through unauthorized compensation and loans.

Most instances of misappropriation of assets involve cash, inventory, fixed assets, and other tangible items. Perpetrators of these frauds are often prosecuted with little fanfare and the public rarely pays attention to the matter. Although these "traditional" misappropriations still occur, advances in information technology have led to a new type of fraud involving a company's data or information systems processing capacity. Although the effects of traditional frauds tend to be limited to the parties directly involved, there may be significant adverse effects on many people when sensitive or confidential data are stolen. For example, consider the possible effects of your personal information being stolen. You may be denied a mortgage, lose a job, be unfairly arrested for crimes you did not commit, and so forth. Now just imagine that a company's information system is compromised and the personal information for 500,000 individuals is stolen. The potential costs are staggering.

According to a recent survey conducted by KPMG, 60 percent of the companies surveyed had experienced misappropriation of assets.[1] These frauds include check fraud, expense account abuse, and payroll fraud. Check fraud, or embezzlement, is sometimes covered up through a technique known as **kiting,** where a fraudster improperly records the transfer of money between bank accounts. Near the end of the month, a check is written from one bank account (the disbursing account) and is deposited into another bank account (the receiving account) just in time for the deposit to be added to the receiving account balance before the end of the month, but not in time for the disbursing account to show the decrease. The result is that the cash balance is temporarily inflated and appears to be larger than it actually is. Because this scheme requires access to company accounting records and bank accounts, it often involves a mid- or high-level member of management. Essentially, kiting is achieved through the increase of one bank account (i.e., the receiving account) resulting from a cash transfer from another bank account (i.e., the disbursing account) without a corresponding decrease in the paying account.

Lapping is another technique used to cover up a theft of cash. This scheme is perpetrated by someone with access to both cash receipts and company accounting records. Lapping is accomplished by stealing, and not recording, the cash received from one customer and covering the shortage with cash received from another customer. The scheme will continue as long as sufficient cash is being received from customers to cover up the stolen cash. However, lapping often fails because the scheme becomes complex relatively quickly as numerous customers' accounts are affected.

Expense account abuse is another common fraud. Employees who travel and receive a travel reimbursement sometimes abuse their expense accounts by reporting inflated or fictitious items. For example, a salesperson may request reimbursement for a round of golf allegedly played with a new customer when the round was actually played with a former college roommate. Another common expense account abuse involves the unreported personal use of company automobiles. Although expense account abuses rarely involve large amounts, the effect usually is a corrosive business environment in which small frauds can lead to bigger frauds.

Causes of Fraud

Objective 2
Describe the fraud triangle and typical causes of fraud

Fraudulent activity results from an interaction of forces both within an individual and the external environment. These forces tend to fit into three general categories that make up what is commonly called the **fraud triangle** (see Exhibit 14-1). These forces include:

- situational pressures and incentives
- opportunities
- personal characteristics and attitudes

---

[1] **Fraud Survey 2003, KPMG** is available at http://www.kpmg.com.

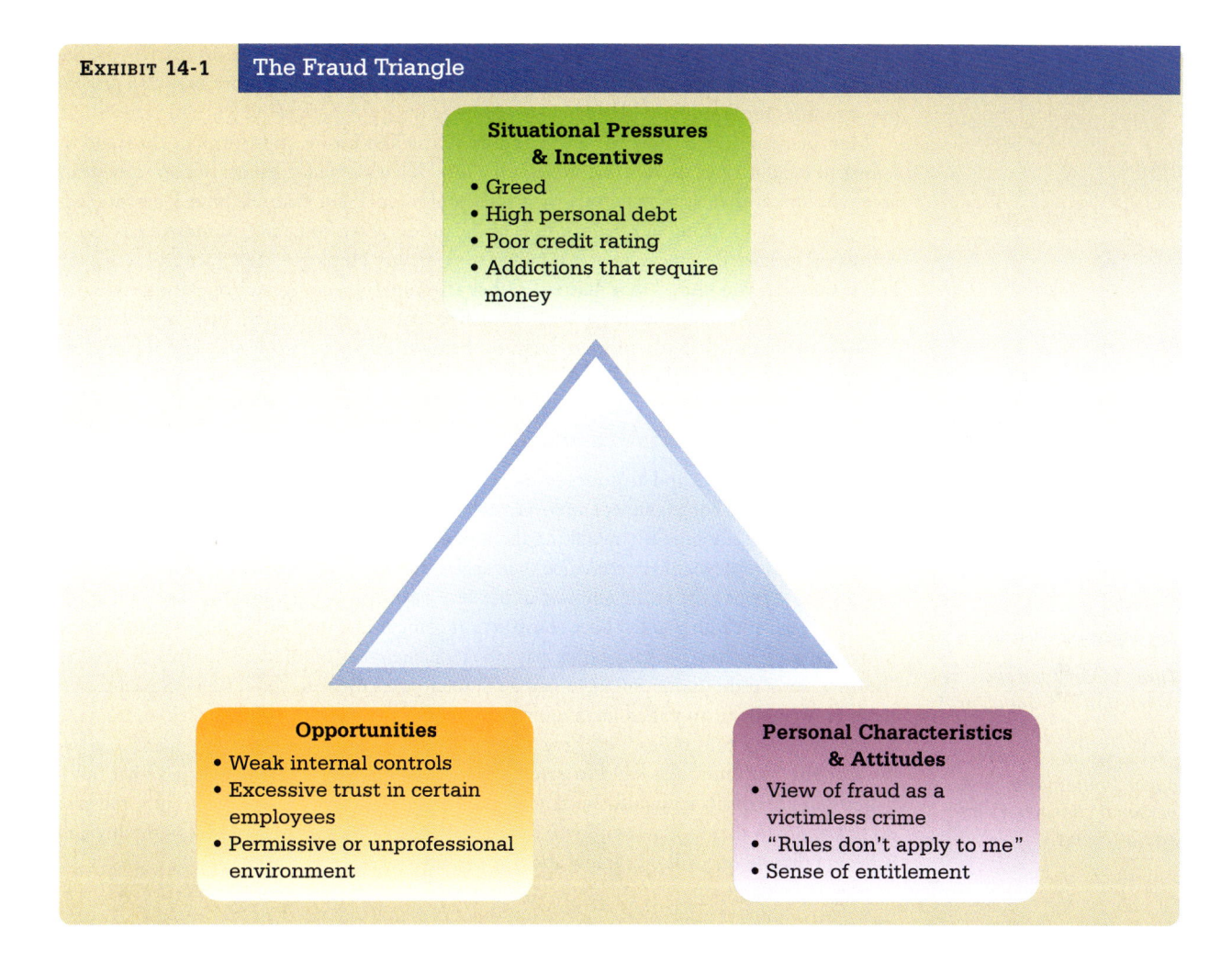

Exhibit 14-1: The Fraud Triangle

Situational Pressures & Incentives
- Greed
- High personal debt
- Poor credit rating
- Addictions that require money

Opportunities
- Weak internal controls
- Excessive trust in certain employees
- Permissive or unprofessional environment

Personal Characteristics & Attitudes
- View of fraud as a victimless crime
- "Rules don't apply to me"
- Sense of entitlement

Situational Pressures and Incentives

Situational pressures and incentives often provide the motivation for employees to commit fraud. Although an employee's motivations vary greatly, they typically result from financial, employment, or other situational pressures. One of the most common financial motivations for fraud is simple greed. This is particularly true of members of management who perpetrate fraud. Other common financial motivations include high levels of personal debt; poor credit ratings; expenses related to addictions to alcohol, drugs, or gambling; and poor performing investments. Situational pressures may be related to employment matters as well. For example, employees occasionally perpetrate fraud because they believe they are underpaid or not appreciated. Other employment-related motivations include general dissatisfaction with work, feeling that there is inadequate recognition for accomplishments, and fear of an impending job loss. Lastly, employees may be motivated to commit fraud because of the perceived challenge of committing and concealing the fraud, family pressures to live a certain lifestyle, and the need to exert control or power over others.

Opportunities

Opportunities are the conditions or circumstances that allow employees to commit fraud. Opportunities usually result from weak or missing internal controls (i.e., policies and procedures that provide reasonable assurance that company's goals and objectives will be achieved). However, management's operating style and philosophy can also provide opportunities for fraud. Regardless, fraud cannot be committed without sufficient opportunity. Separation of duties is a crucial internal control procedure. Insufficient separation of duties is one of the leading reasons that employees ever have the opportunity to commit fraud. At the very least a company should strive to separate the following three duties: transaction approval, recordkeeping, and custody of assets and records. Inadequate documentation of transactions, insufficient authorization procedures, and infrequent independent reviews of employees' work may also provide opportunities for fraudulent behavior.

Management's operating style and philosophy can also create opportunities for fraud by failing to establish the appropriate "tone at the top." That is, management's actions can create an environment that appears permissive and unprofessional. For example, management's lack of commitment to strong internal controls or the promotion of unqualified individuals to positions of authority conveys a clear message to company employees that "it's not what you know, but who you know" that matters. Other attributes of a company's operating style that can lead to fraud include management's excessive trust in certain employees, operating the business in a manner that results in decisions being made in a crisis mode, and insufficient communication of ethical standards.

Personal Characteristics and Attitudes

Personal characteristics and attitudes influence the psychological mind-set that employees rely on to justify fraud. For example, employees may view fraud as a victimless crime. They might say "No one is really hurt by my taking the money. The company doesn't need it like I do." Occasionally, employees may convince themselves that they are "borrowing" the money and they intend to repay the entire amount in the very near future. Such was the case with an elderly payroll clerk who worked for a construction company in the southeastern United States. In her capacity as the company's only payroll clerk, the grandmotherly employee decided to "borrow" several thousand dollars to pay delinquent taxes owed to the Internal Revenue Service. However, the so-called loan quickly ballooned and eventually totaled more than $250,000. When confronted with her crime, the employee admitted to having plans to repay the amount, but found the fraud so easy to commit that she just could not stop. Other rationalizations are equally straightforward and include employees feeling as though rules and laws do not apply to them, or an employee feeling a sense of entitlement from the company and believing that no one will ever know about the fraud.

KEY CONCEPT

Three forces typically contribute to fraudulent behavior: situational pressures and incentives, opportunities, and personal characteristics and attitudes.

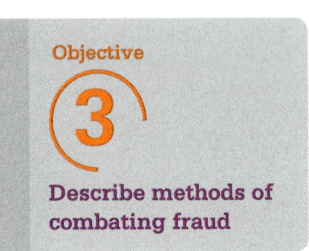

Combating Fraud

All organizations have interests in combating fraud. The cost of fraud can be staggering. According to a 2003 survey, the average cost of fraudulent financial reporting was over $250 million for each company involved.[2] This amount dwarfed the cost of misappropriation of assets, which averaged just $464,000. However, these numbers only tell part of the story. Companies spend significant amounts on antifraud programs and employees devote many hours to the efforts.

Objective 3

Describe methods of combating fraud

Companies have begun implementing a variety of antifraud programs and policies. Most common among the antifraud programs is a review and strengthening of internal controls. Periodic evaluations of controls often reveal gaps in a company's internal controls and can provide a means for management to reduce the opportunities to commit fraud. Companies have begun conducting more frequent audits to ensure that employees are complying with company policies and procedures. This type of audit can provide a powerful incentive for employees to not commit fraud because it serves to put employees on notice that management is actively engaged in fraud detection and prevention. Other techniques used by companies include creating employee hotlines, establishing and publishing a code of conduct for employees, conducting background checks for employees who have budgetary authority, and instituting fraud awareness training programs.

Awareness of factors that contribute to fraud helps companies determine the best ways to combat fraud. A survey of managers revealed that the primary factor contributing to fraud was collusion between employees and third parties such as friends and family who work for suppliers and customers. Other factors included inadequate internal controls and management override of internal controls.[3]

---

[2]Ibid.
[3]Ibid.

The remainder of the chapter focuses on three strategies to combat fraud. The strategies include internal controls, corporate governance policies, and sound ethical business practices. Companies should strive for excellence in each of these areas. Weaknesses in any one of them can reduce the overall effectiveness of a company's antifraud program.

Internal Control

The policies and procedures that provide reasonable assurance that a company's goals and objectives will be achieved are referred to as **internal control**. No one set of policies and procedures is appropriate for every company. Rather, internal control systems must be customized to address the needs and concerns of each company's management. Internal control generally reflects the operating style of management or owners and must be designed so that employees can perform their duties effectively and efficiently. In addition, a company must carefully evaluate internal control to ensure that policies and procedures provide benefits that are sufficient to outweigh the costs. In fact, some companies decide to eliminate controls because their costs outweigh their benefits.

Hershey, the chocolate manufacturer, had a strict policy that prohibited manufacturing employees from taking candy from the plant. However, after experiencing continued inventory losses due to employee pilferage, the company rescinded the policy and announced that each employee would be allowed to take a limited amount of free candy each month. In Hershey's case, the more relaxed policy resulted in a reduction in employee pilferage.

Whether designed for large companies such as Hershey or a small locally owned hardware store, internal control is comprised of five related elements:

- The control environment
- Risk assessment
- Control activities
- Information and communication
- Monitoring

Exhibit 14-2 provides a graphical representation of the relationship among the elements of internal control. Notice how the control environment pervades all of the remaining elements.

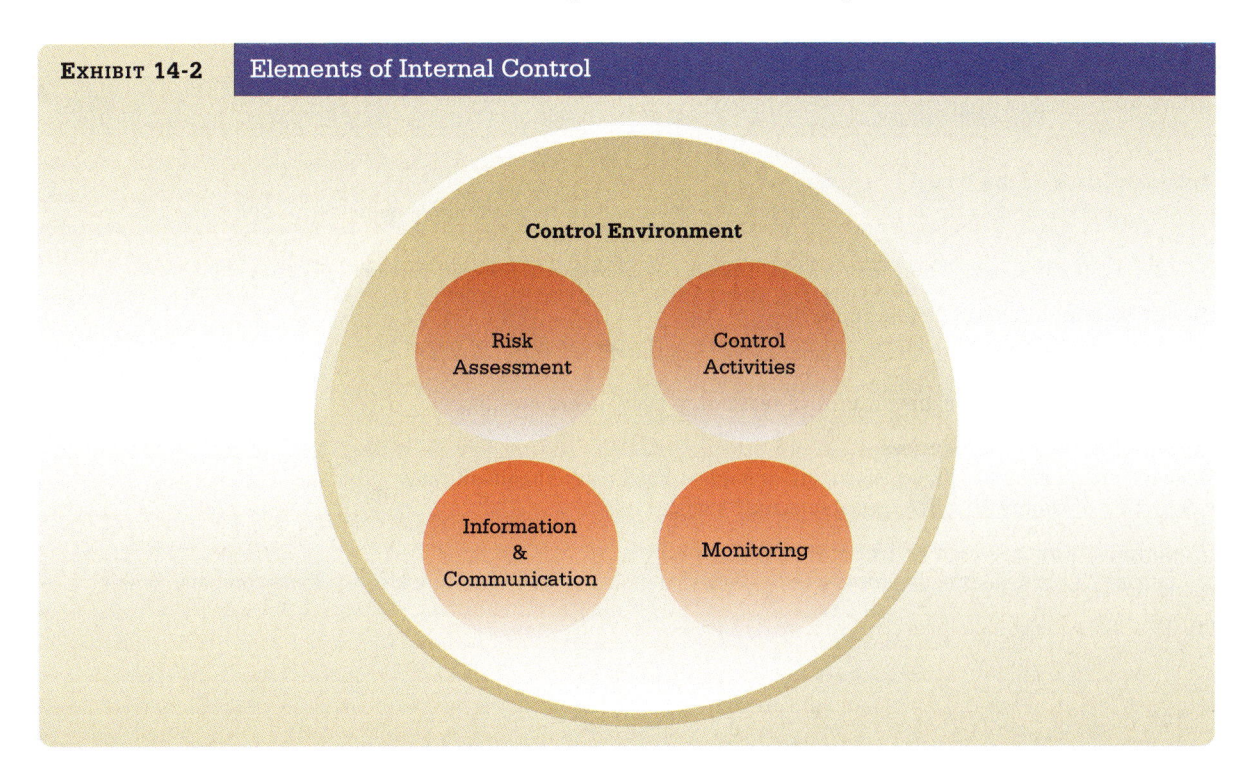

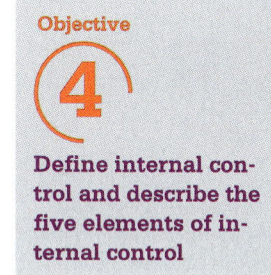

Objective 4
Define internal control and describe the five elements of internal control

EXHIBIT 14-2 Elements of Internal Control

Control Environment
- Risk Assessment
- Control Activities
- Information & Communication
- Monitoring

These elements are part of a framework developed by the Committee of Sponsoring Organizations (COSO) in 1992. COSO is sponsored by the American Accounting Association, the American Institute of Certified Public Accountants, the Financial Executives Institute, the Institute of Internal Auditors, and the Institute of Management Accountants. COSO is comprised of representatives from industry, public accounting, investment firms, and the New York Stock Exchange. The COSO framework is the most widely used internal control framework in the United States.

Control Environment

Owners' and management's attitudes and general philosophy about internal control and accountability are evidenced by company policies and procedures. Collectively these policies and procedures represent the control environment and help to establish the overall tone within a company. For example, if owners and managers believe integrity and ethical behavior are important elements in business, then they will likely establish a well-reasoned and adequately defined set of policies that outline acceptable behaviors for company employees (e.g., a code of conduct). On the other hand, owners and managers who do not view integrity and ethical behavior as important will not likely establish such policies or will not enforce them. Whether a company establishes and enforces policies related to integrity and ethical behavior sets the tone for employees by communicating to them management's expectations of their behavior.

A variety of factors contribute to establishing the control environment. Management that is aggressive and "hungry" generally views internal control as applying only to nonmanagement employees, whereas management that is conservative and measured in its approach to business views internal control as applying to everyone in the organization. Consequently, conservative management tends to establish a more control-conscious environment than their more aggressive counterparts. Other factors that contribute to the control environment include a company's organizational structure, human resource policies, commitment to competence, and oversight by the company's board of directors. Of these factors, the oversight role of a company's board of directors has taken on increasing importance since the passage of the Sarbanes-Oxley Act. As demonstrated in Exhibit 14-3, companies are increasingly diligent about the governance role played by the board of directors.

The boards of directors for public companies are comprised of individuals who possess significant business experience or knowledge and who serve as a liaison between management

> **KEY CONCEPT**
>
> *Internal control is comprised of five elements: the control environment, risk assessment, control activities, information and communication, and monitoring.*

EXHIBIT 14-3 | **Highlights of the Business Roundtable's Corporate Governance Survey**

Independence of the Board of Directors
Almost 85 percent of companies have adopted new standards related to board independence within the last two years.
99 percent of companies report that their boards are comprised of at least 60 percent independent directors.

Board Meetings without Management
All companies expect their outside directors to meet without management present (i.e., in executive session) at least twice during 2004.
61 percent of companies expect executive sessions at every board meeting.

Board of Directors Education
89 percent of companies either encourage or require directors to attend education programs.
19 percent of companies offer special director training.

Communication between Shareholders and Directors
87 percent of companies have procedures to allow shareholders to contact directors regarding company matters.

SOURCE: Business Roundtable, 2003 Corporate Governance Survey.

and stockholders. Directors advise management on strategic decisions and other matters of great importance. For example, directors often advise management on proposed mergers and acquisitions, significant product development issues, and large capital investment decisions. To be most effective, members of the board should not be employed by the company except as directors (i.e., they should be independent) and they should carefully evaluate and question management's decisions. To put it more succinctly, the board of directors should ascertain whether management is looking out for the interests of the company as a whole, and not just its own best interest.

Risk Assessment

A company should take steps to identify and evaluate risks that can adversely affect its ability to successfully conduct business. Constantly changing economic, industry, regulatory, and operating conditions make it necessary for management to regularly assess risks posed by those changing conditions. Management should assess risks that might occur at every level of the company (e.g., employee theft, faulty product design, and fraudulent financial reporting). After risks have been identified, management should evaluate the potential impact and likelihood of the risks adversely affecting the company and also take steps to reduce those risks to an acceptable level. For example, the U.S. Congress may impose strict new guidelines limiting advertising of a particular product such as cigarettes. A tobacco company should have risk assessment processes in place that would allow it to identify this risk as soon as possible and to develop a response that limits the negative effects of the new limits on advertising.

Control Activities

Control activities are often the most visible element of internal control within a company. Control activities are comprised of a company's policies and procedures that aim to reduce risks identified by the company. These activities commonly relate to segregation of duties, transaction authorization, safeguarding of assets, and independent reviews of work.

Segregation of Duties Companies should, whenever possible, segregate duties related to recordkeeping, custody, and authorization. For example, an employee who signs checks should not also be allowed to reconcile the monthly bank statements. Failure to separate the recording of transactions and custody of assets can afford an employee the opportunity to "hide" theft. Similarly, an employee should not maintain custody of assets and authorize transactions because that employee is also in a position to steal from the company and cover up the theft. Of course not all companies will be able to segregate the duties as described because of limited personnel. When such is the case, an active owner/manager can periodically review or "check up" on employees.

Transaction Authorization Every transaction should be authorized to ensure that the company's resources are used only for legitimate business purposes. Companies frequently establish general authorizations for recurring transactions such as inventory purchases, setting credit limits for customers based on some credit score, and so on. Management may require specific authorization for certain nonrecurring transactions that are believed to warrant an evaluation on a case-by-case basis. Examples of transactions that might require specific authorization might include approving special sales discounts for customers, one-time salary adjustments, and selling a piece of production machinery to an employee.

Safeguarding of Assets A company's resources must be safeguarded not only from theft, but also from unauthorized usage. Common controls aimed at protecting a company's assets include locked vaults and safes, locked doors and windows, password-protected computer equipment, and security systems. These and other controls should be devised to not only protect tangible assets such as cash, inventory, and equipment, but also business documents and accounting data. A significant loss of assets and/or data can cripple an otherwise healthy company.

Independent Reviews of Work Independent reviews of work provide a monitoring mechanism that helps companies ensure that all other controls are occurring as intended. To be effective these reviews should be performed on an ongoing basis and should be performed by an employee who is independent from the original control and/or data preparation. For example, one employee should prepare the monthly bank reconciliation for the checking account and another employee should perform an independent review of the reconciliation to ensure that it is complete and accurate. Computerized accounting information systems are commonly used to conduct independent reviews of work. Companies need only to ensure that employees do not gain unauthorized access to the system and that the appropriate controls are enabled in the system.

Information and Communication

The information and communication component of internal control relates to the company's accounting information system, which is used to initiate, record, process, and communicate the company's transactions to managers through performance reports and to stockholders and others via financial statements. Companies can either choose to implement manual or computerized information systems. Large manual information systems were typical in the past, but technology has improved and sophisticated software and hardware have become so widely available that few businesses continue to use such systems. Now even the smallest business can afford to purchase a relatively sophisticated accounting information system. Small businesses sometimes use systems such as Peachtree or Great Plains Business Solutions. Large businesses use much more expensive and sophisticated systems like the ERP systems discussed in Chapter 1. Regardless of their level of sophistication or their purchase price, an accounting information system serves two basic purposes: information collection and reporting.

Monitoring

A company should periodically assess the effectiveness of its internal controls. The periodic assessments relate to both the sufficiency and performance of internal control systems. Management obtains information to perform these assessments via feedback from company employees, customer and supplier complaints, and various other sources. Although monitoring activities can be performed by various company employees, they should be performed by employees who do not record transactions, prepare accounting reports, or perform daily internal control activities. Large companies frequently rely on internal auditors to perform the monitoring function. Internal auditors assist management by evaluating and reporting on employee compliance with company policies and the effectiveness of those policies. For example, internal auditors may evaluate whether employees are adhering to company policies related to personal use of company assets such as delivery trucks. Instances of noncompliance are reported to management, who can then decide on how best to address the violations of company policy.

The Impact of Information Technology on Internal Control

Objective 5
Describe the impact of information technology on internal control

Information technology has dramatically changed the business landscape. Companies now purchase raw materials from suppliers and sell products to customers who are thousands of miles away. In addition, even the smallest companies can often afford highly sophisticated software to manage their businesses. Companies can also leverage the Internet to tell others about their products and services in ways that were unheard of only 10 or so years ago.

While technology has provided companies with many new opportunities, it also introduces new risks. Because more business is now conducted on the Internet than ever before, company data and information are susceptible to being viewed, copied, or altered by nonusers who gain access to the company's network. In short, companies are now faced with threats from sources never before considered. As shown in Exhibit 14-4, threats come from a variety of directions and sources.

Exhibit 14-4: Threats in an E-Information Technology-Intensive Environment

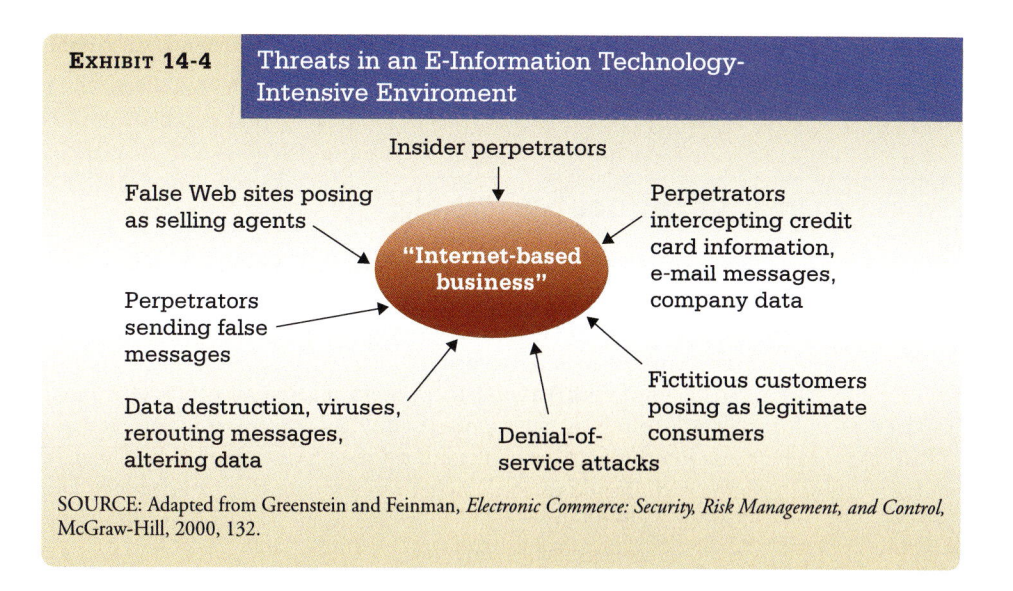

- Insider perpetrators
- False Web sites posing as selling agents
- Perpetrators intercepting credit card information, e-mail messages, company data
- Perpetrators sending false messages
- Fictitious customers posing as legitimate consumers
- Data destruction, viruses, rerouting messages, altering data
- Denial-of-service attacks

SOURCE: Adapted from Greenstein and Feinman, *Electronic Commerce: Security, Risk Management, and Control*, McGraw-Hill, 2000, 132.

Specific risks to companies conducting business in a technology-intensive environment include the following:

- *Customer impersonation.* Fictitious customers can enter a company's computer system and corrupt data or place false orders, using an assumed customer's identification.

- *Denial-of-service attacks.* These are used to destroy, shut down, or severely curtail a system's ability to communicate with legitimate system users. The goal of these attacks is to flood the site with information so that legitimate messages or orders cannot be received or processed.

- *Unauthorized access to data.* Data are particularly vulnerable at intermediate network junctions that handle the transfer of information from one site to another.

- *Sabotage by former employees.* Former employees who are laid off, fired, or leave under unpleasant circumstances are a threat because of their knowledge of the systems and the organization.

- *Threats by current employees.* These types of threats include stealing trade secrets to sell to competitors and embezzling assets from the company.

How does an organization reduce the risks associated with doing business in a technology-intensive environment? Many of the same types of internal controls that we have discussed previously will serve to reduce the risks. However, additional specific internal controls associated with information technology are also necessary. These include the following:

- Passwords to limit access to computer systems
- Firewalls to limit access to computer networks by screening all network traffic and controlling access to critical information
- Encryption of sensitive data to be readable only by persons holding the decryption key
- Moving critical data to a separate server that is not connected to the outside world (i.e., an intranet)
- Shutting off computers during nonbusiness hours
- Staying up-to-date with technology

External auditors also need to consider the impact of e-business activities on the reliability of financial reports. Data that are created and stored electronically may be more vulnerable to

KEY CONCEPT

Conducting business in an information technology-intensive environment introduces new risks and requires new and expanded internal controls.

manipulation. As a result, auditors should pay particular attention to a company's policies and procedures regarding computer security.[4]

Corporate Governance

Objective 6: Describe corporate governance and forces that shape governance systems

Corporate governance is embodied in the processes that companies use to promote corporate fairness, complete and accurate financial disclosures, and management accountability. In other words, corporate governance serves to make management more accountable to employees, stockholders, and others interested in the company.

Both internal and external forces shape a company's system of corporate governance. Internal forces include the board of directors, the various committees of the board (e.g., the audit committee, the compensation committee, and the human resource committee), the internal audit department, compensation and incentive programs, corporate codes of conduct, and conflict of interest policies. External forces include local, state, and federal laws and regulations, generally accepted accounting principles, creditors, and shareholders.

Recent corporate scandals have highlighted the failures of external financial statement auditors, management, and the board of directors to exercise the appropriate level of diligence in fulfilling their respective roles in the corporate governance process. Auditors have been accused of failing to independently, or objectively, evaluate their client's financial statements. Instead, many have accused auditors of having relationships that are too close with their clients leading to an inherent conflict of interest. Scrutiny of management has focused primarily on the charge that they have received significant compensation in the form of stock that they have sold after taking actions to increase their company's stock price in the short term without due regard for the company's long-term prospects. The board of directors has also been criticized for failure to exercise sufficient oversight of management. We now know that boards of directors at companies such as Enron failed to question management on many important decisions, and instead, acted as a rubber stamp too often.

Legislation and regulatory actions by the U.S. Congress and the Securities and Exchange Commission (SEC), as well as the issuance of standards by stock exchanges such as the New York Stock Exchange, have given rise to a host of new requirements impacting corporate boards of directors, management, and external financial statement auditors. For example, it is now common for boards of directors to meet with auditors without members of management present to allow for a free and open discussion about significant accounting and auditing matters. Additionally, certain committees of the board of directors, such as the audit committee, must be composed entirely of independent directors, that is, individuals who have no significant business relationship with the company.

As with internal control, one set of corporate governance processes will not be appropriate for every company. Instead, a company should tailor governance processes to fit the particular circumstances. In addition to the internal and external forces described in the previous paragraphs, a company should consider such matters as management structure, overall size and complexity of operations, stakeholders (i.e., those affected by its decisions), and significant or unique business risks. Exhibit 14-5 shows the components of General Motors' corporate governance system.

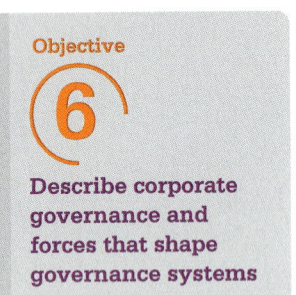

KEY CONCEPT

Corporate governance systems are used by a company to promote corporate fairness, complete and accurate financial disclosures, and accountability.

---

[4]Earp, Ingraham, and Jenkins, "The Newest Technology Tools: (Un)Limited Access?" *The CPA Journal*, January 2000, 58–59.

| EXHIBIT 14-5 | Components of General Motors' Corporate Governance System |

Selection and Composition of the Board
    Board membership criteria
    Selection of new Directors
    Extending the invitation to a potential Director to join the Board
    Director orientation and continuing education

Board Leadership
    Selection of Chairman and Chief Executive Officer
    Chairman of the Directors and Corporate Governance Committee

Board Composition and Performance
    Size of the Board
    Mix of management and independent Directors
    Board definition of what constitutes independence for Directors
    Former Chairman and Chief Executive Officer Board membership
    Directors who change their present job responsibility
    Limits on outside Board memberships
    Term limits
    Retirement age
    Board compensation
    Loans to Directors and executive officers
    Stock ownership by non-employee Directors
    Executive sessions of independent Directors and the role of the Presiding Director
    Access to outside advisors
    Assessing the Board's performance
    Ethics and conflicts of interests
    Board's interaction with advisors, institutional investors, press, customers, etc.

Board Relationship to Senior Management
    Regular attendance of non-Directors at Board meetings
    Board access to senior management

Meeting Procedures
    Selection of agenda items for Board meetings
    Board materials distributed in advance
    Board presentations

Committee Matters
    Number, structure and independence of Committees
    Committee performance evaluation
    Assignment and rotation of committee members
    Frequency and length of committee meetings
    Committee agenda

Leadership Development
    Formal evaluation of the Chairman and Chief Executive Officer
    Succession planning
    Management development

The Need for Ethics

Objective 7
Explain the need to establish an ethical business environment and an ethics program

There is an old saying "It's not personal, it's just business!" To some this suggests that there is no "good and bad" or "right and wrong" in business. Many of the recent corporate scandals suggest that managers sometimes make decisions not on the basis of what is right and what is wrong for the company and its stakeholders, but on the basis of what is best for themselves, their families, and their friends. Frequently these decisions have dire consequences for employees, creditors, suppliers, stockholders, and the local community—that is the broader set of a company's stakeholders. Many business, government, and academic leaders have been calling for a renewed emphasis on business ethics.

Business ethics result from the interaction of personal morals and the processes and objectives of business. That is to say, business ethics are nothing more than our personal views of right and wrong applied in a business setting. For example, some business practices that are viewed as unethical include managers lying to employees, stealing from a company, divulging confidential information, and taking credit for the work of others. Now, consider how these unethical business practices could occur in your personal life. For example, a child might lie to her mother, a roommate may steal money from you while you are in class, a friend may tell another person about a "private" conversation that you and he had, and a group member may contribute nothing to a group project but accept full credit for the project. Business ethics are just an extension of our own personal ethics. Of course the stakes are often much higher. Consider the many billions of dollars that the tobacco industry was forced to pay because it lied to consumers and the government about the ill effects of nicotine. In addition, business managers must consider more stakeholders when they make ethical decisions. A chief executive officer cannot simply make the decision that is best for her without considering the interests of other employees, stockholders, customers, suppliers, creditors, and so forth.

Integrity is the cornerstone of ethical business practices. Just as the control environment pervades a business and establishes a particular level of control consciousness, managing with integrity also tends to create a work environment in which employees expect to be treated honestly. Failure to build a business on integrity carries costs. For example, deceptive business practices may harm a company's standing in the community, decrease employee productivity, reduce customer loyalty, build resentment among employees, increase the likelihood of unethical behavior by other employees, and cause government agencies to scrutinize the business. Although some of these consequences may have costs that are difficult to quantify, there is no doubt that their costs can be substantial.

KEY CONCEPT

Establishing an ethical business environment encourages employees to act with integrity and conduct business in a manner that is just and fair to other stakeholders.

Hitting the Bottom Line.

DOES DOING GOOD ENSURE DOING WELL?

A very basic question that many businesses ask is "Does it pay to be an ethical company?" A research study by Simon Webley and Elise More suggests that the answer to this question is "yes." Webley and More investigated whether the financial performance of companies that have a demonstrable commitment to ethical behavior (i.e., high ethics companies) is different than the performance of companies that do not demonstrate such a commitment (i.e., low ethics companies). Two of the research's more interesting findings relate to wealth creation and profitability. For instance, the study found that high ethics companies created more wealth for investors during the study period than low ethics companies. And second, high ethics companies experienced less volatility in stock price and earnings over time than low ethics companies. According to Webley and More, the study's findings support the contention that high ethics companies are likely to have more stable management and offer greater growth potential over the long run than low ethics companies (Institute of Business Ethics, *Does Business Ethics Pay?* April 2003).

Ethics Programs

Companies frequently create **ethics programs** to establish and help maintain an ethical business environment. Some of the most common elements of ethics programs include written codes of ethics, employee hotlines and ethics call centers, ethics training, processes to register anonymous complaints about wrongdoing, and ethics offices. Ethics programs may include any combination of these elements. However, according to the *2003 National Business Ethics Survey*, it is clear that building an ethics program with multiple elements is more likely to encourage employees to recognize and report wrongdoing. Ultimately a company has to weigh the cost of establishing an ethics program against the potential costs of unethical behaviors of employees and management.

A company may also choose to make the necessary investment in an ethics program for legal reasons. Federal sentencing guidelines established in the early 1990s provide partial relief for companies who have compliance and ethics programs in place. Recently, the standards for the compliance and ethics programs were made more stringent by imposing greater responsibility on boards of directors and management for the oversight and operation of compliance programs. Specifically, directors and management must assume an active leadership role for the content and operation of the programs. Under the new standards, companies that seek to reduce criminal penalties imposed on them must be capable of promoting an organizational culture that encourages a commitment to legal and ethical conduct by all employees.

Codes of Ethics

A fundamental element of every ethics program is a code of ethics. Codes of ethics vary greatly, but fall into three primary types. The first type, often called a code of conduct, lays out specific rules or standards of behavior for various business situations. Codes of conduct tend to be lengthy and somewhat legalistic in their form. The second type describes the vision of a company and is often called a credo or mission statement. Within a mission statement a company generally asserts its commitment to key stakeholders such as employees, customers, suppliers, stockholders, and the community. The third type is a corporate philosophy statement that outlines in broad terms the principles that guide the company in its business endeavors. Exhibit 14-6 shows examples of a mission statement and a corporate philosophy statement.

Objective 8
Describe the types and purposes of codes of ethics

KEY CONCEPT

There are three types of codes of ethics: codes of conduct, mission statements, and corporate philosophy statements.

Purposes of Codes of Ethics Codes of ethics serve a variety of purposes and offer substantial benefits to companies. A well-written code of ethics can reduce the likelihood that matters of "right and wrong" will be left to individual interpretation. Of course, a company must take care to avoid leaving employees with the impression that behaviors not specifically prohibited by the company's code are permitted. A code can establish the tone of the business environment and instill in employees a sense of how to behave even in the absence of specific guidance. A code of ethics serves business interests because unethical behaviors increase the likelihood of government or media scrutiny along with potential legal or reputation costs. A code of ethics also serves as a consensus-building tool that employees can look to for guidance when they believe improper demands are being made of them. Lastly, a code of ethics can be useful in conveying values and beliefs that are important to a company's management or owners. That is, a code can explain the company's reason for being.

Writing Codes of Ethics Given their importance, care must be taken in creating codes of ethics. Without thoughtful consideration, codes of ethics become meaningless and vague. How then should a company write a code of ethics?

Management support is critical to the successful creation of a code of ethics. Company employees must know that management is fully committed to establishing a code of ethics. A company should seek ideas and suggestions from employees at every level of the organization. Including employee input serves to create greater consensus and communicate the importance of the code and the employees' support of it. Legal and regulatory developments should be considered to ensure that the code does not conflict with recently enacted requirements. Also, the code should be written as simply as possible, avoiding excessive legal terminology. Finally, communicate the rationale for various provisions of the code whenever possible. Employees who understand the underlying reasons for the rules are more likely to follow and respect them.

EXHIBIT 14-6 | **Examples of Codes of Ethics**

Johnson & Johnson's Mission Statement

We believe our first responsibility is to the doctors, nurses and patients,
to mothers and fathers and all others who use our products and services.
In meeting their needs, everything we do must be of high quality.
We must constantly strive to reduce our costs in order to maintain reasonable prices.
Customers' orders must be serviced promptly and accurately.
Our suppliers and distributors must have an opportunity to make a fair profit.

We are responsible to our employees, the men and women who work with us throughout the world.
Everyone must be considered as an individual.
We must respect their dignity and recognize their merit.
They must have a sense of security in their jobs.
Compensation must be fair and adequate, and working conditions clean, orderly and safe.
We must be mindful of ways to help our employees fulfill their family responsibilities.
Employees must feel free to make suggestions and complaints.
There must be equal opportunity for employment, development and advancement for those qualified.
We must provide competent management, and their actions must be just and ethical.

We are responsible to the communities in which we live and work and to the world community as well.
We must be good citizens–support good works and charities and bear our fair share of taxes.
We must encourage civic improvements and better health and education.
We must maintain in good order the property we are privileged to use, protecting the environment and natural resources.

Our final responsibility is to our stockholders.
Business must make a sound profit.
We must experiment with new ideas.
Research must be carried on, innovative programs developed and mistakes paid for.
New equipment must be purchased, new facilities provided and new products launched.
Reserves must be created to provide for adverse times.
When we operate according to these principles, the stockholders should realize a fair return.

Levi Strauss & Co.'s Corporate Philosophy Statement

Our values are fundamental to our success. They are the foundation of our company, define who we are and set us apart from the competition. They underlie our vision of the future, our business strategies and our decisions, actions and behaviors. We live by them. They endure. Four core values are at the heart of Levi Strauss & Co.: Empathy, Originality, Integrity and Courage.

Responding to Ethics Violations

The unfortunate reality is that management and company employees violate codes of ethics. The manner in which a company addresses these ethics violations has a significant impact on the future effectiveness of its overall ethics program. For example, employees who know that violators are treated fairly and in accordance with stated policies are more likely to respect the company's ethics program and believe that management is committed to ethics.

So, how should a company react when an employee violates the code of ethics? As with many business decisions there is not one answer to this question, but several principles to follow. First, the apparent violation should be carefully and thoroughly investigated. The goal is to determine whether the employee acted in a manner contrary to the code of ethics. It may be necessary to interview the employee's coworkers to learn details of the suspected violation. It is important that those employees responsible for the investigation are objective and are free of any real or apparent conflicts of interest. Second, the company's reaction should be timely. It is unfair to the suspected violator and the remaining employees for there to be a cloud of distrust or suspicion hanging over the workplace for a long period. Finally, the company should administer sanctions that are appropriate to the violation. Fairness is particularly important. Excessive punishment, as perceived by other employees, can lead to resentment within the workforce and can create a culture in which employees may adopt an "us versus them" mentality. Remember, a primary goal of an ethics program is to encourage employees to act with integrity and in accordance with the company's code of ethics.

> **Objective 9**
> Describe appropriate organizational responses to ethics violations

Summary of Key Concepts

- *Fraud costs businesses and consumers billions of dollars each year. Accordingly, its prevention is of paramount importance. (p. 472)*

- *Fraud may be perpetrated by either management (fraudulent financial reporting) or employees (misappropriation of assets). (p. 474)*

- *Fraud involving upper management can be very difficult, if not impossible to detect. (p. 475)*

- *Three forces typically contribute to fraudulent behavior: situational pressures and incentives, opportunities, and personal characteristics and attitudes. (p. 478)*

- *Internal control is comprised of five elements: the control environment, risk assessment, control activities, information and communication, and monitoring. (p. 480)*

- *Conducting business in an information technology-intensive environment introduces new risks and requires new and expanded internal controls. (p. 483)*

- *Corporate governance systems are used by a company to promote corporate fairness, complete and accurate financial disclosures, and accountability. (p. 484)*

- *Establishing an ethical business environment encourages employees to act with integrity and conduct business in a manner that is just and fair to other stakeholders. (p. 486)*

- *There are three types of codes of ethics: codes of conduct, mission statements, and corporate philosophy statements. (p. 487)*

Key Definitions

Fraud A *knowingly* false representation of a material fact made by a party with the *intent* to deceive and induce another party to justifiably rely on the representation, to his or her detriment. (p. 473)

Fraudulent financial reporting The intentional misstatement of or omission of material, very significant, information from a company's financial statements. (p. 474)

Misappropriation of assets The theft of a company's assets. (p. 475)

Kiting The transfer of money from one bank account to another near the end of a reporting period with the intention of overstating the cash balance. (p. 476)

Lapping A scheme accomplished by stealing, and not recording, the cash received from one customer and covering the shortage with cash received from another customer. (p. 476)

Fraud triangle Three forces typically contribute to fraudulent behavior: situational pressures and incentives, opportunities, and personal characteristics and attitudes. (p. 476)

Internal control The policies and procedures that provide reasonable assurance that a company's goals and objectives will be achieved. (p. 479)

Corporate governance Systems used by a company to promote "corporate fairness, transparency, and accountability." (p. 484)

Ethics programs Programs established to help maintain an ethical business environment. Common elements of ethics programs include written codes of ethics, employee hotlines, ethics call centers, ethics training, processes to register anonymous complaints about wrongdoing, and ethics offices. (p. 487)

Multiple Choice

1. Which of the following statements regarding fraud is not true?
   a. Fraud requires knowledge and intent on the part of the perpetrator.
   b. Management fraud is very easy to detect.
   c. Frauds are often perpetrated by individuals who do not have a criminal background.
   d. Employees often engage in fraudulent activity as a result of situational pressures, opportunities to do so, and personal characteristics.

2. Fraudulent financial reporting is often perpetrated through which of the following means?
   a. Overstating revenue
   b. Understating liabilities
   c. Both a and b
   d. Neither a nor b

3. Which of the following parties is most likely to perpetrate fraudulent financial reporting?
   a. Manufacturing employees
   b. Members of management
   c. Both a and b
   d. Neither a nor b

4. Which of the following characteristics does not describe a possible situational pressure or incentive?
   a. Greed
   b. Fear of an impending job loss
   c. Inadequate recognition for accomplishments
   d. All of the above describe situational pressures or incentives.

5. The three forces that typically contribute to fraudulent behavior include all but which of the following?
   a. Incentives
   b. Psychological deficiencies
   c. Attitudes
   d. Opportunities

6. Which of the following is not a strategy to combat fraud?
   a. Developing strong ethical business practices
   b. Create disincentives for employees to be honest
   c. Establish internal controls
   d. Develop sound corporate governance practices

7. What organization developed the internal control framework that is most widely used by organizations in the United States?
   a. The American Institute of Certified Public Accountants
   b. The Securities and Exchange Commission
   c. The United States Congress
   d. The Committee of Sponsoring Organizations

8. Management's attitudes and general philosophy about internal control are captured in the:
   a. control activities.
   b. control environment.
   c. monitoring of activities.
   d. information and communications processes.

9. Which of the following control activities would most likely reduce the incidence of reporting false hours on employee time cards?
   a. Securing assets through electronic means
   b. Employee background checks
   c. Supervisor review of time cards
   d. None of the above

10. The risks associated with a company that conducts business in a technology-intensive environment include all but which of the following?
    a. Customer impersonation
    b. Earnings management
    c. Unauthorized access to data
    d. Sabotage by former employees

11. Which of the following internal controls would reduce the incidence of unauthorized data access in a technology-intensive environment?
    a. Required vacation time
    b. Timely bank reconciliations
    c. Password controls
    d. Both a and c

12. Corporate governance practices are aimed at promoting:
    a. accurate financial statements.
    b. corporate fairness.
    c. management accountability.
    d. all of the above.

13. Which of the following is not likely to be an element of an ethics program?
    a. Ethics call centers
    b. Employee hotlines
    c. Written codes of ethics
    d. All of the above are possible elements of an ethics program.

14. The three types of codes of ethics used by organizations do not include:
    a. statements of intent.
    b. corporate philosophy statements.
    c. codes of conduct.
    d. mission statements.

15. An organization's response to ethics violations should include/be:
    a. timely.
    b. sanctions that are fair.
    c. a thorough investigation.
    d. all of the above.

Concept Questions

16. *(Objective 1)* Define fraud.
17. *(Objective 1)* What are some of the possible methods of perpetrating fraudulent financial reporting?
18. *(Objective 1)* Explain kiting and describe why a fraudster might use this technique.
19. *(Objective 1)* Explain lapping and describe why the scheme is difficult to maintain.
20. *(Objective 2)* What three categories of factors make up the fraud triangle? Briefly describe each category.
21. *(Objective 3)* Of the three strategies to combat fraud discussed in the chapter, which do you think is most effective? Why?
22. *(Objective 4)* Describe the control environment and explain its importance to an organization.
23. *(Objective 4)* Explain the difference between a general authorization and a specific authorization.
24. *(Objective 5)* Why has information technology increased risks within business?
25. *(Objective 6)* In your opinion, are external forces or internal forces more important in shaping a company's corporate governance system?
26. *(Objective 7)* In your opinion, which elements are most important in a company's ethics program?
27. *(Objective 8)* Explain the difference between a mission statement and a corporate philosophy statement.
28. *(Objective 8)* Briefly discuss the purposes of codes of ethics.
29. *(Objective 9)* Why is it important for an organization's response to an ethics violation to be viewed as fair by other employees?

Exercises

LO 1

30. There are two critical elements to the legal definition of fraud.

Required

Explain each of these elements and why they are critical to the definition.

LO 1

31. There are two different types of fraud: fraudulent financial reporting and misappropriation of assets.

Required

Explain each type of fraud and explain how it differs from the other.

LO 2

32. Each of the following is a factor that might contribute to fraud:
    a. Inadequate documentation of transactions
    b. General dissatisfaction with work
    c. Viewing fraud as a victimless crime
    d. Feeling a sense of entitlement
    e. Insufficient transaction authorization procedures
    f. Fear of an impending job loss

Required

Indicate whether each of the above factors is a situational pressure and incentive, an opportunity, or a personal characteristic and attitude.

33. Senior management at Bigelow Construction has been advised that the present system of internal control needs to be improved. It has recently come to management's attention that the controller, who has almost complete control over cash and the accounting records, is experiencing financial difficulties as the result of a personal tragedy in the family.

Required

What steps should management take to address this potential problem?

34. The internal control framework developed by COSO is comprised of five elements.

Required

Define each of these five elements and indicate which element you believe is most important.

35. Cindy is the vice president of research and development for Big Al's Pizza, Inc. She submits a request for expense reimbursement each month, and Lori, the controller, has noticed that Cindy's requests are always higher than those of anyone else in the company.

Required

What should the controller do? Is this a potential internal control problem?

36. Warren Abraham is the controller of Northern Lights Custom Cabinets. Warren stated, "Northern Lights has very strong internal control. The general ledger must always balance, and this ensures that all transactions are properly transferred to our general ledger."

Required

What do you think of Warren's comment? Does a balanced ledger ensure good internal controls?

37. A regional food wholesaler (a company that sells food to various local grocery stores), Merriman Distributors, established a policy that prohibits its purchasing agents from accepting gifts from food and beverage companies that sell to Merriman. Gifts of nominal amounts less than $25 are permitted and are not considered to create a conflict of interest.

Required

How does such a policy strengthen Merriman's internal control?

38. Irene's Greeting Cards sells custom greeting cards to drugstores across the country. All sales are on credit, and payment is expected within 30 days of the order. The company provides an invoice with each delivery, but does not send subsequent statements. The salespeople who call on the customers are allowed to collect any outstanding invoices.

Required

If the company started sending statements, would that affect the internal control over accounts receivable?

39. Bonnie's Beautiful Lights is a wholesale lighting contractor selling to residential building contractors. The company has very few staff members, so the bookkeeper collects all payments on account, makes the bank deposits, writes checks to pay all accounts payable, and reconciles the bank statement at the end of the month. The company also does not count inventory on a regular basis.

Required

Discuss any internal control weaknesses in the company and suggest possible solutions.

40. At the drive-through window of your local fast-food restaurant, you notice a sign that reads, "If the amount you pay is not the same as your sales receipt, your meal is free."

Required

What is the restaurant trying to accomplish with the sign and policy?

LO 5

41. Dolly's Antiques has decided to add a Web page and go online to sell merchandise. The company's owner, Dolly Praton, has come to you for advice about her new business venture.

Required

What potential control problems might Dolly's face with this type of business? What controls can reduce or eliminate the risks faced by Dolly's Antiques?

LO 6

42. Ted Simpson, vice president of Jerry's Golf Extravaganza, is not supportive of his company's recent move toward strengthening its corporate governance practices. Ted believes that there is no good reason for the efforts because the company is privately owned and is unlikely to be a public company in the near future. On the other hand, Jerry George, the company's founder and chairman of the board believes the company should invest more time and effort in its governance practices.

Required

Explain to Ted why the company should care about good corporate governance practices.

LO 7

43. Heather Hogan, the vice president of a local credit union has always accepted invitations to join credit union members who own skyboxes at the local ball park. She has never paid for the tickets and, in fact, accepts free food and drink provided in the skybox. The credit union has a written policy that states in part: "All employees are strictly prohibited from accepting any gratuities, gifts, donations, or any other remuneration from credit union members for which the fair market value of such gift, gratuity, or donation exceeds $5."

Required

What effect will Heather's actions have on the internal control environment at the credit union?

LO 8

44. Barb Simmons was speaking to Madge Wilcox recently after a management meeting at Clarence Enterprises. Barb told Madge that she was really unimpressed by the company's recently revised code of ethics and really saw no reason that the company should have such a document. After all, she said, everyone knows what's right and wrong. Madge was taken aback by her friend's comment.

Required

What should Madge say to Barb?

Problems

LO 2 4

45. Mark is a sales clerk at a clothing store in the local mall. Mark has been short of cash in the past and has prepared fake sales-return forms and taken money from the cash register equal to those forms. The scheme has not been caught, and now Mark is preparing to take even more money, as the managers seem unaware of the scheme.

Required

A. What internal controls would you suggest to assist management in eliminating this opportunity?
B. In your opinion, is the opportunity to commit theft likely to tempt most employees? Why or why not?

46. Middle managers, those who have authority over daily operations, are often viewed as being particularly prone to perpetrating fraudulent activities.

Required
   A. What are some examples of internal controls that could reduce the likelihood that middle managers perpetrate fraud?
   B. In addition to establishing internal controls, what else can a company do to reduce the likelihood that its managers will perpetrate fraud?

47. Terry is an accountant at Big Time Game Company. Her main function is to prepare production-cost reports for distribution to upper management. Her good friend Tracy is the production supervisor on one of the production lines. While preparing this month's cost report, Terry noticed a substantial increase in production costs on Tracy's production line. To make her friend look better, Terry shifted some of the costs to other lines, thinking that there must be an accounting error somewhere. The shift in costs was never noticed.

Required
   A. Did Terry act appropriately?
   B. Discuss the alternative courses of action that Terry could have taken.

48. LaRue's Machine Shop takes custom orders for metal parts. In order to machine some of the parts, the shop uses various solvents that must be disposed of in compliance with local hazardous-waste rules. For years before the new laws went into effect, LaRue's routinely dumped the solvents in a pit behind the shop. The new law has been in effect for three years, and LaRue's has yet to comply with it.

Required
   A. What risks do you think the company faces by not properly disposing of the solvents?
   B. To what stakeholders does the company have obligations to properly dispose of the solvents?

Case

49. Janco, Inc. is a privately owned business located in the southwestern United States. The company was founded in 1978 as a manufacturer of precision scientific equipment. The company has a strong customer base that is comprised almost entirely of research laboratories and universities. Janco's sales have been solid and the company has experienced significant growth in the last decade. Gordon Jankowski, the company's founder, serves as the company's president and chief scientist. Like others in the industry, Gordon is primarily a scientist. His business experience is solely limited to operating Janco. Given the company's recent success, Gordon would like to take his company public, but knows that the company will need to undergo some corporate changes before that can happen. For example, the company's accounting system has recently undergone a number of changes and is now functioning as a fully operational ERP system. Most employees interface with the system via a secure local network, but some employees do have access to the system through the Internet. Another significant issue relates to the absence of an ethics program. Gordon has never thought it necessary to implement such a program and has not even written a code of ethics for employees.

Required

A. Explain the relevance of internal control to Janco's plan to go public. Is internal control more important to a public company than to a private company?
B. Given the recent change to an ERP system, what additional issues must the company consider in developing internal controls?
C. Based on the very brief description above, what is your impression of Janco's likely approach to corporate governance? Explain your impression to the extent possible.
D. Why should the company establish a formal ethics program? What elements do you think would be most beneficial to a company such as Janco?

Group and Internet Exercises

LO 2, 3, 7, 9

50. There have been a number of frauds at major U.S. corporations in recent years. For examples, frauds have rocked Enron, WorldCom (now MCI), Qwest, Adelphia, Tyco, and HealthSouth. Search the Internet to learn about a company that has undergone a recent scandal. Prepare a one- to two-page paper that summarizes the fraud and describes how the company's environment contributed to the fraud. Describe some of the steps the company has taken to reduce the likelihood that similar frauds could occur again.

LO 7, 8

51. Most large companies are proud to share their views of ethics to employees and other interested parties on their websites. Conduct an Internet search for two or three companies of your choosing to learn about their ethics programs. What elements are in place at the companies? Also, what types of codes of ethics do the companies have?

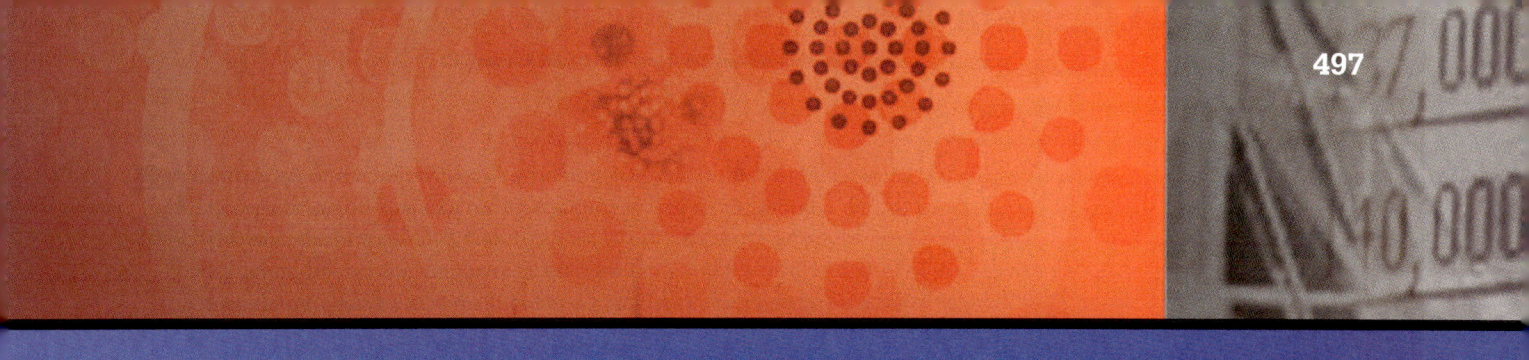

Part 5 — Other Topics

Chapter 15 Financial Statement Analysis

Chapter 16 The Statement of Cash Flows

Chapter 15 Financial Statement Analysis

Financial statement analysis involves the application of analytical tools to financial statements and supplemental data included with the financial statements to enhance the ability of decision makers to make optimal decisions. Investors and creditors need to make decisions to provide a company with loans or other capital. The primary source of information provided to external users is financial statements. The management team also makes decisions using financial statement information. For both groups, the use of financial statement analysis techniques enhances the usefulness of the information contained in the financial statements.

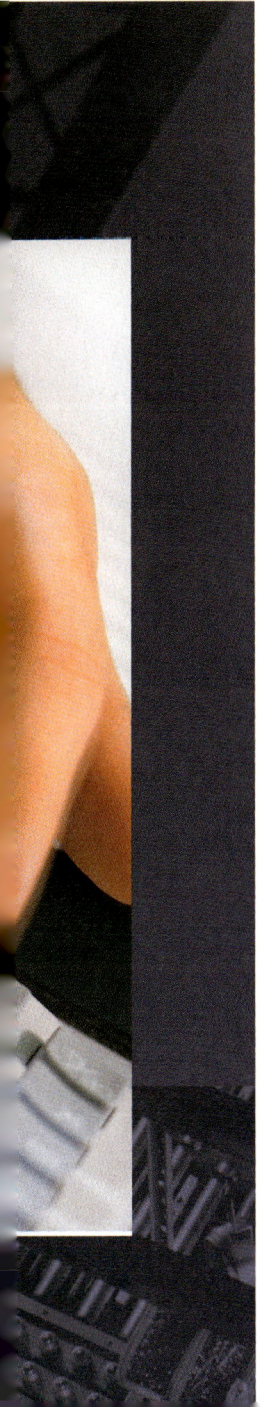

Learning Objectives

After studying the material in this chapter, you should be able to:

1. Explain why decision makers analyze financial statements

2. Recognize the limitations of financial statement analysis

3. Use comparative financial statements to analyze the performance of a company over time (horizontal analysis)

4. Prepare and use common-size financial statements to compare various financial statement items (vertical analysis)

5. Prepare and use liquidity ratios to analyze a company

6. Prepare and use solvency ratios to analyze a company

7. Prepare and use profitability ratios to analyze a company

Introduction

Decision makers need a variety of information in the decision-making process. Bankers and other lenders are interested in the ability of an organization to repay loans. Stockholders or potential stockholders are interested in earning a fair return on their investment. The management team of a company is concerned about these issues and more—the adequacy of cash flow to pay operating expenses, the efficient use of company resources, and how to improve the overall performance of the company. Financial statement analysis is a useful tool for both external and internal users as they make decisions about a company or for a company.

Why Analyze Financial Statements?

Objective 1 — Explain why decision makers analyze financial statements

The most compelling reason to analyze financial statements is simply that it provides useful information to supplement information directly provided in financial statements. Ratio analysis provides additional information necessary to enhance the decision-making ability of the users of the information. Although we will spend some time on the computation of the ratios, the most important aspect of the discussion is what the ratios mean and how to improve performance of the organization by analyzing trends and changes in these ratios. In addition to showing how the company has performed in the past, financial ratios are very useful in predicting the future direction and financial position of organizations.

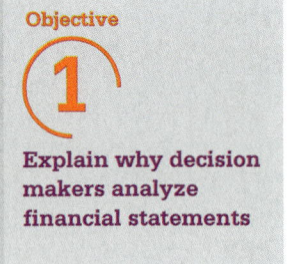

KEY CONCEPT

Ratio analysis provides additional information necessary to enhance the decision-making ability of the users of the information.

THE ETHICS OF BUSINESS
Knowledge is a Dangerous Thing

A company's financial managers often have access to highly sensitive financial information. Such was the case at Duke Energy. F. Barron Stone, a financial analyst with the company, made a complaint on the company's hotline about the accuracy of the company's financial statements, claiming that profits were being understated so state energy regulators would not reduce the company's electricity rates. Investigations by North Carolina and South Carolina officials resulted in a $25 million settlement. So, you might expect Mr. Stone to be the hero; but that is not the way it worked. Instead, Duke eliminated his position as part of a reorganization. He was moved to a nonfinancial position without access to financial data; and he was later not interviewed for a position similar to the one he held prior to making the complaint about understating profits. Unfortunately, Mr. Stone finds himself in the unenviable position of having no recourse under Sarbanes-Oxley because of the dates during which the alleged violations took place and because he chose to report the wrongdoing before the Act was passed into law. Just the same, the lesson here is straightforward—whistleblowing comes at a cost no matter the legal protections.

It's Your Choice—If faced with the knowledge that your employer was engaged in wrongdoing, would you report it to someone inside the company? Would you report the wrongdoing to outsiders such as banks or federal and state law enforcement officials? Why or why not? ("Risk Management: For Financial Whistle-Blowers, New Shield is an Imperfect One: Claims of Employer Reprisal Go to OSHA Investigators Unschooled in Accounting: A Fired CFO Lingers in Limbo," *Wall Street Journal*, A1, October 4, 2004.)

Limitations of Financial Statement Analysis

Financial statements are prepared using generally accepted accounting principles (GAAP). However, GAAP allows financial statement preparers to use a variety of methods, estimates, and assumptions in their preparation. To properly prepare and interpret financial statement ratios, these methods, estimates, and assumptions must be considered. For example, inventory valuation methods include FIFO, LIFO, and other accepted cost flow assumptions. These methods impact the cost of inventory shown on the balance sheet. For example, a company using the LIFO method of inventory costing in a period of rising prices is always selling the most costly inventory purchased (the last inventory purchased is the first to be sold), whereas the inventory shown on the balance sheet is the oldest and least costly. As a result, inventory balances on the balance sheet may be very low and "undercosted" based on today's prices. When comparing companies, differences in accounting methods and cost flow assumptions need to be considered. If accounting methods or assumptions are changed from year to year, comparisons between years can be difficult.

Decision makers using financial statements and the resulting ratios should not place too much emphasis on any single ratio. Ratios must be looked at as a story that cannot be told without all the pieces. Ratios should be compared with prior years' results, with the budget for the current year, and with industry standards. These industry standards can be found in publications by Moody's and Standard & Poor's. These services provide up-to-date information on most industries and regions. Regional differences are very important factors in evaluating performance. In addition, owing to the size and complexity of many companies, industry standards are sometimes useful in evaluating only divisions of a business. For example, hotels that are affiliated with a casino are operated differently from hotels that are only in the hotel business. Rates for rooms are different, as are expectations, and the analysis of the financial ratios must be interpreted in light of these differences.

Objective 2

Recognize the limitations of financial statement analysis

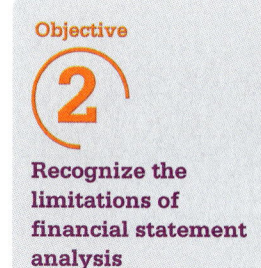

KEY CONCEPT

Rather than focus on a single ratio, decision makers need to evaluate a company by comparing ratios to those of previous years, budgeted amounts, and industry standards.

The Impact of Inflation on Financial Statement Analysis

Financial statements are prepared using historical costs and are not adjusted for the effects of increasing prices. For example, although sales may have increased by 5 percent each year for the past five years, the impact of inflation on changing prices needs to be considered. If inflation averaged 3 percent annually over that same period of time, the real increase in sales dollars is only 2 percent. The impact of changing prices on long-term assets can be even more dramatic. Consider a building purchased 30 years ago for $100,000. If inflation averages 2.5 percent per year over the life of the building, the market value of the building today will be more than double the historical cost used to record the building when purchased. To compound the problem, the building is likely to be almost fully depreciated, so the book value of the building may be very small.

Horizontal Analysis

Analyzing financial statements over time is called **horizontal analysis.** To demonstrate the concept of horizontal analysis, the financial statements for Robyn's Boutique are presented in Exhibit 15-1 and Exhibit 15-2.

Robyn's Boutique is a retail store specializing in children's clothes. The idea behind horizontal analysis is to analyze changes in accounts occurring between years. To facilitate this analysis, dollar changes and percentage changes in each item on the balance sheet are often provided. The percentage changes are the amount of change from the previous year. In the following example, cash increased by $20,000, which is 18.2 percent of the 2004 balance ($\frac{\$20,000}{\$110,000}$).

Looking closely at the balance sheet for Robyn's Boutique, we see two accounts with large percentage changes between 2004 and 2005. Long-term investments have increased by

Objective 3

Use comparative financial statements to analyze the performance of a company over time (horizontal analysis)

KEY CONCEPT

Horizontal analysis is used to analyze changes in accounts occurring between years.

ROBYN'S BOUTIQUE

Exhibit 15-1	Comparative Balance Sheets			
	2005	2004	$Change Increase (Decrease)	% Change Increase (Decrease)
Cash	$130,000	$110,000	$ 20,000	18.2%
Accounts receivable	130,000	120,000	10,000	8.3
Inventory	225,000	215,000	10,000	4.7
Prepaid insurance	25,000	30,000	(5,000)	(16.7)
Total current assets	$510,000	$475,000	$ 35,000	7.4
Long-term investments	110,000	75,000	35,000	46.7
Land	200,000	175,000	25,000	14.3
Property and equipment	215,000	95,000	120,000	126.3
Accumulated depreciation	(105,000)	(80,000)	(25,000)	(31.3)
Total assets	$930,000	$740,000	$190,000	25.7
Accounts payable	60,000	50,000	10,000	20.0
Payroll payable	10,000	8,000	2,000	25.0
Taxes payable	10,000	9,000	1,000	11.1
Total current liabilities	$ 80,000	$ 67,000	$ 13,000	19.4
Notes payable	100,000	80,000	20,000	25.0
Capital stock	500,000	400,000	100,000	25.0
Retained earnings	250,000	193,000	57,000	29.5
Total liabilities and stockholders' equity	$930,000	$740,000	$190,000	25.7

46.7 percent ($\frac{\$35,000}{\$75,000}$), and property and equipment has increased by 126.3 percent ($\frac{\$120,000}{\$95,000}$). Although increases like these are common in growing companies, analysts and others will likely be interested in how Robyn's paid for the acquisitions.

Changes in the income statement for Robyn's Boutique can be analyzed in a similar fashion:

EXHIBIT 15-2 Comparative Statements of Income and Retained Earnings

	2005	2004	$ Change Increase (Decrease)	% Change Increase (Decrease)
Sales revenue	$700,000	$650,000	$50,000	7.7%
Cost of goods sold	500,000	455,000	45,000	9.9
Gross profit	$200,000	$195,000	$ 5,000	2.6
Payroll expense	$ 50,000	$ 42,250	$ 7,750	18.3
Insurance expense	30,000	29,000	1,000	3.4
Rent expense	18,000	18,000	—	—
Depreciation	35,000	15,000	20,000	133.3
Total expenses	$133,000	$104,250	$ 28,750	27.6
Operating Income	$ 67,000	$ 90,750	$(23,750)	(26.2)
Interest expense	$ (7,000)	$ (5,000)	$ (2,000)	40.0
Gain on vehicle sale	25,000	—	25,000	—
Loss on sale of securities	(25,000)	—	(25,000)	—
Interest revenue	75,000	50,000	25,000	50.0
Net income before interest and taxes	$135,000	$135,750	$ (750)	(0.06)
Tax	(40,000)	(40,250)	250	(0.06)
Net income	$ 95,000	$ 95,500	$ (500)	(0.05)
Dividends	(38,000)	(38,000)		
To retained earnings	$ 57,000	$ 57,500		
Retained earnings 1/1	193,000	136,000		
Retained earnings 12/31	$250,000	$193,500		

Sales increased by $50,000 (7.7 percent) from 2004 to 2005. On the surface, this would appear to be a positive sign. However, further analysis shows that the cost of goods sold increased by $45,000, or 9.9 percent, whereas total operating expenses increased by $28,750, or 27.6 percent. Although sales increased, expenses appear to be rising much faster than sales! Note that focusing on net income without looking at other changes in the income statements would be a mistake. Although net income is virtually unchanged from 2004 to 2005, operating income decreased by more than 26 percent.

Horizontal analysis of financial statements can and should include more than just two years of data. Many annual reports include, as supplemental information, up to 10 years of financial data. Using these supplemental reports, readers of financial statements can perform **trend analysis.** Decision makers can use trend analysis to build prediction models to forecast financial performance in the future. Trend analysis can also be used to identify problem areas by looking for sudden or abnormal changes in accounts.

Horizontal analysis can also include the statement of cash flows (see Exhibit 15-3).

Exhibit 15-3: Comparative Statements of Cash Flow

For the years ended December 31

	2005	2004	$ Change	% Change
Cash Flows from Operating Activities				
Cash Receipts From				
Sales on account	$ 690,000	$ 640,000	$ 50,000	7.8%
Interest	75,000	50,000	25,000	50.0
Total cash receipts	$ 765,000	$ 690,000	$ 75,000	
Cash Payments For				
Inventory purchases	$ 500,000	$ 470,000	$ 30,000	6.4
Payroll	48,000	42,250	5,750	13.6
Insurance	25,000	29,000	(4,000)	(13.8)
Interest	7,000	5,000	2,000	40.0
Rent expense	18,000	18,000	—	—
Taxes	39,000	40,250	(1,250)	(3.1)
Total cash payments	$(637,000)	$(604,500)	$ 32,500	5.4
Net cash provided (used) by operating activities	$ 128,000	$ 85,500	$ 42,500	49.7
Cash Flows from Investing Activities				
Sale of note	$ 25,000	—	$ 25,000	—
Sale of vehicle	75,000	—	75,000	—
Purchase of equipment	(180,000)	$ (20,000)	(160,000)	800.0
Purchase of long-term investments	(85,000)	—	(85,000)	
Purchase of land	(5,000)	—	(5,000)	—
Net cash provided (used) by investing activities	$(170,000)	$ (20,000)	$(150,000)	750
Cash Flows from Financing Activities				
Issuance of stock	$ 100,000	—	$ 100,000	—
Payment of cash dividends	(38,000)	$ (38,000)	—	—
Net cash provided (used) by financing activities	$ 62,000	$ (38,000)	$ 100,000	263.2
Net increase in cash	$ 20,000	$ 27,500	$ (7,500)	(27.3)
Cash balance 1/1	110,000	82,500		
Cash balance 12/31	$ 130,000	$ 110,000		
Supplemental Schedule of Noncash Investing and Financing Activities				
Acquisition of land in exchange for note payable	$ 20,000	(2,000)		

Robyn's Boutique shows consistent and increasing cash flows from operations: $765,000 in 2005 and $690,000 in 2004. The company also shows an increase in net cash provided by operating activities of $42,500, or 49.7 percent. These two changes indicate a good trend in cash flows from operating activities. Although the net increase in cash for 2005 was less than the increase in 2004, the decrease can be easily explained by the additional cash used for investing activities in 2005.

Vertical Analysis

Vertical analysis compares financial statements of different companies and financial statements of the same company across time after controlling for differences in size. When comparing companies of different sizes, it is useful to standardize the statements. **Common-size financial statements** are statements in which all items have been restated as a percentage of a selected item on the statements. Common-size financial statements remove size as a relevant variable in ratio analysis and can be used to compare companies that make similar products and that are different in size (such as Boeing and Cessna, both aircraft manufacturers). They also can be used to compare the same company across years.

Common-size comparative balance sheets for Robyn's Boutique are shown in Exhibit 15-4. Note that all asset accounts are stated as a percentage of total assets. Similarly, all liability and stockholders' equity accounts are stated as a percentage of total liabilities and stockholders' equity.

Objective 4

Prepare and use common-size financial statements to compare various financial statement items (vertical analysis)

KEY CONCEPT

Vertical analysis uses common-size financial statements to remove size as a relevant variable in ratio analysis.

Exhibit 15-4 Comparative Balance Sheets

	2005	Percent	2004	Percent
Cash	$130,000	14.0%	$110,000	14.9%
Accounts receivable	130,000	14.0	120,000	16.2
Inventory	225,000	24.2	215,000	29.1
Prepaid insurance	25,000	2.7	30,000	4.1
Total current assets	$510,000	54.8%	$475,000	64.2%
Long-term investments	110,000	11.8	75,000	10.1
Land	200,000	21.5	175,000	23.6
Property and equipment	215,000	23.1	95,000	12.8
Accumulated Depreciation	(105,000)	(11.3)	(80,000)	(10.8)
Total assets	$930,000	100%	$740,000	100%
Accounts payable	$ 60,000	6.5%	$ 50,000	6.8%
Payroll payable	10,000	1.1	8,000	1.1
Taxes payable	10,000	1.1	9,000	1.2
Total current liabilities	$ 80,000	8.7%	$ 67,000	9.1%
Notes payable	100,000	10.8	80,000	10.8
Capital stock	500,000	53.8	400,000	54.1
Retained earnings	250,000	26.9	193,000	26.1
Total liabilities and and stockholders' equity	$930,000	100.0%	$740,000	100.0%

As mentioned earlier, there are two ways to use common-size financial statements. The first is a comparison between years or over a number of years. The second is a comparison of similar companies of different sizes.

When comparing across years, analysts and other decision makers look for critical changes in the composition of accounts. One important measure from the balance sheet is working capital. **Working capital** is defined as the excess of current assets over current liabilities and is a measure of an entity's **liquidity,** or its ability to meet its immediate financial obligations. Robyn's Boutique had current assets and current liabilities in 2005 and 2004 as follows:

	2005	2004
Current assets	$510,000	$475,000
Current liabilities	(80,000)	(67,000)
Working capital	$430,000	$408,000

The amount of working capital has increased by $22,000 from 2004 to 2005, indicating that Robyn's has increased the amount of current assets available to pay current liabilities. However, without information concerning the makeup of working capital, the information is of limited use. If current assets consist primarily of inventory, the company's liquidity could still be in jeopardy. In such a case, a slower conversion to cash would result than it would if current assets consisted primarily of accounts receivable.

Common-size comparative income statements for Robyn's Boutique are presented in Exhibit 15-5. The base on which all income statement accounts are compared is net sales, presented simply as sales revenues in our demonstration.

Exhibit 15-5 Common-Size Comparative Income Statements

	2005	Percent	2004	Percent
Sales revenue	$700,000	100.0%	$650,000	100.0%
Cost of goods sold	500,000	71.4	455,000	70.0
Gross profit	$200,000	28.6%	$195,000	30.0%
Payroll expense	$ 50,000	7.1%	$ 42,250	6.0%
Insurance expense	30,000	4.3	29,000	4.5
Rent expense	18,000	2.6	18,000	2.8
Depreciation	35,000	5.0	15,000	2.3
Total expenses	$133,000	19.0%	$104,250	16.0%
Operating Income	$ 67,000	9.6%	$ 90,750	14.0%
Interest expense	$ (7,000)	(1.0)%	$ (5,000)	(0.8)%
Gain on vehicle sale	25,000	3.6	0	
Loss on sale of securities	(25,000)	(3.6)	0	—
Interest revenue	75,000	10.7	50,000	7.7
Net income before interest and taxes	$135,000	19.3%	$135,750	20.9%
Tax expense	(40,000)	(5.7)	(40,250)	(6.2)
Net income	$ 95,000	13.6%	$ 95,500	14.7%

The common-size income statement points out some interesting but small changes between the two years presented. The gross profit percentage decreased from 30 percent to 28.6 percent. This is a closely watched ratio in many companies and industries.

An important use of common-size financial statements is to compare companies that are in similar lines of business but are of different sizes. The following table shows such a comparison.

Comparison of Robyn's Boutique and Competitor

Account	Robyn's	The Competitor
	Percentage of Total Assets	**Percentage of Total Assets**
Cash	14.0	17.0
Inventory	24.0	20.0
Prepaids	2.7	3.4
Property and equipment (net)	33.3	39.5
Long-term investments	11.8	10.5
	Percentage of Liabilities and Equity	**Percentage of Liabilities and Equity**
Accounts payable	6.5	8.5
Income tax	1.1	2.0
Long-term debt	10.8	13.5
Cost of goods sold	71.4	65.0
Operating expense	19.0	23.5
Net income after tax	13.6	10.5

Ratio Analysis

Financial statement ratios simply refer to a relationship between two financial statement amounts stated as a percentage.

Ratio Analysis and Return on Investment

As discussed in Chapter 11, managers and the investment centers under their control are often evaluated using a measure of return on invested assets. These measures include return on investment (ROI), residual income, and economic value added (EVA). The measures are similar in that they look at performance in relation to the amount of assets or investment under a manager's control. As you will recall from Chapter 11,

KEY CONCEPT

Ratio analysis is useful in assessing the impact of transactions on ROI, residual income, EVA, and other key measures of performance.

$$ROI = \text{Profit margin} \times \text{Asset turnover}$$

where

$$\text{Profit margin} = \frac{\text{Net operating income}}{\text{Sales}}$$

$$\text{Asset turnover} = \frac{\text{Sales}}{\text{Average operating assets}}$$

$$ROI = \frac{\text{Net operating income}}{\text{Sales}} \times \frac{\text{Sales}}{\text{Average operating assets}}$$

The elements of ROI are shown in more detail in Exhibit 15-6.

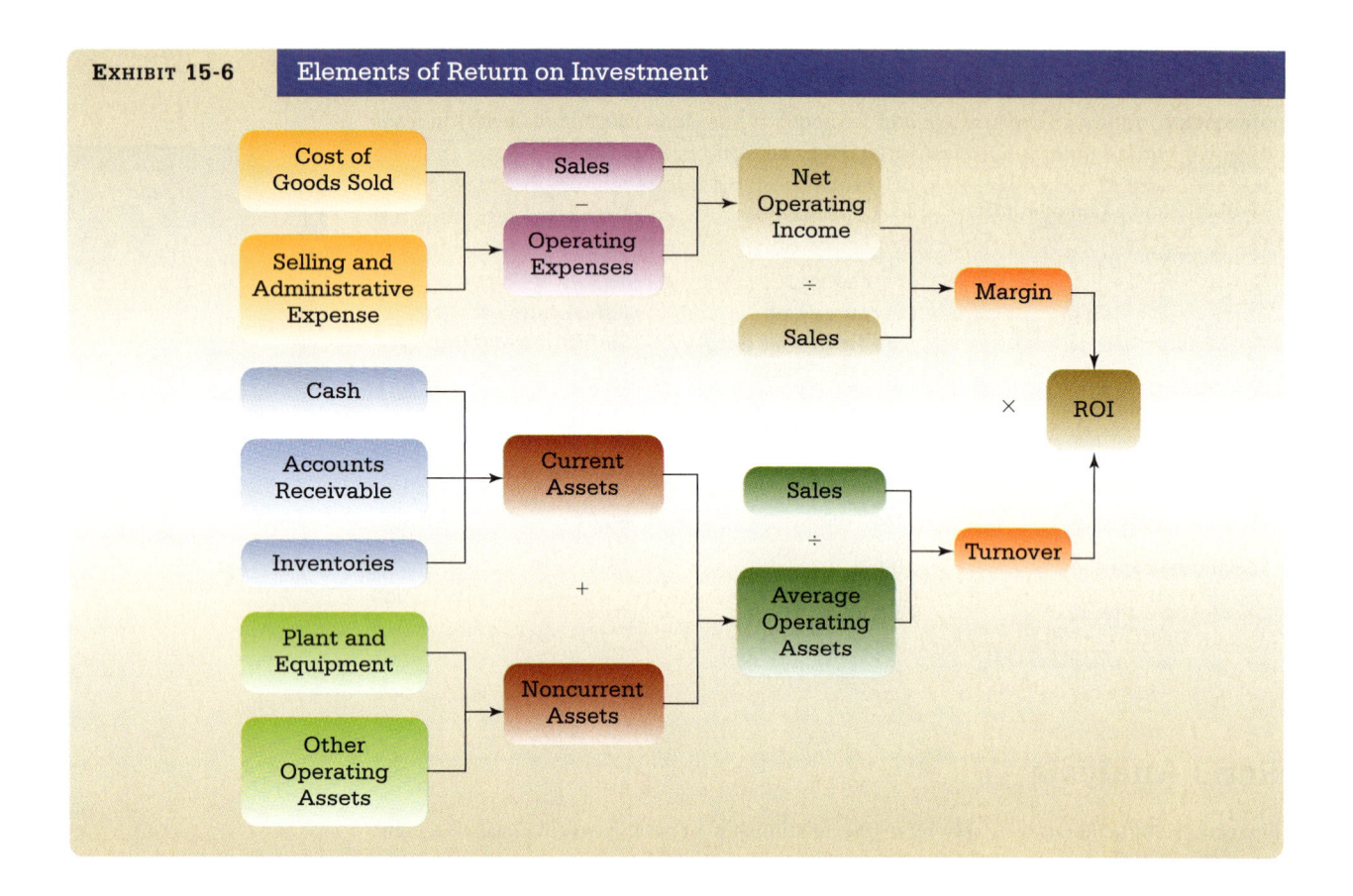

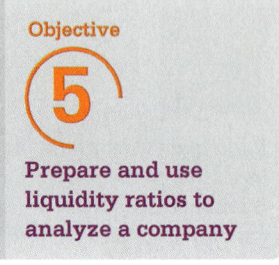

EXHIBIT 15-6 Elements of Return on Investment

Current Ratio

Objective 5
Prepare and use liquidity ratios to analyze a company

The **current ratio,** or working capital ratio, is a measure of an entity's liquidity. The formula for the current ratio is as follows:

$$\text{Current ratio} = \frac{\text{Current assets}}{\text{Current liabilities}}$$

The current ratios for Robyn's Boutique for the past two years are as follows:

2005	2004
$\frac{\$510,000}{\$80,000} = 6.375$	$\frac{\$475,000}{\$67,000} = 7.090$

What does this ratio tell us? In 2005, Robyn's Boutique has $6.38 of current assets for every dollar of current liabilities, and in 2004 the boutique had $7.09 for every dollar of current liabilities. Although high current ratios would appear to be good (if you are a creditor of a company, a high current ratio indicates that you are more likely to be paid), a ratio that is very high may indicate that a company holds too much cash, accounts receivable, or inventory. Historically, a current ratio of 2.0 was considered good. However, many companies strive to maintain current ratios that are closer to 1.0. Internal managers look closely at the current ratio and its composition so that they can better control levels of current assets. As we have discussed elsewhere, holding inventory can be very costly for companies. High levels of accounts receivable may indicate problems collecting cash from customers, and cash held in non-interest-bearing accounts might be more productively used elsewhere.

What is the impact of the current ratio on ROI, residual income, and EVA? The only way to increase the current ratio is to increase current assets or to decrease current liabilities. Although decreasing liabilities has no direct impact on measures of return on investment, increasing current assets with no change in current liabilities will decrease ROI, residual income, and EVA.

Acid-Test Ratio

One way to reduce the concern of the composition of the current accounts when computing the current ratio is to use the quick ratio, or acid-test ratio. The **quick ratio** is a stricter test of a company's ability to pay its current debts with highly liquid current assets. The quick ratio removes inventories and prepaid assets from the current asset amount used in the calculation of the current ratio. These current assets are considered the least liquid. The quick ratio formula is as follows:

$$\text{Quick ratio} = \frac{\text{Quick assets}}{\text{Current liabilities}}$$

Using the amounts from Robyn's Boutique, we can calculate the quick ratio as follows:

2005	2004
$\frac{\$260,000}{\$80,000} = 3.25$	$\frac{\$230,000}{\$67,000} = 3.433$

A quick ratio less than 1.0 should be of concern to both creditors and internal managers, as it indicates that liquid current assets are not sufficient to meet current obligations. On the other hand, Robyn's has unusually high quick ratios. High quick ratios may indicate other problems to management. Unless management has good reasons for holding excess cash (large purchases of property, plant, and equipment, future expansion, etc.), Robyn's should probably try to convert its excess cash into assets generating higher returns.

Cash Flow from Operations to Current-Liabilities Ratio

The current ratio and the quick ratio have two major weaknesses. The first is that all debt payments are made with cash, whereas current assets include noncash assets. The second is that both ratios focus on liquid and current assets at one point in time (the balance sheet date). However, cash, inventories, accounts receivable, and other current assets change over the course of the year. For these reasons, the amount of cash flow from operations (from the statement of cash flows) is sometimes used as the numerator in a ratio, with an average balance of current liabilities in the denominator:

$$\text{Cash flow from operations to current liabilities ratio} = \frac{\text{Net cash provided by operating activities}}{\text{Average current liabilities}}$$

The computation of the 2004 ratios requires the 2003 end-of-year current liability balance. The December 31, 2003, balance sheet for Robyn's Boutique is shown in Exhibit 15-7.

EXHIBIT 15-7   Balance Sheet as of December 31, 2003

Cash	$ 95,000
Accounts receivable	105,000
Inventory	175,000
Prepaid insurance	25,000
Total current assets	$400,000
Long-term investments	$ 45,000
Land	175,000
Property and equipment	85,000
Accumulated depreciation	(60,000)
Total long-term assets	$245,000
Total assets	$645,000
Accounts payable	$ 35,000
Payroll payable	6,500
Income tax payable	7,000
Total current liabilities	$ 48,500
Notes payable	$ 70,000
Total liabilities	$118,500
Capital stock	$400,000
Retained earnings	126,500
Total stockholders' equity	$526,600
Total liabilities and stockholders' equity	$645,000

The ratios for Robyn's Boutique are as follows:

2005	2004
$\dfrac{\$128,000}{\left[\dfrac{(\$80,000 + \$67,000)}{2}\right]} = 1.74$	$\dfrac{\$85,500}{\left[\dfrac{(\$67,000 + \$48,500)}{2}\right]} = 1.48$

Robyn's is generating sufficient cash from operations to pay current obligations.

Accounts Receivable Analysis

The **accounts receivable turnover ratio** is one of the best measures of the efficiency of the collection process. Management's analysis of accounts receivable is very important in monitoring collection and credit-granting policies. The accounts receivable turnover ratio is

$$\text{Accounts receivable turnover ratio} = \frac{\text{Net credit sales}}{\text{Average accounts receivable}}$$

This ratio is known as an activity ratio, which means that it consists of an activity (sales) divided by a related base (accounts receivable). Using the accounts receivable balances in the 2003, 2004, and 2005 balance sheets (Exhibits 15-4 and 15-7), we calculate the ratios for Robyn's Boutique as follows:

2005	2004
$\dfrac{\$700{,}000}{\left[\dfrac{(\$120{,}000 + \$130{,}000)}{2}\right]} = 5.60$	$\dfrac{\$650{,}000}{\left[\dfrac{(\$105{,}000 + \$120{,}000)}{2}\right]} = 5.78$

These ratios tell us that on average, Robyn's Boutique sold on account and subsequently collected accounts receivable almost six times during the year. To convert these amounts to a more understandable measure, consider this question: If you can do something almost six times in a year, how many days did it take you to do it once? The average number of days to collect a credit sale, computed as follows, measures this concept:

$$\text{Number of days sales in receivables} = \frac{\text{Number of days in the period}}{\text{Accounts receivable turnover}}$$

The calculations for Robyn's for 2004 and 2005 are as follows:

2005	2004
$\dfrac{365}{5.6} = 65.18 \text{ days}$	$\dfrac{365}{5.78} = 63.15 \text{ days}$

This ratio tells us that the average time to collect sales on account was 63.15 days in 2004 and 65.18 days in 2005. Is this amount of time to collect sales acceptable? That depends on the credit policy of the particular business and on industry standards. If the accounts are due in 30 days, a collection period in excess of 60 is not good. If the credit policy allows for 60 days, the collection period is in line with existing policy. Large retailers often have collection periods of less than one week.

The accounts receivable turnover ratio will have an impact on ROI and other measures of return on invested assets. One of the key components of ROI is turnover of assets. When turnover is increased, ROI and related measures will also increase.

Inventory Analysis

Analysis of inventory is very similar to the analysis of accounts receivable. The first ratio is the **inventory turnover ratio**:

$$\text{Inventory turnover ratio} = \frac{\text{Cost of goods sold}}{\text{Average inventory}}$$

The ratios for Robyn's for 2004 and 2005 are as follows:

2005	2004
$\dfrac{\$500{,}000}{\left[\dfrac{(\$215{,}000 + \$225{,}000)}{2}\right]} = 2.27$	$\dfrac{\$455{,}000}{\left[\dfrac{(\$175{,}000 + \$215{,}000)}{2}\right]} = 2.33$

These ratios tell us that on average, Robyn's Boutique bought inventory and then subsequently sold it 2.33 and 2.27 times per year in 2004 and 2005. This ratio does not mean that every item in inventory is sold 2.33 times but that the value of inventory was sold 2.33 times. Determining whether inventory turns are good is totally dependent on industry and company standards. Some businesses expect higher inventory turns than others do. For example, a grocery store would expect inventory turns of 50 or even 100 times per year. A bakery may expect inventory turns as high as 200 because it would expect to sell all fresh baked goods the same day they are produced. At the other extreme, furniture stores may expect inventory turns of only 1 or 2 per year. Retail clothing stores should expect to turn over inventory much more frequently than 2 times per year. This is a serious concern for management. Another way to look at inventory turnover is to calculate the number of days inventory is held before it is sold:

$$\text{Number of days inventory is held before sale} = \frac{\text{Number of days in the period}}{\text{Inventory turnover}}$$

On average, Robyn's is holding inventory for more than 150 days in both 2004 and 2005, calculated as follows:

2005	2004
$\frac{365}{2.27} = 160.79$ days	$\frac{365}{2.33} = 156.65$ days

Low turnover ratios and a correspondingly high number of days in which inventory is held for sale can direct management's attention toward a variety of problems. A large amount of obsolete inventory that is not being written off can adversely impact these ratios. These ratios can also indicate problems in the sales department or problems with the product, both of which can cause decreases in sales. As with accounts receivable turnover, if inventory turnover increases, ROI and other measures of return on invested assets will also increase.

Hitting the Bottom Line.

WHERE'S THE CASH COW?

In a survey of over 1,000 U.S. corporations, REL Consultancy Group found some surprising trends on how companies manage their working capital. One observation relates to companies' inefficient use of their working capital. REL found that companies could have, on average, reduced their debt by 36 percent or increased profits by 9 percent, but instead chose to leave the excess working capital in their bank accounts. Not all companies are managing their working capital so poorly. Take Wal-Mart, for example. The company has taken aggressive steps to reduce its working capital. The company's average days in inventory is now 38—meaning that the company has possession of its inventory (merchandise sold in its stores) just over one month on average before it is sold. In addition, Wal-Mart reduced its average collection period by 47 percent to just two days! Another large retailer, Costco Wholesale, reduced its average days in inventory to 29 days, but also saw its average collection period increase to five days. The bottom line for these and other companies is simple—excess working capital must be used profitably!

Cash-to-Cash Operating Cycle Ratio

This ratio measures the length of time between the purchase of inventory and the eventual collection of cash from sales. To calculate this ratio, we combine two measures:

Cash-to-cash operating cycle ratio = Number of days in inventory
 + Number of days in receivables

The cash-to-cash operating cycle ratios for Robyn's Boutique are as follows:

2005	2004
160.79 + 65.18 = **225.97 days**	156.65 + 63.15 = **219.80 days**

On average, it took Robyn's 219.80 days in 2004 and 225.97 days in 2005 to turn purchased inventory into cash.

Solvency refers to a company's ability to remain in business over the long term. Solvency is related to liquidity but differs with respect to time frame. Liquidity measures the ability to pay short-term debt, whereas solvency measures the ability to stay financially healthy over the long run.

Objective 6
Prepare and use solvency ratios to analyze a company

Debt-to-Equity Ratio

The main focus of solvency analysis is capital structure. Capital structure refers to the relationship between debt and stockholders' equity. The **debt-to-equity ratio** is as follows:

$$\text{Debt-to-equity ratio} = \frac{\text{Total liabilities}}{\text{Total stockholders' equity}}$$

Robyn's debt-to-equity ratios for 2004 and 2005 are as follows:

2005	2004
$\frac{\$180,000}{\$750,000}$ = 0.24 to 1	$\frac{\$147,000}{\$593,000}$ = 0.25 to 1

These ratios tell us that for every $1 of capital (capital stock and retained earnings), creditors provided 25 cents in 2004 and 24 cents in 2005. Low debt-to-equity ratios indicate a preference to raise funds through equity financing and a tendency to avoid the higher risk of debt financing. What is considered a good debt-to-equity ratio? As with all other ratios, this is dependent on the business, the industry, and other factors. Although a high debt-to-equity ratio may be of concern to creditors, it may be desirable and necessary for a new business to borrow money. The decision to capitalize a company with debt or equity involves many variables, including the income tax impact of debt versus equity to both a corporation and its shareholders. If management borrows funds at 8 percent and earns a return on investment of 10 percent, the use of debt (leverage) is desirable. But it adds some risk, owing to the obligation to repay the debt and the interest on the debt. This level of risk can be measured by the next ratio, times interest earned.

Times-Interest-Earned Ratio

Times interest earned measures a company's ability to meet current interest payments to creditors by specifically measuring its ability to meet current-year interest payments out of current-year earnings:

$$\text{Times interest earned} = \frac{\text{Net income + Interest expense + Income tax}}{\text{Interest expense}}$$

Both interest expense and income tax expense are added back to net income because interest is deducted from net income to arrive at taxable income. This adjustment gives us a "purer" measure of income available to pay interest. This ratio is especially important to bankers and other lenders. The ratios for times interest earned for Robyn's are as follows:

2005	2004
$\dfrac{\$135{,}000 + \$7{,}000 + 40{,}000}{\$7{,}000} = \textbf{26.0 to 1}$	$\dfrac{\$135{,}750 + \$5{,}000 + 40{,}250}{\$5{,}000} = \textbf{36.2 to 1}$

The ratios for Robyn's Boutique are very good. Robyn's could pay (from current earnings) the interest on debt 36 times in 2004 and 26 times in 2005.

Debt Service Coverage Ratio

Two major weaknesses are associated with the use of the times-interest-earned ratio as a measure of the ability to pay creditors. First, the ratio considers only interest expense. Management and other decision makers must also be concerned about the amount of principal that must be repaid on the currently maturing debt. Second, the ratio does not take into account any noncash adjustments to net income that arise because of accrual accounting. The **debt service coverage ratio** is used to measure the amount of cash generated from operating activities that is available to repay principal and interest in the upcoming year. That ratio is as follows:

$$\text{Debt service coverage ratio} = \frac{\text{Cash flow from operations before interest and taxes}}{\text{Interest and principal payments}}$$

Referring back to the comparative statement of cash flows, we can compute the ratios for Robyn's:

2005	2004
$\dfrac{(\$128{,}000 - \$7{,}000 - 39{,}000)}{\$25{,}000} = \textbf{3.28}$	$\dfrac{(\$85{,}500 - \$5{,}000 - 40{,}250)}{\$25{,}000} = \textbf{1.61}$

These ratios indicate that Robyn's generated $1.61 in cash for every $1 of interest and principal paid in 2004 and $3.28 for every $1 of interest and principal paid in 2005. The 2004 ratio is weak, but the improvement is dramatic.

Cash Flow from Operations to Capital Expenditures Ratio

This ratio measures a company's ability to use cash flow from operations to finance its acquisitions of property, plant, and equipment. The ability to use cash from operations diminishes the need to acquire outside financing, such as debt. The ratio is computed as follows:

$$\begin{matrix}\textbf{Cash flow from operations} \\ \textbf{to capital expenditures ratio}\end{matrix} = \frac{\text{Cash flow from operations} - \text{Total dividends paid}}{\text{Cash paid for acquisitions}}$$

The calculation of these ratios for Robyn's is as follows:

2005	2004
$\dfrac{(\$128{,}000 - 38{,}000)}{\$105{,}000} = \textbf{.86}$	$\dfrac{(\$85{,}500 - 38{,}000)}{\$20{,}000} = \textbf{2.38}$

These ratios tell us that in 2004, Robyn's generated cash from operations approximately 2.4 times greater than what was needed for acquisition of capital assets. In 2005, the ratio shows that Robyn's generated cash from operations to cover only 86 percent of the capital asset needs. Note that the amount used in 2005 to compute the ratio was net assets acquired. Robyn's had acquired $180,000 of new assets but sold a vehicle for $75,000.

Another group of ratios of importance to decision makers are those concerned with profitability analysis. Creditors are concerned with profitability because it indicates an ability to make required principal and interest payments. Stockholders are very interested in profitability because of related increases in stock prices or dividends paid to shareholders. Managers are also concerned with profitability, as it is often related to performance evaluations and tangible rewards from bonus payments and other incentive compensation plans.

Objective 7
Prepare and use profitability ratios to analyze a company

Return on Assets

Return ratios measure the relationship between a return and a specific investment made in the company by various groups of investors, creditors, and owners. **Return on assets (ROA)** considers the return to investors on all assets invested in the company. Because we are measuring a return to investors, net income is often adjusted by interest expense paid to creditors. The formula for computation of return on assets is as follows:

$$\text{ROA} = \frac{\text{Net income} + \text{Interest expense(net of tax)}}{\text{Average total assets}}$$

Assuming a 30 percent tax rate, we calculate ROA as follows:

	2005		2004	
Net income		$ 95,000		$ 95,500
Add back:				
Interest expense	$ 7,000		$ 5,000	
× (1 − Tax rate)	× 0.70	4,900	× 0.70	3,500
Numerator:		$ 99,900		$ 99,000
Assets, beginning of year		$ 740,000		$ 645,000
Assets, end of year		930,000		740,000
Total		$1,670,000		$1,385,000
Denominator:				
Average total assets	$\left(\frac{1,670,000}{2}\right)$	= $835,000	$\left(\frac{1,385,000}{2}\right)$	= $692,500
ROA	$\frac{\$99,900}{\$835,000}$	= **11.96%**	$\frac{\$99,000}{\$692,500}$	= **14.30%**

Interpretation of this ratio is based on the company's required return on assets, industry standards, and trends. In this case, the decline in ROA is likely to be of concern to the owners of Robyn's Boutique.

Like return on investment, ROA can be broken down into margin and turnover components: return on sales and asset turnover. The two ratios are computed as follows:

$$\text{Return on sales} = \frac{\text{Net income} + \text{Interest expense(net of tax)}}{\text{Net sales}}$$

$$\text{Asset turnover ratio} = \frac{\text{Net sales}}{\text{Average total assets}}$$

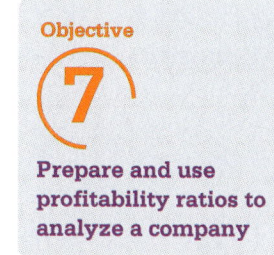

The ratios for Robyn's are as follows:

	2005		2004
Return on sales =	$\dfrac{\$99,900}{\$700,000} = $ **14.27%**		$\dfrac{\$99,000}{\$650,000} = $ **15.23%**
Asset turnover ratio =	$\dfrac{\$700,000}{\$835,000} = $ **0.84 times**		$\dfrac{\$650,000}{\$692,500} = $ **0.94 times**

Both the return on sales (income generated as a percentage of sales) and the asset turnover ratio (sales generated as a percentage of assets) declined from 2004 to 2005. Of particular concern to management is the low asset turnover ratio.

Doing Business.

RETURN ON SALES VS. RETURN ON INVESTMENT

In 2002, Volkswagen announced that the company would de-emphasize return on sales as a measure of performance and rely more heavily on return on investment. The reason? Reliance on the return on sales measure caused problems for some of the company's less expensive brands, including Skoda and Seat. Managers of these brands had felt compelled to develop large and more profitable cars to increase their return on sales, while ignoring the role the lower-priced brands played in the overall strategy of the company. Relying on return on investment signals managers that they need to get the most out of existing capital rather than spending money to increase returns ("Volkswagen to Give More Weight to Return-on-Investment Measure," *Wall Street Journal*, January 28, 2002, A12).

Return on Common Stockholders' Equity

Return on common stockholders' equity (ROCSE) measures the return to common stockholders (net income reduced by preferred dividends) as a percentage of stockholders' equity:

$$\text{ROCSE} = \dfrac{\text{Net income} - \text{Preferred dividends}}{\text{Average common stockholders' equity}}$$

The ROCSE ratios for Robyn's are as follows:

	2005		2004
	$\left[\dfrac{\$95,000}{\dfrac{(\$593,000 + \$750,000)}{2}}\right] = $ **14.15%**		$\left[\dfrac{\$95,500}{\dfrac{(\$526,500 + \$593,000)}{2}}\right] = $ **17.06%**

The ratios indicate that the common stockholders are earning a 17 percent return in 2004 and a 14 percent return in 2005. Adequacy of return on stockholders' equity depends on a number of factors, including the risk of the investment.

Earnings per Share

Current stockholders and potential investors use **earnings per share (EPS)** as a key measure of performance. In contrast to measures of net income, EPS can be used to compare the performance of companies of different sizes. However, it should be used with caution in comparing companies across different industries. EPS is calculated as follows:

$$\text{EPS} = \frac{\text{Net income} - \text{Preferred dividends}}{\text{Average number of common shares outstanding}}$$

The EPS for Robyn's is as follows:

2005	2004
$\text{EPS} = \dfrac{\$95,000}{45,000} = \$2.11$	$\text{EPS} = \dfrac{\$95,500}{40,000} = \$2.39$

Robyn's Boutique has a $10 per share par value, resulting in 40,000 shares outstanding in 2004. In 2005, the boutique sold another 10,000 shares for $100,000, so 50,000 shares were outstanding at the end of 2005. The average number of shares outstanding in 2005 was 45,000 ($\frac{40,000 + 50,000}{2}$).

Price Earnings Ratio

Earnings per share is a very important ratio for investors because of the relationship of earnings to dividends and the market price of a company's stock. Investors are also interested in the current price of a company's stock in comparison to its earnings. The **price/earnings (P/E) ratio** is computed as follows:

$$\text{Price earnings ratio} = \frac{\text{Current market price}}{\text{EPS}}$$

Assuming that the current market price for Robyn's Boutique stock is $13 per share, we can compute the P/E ratio as follows:

2005	2004
$\dfrac{\$13}{\$2.11} = 6.16 \text{ to } 1$	$\dfrac{\$13}{\$2.39} = 5.44 \text{ to } 1$

Doing Business.

How Much is That Stock Worth?

Theoretically, a company's P/E ratio tells us how much an investor is willing to pay for a stock. If a stock has a P/E ratio of 15, it means that the stock is currently selling for 15 times the company's earnings. While you might expect that the P/E ratio of one company would be about the same as the P/E ratio of another, in reality P/E ratios vary greatly from company to company and by industry. For example, as of November 2004, the average P/E ratio for companies in the iron and steel industry was 9.95, the average P/E ratio for a regional bank was 16.60, the average P/E ratio for retail grocery stores was 32.83, and the average P/E ratio for biotechnology and drug companies was 41.81. As such, the P/E ratio is a reflection of an industry's growth prospects in addition to how optimistic investors are about the future of a particular company and its earnings. If a company has a P/E ratio that is higher than the industry average, it typically means that investors think the company will outperform other companies in the industry. Similarly, if a company has a P/E ratio that is lower than the industry average, investors are generally pessimistic about the company's future prospects and earnings compared to other similar companies.

Summary of Key Concepts

- Ratio analysis provides additional information necessary to enhance the decision-making ability of the users of the information. (p. 500)
- Rather than focus on a single ratio, decision makers need to evaluate a company by comparing ratios to those of previous years, budgeted amounts, and industry standards. (p. 501)
- Horizontal analysis is used to analyze changes in accounts occurring between years. (p. 501)
- Vertical analysis uses common-size financial statements to remove size as a relevant variable in ratio analysis. (p. 505)
- Ratio analysis is useful in assessing the impact of transactions on ROI, residual income, EVA, and other key measures of performance. (p. 507)

Key Definitions

Horizontal analysis When financial statements are analyzed over time (p. 501)

Trend analysis Horizontal analysis of multiple years of data (p. 503)

Common-size financial statements Statements in which all items have been restated as a percentage of a selected item on the statements (p. 505)

Working capital The excess of current assets over current liabilities, which is a measure of an entity's liquidity (p. 506)

Liquidity A measure of the ability of a company to meet its immediate financial obligations (p. 506)

Current ratio A measure of an entity's liquidity; also known as working capital ratio (p. 508)

Quick ratio A strict test of a company's ability to pay its current debts with highly liquid current assets (p. 509)

Accounts receivable turnover ratio One of the best measures of the efficiency of the collection process (p. 511)

Inventory turnover ratio A measure of the number of times the value of inventory is sold in one year (p. 511)

Cash-to-cash operating cycle ratio A measure of the length of time between the purchase of inventory and the eventual collection of cash from sales (p. 513)

Debt-to-equity ratio A solvency measure focusing on the amount of capital provided by creditors (p. 513)

Times interest earned A measure of the company's ability to meet current interest payments to creditors (p. 513)

Debt service coverage ratio A measure of the amount of cash generated by operating activities that is available to repay principal and interest in the upcoming year (p. 514)

Cash flow from operations to capital expenditures ratio A measure of a company's ability to use cash flow from operations to finance the acquisition of property, plant and equipment (p. 514)

Return on assets (ROA) A measure of return to investors on all assets invested in the company (p. 515)

Return on common stockholders' equity (ROCSE) A measure of return to common stockholders as a percentage of stockholders' equity (p. 516)

Earnings per share (EPS) A key measure of performance that is often used to compare companies of different size (p. 517)

Price/earnings (P/E) ratio A measure of the current price of a company's stock in comparison to its earnings. Theoretically, the P/E ratio tell us something about how investors think a company's stock will perform in the future compared to other companies (p. 517)

Multiple Choice

1. Which of the following statements about ratio analysis is *not* true?
   a. Financial ratios can show how a company has done in the past but is not very useful in predicting its future direction and financial position.
   b. The most compelling reason to analyze financial statements is simply that it provides useful information to supplement information directly provided in financial statements.
   c. Financial statement analysis involves the application of analytical tools to financial statements and supplemental data included with the financial statements to enhance the ability of decision makers to make optimal decisions.
   d. For both internal and external users, financial statement analysis enhances the usefulness of the information contained in the financial statements.

2. Which of the following is *not* a limitation of financial statement analysis?
   a. When comparing companies, you need to take into consideration differences in accounting methods and cost flow assumptions.
   b. Financial statement analysis involves the application of analytical tools to financial statements and supplemental data included with the financial statements to enhance the ability of decision makers to make optimal decisions.
   c. In order to properly prepare and interpret financial statement ratios, these methods, estimates, and assumptions must be taken into consideration.
   d. Ratios must be looked at as a story that can't be told without all the pieces.

3. To perform horizontal analysis:
   a. dollar changes and percentage changes in each item on the balance sheet are often provided.
   b. common-size financial statements are prepared.
   c. return on investment (ROI), residual income, and economic value added (EVA) are computed.
   d. each of the above is true.

LO 3

4. Which of the following statements regarding trend analysis is *not* true?
   a. Many annual reports include, as supplemental information, up to 10 years of financial data that can be used to perform trend analysis.
   b. Decision makers can use trend analysis to build prediction models to forecast financial performance.
   c. Trend analysis is also known as vertical analysis.
   d. Trend analysis can be used to identify problem areas by looking for sudden or abnormal changes in accounts.

LO 4

5. Achmed's Animations had current assets and current liabilities in 2005 and 2004 as follows:

	2005	2004
Current assets	$500,000	$475,000
Current liabilities	60,000	67,000

The amount of working capital from 2004 to 2005 has:
a. increased by $25,000.
b. decreased by $7,000.
c. increased by $32,000.
d. decreased by $32,000.

LO 5

6. Carla's Creations had sales of $950,000 and net operating income of $575,000. If operating assets during the year average $450,000, Carla's Creations' asset turnover is:
   a. 0.605
   b. 0.783
   c. 1.277
   d. 2.111

Use the following information from Paddington's 12/31/05 financial statements to answer questions 7 and 8:

Cash	$150,000	Accounts payable	$ 60,000
Accounts receivable	130,000	Payroll payable	10,000
Inventory	125,000	Taxes payable	10,000
Prepaid insurance	25,000	Total current liabilities	$ 80,000
Total current assets	$430,000	Notes payable	50,000
Long-term investments	110,000	Capital stock	500,000
Land	200,000	Retained earnings	220,000
Property and equipment	215,000	Total liabilities and stockholders' equity	$850,000
Accumulated depreciation	(105,000)		
Total long-term assets	$420,000		
Total assets	$850,000		

Current liabilities (12/31/04)	$ 70,000
Net cash provided by operating activities	120,000
Accounts receivable (12/31/04)	120,000
Net cash provided by investing activities	100,000
Inventory (12/31/04)	100,000
Net cash provided by financing activities	80,000
Net credit sales	500,000
Cost of goods sold	380,000

7. Paddington's current ratio is:
   a. 5.375
   b. 3.81
   c. 3.50
   d. It cannot be determined from the information provided.

8. Paddington's debt-to-equity ratio is:
   a. 0.10
   b. 0.11
   c. 0.18
   d. It cannot be determined from the information provided.

9. The following information was obtained from Chandler's 12/31/05 financial statements:

Cash	$250,000	Accounts payable	$160,000
Accounts receivable	110,000	Payroll payable	110,000
Inventory	125,000	Taxes payable	110,000
Prepaid assets	25,000	Total current liabilities	$380,000
Total current assets	$510,000	Notes payable	50,000
Long-term investments	$110,000	Capital stock	400,000
Land	200,000	Retained earnings	90,000
Property and equipment	205,000	Total liabilities and stockholders' equity	$920,000
Accumulated depreciation	(105,000)		
Total long-term assets	$410,000		
Total assets	$920,000		
Current liabilities (12/31/04)	$270,000		
Net cash provided by operating activities	120,000		
Accounts receivable (12/31/04)	120,000		
Net cash provided by investing activities	100,000		
Inventory (12/31/04)	100,000		
Net cash provided by financing activities	80,000		
Net credit sales	450,000		
Cost of goods sold	380,000		

Chandler's return on common stockholders' equity is:
a. 0.18
b. 0.14
c. 1.25
d. It cannot be determined from the information provided.

10. Brown's Breads had the following financial statement information for 2005:

Net sales	$1,500,000
Gross profit margin	1,250,000
Interest expense (net of tax)	240,000
Net income	900,000
Total assets, 12/31/04	1,010,000
Total assets, 12/31/05	1,200,000
Total liabilities, 12/31/05	260,000
Stockholders' equity, 12/31/04	650,000
Stockholders' equity, 12/31/05	750,000
Preferred dividends	100,000
Average number of shares outstanding	1,000,000

The return on common stockholders' equity for Brown's Breads is:
a. 1.14
b. 1.20
c. 1.38
d. It cannot be determined from the information provided.

Concept Questions

11. *(Objective 1)* Explain the purpose of financial statement analysis.
12. *(Objective 2)* Explain the limitations of financial statement analysis.
13. *(Objective 3)* Why would individuals want to perform a trend analysis?
14. *(Objective 3)* Is it better to use more or fewer years when performing a trend analysis? Why?
15. *(Objective 4)* Why are common-size financial statements useful?
16. *(Objective 4)* Why should companies monitor their working capital?
17. *(Objective 5)* What is the formula to compute accounts receivable turnover?
18. *(Objective 5)* A company has a current ratio of 3 to 1 but would like to decrease the ratio. What types of options does it have to accomplish this?
19. *(Objective 5)* At the beginning of 2005, the Golden Eagle Company had a current ratio of 2 to 1. What could Golden Eagle do to increase this ratio?
20. *(Objective 6)* What does the debt-to-equity ratio tell about a company?
21. *(Objective 7)* If sales are $475, beginning assets are $420, and ending assets are $480, what is the asset turnover ratio?

Exercises

22. Information taken from recent annual reports of two retailers follows (amounts in millions). Dan's Duds and Handsome Hal's both sell men's clothing. The income tax rate is 34 percent.

	Dan's Duds	Handsome Hal's
Sales	$4,071	$20,649
Interest expense	64	136
Net income	245	837
Average total assets	2,061	5,746

LO 4

✓ Dan's ROA: 13.91%

Required

Indicate which of these companies is the discount store and which is the specialty retailer. Explain your answer.

23. Annual reports of Kellogg's and Quaker Oats reveal the following for a recent year (amounts in millions):

	Kellogg's	Quaker Oats
Sales	$3,793	$3,671
Accounts receivable, January 1	219	505
Accounts receivable, December 31	275	537

LO 5

✓ Kellogg's A/R turnover: 15.4 times

Required

A. Compute the accounts receivable turnover for each company.
B. Compute the average number of days that accounts receivable are outstanding for each company.
C. Which of these two companies is managing its accounts receivable more efficiently?

24. The following relates to the activities of Eli Lilly, a pharmaceutical company (amounts in millions):

	Year 5	Year 6	Year 7	Year 8
Sales	$3,271	$3,720	$3,644	$4,070
Cost of goods sold	1,175	1,346	1,303	1,337
Average inventory	662	694	655	645

LO 5

✓ Year 6 inventory turnover: 1.9

Required

A. Compute the inventory turnover for each year.
B. Compute the average number of days that inventories are held each year.
C. Compute the cost of goods sold to sales percentage for each year.
D. How well has the company managed its inventories over the four years?

25. The following information relates to a manufacturer of CD players (amounts in millions):

	Year 2	Year 3	Year 4
Sales	$210	$538	$1,051
Average total assets	70	145	256
Net income	36	87	137

LO 5

✓ Year 2 asset turnover: 3.0

Required

A. Compute the asset turnover ratio for each year.
B. How well has the company managed its investment in plant assets over the three years?

26. Recent annual reports of Coca-Cola and PepsiCo reveal the following for year 3 (in millions):

	Coca-Cola	PepsiCo
Revenues	$8,338	$13,007
Interest expense	199	345
Net income	1,045	762
Average total assets	8,028	10,079

The income tax rate for year 3 is 34 percent.

Required

A. Calculate the rate of return on assets for each company.
B. Break the rate of return on assets into return on sales and total asset turnover.
C. Comment on the relative profitability of the two companies for year 3.

27. The following data show five items from the financial statements of three companies for a recent year (amounts in millions):

	Company A	Company B	Company C
For the Year			
Revenues	$8,824	$9,000	$11,742
Income before interest and related taxes[1]	615	1,043	611
Net income to common shareholders[2]	477	974	503
Average during the Year			
Total assets	9,073	6,833	7,163
Common shareholders' equity	2,915	3,494	2,888

[1] Net income + Interest expense × (1 − tax rate)
[2] Net income − Preferred stock dividends

✓ Company B's ROA: 15.31%

Required

A. Compute the rate of return on assets for each company. Separate the rate of return on assets into the return on sales and the asset turnover ratio.
B. The three companies are American Airlines, Johnson & Johnson, and May Department Stores. Which of the companies corresponds to A, B, and C? What clues did you use in reaching your conclusions?

✓ PepsiCo ROA: 9.8%

Problems

28. Avantronics is a manufacturer of electronic components and accessories, with total assets of $20,000,000. Selected financial ratios for Avantronics and the industry averages for firms of similar size are as follows:

	Avantronics 2003	Avantronics 2004	Avantronics 2005	Industry Average
Current ratio	2.09	2.27	2.51	2.24
Quick ratio	1.15	1.12	1.19	1.22
Inventory turnover	2.40	2.18	2.02	3.50
Profit margin	0.14	0.15	0.17	0.11
Debt-to-equity ratio	0.24	0.37	0.44	0.35

Avantronics is being reviewed by several entities whose interests vary, and the company's financial ratios are a part of the data being considered. Each of the following parties must recommend an action based on its evaluation of Avantronics' financial position.

MidCoastal Bank. The bank is processing Avantronics' application for a new five-year term note. MidCoastal has been the banker for Avantronics for several years but must reevaluate the company's financial position for each major transaction.

Ozawa Company. Ozawa is a new supplier to Avantronics and must decide on the appropriate credit terms to extend to the company.

Drucker & Denon. A brokerage firm specializing in the stock of electronics firms that are sold over the counter, Drucker & Denon must decide whether it will include Avantronics in a new fund being established for sale to Drucker & Denon's clients.

Working Capital Management Committee. This is a committee of Avantronics' management personnel chaired by the chief operating officer. The committee is responsible for periodically reviewing the company's working capital position, comparing actual data against budgets, and recommending changes in strategy as needed.

Required

A. Describe the analytical use of each of the five ratios just presented.
B. For each of the four entities described, identify the financial ratios, from those ratios presented, that would be most valuable as a basis for its decision regarding Avantronics.
C. Discuss what the financial ratios presented in the question reveal about Avantronics. Support your answer by citing specific ratio levels and trends as well as the interrelationships among these ratios.

29. Following are the income statements for Martha's Miscellaneous for 2004 and 2005.

Martha's Miscellaneous Comparative Statements of Income and Retained Earnings

	2005	2004	$ Change	% Change
Sales revenue	$700,000	$650,000		
Cost of goods sold	500,000	455,000		
Gross profit	$200,000	$195,000		
Payroll expense	$ 50,000	$ 42,250		
Insurance expense	30,000	29,000		
Rent expense	18,000	18,000		
Depreciation	35,000	15,000		
Total expenses	$133,000	$104,250		
Operating income	$ 67,000	$ 90,750		
Interest expense	(7,000)	(5,000)		
Gain on vehicle sale	25,000	—		
Loss on sale of securities	(25,000)	—		
Interest revenue	75,000	50,000		
Net income before interest and taxes	$135,000	$135,750		
Income taxes	40,000	40,250		
Net income	$ 95,000	$ 95,500		
Dividends	38,000	38,000		
Total retained earnings	$ 57,000	$ 57,500		
Retained earnings 1/1	193,000	136,000		
Retained earnings 12/31	$250,000	$193,000		

Required

Complete the comparative income statement by computing dollar change ($ change) and percentage change (% change).

30. Following are the balance sheets for Howard's Hammocks for December 31, 2005 and 2004.

Howard's Hammocks Comparative Balance Sheets

	2005	2004
Cash	$130,000	$110,000
Accounts receivable	130,000	120,000
Inventory	225,000	215,000
Prepaid insurance	25,000	30,000
Total current assets	$510,000	$475,000
Long-term investments	$110,000	$ 75,000
Land	200,000	175,000
Property and equipment	215,000	95,000
Accumulated depreciation	(105,000)	(80,000)
	$420,000	$265,000
Total assets	$930,000	$740,000
Accounts payable	$ 60,000	$ 50,000
Payroll payable	10,000	8,000
Taxes payable	10,000	9,000
Total current liabilities	$ 80,000	$ 67,000
Notes payable	100,000	80,000
Capital stock	500,000	400,000
Retained earnings	250,000	193,000
Total liabilities and stockholders' equity	$930,000	$740,000

Required

Using the preceding income statement figures, prepare common-size statements for 2005 and 2004.

31. Using the following financial statements for Eagle Company, compute the required ratios:

✓ 2005 current ratio: 1.45

Eagle Company Balance Sheet as of December 31 (in millions)

	2003	2004	2005
Assets			
Cash	$ 2.6	$ 1.8	$ 1.6
Government securities	0.4	0.2	0.0
Accounts and notes receivable	8.0	8.5	8.5
Inventories	2.8	3.2	2.8
Prepaid assets	0.7	0.6	0.6
Total current assets	$14.5	$14.3	$13.5
Property, plant, and equipment (net)	4.3	5.4	5.9
Total assets	$18.8	$19.7	$19.4

	2003	2004	2005
Liabilities and Shareholders' Equity			
Notes payable	$ 3.2	$ 3.7	$ 4.2
Accounts payable	2.8	3.7	4.1
Accrued expenses	0.9	1.1	1.0
Total current liabilities	$ 6.9	$ 8.5	$ 9.3
Long-term debt, 6% interest	3.0	2.0	1.0
Total liabilities	$ 9.9	$10.5	$10.3
Shareholders' equity	8.9	9.2	9.1
Total liabilities and shareholders' equity	$18.8	$19.7	$19.4
Income Statement for the Year Ended December 31 (in millions)			
Net sales	$24.2	$24.5	$24.9
Cost of goods sold	(16.9)	(17.2)	(18.0)
Gross margin	$ 7.3	$ 7.3	$ 6.9
Selling and administrative expenses	(6.6)	(6.8)	(7.3)
Earnings (loss) before taxes	$ 0.7	$ 0.5	$ (0.4)
Income taxes	(0.3)	(0.2)	0.2
Net income	$ 0.4	$ 0.3	$ (0.2)

Required

A. What is the rate of return on total assets for 2005?
B. What is the current ratio for 2005?
C. What is the quick (acid-test) ratio for 2005?
D. What is the profit margin for 2004?
E. What is the profit margin for 2005?
F. What is the inventory turnover for 2004?
G. What is the inventory turnover for 2005?
H. What is the rate of return on stockholders' equity for 2004?
I. What is the rate of return on stockholders' equity for 2005?
J. What is the debt-equity ratio for 2005?

32. The 2005 financial statements for the Griffin Company are as follows:

Griffin Company
Statement of Financial Position

	12/31/05	12/31/04
Assets		
Cash	$ 40,000	$ 10,000
Accounts receivable	30,000	55,000
Inventory	110,000	70,000
Property, plant, and equipment	250,000	257,000
Total assets	$430,000	$392,000

Liabilities and Stockholders' Equity		
Current liabilities	$ 60,000	$ 50,000
5% mortgage payable	120,000	162,000
Common stock (30,000 shares)	150,000	150,000
Retained earnings	100,000	30,000
Total liabilities and stockholders' equity	$430,000	$392,000

Griffin Company
Income Statement for the Year Ended December 31, 2005

Sales on Account		$420,000
Less Expenses		
Cost of goods sold	$214,000	
Salary expense	50,000	
Depreciation expense	7,000	
Interest expense	9,000	
Total expenses		$280,000
Income before taxes		$140,000
Income tax expense (50%)		70,000
Net income		$ 70,000

Required

Compute the following ratios for the Griffin Company for the year ending December 31, 2005:
A. Profit margin ratio (before interest and taxes)
B. Total asset turnover
C. Rate of return on total assets
D. Rate of return on common stockholders' equity
E. Earnings per share of stock
F. Inventory turnover
G. Current ratio
H. Quick ratio
I. Accounts receivable turnover
J. Debt-to-equity ratio
K. Times interest earned

Group and Internet Exercises

33. Search the Internet and locate the financial statements for three companies in the same industry. Compare the financial performance of the companies, using liquidity ratios, solvency ratios, and profitability ratios as described in the chapter. What surprises did you uncover? Were the companies more or less similar than you expected?

34. Conduct a search on the Internet to find companies that perform financial statement analysis for consumers and businesses. What types of services do these companies provide? How could you personally use these services? Do you think the information provided by these companies is reliable?

Chapter 16: The Statement of Cash Flows

In this chapter, we present an in-depth discussion of the preparation and use of the statement of cash flows. Although this statement is used primarily by those external to the organization, the statement of cash flows and the related cash budget (discussed in Chapter 9) are also useful tools for managerial decision making.

Learning Objectives

After studying the material in this chapter, you should be able to:

① Recognize the purpose of a statement of cash flows and explain why accrual accounting creates a need for the statement of cash flows

② Discuss the types of transactions that result from operating, investing, and financing activities and how they are presented on the statement of cash flows

③ Discuss the difference between the direct and the indirect methods of computing cash flow from operating activities

④ Prepare a statement of cash flows

⑤ Analyze the statement of cash flows and use the information in decision making

Introduction

The statement of cash flows reports the impact of a firm's operating, investing, and financing activities on cash flows during the accounting period. Along with the balance sheet, income statement, and the statement of changes in stockholders' equity, this statement is a required component of a company's external financial statements.

Users of financial statements have made the statement of cash flows one of the most important of the four required financial statements. In today's highly competitive global environment, users of financial accounting information have learned that cash flows may be a better indicator of financial performance than net income or earnings per share.

Doing Business.

YOU HAVE TO HAVE ENOUGH CASH TO PAY YOUR BILLS

During the 1990s, numerous companies failed that appeared financially healthy and profitable in the years immediately preceding the failures. Among those businesses are some very well-known companies, such as Boston Market, United Press International, Montgomery Ward, and Filene's Basement. However, each of these companies filed for bankruptcy protection owing to the company's inability to generate sufficient cash flow to cover operating costs, capital expansion, and debt repayment. Investors and others sometimes learn too late that to be successful, companies must generate sufficient cash to pay their bills!

Purpose of the Statement of Cash Flows

Objective 1

Recognize the purpose of a statement of cash flows and explain why accrual accounting creates a need for the statement of cash flows

The main purpose of the statement of cash flows is to provide information to decision makers about a company's cash inflows and outflows during the period. The statement of cash flows provides information relating to the change in cash balances between two balance sheet dates. Balance sheets provide a "snapshot" of the financial position of a company at a particular point in time, whereas the statement of cash flows reports changes over time. The statement of cash flows should be viewed as an explanation of the changes to the cash balance reported on the balance sheet. The statement of cash flows also discloses items that affect how the balance sheet changed but that don't show up in the income statement, such as issuance of stock or acquisitions of property, plant, and equipment.

The Composition of the Statement of Cash Flows

The statement of cash flows summarizes and explains all major cash receipts (inflows) and cash payments (outflows) during the period and categorizes the changes as resulting from operating, investing, or financing activities.

Operating Activities

Operating activities include acquiring and selling products in the normal course of business. Different types of businesses will have different transactions that are included in cash flows from operating activities. Typical types of items reported in this section of the statement of cash flows as inflows are cash from sales to customers, collection of cash from past sales that were made on credit, and interest and dividends received. Typical outflows of cash from operating activities are purchases of merchandise for sale or materials to manufacture products, payments for operating expenses, interest on debt, payments for services, and payments of taxes.

Investing Activities

Cash flows from **investing activities** include cash inflows from the sale of property, plant, and equipment; the sale of securities (stocks and bonds) of other companies; and the receipt of loan payments. Cash outflows include the purchase of property, plant, and equipment; the purchase of securities; and making loans as investments. Loans directly related to the sale of products or services are likely classified as operating activities. The interest on loans included as an investing activity is also classified as a cash flow from operating activities.

Financing Activities

Cash flows from **financing activities** include cash inflows from selling stock or from issuing bonds (see Exhibit 16-1). Cash inflows from financing activities also include contributions from owners and borrowing from banks on a long-term basis. Cash outflows from financing activities include repayment of notes and bonds, cash payments to repurchase stock (Treasury stock), and the payment of dividends. Once again, all interest payments are included in cash flows from operating activities.

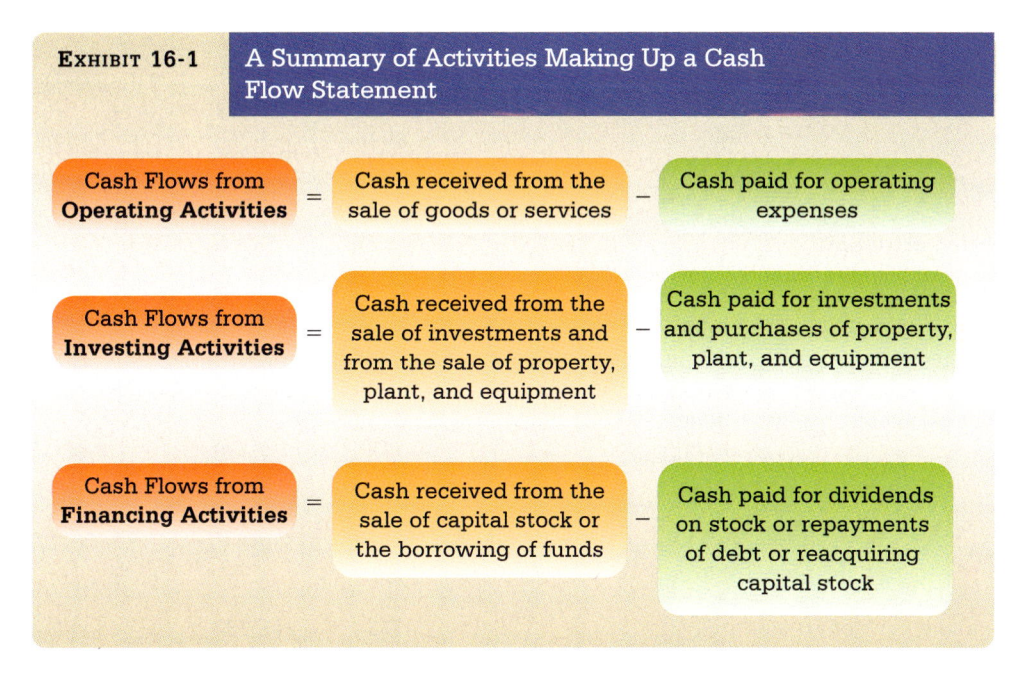

EXHIBIT 16-1 A Summary of Activities Making Up a Cash Flow Statement

Cash Flows from Operating Activities =	Cash received from the sale of goods or services	− Cash paid for operating expenses
Cash Flows from Investing Activities =	Cash received from the sale of investments and from the sale of property, plant, and equipment	− Cash paid for investments and purchases of property, plant, and equipment
Cash Flows from Financing Activities =	Cash received from the sale of capital stock or the borrowing of funds	− Cash paid for dividends on stock or repayments of debt or reacquiring capital stock

As an example, consider Hasbro, whose Consolidated Statements of Cash Flows are presented in Exhibit 16-2. Note than even though Hasbro's 2003 earnings were almost $158 million, cash and cash equivalents increased by only $25.4 million. Likewise, between 2001 and 2002, when the company experienced a loss of $170.7 million, cash increased by $262.3 million.

The increase in cash in 2002 appears to have resulted from a combination of things. Net cash provided by operating activities was much higher in 2002 ($473.1 million) than in 2001 ($372.5 million). Likewise, net cash utilized by financing activities was lower in 2002 ($159.3 million) than in 2001 ($202.7 million).

EXHIBIT 16-2   Consolidated Statements of Cash Flows (Hasbro, Inc.)

Fiscal Years Ended in December (Thousands of Dollars)	2003	2002	2001
Cash flows from operating activities			
Net earnings (loss)	$ 157,664	$ (170,674)	$ 59,732
Adjusting to reconcile net earnings (loss) to net cash provided by operating activities:			
Cumulative effect of accounting change, net of tax	17,351	245,732	1,066
Depreciation and amortization of plant and equipment	88,070	89,262	104,247
Other amortization	76,053	94,576	121,652
Loss on early extinguishment of debt	20,342	—	—
Loss on impairment of investment	—	42,902	—
Change in fair value of liabilities potentially settleable in common stock	13,630	—	—
Deferred income taxes	22,774	5,441	38,697
Compensation earned under restricted stock programs	172	1,770	2,532
Change in operating assets and liabilities (other than cash and cash equivalents):			
(Increase) decrease in accounts receivable	(13,202)	33,653	99,474
Decrease in inventories	34,846	38,783	109,002
Decrease in prepaid expenses and other current assets	7,845	184,988	45,936
Increase (decrease) in accounts payable and accrued liabilities	16,707	22,863	(195,691)
Other, including long-term advances	11,903	(116,157)	(14,272)
Net cash provided by operating activities	$ 454,155	$ 473,139	$ 372,475
Cash flows from investing activities			
Additions to property, plant and equipment	$ (63,070)	$ (58,661)	$ (50,045)
Investments and acquisitions, net of cash acquired	—	(7,419)	—
Other	(1,809)	3,766	(7,734)
Net cash utilized by investing activities	$ (64,879)	$ (62,314)	$ (57,779)
Cash flows from financing activities			
Proceeds from borrowings with original maturities of more than three months	—	—	$ 250,000
Repurchases and repayments of borrowings with original maturities of more than three months	$(389,279)	$ (126,970)	(250,127)
Net proceeds (repayments) of other short-term borrowings	309	(14,695)	(190,216)
Purchase of common stock and other equity securities	(3,378)	—	—
Stock option transactions	39,892	3,100	8,391
Dividends paid	(20,851)	(20,772)	(20,709)
Net cash utilized by financing activities	$(373,307)	$ (159,337)	$ (202,661)
Effect of exchange rate changes on cash	$ 9,406	$ 10,789	$ (6,055)
Increase in cash and cash equivalents	$ 25,375	$ 262,277	$ 105,980
Cash and cash equivalents at beginning of year	495,372	233,095	127,115
Cash and cash equivalents at end of year	$ 520,747	$ 495,372	$ 233,095
Supplemental information			
Interest paid	$ 64,189	$ 77,840	$ 103,437
Income taxes paid (received)	$ 28,354	$ (41,378)	$ (34,813)

THE ETHICS OF BUSINESS
It's All About Categorization

WorldCom (now MCI) was embroiled in an accounting scandal over the decisions made by some of the company's executives about how to treat certain expenditures. The company's former chief financial officer, Scott Sullivan, reclassified certain items from expenses (i.e., operating activities) to fixed asset purchases (i.e., investing activities). This reclassification had two significant implications for the company's financial statements. First, by reducing expenses and increasing purchases of fixed assets, WorldCom reported higher profits than would otherwise have been reported. And, second, the company's statement of cash flows reported lower cash flows from operating activities than was the case. Instead, the expenditures were reported as cash flows in the investing section of the statement. Clearly, these two effects gave investors the wrong impression of the company's actual financial performance.

It's Your Choice Is the reclassification of expenditures as described above unethical? Why or why not? Who is harmed by the actions of executives such as Scott Sullivan who make such decisions? Can you imagine circumstances that might motivate you to participate in such activities as those described at WorldCom?

The Definition of Cash: Cash and Cash Equivalents

Before we begin our discussion of the preparation of the statement of cash flows, it is important to be specific about exactly what is meant by cash. Accounting standards define certain items as equivalent to cash, which are combined with cash on the balance sheet and the statement of cash flows.

Commercial paper (short-term notes issued by corporations), money market funds, and Treasury bills are examples of cash equivalents. A **cash equivalent** is an item that can be readily converted to a known amount of cash and has an original maturity to the investor of three months or less. For example, a three-year Treasury bill purchased three years before maturity is not a cash equivalent, but if that same Treasury bill is purchased three months prior to maturity, it would be a cash equivalent.

Noncash Transactions

It is not uncommon for organizations to have exchange transactions that do not directly involve cash inflows or outflows but still warrant disclosure on a statement of cash flows. These transactions are primarily in the financing and investing areas. For example, if an exchange were made of stock for an asset, the transaction would require an accounting entry to record the issuance of the stock and the addition of the asset. This transaction would not directly affect cash flows. However, if the company sold the stock on the open market and then used that cash to purchase the asset, the transaction would directly impact cash and be shown on the statement of cash flows. The sale of stock would show up as an inflow in the financing activities section, and the purchase of the asset would show up as an offsetting outflow in the investing activities section of the statement of cash flows. The key point is that the form of the transaction differs between the two transactions (exchange versus sale and purchase), whereas the substance (or result) of the two transactions is the same. Both transactions result in the same impact on the financial statements. Because we are more concerned with the substance of accounting transactions and full disclosure to users of the information, generally accepted accounting principles require that any significant noncash transaction be reported either in a separate schedule or in a footnote to the financial statements.

> **Objective 2**
>
> Discuss the types of transactions that result from operating, investing, and financing activities and how they are presented on the statement of cash flows

Objective 3

Discuss the difference between the direct and the indirect methods of computing cash flow from operating activities

Cash Flows from Operating Activities

Organizations use two methods (direct and indirect) to report cash flows from operating activities. The **direct method** reports major classes of gross cash receipts and payments. For example, the direct method would report cash collected from customers, cash paid for inventory, cash paid for salaries and wages, and so on. The **indirect method,** in comparison, starts with net income and then removes the effect of all noncash items resulting from accruals or noncash expenses, such as depreciation. In other words, the indirect method essentially converts the accrual-basis income statement to a cash-basis income statement by taking out noncash items, such as depreciation, and nonoperating items, such as accruals.

In order to compare the two methods, consider the income statement and balance sheet below. The company began operations on January 1, 2005, with the owners investing $100,000 in cash. The financial statements for the year ending December 31, 2005, are as follows:

Income Statement For the Year Ended December 31, 2005

Sales revenues	$800,000
Operating expenses	640,000
Income before tax	$160,000
Income tax expense	40,000
Net income	$120,000

Balance Sheet As of December 31, 2005

Assets		Liabilities and Stockholders' Equity	
Cash	$150,000	Accounts payable	$ 60,000
Accounts receivable	130,000	Capital stock	100,000
		Retained earnings	120,000
Total assets	$280,000	Total liabilities and stockholders' equity	$280,000

Direct Method

When using the direct method, each item on the income statement must be looked at to determine how much cash each of these activities either generated or used during the year. As an example, if all sales were for cash, cash collections from customers would be equal to sales revenue. However, if sales are made on account, sales revenue must be adjusted for changes in accounts receivable:

> Sales revenue + Beginning accounts receivable
> − Ending accounts receivable = Cash collections from customers

or

> Cash collections from customers = Sales ± Decrease (Increase) in accounts receivable

In this case, the company had a beginning accounts receivable balance of $0. The ending accounts receivable balance is $130,000, so cash collections from customers equal $670,000 ($800,000 + $0 − $130,000).

Applying the same concept, if all operating expenses are paid in cash, cash outflows for operating expenses will equal $640,000. However, if some of the expenses are incurred on account, expenses must be adjusted for any changes in related accounts payable balances:

> Cash outflows for operating expenses = Operating expenses
> + Beginning accounts payable − Ending accounts payable

Therefore, the cash outflow from operating expenses is $580,000 ($640,000 + $0 − $60,000). Assuming that the company's tax payments are made in cash (note that there is no liability for taxes payable), cash flows from operating activities are as follows:

Cash Flows from Operating Activities (Direct Method)

Cash collected from customers	$670,000
Cash payments for operating activities	(580,000)
Cash payments for taxes	(40,000)
Net cash inflow from operating activities	$ 50,000

Indirect Method

The indirect method of preparing the cash flows from operating activities starts with the net income for the period, which is $120,000. This amount is then adjusted to arrive at the amount of cash provided by operating activities. The first adjustment to net income will be the change in accounts receivable. In this case, the increase of $130,000 will be subtracted from revenue. The next adjustment will be for the decrease in accounts payable ($60,000). The increase in accounts receivable means that some of the sales were not collected so did not result in cash flows. The decrease in accounts payable means that cash in excess of current period expenses (shown on the income statement) was used to pay expenses from prior periods. Using the indirect method, cash flows from operations are presented as follows:

KEY CONCEPT

The only difference between the direct and indirect methods is in the presentation of the cash flows from operating activities. Cash flows from investing activities and cash flows from financing activities are calculated in exactly the same way.

Cash Flows from Operating Activities (Indirect Method)

Net income	$120,000
Adjustments to Reconcile Net Income to Net Cash	
Increase in accounts receivable	(130,000)
Increase in accounts payable	60,000
Net cash inflow from operating activities	$ 50,000

Proponents of the direct method point to the straightforward presentation of the cash flows from operating activities and point out that anyone, even someone with no training in accounting, can very easily use this information in decision making. Proponents of the direct method also argue that this method provides more useful information for evaluating operating efficiency.

Supporters of the indirect method argue that it focuses attention on differences between the cash and accrual basis of accounting, which is very important for decision making. They also point out that if the direct method is used, the indirect schedule must still be prepared. Consequently, more companies choose to report using the indirect method.

The Statement of Cash Flows and the Accounting Equation

The basic accounting equation as presented in your financial accounting course is

$$\text{Assets} = \text{Liabilities} + \text{Owners' equity}$$

In more detail,

$$\text{Cash} + \text{Noncash current assets} + \text{Long-term assets} = \text{Current liabilities}$$
$$+ \text{Long-term liabilities} + \text{Capital stock} + \text{Retained earnings}$$

We can rearrange the equation so that cash is on the left side and all other items are on the right side:

Cash = Current liabilities + Long-term liabilities + Capital stock
+ Retained earnings − Noncash current assets − Long-term assets

Using this equation, we see that any changes in cash (the left side of the equation) must be accompanied by a corresponding change on the right side of the equation. For example:

Transaction	Activity	Left Side	Right Side
Collect accounts receivable	Operating	+ Cash	− NCCA
Prepay insurance	Operating	− Cash	+ NCCA
Collect customer's deposit	Operating	+ Cash	+ Current liabilities
Pay suppliers	Operating	− Cash	− Current liabilities
Make a cash sale	Operating	+ Cash	+ RE
Sell equipment	Investing	+ Cash	− Long-term assets
Buy equipment	Investing	− Cash	+ Long-term assets
Issue bonds	Financing	+ Cash	+ Long-term liabilities
Retire bonds	Financing	− Cash	− Long-term liabilities
Issue capital stock	Financing	+ Cash	+ Capital stock
Buy treasury stock	Financing	− Cash	− Capital stock
Pay dividends	Financing	− Cash	− Retained earnings

Preparing the Statement of Cash Flows

To prepare the statement of cash flows, we must gather appropriate information, which includes comparative balance sheets (last year's and this year's), the current income statement, and additional information needed to analyze noncash transactions. After gathering the preceding information, we must complete six steps in preparing the statement of cash flows.

1. Compute the net change in cash (increase or decrease)
2. Compute net cash provided or used by operating activities
3. Compute net cash provided or used by investing activities
4. Compute net cash provided or used by financing activities
5. Compute net cash flow by combining the results from operating, investing, and financing activities
6. Report any significant noncash investing and/or financing activities in a separate schedule or a footnote

Objective 4
Prepare a statement of cash flows

As an example, consider the financial statements for Robyn's Bourique, which retails children's clothes.

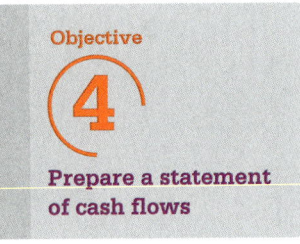

Robyn's Boutique
Income Statement
For the Year Ended December 31, 2005

Revenues and Gains		
Sales revenue	$700,000	
Interest income	75,000	
Gain on sale of vehicle	25,000	
Total revenues and gains		$800,000
Expenses and Losses		
Cost of goods sold	$500,000	
Payroll expense	50,000	
Insurance expense	30,000	
Interest expense	7,000	
Rent expense	18,000	
Depreciation	35,000	
Loss on sale of long-term investments	25,000	
Income tax expense	40,000	
Total expenses and losses		705,000
Net income		$ 95,000

Robyn's Boutique
Comparative Balance Sheets

	12/31/2005	12/31/2004
Cash	$130,000	$110,000
Accounts receivable	130,000	120,000
Inventory	225,000	215,000
Prepaid insurance	25,000	30,000
Total current assets	$510,000	$475,000
Long-term investments	$110,000	$ 75,000
Land	200,000	175,000
Property and equipment	215,000	95,000
Accumulated depreciation	(105,000)	(80,000)
Total long-term assets	$420,000	$265,000
Total assets	$930,000	$740,000
Accounts payable	$ 60,000	$ 50,000
Payroll payable	10,000	8,000
Income tax payable	10,000	9,000
Total current liabilities	$ 80,000	$ 67,000
Notes payable	400,000	380,000
Total liabilities	$480,000	$447,000
Capital stock	200,000	100,000
Retained earnings	250,000	193,000
Total liabilities and stockholders' equity	$930,000	$740,000

Additional information

1. Long-term investments were purchased for $85,000.
2. Long-term investments were sold for $25,000, with a book value of $50,000, resulting in a loss of $25,000.
3. Land was purchased for $25,000. $5,000 of the purchase price was paid in cash. The remaining $20,000 was borrowed from the seller.
4. Equipment was purchased for $180,000.
5. A vehicle with an original cost of $60,000 and a book value of $50,000 was sold for $75,000, resulting in a gain of $25,000.
6. Capital stock was issued for cash of $100,000.
7. Dividends of $38,000 were paid.

Step 1: Compute the Net Change in Cash The net change in cash as shown on the balance sheet is $20,000.

Step 2: Compute Net Cash Provided or Used by Operating Activities

Direct Method

Operating activities generating cash inflows for Robyn's Boutique include selling goods and services and collecting interest income. Sales revenue was reported as $700,000. However, we must consider the change in accounts receivable to determine how much cash was actually collected from sales. Using the formula on page 536, cash collections are equal to $690,000 ($700,000 sales + $120,000 beginning accounts receivable − $130,000 ending accounts receivable). Interest income reported on the income statement is $75,000. How can we tell whether the entire $75,000 was collected in cash? In this case, because there is no "interest receivable" account on the balance sheet, the entire amount must have been collected in cash.

Operating activities generating cash outflows include buying merchandise for resale to customers, making payments to employees, and making payments for other operating expenses, such as insurance, interest, rent, and taxes. Cost of goods sold is reported at $500,000. However, cash outflows for purchases of inventory may be different. To determine the amount of cash expended to purchase inventory, we must analyze changes in the inventory account as well as changes in accounts payable because inventory purchases are normally made on credit. Using the cost of goods sold model for a merchandising company developed in Chapter 2 (see page 42):

$$\text{Beginning inventory} + \text{Cost of goods purchased} - \text{Ending inventory} = \text{Cost of goods sold}$$

Consequently, the cost of goods purchased equals the following:

$$\text{Cost of goods purchased} = \text{Cost of goods sold} - \text{Beginning inventory} + \text{Ending inventory}$$

Therefore, the cost of goods purchased by Robyn's is $510,000 ($500,000 − $215,000 + $225,000). However, we still don't know whether all these purchases were for cash. Using the formula developed earlier for analyzing cash expenditures for operating expenses:

$$\text{Cash outflows for purchases} = \text{Cost of goods purchased} + \text{Beginning accounts payable} - \text{Ending accounts payable}$$

Robyn's cash outflows for purchases equals $500,000 ($510,000 + $50,000 − $60,000).

Next, consider payroll expense of $50,000. Once again, if any payroll expense is accrued at the end of the year for employees who are owed wages but not paid by year-end, the payroll expense must be adjusted by changes in payroll liabilities to determine the cash outflows for payroll. The formula is as follows:

Cash outflows for payroll = Payroll expense + Beginning payroll payable
− Ending payroll payable

Cash outflows for payroll are therefore $48,000 ($50,000 + $8,000 − $10,000).

Another way to look at the cash outflow for payroll is to assume that Robyn's paid the amount owed from last year ($8,000) plus all this year's expense ($50,000) except the amount owed at the end of the current year ($10,000)—in other words, $8,000 + $50,000 − $10,000 = $48,000.

The next item on the income statement is insurance expense. Although there are no liabilities for insurance at the end of 2004 or 2005, you will note that the balance sheet does include an asset called prepaid insurance with a beginning-of-year balance of $30,000 and an end-of-year balance of $25,000. The $30,000 beginning balance represents prepayments that were made in 2004 for insurance coverage provided in 2005. This $30,000 was expensed on the income statement in 2005 as insurance coverage was provided for Robyn's Boutique. Likewise, the $25,000 prepaid balance at the end of 2005 represents cash outflows for insurance that occurred in 2005. This amount will be expensed on the income statement for the year ended December 31, 2006.

Cash outflows for interest expense and rent expense are equal to $7,000 and $18,000, respectively. Note that Robyn's must have paid for these items in cash because no related liabilities or assets appear on the balance sheet. Although Robyn's also reports depreciation expense of $35,000, depreciation does not result in a cash outflow. The cash outflow occurs at the time the depreciable property is purchased and is shown in the investing activities section of the cash flow statement. Finally, income tax expense is equal to $40,000. Adjusting for related increases in income tax liabilities on the balance sheet, cash outflows for income taxes during the year must have been $39,000 ($40,000 income tax expense + Beginning income tax payable balance of $9,000 − Ending income tax payable balance of $10,000).

Net Cash Flows from Operating Activities (Direct Method)

Cash Receipts From	
Sales on account	$690,000
Interest	75,000
Cash Payments For	
Inventory purchases	(500,000)
Payroll	(48,000)
Insurance	(25,000)
Interest	(7,000)
Rent expense	(18,000)
Taxes	(39,000)
Net cash provided (used) by operating activities	$128,000

Indirect Method

The indirect method reconciles net income to net cash flow from operating activities by taking the income statement amounts of revenues and expenses and adjusting for changes in related noncash assets and liabilities:

Income statement amount
+ Increases in related liabilities
+ Decreases in related noncash assets
− Increases in related noncash assets
− Decreases in related liabilities
= Cash flow amount

> **KEY CONCEPT**
>
> When using the indirect method, increases (decreases) in asset (liability) accounts during the year must be deducted from net income. When asset (liability) accounts decrease (increase) during the year, the amount of decrease or increase must be added to net income in arriving at net cash provided by operating activities.

Additions to Net Income	Deductions from Net Income
Decrease in accounts receivable	Increase in accounts receivable
Decrease in inventory	Increase in inventory
Decrease in prepaid assets	Increase in prepaid assets
Increase in accounts payable	Decrease in accounts payable
Increase in accrued liabilities	Decrease in accrued liabilities

In addition, gains (losses) on sales of assets and securities must be deducted (added) to net income because these amounts are not operating cash flows. Although the cash received from the sale will affect cash flow, it will be reported in the investing activities section of the cash flow statement rather than in the operating activities section. Likewise, because depreciation expense does not affect cash flow, it must be added back to net income, using the indirect method.

With the indirect method, the net cash provided by the operating activities section of the cash flow statement for Robyn's Boutique would appear as follows:

Robyn's Boutique
Net Cash Flows from Operating Activities (Indirect Method)

Net income	$ 95,000
Adjustments to Reconcile Net Income to Net Cash Provided (Used) by Operating Activities	
Increase in accounts receivable	(10,000)
Increase in inventory	(10,000)
Decrease in prepaid insurance	5,000
Increase in accounts payable	10,000
Increase in payroll payable	2,000
Increase in income taxes payable	1,000
Gain on sale of vehicle	(25,000)
Loss on the sale of securities	25,000
Depreciation expense	35,000
Net cash provided (used) by operating activities	$128,000

Step 3: Compute Net Cash Provided or Used by Investing Activities Investing activities for Robyn's Boutique include cash inflows from the sale of a vehicle and the sale of long-term investments and cash outflows for purchases of land, equipment, and long-term investments. As shown on the income statement, the sale of the vehicle (shown on the balance sheet as property and equipment) generated a gain of $25,000. However, the actual cash generated from the sale was the sales price of $75,000.

The vehicle that was sold had a book value of $50,000 and originally cost $60,000, which means that accumulated depreciation was $10,000 ($60,000 − $50,000). Likewise, the sale of securities generates cash inflows equal to the amount of cash that was received ($25,000), not the loss on securities sold.

Long-term investments increased by $35,000 during the year (from $75,000 to $110,000). However, just looking at the net change in the accounts does not really tell the complete story of what happened during the year. During the year, long-term investments were purchased for $85,000 cash (increasing the asset account by $85,000), and investments with a book value of $50,000 were sold.

Equipment was purchased for $180,000. Land was also purchased for $25,000. However, the land purchase was made by paying $5,000 in cash and borrowing the remaining $20,000 from the seller.

Net Cash Flows from Investing Activities

Cash Inflows From	
Sale of note	$ 25,000
Sale of vehicle	75,000
Cash Outflows For	
Purchase of long-term investments	(85,000)
Purchase of equipment	(180,000)
Purchase of land	(5,000)
Net cash provided (used) by investing activities	$(170,000)

The information on the acquisition of land in exchange for the note payable is disclosed on a supplemental schedule of noncash investing and financing activities as follows:

Supplemental Schedule of Noncash Investing and Financing Activities

Acquisition of land in exchange for note payable	$20,000

Step 4: Compute Net Cash Provided or Used by Financing Activities Activities reported in this section include a $100,000 increase in capital stock and payment of dividends of $38,000.

Net Cash Flows from Financing Activities

Cash Inflows From	
Issuance of stock	$100,000
Cash Outflows For	
Payment of cash dividends	(38,000)
Net cash provided (used) by financing activities	$ 62,000

Step 5: Compute Net Cash Flow by Combining the Results from Operating, Investing, and Financing Activities Combining all the information contained in the three schedules of operating, investing, and financing activities and adding the supplemental schedule, we can easily prepare the completed statement of cash flows for Robyn's Boutique for the year ended December 31, 2005.

Robyn's Boutique
Statement of Cash Flows (Direct Method)
for the Year Ended December 31, 2005

Cash Flows from Operating Activities		
Cash Receipts From		
Sales	$ 690,000	
Interest	75,000	
Total cash receipts		$ 765,000
Cash Payments For		
Inventory purchases	$ 500,000	
Payroll	48,000	
Insurance	25,000	
Interest	7,000	
Rent expense	18,000	
Taxes	39,000	
Total cash payments		$(637,000)
Net cash provided (used) by operating activities		$ 128,000
Cash Flows from Investing Activities		
Sale of securities	$ 25,000	
Sale of vehicle	75,000	
Purchase of equipment	(180,000)	
Purchase of long-term investments	(85,000)	
Purchase of land	(5,000)	
Net cash provided (used) by investing activities		$(170,000)
Cash Flows from Financing Activities		
Issuance of stock	$ 100,000	
Payment of cash dividends	(38,000)	
Net cash provided (used) by financing activities		$ 62,000
Net increase in cash		$ 20,000
Cash balance 12/31/04		110,000
Cash balance 12/31/05		$ 130,000

Step 6: Report Any Significant Noncash Investing or Financing Activities in a Separate Schedule or a Footnote

Supplemental Schedule of Noncash Investing and Financing Activities	
Acquisition of land in exchange for note payable	$20,000

Objective 5

Analyze the statement of cash flows and use the information in decision making

Using the Cash Flow Statement in Decision Making

The statement of cash flows is a major source of information to investors and creditors. Many users view the statement of cash flows as the most important of the three main financial statements. Many investors and bankers focus on cash flows as opposed to net income because they are concerned about the ability of the company to meet its short-term obligations. Accrual accounting is felt to mask cash flow problems. Sophisticated users of financial statements may determine the cash flows of a business by using only the income statement and balance sheet through such details as purchases of property, plant, and equipment, and details of financing and investing activities may not be evident without the separate statement of cash flows.

Cash Flow Adequacy

Creditors are concerned about the ability of the organization to repay its debts and meet its interest payments. **Cash flow adequacy** is a measure designed to help users of the financial statements make better lending decisions. Cash flow adequacy measures the cash available to meet future debt obligations after payment of interest and taxes and any long-term expenditures. Analysts are concerned about the amount of cash available to repay debt after the company has replaced or updated its existing property, plant, and equipment. Cash flow adequacy is computed as follows:

$$\text{Cash flow adequacy} = \frac{\text{Cash flow from operating activities} - \text{Capital expenditures}}{\text{Average amount of debt maturing over the next five years}}$$

How is this measure used in decision making? In general, if the ratio is less than 1, it indicates that cash flow is insufficient to repay average annual long-term debt over the next five years. Any ratio above 1 would indicate sufficient cash flow to repay long-term debt. However, as with any ratio, the results should not be used without looking at the previous year's ratios to determine trends and also to compare with industry standards. Short-term flutuations from positive to negative are common.

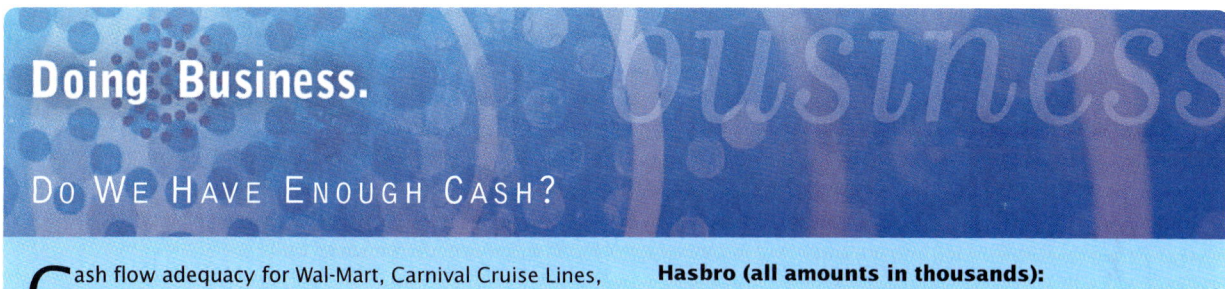

Doing Business.

DO WE HAVE ENOUGH CASH?

Cash flow adequacy for Wal-Mart, Carnival Cruise Lines, and Hasbro are reported below. The data used in the calculation comes from the cash flow statement and information from the required footnote on long-term debt.

Wal-Mart (all amounts in millions):
Cash flow adequacy (2004) =
$15,996 − 10,308 / 2,124 = 2.68

Carnival Cruise Lines (all amounts in millions):
Cash flow adequacy (2003) =
$1,933 − 2,516 / 1,147 = −.51

Hasbro (all amounts in thousands):
Cash flow adequacy (2003) =
$454,155 − 63,070 / 56,719 = 6.90

Before we jump to conclusions about Carnival's negative cash flow adequacy ratio in 2003, we should look at trends. However, Carnival's cash flow adequacy ratio in 2002 was also negative indicating potential cash flow problems over the next few years.

Some investment analysts prefer using cash flow per share as a measure of financial health as opposed to earnings per share. Among other things, "it ignores accounting tricks and shows the true health of companies."[1] The accounting profession has expressly forbidden reporting information on cash flow per share in external financial statements. The profession believes that this type of information is not an acceptable alternative to earnings per share as an indicator of company performance. As is the case in a lot of areas of accounting disclosure, there is disagreement on what is the most useful information to disclose. Individuals will use the information that best serves their needs for each specific decision situation.

---

[1] "Analysts Increasingly Favor Using Cash Flow over Reported Earnings in Stock Valuations," *Wall Street Journal*, April 11, 1999, C2.

Hitting the Bottom Line.

"What Do We Do With All of This Money?"

As of June 30, 2004, the federal government estimated that U.S. corporations (excluding farming and finance companies) had liquid assets, cash and assets that are easily convertible into cash, of $1.27 trillion—a 25 percent increase from two years earlier. Nonetheless, companies are showing tremendous reluctance to invest this cash. Illinois Tool Works Inc., a manufacturer with annual sales of $10 billion, typically generates $1 billion in cash flow each year. And, although the company has $1.8 billion and is not planning to make investments any time soon. So, what is the company doing with all this cash? According to the company's vice president of investor relations, the cash is used to repair existing machinery and replace old machinery with more productive machines. And, even though sales are improving and the company's manufacturing facilities currently have excess capacity, there is no compelling reason to make investments in productive assets. In fact, the company has decided to return much of the cash to stockholders through a stock buyback plan. Other companies are acting similarly. Microsoft announced plans in 2004 to pay cash dividends in excess of $30 billion to its stockholders and Cisco has spent almost $2 billion in its own stock buyback plan ("Despite Piles of Cash, Businesses Get Stingy 1," *Wall Street Journal*, A1, A13, October 11, 2004).

Summary of Key Concepts

- The only difference between the direct and indirect methods is in the presentation of the cash flows from operating activities. Cash flows from investing activities and cash flows from financing activities are calculated in exactly the same way. (p. 537)

- When using the indirect method, increases (decreases) in asset (liability) accounts during the year must be deducted from net income. When asset (liability) accounts decrease (increase) during the year, the amount of decrease or increase must be added to net income in arriving at net cash provided by operating activities. (p. 542)

Key Definitions

Operating activities Include acquiring and selling products in the normal course of business (p. 533)

Investing activities Include the purchase and sale of property, plant, and equipment; the purchases and sales of securities; and loans made as investments (p. 533)

Financing activities Include cash flows from selling or repurchasing capital stock, long-term borrowing, and contributions from owners (p. 533)

Cash equivalent An item that can be readily converted to a known amount of cash and has an original maturity to the investor of three months or less (p. 535)

Direct method Reports cash collected from customers and cash paid for inventory, salaries, wages, and so on (p. 536)

Indirect method Starts with net income and removes the impact of noncash items and accruals (p. 536)

Cash flow adequacy A measure of cash available to meet future debt obligations (p. 545)

Multiple Choice

1. Which of the following statements is *not* true?
    a. Even companies that appear financially healthy and profitable can become business failures owing to an inability to generate sufficient cash flow.
    b. The statement of cash flows provides information relating to the change in cash and receivable balances between two balance sheet dates.
    c. The statement of cash flows reports the impact of a firm's operating, investing, and financing activities on cash flows during the accounting period.
    d. Along with the balance sheet, income statement, and the statement of changes in stockholders' equity, the statement of cash flows is a required component of a company's external financial statements.

2. Which of the following statements regarding financial statements is *not* true?
    a. Balance sheets report the financial position of a company at a particular time.
    b. The income statement discloses items that affect how the balance sheet changed but that don't show up on the statement of cash flows.
    c. The statement of cash flows discloses items that affect how the balance sheet changed but that don't show up in the income statement.
    d. Along with the balance sheet, income statement, and the statement of changes in stockholders' equity, the statement of cash flows is a required component of a company's external financial statements.

3. Cash flows from financing activities are equal to:
    a. cash received from the sale of goods and services less cash paid for operating expenses.
    b. cash received from the sale of investments and property, plant, and equipment less cash paid for investments and purchases of property, plant, and equipment.
    c. cash received from the sale of property, plant, and equipment less cash paid for operating expenses.
    d. cash received from the sale of capital stock or the borrowing of funds less cash paid for dividends on stock or repayments of debt or reacquiring capital stock.

4. Cash flows from investing activities are equal to:
    a. cash received from the sale of goods and services less cash paid for operating expenses.
    b. cash received from the sale of investments and property, plant, and equipment less cash paid for investments and purchases of property, plant, and equipment.
    c. cash received from the sale of property, plant, and equipment less cash paid for operating expenses.
    d. cash received from the sale of capital stock or the borrowing of funds less cash paid for dividends on stock or repayments of debt or reacquiring capital stock.

5. Cash flows from operating activities are equal to:
    a. cash received from the sale of goods and services less cash paid for operating expenses.
    b. cash received from the sale of investments and property, plant, and equipment less cash paid for investments and purchases of property, plant, and equipment.
    c. cash received from the sale of property, plant, and equipment less cash paid for operating expenses.
    d. cash received from the sale of capital stock or the borrowing of funds less cash paid for dividends on stock or repayments of debt or reacquiring capital stock.

6. Which of the following statements about the direct and indirect methods of reporting cash flows is *not* true?
    a. Proponents of the direct method point to the straightforward presentation of the cash flows from operating activities.
    b. Proponents of the direct method argue that this method provides more useful information for evaluating operating efficiency.
    c. Supporters of the indirect method argue that it focuses attention on differences between the cash and accrual basis of accounting, which is very important for decision making.
    d. Supporters of the indirect method point out that if the indirect method is used, the direct schedule must still be prepared.

7. The only difference between the direct method and the indirect method statement of cash flows relates to the calculation of cash flows from:
   a. investing activities.
   b. financing activities.
   c. operating activities.
   d. all three types of activities.

8. Clario Corporation's accounts payable balance decreased during the year from $1,400,000 to $1,240,000. Which of the following statements is correct?
   a. Cash paid to suppliers was greater than the value of the goods purchased from them.
   b. Cash paid to suppliers was less than the value of the goods purchased from them.
   c. Cash paid to suppliers was equal to the value of the goods purchased from them.
   d. None of the above.

9. Carlton Company had the following information related to sales last year:

Cash sales	$125,000
Credit sales	120,000
Accounts receivable, beginning	145,000
Accounts receivable, ending	135,000

   What amount would be recorded as "cash collections from customers" on the direct statement of cash flows?
   a. $125,000
   b. $120,000
   c. $245,000
   d. $255,000

10. Cane Company had the following information related to purchases last year:

Cost of goods purchased	$250,000
Accounts payable, beginning	175,000
Accounts payable, ending	185,000

   What amount would be recorded as "cash outflows for purchases" on the direct statement of cash flows?
   a. $250,000
   b. $240,000
   c. $260,000
   d. It cannot be determined from the information provided.

11. Webster Company has no liabilities for insurance at the end of 2004 or 2005, but you note that the 12/31/04 balance sheet does include an asset called prepaid insurance with a balance of $30,000 and a 12/31/05 balance of $25,000. The $30,000 balance represents prepayments that were made in 2004 for insurance coverage provided in 2005. The $25,000 prepaid balance at the end of 2005 represents cash paid in 2005 for insurance that will be used in 2006.

   What are the cash outflows in 2005 for insurance?
   a. $25,000
   b. $30,000
   c. $50,000
   d. $55,000

12. The amount of "cost of goods purchased" to be included in the statement of cash flows prepared on the direct method should be calculated with which of the following:
    a. Beginning accounts payable − Ending accounts payable + cost of goods sold
    b. Ending accounts payable + Beginning accounts payable + cost of goods manufactured
    c. Cost of goods sold − Beginning inventory + Ending inventory
    d. None of the above

13. Cable Car Company had the following information available from its 2005 financial statements:

Cash flow from operating activities	$175,000
Cash flow from financing activities	75,000
Cash flow from investing activities	25,000
Interest	10,000
Taxes	8,000
Capital expenditure	15,000
Average amount of debt maturing over the next five years	150,000

    Cable Car Company's cash flow adequacy ratio is:
    a. 0.50
    b. 0.947
    c. 1.056
    d. 1.613

14. Capitol Company had the following information available from its 2005 financial statements:

Cash flow from operating activities	$197,000
Cash flow from financing activities	125,000
Cash flow from investing activities	75,000
Interest	15,000
Taxes	0
Capital expenditures	25,000
Average amount of debt maturing over the next five years	175,000

    Capitol Company's cash flow adequacy ratio is:
    a. 0.20
    b. 0.947
    c. 0.897
    d. 0.486

15. The cash flow adequacy ratio provides a measure of:
    a. a company's ability to pay employees and suppliers.
    b. a company's ability to pay interest and taxes due in the future.
    c. a company's ability to pay average annual long-term debt over the next five years.
    d. none of the above.

Concept Questions

16. *(Objective 1)* What is the purpose of the statement of cash flows?
17. *(Objective 1)* Discuss how the statement of cash flows differs from an income statement.
18. *(Objective 2)* What is a cash equivalent? How is it used in preparation of the statement of cash flows?

19. *(Objective 3)* How is depreciation expense handled on the statement of cash flows?
20. *(Objective 3)* Explain why, when a company uses the indirect method to prepare the operating activities section of the statement of cash flows, a decrease in a current asset is added back to net income.
21. *(Objective 1, 2 and 3)* "To prepare a statement of cash flows, all you have to do is compare the beginning and ending balances in cash on the balance sheet and compute the net inflow or outflow of cash." Do you agree with this statement? Why or why not?
22. *(Objective 1 and 4)* "The statement of cash flows is the easiest of the basic financial statements to prepare because you know the answer before you start." Do you agree with this statement? Why or why not?
23. *(Objective 3 and 5)* Which method for preparing the operating activities section of the statement of cash flows—the direct or the indirect method—provides the most information to users of the statement? Explain your answer.
24. *(Objective 5)* Can a company show an increase in cash even if reporting a net loss? Why?

Exercises

25. Each of the following is an independent situation.

✓ Total cash collections for Case 1: $350,000

Case 1	
Accounts receivable, beginning balance	$250,000
Accounts receivable, ending balance	200,000
Credit sales for the year	275,000
Cash sales for the year	160,000
Uncollectible accounts written off	135,000
Total cash collections for the year	?

Case 2	
Inventory, beginning balance	$180,000
Inventory, ending balance	155,000
Accounts payable, beginning balance	125,000
Accounts payable, ending balance	115,000
Cost of goods sold	275,000
Cash payments for inventory (assume that all purchases are on account)	?

Case 3	
Prepaid insurance, beginning balance	$ 27,000
Prepaid insurance, ending balance	30,000
Insurance expense	25,000
Cash paid for new insurance	?

Case 4	
Interest payable, beginning balance	$105,000
Interest payable, ending balance	125,000
Interest expense	300,000
Cash payments for interest	?

Case 5	
Income taxes payable, beginning balance	$ 55,000
Income taxes payable, ending balance	75,000
Income tax expense	100,000
Cash payments for income taxes	?

Required

Determine the missing amount for each individual case.

26. Vardy Toys, Inc. prepays insurance in January of each year on various policies. The beginning balance in prepaid insurance was $12,500, and the ending balance was $10,000. The income statement reports insurance expense of $65,000.

Required

Under the direct method, what amount would appear for cash paid for insurance in the operating section of the statement of cash flows?

27. Williams Media, Inc.'s comparative balance sheets included accounts receivable of $100,000 at December 31, 2004, and $125,000 at December 31, 2005. Sales of consulting services reported by Williams Media on its 2005 income statement amounted to $2,000,000.

Required

What is the amount of cash collections that Williams Media should report in the Operating section of its 2005 statement of cash flows, assuming that the direct method is used?

28. Workman-Smith Company's comparative balance sheets included inventory of $120,000 at December 31, 2004, and $110,000 at December 31, 2005. Workman-Smith's comparative balance sheets also included accounts payable of $60,000 at December 31, 2004, and $55,000 at December 31, 2005. Workman-Smith's accounts payable balances are composed solely of amounts due to suppliers for purchases on inventory. Cost of goods sold, as reported by Workman-Smith on its 2005 income statement, amounted to $850,000.

Required

What is the amount of cash payments for inventory that Workman-Smith should report in the Operating Activities section of its 2005 statement of cash flows assuming that the direct method is used?

29. The following transactions occurred for a company that uses the direct method to prepare its statement of cash flows.
  a. _____ A company purchases its own common stock in the open market and immediately retires it.
  b. _____ A company issues common stock in exchange for land.
  c. _____ A six-month bank loan is obtained.
  d. _____ Thirty-year bonds are issued.
  e. _____ A customer pays the balance in an open account.
  f. _____ Income taxes are paid.
  g. _____ Cash sales are recorded.

h. _____ Cash dividends are declared and paid.
i. _____ A creditor is given common stock in exchange for a long-term note.
j. _____ A new piece of machinery is acquired for cash.
k. _____ Stock of another company is acquired as an investment.
l. _____ Interest is paid on a bank loan.
m. _____ Workers are paid for one week's wages.

Required

For each of the above transactions, fill in the blank to indicate whether it would appear in the Operating Activities section (O), in the Investing Activities section (I), or in the Financing Activities section (F). Put an (S) in the blank if the transaction does not affect cash but is reported in a supplemental schedule of noncash activities.

30. Tiffany Company uses the indirect method to prepare the Operating Activities section of the statement of cash flows. The following activities occurred during the year at Tiffany Company.
  a. Depreciation expense _____
  b. Gain on the sale of used delivery truck _____
  c. Bad debt expense _____
  d. Increase in accounts payable _____
  e. Purchase of a new delivery truck _____
  f. Loss on retirement of bonds _____
  g. Increase in prepaid rent _____
  h. Decrease in inventory _____
  i. Increase in investments _____
  j. Amortization of patents _____

Required

For each of the above items, fill in the blank to indicate whether it would be added to net income (A), deducted from net income (D), or not reported in this section of the statement under the indirect method (NR).

31. The account balances for the noncash current assets and current liabilities of Abraham Music Company are as follows:

	December 31 2004	December 31 2005
Dividends payable	$ 50,000	$ 40,000
Retained earnings	545,000	375,000

Other information for 2005:
  a. Abraham reported $375,000 in net income for 2005.
  b. The company declared and distributed a stock dividend of $85,000 during the year.
  c. The company declared cash dividends at the end of each quarter and paid them within the first 30 days of the next quarter.

Required

  A. Determine the amount of cash dividends paid during the year for presentation in the Financing Activities section of the statement of cash flows.
  B. Should the stock dividend appear on a statement of cash flows? Explain your answer.

32. Van Buren Company acquires a piece of land by signing a $100,000 promissory note and making a $30,000 down payment.

Required

How should this transaction be reported on the statement of cash flows?

33. Van Patten, Inc. made two purchases during September. One was a $25,000 certificate of deposit that matures in 90 days. The other was a $50,000 investment in Microsoft common stock that will be held indefinitely.

✓ Cash dividends paid: $470,000

Required

How should each of these transactions be treated on the statement of cash flows?

34. Walden Book Buyers buys 5,000 shares of its own common stock at $25 per share. The company purchases the shares as Treasury stock.

Required

How is this transaction reported on the statement of cash flows?

35. Washburn Delivery Company sold a company car for $12,000. Its original cost was $35,000, and the accumulated depreciation at the time of sale was $20,000.

Required

How does the transaction to record the sale appear on a statement of cash flows prepared using the indirect method?

36. Whitney R.V.'s Inc. has invested its excess cash in the following instruments during December 2004:

Certificate of deposit, due Jan. 31, 2005	$100,000
Certificate of deposit, due May 31, 2005	150,000
Investment in City of Portland bonds, due June 30, 2005	110,000
Investment in Sheetz Inc. stock	125,000
A money market fund	225,000
90-day Treasury bills	125,000
Treasury note, due December 2005	200,000

Required

A. What should be included in cash equivalents at year-end 2004?
B. Where should the amount of cash equivalents be disclosed?

37. The following transactions occurred for a company during the year.
   a. Purchased a six-month certificate of deposit
   b. Purchased a 90-day Treasury bill
   c. Issued 10,000 shares of common stock
   d. Purchased 5,000 shares of stock of another company
   e. Purchased 10,000 shares of its own stock to be held in the treasury
   f. Invested $10,000 in a money market fund
   g. Sold 1,500 shares of stock of another company
   h. Purchased 10-year bonds of another company
   i. Issued 20-year bonds
   j. Repaid a nine-month bank note

Required

Use the following legend, indicate how each of the above transactions would be reported on the statement of cash flows.

II = inflow from investing activities

OI = outflow from investing activities

IF = inflow from financing activities

OF = outflow from financing activities

CE = classified as a cash equivalent and included with cash for purposes of preparing the statement of cash flows

Problems

38. The following account balances are for the noncash current assets and current liabilities of Wynn Bicycle Company for 2004 and 2005:

	December 31 2004	December 31 2005
Accounts receivable	$ 4,000	$ 6,000
Inventory	30,000	20,000
Office supplies	5,000	8,000
Accounts payable	10,000	7,000
Salaries and wages payable	2,500	4,000
Interest payable	1,500	2,500
Income taxes payable	5,500	2,500

In addition, the income statement for 2005 is as follows:

Sales revenue	$110,000
Cost of goods sold	85,000
Gross profit	$ 25,000
General and administrative expense	$ 9,000
Depreciation expense	2,000
Total operating expenses	$ 11,000
Income before interest and taxes	$ 14,000
Interest expense	2,000
Income before tax	$ 12,000
Income tax expense	4,800
Net income	$ 7,200

Required

A. Prepare the Operating Activities section of the statement of cash flows, using the indirect method.

B. What does the use of the direct method reveal about a company that the indirect method does not?

39. The account balances for the noncash current assets of Allen Company are as follows:

	December 31 2004	December 31 2005
Accounts receivable	$ 45,000	$ 38,000
Inventory	40,000	50,000
Prepaid insurance	21,000	17,000
Total current assets	$106,000	$105,000

Net income for 2005 is $35,000. Depreciation expense is $22,000. Assume that all sales and all purchases are on account.

Required

A. Prepare the Operating Activities section of the statement of cash flows, using the indirect method. Explain why cash flow from operating activities is more or less than the net income for the period.
B. What additional information do you need to prepare the Operating Activities section of the statement of cash flows using the direct method?
C. Explain the usefulness of each method for managerial decision making.

40. The following account balances are taken from the records of Roadhouse Corporation for the past two years:

	December 31 2005	December 31 2004
Plant and equipment	$750,000	$500,000
Accumulated depreciation	160,000	200,000
Patents	92,000	80,000
Retained earnings	825,000	675,000

Other information available for 2005 follows:
a. Net income for the year was $200,000.
b. Depreciation expense on plant and equipment was $50,000.
c. Plant and equipment with an original cost of $150,000 was sold for $64,000 (you will need to determine the book value of the assets sold).
d. Amortization expense on patents was $8,000.
e. Both new plant and equipment and patents were purchased for cash during the year.

Required

Indicate, with amounts, how all items related to these long-term assets would be reported in the 2005 statement of cash flows, including any adjustments in the Operating Activities section of the statement. Assume that Roadhouse Corp. uses the indirect method.

Group and Internet Exercises

41. Within small groups perform an Internet search to find the statement of cash flows for three companies of your choosing. Try to select companies that are in different industries so that you can compare and contrast the sources and uses of cash. Where do the companies get most of their cash? Where do the companies spend most of their cash? Are you surprised by the information you found on the statement of cash flows? Why or why not? How does each company's cash flows compare to its net income? What could explain such differences? Prepare a brief memo to compare and contrast the statements of cash flows and answer the questions above.

42. Within small groups perform an Internet search to find the statement of cash flows for a company of your choosing for each of the last four years. Your group should compare and contrast the company's statement of cash flows over these years. Where does the company get most of its cash? Where does the company spend most of its cash? How has the company's sources and uses of cash changed over the four year period? Are you surprised by the changes? What could explain these changes? Prepare a brief memo to compare and contrast the statements of cash flows and answer the questions above.

Glossary

Abnormal spoilage Spoilage resulting from unusual circumstances, including improper handling, poorly trained employees, faulty equipment, and so on (p. 69)

Absorption (full) costing A method of costing in which product costs include direct material, direct labor, and fixed and variable overhead; required for external financial statements and for income tax reporting (p. 194)

Accounting information system (AIS) A transaction processing system that captures financial data resulting from accounting transactions within a company (p. 4)

Accounts receivable turnover ratio One of the best measures of the efficiency of the collection process (p. 511)

Activities Procedures or processes that cause work to be accomplished (p. 105)

Activity-based costing (ABC) A system of allocating overhead costs that assumes that activities, not volume of production, cause overhead costs to be incurred (p.105)

Activity-based management (ABM) A system that focuses on managing activities to reduce costs and to make better decisions (p. 457)

Actual costing A product costing system in which actual overhead costs are entered directly into work in process. (p. 38)

Allocation The process of finding a logical method of assigning overhead costs to the products or services a company produces (p. 71)

Annuity A series of cash flows of equal amount paid or received at regular intervals (p. 273)

Appraisal (detection) costs Costs incurred to inspect finished products or products in the process of production (p. 418)

Asset turnover The measure of activity used in the ROI calculation; it measures the sales that are generated for a given level of assets (p. 382)

Backflush costing A costing system in which manufacturing costs are directly flushed into cost of goods sold instead of flowing through inventory (p. 81)

Balanced-scorecard approach Uses a set of financial and nonfinancial measures that relate to the critical success factors of any organization (p. 414)

Batch-level Costs that are incurred each time a batch of goods is produced. (p. 105)

Bottlenecks Production-process steps that limit throughput or the number of finished products that go through the production process (p. 226)

Break-even point The level of sales at which contribution margin just covers fixed costs and net income is equal to zero (p. 185)

Budget variance The difference between the amount of fixed overhead actually incurred and the flexible budget amount; also known as the spending variance (p. 350)

Budgets Plans dealing with the acquisition and use of resources over a specified time period (p. 296)

Capital investment decisions Long term decisions involving the purchase (or lease) of new machinery and equipment and the acquisition or expansion of facilities used in a business (p. 248)

Cash disbursements budget Used to project the amount of cash to be disbursed during the budget period (p. 309)

Cash equivalent An item that can be readily converted to a known amount of cash and has an original maturity to the investor of three months or less (p. 535)

Cash flow adequacy A measure of cash available to meet future debt obligations (p. 545)

Cash flow from operations to capital expenditures ratio A measure of a company's ability to use cash flow from operations to finance the acquisition of property, plant and equipment (p. 515)

Cash receipts budget Used to project the amount of cash expected to be received from sales and cash collections from customers (p. 309)

Cash-to-cash operating cycle ratio A measure of the length of time between the purchase of inventory and the eventual collection of cash from sales (p. 513)

Common costs Indirect costs that are incurred to benefit more than one segment and cannot be directly traced to a particular segment or allocated in a reasonable manner (p. 378)

Common-size financial statements Statements in which all items have been restated as a percentage of a selected item on the statements (p. 505)

Compound interest Interest on the invested amount plus interest on previous interest earned but not withdrawn (p. 266)

Constraint A restriction that occurs when the capacity to manufacture a product or provide a service is limited in some manner (p. 224)

Contribution margin per unit The sales price per unit of product less all variable costs to produce and to sell the unit of product; used to calculate the change in contribution margin resulting from a change in unit sales (p. 177)

Contribution margin ratio The contribution margin divided by sales; used to calculate the change in contribution margin resulting from a dollar change in sales (p. 179)

Control Involves ensuring that the objectives and goals developed by the organization are being attained; often involves a comparison of budgets to actual performance and the use of budgets for performance evaluation purposes (p. 296). Involves the motivation and monitoring of employees and the evaluation of people and other resources used in the operations of the organization (p. 338)

Controlling activities The motivation and monitoring of employees and the evaluation of people and other resources used in the operations of the organization (p.9)

Corporate governance Systems used by a company to promote "corporate fairness, transparency, and accountability." (p. 484)

Cost behavior How costs react to changes in production volume or other levels of activity (p. 142)

Cost center An organizational segment, or division, in which the manager has control over costs but not over revenue or investment decisions (p. 377)

Cost drivers Factors that cause, or drive, the incurrence of costs (p. 72)

Cost of capital What the firm would have to pay to borrow (issue bonds) or raise funds through equity (issue stock) in the financial marketplace (p. 250)

Cost leadership strategy A strategy used when a company's goal is to provide the same or better value to customers at a lower cost than its competitors. (p. 446)

Cost pools Groups of overhead costs that are similar; used to simplify the task of assigning costs to products using ABC costing (p. 72)

Cost-plus pricing A method of pricing in which managers determine the cost of the product or service and then add a markup percentage to that cost to arrive at the sales price (p. 449)

Cost-volume-profit (CVP) analysis A tool that focuses on the relationship between a company's profits and (1) the prices of products or services, (2) the volume of products or services, (3) the per unit variable costs, (4) the total fixed costs, and (5) the mix of products or services produced (p. 176)

Current ratio A measure of an entity's liquidity; also known as working capital ratio (p. 508)

Customer relationship management (CRM) Designed to bring a company closer to its customers in order to serve them better (p. 456)

Customer response time The time it takes to deliver the product or service after the order is received (p. 426)

Data Reports, such as financial statements, customer lists, inventory records, and so on (p. 4)

Data mining A process of searching and extracting information from data (p. 5)

Data warehouses Central depositories for electronic data (p. 5)

Decentralized organization An organization in which decision-making authority is spread throughout the organization (p. 374)

Decision making The process of identifying alternative courses of action and selecting an appropriate alternative in a given decision-making situation (p. 12)

Dependent variable The variable in regression analysis that is dependent on changes in the independent variable (p. 151)

Depreciation tax shield The tax savings from depreciation. (p. 257)

Debt service coverage ratio A solvency measure focusing on the amount of capital provided by creditors (p. 513)

Debt to equity ratio A measure of cash available to meet future debt obligations (p. 545)

Direct costs Costs that are directly attachd to the finished product and can be conveniently traced to the product. (p. 31)

Direct labor Labor that can easily and conveniently be traced to particular products (p. 32)

Direct labor budget Used to project the dollar amount of direct labor cost needed for production (p. 305)

Direct materials Materials that can easily and conveniently be traced to the final product (p. 32)

Direct method Reports cash collected from customers and cash paid for inventory, salaries, wages, and so on (p. 536)

Discount rate Used as a hurdle rate, or minimum rate of return in calculations of the time value of money; adjusted to reflect risk and uncertainty (p. 250)

Diverse Products Products that consume resources in different proportions (p. 115)

Earnings per share (EPS) A key measure of return to investors on all assets invested in the company (p. 517)

Economic value added (EVA) A contemporary measure of performance focusing on shareholder wealth (p. 386)

Elastic demand A price increase (decrease) of a certain percent lowers (raises) the quantity demanded by more than that percentage. (p. 447)

Electronic data interchange (EDI) The electronic transmission of data, such as purchase orders and invoices (p. 7)

Enterprise resource planning (ERP) systems Systems used to collect, organize, report, and distribute organizational data and transform that data into critical information and knowledge (p. 4). Used to collect, organize, report, and distribute data from all aspects of a company's business and to transform that data into useful knowledge (p. 422)

Environmental costs The costs of producing, marketing, and delivering products and services- including any postpurchase costs caused by the use and disposal of products- that may have an adeverse affect on the environment. (p. 424)

Equivalent units The number of finished units that can be made from the materials, labor, and overhead included in partially completed units (p. 81)

Ethics programs Programs established to help maintain an ethical business environment. Common elements of ethics programs include written codes of ethics, employee hotlines, ethics call centers, ethics training, processes to register anonymous complaints about wrongdoing, and ethics offices. (p. 487)

External failure costs Costs incurred when a defective product is delivered to a customer (p. 419)

External linkages Relationships between a company's own value-chain activities and those of its suppliers and customers. (p. 454)

External Users Stockholders, potential investors, creditors, government taxing agencies and regulators, suppliers and customers. (p. 8)

Facility-level costs Costs that are incurred to sustain the overall manufacturing process. (p. 105)

Finance function It is responsible for managing the financial resources of the organization. (p. 10)

Financial Accounting The area of accoutning primarily concerned with the preparation of general use financial statements for use by creditors, investors and other users outside of the company (external users). (p.8)

Financing activities Include cash flows from selling or repurchasing capital stock, long-term borrowing, and contributions from owners (p. 533)

Finished-goods inventory Inventory of finished product waiting for sale and shipment to customers (p. 29)

Fixed costs Costs that remain the same in total when production volume increases or decreases but vary per unit (p. 142)

Flexible budget variance The difference between the flexible budget operating income and actual operating income (p. 342)

Flexible budgets Take differences in spending owing to volume differences out of the analysis by budgeting for labor (and other costs) based on the *actual* number of units produced (p. 319)

Focusing Strategy A strategy involving selecting or emphasizing a market or customer segment in which to compete. (p. 446)

Fraud A *knowingly* false representation of a material fact made by one party with the intent to deceive and induce another party to justifiably rely on the fact to his or her detriment (p. 473)

Fraud triangle Three forces typically contribute to fraudulent behavior: situational pressures and incentives, opportunities, and personal characteristics and attitudes. (p. 476)

Fraudulent financial reporting The intentional misstatement of *or* omission of material, very significant, informaiton from a company's financial statements. (p. 474)

Fringe benefits Payroll costs in addition to the basic hourly wage (p. 70)

Gross profit The difference between sales and cost of goods sold (p. 176)

Horizontal analysis When financial statements are analyzed over time (p. 501)

Human resource function It is concerned with the utilization of human resources to help an organization reach its goals. (p. 10)

Ideal standard A standard that is attained only when near-perfect conditions are present (p. 339)

Idle time Worker time that is not used in the production of the finished product (p. 70)

Independent variable The variable in regression analysis that drives changes in the dependent variable (p. 151)

Indirect costs Costs that are attached to the product but cannot be conveniently traced to each separate product. (p. 31)

Indirect labor Labor used in the production of products but not directly traceable to the specific product (p. 33)

Indirect materials Materials used in the production of products but not directly traceable to the specific product (p. 33)

Indirect method Starts with net income and removes the impact of noncash items and accruals (p. 536)

Inelastic demand Demand is not greatly affected by an increase or decrease in price. (p. 447)

Information Data that have been organized, processed, and summarized (p. 4)

Internal control The policies and procedures that provide reasonable assurance that a company's goals and objectives will be achieved. (p. 479)

Internal failure costs Costs incurred once the product is produced and then determined to be defective (p. 418)

Internal linkages Relationships among activities that are performed within a company's portion of the value chain. (p. 454)

Internal rate of return (IRR) The actual yield, or return, earned by an investment (p. 251)

Internal Users Includes individual employees as well as teams, departments, regions, and top management of an organization. Internal users are often just referred to as managers. (p. 9)

Inventory turnover ratio A measure of the number of times the value of inventory is sold in one year (p. 511)

Investing activities Include the purchase and sale of property, plant, and equipment; the purchases and sales of securities; and loans made as investments (p. 533)

Investment center An organizational segment, or division, in which the manager has control over costs, revenue, and investment decisions (p. 377)

ISO 9000 A set of guidelines for quality management focusing on the design, production, inspection, testing, installing, and servicing of products, processes, and services (p. 417)

Job costing A costing system that accumulates, tracks, and assigns costs for each job produced by a company (p. 66)

Just-in-time (JIT) production systems The philosophy of having raw materials arrive just in time to be used in production and for finished-goods inventory to be completed just in time to be shipped to customers (p. 29)

Kaizen A system of improvement based on a series of gradual and often small improvements (p. 416)

Kiting The transfer of money from one bank account to another near the end of a reporting period with the intention of overstating the cash balance. (p. 476)

Knowledge Information that is shared and exploited so that it adds value to an organization (p. 4)

Knowledge warehouses Used to store and provide access to a wide variety of qualitative data (p. 6)

Lapping A scheme accomplished by stealing, and not recording, the cash received from one customer and covering the shortage with cash received from another customer. (p. 476)

Life-cycle cost The costs accumulated over the entire life cycle of a product (p. 449)

Life-cycle costing Includes all the costs incurred throughout a product's life, not just in the manufacturing and selling of the product (p. 34)

Liquidity A measure of the ability of a company to meet its immediate financial obligations (p. 506)

Make-or-buy decision A short-term decision to outsource labor or purchase components used in manufacturing from another company rather than to provide services or to produce components internally. (p. 219)

Management by exception The process of taking action only when actual results deviate significantly from planned (p. 338)

Managerial Accounting The area of accounting primarily concerned with generating financial and nonfinancial information for use by managers in their decision-making roles within a company (internal users). (p. 8)

Manufacturing companies Companies that purchase raw materials from other companies and transform those raw materials into a finished product (p. 28)

Manufacturing costs Costs incurred in the factory or plant to produce a product; typically consists of three elements: direct materials, direct labor, and manufacturing overhead (p. 31)

Manufacturing overhead Indirect material and labor and any other expenses related to the production of products but not directly traceable to the specific product (p. 33)

Manufacturing-cycle efficiency (MCE) The value-added time in the production process divided by the throughput, or cycle, time (p. 427)

Manufacturing-cycle time The total time a product is in production, which includes process time, inspection time, wait time, and move time; cycle time will include both value-added and non-value-added time (p. 427)

Manufacturing-overhead budget Used to project the dollar amount of manufacturing overhead needed for production (p. 305)

Margin For each sales dollar, the percentage that is recognized as net profit (p. 382)

Marketing function It is involved with the process of developing, pricing, promoting and distributing goods and services sold to customers. (p. 10)

Mater budget Consists of an interrelated set of budgets prepared by a business. (p. 298)

Material price variance The difference between the actual price and the standard price times the actual volume purchased (p. 345)

Maternal purchases budget Used to project the dollar amount of raw material purchased for production. (p. 303)

Merchandising companies Companies that sell products that someone else has manfactured (p. 28)

Misappropriation of assets The theft of a company's assets. (p. 476)

Mixed costs Costs that include both a fixed and a variable component, making it difficult to predict the behavior of a mixed cost as production changes unless the cost is first separated into its fixed and variable components (p. 148)

Net operating income Net income from operations before interest and taxes (p. 383)

Net present value (NPV) A technique for considering the time value of money whereby the present value of all cash inflows associated with a project is compared with the present value of all cash outflows (p. 250)

Nonmanufacturing costs Costs that include selling and administrative costs (p. 33)

Non-value-added activities Activities that can be eliminated without affecting the quality or performance of a product (p. 458.)

Normal costing A product costing system in which estimated or predetermined overhead rates are used to appl overhead to work in process. (p.38)&(p. 76)

Normal spoilage Spoilage resulting from the regular operations of the production process (p. 69)

Operational activities Involve the day-to-day activities undertaken as a product is manufactured or a service is provided. (p. 454)

Operational planning Teh development of short-term objectives and goals (typically achieved in less than one year) (p. 9)

Operating Involves day-to-day decision making by managers, which is often facilitated by budgeting (p. 296)

Operating activities The day-to-day operations of a business (p. 9). Include acquiring and selling products in the normal course of business (p. 533)

Operating assets Typically include cash, accounts receivable, inventory, and property, plant, and equipment needed to operate a business (p. 383)

Operating budgets Used to plan for the short term (typically one year or less) (p. 301)

Operating leverage The contribution margin divided by net income; used as an indicator of how sensitive net income is to the change in sales (p. 192)

Operations and production function It produces the products of services that an organization sells to its customers. (p. 10)

Operations costing A hybrid of job and process costing; used by companies that make products in batches (p. 67)

Opportunity costs The benefits forgone by choosing one alternative over another (p. 14)

Organizational activities Involve decisions concerning how a company is organized and how decisions are made within the company. (p. 453)

Overapplied overhead The amount of applied overhead in excess of actual overhead (p. 77)

Overtime premiums An additional amount added to the basic hourly wage owing to overtime worked by the workers (p. 71)

Payback period The length of time needed for a long-term project to recapture, or pay back, the initial investment (p. 263)

Penetration pricing The pricing of a new product at a low initial price to build market share quickly or to establish a customer base. (p. 451)

Performance report Provides key financial and nonfinancial measures of performance for a particular segment (p. 377)

Period costs Costs that are expensed in the period incurred; attached to the period as opposed to the product (p. 34)

Planning The development of both the short-term (operational) and the long-term (strategic) objectives and goals of an organization and an identification of the resources needed to achieve them (p. 9). The cornerstone of good management; involves developing objectives and goals for the organization, as well as the actual preparation of budgets (p. 296)

Practical standard A standard that should be attained under normal, efficient operating conditions (p. 339)

Predatory pricing Setting prices below cost for the purpose of injuring competitors and eliminating competition. (p. 451)

Predetermined overhead rates Used to apply overhead to products; calculated by dividing the estimated overhead for a cost pool by the estimated units of the cost driver (p. 76)

Preference decisions Decisions that involve choosing between alternatives (p. 253)

Present value (PV) The amount of future cash flows discounted to their equivalent worth today (p. 265)

Prevention costs Costs incurred to prevent product failures from occurring, typically related to design and engineering (p. 418)

Price discrimination Charging different prices to different customers with no justification based on the competitive situation or identifiable cost savings. (p. 451)

Price/earnings (P/E) ratio A measure of current price of a company's stock in comparision to its earning. Theoretically, the P/E ratio tell us something about how investors think a company's stock will perform in the future compared to other companies (p. 517)

Price gouging Setting prices higher for unusual situations. (p. 452)

Price skimming Charging a higher price when a product or service is first introduced. (p. 451)

Price Vanance the difference between the actual price and the standard prices times the actual volume purchased (p. 345)

Pro forma financial statements Budgeted financial statements that are sometimes used for internal planning purposes but more often are used by external users (p. 308)

Process costing A costing system that accumulates and tracks costs for each process performed and then assigns those costs equally to each unit produced (p. 65)

Product costs Costs that attach to the products as they go through the manufacturing process; also called inventoriable costs (pg. 33)&(p. 43)

Product differentiation strategy A strategy used when a company's goal is to distinguish the product or service offered by a company from those of its competitors. (p. 446)

Product-level costs Costs that are incurred as needed to support the production of each tpe of product. (p. 105)

Product life cycle The time a product exists through the entire value chain. (p.301)

Production budget Used to forecast how many units of product to produce in order to meet the sales projections (p. 297)

Productivity A measure of the relationship between outputs and inputs (p. 425)

Profit center An organizational segment, or division, in which the manager has control over both costs and revenue but not investment decisions (p. 377)

Profitability index (PI) Calculated by dividing the present value of cash inflows by the initial investment (p. 255)

Qualitative Deals with nonnumerical attributes or characteristics (p. 13)

Quality Usually defined as meeting or exceeding customers' expectations (p. 416)

Quantitative Can be expressed in terms of dollars or other quantities (units, pounds, etc.) (p. 13)

Quick ratio A strict test of a company's ability to pay its current debts with highly liquid current assets (p.509)

R square (R^2) A measure of goodness of fit (how well the regression line "fits" the data) (p. 154)

Raw materials inventory Inventory of materials needed in the production process but not yet moved to the production area (p. 29)

Regression analysis The procedure that uses statistical methods (least squares regression) to fit a cost line (called a regression line) through a number of data points (p. 151)

Relevant costs Those costs that differ between alternatives (p. 14)

Relevant range The normal range of production that can be expected for a particular product and company (p. 145)

Residual income The amount of income earned in excess of a predetermined minimum level of return on assets (p. 385)

Return on common assets A measure of return to investors on all assets invested in the company (p. 515)

Return on common stockholders' equity (ROCSE) A measure of return to common stockholders as a percentage of stockholders' equity (p. 516)

Resource utilization decision A decision requiring an analysis of how best to use a resource that is available in limited supply (p. 224)

Responsibility accounting An accounting system that assigns responsibility to a manager for those areas that are under that manager's control (p. 376)

Restricted stock A form of management compensation in which employees receive shares of stock with restrictions such as requirements to stay with the company for a set period of time of requirements to meet established performance measures. (p. 392)

Return on investment (ROI) Measures the rate of return generated by an investment center's assets (p. 382)

Revenue center An organizational segment, or division, in which the manager has control over revenue but not costs or investment decisions (p. 377)

Risk The likelihood that an option chosen in a decision situation will yield unsatisfactory results (p. 16)

Sales budget Used in planning the cash needs for manufacturing, merchandising, and service companies (p. 300)

Sales forecast Combines with the sales budget to form the starting points in the preparation of production budgets for manufacturing companies, purchases budgets for merchandising companies, and labor budgets for service companies (p. 300)

Sales price variance Computed by comparing the actual sales price to the flexible budget sales price times the actual sales volume (p. 343)

Sales volume variance The difference between the actual sales volume and the budgeted sales volume times the budgeted contribution margin (p. 341)

Screening decisions Decisions about whether an investment meets a predetermined company standard (p. 253)

Segment costs All costs attributable to a particular segment of an organization but only those costs that are actually caused by the segment (p. 378)

Segment margin The profit margin of a particular segment of an organization, typically the best measure of long-run profitability (p. 380)

Segmented income statements Calculate income for each major segment of an organization in addition to the company as a whole (p. 378)

Sensitivity analysis The process of changing the values of key variables to determine how sensitive decisions are to those changes (p. 15). Used to highlight decisions that may be affected by changes in expected cash flows (p. 262)

Service companies Companies that do not sell tangible product as their primary business. (p. 28)

Simple interest Interest on the invested amount only (p. 265)

Special-order decisions Short-run pricing decisions in which management must decide what sales price is appropriate when customers place orders that are different from those placed in the regular course of business (larger quantity, one-time sale to a foreign customer, etc.) (p. 216)

Standard cost A budget for a single unit of product or service (p. 338)

Standard price The budgeted price of the material, labor, or overhead for each unit (p. 338)

Standard quantity The budgeted amount of material, labor, or overhead for each product (p. 338)

Static budgets Budgets that are set at the beginning of the period and remain constant throughout the budget period (p. 317)

Step costs Costs that vary with activity in steps and may look like and be treated as either variable costs or fixed costs; step costs are technically not fixed costs but may be treated as such if they remain constant within a relevant range of production (p. 147)

Stock option The right to buy a share of stock at a set price (called the option price or strike price) at some point in the future. (p. 391)

Strategic business unit (SBU) Another term for investment center (p. 377)

Strategic planning Addresses long-term questions of how an organization positions and distinguishes itself from competitors. (p. 9)

Strategy The set of policies, procedures and approaches to business that relate to the long-term success of a business. (p. 446)

Structural activites Involve fundamental decisions concerning a company's size and scope of operations. (p. 453)

Summary cash budget Consists of three sections: (1) cash flows from operating activities, (2) cash flows from investing activities, and (3) cash flows from financing activities; these three sections are the same as used in the cash flow statement prepared under generally accepted accounting principles (GAAP) (p. 311)

Sunk costs Costs that have already been incurred (p. 14)

Supply-chain management Includes a variety of activities centered on making the purchase of materials and inventory more efficient and less costly (p. 454)

Target pricing A pricing method used when a price is preset by market conditions or when a company wishes to set a price in order to capture a predetermined market share or to meet other marketing goals (p. 448)

Task analysis A method of setting standards that also examines the production process in detail to determine what it should cost to produce a product (p. 339)

Theory of constraints A management tool for dealing with constraints; identifies and focuses on bottlenecks in the production process (p. 226)

Throughput The amount of product produced in a given amount of time, such as a day, week, or month (p. 427)

Time and material pricing A pricing method often used in service industries, in which labor is the primary cost incurred (p. 451)

Time value of money The concept that a dollar received (paid) t0day is worth more (less) than a dollar received (paid) in the future (p. 248)

Transfer price The price charged by one segment, or division, to another segment, or division, within the same organization for the transfer of goods or services (p. 393)

Trend analysis Horizontal analysis of multiple years of data (p. 503)

Underapplied overhead The amount of actual overhead in excess of applied overhead (p. 77)

Unit-level costs costs that are incurred each time a unit is produced (p. 104)

Usage variance The difference between the actual quantity and the standard quantity times the standard price (p. 345)

Value chain The set of activities that increase the value of an organization's products and services: research and development, design, production, marketing, distribution, and customer service activities (p. 34) & (p. 452)

Value chain analysis Involves identifying and taking advantage of internal and external linkages with the objective of strengthening a firm's strategic position. (p. 454)

Value pricing A pricing method that bases the price of services on the perceived or actual value of the service provided to a customer (p. 453)

Variable costs Costs that stay the same per unit but change in total as production volume increases or decreases (p. 142)

Variable (direct) costing A method of costing in which product costs include direct material, direct labor, and variable overhead; fixed overhead is treated as a period cost; consistent with CVP's focus on cost behavior (p. 194)

Variance analysis Allows managers to see whether sales, production, and manufacturing costs are higher or lower than planned and, more important, *why* actual sales, production, and costs differ from budget (p. 338)

Vertical integration Accomplished when a company is involved in multiple steps of the value chain (p. 219)

Volume variance The difference between the flexible budget and the fixed overhead applied to a product (p. 350)

Working capital The excess of current assets over current liabilities, which is a measure of an entity's liquidity (p. 506)

Work-in-process inventory Inventory of unfinished product (in other words, what is left in the factory at the end of the period) (p. 29)

Zero-based budgeting Requires managers to build budgets from the ground up each year (p. 296)

Company Index

A
Ace Putters Inc., 221-22, 227
Adelphia, 472
Amazon, 298
Amber Valley Ski Resort, 259–64
American Airlines, 151
American Red Cross, 4, 8
Apple Computer, 446
Arthur Andersen, 472–73

B
Bassett Furniture, 28, 45–46
Ben & Jerry's, 9, 76
Big Al's Pizza Emporium, 383–86, 421, 424–25, 428–29
Birdie-Maker Golf Inc., 220-22, 225–27, 448
Boston Market, 532
Bristol-Myers Squibb, 475
Bud and Rose's Flower Shop, 265

C
Camelback Mountain Community Bank, 378-79
Carnival Cruise Lines, 545
Charles Custom Furniture, 66–72, 76–78
Cheri's Chips, 177
Cheryl's Bike Shop, 42
Chrysler, 184, 306
Clayton Herring Tire Co., 223–24
Coca-Cola, 355, 419
Corinne's Country Rockers, 340–53

D
Daimler Chrysler, 220, 378, 426
Dell Computer,, 30, 32, 183, 446
DuPont, 382

E
Enron, 391, 472–74

F
Fed Ex, 4
Filene's Basement, 532
Ford Motor Company, 4, 32, 143, 184, 220, 248, 300, 374, 426, 446

G
Garcia And Buffet CPAs, 379–80, 421, 428–29
General Electric, 248

General Motors, 9, 184, 220, 300, 375–76, 426, 487f
Georgia-Pacific, 424
Gillette, 198

H
Happy Daze Game Company, 179–82, 185–91
Harbourside Hospital, 252–53
Hasbrow, 533–34, 545
HealthSouth, 472
Hershey Foods, 6, 479
Honda, 426

I
IBM, 219, 446
Internal Revenue Service, 4

J
J.C. Penney, 300, 455
Johnson & Johnson, 488

K
KenCor Pizza Emporium, 145–56

L
Levi Strauss & Co., 488
Liz Claiborne, 456
L.L. Bean, 454
Luen Thai Holdings, Ltd., 456

M
Marks & Spencer, 458
McKesson-Robbins, 475
Microsoft, 389
Mitsubishi, 419, 422
Montgomery Ward, 532

N
Nabisco, 7
Nike, 15, 453
Nissan, 426
Northern Lights Custom Cabinets, 36–41, 421, 424–25, 428–29, 449
Northrop Grumman, 450

P
Parker Brothers, 453

R
Ralph Lauren, 456
Reebok, 453
Robyn's Boutique, 501–17
Royal Dutch/ Shell, 16

S
Sara Lee, 446
Southwest Airlines, 446
Sunset Airlines, 216–18
Superior Industries International, 220

T
Target, 28
Tina's Fine Juices, 301–8, 310–14, 319
TopSail Construction, 108–114, 450
Toyota, 28, 417, 426
Tyco, 472, 474

U
United Parcel Service, 340
United Press International, 532

W
Wal-Mart, 4, 7, 28, 45–46, 223, 248, 300, 446, 545
Waste Management, 474
Winn-Dixie, 223
WorldCom, 44, 472

Z
ZIA Motors, 183–84

Subject Index

A

ABC. *See* activity-based costing
abnormal spoilage, 69–70. *See also* spoilage
absorption costing, 194–97, 312–13
accounting,
    defition of, 3
    equation, 537–38
    financial, 4–8
    information, 4–5, 8–12
    net income, 248
    primary role of, 3
accounts receivable ratio, 511
action-based costing, 448
activities, 105
activity-based, costing, 105
    to allocate costs, 114
    to allocate overhead costs, 113
    and cost flows, 108
    its effect on flexible budgets, 319
    flexible overhead budget with
        variance analysis, 352
    and important benefit of, 458
    and Just-In-Time, 106–7
    for nonmanufacturing activities, 114
    and relevant-cost analysis, 229
    for service providers, 114
    standard activity rate, 351
    systems, 115–116
    traceable or common costs, 381
    and traditional overhead allocation, 108
    as used by TopSail Construction,
        110–12
    See cross subsidies
activity-based management,
    value chain, 457–59
        benefits of, 459
        cost dimension, 457
        goal of, 458
        non-value added activity, 458
        process dimension, 457
        value-added activities, 458
actual costing, 38
AIS. *See* accounting information system
allocation, 71
application of overhead, 76
art.com, 107
asset turnover, 382–83
automating production processes, 262–63
automation, 143

B

backflush costing, 81–82
balance sheets, 44–45
basic process costing, 80–81
batch-level costs, 105
bottlenecks, 226–27
break-even,
    analysis, 185
        calculations with multiple products,
            186–87
        formula for a company with
            multiple products, 187
        point, 185, 187, 193
    calculations using activity-based
        costing, 188–89
    conventional analysis and activity-based costing, 189
    equation when using activity-based costing, 188
    formulas, 190
budget,
    flexible, 341
    static, 341
budgeted,
    balance sheet, 314
    contribution margin per unit, 341
    financial statements. *See* pro forma
        financial statements
budgeting,
    advantages of, 298
    as a control tool, 338
    defined, 296
    flexible, 337
    focus of, 295
    in an international environment, 316–17
    main focus of for service companies, 315
    process, 298
    purpose of, 295
    for sales, 300
    zero-based, 296
budgets,
    cash, 308–311
    development process, 296
    direct labor, 305
    financial and nonfinancial, 316
    managers' use of, 296–97
    manufacturing overhead, 305–06
    Master, The, 298–99
    material purchases, 303–4, 306
    of manufacturing companies, 315
    of merchandising companies, 315–16
    selling and administrative, 308
    of service companies, 315–16
    static vs. flexible, 317–19
    to be successful, 296
    summary cash, 311–12
    time, 317

business environments, 4
    elements of internal control, 479–82
        control activities, 481–82
        control environment, 480–81
        corporate governance, 484–85
        information technology, 482–84
        need for ethics, 486
        risk assessment, 481
capital investment decisions, 247–54
    analysis of costs and benefits, 248–54
    the effect of raising the discount rate, 261
    the impact of the new manufacturing environment, 262–63
    impact of taxes on, 256–61
    impact of uncertainty, 261–62
    internal rate of return, 251–54, 260–61
    net present values, 249–54, 260–61
    payback method vs. cash flow methods, 263
    preference decisions, 253–56
    problems addressed in, 254
    screening decisions, 253–56
capital structure, 513
cash,
    equivalent, 535
    flow, 32
    adequacy, 545
    and budgets, 308
    discounted analysis, 249–53
    the effect of raising the discount rate on, 261
    focus on, 248–49
        from operations to capital
            expenditures ratio, 514–515
        from operations to current-liabilities
            ratio, 509–10
    from operating, investing, and
        financing activities, 311–12
    on financial statements, 504–05
    payback calculations with uneven, 264
    and the payback method, 265
    problem of uneven, 252–53
        profitability index, 255
    and sensitivity analysis, 262
    and small businesses, 309
    and small business profitability, 264
        taxes as a source of, 256–57
        vs. earnings per share, 547
Certified Public Accounting firms, 381
closely held companies, 8
codes of ethics, 487
    and company performances, 486
    manners in addressing violations, 489
    purposes of, 487
    three types of, 487
        codes of conduct, 487
        corporate philosophy statement, 487
        mission statements, 487
coefficient of determination, 154

Committee on Sponsoring Organizations, The, 480
common-size,
  balance sheets, 505–06
  comparative income statements, 507t–08
  financial statements, 505–06
competition, 339
constraints, 226–27
continuous improvement, 416–17
contribution margin, 184–87, 225–26
  definition and use of, 380
  income statement, 176–77, 179
  its uses, 179–80
  per unit, 177–178
  per unit in the break-even formula, 188
  ratio, 179
control, 538–39
controlling activities, 9
correlation coefficient, 154
COSO. *See* Committee of Sponsoring Organizations
cost,
  behavior, 142
    and relevant costs, 156–57
    as useful for decision-making, 147
  drivers, 156
    for activities, 106
    choice of, 72
    equation, 145
    for overhead, 72
    single, 73
  flows,
    a comparison of, 82
    in a JIT environment, 41
    in job costing vs. process costing, 80–81
    in a traditional environment, 35
    See also statement of cash flows
  information, 66
costing, 28
cost of capital, 250–54
cost-of-goods-sold model, 36–41
cost pools, 72
costs,
  and decision-making, 214–29
  direct vs. indirect, 31
  and long-term decisions, 247–53
  of goods sold, 449
  life-cycle, 34–35
  management and strategy, 452–57
  manufacturing, 33
  manufacturing vs. nonmanufacturing, 31–34
  and prices, 450
  selling and administrative, 449
  standard, 337–39
  structure, 192–94
  uses as bases, 450
  variable, 449
  See also estimates
customer response time, 426–27
cost-volume-profit analysis, 176, 183–184
  assumptions of, 191–192
  and decisions to increase net income using, 180–182
  and net income, 189–194
  to increase profit, 183

to make decisions on price and income, 182
  vs. activity-based costing, 188
CPA firms. *See* Certified Public Accounting firms
cross subsidies, 113
customer-relationship management, 456–57
CVP. *See* cost-volume-profit analysis

D

data, 4
  mining, 5–6
  software, 6
  techniques, 6
  warehouses, 5
decentralization, 374–75, 389
decision-making, 11–16
  control, 338
  in decentralized organizations, 373–96
  defined, 12
  and ethics, 15–16
  a model, 354–55
  objectives of, 13
  relevant factors and costs, 14–15
  and risk, 15
decisions. *See* capital investment decisions
  make-or-buy, 218–23
  outsourcing, 218–20
  resource utilization, 224–26
  to drop a product or service, 223–24
  to sell or process further, 227–28
defects, 417, 420–22
dependant variable, 151
depreciation tax shield, 258
direct,
  costing. *See* variable costing
  labor, 32–33, 68
    as a variable cost, 132–43
    compared to overhead, 70–71
    costs of, 70
    costs in heavily automated manufacturing environments, 74–75
    examples of, 68
    historical development of, 104
    measuring and tracking, 70
    under basic process costing, 80
    See also variable costs
  materials, 33
    compared to overhead, 71
    costs, 33
    measuring and tracking, 66–68
    under basic process costing, 86
    See also variable costs
dot.coms, 107

E

earnings per share, 517
economic value added, 386–88, 424
EDI. *See* electronic data interchange
electronic data interchange, 7, 455
employee empowerment, 417
energy efficiency of household appliances, 422
enterprise resource planning, 296
  in decentralized organizations, 375
  facilitates customer-relationship management, 456

and supply chain management, 455
  systems, 4, 6–7
environmental costing, 423–24
EPS. *See* earnings per share
equivalent units, 81
ERP. *See* enterprise resource planning
estimates, 75–79
ethics programs, 487
EVA. *See* economic-value added
evaluation of managers, 374–78
exchange rates, 318, 389

F

facility-level costs, 105
finance, 10
financial,
  accounting, 8
  statement analysis,
    defined, 499
    horizontal analysis, 501–05
    impact of inflation on, 501
    limitations of, 501
    purpose of, 500
    trend analysis, 503
    vertical analysis, 505–07
  statements, 532
finished-goods inventory, 29
First-In, First-Out, 81–83
fixed,
  costs, 142, 156–57
    compared to mixed cost, 149
    and gross profits, 176
    a large proportion relative to variable costs, 192
    and net income, 184
    manufacturing overhead, 197
  overhead, 194–195
flexible budgets, 340–41
  the efficient use of the cost driver in, 348
  for variable overhead, 344
fraud, 472
  causes of: the fraud triangle, 477
  defined, 473
    opportunities, 477
    personal characteristics and attitudes, 478
    situational pressures and incentives, 477
  three strategies for combatting, 478–79
    corporate governance, 484
    internal controls, 479
  types of, 473–76
    channel stuffing, 475
    check fraud, 476
    expense account abuse, 476
    kiting, 476
    lapping, 476
    management (fraudulent financial reporting), 475, 478
    (misappropriation of assets), 475, 478
    sound business ethics, 486
fringe benefits, 70
full costing. *See* absorption costing

G

GAAP. *See* Generally Accepted Accounting Principles
general authorizations, 481
Generally Accepted Accounting Principles, 28, 387, 475
    and financial statements, 501
    noncash transactions, 535
gross,
    book value, 383
    margin, 35
    profit, 35, 176

H

Hejunka, 417
high/low method, 155–156
human resources, 10

I

ideal standard, 339
idle time, 70
income,
    statements, 176
    in equation form, 184
    and profits, 198
    tax impact, 190–191
independent variable, 151
indirect,
    examples of labor, 70
    materials, 33
information, 4–5
    needs of internal and external users, 11
    role of managerial accountants in providing, 11
    technology, 482–84
inspection and testing, 418
interest rate formula, 251
internal,
    control of inventory, 479
    rate of return, 247–54
    and taxes, 258–61
    use of as a screening tool, 254
inventory analysis, 511–12
investment,
    center managers, 381
    center performance,
    economic value added, 386–88
IRR. *See* internal rate of return
ISO,
    9000 certification, 417
    14000, 423
    See ISO 9000 certification

J

JIT (Just-in-time),
    companies, 315
    inventory management, 32
    manufacturing advantages and problems, 31
    manufacturing system success, 455
    production systems, 29
job-costing systems, 36, 66–67, 81
Just-in-time. *See* JIT

K

kaizen, 416–17, 449
knowledge, 4–5
    management, 3, 5–7
    warehouses, 6

L

least squares regression, 151, 156
life-cycle costing, 34–35
liquidity, 506–08, 513
long-term purchasing decisions, 248

M

management, 10
    by exception, 338, 354
    performance and compensation, 390
        cash compensation, 390–91
        in a multinational environment, 372
        non cash benefits and perks, 392
        recommendations about, 392
        stock compensation, 391–92
managerial,
    accountants, 66
    accounting, 8, 11
    decision-making, 176
manufactured products, 35
manufacturing,
    cells, 30
    companies, 28–31, 39–41, 45–46
    costs, 31–35
    in a JIT environment, 29–31
    overhead, 33f, 69, 77
    in a traditional environment, 28–29
    See also abnormal spoilage
margin, 382–83
marketing, 10
markups, 449
Master Budget, The, 298–99
merchandising companies, 28
    and the cost of products, 42
        calculation of cost of goods sold, 42
        income statement, 43
    example of a,
        balance sheet of a, 45
        income statement of a, 45–46
mixed costs, 148–149
    computing the variable-cost component, 156
    separation of, into fixed and variable components, 155
multiple,
    R, 154
    regression, 154

N

net,
    book value, 383
    income, 180–182
        higher due to absorption costing, 195
        impact of changes in cost, sales volume, and price, 189–194
        and operating leverage, 193
        using a variable-costing approach, 197
    operating income, 383. *See also* residual income
    present value, 247–54
        and IRR vs. payback method, 265
        and taxes, 258, 260–61
        use of as a screening tool, 254
        vs. internal rate of return method, 255–56
nonmanufacturing costs, 33–34
nonprofit organizations, 8
normal costing, 38, 76
normal spoilage, 69
NPV, *See* Net Present Value

O

One to One Manager, The, 456
operating
    activities, 9
    budgets, 301
    cycles, 32, 297
    leverage, 192–194
operational planning, 9
operations,
    costing, 66–67
    and productions, 10
opportunity costs, 14, 217, 221–23
orders requiring specials, 216
outliers, 155
outsourcing, 218–20
overapplied overhead, 77–79
overhead,
    allocation,
        using direct labor hours as the cost driver, 73
        using departmental overhead rates, 75
    as volume based, 72
    based on direct labor or machine time, 74
    calculating rates, 72
    calculation of applied, 77
    consists of, 71–72
    costs, 33, 65, 67–68, 103
    costs,
        and Cooper's Hierarchy, 105
        as a portion of the total costs of products, 74–75
        estimates of, based on the regression equation, 154
        in a JIT environment, 71
        in an ABC system, 103–104
        in heavily automated manufacturing environments, 74–75
        See also mixed costs; regression line
    departmental rates, 73–75
    examples of costs, 71–72
    in the past, 104
    manufacturing, 77–78
    plantwide rates, 72–73
    rate, 74–75
overtime premiums, 70–71

P

payback period, 263
performance measurement, 413
    balanced scorecard approach to, 414, 446
        customer perspective of, 415, 426

efficiency and timeliness, 426
environmental costing, 423–24
financial perspective, 415
internal business perspective, 415
learning and growth perspective, 415
earnings per share, 517
efficiency and timeliness, 426–28
environmental costs, 423–24
financial measures, 414
manufacturing-cycle efficiency, 427–28
manufacturing-cycle time, 427–28
marketing effectiveness, 429
nonfinancial measures of, 429
non-value added time, 428
productivity, 425
quality, 416
    appraisal (detection) costs, 418
    external failure costs, 419
    internal failure costs, 418–19
    prevention costs, 418
throughput, 427–28
period costs, 44, 194
planning, 9, 99
practical standard, 339
predetermined overhead rates, 76
present value of an annuity, 251
price setting, 66
prices and net income, 182
pricing, 447–52
    cost-plus, 449–50
    costs and, 447–48
    discrimination, 451
    dumping, 451
    economic concepts and, 447
        elastic demand, 447
        inelastic demand, 447
    gouging, 452
    legal and ethical issues in, 451–52
    market, 452
    of time and materials, 451
    penetration, 451
    predatory, 451
    price skimming, 451
    target, 448–49
    value, 451
process costing, 67, 81, 82–83
product and service costing, 27
product costs, 35, 43–44, 194
production,
    budget model, 301–03
    process, 28
productivity, 425
product-level costs, 105
profit,
    as related to factory productivity, 428
    as the goal of every enterprise, 415
    asset turnover ratio, 516
    and changes in sales volume, 192
    earnings per share, 517
    increasing, 184
    a model, 449–50
    price/earnings ratio, 517
    return on assets, 515–16
    return on common stockholders' equity, 516–17
    return on sales, 516
    See gross profit

pro forma financial statements, 312–14
PVA. See present value of an annuity

Q

quality, 416
    costs, 418–19
        appraisal (detection) costs, 418–49
        external failure costs, 418–21
        for nonmanufacturing companies, 423
        internal failure costs, 420–21
        minimizing, 419–21
    products and services, 417
ratios analysis, 500
    accounts receivable turnover ratio, 511
    acid-test ratio, 509
    activity ratio, 511
    and return on investment, 507–08
    cash flow adequacy ratio, 545
    cash-to-cash operating cycle, 513
    current ratio, 508–09
    debt service coverage ratio, 514
    debt-to-equity, 513
    inventory turnover ratio, 511
    quick ratio, 509
    prevention costs, 418–21
    times-interest-earned ratio, 513–14
    to current liabilities ratio, 509–12
    to capital expenditures ratio, 515–20
raw materials inventory, 29
regression,
    analysis, 151–155
        line, 151, 154– 155
        other uses of, 155
    equation, 154
    results with the high/low method, 155–56
    statistics, 154–155
relevant,
    costs, 156–57
    range, 145
reporting of expenditures, 44
residual income, 385
responsibility accounting, 376–77
restricted stock, 392
return on common stockholders' equity, 516–17
return on investment, 382–85
    effect of financial measures of performance, 414
    net book value method, 384
    to increase, 384
    vs. residual income, 386
    when,
        operating assets decrease, 385
        operating costs decrease, 384
        sales volume or price increases, 384
risk, 15
ROCSE. See return on common stockholders' equity
ROI. See return on investment
R square, 154
R2. See R square
rush orders, 216

S

sales,
    and the break-even point, 187
    budget, 300–02

    forecast, 300–02
    incentives, 181
    mix, 186
sampling, 418
Sarbanes-Oxley Act, 472–73, 480
SAS Institute, 457
scrap, 417
segmented income statements, 379–80
segment margin, 379–80
segments, 374–75
    in a multinational company, 389
    measuring the performance of a, 390
    performance and transfer pricing, 393
    See also segmented income statements
sensitivity analysis, 15–16
service companies, 28, 312
    and the cost of services, 43
setting standards, 339
solvency, 513
special orders, 216–18
    decision to accept, 218
    fixed costs can be relevant, 218
specific authorizations, 481
spoilage, 69
standard,
    costing,
        and competitiveness, 339
        use of, by nonmeanufacturing organizations, 340
    costs, 337, 340
        as the basis of flexible budgets, 340–41
        defined, 338
        determining, 339
        use of behavioral considerations, 355
        where they are most effective, 353
    price, 338, 340
    quantity, 338, 340
standards,
    ideal, 339
    practical, 339
    use of by nonmanufacturing organizations, 340
    use of is common, 340
statement of cash flows
    and the accounting equation, 537–38
    as an indicator of financial performance, 532
    composition of the, 532
        financing of the, 533, 543–44
        investing activities, 532, 542–43
        operating activities, 533, 540–43
    noncash transactions, 535
    purpose of the, 532
    steps in preparing, 538–44
    use of in decision-making, 544
step costs, 147–48
stock option, 391
strategic planning, 9
strategy, 446
    and creating a competitive advantage, 446–47
    cost leadership, 446
    focusing, 446
    product differentiation, 446
sunk costs, 14, 216, 227–28
supply-chain,
    cities, 456
    management, 454–56

T

target,
    costing, 448–49
    pricing, 448–49
    profit analysis, 189–90
task analysis, 339
taxes,
    costs and decision-making,
        after-tax costs and revenues, 157–58
        before-and-after tax income, 158
        impact of, 157–58
        laws concerning, 158
    impact of on capital investment decisions, 256–58, 260–61
theory of constraints, 226–27
"time and a half", 70
transfer prices, 393–96
    impact of an after-tax profit, 396
    international aspects of, 395
    multinationals and taxes, 396

U

underapplied overhead, 77–79
unit-level costs, 105.
    See also variable costs
US Olympic coins, 188
utility costs, calculating, 71–72

V

value,
    chain, 34–35, 380
    engineering, 448
variable,
    costing, 194-97
    costs, 142, 156, 176, 180–81
variance analysis, 315, 337
    and activity-based costing, 345
    analyzing variable manufacturing cost variances, 345
    and costing, 337
    and the limitations of standard costing, 337
    defined, 338
    in an ABC environment, 337
    interpreting and using, 353–54
    interpreting favorable and unfavorable, 354–55
    overhead variance analysis using activity-based costing, 351–52
    real-time at Coca-Cola, 354
    use of behavioral consideration, 355
    See also flexible budgeting
variances, 337
    as a measure of performance, 354–55
    budget, 350
    direct labor, 347–48
    direct material, 345–47
    factoring cost, 343–344
    fixed overhead, 351–52
    flexible budget, 342–43
    labor, 347–48
    material, 353
    of the sales volume, 341–42
    price, 345
    sales price, 343
    selling and administrative expense, 352–53
    spending and efficiency, 353
    summary of, 351
    usage, 345
    variable,
        manufacturing cost, 343–44
        overhead, 348–49
        overhead spending, 351
    unfavorable,
        direct labor efficiency, 354
        direct material price variance, 355
        direct material usage, 354
        material price variance, 354–55
    volume, 350
vendor-managed inventory, 455
vertical integration, 219–20
volume -based overhead,
    allocation system, 109
    compared to activity-based costing, 112–113
    costing, 112–113

W

weighted average method, 85–87
WIP. *See* work-in-process inventory
"working against the clock", 317
working capital, 506
work-in-process inventory, 29

WAKE TECHNICAL COMMUNITY COLLEGE LIBRARY
9101 FAYETTEVILLE ROAD
RALEIGH, NORTH CAROLINA 27603

WITHDRAWN

DATE DUE

OCT 2 1 2008			
OCT 2 0 2010			
JUL 0 2 2012			
AUG 8 2012			
MAR 0 1 2013			

GAYLORD | | | PRINTED IN U.S.A.

JUN 06

Present Value of $1 Due in n Periods

Factor $= \dfrac{1}{(1+r)^n}$

Period	1%	2%	3%	4%	5%	6%	7%	8%	9%	10%	12%	14%	15%	16%	18%	20%	24%
1	0.9901	0.9804	0.9709	0.9615	0.9524	0.9434	0.9346	0.9259	0.9174	0.9091	0.8929	0.8772	0.8696	0.8621	0.8475	0.8333	0.8065
2	0.9803	0.9612	0.9426	0.9426	0.9070	0.8900	0.8734	0.8573	0.8417	0.8264	0.7972	0.7695	0.7561	0.7432	0.7182	0.6944	0.6504
3	0.9706	0.9423	0.9151	0.8890	0.8638	0.8396	0.8163	0.7938	0.7722	0.7513	0.7118	0.6750	0.6575	0.6407	0.6086	0.5787	0.5245
4	0.9610	0.9238	0.8885	0.8548	0.8227	0.7921	0.7629	0.7350	0.7084	0.6830	0.6355	0.5921	0.5718	0.5523	0.5158	0.4823	0.4230
5	0.9515	0.9057	0.8626	0.8219	0.7835	0.7473	0.7130	0.6806	0.6499	0.6209	0.5674	0.5194	0.4972	0.4761	0.4371	0.4019	0.3411
6	0.9420	0.8880	0.8375	0.7903	0.7462	0.7050	0.6663	0.6302	0.5963	0.5645	0.5066	0.4556	0.4323	0.4104	0.3704	0.3349	0.2751
7	0.9327	0.8706	0.8131	0.7599	0.7107	0.6651	0.6227	0.5835	0.5470	0.5132	0.4523	0.3996	0.3759	0.3538	0.3139	0.2791	0.2218
8	0.9235	0.8535	0.7894	0.7307	0.6768	0.6274	0.5820	0.5403	0.5019	0.4665	0.4039	0.3506	0.3269	0.3050	0.2660	0.2326	0.1789
9	0.9143	0.8368	0.7664	0.7026	0.6446	0.5919	0.5439	0.5002	0.4604	0.4241	0.3606	0.3075	0.2843	0.2630	0.2255	0.1938	0.1443
10	0.9053	0.8203	0.7441	0.6756	0.6139	0.5584	0.5083	0.4632	0.4224	0.3855	0.3220	0.2697	0.2472	0.2267	0.1911	0.1615	0.1164
11	0.8963	0.8043	0.7224	0.6496	0.5847	0.5268	0.4751	0.4289	0.3875	0.3505	0.2875	0.2366	0.2149	0.1954	0.1619	0.1346	0.0938
12	0.8874	0.7885	0.7014	0.6246	0.5568	0.4970	0.4440	0.3971	0.3555	0.3186	0.2567	0.2076	0.1869	0.1685	0.1372	0.1122	0.0757
13	0.8787	0.7730	0.6810	0.6006	0.5303	0.4688	0.4150	0.3677	0.3262	0.2897	0.2292	0.1821	0.1625	0.1452	0.1163	0.0935	0.0610
14	0.8700	0.7579	0.6611	0.5775	0.5051	0.4423	0.3878	0.3405	0.2992	0.2633	0.2046	0.1597	0.1413	0.1252	0.0985	0.0779	0.0492
15	0.8613	0.7430	0.6419	0.5553	0.4810	0.4173	0.3624	0.3152	0.2745	0.2394	0.1827	0.1401	0.1229	0.1079	0.0835	0.0649	0.0397
16	0.8528	0.7284	0.6232	0.5339	0.4581	0.3936	0.3387	0.2919	0.2519	0.2175	0.1631	0.1229	0.1069	0.0930	0.0708	0.0541	0.0320
17	0.8444	0.7142	0.6050	0.5134	0.4363	0.3714	0.3166	0.2703	0.2311	0.1978	0.1456	0.1078	0.0929	0.0802	0.0600	0.0451	0.0258
18	0.8360	0.7002	0.5874	0.4936	0.4155	0.3503	0.2959	0.2502	0.2120	0.1799	0.1300	0.0946	0.0808	0.0691	0.0508	0.0376	0.0208
19	0.8277	0.6864	0.5703	0.4746	0.3957	0.3305	0.2765	0.2317	0.1945	0.1635	0.1161	0.0829	0.0703	0.0596	0.0431	0.0313	0.0168
20	0.8195	0.6730	0.5537	0.4564	0.3769	0.3118	0.2584	0.2145	0.1784	0.1486	0.1037	0.0728	0.0611	0.0514	0.0365	0.0261	0.0135
21	0.8114	0.6598	0.5375	0.4388	0.3589	0.2942	0.2415	0.1987	0.1637	0.1351	0.0926	0.0638	0.0531	0.0443	0.0309	0.0217	0.0109
22	0.8034	0.6468	0.5219	0.4220	0.3418	0.2775	0.2257	0.1839	0.1502	0.1228	0.0826	0.0560	0.0462	0.0382	0.0262	0.0181	0.0088
23	0.7954	0.6342	0.5067	0.4057	0.3256	0.2618	0.2109	0.1703	0.1378	0.1117	0.0738	0.0491	0.0402	0.0329	0.0222	0.0151	0.0071
24	0.7876	0.6217	0.4919	0.3901	0.3101	0.2470	0.1971	0.1577	0.1264	0.1015	0.0659	0.0431	0.0349	0.0284	0.0188	0.0126	0.0057
25	0.7798	0.6095	0.4776	0.3751	0.2953	0.2330	0.1842	0.1460	0.1160	0.0923	0.0588	0.0378	0.0304	0.0245	0.0160	0.0105	0.0046
26	0.7720	0.5976	0.4637	0.3607	0.2812	0.2198	0.1722	0.1352	0.1064	0.0839	0.0525	0.0331	0.0264	0.0211	0.0135	0.0087	0.0037
27	0.7644	0.5859	0.4502	0.3468	0.2678	0.2074	0.1609	0.1252	0.0976	0.0763	0.0469	0.0291	0.0230	0.0182	0.0115	0.0073	0.0030
28	0.7568	0.5744	0.4371	0.3335	0.2551	0.1956	0.1504	0.1159	0.0895	0.0693	0.0419	0.0255	0.0200	0.0157	0.0097	0.0061	0.0024
29	0.7493	0.5631	0.4243	0.3207	0.2429	0.1846	0.1406	0.1073	0.0822	0.0630	0.0374	0.0224	0.0174	0.0135	0.0082	0.0051	0.0020
30	0.7419	0.5521	0.4120	0.3083	0.2314	0.1741	0.1314	0.0994	0.0754	0.0573	0.0334	0.0196	0.0151	0.0116	0.0070	0.0042	0.0016